Workable Competition and Antitrust Policy

George W. Stocking

VANDERBILT UNIVERSITY PRESS
NASHVILLE
1961

Copyright © 1961 by Vanderbilt University Press

"Saving Free Enterprise from Its Friends"
Copyright 1953 Southern Economic Association

"The Rule of Reason, Workable Competition, and the Legality of Trade Association Activities"
Copyright 1953 by the University of Chicago

"The Rule of Reason, Workable Competition, and Monopoly"
Copyright 1954-1955 by the Yale Law Journal Company, Inc.

"The Attorney General's Committee's Report: The Businessman's Guide through Antitrust"
Copyright 1955 by The Georgetown Law Journal Association

"On the Concept of Workable Competition as an Antitrust Guide"
Copyright © 1956 by Federal Legal Publications, Inc.

"Economic Tests of Monopoly and the Concept of the Relevant Market"
Copyright © 1957 by Federal Legal Publications, Inc.

"Business Reciprocity and the Size of Firms"
Copyright 1956 by the University of Chicago

"The Du Pont-General Motors Case and the Sherman Act"
Copyright 1958 The Virginia Law Review Association, Charlottesville, Virginia

"Economic Change and the Sherman Act: Some Reflections on 'Workable Competition'"
Copyright 1958 The Virginia Law Review Association, Charlottesville, Virginia

"Institutional Factors in Economic Thinking"
Copyright 1959 by American Economic Association

Material reprinted by permission of the copyright holders

Printed in the United States of America
by the Parthenon Press, Nashville, Tennessee
Library of Congress catalog card number 61-6406

To D. R. S.
who has made it all worthwhile

Preface

To classical and neoclassical economists markets fell into two relatively simple categories, competitive and monopolistic, and they developed a lucid and logical explanation as to how price was determined in each and how it functioned in the allocation of resources and the distribution of income. As their theories gained in refinement and precision, they lost in reality. Edward Chamberlin was the first in this country to give systematic expression to a logic better adapted to the market structures of contemporary industrial society. But Chamberlin's theory of oligopolistic competition was a disturbing doctrine. He suggested that oligopolists making homogeneous and identical products, confronted with similar costs and reaching similar judgments on market demand, if rational would without conspiring behave like monopolists. This was disconcerting to both friends and critics of the antitrust laws. The Sherman Act, which forbids conspiracy to monopolize and restrain trade, must either prove inadequate to cope with oligopolistic market structures or, if so interpreted as to bring them within its reach, would call for a major reconstruction of industrial markets. Confronted with such a dilemma, economists reconstructed their thinking. John Maurice Clark pointed the way "Toward a Concept of Workable Competition" in his scholarly paper presented to the American Economic Association in 1939. Other economists were quick to nurture Clark's idea, and it was not long before some economists and more lawyers were insisting that workable competition be adopted as a standard for determining violations of the antitrust laws.

Most of the essays in this book are concerned with the significance of this proposal to antitrust policy. Although initially written as separate essays, they were conceived as parts of a systematic and book-length discussion of the proposal. When I began the task of transforming them into a book I found myself writing a new one, *The Evolution of Federal Antitrust Policy*. That book, which I hope to complete early in 1962, will include none of the original essays. Numerous requests for reprints have persuaded me to publish the original papers independently in book form. I am indebted to the following publications and publisher for permission

Workable Competition and Antitrust Policy

to do so: *American Economic Review, Antitrust Bulletin, Georgetown Law Journal, Journal of Business of the University of Chicago* and the University of Chicago Press, *Southern Economic Journal, University of Chicago Law Review, Virginia Law Review,* and *Yale Law Journal.*

I have included all of the articles that I have written on the subject of workable competition during the last six years except "The Cellophane Case and the New Competition," published in the *American Economic Review* in March 1955 and written in collaboration with Willard F. Mueller, formerly a graduate student at Vanderbilt University and now an associate professor at the University of Wisconsin. I excluded this article because it has since been republished in the American Economic Association's *Readings in Industrial Organization and Public Policy.*

I wish to acknowledge Professor Mueller's joint authorship of the paper on "Business Reciprocity and the Size of Firms." I also wish to acknowledge gratefully the criticisms that were made of various papers by George H. Hildebrand, James W. McKie, Irving H. Siegel, and Collis A. Stocking, and the help of Elizabeth R. Post in the preparation of all of these articles and particularly in preparing them for publication in book form. I am grateful to the Rockefeller Foundation for a grant to the Institute of Research in the Social Sciences at Vanderbilt University that has greatly facilitated the research on which these papers are based.

GEORGE W. STOCKING

Nashville, Tennessee
August 8, 1960

Table of Contents

1. SAVING FREE ENTERPRISE FROM ITS FRIENDS — 1
2. THE RULE OF REASON, WORKABLE COMPETITION, AND THE LEGALITY OF TRADE ASSOCIATION ACTIVITIES — 18
3. THE RULE OF REASON, WORKABLE COMPETITION, AND MONOPOLY — 119
4. THE ATTORNEY GENERAL'S COMMITTEE'S REPORT: THE BUSINESSMAN'S GUIDE THROUGH ANTITRUST — 185
5. ON THE CONCEPT OF WORKABLE COMPETITION AS AN ANTITRUST GUIDE — 241
6. ECONOMIC TESTS OF MONOPOLY AND THE CONCEPT OF THE RELEVANT MARKET — 273
7. BUSINESS RECIPROCITY AND THE SIZE OF FIRMS — 287
8. THE DU PONT-GENERAL MOTORS CASE AND THE SHERMAN ACT — 319
9. ECONOMIC CHANGE AND THE SHERMAN ACT: SOME REFLECTIONS ON "WORKABLE COMPETITION" — 357
10. INSTITUTIONAL FACTORS IN ECONOMIC THINKING — 401

TABLE OF CASES — 425
INDEX — 429

1
Saving Free Enterprise
From Its Friends

MOST AMERICANS, I BELIEVE, would profess to be friends of free enterprise; but in acknowledging that friendship, most would find it difficult to define what they befriend; for free enterprise is rapidly becoming a slogan of propaganda, a shibboleth of politics, an emblem for a crusade, around which to marshall public sentiment against the wickedness of the "welfare state."

That free enterprise has become a fighting slogan reflects the profound influence which the American environment has exerted on its citizenry. Many elements have gone into the making of the American character. Our wide open spaces made our population mobile and gave us a sense of grandeur; our frontier created an atmosphere of independence and egalitarianism; a shortage of labor and capital encouraged ingenuity and contrivance; our tremendous natural resources created opportunities, invited enterprise, and fomented a spirit of optimism. American ideology conspired with our affections and interests to create a faith. American property owners, who today expound vigorously the doctrine of rugged individualism, are the spiritual descendants of our pioneer forefathers, who were forced to practice what their spiritual heirs so fervently preach.

But free enterprise as a way of life is something different from free enterprise as a habit of thought. While in the egalitarian climate of American thought, one man's opinion may be as good as another's—or perhaps a little bit better—economists should have a special competence to indicate what is meant by a system of free enterprise, a term which they contributed to popular usage. We mean by it, of course, an economy the members of which rely on the forces of competitive markets to allocate

Note: Presidential address delivered at the Silver Anniversary Meeting of the Southern Economic Association, Jacksonville, Florida, Nov. 15, 1952. Reprinted from the *Southern Economic Journal,* Vol. 19, No. 4 (April 1953).

Workable Competition and Antitrust Policy

resources and organize the productive processes. The members of such a society, as producers or workers, are free within the limits of their talents to choose their occupations; and as consumers making free choices in the market place, they have the power to guide productive processes and allocate resources. In short, they determine what shall be produced and in what amounts.

The essence of free enterprise is decentralized decision-making or, stated negatively, the lack of concentration of power. Competitive models as contrived by the theorists are abstractions, but they are useful as standards by which to measure performance and by which to shape policies. We are all aware of the gaps between the theoretical models and a practically achievable economy of workable competition. I have little patience with those economists who criticize other economists because they would atomize American industry. I know no advocates of atomization. Students of industrial concentration differ as to how far industrial concentration as measured by "concentration ratios" has gone, and on whether or not the last fifty years have witnessed a decline in competition. I do not wish to revive that controversy here. Rather, I wish to point out that since the laissez-faire ideology of Herbert Spencer was wed with our affections and interests to give birth to the common-sense bias of contemporary defenders of free enterprise, two great institutional changes have transformed the structure of the American economy—trade unionism and collective bargaining on the one hand, and the modern corporation on the other. Industrial workers no longer sell their own labor as individuals to the owners of relatively small business firms who manage them for their own benefit. On the contrary, the managers of powerful trade unions, frequently speaking directly or indirectly for all the workers in an industry, sit down around the conference table and bargain on wages and working conditions with the managers of one or more great corporations who directly or indirectly may be speaking for all the corporate managers of that industry. This, of course, has not become a universal practice, but it is the end toward which labor is working and toward which circumstances are driving the managers of industry.

Every literate person is familiar with this development; and although some deplore it, most people ardently defend as inevitable, if not, indeed, desirable, one or both of the institutions without which it would have been impossible. Few would dispute that big business and big labor are here to stay.

As a student of economic history I should like to review quite briefly, hence necessarily inadequately, how big labor and big business came

Saving Free Enterprise from Its Friends

about and to raise the question where they are leading us. I take this brief excursion into history because I agree with Winston Churchill that the longer you look backwards, the farther you can see forwards.

THE RISE OF BIG LABOR

The fundamental object of trade unionism, according to two of its most competent and sympathetic early analysts, Sidney and Beatrice Webb, is "the deliberate regulation of the conditions of employment in such a way as to ward off from the manual-working producers the evil effects of industrial competition...."[1]

Students of American economic history also recognize that early trade unionism in the United States was designed to isolate workers, primarily skilled workers, from the free and ruthless play of competitive forces. To acknowledge this is not to deplore it. I accept the verdict of most students of labor that trade unions, by equalizing bargaining power between workers and employers, have improved the workers' lot; that they have given workers a weapon with which they could fight the boycott, the black list, the labor spy; that they have helped particular labor groups escape from what they regarded as intolerable conditions; that they have protected their membership from arbitrary and capricious discrimination by petty bosses; that they have brought greater security and dignity to the worker and his job; and that they may even have contributed to a sense of responsibility to management and the community.

But merely to admit that trade unionism may have done these things is to obscure the significance of the modern trade union movement to the preservation of a free enterprise society. Modern trade unions have become powerful instruments of social and economic control. They are frequently captained by ambitious leaders who aspire to power both for what they can do with it and for its own sake. John L. Lewis affords perhaps the best illustration in point. Under his aggressive leadership the average hourly wage of bituminous coal miners advanced from 41 cents in 1933 to over $2.00 in 1952. Average weekly earnings for bituminous coal miners advanced from $13.32 to $68.68, while the basic work day was materially shortened by payment for travel time under the portal-to-portal principle. Meanwhile, to protect miners from the insecurity of old age, the union, through a tax currently levied on consumers of coal at the rate of 30 cents a ton, has been accumulating a welfare fund at the rate of over

---

1. Sidney and Beatrice Webb, *Industrial Democracy* (London: Longmans, Green, 1924 edition), p. 807.

Workable Competition and Antitrust Policy

$100 million annually. Truly, miners have never had it so good; and who is to say they have not deserved it? Coal mining, to borrow a phrase from John Masefield's description of trench warfare in World War I, is damned dull, damned dirty, and damned dangerous. But in getting it so good, the union acquired power so great that time and again it has audaciously defied the federal government and flagrantly flouted its statutes. In 1941 Mr. Lewis successfully challenged the National Defense Mediation Board; and, on the very day of Pearl Harbor, from a governmental official sitting as an impartial arbitrator, he obtained for his union the closed shop in captive mines, which he had wrecked the Board for having refused. Time and again he defied its successor, the National War Labor Board, and undermined the government's wage and price stabilization program by ignoring its rulings. In his most recent ruthless display of power, Mr. Lewis, after having obtained for his miners a raise in their basic daily wage of $1.90 and an additional levy of 10 cents a ton for the union's welfare fund in what he characterized as a "triumph of collective bargaining," called a strike against the coal operators because they refused to disobey the wage stabilization law, which requires approval of the wage increase by the Wage Stabilization Board before operators can put it into effect. And eventually, to insure industrial peace, the President of the United States bowed to Mr. Lewis' demands, overruling and wrecking his Wage Stabilization Board and emasculating if not junking the wage stabilization program to which he was committed. Other unions have not acquired a power so great, but their failure is not due to a lack of ambition. They deserve an *A* for effort. Both Mr. Lewis' power and the way he uses it are the envy of many lesser lords of labor kingdoms.

Nor should the credit or blame for this condition fall exclusively on labor. Trade union membership has had three periods of rapid growth: 1897–1904, 1914–1920, 1933–1948. During the prosperity of the first period, under Gompers' leadership, the American Federation of Labor increased its membership fourfold, a rate never again duplicated. During World War I and its inflationary aftermath, trade union membership increased from 2,500,000 to 5,200,000. During the prosperity of the 1920's with its antiunion drives in which employers enlisted public support under a slogan of Americanism, union membership declined. The Great Depression accentuated the trend. The New Deal reversed it. AFL unions increased their membership from about 2,100,000 in 1933 to 7,250,000 in 1948. Meanwhile, the Congress of Industrial Organizations was born and by

Saving Free Enterprise from Its Friends

1948 had become a lusty giant with approximately 6,000,000 members. Independent unions accounted for 2,250,000 more.

The recent rapid increase in trade union membership and power was a result of deliberate governmental policy, and many count it one of the New Deal's great and lasting achievements. During the 1920's organized labor had been stunted in part by its lack of foresight, in part by the foresight of management in introducing its own welfare program, and in part by management's having enlisted the power of the state through the use of the injunction in its battle with unionism. The Norris–La Guardia Act, a pre–New Deal measure, deprived management of the injunction as a weapon in its fight with labor. In the struggle between labor and capital the state announced its neutrality. It in effect insured labor and management a free field in which to fight out their battles, which, despite their repercussions on the whole economy, were still regarded as private disputes.

The New Deal changed this. With the support, in truth at the behest, of both labor and capital, it formally abandoned reliance on free markets to guide the economy. As a cost of the privilege of collaborating on price and production policies under a virtual suspension of the antitrust laws, business accepted a labor policy designed to match its power with that of the union. Under the National Industrial Recovery Act, and the Wagner Act which superseded it, the federal government in effect placed its authority behind unions in their effort to organize American workmen. The rules were so drawn that trade union management through persuasion and, when persuasion failed, through coercion could mobilize industrial workers under its banner free from molestation or interference. The law freed labor's hand; it tied management's. Again, to record history is not to decry it. As the remorseless forces of the Great Depression shrank output and earnings, devalued assets, and threatened bankruptcy and ruin all around the place, businessmen themselves lost confidence in private enterprise. That management got rather more than it bargained for when the courts invalidated the NIRA and Congress came to the support of labor reflects an alerted public sympathy for the common man, to which category the Great Depression had reduced so many Americans. It reflected a deepening conviction that the power of big business must be matched by the power of labor if all private interests were to be protected and if the public welfare were to be promoted.

I do not mean to imply that trade union power has been exclusively a reaction to the power of big business, although it has been that in considerable part. Labor's right to bargain collectively is as secure in dealing with

Workable Competition and Antitrust Policy

little business as with big business, and in the exercise of that right labor has not restricted its use of collective power to that of the labor force of a single firm. It has sought rather to unite in a solid front all the workers of a craft, occupation, or even an industry within a particular labor market and to impose upon each employer within that market the conditions under which it would supply management with labor. So lopsided did the struggle between individual managements and united labor become that the employers of the San Francisco market area eventually united and demanded of labor the right to bargain collectively with it. The first president of San Francisco Employers' Council in 1939 expressed the Council's philosophy as follows:

> Collective bargaining is primarily a pressure game. Labor unions have been effectively organized into city-wide councils and national organizations. By and large they are well staffed and financed. They have definite programs and objectives, and they are eternally on the job to secure concessions for their members and to strengthen their position. . . . When one is engaged in a pressure game with a competitor who is well organized and financed and knows where he is going, it is simply good common sense to meet organization with organization, and this is exactly what we propose to do in San Francisco through the agency of the San Francisco Employers' Council. In the vernacular of the water front, we expect to "Match Heat with Heat."

Group action was to generate the heat. As the president of the Council put it:

> . . . the great majority of employers in San Francisco have abandoned any hope of dealing with labor unions on a basis of rugged individualists who do not require the aid of their fellow employers. Whether we like it or not we have reached the point where we are prepared to admit that the rugged individualist has largely passed from the San Francisco labor relations picture.[2]

World War II both harnessed and enhanced the power of trade unions locally and nationally. In return for limitations on labor's right to strike, the government undertook to increase and maintain union membership. To preserve the peace, it forced both labor and management to accept what in reality, if not formally, was compulsory arbitration of labor disputes. It put genuine collective bargaining on ice for the emergency. When it was brought out of cold storage, labor's power to use it had grown to its present dimensions.

2. Almon E. Roth, *Objectives of the San Francisco Employers' Council* (New York: American Management Association, 1939), quoted by Clark Kerr and Lloyd H. Fisher in "Multi-Employer Bargaining: The San Francisco Experience," published in *Insights into the Labor Issue*, ed. Richard A. Lester and Joseph Shister (New York: Macmillan, 1948), p. 56.

Saving Free Enterprise from Its Friends

THE RISE OF BIG BUSINESS

In discussing the rise of big business, it is important to distinguish between big plants, big firms, and big industries. No industrial society can endure without using modern industrial technology. Modern technology necessitates large industrial establishments using mass production methods. To utilize modern technology in large industrial establishments in a private enterprise economy requires a business mechanism. The modern corporation is that mechanism. It is the instrument by which capital can be mobilized and, with the other factors of production, organized into a productive process. The mechanism must be large enough to encompass and coordinate resources on a scale essential to command, utilize, and, in a progressive society, enlarge and improve the technology. But this principle gives us no precise yardstick by which to measure the size of the optimum firm. Doubtless, this differs from industry to industry; but economists and most articulate businessmen agree that the optimum firm falls within a fairly wide range of magnitudes rather than at a point on a scale. That is to say, many firms may in fact be larger than they need be for efficiency, and evidence exists to support the proposition that some have gotten too large to remain efficient.[3]

To raise the level of living of a large and growing population and, more particularly, to give it national security requires large and efficient industries, industries generally far larger than plants or firms need be. Obviously, without America's large steel industry, made up of many large and efficient plants, the Allies could not have won World War II. But no single firm, however large it may have been, was essential as such to American military success. A great steel industry must be larger than the firms that comprise it and the firms may be larger than the industrial establishments that they command. But big firms alone do not guarantee an efficient industry. Before World War II the United States Steel Corporation, with one third of America's steel ingot capacity, could produce about as much steel as could all of the steel firms of England, Belgium, and France combined, but that is not what made America's steel industry great. Other integrated firms with only a fraction of the corporation's steel ingot capacity were making proportionately more high grade steel and apparently making it at a lower cost than was the Steel Corpora-

---

3. See, for example, *Hearings before the Subcommittee on Study of Monopoly Power of the House Committee on the Judiciary,* 81st Cong., 2d Sess., ser. 14, pt. 4A, testimony of Benjamin Fairless, at 615–711 *passim,* and my testimony, at 961–91 (1950).

Workable Competition and Antitrust Policy

tion.[4] But obviously we needed every ton of America's steel capacity to do the job we did.

Although big business, i.e., the modern giant corporation, preceded big labor, the rise of both contains some striking parallels. Like trade unions, the modern corporation has been an instrument of control. Both trade unions and corporations have grown most rapidly in boom times; both have been nourished by war; and both owe their power in considerable part to the state. The Great Combination Movement culminated during the prosperous years of the turn of the century. Although economists do not agree on the relative weight of the specific forces which actuated it, they recognize that professional promoters and investment bankers interested in profiting by creating and maintaining security values engineered it. Few will deny that it changed greatly the structure of the American economy. I believe that in institutional importance it compares with the breakdown of the feudal system, the rise of towns, or the appearance of mercantilism—movements that extended over hundreds of years. Perhaps never in so short a peacetime period have such great structural changes taken place in any other economic system.

The state of New Jersey, containing only 2 per cent of the country's population and 1.3 per cent of its wealth, took the lead in providing an effective instrument for extending the area over which business firms could exert private power. Other states, envious of the contribution of New Jersey corporations to the state's finances, quickly followed suit. The modern corporation was their handiwork. Together the states shaped a corporate instrument of business control without which industrial concentration on the scale that we know it would have been impossible.

Contemporaries viewed this development with skepticism or even alarm, one economist making the bold claim that New Jersey by its corporation law had nullified the antitrust statutes of every state that had passed them.[5] And, indeed, the Supreme Court in the first case to come before it involving the use of the New Jersey holding corporation as a device for eliminating competition among rival manufacturers recognized that in grappling with the monopoly problem the power of Congress was subordinate to that of the New Jersey legislature. In passing the Sherman Act, the Court said, Congress had not attempted "to assert the power to deal with monopoly directly as such; or to limit and restrict the rights of

4. *Ibid.*
5. Edward S. Mead, *Trust Finance* (New York: Appleton, 1903), p. 39.

Saving Free Enterprise from Its Friends

corporations created by the States or the citizens of the States in the acquisition, control, or disposition of property. . . ."[6]

Alexander Pope seems to have expressed a sound sociological principle in these poetic lines:

> Vice is a monster of so frightful mien,
> As, to be hated, needs but to be seen;
> Yet seen too oft, familiar with her face,
> We first endure, then pity, then embrace.

At any rate, many contemporary students of institutional arrangements now approve New Jersey's contribution to our industrial structure, counting the holding corporation as a manifestation of the genius of American businessmen for organizational and managerial achievement. All of us can point with pride to the twentieth-century accomplishments of American private enterprise, overlooking, of course, the dreary decade of the 1930's and ignoring the role of wartime inflation under a centrally managed economy in contributing to it. But no one has offered convincing evidence that American industry would have been less efficient had the scope of corporate ownership been more restricted. And there are both *a priori* reasons and empirical evidence to indicate that in some instances it might have been more efficient had firms remained smaller.

The Great Combination Movement gave birth to big business as a managerial and organizational phenomenon. The prosperity of the 1920's provided a climate which nourished it. Economic historians and theorists alike are familiar with these facts; but troubled by what some students of industrial structure believe the merger movements signify to corporate greatness, economists are now trying to determine statistically the relative importance of internal expansion (i.e., all growth except that occasioned by absorbing independent firms or buying their properties) and external expansion (i.e., growth by mergers) as a factor in corporate size.

J. Fred Weston, of the University of California at Los Angeles, in an as yet unpublished study concludes that only

approximately one-fourth of the growth of the 74 firms studied was directly accounted for by mergers. If assets of the initial year for firms which were formed by combinations are classified as acquisitions, about one-third of the growth then becomes external growth. At least 70 per cent of the firms studied grew by internal expansion to the extent of more than half of their total growth. Acquisitions accounted for less than 25 per cent of the growth of one-half of the firms.[7]

6. United States v. E. C. Knight Co., 156 U.S. 1, 16 (1895).
7. J. Fred Weston, "Mergers and Oligopoly" (University of California), p. 52. In

Workable Competition and Antitrust Policy

Some uncritical students may use Weston's findings to discredit the hypothesis that the Great Combination Movement has had a significant effect on the structure of the American economy. Weston himself avoids this error. He correctly points out, despite the apparent paradox, that internal growth has not been the major cause of industrial concentration. He recognizes that at the turn of the century the merger movement occasioned a high degree of concentration in a great many industries and that "although the *absolute* size of present day oligopolists is due only in small part to either earlier or late acquisitions, the *relative* position of these firms is accounted for by the *earlier* acquisitions."[8] Weston also recognizes that although the combined assets of original mergers today represent a relatively small part of the total assets of the merged companies, the assets of the many separate companies that were combined might well have shown, if the merger movement had not taken place, a rate of growth comparable to that of the combination; and he recognizes that in the absence of the merger movement assets as large as those now under the control of a single company might well have been under the control of as many companies as went into a particular merger. In short, he recognizes that the potential internal expansion of each of the merged companies has been merged into the actual internal expansion of the combination, and hence that the merger may be indirectly responsible for the overwhelming size of many present-day corporations which ostensibly have grown primarily by internal expansion.

Unfortunately, Weston's study discloses changes in the size of assets of the corporations studied only between his terminal dates (i.e., between the year of the initial merger and 1948). I venture the hypothesis that our two world wars, particularly World War II, witnessed the most rapid rate of growth in the firms studied by Weston. World War II, as everyone knows, taxed American production facilities to the limit. To get what it needed to win the war without lowering consumption levels, the government by persuasion and subsidy encouraged private enterprise to expand production facilities; where necessary, the government built its own industrial plants with the cooperation and under the supervision of the private corporations which managed them. Many of the plant facilities were necessarily so-called "scrambled facilities," of little value except to the firms that operated them and subsequently acquired them at bargain prices.

1953 this study was published under the title *The Role of Mergers in the Growth of Large Firms* (Berkeley: University of California Press). See p. 30 for the passage quoted.

8. *Id.* at 85. Emphasis in original.

Saving Free Enterprise from Its Friends

The emergency of a world war necessitates immediate expansion of production facilities. Although it brings opportunities to new producers, a government must look for the most part to existing firms to carry out its expansion program. Necessarily it must follow the Biblical maxim, "To him that hath shall be given." Had the tremendous expansion in consumption occasioned by World War II been distributed over a longer period of normal peacetime growth, it might well have encouraged the birth of many more new firms in basic industries.

Obviously, private enterprise is to be praised, not censured, for its willingness to cooperate with the government in its program of industrial expansion. But although small and intermediate-sized firms, some new, shared in the government's program of industry expansion, the great bulk of the war contracts went to a handful of giant corporations, most of which were born through combinations; despite their having sublet many thousands of contracts, they emerged from the war far larger and, to the extent that size brings power, more powerful than when they went into it.[9]

While economists agree that the Great Combination Movement—which apparently is the most significant factor accounting directly for the relative size of corporations in many industries and indirectly for their absolute size—wrought profound changes in the structure of the American economy, they do not agree as to what this has meant for market behavior. I cannot recount the details of the controversy here, but I believe that nearly all economists would subscribe to the following two propositions: first, that the combination movement has reduced significantly the number of sellers in many markets; and second, that fewness of sellers encourages monopoly-like behavior. The second of these propositions is true for two reasons: (1) the Chamberlinian theory that rational behavior by oligopolists who take account of the indirect as well as the direct consequences of their decisions results in monopoly prices, is not only logically consistent but may have some practical significance in the market (although I believe this has been overemphasized); and (2) fewness of sellers makes it easy for business rivals to reap the fruits of conspiracy without paying its legal penalties.

Moreover, as Corwin Edwards has pointed out, the giant conglomerate firm, even though it falls far short of monopoly in any technical sense, may jeopardize the interests of smaller suppliers, competitors, or custo-

9. I use the term "power" broadly. As indicated below it means more than power over the market. I do not believe anyone can assert what the precise effects of an increase in the absolute size of the very large corporations will be on market behavior.

mers.[10] Large firms, because they are large, have financial resources that enable them to "outbid, outspend, or outlose" smaller rivals. They can command the best talents; they can buy the best sites; by integrating backwards and controlling their own raw materials, they can free themselves from the fortuities of the market; by integrating forward, they can obtain a more certain and dependable outlet for their finished goods. In dealing with suppliers, they can obtain better terms than can smaller rivals. In times of shortage of supplies it is the little firm that finds the going toughest. On the significance of these facts to policy, economists may disagree, but few will deny that they are facts.

Big firms have developed among themselves an *esprit de corps,* a spirit of live-and-let-live, codes of ethics, commercial interrelationships, an interchange of patent rights, a reciprocal recognition of priorities of interest, all of which tend to lessen the vigor of competitive rivalry and to develop spheres of influence which at times may prove as effective as formal cartels in regulating markets.

Finally, modern techniques of mass communication—popular magazines, radio, television, and the privately distributed motion-picture film—are bringing to the great corporations and to a lesser extent to trade unions an opportunity to wield a new and subtle, if not ominous, power—a power over the human mind. This enterprise is not entirely new, but its tools are. Radio and television, the press, and the privately distributed motion-picture film enable those with adequate finances and a vested interest in institutional arrangements to shape attitudes, arouse prejudices, coin good will, mold public opinion, and create habits of thought with readers or listeners, who are unaware that their ideas are being fabricated for them. No one can blame big business or big labor for trying to sell themselves to the American public as essential elements in a free enterprise system. And no lover of democratic institutions would deny to business, big or little, or to labor, freedom of thought and freedom of expression. But students of social institutions cannot blind themselves to the processes that go on before them; and sound public policy towards bigness, whether of labor or business, must rest upon an understanding of its social as well as its economic significance.

Indeed, the last fifty years have brought significant changes in the struc-

---

10. Corwin D. Edwards, "The Conglomerate Firm," paper presented to the Conference on Business Concentration and Price Policy conducted by Universities–National Bureau Committee for Economic Research, June 17–19, 1952. In 1955 this paper was published under the title "Conglomerate Bigness as a Source of Power" in *Business Concentration and Price Policy* (Princeton: Princeton University Press), pp. 331–52.

Saving Free Enterprise from Its Friends

ture of the American economy. Big trade unions now sell labor under monopoly or near-monopoly conditions. Big corporations buy it. Compromise, not competition, determines what it sells for. To analyze the significance of the power that unions exert in selling labor and of the power that the very large corporations may independently exert in selling the things they make to the price structure and to the level of output and employment would lead us into a controversial field which I cannot explore here. To suggest what these developments may mean to the future of free enterprise is an easier task, although it may be a thankless one. But first, let us examine what the optimists are saying about it. Time permits only passing reference to Lilienthal's artful and artistic encomium of big business and only brief generalization on a panegyric of a professional scholar of high repute and unquestioned competence.

The Concept of Countervailing Power

Recognizing the inadequacy of orthodox price theory to explain the pricing process in the contemporary economy and impressed by the gap between theory and practice, economists have generally felt the need of a more realistic explanation of economic processes. Perhaps influenced unconsciously by the spirit of transcendentalism, perhaps confusing change with progress, or even perhaps with a wisdom born of experience and thought, Professor Galbraith, believing that we are captives of economic doctrines that no longer apply to our current life, in 1952 presented a systematic and comforting logic to explain market behavior where large buyers and large sellers confront each other. He developed it in a challenging and sparkling manner in his *American Capitalism,* published under the captivating subtitle, "The Concept of Countervailing Power," and described on its jacket as a "bold new concept of balance of power in the last refuge of private capitalism."

Galbraith's doctrine of countervailing power can be stated succinctly, although as usual brevity means oversimplification. His study contains little that is new except its strikingly optimistic evaluation of the significance of bigness and the brilliance and originality with which it develops and integrates the doctrine of countervailing power with Neo-Keynesian, Chamberlinian, and Schumpeterian theory.

Galbraith recognizes that a handful of firms have pre-empted the market in many American industries, and he believes that in such markets businessmen reject price competition as a means of maximizing profits. But

Workable Competition and Antitrust Policy

he does not think that they are content to sit on their hands. If they behave rationally, we might expect them to try to make more by selling less. Fortunately, their urge to sabotage is circumvented by their urge to innovate. Fortunately also, large firms (and Galbraith thinks *only* large firms) can command research facilities on a scale essential for manipulating effectively modern technology and improving it. As Galbraith puts it, an industry must contain "some element of monopoly . . . if it is to be progressive." [11] ". . . There can be little doubt," he tells us, that oligopoly, both in theory and in fact, "is strongly oriented towards change." [12]

At this point one may think he is hearing the distant roar of Schumpeter's "Perennial Gale of Creative Destruction"—a gale that will eventually wreck the structure of monopoly and insure the consumers better things for living at prices they can afford. But it is only a false echo. It is countervailing power that will force from the technological horn of plenty a plethora of novel and better things for all of us. Countervailing power—the matching of the power of big sellers with the power of big buyers, the power of big business with the power of big labor—provides a streamlined twentieth-century mechanism to replace the technologically obsolete mechanism of competitive markets in promoting the public welfare. As Galbraith puts it:

> To begin with a broad and somewhat too dogmatically stated proposition, private economic power is held in check by the countervailing power of those who are subject to it. The first begets the second. The long trend towards concentration of industrial enterprise in the hands of relatively few firms has brought into existence not only strong sellers, as economists have supposed, but also strong buyers as they have failed to see. The two develop together, not in precise step but in such manner that there can be no doubt that the one is in response to the other. . . . In the ultimate sense it was the power of the steel industry, not the organizing abilities of John L. Lewis and Philip Murray, that brought the United Steel Workers into being.[13]

(The New Deal, I take it, was merely the proximate force through which the ultimate was realized, after a third of a century.)

In more technical language, competition has been succeeded by bilateral monopoly, and the conflicting interests of buyer and seller guarantee consumers substantially the same protection that competition used to afford. The unseen hand has not forsaken us. Tennyson has put it more poetically:

11. John K. Galbraith, *American Capitalism* (Boston: Houghton Mifflin, 1952), p. 93.
12. *Id.* at 95.
13. *Id.* at 118 and 121.

Saving Free Enterprise from Its Friends

> Yet I doubt not through the ages one increasing purpose runs,
> And the thoughts of men are widened with the process of the suns.

Galbraith believes that although bigness on one side of the market tends to beget bigness on the other, if a hostile environment stifles the secondary growth the government is obligated to provide a new environment. If necessary, the government must lay the egg, hatch the ostrich, and nurse it to maturity. This the government has done in providing parity for farm prices.

Galbraith regards countervailing power as capitalism's salvation, but he sees a devil lurking in the wood pile. He believes that the forces of inflation dissipate countervailing power and that during the upswing of the business cycle the strong arm of the state must protect the public welfare by setting up arbitrary controls over costs and prices. It is in depression that countervailing power really comes into its own. A mild recession makes of it a system of checks and balances protecting the interests of all of us.

With much of what Galbraith says in two hundred scintillating pages many economists will agree. With much some have found fault. While avoiding controversy on details, I want to challenge the institutional implications of the Galbraithian doctrine. Far from finding it the last bulwark against "creeping socialism," I believe that the private power which permeates our economy invites nationalization of our basic industries or regimentation on a scale so vast that enterprise would cease to be either free or private. The 1952 steel strike may have been a dress rehearsal for the real show. When the conflicting demands of two power groups brought not compromise, but stalemate, a stalemate that threatened to deadlock a whole economy, the President without constitutional or legislative authority seized the industry; and when the courts struck down the reckless abuse of executive power, he asked Congress to grant him the power which the Constitution had denied him. That Congress did not do so does not guarantee that another Congress confronted with a similar crisis will not do so. A democratic society is unlikely to leave such power in private hands forever. Stalemate as well as compromise is a continuing promise of countervailing power.

Moreover, countervailing power does not guarantee the fruits of workable competition even in recession. Galbraith's chief ground for optimism about the workability of countervailing power is the remarkable performance of capitalism since the outbreak of World War II. Capitalism thrives in an expansionist environment. When customers, public and private,

Workable Competition and Antitrust Policy

clamor for more goods than they can get at prevailing prices, business, big and little, makes money and everyone loves free private enterprise. When recession brings a competition so vigorous that it threatens to diminish or undermine capital values, business, big and little, seeks refuge in monopolistic schemes of one sort or another. Surely the 1930's with the NRA and its aftermath have not been forgotten. With increasing frequency economists have been calling on the mythical man from Mars to testify to the wonders of American capitalism. Why they should do so without having exhausted earthly witnesses constantly puzzles me, but I note that it is the output during the war and the postwar period of inflation that is expected to excite the admiration of our cosmic visitors. During the dreary days of the 1930's, when countervailing power brought both domestic and international conspiracy or government-sponsored cartels, neither the Earthians nor the Martians acclaimed the vigors of unfettered free enterprise. Whether a recession brings compromise or conspiracy no doubt depends on its amplitude and duration; but the longer it lasts and the deeper it gets, the less trustworthy private countervailing power will become as a guarantee of socially salutary compromise; and always it invites countervailing power in government.

WHAT CAN BE DONE ABOUT IT?

We have built power blocs into our economic structure with a political cement that is difficult to loosen. Captains of power are always reluctant to relinquish it. Few labor leaders or corporate managers would care to preside at the liquidation of their empires. Perhaps policy makers, backed by the people, i.e., all of us, can develop the determination, insight, and sagacity essential to create an environment more conducive to decentralization of economic power. The aim of such policy should be to nurture the dynamic elements in private capitalism. Power which impedes market forces should be curtailed, not strengthened. Limiting the power of trade unions is a delicate task of political surgery; and if the power of corporations is not similarly curtailed, it might endanger the health of the economy. Limiting the power of big business is equally delicate and more complex. An indiscriminate program of disintegration is neither economically feasible nor politically expedient. Case-by-case procedure is essential. Industrial structure and market behavior need careful analysis before the use of the surgical knife. Since a dynamic capitalism relies on the profit motive, penalization of mere bigness might well prove fatal. Hope lies more in guiding the future than in undoing the past. A practical program

Saving Free Enterprise from Its Friends

might include not merely limiting the power of trade unions, but, among other things, centralizing the power to charter corporations doing business in interstate commerce; limiting appropriately the use of holding companies; modifying our patent laws to insure a more competitive exploitation of technological innovations without impairing incentive; sponsoring technical research at public expense more liberally and making its fruits available for exploitation on a competitive basis; revising the tax laws so as to encourage large firms to obtain funds for expansion not by reinvesting earnings but by competing for funds in the private capital market; and finally, so modifying and enforcing our antitrust laws as not merely to prevent conspiracy but to increase the number and viability of moderate-sized independent firms.

Such a program is unlikely to appeal to persons with vested interests, who correctly insist that one can't set back the hands of the clock. But that is not the issue. The issue is whether the hands will move forward with the steadiness and regularity essential to progress and stability, or be retarded by the dead weight of vested interests, or eventually be accelerated by the impatient forces of political radicalism. Only time will resolve it.

2
The Rule of Reason, Workable Competition, And the Legality of Trade Association Activities

A DETERMINED MOVEMENT to change the antitrust laws[1] is now under way.[2] Businessmen, lawyers, and students of public policy have joined in it. Such a movement is not unique to our time. Dissatisfaction with the administration and interpretation of the antitrust laws is about as old as the Sherman Act itself. Emotions aroused by this issue have ranged from discouragement to alarm. In the first antitrust case to come before it, the Supreme Court, in holding that Congress lacked jurisdiction to ban monopolies in the manufacturing field, discouraged and disturbed

Note: Reprinted from the *University of Chicago Law Review*, Vol. 21, No. 4 (Summer 1954).

1. The four basic antitrust laws are the Sherman Act, 26 Stat. 209 (1890), as amended, 15 U.S.C. §§ 1-7 (1958); the Clayton Act, 38 Stat. 730 (1914), as amended, 15 U.S.C. §§ 12 *et seq.* (1958); the Robinson-Patman Act, 49 Stat. 1526 (1936), 15 U.S.C. §§ 13 *et seq.* (1958); and the Federal Trade Commission Act, 38 Stat. 717 (1914), as amended, 15 U.S.C. §§ 41 *et seq.* (1958). The Antitrust Division of the Department of Justice is also responsible for the enforcement of some fifty related laws, but this study will examine only the application of the basic antitrust statutes to trade association activities.
2. The movement took official form in the Attorney General's Committee to Study the Antitrust Laws, which was organized in August 1953. As indicated in the *Note* above, this paper was first published in 1954; the *Report of the Attorney General's National Committee to Study the Antitrust Laws* was published March 31, 1955. Judge Stanley N. Barnes, then Assistant Attorney General in charge of the Antitrust Division of the Department of Justice, and Professor S. Chesterfield Oppenheim of the University of Michigan Law School were co-chairmen of the committee, which consisted of fifty-eight experts in antitrust problems, most of them lawyers or economists. Trade Practice Bulletin, August 1953, pp. 1, 6; *id.*, September 1953, pp. 1, 6. Oppenheim's article, "Federal Antitrust Legislation: Guideposts to a Revised National Antitrust Policy," 50 Mich. L. Rev. 1139 (1952), is an important reflection of and contribution to the movement. *Effective Competition: Report to the Secretary of Commerce by His Business Advisory Council,* published by the Department of Commerce Dec. 18, 1952, reflects the dissatisfaction of some businessmen with what they consider inconsistencies in the antitrust statutes as they are

those who feared the power of big business and regarded monopolies as a threat to the American way of life.[3] And well it might have, for the decision served as a green light to the Great Combination Movement [4] that was just gaining momentum. On the other hand, businessmen re-

interpreted. Similar ideas are expressed by Blackwell Smith, "Effective Competition: Hypothesis for Modernizing the Antitrust Laws," 26 N.Y.U.L. Rev. 405 (1951). For varying points of view on this problem, see also Morris A. Adelman, "Effective Competition and the Antitrust Laws," 61 Harv. L. Rev. 1289 (1948); Arthur R. Burns, *The Decline of Competition* (New York: McGraw-Hill, 1936); John T. Cahill, "Some Recent Trends and Developments in the Anti-trust Laws," 1 The Record (N.Y.C. Bar) 201 (1946); John M. Clark, "Toward a Concept of Workable Competition," 30 Am. Econ. Rev. (Proceedings of the American Economic Ass'n) 241 (1940); Clark, "The Orientation of Antitrust Policy," 40 Am. Econ. Rev. (Proceedings of the American Economic Ass'n) 93 (1950); Corwin D. Edwards, "An Appraisal of the Antitrust Laws," 36 Am. Econ. Rev. (Proceedings of the American Economic Ass'n) 172 (1946); Edwards, *Maintaining Competition* (New York: McGraw-Hill, 1949); Clare E. Griffin, *An Economic Approach to Antitrust Problems* (New York: American Enterprise Association, 1951); Milton Handler, *A Study of the Construction and Enforcement of the Federal Antitrust Laws* (TNEC Monograph No. 38, 1941); Handler, "Anti-Trust—New Frontiers and New Perplexities," 6 The Record (N.Y.C. Bar) 59 (1951); *Hearings before the Subcommittee on Study of Monopoly Power of the House Committee on the Judiciary,* 81st Cong., 1st Sess. (1949); Dexter M. Keezer, ed., "The Effectiveness of the Federal Antitrust Laws: A Symposium," 39 Am. Econ. Rev. 689 (1949); Edward H. Levi, "The Antitrust Laws and Monopoly," 14 Univ. Chi. L. Rev. 153 (1947); David E. Lilienthal, "Our Anti-Trust Laws Are Crippling America," Collier's, May 31, 1952, p. 15; Lee Loevinger, *The Law of Free Enterprise* (New York: Funk & Wagnalls, 1949); Edward S. Mason, "The Current Status of the Monopoly Problem in the United States," 62 Harv. L. Rev. 1265 (1949); Oppenheim, "A New Look at Antitrust Enforcement Trends," in Commerce Clearing House, *Antitrust Law Symposium* (1950), p. 69; Eugene V. Rostow, "The New Sherman Act: A Positive Instrument of Progress," 14 Univ. Chi. L. Rev. 567 (1947); Joseph A. Schumpeter, *Capitalism, Socialism, and Democracy* (New York: Harper, 1942); George W. Stocking and Myron W. Watkins, *Monopoly and Free Enterprise* (New York: Twentieth Century Fund, 1951); Thomas E. Sunderland, "Changing Legal Concepts in the Antitrust Field," 3 Syracuse L. Rev. 60 (1951); *United States Versus Economic Concentration and Monopoly: A Staff Report to the Monopoly Subcommittee of the House Committee on Small Business,* H. Res. 64, 79th Cong. (1946); David McCord Wright, "Toward Coherent Anti-Trust," 35 Va. L. Rev. 665 (1949).

3. United States v. E. C. Knight Co., 156 U.S. 1 (1895). Former President Taft writing in 1914 had the following to say about this decision: "The effect of the decision . . . upon the popular mind, and indeed upon Congress as well, was to discourage hope that the statute could be used to accomplish its manifest purpose and curb the great industrial trusts. . . . So strong was the impression . . . that both Mr. Olney and Mr. Cleveland concluded that the evil must be controlled through State legislation, and not through a national statute, and they said so in their communications to Congress." William H. Taft, *The Anti-Trust Act and the Supreme Court* (New York: Harper, 1914), p. 60.

4. The Great Combination Movement took place between 1897 and 1904, when many of the railroad and industrial consolidations which today dominate the national

Workable Competition and Antitrust Policy

garded the Court's rejection of the rule of reason in the freight association cases [5] a couple of years later not only as a threat to their constitutional liberties—freedom of contract in their business pursuits—but as a threat to the free-enterprise system itself. As William D. Guthrie, a contemporary lawyer, put it: "It is . . . not surprising that the realization of the intended scope and legal effect of this statute should have caused dismay in the commercial world, and have created profound misgiving as to the future." [6] Guthrie was perhaps even more disturbed than the businessmen, for he predicted the flight of capital to Canada as a consequence of this "arbitrary and socialistic" measure. The private-enterprise economy survived and so did the clamor to change the law.

The 1914 Legislation

Twelve years later Congress rejected a bill that would have incorporated the rule of reason into the Sherman Act,[7] but in 1911 the Supreme Court did by interpretation what Congress had refused to do by legislation.[8] The 1911 decisions precipitated another move to amend the Sher-

---

economy were formed. Among these were United States Steel Corp., Standard Oil Co. of New Jersey, American Tobacco Co., International Harvester Co., American Can Co., and United Shoe Machinery Corp. Harry Leslie Purdy, Martin L. Lindahl, and William A. Carter, *Corporate Concentration and Public Policy* (2d ed.; New York: Prentice-Hall, 1950), p. 25.

5. United States v. Trans-Missouri Freight Ass'n, 166 U.S. 290 (1897); United States v. Joint Traffic Ass'n, 171 U.S. 505 (1898).

6. "Constitutionality of the Sherman Anti-Trust Act of 1890," 11 Harv. L. Rev. 80 (1897).

7. In 1909, S. 6440, introduced in the 60th Congress, 2d Session, proposed to amend the Sherman Act to give all corporations except railroad companies (already subject to the Interstate Commerce Act) immunity from antitrust prosecution unless notified within thirty days by the Commissioner of Corporations, with the concurrence of the Secretary of Commerce and Labor, that any proposed contract or combination filed with the Commissioner of Corporations was in unreasonable restraint of trade. It would have limited the amount of recovery in a civil action for injury to business under Section 7 to single instead of threefold damages and, according to the Senate Judiciary Report on it, would have provided "that no prosecutions under the first six sections of the act shall be maintained for past offenses unless the contract, or combination, be in *unreasonable* restraint of trade. . . ." Sen. Rep. No. 848, 60th Cong., 2d Sess. 9 (1909). The Senate Judiciary Committee rejected the proposed amendment, saying that to make "civil and criminal prosecution hinge on the question of reasonableness or unreasonableness . . . destroys . . . the provisions of the act as to criminal prosecutions, and renders them nugatory, and opens the door wide to doubt and uncertainty as to civil prosecutions. . . . The defense of reasonable restraint would be made in every case and there would be as many different rules of reasonableness as cases, courts, and juries." *Id.* at 9–11.

8. Standard Oil Co. v. United States, 221 U.S. 1 (1911); United States v. American Tobacco Co., 221 U.S. 106 (1911).

man Act. They disturbed Congressmen, "unwilling to repose in . . . any . . . court, the vast and undefined power which it must exercise in the administration of the statute under the rule which it has promulgated." [9]

In reinterpreting the Sherman Act to include the rule of reason, while at the same time finding against the Standard Oil Company and the American Tobacco Company, the Supreme Court had placed great emphasis on the role which predatory practices had played in gaining for these companies monopolies in their respective fields. Students of the monopoly problem awoke to the fact that outlawing monopolies and contracts in restraint of trade was not enough to prevent their growth, and they urged that to preserve competition Congress must outlaw business practices which threatened to destroy it. Brandeis was the chief spokesman for a group who took the position that large combinations of capital "are inherently uneconomic and wasteful" [10] and that they gain their power through well-known exclusionary practices. Woodrow Wilson had written that anybody who read the newspapers knew what these practices were and that "any decently equipped lawyer" could suggest legislation "by which the whole business can be stopped." [11]

Reformers were not alone in demanding change in the statutes. Businessmen, convinced that unrestrained competition was bad for industry, uncertain as to what they could lawfully do to check it, and fearful that bigness alone laid business open to attack, also wanted the statutes changed. Judge Elbert H. Gary, president of the United States Steel Corporation, testified before the Stanley Committee in 1911 that competition was ruinous, that it served the interests of neither industry nor the public, that it must give way to cooperation under government supervision, and that the Sherman Act was an archaic law inadequate to deal with the

---

9. This is the language of the Senate Committee on Interstate Commerce, Sen. Rep. No. 1326, 62d Cong., 3d Sess. xii (1913).

10. Gerard C. Henderson, *The Federal Trade Commission* (New Haven: Yale University Press, 1924), p. 18. Louis D. Brandeis' testimony before the Senate Committee on Interstate Commerce in its investigation of proposed revisions of the antitrust laws reflected his intimate knowledge of the causes and effects of combination in the steel, shoe machinery, oil, and tobacco industries. *Hearings before the Senate Committee on Interstate Commerce Pursuant to Sen. Res. 98,* 62d Cong. 1146–94, 1196–1291 (1911).

11. Woodrow Wilson, *The New Freedom* (New York: Doubleday, Page, 1913), p. 172. Support for a commission of experts to adapt antitrust laws to the changing needs of a dynamic economy rested, according to Henderson, *op. cit. supra* note 10, at 18, on "a more vivid appreciation of the inherent difficulties of the situation. The forms of unfair and oppressive competition are myriad. By the time Congress has discovered and defined a dozen, a dozen more will be devised and put in operation."

Workable Competition and Antitrust Policy

problems of competition and combinations.[12] George W. Perkins, a former member of J. P. Morgan & Company, testified before the Senate Committee on Interstate Commerce in 1912 that fear engendered by the prosecutions under the Sherman Act was retarding capital investments in the United States, that a businessman did not know "when he is right or when he is wrong . . . until he is prosecuted and his case reaches a court," and that business needed "immediate relief . . . from the uncertainty in which every businessman who is doing anything that approaches a large business finds himself." [13]

In the presidential campaign of 1912 the political parties responded to pressure from the right and from the left, and the antitrust issue obtained a place on all three party platforms.[14] The agitation culminated in the

---

12. *Hearings before the House Committee on Investigation of the United States Steel Corporation*, 62d Cong., 2d Sess. 79, 99 (1911). On February 3, 1912, Judge Gary presented to the Senate Committee on Interstate Commerce his draft of a federal licensing bill requiring all corporations owning $10,000,000 or more in capital stock or assets to apply to a federal corporation commission for a license before doing business in interstate or foreign commerce. The bill would make the issuance of a license depend on the commission's finding that no "unlawful restraint of trade" or "monopoly or attempt to monopolize" was involved in the organization and business of the applicant. A corporation that violated the Sherman Act would forfeit its license or be enjoined from continuing the violation. The federal corporation commission would be authorized to make advance orders on any proposed action and to fix the maximum prices of any product affected while the order was in effect if the commission considered this necessary to prevent monopoly or undue restraint of trade. *Hearings before the Senate Committee on Interstate Commerce Pursuant to Sen. Res. 98*, 62d Cong. 2407 et seq. (1912).

13. *Hearings before the Senate Committee on Interstate Commerce Pursuant to Sen. Res. 98*, 62d Cong. 1092 (1911). Perkins proposed the creation in the Department of Commerce and Labor of "a business court or controlling commission, composed largely of experienced businessmen," authorized to license corporations engaged in interstate or foreign commerce on prescribed conditions and regulations, after which their legality could not be questioned. Violations of this commission's rules and regulations would be punishable by the imprisonment of the individuals responsible "rather than by the revocation of the license of the company." *Id.* at 1091, 1092. Perkins favored giving his proposed commission "very broad power that in practical business questions would be analogous to the power, so to speak, of the Supreme Court. . . ." He felt businessmen wanted not "unnatural contraction of trade" but permission to bring about "a certain proper restraint of competition" that "might mean expanding trade." *Id.* at 1102, 1103. He favored "proper government regulation" and felt that a regulatory commission for large-scale companies "would very soon come to recognize the enormous advantages" of large scale and "a large and scattered public ownership." *Id.* at 1111. He believed "monopoly comes more from methods than it does from the percentage of business," and that instead of the dissolution of consolidations "complete publicity, required by governmental authority and submitted to the people, about these concerns would largely regulate or would be largely a corrective in itself." *Id.* at 1113, 1114.

14. The Republicans stood for legislation to outlaw "those specific acts that uni-

passage of the Clayton and the Federal Trade Commission Acts under a Democratic administration.[15] These acts inaugurated a new policy, a policy designed to preserve competition by regulating it. Aside from the short-lived NRA aberration, which might appropriately be characterized as an attempt to preserve private enterprise by letting it regulate itself, this has remained national policy. But it has not brought businessmen the relief they sought. As the statutes have been interpreted they have not alleviated the feeling of insecurity expressed by big business nor made more certain what businessmen may do to restrain the excesses of competition. Moreover, they have reputedly given to small business protection against a hard competition that threatened its survival.[16]

formly mark attempts to restrain and monopolize trade, to the end that those who honestly intend to obey the law may have a guide to their action and that those who aim to violate the law may the more surely be punished"; and they favored a "federal trade commission" to assure promptness in the administration of the antitrust law and to "avoid delays and technicalities incidental to court procedure." *Republican Campaign Text Book* (1912), pp. 272, 273 quoted by Henderson, *op. cit. supra* note 10, at 16. The Democratic platform enumerated the evils most in need of correcting as holding companies, interlocking directors, stock watering, price discrimination, and "the control by any one corporation of so large a proportion of any industry as to make it a menace to competitive conditions." *Republican Campaign Text Book* at 279, quoted by Henderson, *op cit. supra* note 10, at 17. The Progressives advocated establishment of a federal trade commission and the prohibition of "agreements to divide territory or limit output; refusing to sell to customers who buy from business rivals; to sell below cost in certain areas while maintaining higher prices in other places; using the power of transportation to aid or injure special business concerns; and other unfair trade practices." Roosevelt, *Progressive Principles,* Appendix 318, 319, quoted by Henderson, *op. cit. supra* note 10, at 17, 20.

15. Professor J. A. McLaughlin of the Harvard Law School in 1936 said of the Clayton Act that it "was passed in large part as the outgrowth of controversies started by the promulgation of the so-called 'rule of reason' in 1911. Business men, complaining that they should be told more definitely by congress what they might do, received congressional assistance to the extent that they might at least know certain particular kinds of things which they should not do. It was thought that any legislative policy which merely prohibited certain accurately defined acts and declared all else to be lawful, would simply be inviting evasion. Four sections of the Clayton Act may be regarded as specifications of the kind of practices violative of the policy of the Sherman Act. This does not mean that the Clayton Act was merely declaratory and rendered nothing unlawful which was not unlawful before. Although such an argument was forcefully made by the corporation bar, the second *Shoe Machinery* case established the contrary." "Legal Control of Competitive Methods," 21 Iowa L. Rev. 274, 280–81 (1936).

16. William Simon, *Geographic Pricing Practices* (Chicago: Callaghan, 1950), p. 95; George W. Stocking, "The Law on Basing Point Pricing: Confusion or Competition," 2 J. Pub. Law 1, 14 n. 41 (1953); Stocking and Watkins, *op. cit. supra* note 2, at 369 n. 70; Thomas E. Sunderland, "Save the Sherman Act from Its 'Friends,'" 1950 *Institute on Antitrust Laws and Price Regulations* (Dallas: Southwestern Legal Foundation) at 211, 214–16, 218.

Workable Competition and Antitrust Policy

The Rule of Reason

As the clamor to change the laws has intensified it has not lost its familiar ring. But public-spirited lawyers and economists have contributed a new note. They have developed a set of principles in accordance with which the amended laws are to be administered: the rule of reason and the principle of workable competition.

Basically, of course, the rule of reason is old. In the quarter-century after the *Standard Oil* [17] and *American Tobacco* [18] cases it developed into a settled principle of law in testing the legality of combinations, that, however short of monopoly they may have fallen, changed greatly the structure of American industry and influenced directly the behavior of markets. Under this principle, combinations which restricted competition were held to be lawful as long as the restraint was not unreasonable. Since there is no precise economic standard by which the reasonableness of a restriction on competition can be measured, the courts examined the practices pursued by a corporate giant in achieving and maintaining its position in the market. Predatory practices were indicative of an intent to monopolize the market, and a corporate combination which achieved dominance by indulging in them might be dissolved. Those which behaved in a more exemplary manner, even though their size gave them power over the market, did not transgress the law.[19]

But while the courts thus distinguished between the use and abuse of power achieved by combinations, they steadfastly refused to apply the

17. Standard Oil Co. v. United States, 221 U.S. 1 (1911).
18. United States v. American Tobacco Co., 221 U.S. 106 (1911). United States v. E. I. du Pont de Nemours & Co., 188 Fed. 127 (C.C. Del., 1911), followed shortly in time and closely in principle. In this case the corporate combination under attack had grown out of thirty years' experience in trade association agreements. Seven years after the "rule of reason" opinions Justice Brandeis expounded the rule more concisely: ". . . the legality of an agreement or regulation cannot be determined by so simple a test, as whether it restrains competition. . . . The true test of legality is whether the restraint imposed is such as merely regulates and perhaps thereby promotes competition or whether it is such as may suppress or even destroy competition. To determine that question the court must ordinarily consider the facts peculiar to the business to which the restraint is applied; its condition before and after the restraint was imposed; the nature of the restraint and its effect, actual or probable. The history of the restraint, the evil believed to exist, the reason for adopting the particular remedy, the purpose or end sought to be attained, are all relevant facts." Chicago Board of Trade v. United States, 246 U.S. 231, 238 (1918).
19. The most notable examples of this treatment—"the law does not make mere size an offense"—of course are United States v. United States Steel Corp., 251 U.S. 417 (1920), and United States v. International Harvester Co., 274 U.S. 693, 708 (1927). More recent cases dealing with dominance of a market where no continuing

24

Legality of Trade Association Activities

principle of reasonableness to conspiracies to fix prices. These were per se unlawful.[20] Moreover, both the courts and administrative agencies have rejected the rule of reason in determining the legality of certain types of contracts or conspiracies and have sought to ban them without any specific finding as to their economic consequences.[21] This has made the administration of the statutes simpler and more certain, but it has also restricted business operations. Some think it has hindered, not promoted, business enterprise.[22]

Businessmen, while seeking escape from the uncertainties of a law which for the most part has been applied on a case-by-case basis, are paradoxically demanding that the per se principle be renounced. They want every alleged violation of the antitrust statute to be examined in all of its economic implications and a determination made on a basis of its reasonableness as a restraint on competition. Lawyers, sympathetic with

predatory practices were proved reflect a different view: United States v. Aluminum Co. of America, 148 F. 2d 416, 432 (2d Cir. 1945)—"no monopolist monopolizes unconscious of what he is doing"—and American Tobacco Co. v. United States, 328 U.S. 781, 814 (1946).

20. The classic expression of the principle appears in United States v. Trenton Potteries, 273 U.S. 382, 398 (1927), where the Supreme Court, referring to the *Trans-Missouri Freight Association* case, 166 U.S. 290 (1897), said: ". . . it has since often been decided and always assumed that uniform price-fixing by those controlling in any substantial manner a trade or business in interstate commerce is prohibited by the Sherman Law, despite the reasonableness of the particular prices agreed upon." It should not be overlooked that the *Standard Oil* opinion expressly recognized that certain combinations are *inherently* unreasonable and that it included the freight association rate-fixing cases in this category, saying that there the contracts, which were "fully referred to," created a "conclusive presumption which brought them within the statute." Standard Oil Co. v. United States, 221 U.S. 1, 64, 65 (1911). The per se illegality of price-fixing agreements is the rule of decision in United States v. New Wrinkle, Inc., 342 U.S. 371 (1952); Kiefer-Stewart Co. v. Seagram & Sons, Inc., 340 U.S. 211 (1951); United States v. National Ass'n of Real Estate Boards, 339 U.S. 485 (1950); United States v. United States Gypsum Co., 333 U.S. 364 (1948); United States v. Bausch & Lomb Optical Co., 321 U.S. 707 (1944); United States v. Masonite Corp., 316 U.S. 265 (1942); United States v. Univis Lens Co., 316 U.S. 241 (1942); United States v. Socony-Vacuum Oil Co., 310 U.S. 150 (1940); Ethyl Gasoline Corp. v. United States, 309 U.S. 436 (1940).

21. Section 3 of the Clayton Act forbids the use of tying clauses and exclusive dealing arrangements in sales or leases where their effect "may be to substantially lessen competition or tend to create a monopoly in any line of commerce." 38 Stat. 731 (1914), 15 U.S.C. § 14 (1958). In two important cases to reach the Supreme Court under this section the Court has taken the position that to "foreclose competitors from any substantial market" or to eliminate competition "in a substantial share of the line of commerce affected" establishes a violation of the Act. International Salt Co. v. United States, 332 U.S. 392, 396 (1947); Standard Oil Co. of California v. United States, 337 U.S. 293, 314 (1949).

22. Oppenheim, *supra* note 2; Smith, *supra* note 2; Sunderland, *supra* note 16.

Workable Competition and Antitrust Policy

the problems which antitrust enforcement creates for business and conscious of the vast changes in technology and industrial structure which have taken place since the rule of reason was laid down, find hope in a broader application of the rule. They believe that a statutory requirement that courts and administrative agencies follow the rule of reason in every antitrust case would be better adapted to the needs of the contemporary economy than the varying methods of approach now employed. Oppenheim is one of the most vigorous expositors of this theory. As he puts it, "The Rule of Reason would provide the central artery of a procedural device for considering all relevant legal and economic factors in any given factual situation."[23] Oppenheim proposes to supplement this extension of the judicial process with a statutory requirement that antitrust cases be judged by the principle of workable competition.[24] In this demand some economists have joined.

The Principle of Workable Competition

Economists, schooled in classical theory, have long been disturbed by the discrepancies between the theoretical models they created and the actual structure of the contemporary economy. They have become increasingly aware of the futility of any public policy which aims at creating an industrial structure within which competition works with perfection. They realize not only that imperfect knowledge of markets interferes with the smooth functioning of competition but that mass production and distribution inevitably inject an element of monopoly into modern business. Competition is neither pure nor perfect. So remote from reality had become the neoclassical theory of price competition that Piero Sraffa writing in 1926 said of it:

It is essentially a pedagogic instrument, somewhat like the study of classics, and, unlike the study of the exact sciences and law, its purposes are exclusively those of training the mind, for which reason it is hardly apt to excite the passions of men, even academical men—a theory, in short, in respect to which it is not worthwhile departing from a tradition which is finally accepted."[25]

23. Oppenheim, *supra* note 2, at 1145.
24. Oppenheim explains the manner in which the two concepts interact as follows: "This writer believes that the main bridge for connecting economic and legal concepts with realistic national antitrust policy should be built on the engineering foundation of the Rule of Reason applied through utilization of the concept of Workable Competition." Oppenheim, *supra* note 2, at 1187.
25. "The Laws of Returns under Competitive Conditions," 36 Econ. J. 535–36 (1926).

Legality of Trade Association Activities

Growing recognition of the inadequacy of price theory to explain price behavior eventually produced new doctrines more appropriate to the realities of business organization and operation. Specifically, in 1933 it brought forth in this country Edward Chamberlin's *The Theory of Monopolistic Competition* and in England Joan Robinson's *The Economics of Imperfect Competition*. While these doctrines differ in the details of their logic, they are alike in their recognition of the departure of the contemporary economy from the neoclassical models and in their implications for public policy.

Chamberlinian Theory

Chamberlin's theory, which is more relevant to domestic policy, was concerned with two major problems: How are prices determined in markets occupied by a few sellers selling a standardized product? How are prices determined in markets occupied by few or many sellers selling differentiated products? Both of these situations are typical of modern business and in both, according to the Chamberlinian theory, prices are apt to behave as they would in monopoly markets. Specifically, Chamberlin concluded, on the basis of his very rigorous assumptions—few sellers, a standardized product, identical demand and cost curves—that such sellers, if fully informed and rational (taking account of the indirect as well as the direct consequences of their decisions), would, acting independently, behave like monopolists.[26] They would maximize profits by restricting output and keeping prices at the monopoly level. The public would get less and would pay more for what it got, other things being equal, than it would in a market of many sellers. Chamberlin also concluded that many sellers selling a differentiated product would get more for it and produce less of it at a higher cost than would an equal number of sellers selling a standardized product. Chamberlin is primarily a theorist and as such has been only incidentally concerned with policy, but the policy implications of his theory of monopolistic competition are clear. Rational behavior in competitive markets of the neoclassical models promoted the public welfare by insuring that prices would in the long run cover the average cost of efficient producers and guide resources into economical

---

26. As Chamberlin put it: "If each [of two or a few sellers] seeks his maximum profit rationally and intelligently ... the equilibrium result is the same as though there were a monopolistic agreement between them." Chamberlin, *The Theory of Monopolistic Competition* (7th ed.; Cambridge: Harvard University Press, 1957), p. 48.

channels. Rational behavior in markets of "monopolistic competition" results in output restriction, higher prices, and an uneconomical utilization of resources.

These unhappy implications, coupled with the contention of other economists that modern technology necessitates only a small number of large firms in many markets, created a dilemma.[27] To obtain the economies of mass production we need only a few firms in major sectors of our economy; but when only a few firms occupy a market, they behave like monopolists.

Clark's Concept of Workable Competition

But economists are a resourceful lot. Having created a dilemma, they resolved it. They did so by developing the concept of workable competition. Numerous economists have contributed to the concept, but in its initial formulation John M. Clark pioneered.[28] Clark, recognizing the impossibility of achieving perfect competition in our economy, argued that (1) some unavoidable departures from the competitive norm may justify other departures;[29] (2) in the long run potential competition and the competition of substitutes may force sellers, even when they are few in number, to behave like competitors; and (3) unrestrained competition in periods of weak demand which forces prices down to marginal costs may prove disastrous in the long run, because prices in periods of strong demand will not rise enough above average cost to insure that average cost will be covered over both phases of the cycle.

In brief, Clark argued that in the long run rivalry among few sellers approximates the competitive solution, and that in the short run the power of oligopolists to influence prices performs a socially salutary function by holding prices above marginal cost in times of weak demand. He also argued that quality competition among sellers of differentiated products may serve the public as well as or better than price competition. Clark recognized that no two markets are alike, that they vary in the degree and kind of competition, and that the social acceptability of any market situation must be judged by its performance. The workability of a particular industrial situation is to be judged by available alternatives.

27. Burns, *op. cit. supra* note 2, especially chap. 1.
28. Clark, "Toward a Concept of Workable Competition," 30 Am. Econ. Rev. (Proceedings of the American Economic Ass'n) 241 (1940).
29. For example, where two-way mobility of capital is lacking in a period of slack demand, the presence of many sellers in a market might result in ruinous competition and a sick industry. *Id.* at 242.

Legality of Trade Association Activities

But he contended that even though in some markets sellers may have some degree of monopoly power, no better alternative may be available and such power as they have has a positive social value.[30]

Since the concept of workable competition is applicable to quasi-monopolistic situations, a more precise term might be "workable monopoly," but this is not a concept around which public loyalty may readily be developed.

Modifications of Clark's Concept

Taking Clark's notions as a point of departure, other economists have tried to enumerate and define the conditions and describe the behavior which make quasi-monopolistic markets socially acceptable.[31] On some characteristics they agree; on some they do not. Few theorists, if any, would dispute that the departures from competition are socially unacceptable if they are the product of collusion or conspiracy. In short, few economists would defend rigging the market, but no doubt they would disagree on what constitutes market-rigging. Most would insist that any market situation that is acceptable must provide two or more independent sources of supply for any particular product, or make available satisfactory substitutes on equally attractive terms. Outright monopoly is not workably competitive. Most economists would hold that for competition to be workable no artificial obstacles must block entry;[32] most would hold

---

30. In another work Clark has qualified his position on this point. He recognizes that monopolists cannot always be relied on to promote the public welfare. As he puts it, "A monopolist does not typically price for the utmost possible immediate profit that curves of demand and cost permit, but seeks expanding business at a profit that seems to him reasonable. It is not exactly safe to let him be the sole judge of reasonableness in his own case; in fact, it is thoroughly unsound. . . . The trouble with monopoly is not that it always leads to the kind of pricing which theory assumes, but rather that it can do so, and is virtually sure to distort pricing in that direction, leaving the monopolist too wide a range of arbitrary discretion." Clark, *Alternative to Serfdom* (Oxford: B. Blackwell, 1948), pp. 65, 66.

31. Adelman, *supra* note 2; Joe S. Bain, "Workable Competition in Oligopoly," 40 Am. Econ. Rev. (Proceedings of the American Economic Ass'n) 35 (1950); Edwards, *Maintaining Competition,* at 9–10; Jesse W. Markham, "An Alternative Approach to Workable Competition," 40 Am. Econ. Rev. 349 (1950); Edward S. Mason, "Methods of Developing a Proper Control of Big Business," 18 Acad. Pol. Sci. Proc. (No. 2) 40 (1939); Mason, "The Current Status of the Monopoly Problem in the United States," 62 Harv. L. Rev. 1265 (1949); George J. Stigler, "The Extent and Bases of Monopoly," 32 Am. Econ. Rev. (No. 2, Supplement, Pt. 2) 2, 3 (1942); Clair Wilcox, *Competition and Monopoly in American Industry* (TNEC Monograph 21, 1940).

32. But Bain argues that complete freedom of entry in oligopolistic markets would contribute to inefficiency and an unstable market. Bain, *supra* note 31, at 43.

Workable Competition and Antitrust Policy

that there must be a "considerable" or a "sufficient" number of firms, but according to Adelman competition is compatible with "many small firms . . . with a few large ones . . . and with large and small ones together." [33] Other economists stress performance rather than structure in giving content to the term "workable competition." According to their approach the workability of imperfect competition depends on the flexibility of prices with changing costs, the presence of interindustry competition, the rate of product and process improvement, the level of profits, the role of selling expenditures, and cost-price and capacity-output relationships.

Certainly the concept is vague and the standard of performance by which it is to be determined is imprecise. Markham's somewhat abstruse definition illustrates the difficulty which economists experience in determining whether any particular industrial situation is workably competitive:

> An industry may be judged to be workably competitive when, after the structural characteristics of its market and the dynamic factors that shaped them have been thoroughly examined, there is no clearly indicated change that can be effected through public policy measures that would result in greater social gains than social losses.[34]

Just as economists find it hard to define accurately workable competition or to establish criteria by which it can be readily recognized, so they find it difficult to formulate policy about it which lends itself to easy administration. As early as 1937 Mason stated the problem when he said that the formulation of public policy requires "a distinction between situations and practices which are to be approved as in the public interest and those which are to be disapproved. . . ." [35] More recently he recognized how difficult this goal is when he said:

> The relative importance to be assigned to the objective of establishing appropriate market limitations on the scope of action of firms as against the objective of encouraging efficient performance in the use of economic resources no doubt presents serious difficulties. It seems probable that individual judgments will always be influenced to some extent by ideological considerations.[36]

In short, if economists are to appraise industrial arrangements, judgments on their competitive workability are apt to be greatly influenced by the preconceptions of the appraisers.[37]

33. Adelman, *supra* note 2, at 1303.
34. Markham, *supra* note 31, at 361.
35. Mason, "Monopoly in Law and Economics," 47 Yale L. J. 34 (1937).
36. Mason, "The Current Status of the Monopoly Problem in the United States," 62 Harv. L. Rev. 1265, 1283 (1949).
37. Perhaps my preconceptions will be known to some readers, but I should like

Legality of Trade Association Activities

TRADE ASSOCIATION ACTIVITIES

I propose to examine the development of antitrust law in its application to one sector of the economy, the activities of trade associations, in the light of the rule of reason and the principle of workable competition. I have chosen this sector not because of its current importance but because it becomes important whenever the economy moves from a sellers' into a buyers' market. During World War II and the decade after, businessmen found it easy to sell goods at continuously higher prices. An inflationary economy provided an environment friendly to competition. With nearly everybody making money, trade rivals need not act collectively to improve their individual lot. But when the going gets tough, if precedent can be relied on, they may seek mutual aid through cooperation. Adjusting to new demand-supply relationships frequently brings financial hardships. As competition becomes keener businessmen are apt to regard it as less trustworthy. While extolling the virtues of an individualistic economy businessmen may resent the ruthlessness of impersonal market forces. George Shea, writing in the *Wall Street Journal* in 1953, put it this way:

Like the fight against weeds in a country garden, the fight against monopoly in the business system is never ended. No one anywhere holds stronger antitrust opinions than the American business man. To the banner of free, merciless competition he owns an allegiance second only to his love for his country's flag. But when his sales prices are undercut, he often gives vent to an expression of moral indignation.[38]

Sometimes he also takes positive steps to alleviate his lot. These may range from such extreme action as that taken in 1953 by the rug merchants in Albany, New York, in organizing a "vigilante committee" which, according to a report in *Retailing Daily*, was "determined to try to put cut-rate floor coverings houses out of business in this area,"[39] to the more restrained activities of trade associations anxious to steer a safe course between the Scylla of antitrust and the Charybdis of insolvency.

to restate them. I believe in a free-enterprise economy, and I view with suspicion arrangements designed to subject market forces to concerted control through either governmental or private action. I do not believe in laissez faire. I think the government has a responsibility to create an economic and political environment favorable to free enterprise and that society cannot rely solely on competition to achieve economic stability.
38. Wall Street Journal, Nov. 16, 1953, p. 1, col. 5.
39. Retailing Daily, October 16, 1953, p. 16, col. 5. The president of Capital District Floor Coverings Association in announcing the formation of a "vigilante committee" outlined the steps the committee would take. The committee would act as "moral guiders" to price cutters but, if this proved insufficient, would request

Workable Competition and Antitrust Policy

In tracing the development of the law on trade associations I shall be concerned with the specific question: Was the arrangement under governmental attack a workably competitive one, or did it transgress the principles of workability and hence become an appropriate object of condemnation? To facilitate judgment on this issue, I shall first analyze in general terms the economics of trade association market-reporting activities and lay down a specific standard by which their competitive workability may be judged. The reader will thereby have an intelligent basis for agreeing or disagreeing with my conclusions.

The Function of Price in a Competitive Economy

To understand the significance of trade association activities in the operation of an effectively competitive economy, it is necessary to keep in mind the function of price in such an economy. Price is a mechanism by which to organize economic activity.[40] In a price economy cost-price relationships guide the use of a community's productive factors. They reflect the relative urgency of the demand for the myriad of commodities and services which a division of labor makes possible and for which consumers spend their incomes. When cost and price get out of balance, too little or too much of a commodity is being produced. The imbalance is repaired by the movement of economic resources away from or toward the point of instability. "High" prices serve as a magnet to pull resources into an industry whose goods are in relatively strong demand; "low" prices, as a repellent to push resources out of an industry that is producing in "overabundance." The adjustments are automatic. They are not made by a central planning agency whose directives are authoritative and which wants to promote the general welfare. On the contrary, they result from the voluntary decisions of rational businessmen who want to make money by selling goods.

To state these principles reflects no naïve and unsophisticated faith in

the mill representative supplying the price cutters to stop selling to them; the next step would be to persuade members of the association to stop dealing with the manufacturer who supplied the price cutters. Since manufacturers as well as retailers were members of the association, action by its committee was expected to be effective.

40. For discussions of this point see Kenneth E. Boulding, *Economic Analysis* (rev. ed.; New York: Harper, 1948) pp. 117–20; Frank H. Knight, *The Economic Organization* (mimeographed reprint, University of Chicago, 1933), chap. VIII, "The Price System and the Economic Process"; Stigler, *The Theory of Price* (rev. ed.; New York: Macmillan, 1952) p. 8; Stocking and Watkins, *op. cit. supra* note 2, at 6–9, 100–2.

Legality of Trade Association Activities

an invisible hand guiding economic activities toward remote but beautiful goals. Competitive forces in a machine society work imperfectly. Serious obstacles and frictions impede the movement of resources. These obstacles cannot always be overcome without someone's being hurt. Getting into an industry may not be easy and getting out is likely to be harder. Where entry is blocked, those already in may reap abnormal rewards in the face of strong demand. Where egress is blocked, those in may suffer hardship or even disaster when demand falls off. The fortunate like price competition; the unfortunate despise their misfortune and seek to escape it. And who can blame them? But while some may suffer from competitive readjustments, society may benefit from a more economical use of limited resources.

A dynamic society is subject to frequent disturbances. Some of these are the inevitable consequences of changes in the tastes and habits of consumers or changes in the ways in which their tastes and habits are satisfied. When such changes take place, they affect cost and consumption "functions"—to use the jargon of my profession—and they necessitate corrective changes in the use of resources. The difficulty in making the indicated adjustments is a function of the state of business activity: when business is expanding the adjustments are relatively easy; when it is contracting they are more difficult. In truth, the forces making for change in the general level of economic activity may conceal the forces making for readjustments within a particular industry. And this may confuse the government in the exercise of its responsibility toward economic change. Businessmen, however wise they may be, are unlikely ever by independent action to eliminate the excessively rhythmical character of business activity. The government by sound monetary and fiscal policies may learn to ameliorate if not to eliminate it; and if democratic states are to survive, I suspect they must learn to do so.

But the state's obligation toward the specific maladjustments within particular industries occasioned by changes in methods of production, the discovery of new sources of raw materials, the development of new products, changes in consumers' tastes and wants, and the like, is of a different order. If society is to progress, the state should aim at facilitating, not at blocking, such readjustments. It should also try to create an environment within which businessmen can make informed decisions and thereby fewer mistakes.

This leads us to a more specific consideration of the competitive nature of markets and of the role that trade associations may play in them.

Workable Competition and Antitrust Policy

The Nature of Markets

A market is an area within which the forces of demand and supply converge to establish a price. In the perfectly competitive market as the economists have conceived it the buyers and sellers of a standardized commodity are so numerous and so well informed that none has any influence on the price for which the product sells. Sellers are free to sell or withhold their products from the market as best suits the interest of each. Buyers are free to buy or to refrain from buying according to their several judgments. But sellers who sell and buyers who buy do so at identical prices at any moment of time. The prevailing price is one at which the amount offered equals the amount which buyers will take. It clears the market. It is the equilibrium price of the economic theorists.

But real markets differ from the economic models. Save in the produce market, sellers generally quote a price and sell what they can at that price. Their job is to insure a continuous flow of goods through sellers to consumers. They will not continue at it unless in the long run they can cover their costs. They must inevitably look to the future as well as the present, and they try so to order their business that they will survive. To do this they need to acquaint themselves with all available information which affects market behavior. Buyers similarly need access to market information if they are to buy wisely. Whether they buy as ultimate consumers or as intermediaries themselves engaged in the production of goods and services for sale, buyers want to get the best bargain they can, in one case to maximize satisfactions, in the other to minimize costs. Both buyers and sellers, therefore, have a legitimate interest in such market statistical data as current output, inventories, orders, shipments, prices, and the like. Rational entrepreneurs not only live in the present; they plan for the future. The market aids them in their planning, for it is not only a mechanism by which the forces of demand and supply are brought into equilibrium, it is a means of communication by which buyers and sellers learn significant facts essential for wise decisions. Businessmen continuously reshape their plans and modify their production programs on a basis of what they learn about market behavior. It is only by doing so that they can perform efficiently their function of coordinating the means of production and allocating economically society's limited productive factors.

Eddy's The New Competition

Society has an interest in removing obstacles to the dissemination of

Legality of Trade Association Activities

basic market data among both buyers and sellers and in facilitating their easy and continuous flow. Trade associations are appropriate mechanisms for spreading the necessary information, and they may make competition more workable. Arthur Jerome Eddy, a distinguished corporation lawyer, recognized this almost fifty years ago and not only became a professional organizer of "open-price associations" but developed a philosophy in justification of them. His *The New Competition,* published in 1912, became a sort of bible to businessmen who recognized the need to cooperate in informing each other about the market. Eddy, however, apparently aimed at something more than mere dissemination of market information as a basis for independent, informed decision-making by trade rivals, for he denounced competition as war and war as hell. He condemned as "inhuman" the struggle which permits only the fittest to survive, and he advocated the thoroughgoing replacement of competition by cooperation. He encouraged a live-and-let-live policy under the umbrella of which business units, big and little, efficient and inefficient, would survive. About this he said:

> So far from promoting progress, competition stays and hinders. . . . Rightfully viewed, there is not a single good result accomplished by man in . . . economics . . . that should not be attained by intelligent and far-sighted cooperation.[41]

But despite his comprehensive condemnation of competition, his advocacy of "open pricing" as a basis for rational behavior is, as Fetter pointed out many years ago, "in some respects in harmony both with the lessons of the history of markets and with contemporary needs for recreating effectual competitive conditions."[42]

The economic standard for judging the propriety of the cooperative interchange of market data by trade rivals in a free-enterprise economy should be: Is it designed to promote informed but *independent* decisions by trade rivals and by their customers in order that they may adjust their operations more intelligently to the vagaries of the market, or is it designed to achieve a common judgment among business rivals about their business policies and a common pattern of behavior which will bring security to all of them? Setting up this standard means, of course, resort to reason in the administration and application of the antitrust statutes. It necessitates a review of all the relevant factors and a determination of whether the fact-spreading activities of a particular trade association

41. Arthur J. Eddy, *The New Competition* (New York: Appleton, 1912), p. 26.
42. Frank A. Fetter, *The Masquerade of Monopoly* (New York: Harcourt, Brace, 1931), p. 209.

Workable Competition and Antitrust Policy

are designed to promote the public welfare by making competition workable or to promote business welfare by making cooperation work. This should be the test.

I propose, then, to re-examine the leading open-price-association cases and to test the validity of the courts' disposition of them in the light of the principle I have set up. The specific question I shall try to answer is, were the activities designed to overcome market imperfections and insure rational, independent, and informed decisions by business rivals—who have assumed the risks of private enterprise—and thereby to make competition more effective; or were they designed to substitute for individual competitive effort cooperation on business policies and practices in an attempt to eliminate risks and bring greater security to businessmen who have associated themselves for those purposes? I shall deal briefly with the cases in which I think the courts' opinions are in harmony with this principle and in greater detail with the cases in which I think they conflict with it.

Hardwood Lumber Manufacturers Association

The Hardwood Lumber Manufacturers Association's "open competition plan" was a forthright experiment in Eddy's new competition. Members of the plan borrowed their slogan—"Cooperation, not Competition, is the Life of Trade" [43]—from Eddy and patterned their statistical activities along the lines laid down by him. A manager of statistics collected from each member of the plan monthly data on stocks, current production, and estimates of future production. On the first of each month each member filed his price list with the manager of statistics and reported promptly all departures from list. Each member reported daily all sales, showing to whom the lumber was sold, at what price, and on what terms. To verify his report each member sent with it an exact copy of each invoice sent to a customer and subjected his books and records to a detailed audit by representatives of the association. The manager of statistics sent all members monthly reports showing each member's production, stocks on hand, and official price lists. He also furnished weekly reports covering sales and shipments, showing to whom each sale was made, by whom, and at what price. He reported to all members every departure from list prices made by any member.

43. United States v. American Column & Lumber Co., 263 Fed. 147, 149 (1920). The description in the text of the open-price plan is based on the district court's decision and the Supreme Court's opinion, American Column & Lumber Co. v. United States, 257 U.S. 377 (1921).

Legality of Trade Association Activities

The association's plan did not include supplying this information to buyers, and the information was in far greater detail than necessary for independent decision-making by lumber manufacturers who merely wanted to plan their own production programs wisely. What businessmen need for intelligent decisions in competitive markets is general information which reveals the strength of market forces and the direction of their movement. Detailed information mutually exchanged by rival sellers, identifying each seller, each buyer, the quality of lumber, and the price and terms of sale, is more essential for cooperative than for independent decision-making. Moreover, the plan did not permit each member independently to evaluate the significance of his own market policy of other business transactions. Rather, it provided machinery for translating specific market data into a common market policy. At periodic meetings the members discussed the statistical position of the industry and the price and production policies necessary to exploit it fully. The manager of statistics sent members a monthly market letter in which he indicated the policy implications of the market information supplied members. As he put it on one occasion: "With this information before him it is difficult to see how any intelligent hardwood manufacturer can entertain any hesitation as to *the proper course for him to pursue* in selling his lumber." [44]

Clearly the association's activities were not designed to insure an intel-

---

44. American Column & Lumber Co. v. United States, 257 U.S. 377, 405 (1921). Each member of the plan subscribed to the principle that "[k]*nowledge regarding prices actually made is all that is necessary to keep prices at reasonably stable and normal levels.*" *Id.* at 393. But members did not rely on independent interpretations of market data to insure this result. One of the chief duties of their manager of statistics was to make a "harmonized" interpretation of the confidential reports coming to him. On paper the plan provided for monthly meetings of district groups of members, but in practice the members met almost weekly during the period January 31, 1919, to February 19, 1920. Before each meeting the manager of statistics sent out a questionnaire in which he asked each member eleven questions, including the member's estimate of his production for the next two months and his view of market conditions for the next few months, with his reasons. On the basis of members' answers the manager of statistics distributed *his* estimate of prospective market conditions to members at the meeting and mailed it to those not present. The minutes of the meetings and the sales reports contained repeated warnings against overproduction, which would be "killing the goose that laid the golden egg," would "spell disaster," be "criminal folly," and "commercial suicide." *Id.* at 403. Constant exhortations at the meetings and in the sales reports and market letters worked to build up an expectation of higher prices and a common determination to demand them. For example, in the market letter of April 26, 1919, after pointing out that stocks were less than 75 per cent of normal, production was about 60 per cent of normal, and demand was far in excess of supply, the manager of statistics rejoiced: "The demand is with us, the supply inadequate, therefore, values must increase, as our competition in hardwoods is only among ourselves." *Id.* at 406.

ligent and informed business rivalry by which competitive cost-price relationships could be established and an economical allocation of resources and distribution of income could be effected. On the contrary, association members engaged in a cooperative interpretation of market data and a coordination of market policy designed to bring security and profits to them at the expense of those who bought their lumber. It is not surprising, therefore, that the Supreme Court said of the "plan":

> Genuine competitors do not make daily, weekly and monthly reports of the minutest details of their business to their rivals, as the defendants did; they do not contract, as was done here, to submit their books to the discretionary audit and their stocks to the discretionary inspection of their rivals for the purpose of successfully competing with them; and they do not submit the details of their business to the analysis of an expert, jointly employed, and obtain from him a "harmonized" estimate of the market as it is and as, in his specially and confidentially informed judgment, it promises to be. This is not the conduct of competitors but is so clearly that of men united in an agreement, express or implied, to act together and pursue a common purpose under a common guide that, if it did not stand confessed a combination to restrict production and increase prices in interstate commerce and as, therefore, a direct restraint upon that commerce, as we have seen that it is, that conclusion must inevitably have been inferred from the facts which were proved. To pronounce such abnormal conduct on the part of 365 natural competitors, controlling one-third of the trade of the country in an article of prime necessity, a "new form of competition" and not an old form of combination in restraint of trade, as it so plainly is, would be for this court to confess itself blinded by words and forms to realities which men in general very plainly see and understand and condemn, as an old evil in a new dress and with a new name."[45]

I do not see how an application of the rule of reason supplemented by the principle of workable competition as this study has formulated it could have led to any other conclusion.

LINSEED CRUSHERS COUNCIL

My judgment of the *Linseed Oil* case [46] is similar. Here the evidence is very clear that the purpose of the Linseed Crushers Council was to subordinate independent decision-making by which informed competitors might facilitate the operation of market forces and to promote group action serving private interests at the expense of the public welfare. The market data which the Armstrong Bureau of Related Industries collected

---

45. *Id.* at 410.
46. United States v. American Linseed Oil Co., 275 Fed. 939 (N.D. Ill. 1921), *rev'd*, 262 U.S. 371 (1923).

Legality of Trade Association Activities

and disseminated for the Linseed Crushers Council was for the *exclusive* use of the sellers of linseed products. Buyers did not get it. On their face the details of the information supplied by and disseminated to members of the council were designed to discourage, not to encourage, independent decision-making by trade rivals. They were the foundation on which group action could be built. By contracting to supply each other with price lists, to reveal all quotations or sales below list, and to forfeit Liberty bonds for failure to comply with any provision of the contract, council members revealed a purpose to cooperate in exploiting the market for linseed products. As the Supreme Court put it in condemning the association:

> With intimate knowledge of the affairs of other producers and obligated as stated, but proclaiming themselves competitors, the subscribers went forth to deal with widely separated and unorganized customers necessarily ignorant of the true conditions. Obviously they were not *bona fide* competitors; their claim in that regard is at war with common experience and hardly compatible with fair dealing.[47]

Maple Flooring Manufacturers Association

Lacking conspiratorial arrangements, maple-flooring manufacturers would find it difficult to restrict competition. Although not conforming precisely to the economists' model of perfect competition, this industry approximates it. Over the centuries God, not man, has created the potential supply of maple lumber and its kindred products beech and birch, and long ago He made them abundantly. Monkeys used them before man. The learned brief of the defendants in the *Maple Flooring* case [48] tells us that all three woods date back to the Miocene era, "long before man's prehuman ancestors had abandoned their arboreal habits. . . . [These woods] preceded the Tool-maker and Dreamer by at least some 500,000 years." [49] And when the North American Dreamer began to fashion them to his imaginative needs, they were here in profusion. When he ran afoul of the law in 1923, the maple, beech, and birch stand in the continental United States totalled an estimated 86,000,000,000 board feet, distributed unevenly but widely among the New England, Middle Atlantic, South Atlantic, Lower Mississippi, Central, and Lake States.[50]

Our domestic "Tool-makers and Dreamers" had not got around to using

---

47. United States v. American Linseed Oil Co., 262 U.S. 371, 389–90 (1923).
48. Maple Flooring Manufacturers Ass'n v. United States, 268 U.S. 563 (1925).
49. Brief and Argument for Appellants, at 25 n. 5. All references to "Record," briefs, and exhibits in this section apply to the *Maple Flooring* case.
50. Defendants' Exhibit DD, Record, Vol. IV, at 838.

Workable Competition and Antitrust Policy

these woods extensively until the 1890's. Their very excellence delayed their use. They are very hard and therefore hard to fashion. Until cutting tools had been perfected, lumberers preferred to work on softer materials. But when the tools became available, the "Tool-makers and Dreamers" and even the less imaginative (but possibly more aggressive) tool users, the hard-boiled lumberjacks, tutored in the stern realities of the craft, found it relatively easy to get into the business. The required tools were relatively cheap and the know-how was simple.

Processes in Making Flooring

Making flooring involves three major operations.[51] The first stage includes felling the trees, cutting the logs into suitable lengths, and skidding them to a loading point. The second step involves the making of rough lumber. From the loading point trucks or trains transport the logs to a mill where they are dumped in a pond of water (heated in the winter) to cleanse them of sand. Removed to the sawmill, the logs are machine-sawed into the desired thickness and width and the larger defects are removed. They are then graded, cross-piled, and air-dried for from nine to eighteen months. Seasoning is a meticulous business, and after air-drying the lumber is dried in kilns—generally concrete or brick structures but occasionally wood, customarily about a hundred feet long by eighteen feet wide—through which the lumber slowly moves on steel trucks. The trip through the kiln requires from six to seven days. As the logs journey forward, the moisture content of the air in the kiln is gradually reduced. The lumber is eventually discharged into a cooling room where it remains until its temperature has been reduced to that of the finishing mill.

The third stage yields finished flooring. In the finishing mills the flooring is ripped to desired widths, double-surfaced, tongued and grooved, and polished. It is then graded and warehoused in steam-heated storage rooms ready for shipment to lumber dealers and building contractors.[52]

An Industry Easy to Enter

Obviously, integrated firms conducting these several operations and owning their own lumber may have a relatively large investment, depending on the size of their live timber reserves and their scale of operations.

---

51. This description of the processes in making flooring is based on the record in the *Maple Flooring* case and may be out of date.
52. Record, Vol. I, at 199; Vol. II, at 512–16.

Legality of Trade Association Activities

But most mills specialize in either the making of rough lumber or the making of finished flooring. Although 14 of the 22 members of the Maple Flooring Manufacturers Association in 1923 owned timber,[53] in 1920 in Michigan and Wisconsin alone 476 sawmill operators and in the entire country more than 4,000 operators produced rough maple lumber.[54] Precise data on the number of makers of finished flooring are not available, but the number must have been large. To say that the basic capital equipment consisted of a buzz saw and a place to put it is to oversimplify. But such oversimplification reflects the ease with which businessmen could get into the maple-flooring industry. An economist for the association testified that data obtained from various members indicated that $30,000 would command the capital equipment for making maple, beech, and birch flooring and that the equipment could be bought on a free market.[55] His statement was neither challenged nor rejected. Every lumber dealer is a potential flooring manufacturer, and some dealers do in fact saw their own lumber. A representative of the Brown Lumber Company of Traverse City, Michigan, testified that in 1920 his company bought for $5,000 the essential equipment for making maple flooring, exclusive of installation costs, and produced 1,200,000 feet of maple flooring in 1922.[56] Moreover, the makers of some other kinds of flooring, oak and fir, for example, use the same kind of equipment and can and do shift production from one product to another in response to market forces. When it pays to shift from one branch of production to another, some of them shift.[57]

Joint Costs

But not only do flooring makers find it easy to get into the business, once they get there they produce a variety of floorings under joint costs. This makes it difficult to determine average or marginal cost for any particular grade of flooring and hence complicates the pricing problem. One of the positive achievements of the Maple Flooring Manufacturers Association has been its standardization of grades. Under its standardization program rough maple, beech, and birch lumber fall into the following grades in order of excellence: firsts, seconds (or clear), selects, No. 1 common, No. 2 common, No. 3-A common, No. 3 common.[58] Firsts and sec-

53. Defendants' Exhibit DD-1, Record, Vol. IV, at 839.
54. Defendants' Gordon Exhibit 5, Record, Vol. V, at 897.
55. Record, Vol. II, at 632.
56. Record, Vol. I, at 91–92.
57. Record, Vol. I, at 84, 88, 137; Vol. II, at 526, 771.
58. Record, Vol. I, at 197; Vol. II, at 511–12.

Workable Competition and Antitrust Policy

onds, selects, and better grades of common No. 1 are used primarily in automobiles and similar durable goods requiring the best of materials. The common grades account for most of the flooring. Just as the rough maple lumber has been graded to meet different requirements, so maple, beech, and birch flooring falls into three grades, clear, No. 1, and factory. Not only do floorings differ in quality, but they differ in width and thickness, and these have been similarly standardized. Unfortunately, nature has circumscribed the discretion of the flooring manufacturer in determining what grades and sizes of flooring he will make. In truth, he must ordinarily make all three grades and a variety of widths if he is to avoid costly wastage.[59] This makes a flooring manufacturer peculiarly vulnerable to the shifts in consumer requirements. In meeting the demand for flooring of any particular grade and size, other grades and sizes must be produced. It is costly to warehouse them and, as one maker expressed it, it may be "necessary for us to sell . . . [certain] widths in the markets where they are used, regardless of price, when our surplus gets to a point where we feel that we must unload." [60]

Flooring Industry Resembles Competitive Model

Finally, the buyers of flooring are for the most part informed and experienced. They are wholesale and retail lumber dealers who through trade journals and market representatives learn promptly at what prices lumber is available. The large buyers customarily send out inquiries by mail or wire to many rival sellers asking for prices on specified quantities and grades, and they buy where they can buy cheapest.[61]

In short, both the structure of the flooring industry and the structure of the market for flooring contribute to vigorous competition in its sale. When demand is strong and profits are high, supply is likely to respond promptly. A decline in demand is likely to bring about sharp competition and a decline in prices and ultimately to force a contraction in production facilities. Thus, as previously stated, while not conforming precisely to the theorists' model of perfect competition, the floormaking industry closely approximates it. Sellers are many, entrance is easy, the product has been

---

59. Record, Vol. I, at 94. In the language of one witness, "The manufacturer has no choice as to the grades that he will produce. All three grades of flooring can be manufactured from cull lumber. We cannot, for instance, manufacture Clear flooring at one time, No. 1 at another, and Factory at another." Record, Vol. I, at 199.
60. *Ibid.*
61. Record, Vol. I, at 291–92, 410–27, 429, 436–48; Vol. II, at 450–61, 466–69, 530–38, 560, 564, 571–77, 578, 581, 584, 588, 597, 605, 617–24.

Legality of Trade Association Activities

standardized, buyers and sellers are well informed. In the absence of collusive arrangements that prevent it, prices are likely to be exceedingly flexible, responding promptly to changes in cost and changes in the intensity of demand.

Government Alleges Conspiracy

In a complaint filed on March 5, 1923, in the District Court for the Western District of Michigan the United States alleged such collusive arrangements. It charged the Maple Flooring Manufacturers Association and its several members with having conspired to fix the price of maple, beech, and birch flooring in violation of Section 1 of the Sherman Antitrust Act. The government alleged that the defendants carried out the conspiracy through the association's activities, chief of which were its statistical program covering costs, freight rates, and market conditions, and through association meetings at which these matters were discussed and views about them exchanged. The district court found the defendants guilty and in doing so rejected their plea that relief be confined to an injunction against "the specific transactions which may be found to be objectionable." [62] In rejecting the defendants' plea the court concluded that "the evidence . . . shows clearly that the fundamental and primary purposes and objects of this combination are unlawful and relief short of terminating its existence and restraining defendants from entering into other agreements or combinations of like character would be insufficient and inadequate." [63]

Supreme Court Finds Arrangement Legal

Had this decision stood, contemporary proponents of the rule of reason and of the principle of workable competition as a guide to administrative agencies and the courts in enforcing antitrust statutes might have found a reasonable basis for demanding a change in the statutes. But the decision did not stand. The Supreme Court in overruling it gave its unqualified approval to trade association activities of the sort which businessmen recognize as essential to sound decision-making in competitive markets. The Court said:

We decide only that trade associations or combinations of persons or corpo-

62. District court's opinion, United States v. Maple Flooring Manufacturers Ass'n (W.D. Mich. 1923) (unreported), Record, Vol. I, at 52, 60.
63. Ibid.

rations which openly and fairly gather and disseminate information as to the cost of their product, the volume of production, the actual price which the product has brought in past transactions, stocks of merchandise on hand, approximate cost of transportation from the principal point of shipment to the points of consumption, as did these defendants, and who, as they did, meet and discuss such information and statistics *without however reaching or attempting to reach any agreement or any concerted action with respect to prices or production or restraining competition*, do not thereby engage in unlawful restraint of commerce.[64]

What more could businessmen who believe in competition want? Indeed it is possible that in the *Maple Flooring* case they got more than they were entitled to under antitrust statutes designed to keep competition workable and preserve free enterprise. About this economists like judges are apt to disagree. But to test the above statement requires a brief résumé of the history of trade associations in the maple-flooring industry. Such a history will reveal purpose and method. Effect is doubtless of greater significance in determining the acceptability of any control scheme that is to be judged by the standards of "workable" competition, but as to effects opinions may frequently differ. "By their fruits ye shall know them" may be a good botanical guide, but the fruits of economic arrangements are not always so readily identifiable. It may help, therefore, to see what was planted.

Earlier Associations

Trade associations in the maple-flooring industry date back to about 1900 [65] and with frequent modifications in their provisions have operated continuously or with brief interruptions from that date until this. Between 1905 and March 1923, when the government's suit was filed, seven different associations had come and gone. But judged by their general

64. Maple Flooring Manufacturers Ass'n v. United States, 268 U.S. 563, 586 (1925). Emphasis supplied. The record indicates that the association's statistical activities went beyond the open gathering and dissemination approved by the Court. Only members who made a weekly sales report to the secretary received the association's composite report showing the details of each significant sale reported; and only a *summary* of the *average* prices, delivered and net, realized during the week was reported to the public. See testimony of George W. Keehn, the association's secretary, Record, Vol. I, at 125–26.

65. Counsel for the maple-flooring manufacturers stated that association methods had followed "a more or less orderly evolution" since 1897. Appellants' Supplemental Reply Brief at 22. The district court's opinion referred to 1895 as the first year of trade association activity. Record, Vol. I, at 55. The Government's Brief before the Supreme Court, at 11, stated: "So far as the record shows the first trade association was organized in 1905."

Legality of Trade Association Activities

spirit and purpose and to a lesser extent by their membership [66] and specific provisions, they were like the little babbling brook which the poet heard say,

>For men may come and men may go,
>But I go on forever.

Counsel for the defendants objected to including in the record evidence on the activities of the forerunners of the association against which the complaint ran. As counsel put it: "[T]he purpose of the petitioner in bringing into this case long-extinct associations and plans which had been abandoned years before the institution of this suit, was to prejudice the *present association* and confuse the issues." [67] This criticism may be appropriate in a lawsuit, but it does not apply here. I am not here interested in determining the legality of the arrangements engaged in by maple-flooring manufacturers but in assessing their economic significance.

Agreement Provides for Sales Quotas

The earlier associations may appropriately be characterized as cartels, that is, as arrangements "among, or on behalf of, producers engaged in the same line of business, with the design or effect of limiting competition among them." [68] Full details about the earlier associations are missing, but the 1913 agreement clearly indicates that its purpose was to curb competitive rivalry among association members in selling maple flooring. Its provisions if adhered to no doubt restrained the eagerness of rivals to get business. They did so by allotting each member of the association a percentage of total sales by association members and penalizing those who exceeded their quotas and rewarding those who fell short of them. Specifically, the agreement provided that members be assessed $3.00 a thousand

---

66. Of the twenty-two members of the association against which the government's suit ran, the articles of which were adopted in March 1922, sixteen were members of the association whose articles became effective January 1, 1913 (Record, Vol. I, at 73); seventeen were members of the association operating under these articles as extended with modifications from January 1, 1916, to January 1, 1919; fourteen signed the Minimum Price Plan of June 27, 1916 (Record, Vol. III, at 78–81, Vol. IV, at 798); twenty-one were members of the association operating under articles in effect from January 1 to July 1, 1919 (Record, Vol. I, at 76); and eighteen signed the Minimum Price Basis plan of January 6, 1921 (Record, Vol. III, at 92–94 *et seq.*).

67. Brief and Argument for Appellants, at 7.

68. Stocking and Watkins, *Cartels or Competition?* (New York: Twentieth Century Fund, 1948), p. 3.

board feet for all lumber shipped in excess of their allotments, that assessments be placed in a special fund, and that they be returned at the rate of $3.00 a thousand feet for the amount by which a member undersold his quota down to 75 per cent of his allotted share. For curtailing below that percentage, members received no reward. Members selling more than their allotments received no return.[69] In effect they were fined on all their sales for exceeding their allotment by whatever amount.[70]

Allotment Plan Abandoned

The allotment feature of the 1913 association was carried over into subsequent agreements and admittedly was not abandoned until the District Court for the Western District of Tennessee found the plan of the American Hardwood Lumber Association unlawful.[71] But association members in abandoning the allotment plan did not abandon their effort to restrain competition. At its expiration on January 1, 1916, the 1913 plan was continued with few changes until January 1, 1919.[72] The precise date on which the association abandoned its allotment plan is not clear. Keehn, the association's secretary, testified that on advice of counsel the association discontinued the allotment plan on March 31, 1920, but the minutes of neither the association nor the board of trustees disclosed the date of discontinuance. The tentative draft of new articles of association covering the period October 1, 1921, to July 1, 1922, which was never put into effect because of the failure of several manufacturers to sign, contained the allotment feature.[73]

69. Record, Vol. III, at 6.
70. Assessments were required to be paid within five days after members had been notified. The trustee of the special fund set up to guarantee performance of association agreements was authorized to draw on a member's undistributed share of the special fund to pay any delinquent assessment. Failure to restore such withdrawals brought forfeiture of membership and of all claims against the special and the general funds. *Ibid.*
71. United States v. American Column and Lumber Co., 263 Fed. 147 (1920), discussed previously in the text; Appellants' Supplemental Reply Brief, at 22.
72. Record, Vol. I, at 74–75; Government Exhibit 2, Record, Vol. III, at 14–21.
73. Government Exhibit 5, Record, Vol. III, at 49–56. Keehn testified that "upon the advice of our attorney we suspended all Association activities beginning in April, 1920, and running about four months thereafter on account of the Memphis case . . . then we resumed afterwards in August, 1920, our statistical work, but we never resumed any allotment contracts. . . ." Record, Vol. I, at 77. See also Record, Vol. I, at 143–44, 146; Vol. II, at 794. The government offered in evidence a letter to association members dated September 16, 1921, which said in part: "It would seem that the allotments as agreed upon in our present Articles of Association, which allotments were to be in force from July 1, 1919 to July 1, 1922, should govern from

Legality of Trade Association Activities

Minimum Price Plan and Minimum Price Basis

Before the association formally abandoned the allotment plan, it adopted, on July 1, 1916, a "Minimum Price Plan" [74] and on January 6, 1921, a "Minimum Price Basis," [75] apparently designed to place a floor under maple-flooring prices. The two plans were similar in all important respects save for the provision of penalties. The minimum price plan provided that association members selling below the association's minimum prices were to pay penalties; the minimum price basis proclaimed a "scientific principle" for pricing maple flooring but provided no penalties for failure to observe it or procedure for enforcing conformance. Both apparently contemplated that association members should sell flooring above an average cost, the elements of which were both described and determined. These included:

(a) The actual market value of the raw material;
(b) The average cost and expense of manufacturing and selling flooring;
(c) Interest on the capital actually invested in the flooring business at the rate of five (5) per cent per annum [six per cent under the minimum price basis];
(d) Annual depreciation of plant; and
(e) The usual overhead charges incurred in carrying on the flooring business.[76]

The association's Market Conditions Committee averaged the surveys of manufacturing and marketing costs sent in by members and the results of "test runs" made by certain members and on the basis of these recommended changes from time to time in minimum prices.[77] Under the mini-

October 1, 1921 to July 1, 1922, because each member has already agreed to his allotment to run to July 1, 1922, and if we begin changing allotments, there will be no end to it." Government Exhibit 6, Record, Vol. III, at 61. The government contended that although suspended for business reasons from April 1, 1920, to October 1, 1921, the allotment plan was not formally abandoned until March 1922, when association members adopted the plan against which the government's complaint specifically ran. Government's Brief, at 17–19.

74. Government Exhibit 11, Record, Vol. III, at 78–81; minimum price plan as revised January 1, 1919, Government Exhibit 12, Record, Vol. III, at 84–89.

75. Government Exhibit 13, Record, Vol. III, at 92–94.

76. Minimum price plan: Record, Vol. III, at 78–79, 84–85; minimum price basis: Record, Vol. III, at 92.

77. Government Exhibits 18-U and 18-V, Record, Vol. III, at 246–51. Apparently at times association policy aimed at keeping prices down. For example, on August 21, 1919, the Market Conditions Committee reported to members that an advance in the price of rough flooring lumber justified an advance of $10.50 in the minimum price plan but that it recommended advances of only $6.00 on two grades of flooring and of $5.00 on certain other grades. Record, Vol. III, at 250–51. Apparently the relative strength of demand for different grades of flooring, more

Workable Competition and Antitrust Policy

mum price plan it was agreed that minimum prices should not yield more than 10 per cent profit over the average actual cost,[78] and under the minimum price basis agreement, not over 5 per cent.[79] Under both plans the association sent to members "Tables of Values Based Upon Average Cost" and supplemented these from time to time with a list showing the "Application of Minimum Prices" [80] or "Concessions and Additions." [81]

As indicated, the minimum price basis carried no specific procedure for enforcement and provided no penalties. It left final discretion with each flooring manufacturer on the prices he would charge, but while it was in operation each member reported weekly to the association on actual prices charged and through the association to all the members.[82] On advice from the Assistant Attorney General in charge of the Antitrust Division that the minimum price basis and the freight rate book used with it constituted a violation of the criminal provisions of the Sherman Act, the association on February 25, 1921, formally abandoned it.[83]

Recession Calls for Cooperation

Meanwhile the 1920–21 business recession, accompanied as it was by a severe contraction in building, had created "deplorable conditions" in the flooring industry.[84] These apparently precipitated a demand for a renewal of cooperation among flooring manufacturers to stabilize conditions [85] and

than actual cost changes, may have influenced the cost figures which were distributed. For example, in estimates of average manufacturing and marketing costs covering the first half of 1921 spreads of as much as $35.00 between various dimensions of the same grade of flooring were reported, although the cost of lumber must have been about the same for all dimensions. Government Exhibits 25-A, 26, and 27, Record, Vol. III, at 280, 284, 287. In one case a reported increase in the average cost of rough lumber was distributed among three dimensions of flooring and the cost of one dimension was *reduced*. Government Exhibits 25-A and 26, Record, Vol. III, at 280, 284. Keehn testified that the cost differential between two grades of beech was not a continuing one because "it depends upon the supply and demand of these different floorings, to what a man's stock conditions are, and the cost of it, too." Record, Vol. I, at 153–54.

78. Record, Vol. III, at 79.
79. Record, Vol. III, at 92–93.
80. Government Exhibit 31-M, Record, Vol. III, at side folio p. 533.
81. Government Exhibit 34-M, Record, Vol. III, at 326.
82. Government Exhibits 14-B and 14-I, Record, Vol. III, at 98–99, 102.
83. Defendants' Exhibit C, Record, Vol. IV, at 799–810, especially p. 804.
84. The minutes of a special meeting of association members held April 27, 1921, used this term in describing the plight of the industry. Government Exhibit 15-Q, Record, Vol. III, at 134.
85. A letter of August 11, 1921, calling a meeting of members August 19, 1921,

for adoption of new articles of association to implement cooperation. The minutes of the August 19, 1921, meeting state: "After a prolonged discussion of the demoralized conditions in the flooring industry, the Secretary was instructed to prepare a draft revising the Articles of Association with the view of securing greater cooperation in the industry. . . ." [86] Apparently the association looked to cooperation, not competition, to solve the industry's troubles.

The 1922 Agreement

The outcome was the adoption of new articles of association in March 1922, some three months before the old articles formally expired, but dating them back to January 1, 1922.[87] These articles were to govern association activities until January 1, 1925.[88] It was against the association's activities as conducted under these articles that the government's complaint ran in the antitrust proceedings initiated March 5, 1923. These articles are strikingly similar in their more basic features to those which preceded them. They had four major features:

(1) Provision for calculating an average cost of production;
(2) Provision for a freight rate book showing freight rates from Cadillac, Michigan, to all the leading buying centers for maple flooring;
(3) Provision for computation and distribution of trade statistics; and
(4) Provision for meetings at which the statistics and market conditions were to be discussed.[89]

said: "Our Weekly Sales Reports indicate considerable *demoralization* in the flooring situation and it seems absolutely necessary that every member should be represented at the meeting so that greater cooperation can be assured and conditions in the industry, which are now much disturbed, can be stabilized." Record, Vol. IV, at 566–67. Emphasis supplied.
  86. Record, Vol. III, at 138.
  87. Keehn's testimony, Record, Vol. I, at 78.
  88. Government Exhibit 8, Record, Vol. III, at 64–74.
  89. The January 22, 1913, annual meeting of the association had authorized the Market Conditions Committee to "figure out what the selling values of flooring would be if a logical and scientific method of determining values of flooring were used, that is: if the selling values of flooring were based upon the cost of raw material plus manufacturing and selling costs and plus a reasonable profit." Government Exhibit 15, Record, Vol. III, at 106, 108. The first "Scientific List" was made up in February 1913 (Record, Vol. III, at 114, 230), and a "Table of Delivered Values" was printed May 21, 1913 (Record, Vol. III, at 213, 215, 222, 238). Keehn, the association's secretary, testified that throughout the period 1913–23 he distributed to association members from time to time lists of what in 1923 were called "average costs" and that these were based on changes in the market value of

Workable Competition and Antitrust Policy

Association Compiles Average Costs

The new articles recognized, as had earlier articles, that if makers of flooring are to conduct their business "scientifically," they must carefully consider their costs in making and selling it.[90] To aid them in doing this the association provided its members with a table of costs showing "average costs" for each grade and dimension of flooring. These replaced the "Scientific Price List" and "Table of Values" provided by earlier associations. They were calculated in much the same way. The average costs distributed by the association to its members were based on market prices of raw lumber, an average of the costs of making and selling flooring as reported by association members to the association, interest on capital at 6 per cent, annual depreciation of plant as "usually allowed" by the government, "usual" overhead charges, and an allowance for contingencies at 5 per cent of average total cost.[91]

By its costing program the association apparently provided a uniform system of cost accounting which could not have been otherwise achieved. But it did more than this. It provided standardized cost figures which afforded a basis for identical f.o.b. pricing if members chose so to use it.[92]

rough lumber and changes in manufacturing and marketing costs. Record, Vol. I, at 110.

The successive associations each had a committee to advise on costs; at first the Market Conditions Committee reported directly to members on both costs and selling prices, but under the 1922 articles of association the Cost Surveys Committee merely determined what cost information should be included in Keehn's reports to members. Record, Vol. I, at 104–5, 396.

Each of the five association agreements in effect between 1913 and 1922 provided for an annual meeting and from three to five regular meetings, for daily reports to the association secretary of all shipments and deliveries made except those made to other members, and for a monthly summary of the daily reports. Government Exhibits 1, 2, 3, 4, 8, Record, Vol. II, at 1–8, 14–21, 25–32, 37–44, 64–74.

90. Art. XIV, § 1, of the January 1, 1922, Articles of Association, Record, Vol. III, at 69.

91. Art. XIV, § 3, *id.* The Supreme Court's opinion noted that the allowance for contingencies was discontinued by the association on July 19, 1923 (four months after the government filed its complaint). Maple Flooring Manufacturers Ass'n v. United States, 268 U.S. 563, 569 (1925).

92. The appellants denied this, contending that the members' diversity of output and position in the market made it impossible for them to take concerted action in production and sales policies and that the association could not undertake to furnish members with the cost of producing and selling flooring, but only to place before each member the average of the costs reported by members, leaving each member free to sell his flooring at any price he chose. Brief and Argument for Appellants, at 66–75, 244–45. The government analyzed the estimates of average cost which

Legality of Trade Association Activities

The Freight Rate Book and the Weekly Reports

To make it easy to calculate a delivered price to any point to which maple flooring might be shipped, the association compiled and distributed a freight rate book. The "freight" book, which with occasional changes the successive associations had apparently used continuously since 1905,[93] contained freight rates on flooring from Cadillac, Michigan, to several thousand destinations throughout the nation. The last book issued before the government filed its complaint was dated February 15, 1923, and contained freight rates from Cadillac to some 7,600 towns throughout the country.[94] The book contained an average cost chart showing f.o.b. average cost of maple flooring of specified grades and dimensions, a table of freight rates, and a delivered cost chart, formerly called a "Table of Values," showing a delivered cost or price made up of the average cost and the freight from Cadillac to destination.[95] It stated "differentials" from which association members could calculate the average cost of beech and birch flooring of varying grades and dimensions, and it published standardized terms of discount. In brief, it gave association members all the data they needed to insure their quoting identical delivered prices for the varying grades of flooring if they wished to do so.[96] It did not guarantee that members would so use it.

were offered in evidence and argued that "the distribution of the increase or decrease of the so-called cost of production between the different grades and dimensions has no relationship whatever to the advance or decrease in cost; but is based entirely upon other influences, which unquestionably are the prevailing and prospective conditions of the market. In other words, the secretary of the association, aided to some extent by the [Cost Surveys] Committee, surveys the entire situation and makes up a price list which, so far as the relative price of grades and dimensions is concerned, is wholly arbitrary and not controlled in the least by any of the elements that appear in the cost of production." Government's Brief, at 78.

93. Record, Vol. I, at 111.

94. Government Exhibit 37, Record, Vol. III, at 329, side folio pp. 909–29.

95. After the government filed its complaint, the association quit publishing a delivered price but continued to present its average cost table and freight rates from Cadillac. This left to association members the problem of addition to arrive at identical delivered costs or prices. Keehn's testimony, Record, Vol. I, at 118.

96. A flooring salesman testified that he was not very familiar with the activities of the Maple Flooring Manufacturers Association "except that they issue a price book and rate book, which practically everybody uses, to determine delivered prices in various parts of the country." Record, Vol. II, at 575. The defendants offered testimony by a number of manufacturers that they used the freight rate book only to quote a delivered price promptly upon request and that the customer deducted the freight actually paid when remitting for his flooring. Record, Vol. I, at 228–35, 384.

Workable Competition and Antitrust Policy

Association Reports

The association collected and distributed statistical information reflecting conditions in the flooring market.[97] It collected monthly from each of its members data showing stocks on hand, unfilled orders, shipments, production, new orders booked, and "average price realized." From the individual reports the association's secretary compiled tables giving total figures for each of these items and showing the absolute and percentage changes from the previous month's report and the previous year's report for the same month.[98] The association's reports also presented similar data for each member individually. In short, the monthly reports enabled each member to see the market picture as a whole and the position of each member in it.

The weekly report covered all sales by each member, showing date of sale, exact quantity of each dimension and grade sold, the delivered price, the freight rate from Cadillac to destination, commissions allowed, if any, and the member making the sale. Several months after the government challenged the legality of the association's activities, the association stopped identifying the particular mill reporting each sale [99] but thereafter presented the data by groups of mills so arranged that alert and informed members might readily identify the individual reports.

The weekly reports, supplementing as they did the monthly reports, not only gave members more frequent pictures of the flooring market and the position of each member in it, but a more exact one. Specifically, a member could compare his own stock, shipments, orders, production, prices, and trends in each, with those of each other member and with the aggregate of all members.[100]

---

97. Perhaps the chief value of the statistics on price was to enable a seller to test the accuracy of buyers' claims that other sellers were offering for less. See various Market Conditions Committee Reports between 1913–15 and one dated October 28, 1921, and a letter dated December 3, 1921, from Keehn to three members who were not then making weekly sales reports. Record, Vol. III, at 203, 207–8, 331–32, 205, 219–20, 116, 233, 124, 254–55; Vol. IV, at 535–36.

98. Government Exhibit 40-RRRRR, Vol. III, at 350, side folio pp. 2049–59. After July 1923 the association reported these data for groups of members. District court's opinion of December 19, 1923 (unreported), Record, Vol. I, at 52, 57.

99. Record, Vol. I, at 127. The weekly sales report for July 21, 1923 (Government Exhibit 43-AAAAAA, Vol. III, at 398–402), does not show the reporting members' identifying numbers.

100. The Supreme Court described the association's exchange of trade information substantially as it has been described here, but it characterized the significance of the information altogether differently. It chose to emphasize that the association had *ceased* identifying individual members and did not exchange certain kinds of

Legality of Trade Association Activities

Association Meetings

All of the articles of association back to 1913 provided for regular association meetings. In addition, the association's secretary called meetings from time to time. During the life of the articles under attack by the government, meetings were held about once a month. What transpired at these meetings is not clear, but what is clear is that the meetings gave members an opportunity to discuss and analyze the statistical information compiled and distributed by the association and to relate this information to sound policy on production and prices. The report of the association's Market Conditions Committee issued shortly before the association's meeting in November 1921 recommended that to obtain greater cooperation among members the secretary's monthly report be mailed promptly so that members "will receive the October statistics in advance of the meeting and have an opportunity to analyze them and can come to the meeting fully informed respecting trade conditions as reflected by the statistical reports." [101] The secretary in July 1922, in urging association members to send in their monthly reports promptly so that market data might be compiled before the next association meeting, advised members, "This will save time and give you a better opportunity to consider the relations of supply and demand as reflected by the data than if the matter is delayed by our not getting these reports until the members arrive in Chicago and then not getting them compiled until late in the afternoon." [102] Writing again on August 10, 1922, Secretary Keehn urged members to bring the flooring data to the meeting "so that you will have as complete information as possible regarding statistical conditions on the day of the meeting." [103] And again, writing in October 1922, Secretary Keehn noted that two months had elapsed without a "gathering of the clan" and expressed the hope "that every member of the Association will be represented at the meeting so that trade conditions and the relations of supply and demand for flooring can be discussed and considered." [104]

information, such as current prices, names of customers, names of members with surplus stock, etc. By looking at the even more revealing information that the association *might* have exchanged, the Court decided that the information actually exchanged did not show every member "the exact market condition generally" and "the exact condition of the business of each of his fellow members." Maple Flooring Manufacturers Ass'n v. United States, 268 U.S. 563, 573 (1925).
101. Record, Vol. III, at 255.
102. *Id.* at 175.
103. *Id.* at 181.
104. *Id.* at 185.

Workable Competition and Antitrust Policy

No Signed Agreement to Fix Prices

The articles of association of January 1, 1922, contained no agreement not to sell below minimum prices fixed by the association, and apparently this was the decisive element in the Supreme Court's decision of the case;[105] but as late as September 16, 1921, association members were furnished with three rough drafts of a "Declaration of Our Business Policy," under Form 2 of which members would voluntarily agree to pay the association 10 per cent of any and all flooring sold below "the average cost of production, plus the average cost of freight to destination, as ascertained from time to time by the Maple Flooring Manufacturers Association's Survey of Costs and Tables of Values Based Upon Average Cost"[106] (after allowing a commission to certain wholesalers and dealers not to exceed $2.00 per thousand feet). The record does not show that any declaration of business policy was adopted.

The Supreme Court, far from finding any attempt to violate the spirit of the antitrust laws while seeking to appear to obey them, praised the association members for "steadily" indicating "a purpose to keep within the boundaries of legality as rapidly as those boundaries were marked out by the decisions of courts interpreting the Sherman Act."[107]

The Association's Goal

The successive articles of association indicate clearly that the association aimed to restrain competition. It sought to substitute concerted action among the leading maple-flooring makers for the unrestrained forces of a free market. Its allotment plan, its minimum price plan, its minimum price basis could have had no other purpose. Clearly also the association tried to avoid carrying concerted action to the point of an unlawful restraint on trade. In an effort to stay within the law it from time to time revised its articles and modified its program. In response to the shifting winds of legal interpretation it tacked sail in an effort to steer clear of the administrative shoals and legislative reefs which might otherwise have wrecked it. But it did not abandon its goal.

105. Maple Flooring Manufacturers Ass'n v. United States, 268 U.S. 563, 572, 575, 586 (1925).
106. Record, Vol. IV, at 568.
107. Maple Flooring Manufacturers Ass'n v. United States, 268 U.S. 563, 577 (1925).

Legality of Trade Association Activities

Effects of the Association's Activity

But did the association achieve it? The defendants introduced expert testimony to prove that it did not. In truth, they denied any intent to interfere with competitive forces, characterizing the association's activities not merely as innocent but as socially salutary. Counsel for defendants argued and witnesses testified that the association had standardized and graded the flooring made by its members and that, to insure that the grades would comply with the standards set, it provided an inspection service. By doing this it had made it possible for buyers to buy what they wanted and to get what they bought. Scores of witnesses testified to the dependability of association members' products and to their preference for them.[108] Counsel for defendants clinched their argument that the association's standardization program represented a public service by quoting from the Department of Commerce's Tenth Annual Report in which Secretary Hoover recognized the importance of standardization to the elimination of waste and urged that it be voluntarily established by private industry.[109] The association, according to its counsel, had conducted an extensive advertising campaign beneficial to the entire industry and beyond the ability of any single firm to finance. This had given some security to maple-flooring makers who otherwise would have lost business to rival products.[110] Numerous witnesses testified that members' prices for maple, beech, and birch flooring had been "fair and reasonable," and lumber dealers testified that they found it cheaper to buy flooring than to make their own.[111]

In defense of the association's calculations of the average cost of producing flooring, counsel for defendants with great erudition outlined the development of cost accounting and through the writings of renowned economists showed its significance to business stability and economic survival. They cited authorities on the theory and practice of accounting to justify the content of the association's cost figures;[112] the Federal Trade Com-

---

108. Record, Vol. I, at 94, 140, 141, 293, 307, 427, 430–31; Vol. II, at 455, 459–60, 462, 466–67, 522–23, 538, 562, 565–66, 574, 579, 583, 584–86, 593, 604, 610, 618.
109. Brief and Argument for Appellants, at 191.
110. *Id.* at 165–66.
111. Record, Vol. I, at 86–87, 93, 427–32, 435–36, 446; Vol. II, at 462, 466–67.
112. Brief and Argument for Appellants, at 235–40, quoting from or citing Leon Carroll Marshall, *Readings in Industrial Society* (Chicago: University of Chicago Press, 1918), pp. 404–5, 408, 412; John A. Hobson, *The Evolution of Modern Capitalism* (new ed.; New York: Scribner, 1898), p. 1; William James Ashley, *The Economic Organization of England* (1st ed.; London: Longmans, Green, 1914),

mission, to show the importance of proper cost accounting and the inadequacy of customary cost-accounting procedures among small business firms;[113] and the Department of Commerce, to justify association activities in sponsoring standard cost-accounting procedures.[114]

A score of witnesses testified that they used their own discretion in pricing flooring and that in doing so they took account of the general market for flooring and their position in it. When demand was weak and their stocks large, they cut prices to move their goods. When demand was strong and their stocks small, they raised prices.[115] Defendants supplemented the testimony of distributors and manufacturers by expert testimony.

Long-run Price Movements

Two young Harvard-trained economists, Edward B. Gordon and Grant Keehn, supported the defendants' contention that market forces, not trade association activity, accounted for maple-flooring prices and movements therein.[116] They made an analysis, too comprehensive and detailed to reproduce here, of relevant statistical data bearing on the demand for and supply of maple flooring. It was impressive. Much of their testimony centered around the relative movements over a ten-year period (1913–23) of indexes of maple-flooring prices, the wholesale prices of all commodities, the prices of building materials, and the prices of raw lumber. These data, presented on a logarithmic chart, showed that the several indexes had in general moved in the same direction at roughly the same time.[117] The economists concluded that the price movements reflected market forces, not association manipulations. Using stocks on hand as a measure-

pp. 35–36; Irving Fisher, *Elementary Principles of Economics* (3d ed.; New York: Macmillan, 1912).

113. Brief and Argument for Appellants, at 240–42, quoting from Franklin D. Jones, *Trade Association Activities and the Law* (New York: McGraw-Hill, 1922), p. 62, and an address by Edward N. Hurley, vice chairman of the Federal Trade Commission, before the Boston Commercial Club, March 28, 1916.

114. Brief and Argument for Appellants, at 243, quoting from *Trade Association Activities* (1923), a study by the Department of Commerce, p. 4, Defendants' Exhibit NN-1 (omitted in printing the record).

115. Record, Vol. I, at 84–86, 88–89, 92, 94, 198–201, 208–9, 210–16, 221–22, 227–29, 230–31, 236–38, 260–63, 268–85, 289–93, 322–27, 336–37, 385–91, 393–95, 410–12.

116. For Gordon's testimony see Record, Vol. II, at 624–76; for Grant Keehn's, see pp. 677–722. Grant Keehn was the son of George W. Keehn, secretary of the successive associations.

117. Defendants' Gordon Exhibit 6, Record, Vol. V, at 899.

Legality of Trade Association Activities

ment of supply and unfilled orders as reflecting the intensity of demand, Grant Keehn concluded that the price of maple flooring moved with only natural lags "in accord with the factors of supply and demand." [118] In short, the economists contended that markets, not men, made maple-flooring prices. Gordon and Grant Keehn, fresh out of Harvard's graduate school of business administration, did a competent job; and their more mature professors, Homer B. Vanderblue and Albert J. Hettinger, Jr., backed them in it.[119] I have no desire to quarrel with the long-run implications of their findings.

But clearly the association had aimed at market control. Clearly also the structure and ownership patterns of the industry (the association accounted for only 70 per cent of maple-flooring output and for a far smaller percentage of potential output) and the nature of the demand and long-run supply (particularly the ease of entry), made it difficult if not impossible for the association to block the operation of long-run market forces. Only a close-knit cartel of the European variety, operating in a friendly legal environment, could have hoped to do this. American NRA and European experiences indicate that even with the law behind them cohesive cartel members may be unable to stem for long a decline in the price of an easily produced commodity in the face of an abrupt and prolonged decrease in demand.

Short-run Price Behavior

In the short run they may do better. I note that the price index for maple flooring [120] moved upward during 1918, when unfilled orders, which were abnormally low, were moving downward, and that it responded with alacrity and great strength to the 1919 increase in unfilled orders.[121] So fast and far did it move that it overtook and passed by a substantial margin the price indexes for all commodities, all building materials, and raw lumber. Moreover, it remained close to its peak throughout most of 1920 despite a sharp decline in unfilled orders. When the break came late in 1920, it fell further and faster than the other three indexes, which had moved down more promptly; but it never sank to its prewar position below the other three indexes. Whether the association's activities alone were

---

118. Record, Vol. II, at 712.
119. For Professor Vanderblue's testimony see Record, Vol. II, at 740–69; for Professor Hettinger's, see pp. 722–39.
120. Defendants' Gordon Exhibit 6, Record, Vol. V, at 899.
121. Defendants' Grant Keehn Exhibit 24, Record, Vol. V, at 959.

responsible for its relatively better performance over the period 1918–23 is not clear, but its performance is consistent with that inference. Moreover, witnesses for both the government and the defendants offered testimony which supports the proposition that association activities affected prices in the short run. Grant Keehn, for example, in commenting on the failure of maple-flooring prices to decline in 1918 and early in 1919 when "demand was decreasing and supply was increasing," noted that raw materials, manufacturing and marketing costs, and commodity prices were "on a higher relative level than the prices of the product [maple flooring] ... and after the close of the War there was a condition of uncertainty."[122] But uncertainty would contribute to price weakness, not strength. Grant Keehn recognized as more important than the above factor in raising maple-flooring prices when demand for maple flooring was declining "the fact that during the latter half of 1918, there were restrictions placed upon building. Because of these restrictions people could not build, even though they so desired. A cut in price of the product at that time, therefore, would not have stimulated demand."[123] Failure to cut prices in the face of a decline in demand would be a profitable policy for a monopolist or a cartel to follow, but it is not a very satisfactory explanation for competitive price behavior. On the contrary it suggests that the association as a price-control agency was doing very well indeed.

Realized Prices and "Average Cost"

The government's evidence of the association's influence on maple-flooring prices was based largely on the weekly sales reports of association members. Its analysis of these materials covered the period November 19, 1921, to June 30, 1923. After analyzing the weekly reports the government contended that the average cost figures compiled by the association and distributed to its members were in fact its suggested minimum prices below which association members should not sell. In accordance with this hypothesis, it calculated the percentage (by volume in board feet) of weekly sales of $13/16'' \times 2\frac{1}{4}''$ clear maple flooring made at, below, or above the association's average cost figures over a period of nineteen months. The average cost when combined with the rate book, as previously indicated, provided a convenient device for arriving at a minimum delivered price.

The government summarized the results of its analysis in four periods:

122. Record, Vol. II, at 707.
123. *Ibid.*

Legality of Trade Association Activities

November 19, 1921–March 25, 1922; April 1, 1922–June 30, 1923; October 28, 1922–June 30, 1923; and November 19, 1921–June 30, 1923. During the period November 19, 1921—March 25, 1922, which the government appropriately characterized as a period of confusion, it being a portion of the interim between the abandonment of the minimum price basis and the adoption of new articles, association members sold 57.5 per cent of their 13/16" × 2¼" clear maple flooring below the association's average cost figures for that period. During the period from the date the new articles were adopted until the government's suit was filed (April 1, 1922, to June 30, 1923) association members sold only 12.4 per cent of this grade of flooring below the association's average cost. Over the whole period studied by the government (November 19, 1921, to June 23, 1923, which included the period of "confusion") they sold only 18.4 per cent of it below the association's average cost. During the period when the plan had passed its trial stage (October 28, 1922, to June 30, 1923), members sold only 8.8 per cent of their clear-grade maple flooring below the association's average cost figures or—as the government characterized them—suggested minimum prices.[124]

When it is recalled that the association's average cost included cost of raw lumber, cost of processing, depreciation, insurance and taxes, marketing costs, usual overhead, 5 per cent for contingencies, and interest on capital at 6 per cent (or what economists would regard as a normal profit), these findings support the government's contention that the association's average cost was designed to place a floor under maple-flooring prices.[125]

Weekly and monthly data drawn from members' weekly sales reports also support the government's position. In November 1921, before the new articles were adopted, association members sold 86.6 per cent of their 13/16" × 2¼" clear maple flooring below the association's average cost figure. In October 1922, six months after the adoption of the new articles and immediately preceding an increase in the association's average cost figure, they sold only 2.4 per cent below it. During November 1922, fol-

---

124. Government's Brief, at 198.
125. The association's contingency allowance was calculated by adding the cost of raw lumber (adjusted for waste) to the average manufacturing and marketing costs per thousand feet of flooring and taking 5 per cent of this amount. Its per unit allowance for interest, insurance and taxes, and depreciation was calculated on a basis of actual production over some specified period. The association's "Survey of Costs" questionnaire instructed members to divide one-fourth of the annual amounts of these items by the quantity of flooring produced during the previous quarter. George W. Keehn's testimony, Record, Vol. I, at 108; Government Exhibit 25, Record, Vol. III, at 279.

Workable Competition and Antitrust Policy

lowing the increase, they sold 14 per cent of this grade of flooring below the association's average cost figure. The percentage declined to 7.3 per cent in February 1923, and a new advance was announced on February 15. In the following week members sold 14.3 per cent of their 13/16" × 2¼" clear maple flooring below the new average cost figure; by the week ending March 24, 1923, they sold only 7.9 per cent of it below. The association announced another advance on March 24, 1923, and in the week following members sold 56.9 per cent of this flooring below it; but on May 26, 1923, they were selling only 2.5 per cent below the association's average cost figure.[126]

126. The government derived these comparisons from members' individual weekly sales reports appearing in the Record, Vol. IV, at 583–796. For a detailed discussion of the government's procedure, see Government's Brief, at 170–210. The government tabulated from the weekly sales reports of association members the following data: (1) date of order, (2) number of mills making sales, (3) quantity, (4) delivered price per thousand feet, (5) freight rate, (6) the average freight charge (freight from Cadillac), and (7) commissions. By deducting the freight charge from the delivered price the government calculated an f.o.b. mill price. By comparing the price thus determined with the average cost furnished to association members (which the government contended was a recommended minimum selling price), the government calculated the percentage of sales made at, below, or above the average cost. The defendants challenged this procedure, alleging that variations in commissions charged by different members reflected price competition and contending that to calculate a proper net factory price with which to compare the association's average cost the government should have deducted commissions as well as freight from the delivered price. Brief and Argument for Appellants, at 342. The defendants' proposed procedure would have increased substantially the percentage of sales below the association's average cost (Appellants' Brief, Appendix T, at 24) and would have weakened accordingly the government's hypothesis.

The government justified its inclusion of commissions in its calculated f.o.b. mill price on the following grounds: (1) The questionnaire on which members reported their costs to the association and from which the association calculated its average cost figure asked for both marketing costs in general and commissions specifically. Government Exhibit 25, Record, Vol. III, at 279. Hence to deduct commissions from the delivered prices would be to double-count. (2) The testimony showed no evidence that commissions were used for competitive purposes. They were merely a marketing cost, generally paid to wholesalers, commission men, or traveling salesmen. Retail dealers, so far as the record shows, never received them. Record, Vol. II, at 449–72. (3) The association's secretary in sending instructions to members on the meaning of the "Delivered Cost Charts" explained that "the Average Cost of Freight is added to the Average Cost of the flooring F.O.B. cars at flooring mills to illustrate what the Delivered Cost would be at destination." Government Exhibit 28-Q, Record, Vol. III, at 319. (4) The minimum price plan of January 1919 had made clear that payments of commissions to registered special representatives, wholesalers, and commission men were appropriately to be regarded as costs, not as evidence of deviations from the plan's minimum price subject to penalties. Government Exhibit 13, Record, Vol. III, at 94. These facts and arguments are convincing.

The Government's analysis covered only reported sales of 13/16" × 2¼" clear-grade maple flooring, which represented only 35 per cent of all grades sold.

Legality of Trade Association Activities

Conclusion

These figures do not prove but they certainly support the government's contention that the 1922 plan was in reality but a thinly disguised replica of its predecessors. The record is barren of any evidence that its objective had changed from that of lessening the rigors of competition for the benefit of its members. The association was faithful in its effort to avoid the appearance of evil, but apparently it sought the fruits of conspiracy while trying to escape its legal consequences. And apparently it succeeded in part; not so well as might have been desired, but well enough to justify members' adherence.

Analysis of the record indicates that the association influenced the short-run price of maple flooring to the disadvantage of buyers. I believe that such arrangements are contrary to the interests of the buying public and that a government which protects and nurtures them is contributing to the death, not the survival, of a free private-enterprise economy. In saying this I do not want to seek refuge in semantics.

Economists who would defend such collective efforts to interfere with market forces probably fall into two groups: those who, like the defendants' consultants, Gordon and Grant Keehn, believe that the program failed; and those who believe that unrestrained competition in an industry like the manufacture of maple flooring prejudices the general welfare.

On the first issue I can say only that failure is poor justification for trade association activity designed to restrain competition. On the second, I shall say more below.

CEMENT MANUFACTURERS PROTECTIVE ASSOCIATION AND THE CEMENT INSTITUTE

The Cement Manufacturers Protective Association, organized in 1916 after a price war, by nineteen leading cement manufacturers in the Northeast,[127] performed four major services for its members: (1) it collected from each and distributed to all of its members information on specific job

---

127. The chairman of the organizational meeting expressed its purpose as follows: "Of course you understand that the idea of this thing is cooperation, and I think it is not necessary to say anything more on that point. We all agree that the necessity of cooperation is acknowledged by everybody in the industry. The only question now we have to determine is how best we can make use of cooperation." Record, at 401, Cement Manufacturers Protective Ass'n v. United States, 268 U.S. 588 (1925). References in this section to "Record," exhibits, and briefs are to this case unless otherwise specified.

contracts; (2) it acted as a credit clearinghouse, collecting and distributing information on accounts owed its members; (3) it compiled and distributed a freight rate book showing the freight rate from the nearest basing point to each of the numerous delivery points in the northeastern area; and (4) it collected, compiled, and distributed monthly statistics relating to the supply and demand for cement.

On July 30, 1921, the Department of Justice filed a complaint in the District Court for the Southern District of New York alleging that the association constituted a combination in restraint of trade within the meaning of Section 1 of the Sherman Act and petitioning that it be dissolved. On October 23, 1923, Judge John C. Knox sustained the government's charges and ordered the association to dissolve.[128] Defendants appealed, and on June 1, 1925, the Supreme Court in a six-to-three decision reversed the lower court.[129]

Specific Job-contract Information

The association's activities relating to specific job contracts and customer credit were ostensibly designed merely to protect association members against exploitation by unreliable or financially irresponsible customers, and the Supreme Court so found. The reports on specific job contracts aimed at correcting what the industry regarded as a serious abuse of a necessary business practice. Construction contractors wanted to be assured of an adequate supply of cement at a fixed price. They customarily contracted with a cement producer, frequently through a dealer, to purchase at a fixed price a designated amount of cement for future delivery for a specific construction job. Frequently dealers or contractors entered into several such contracts with different cementmakers. If cement prices went down, they cancelled all their contracts except that needed for the specific job. If the price of cement advanced, they accepted delivery under all the contracts. This supplied them with cheap cement which competed with the dearer cement otherwise generally available from cementmakers and gave them an advantage over less fortunately situated rivals. It also tended to check the price rise. As cement for specific job contracts constituted about 35 to 40 per cent of all cement sold, these practices tended to intensify competition in the sale of cement. To pre-

128. United States v. Cement Manufacturers Protective Ass'n, 294 Fed. 390 (S.D.N.Y. 1923).
129. Cement Manufacturers Protective Ass'n v. United States, 268 U.S. 588 (1925).

Legality of Trade Association Activities

vent this abuse, association members obligated themselves to report promptly to the association the details of all their specific job contracts and the association undertook to mail a compilation of this information to all members on the day received.[130] Members' reports on specific job contracts were detailed. They designated the purchaser and his address, described the construction job and its location, and specified the contractor, the amount of cement contracted for, and the *contract price*.[131]

In addition to the daily reports on specific job contracts, the association sent each member a daily, a monthly, and a quarterly cumulative report.[132] From these reports members could readily identify each specific job and refuse delivery on a contract which duplicated a rival's or called for more cement than the job required. But, as indicated, the reports served a broader purpose. They constituted a price-reporting system, a function quite irrelevant to preventing duplication of specific job contracts. Since contractors customarily got cement at 10 cents a barrel above the dealer price, the specific job contract reports informed each member of the prices which other members were charging on sales to dealers as well.[133] In this

---

130. There was no specific deadline for filing these reports. Mary Belle Phalen, the association's secretary, testified, "It was usual for them to be sent in within a very few days" after a contract was closed. Record, at 155. From this information the association made up a report "sometime during the day and mailed it out that night every day except Sundays and holidays." Record, at 156.

131. This information on new contracts was reported on Form 20. Subsequent changes in these contracts were reported on Form 21. Form 21 provided a place for reporting cancellation of a contract, a decrease or an incease in the amount of cement called for, and the balance still due if the contract was increased. Government Exhibits 14 and 15, Record, at 460.

132. The data reported to the association by each member on Forms 20 and 21 were sent to all members daily on Form 7. Record, at 156–58. Form 8, also sent to members daily, reported for each company the number of new contracts reported that day and since the first of the month, the number of contracts reported cancelled that day and since the first of the month, the amount of cement involved, and contractual requirements reported reinstated, increased, or decreased that day and since the first of the month. Government Exhibit 17, Record, at 360, side folio p. 655. Form 9, sent monthly to all members, presented this same information as reported since the first of the year. Government Exhibit 405, Record, at 706, side folio p. 1463. Form 10 was a complete recapitulation for the quarter of the detailed information reported daily by the members. Government Exhibit 26, Record, at 364, side folio p. 64.

133. Apparently cement company salesmen, eager for business, connived in the duplication and padding of dealer contracts. To stamp out this practice the association supplemented its reporting system by employing checkers or "auditors" to investigate the amount of cement delivered under the specific job contracts about which members were suspicious. Government Exhibits 82, 85, and 86, Record, at 376–78, 380, 381. The government irreverently characterized this as a spy system. Brief and Argument on Behalf of the Government, at 96–110.

Workable Competition and Antitrust Policy

way the specific job contract reports, supplemented by the association's freight rate books, enabled members to quote identical delivered prices on all sales of cement at any destination.

Other Association Activities

The association's other statistical activities supplied members with market information essential for wise production planning. The association collected, compiled, and distributed monthly statistics on cement and clinker production, stocks, and cement shipments.[134] It supplied quarterly statistics on returned bags.[135]

The record indicates that association members made a concerted effort to conduct their operations in accordance with the law. The association's by-laws provided for monthly meetings and for special meetings at the call of the president on request of five members.[136] The association kept a stenographic report of all discussions and actions taken, and counsel exercised constant surveillance at meetings to guard against transgression of the law. The minutes disclose no agreement on or even discussion of prices, but they do reflect a concern by members about lack of uniformity in certain price-affecting practices—allowances for returned bags, terms of discount, use of trade acceptances, bin charges, and the like.[137]

---

134. Form 12 reported statistics on these items for the current month and for the same month in the preceding year, together with statistics for the year to date and for the same period in the preceding year. In both cases the percentage increase or decrease in activity was given. Government Exhibit 34, Record, at 366, side folio p. 679.

135. These were reported on Form 19. Record, at 161. About its four major activities, policing specific job contracts, clearing credit risks, supplying market statistics, and publishing freight rate books for members, the association's secretary testified: "The business of the Association is carried out by getting certain information as to those four subjects, putting that information on printed or mimeographed reports and sending these reports to the members. The Association simply repeats or tabulates this information without drawing any conclusions from the information or making any suggestions in connection with those subjects. The Association is in substance simply a mechanical multiplying and tabulating machine." Record, at 162.

136. By-Laws § 7, Record, at 358.

137. Members discussed at length their differences in policy on giving credit for returned bags; some were accepting bags which others rejected as unusable, and some were granting credit for returned bags as of the date of shipment by customers, while others insisted on prior receipt before crediting. Government Exhibits 129, 162, and 166, Record, at 493–94, 575, 596–97. At least one member felt the variations occurred because "with some companies the sales department has too much to say regarding bag credits." Record, at 597. All agreed to allow five cents a barrel discount for cash payment within ten days, but members continued to be disturbed by variations in some companies' methods of computing the ten-day period, in granting the

Legality of Trade Association Activities

The Freight Rate Books

The association's activity that most clearly affected the industry's pricing was its compilation and distribution of freight rate books. The association's by-laws provided that the secretary prepare and distribute among its members a complete schedule of freight rates on cement and advise all members of changes in freight rates.[138] Members used these books for pricing cement, customarily quoting a delivered price equal to the governing base price plus cost of sacks and the freight rate from the governing base to the destination.[139] The record indicates that members understood these books were to be used in pricing cement rather than in determining freight rates. Under this pricing system each seller quoted identical prices to all destinations. A memorandum by an official of the Atlas Company under date of March 1, 1916, had this to say about the freight rate books: "These books, as I understand it, are to be used in making prices, whether the rates are correct or not."[140]

At an association meeting for sales managers a cementmaker, in discussing the importance of keeping the freight books out of the hands of dealers, stated:

[A]bout a year ago I was requested by a dealer in Baltimore for a freight rate book, and before I gave it any thought, I sent him one, and it was but a short time before I learned that he was making prices at different points down on the eastern shore there, and he had those freight rate books which he was using to upset the business that we had with the different dealers, and it all started from letting him have one of those freight rate books.[141]

Members agreed that the books should be kept from dealers, and the president of the association summed up the matter with these remarks: "I think this information should be kept for the members of the Associa-

---

discount for payment by note, and in granting the discount to customers with past-due accounts. Goverment Exhibits 123, 124, 127, and 136, Record, at 447–52, 457, 482–84, 510–12. Attempts were made to adopt a standard trade acceptance, but these failed. Government Exhibit 129, Record, at 488–93. After rejecting a proposal to adopt a uniform bin charge, members agreed to report to the association when a price included such a charge. Government Exhibit 124, Record, at 456–59.

138. By-Laws § 8(4), Record, at 359.
139. Record, at 146–47, 152, 675; Government Exhibit 337, Record, at 684. Defendants in their answer to the government's complaint acknowledged this method of pricing but justified it as a means of meeting competition. Answer, Record, at 101–8.
140. Government Exhibit 687, Record, at 969.
141. Government Exhibit 124, Record, at 461.

65

Workable Competition and Antitrust Policy

tion, and not for its customers." [142] Members, although aware of errors in the freight book, advised salesmen to use it in quoting prices.[143]

Economists' Views Differ

A distinguished economist, Professor Thomas S. Adams of Yale University, testified that the identical delivered prices at which rivals sold cement under this system were a reflection of the effectiveness of competition, and he cited a score or more of economists from Jevons to Fetter in support of his position.[144] His reference to Fetter is particularly striking since it came at about the same time that Fetter himself was testifying on behalf of the government in the *Pittsburgh Plus* proceedings before the Federal Trade Commission [145] that Pittsburgh Plus pricing was monopolistic and discriminatory.[146] In his subsequent writings Fetter became one of the country's most vigorous critics of systematic basing point pricing, contending that it could be maintained only through conspiracy and advocating compulsory f.o.b. pricing as the appropriate remedy.

Commission v. Cement Institute

While Fetter's view has not wholly prevailed, it influenced greatly the work of the Federal Trade Commission, which on July 2, 1937, issued a complaint against the Cement Institute and seventy-four producers of cement,[147] charging them with having conspired to use a basing point pricing system in violation of Section 5 of the Federal Trade Commission Act and with having discriminated in pricing in violation of Section 2 of

---

142. *Id.*
143. Government Exhibit 687, Record, at 969.
144. Record, at 294–308. W. Stanley Jevons' *Theory of Political Economy* (New York: Macmillan, 1871), Fetter's *Economic Principles* (New York: Century, 1915), and the other works referred to by Adams undoubtedly support his contention that in any market under conditions of perfect competition a single price will prevail. Fetter defines a competitive market as "a group of closely communicating traders whose valuations, however diverse before they meet, unite for a moment into a single price." Fetter, *Economic Principles* at 59. When, however, sellers possess market knowledge withheld from the buyers, a market becomes imperfect and "different prices may exist at the same moment...." *Id.* at 60. Recent developments in economic thought make Adams' testimony sound quaint. When he testified, economists had not yet developed the theory of oligopolistic pricing or the concept of workable competition. See note 152 *infra.*
145. United States Steel Corporation, 8 F.T.C. 1 (1924).
146. N.Y. Times, Dec. 12, 1923, p. 33, col. 3.
147. Cement Institute, 37 F.T.C. 87 (1943).

Legality of Trade Association Activities

the Clayton Act as modified by the Robinson-Patman Act. The Commission found respondents guilty and ordered them to cease and desist.[148] Respondents appealed and the United States Court of Appeals for the Seventh Circuit reversed the Commission.[149] The Commission carried the case to the Supreme Court, which found for the Commission.[150] The Commission's proceedings in the case were prolonged and the record was profuse. It revealed a long history of concerted action in the cement industry to lessen the rigor of competition.[151]

Basing Point Pricing, Not Open Price Reporting, the Real Issue

The *Cement* cases do not throw much light on either the economic or the legal significance of open price-reporting activities conducted by trade associations. The market information disseminated by the Cement Manufacturers Protective Association—statistics on production, stocks, and shipments—is the sort of information which sellers need for wise decisions in

148. Specifically, the Commission ordered respondents to cease and desist from entering into, continuing, cooperating in, or carrying out "any planned common course of action, understanding, agreement, combination, or conspiracy" to quote or sell cement "at prices calculated or determined pursuant to or in accordance with the multiple basing-point delivered-price system. . . ." *Id.* at 260. The Commission prohibited some sixteen kinds of concerted action in aid or support of a basing-point delivered-pricing system, such as refusing to sell or quote f.o.b. mill and permit customers to provide transportation; quoting f.o.b. mill prices which when added to freight charges will systematically produce identical delivered prices by all sellers at any given destination; quoting or selling at delivered prices systematically equivalent to a price at and freight from some point other than the actual shipping point; quoting or selling at delivered prices which systematically include an artificial freight factor; quoting or selling at destination-cost prices but making specified deductions in invoicing; circulating freight rate information to be used as a factor in the price of cement; agreeing on a classification of customers; agreeing on certain uses for which or purchasers to whom cement will not be sold; exchanging statistical data which reveal an individual respondent's production, stocks, sales, or shipments; maintaining a spy system to police the use of imported cement; or agreeing on terms and conditions of sale. The Commission also ordered respondents to cease cooperating in price discrimination among their customers by charging and accepting mill net prices which vary by the amount necessary to produce delivered prices identical with their rivals' prices to such customers. *Id.* at 261.
149. Aetna Portland Cement Co. v. Federal Trade Commission, 157 F. 2d 533 (7th Cir. 1946).
150. Federal Trade Commission v. Cement Institute, 333 U.S. 683 (1948).
151. This history cannot be summarized adequately here. It has produced a considerable body of literature. See Earl Latham, "Giantism and Basing Points: A Political Analysis," 58 Yale L. J. 383 (1949); Fritz Machlup, *The Basing-point System* (Philadelphia: Blakiston, 1949), pp. 40–41, 78–83, 92; Vernon A. Mund, *Government and Business* (New York: Harper, 1950), pp. 386–90; Stocking and Watkins, *Monopoly and Free Enterprise*, at 193–216.

Workable Competition and Antitrust Policy

planning production. Even the information on prices, disseminated as a part of the association's program on specific job contracts, covered prices on closed transactions and is the sort of information essential to wise decision-making by business rivals. An objection to the association's activities in collecting and disseminating market information is, of course, that it went only to sellers and that the price information was specific rather than general in character.

Basing point pricing, on the other hand, as *practiced by the cement industry* was an effective device for weakening competition; and when the Federal Trade Commission challenged, on the ground of conspiracy, the industry's use of systematic basing point pricing, it won its case.

To discuss this issue would carry this study beyond an appropriate scope.[152] It may be relevant, however, to reproduce a forthright and oft-quoted statement about the competitive significance of systematic basing

---

152. The literature on the economic and legal significance of basing-point pricing is voluminous. The more important discussions include: Burns, *op. cit. supra* note 2, at 280–90, 329–71; Clark, "Basing Point Methods of Price Quoting," 4 Can. J. Econ. and Pol. Sci. 477 (1938); Clark, "Imperfect Competition Theory and Basing-Point Problems," 33 Am. Econ. Rev. 283 (1943); Clark, "The Law and Economics of Basing Points: Appraisal and Proposals," 39 Am. Econ. Rev. 430 (1949); Clark, "Machlup on the Basing-Point System," 63 Q. J. Econ. 315 (1949); Carroll R. Daugherty, Melvin G. deChazeau, and Samuel S. Stratton, *The Economics of the Iron and Steel Industry* (Bureau of Business Research, University of Pittsburgh; New York: McGraw-Hill, 1937), pp. 533–732; Edwards, "The Effect of Recent Basing-Point Decisions upon Business Practices," 38 Am. Econ. Rev. 828 (1948); Edwards, "Geographic Price Formulas and the Concentration of Economic Power," 37 Georgetown L. J. 135 (1949); Fetter, *The Masquerade of Monopoly, passim;* Fetter, "The New Plea for Basing-Point Monopoly," 45 J. Pol. Econ. 577 (1937); Fetter, "Exit Basing Point Pricing," 38 Am. Econ. Rev. 815 (1948); E. B. George, "The Law and Economics of Basing Points," 56 Dun's Review 14 (September 1948); *id.* at 11 (October 1948); *id.* at 22 (November 1948); William Summers Johnson, "The Restrictive Incidence of Basing-Point Pricing on Regional Development," 37 Georgetown L. J. 149 (1949); Carl Kaysen, "Basing Point Pricing and Public Policy," 63 Q. J. Econ. 289 (1949); Robert Kraemer, ed., "Delivered Pricing: A Symposium," 15 Law and Contemp. Prob. 123–310 (1950); Latham, *op. cit. supra* note 151; Machlup, *op. cit. supra* note 151; Mund, *Open Markets* (New York: Harper, 1948), pp. 165 et seq.; Mund, "Monopolistic Competition and Public Price Policy," 32 Am. Econ. Rev. 727 (1942); Mund, "Application of Economic Analysis to Antitrust Law Policy," in Proceedings of Twentieth Annual Conference of the Pacific Coast Economic Association (1941), p. 75; Mund, "The 'Freight Allowed' Method of Price Quotation," 54 Q. J. Econ. 232 (1940); Alfred Nicols, "The Economic Consequences of Some Recent Antitrust Decisions: The Cement Case," 39 Am. Econ. Rev. (Proceedings of American Economic Ass'n) 297, 311–21 (1949); George H. Sage, *Basing-Point Systems under the Federal Antitrust Laws* (St. Louis: Thomas Law Book Co., 1951); Simon, *op. cit supra* note 16; Arthur Smithies, "Aspects of the Basing-Point System," 32 Am. Econ. Rev. 705 (1942); Stocking, *Basing Point Pricing and Regional Development*

Legality of Trade Association Activities

point pricing which apparently reflects its real character. An industry spokesman put it this way:

> Do you think any of the arguments for the basing point system, which we have thus far advanced, will arouse anything but derision in and out of the government? I have read them all recently. Some of them are very clever and ingenious. They amount to this however: that we price this way in order to discourage monopolistic practices and to preserve free competition, etc. This is sheer bunk and hypocrisy. The truth is of course—and there can be no serious, respectable discussion of our case unless this is acknowledged—that ours is an industry above all others that cannot stand free competition, that must systematically restrain competition or be ruined.[153]

Cement Cases Reflect Difficulty of Determining When Competition Is Workable

The usefulness of the cement cases is not in drawing a line between economically desirable and undesirable price-reporting activities, but in showing how treacherous is the principle of workable competition as a guide to public policy when set up as a standard by which to judge an industry's performance. In the *Cement Institute* proceedings both the Commission and the industry utilized economic experts in developing their case. Economists called by the industry [154] testified that the identical delivered prices charged under the industry's pricing system were a reflection of normal, healthy, competitive business rivalry. Economists called by the Commission testified that basing point pricing was discriminatory and incompatible with a free market. About its significance to the general welfare Jacob Viner, then professor of economics at the University of Chicago, testified: "[I]n thinking about the structure, I have not been able to see how you could design any worse one, from the point of view of national economy, assuming we have free choice." [155]

(Chapel Hill: University of North Carolina Press, 1954); United States Steel Corp., *TNEC Papers* III, "The Basing Point Method" (New York [?] United States Steel Corp., 1940); Walter B. Wooden and Hugh E. White, "An Analysis of the Basing-Point System of Delivered Prices as Presented by United States Steel Corporation in 'Exhibits Nos. 1410 and 1418,' " p. 91 (TNEC Monograph No. 42, 1941).

153. Letter of May 17, 1934, from John Treanor to B. H. Rader, Chairman of the Code Authority for the Cement Industry, Brief for Respondent, at 127, Aetna Portland Cement Co. v. Federal Trade Commission, 157 F. 2d 533 (7th Cir., 1946).

154. These included Fairchild, Grether, Griffen, Vaile, and Westerfield. Brief of Respondents-Petitioners, A Topical Digest of the Evidence, Appendix A, at 3005–82, Aetna Portland Cement Co. v. Federal Trade Commission, 157 F. 2d 533 (7th Cir., 1946).

155. Brief for Respondent, at 89, citing Record 5225, Aetna Portland Cement Co.

Workable Competition and Antitrust Policy

The *Cement* cases lend convincing support to Mason's observation that on the issue of the workability of any competitive arrangement judgment is apt to reflect the preconceptions of the judges.[156] The standard here proposed for judging the economic significance of open price-reporting systems has the advantage of relative simplicity, and it should appeal to those who are willing to rely primarily on market forces to guide the economy. Determining whether an arrangement reflects or interferes with competition is not always easy, but it is easier than determining whether an arrangement that interferes with competition promotes the general welfare.[157]

THE SUGAR INSTITUTE

When the American Sugar Refining Company acquired the stock of four Philadelphia sugar companies in the early nineties,[158] it boosted its control of domestic sugar output to 98 per cent of the country's total. Few monopolies have been more complete. Despite the Court's blessing in the *E. C. Knight* case, the sugar monopoly was short-lived. Competition sprang up all around the place [159] and a quarter-century later had become, from

v. Federal Trade Commission, 157 F. 2d 533 (7th Cir., 1946). Other economists expressed similar points of view: Duddy, Fetter, Hibbard, Nourse. *Id.* at 87–107.

156. See p. 30 *supra.*

157. In 1938 Clark expounded a theory to explain the origins of basing-point pricing which I have characterized as a theory of spontaneous evolution. See Clark, "Basing Point Methods of Quoting Prices," 4 Can. J. Econ. and Pol. Sci. 477 (1938); Stocking, "The Economics of Basing Point Pricing," 15 Law and Contemp. Prob. 159, 162–64 (1950). In writing on this subject at a later date Clark implied, without specifically saying so, that conspiracy may exert a considerable influence in *establishing* a basing-point pricing system. Clark, "The Law and Economics of Basing Points: Appraisal and Proposals," 39 Am. Econ. Rev. 430, especially 439 (1949). But he implied also that in *setting* base prices rivals act independently, taking account of the indirect as well as the direct consequences of their decisions. This leads to identical pricing. If this view is correct, it means that by conspiring to use a basing-point pricing system, oligopolists place themselves in a position better to reap the fruits of oligopolistic pricing in accordance with the Chamberlinian principle.

158. The Antitrust Division instituted proceedings to enjoin these purchases but, as indicated in the text at the beginning of this article, the Supreme Court ruled that the Sherman Act did not apply to monopolies in manufacture. United States v. E. C. Knight Co., 156 U.S. 1 (1895). See note 3 *supra.*

159. As rivals appeared in the market, American continued for a decade or more its practice of trying to block or control competition. In 1903, when the Pennsylvania Sugar Refining Company was about to open a new refinery, representatives of American by a series of legal and financial moves against its principals succeeded in blocking it. By 1911 American had bought an average of 41 per cent stock interest in eleven companies refining about one-half the country's beet sugar output. It had also acquired substantial stock interests in the National, the Great Western,

Legality of Trade Association Activities

the industry's point of view, intolerably severe. By 1927 the American Sugar Refining Company produced only one-fourth of the domestically refined cane sugar. It was still the country's largest refiner but only by a small margin, National Sugar Refining Company refining 22 per cent. Thirteen other refineries, only one of which refined as much as 10 per cent of the total, accounted for the balance.[160] Moreover, domestically refined cane sugar met the competition of beet sugar and of "off-shore" refined cane sugar.[161] The rise of competition promptly brought a decrease in refiners' margins, but World War I reversed the trend and brought great but temporary prosperity.[162] The depression reversed a long upward trend in the per capita consumption of sugar. The "slimness campaign" of 1927 accentuated the reversals. Hard times precipitated what the district court described as "highly unfair and otherwise uneconomic competitive conditions." [163] As the court put it,

[A]rbitrary, secret rebates and concessions were the rule, and the widespread knowledge of market conditions which the courts and economists have recognized as necessary for intelligent fair competition were lacking. . . . [T]he refiners . . . were disturbed economically and morally over the then prevailing conditions. . . . [A]t least American was concerned at the possibility of liability under the Clayton Act because of the discriminations resulting from the various concessions.[164]

Refiners Organize Sugar Institute

To remedy this situation the domestic cane-sugar refiners in December 1927 organized the Sugar Institute, drew up a "Code of Ethics," and inaugurated a program ostensibly designed primarily to eliminate secret

and the Michigan Sugar companies. A government suit resulted in a consent decree in 1922 limiting its stock interest in these three companies to 25, 31, and 34 per cent, respectively. United States v. American Sugar Refining Co., U.S.D.C., Dkt. No. 7–8 (S.D.N.Y. May 9, 1922). See Charles A. Pearce, *Trade Association Survey* (TNEC Monograph No. 18, 1914), p. 111.
  160. *Id.* at 112.
  161. Defendants' Exhibit D-15, reproduced in the district court's opinion in United States v. Sugar Institute, 15 F. Supp. 817, 823 (S.D.N.Y. 1934), showed that in 1927, 82.5 per cent of the country's sugar supply was domestically refined cane, 14.4 per cent consisted of domestic beet sugar, and 2.8 per cent represented foreign- and insular-refined cane sugar. Institute members refined between 70 and 80 per cent of the domestically refined sugar. *Id.* at 822.
  162. Pearce, *op. cit. supra* note 159, at 113.
  163. United States v. Sugar Institute, 15 F. Supp. 817, 826 (S.D.N.Y. 1934).
  164. *Id.* at 826–27. The Supreme Court approved this finding and reproduced it in substantially this form in its opinion. Sugar Institute v. United States, 297 U.S. 553, 575 (1936).

concessions and rebates.[165] The core of the institute's program was the basic agreement that "[a]ll discriminations between customers should be abolished. To that end, sugar should be sold only upon open prices and terms publicly announced."[166]

On March 30, 1931, in the District Court for the Southern District of New York, the government filed a petition for the dissolution of the institute and an injunction against its members on the grounds of conspiracy to restrain interstate commerce in sugar. The district court on March 7, 1934, and the Supreme Court on March 30, 1936, handed down opinions holding that the arrangement complained against constituted an unlawful combination and conspiracy in restraint of trade and enjoining forty-odd specific collusive practices which represented essential elements in the broader conspiracy.[167]

The Supreme Court found nothing new or objectionable in the industry's method of announcing prices. What it did object to was the refiners' agreement to adhere to their prices and terms as publicly announced and to the ancillary arrangements designed to convert an innocent price-reporting program into a device for eliminating competition among the sugar refiners. Both the facts and the logic of this case are well known and can be dealt with briefly. The Court's decision in this case conforms to a sound application of the rule of reason and the principle of workable competition, although the logic by which it reaches its decision does not always do so.

Court Approves the Principle of Cooperation to End Abuses

The Supreme Court recognized the propriety of cooperation among businessmen to bring health to a sick industry by eliminating unsavory business practices. Citing its opinion in the *Appalachian Coals* case,[168] the Court put it this way:

165. A few months later the beet-sugar manufacturers organized a similar trade association, the Domestic Sugar Bureau, with a substantially identical "Code of Ethics." The two organizations enjoyed a high degree of cooperation and sometimes held joint meetings and took joint action. The district court found that although domestic refined sugar's price differential of 20 cents per hundred pounds over beet sugar prevailed more consistently after the organization of the two trade associations than before, the evidence did not establish an agreement between them. United States v. Sugar Institute, 15 F. Supp. 817, 824 (S.D.N.Y. 1934).

166. *Id.* at 828.

167. United States v. Sugar Institute, 15 F. Supp. 817 (S.D.N.Y. 1934), *aff'd*, Sugar Institute v. United States, 297 U.S. 553 (1936).

168. Appalachian Coals, Inc. v. United States, 288 U.S. 344, 373, 374 (1933).

Legality of Trade Association Activities

Voluntary action to end abuses and to foster fair competitive opportunities in the public interest may be more effective than legal processes. And cooperative endeavor may appropriately have wider objectives than merely the removal of evils which are infractions of positive law. Nor does the fact that the correction of abuses may tend to stabilize a business, or to produce fairer price levels, require that abuses should go uncorrected or that an effort to correct them should for that reason alone be stamped as an unreasonable restraint of trade. Accordingly we have held that a cooperative enterprise otherwise free from objection, which carries with it no monopolistic menace, is not to be condemned as an undue restraint merely because it may effect a change in market conditions where the change would be in mitigation of recognized evils and would not impair, but rather foster, fair competitive opportunities.[169]

This is a principle which reasonable men are apt to approve. In truth, their approving it is likely to be regarded as evidence of their reasonableness. But it fails to recognize the nature of the sugar industry's sickness. It confuses the disease with its symptoms. The sugar industry had come upon hard times. World War I had brought an artificial prosperity and had expanded capacity. The postwar slump was followed by a change in the eating habits of millions of people. People demanded less sugar and this called for a readjustment in the use of resources. The price system's method of effecting such readjustments is a cruel one. Unprofitable cost-price relationships cause bankruptcies. A readjustment in profits was taking place in the sugar industry in the years immediately preceding the organization of the institute.[170] That businessmen should want to collaborate to make prices more stable in the face of a declining demand is understandable, but it is not a very promising method of forcing economic readjustments.[171]

169. Sugar Institute v. United States, 297 U.S. 553, 598 (1936).
170. It was the "unethical" (price-cutting) refiners who took the lead in organizing the Sugar Institute, but they implied that in doing so they were trying to save their more "ethical" rivals. The district court's opinion quoted from the defendants' brief: "[T]he refiners who did not indulge in concessions were well on their way to becoming martyrs . . . their problem was how long they could survive." United States v. Sugar Institute, 15 F. Supp. 817, 826 (S.D.N.Y. 1934). The court took a different view of the matter, observing: "While the 'ethical' refiners may have been inconvenienced through the sales methods of some of their competitors and probably believed its effect on them to be harmful, they had no part in the first steps taken to form the Institute and were in no danger of being eliminated from the industry. . . . Moreover, despite the 'fair competition' inaugurated by the Institute, two of the 'ethical' companies showed substantially less profits for the post-Institute period, 1928 to 1931, than for the pre-Institute years of 1925 to 1927, while the profits of several of the 'unethical' companies increased substantially in the post-Institute period." Ibid.
171. For a contrary view see Clark, *Guideposts in Time of Change* (New York: Harper, 1949), pp. 119–21. Clark denies that price changes are necessary to allocate

Workable Competition and Antitrust Policy

Price Discrimination Performs an Economic Function

In an effort to survive, refiners had made concessions to get business. They made them secretly because, with sugar a standardized product, to have made them openly would have forced all prices down to the level of the concessions. Price discrimination is difficult to justify on ethical grounds, and the refiners who regularly discriminated were dubbed "unethical." To the layman it may seem hard to justify on economic grounds; and where the discrimination may tend to lessen competition substantially, there is a law against it.[172] The Supreme Court's opinion lends approval to cooperative action to insure compliance with legal obligations so long as the cooperation itself does not become illegal, and this, too, is apt to strike reasonable men as reasonable. But economists have come to realize that price discrimination may serve an economic function in an economy of imperfect competition. In markets of few sellers it may contribute to that degree of price flexibility essential to efficient economic readjustments. The secret concessions may reflect economic pressures that eventually will undermine a price level not justified by supply-demand relationships. In short, they may convert quasi-monopoly prices into competitive prices.[173]

To permit businessmen to conspire to eliminate price discrimination because it may violate the Clayton Act is to invite them to violate the

resources economically and believes that changes in the volume of sales are sufficient. For a discussion of this point see Stocking and Watkins, *Monopoly and Free Enterprise*, at 100 n. 42.

172. The sugar refiners who organized the Sugar Institute in 1927 to abolish price discriminations among customers had little to fear from the courts' interpretation of the Clayton Act. Although Section 2 outlawed price discrimination which might substantially lessen competition in *any* line of commerce, at least two decisions had ruled that the act did not apply to competition at the secondary level. National Biscuit Co. v. Federal Trade Commission, 299 Fed. 733 (2d Cir. 1924), *cert. denied*, 266 U.S. 613; Mennen Co. v. Federal Trade Commission, 288 Fed. 774 (2d Cir. 1923), *cert. denied*, 262 U.S. 759. The Clayton Act was not applied to injury to competition among purchasers until 1929, in a triple-damages action between private litigants. Van Camp & Sons v. American Can Co., 278 U.S. 245 (1929). The Sugar Institute's encounter with the law arose from another cause—conspiracy under the Sherman Act—five years before the Robinson-Patman amendment to the Clayton Act made it unmistakably clear that Section 2 applies to injuries to competition among the buyers from a price-discriminating seller.

173. Monopoly prices are not necessarily profitable prices. Monopolists and oligopolists in the face of declining demand cannot always so restrain output as to insure profitable operations. Whether or not they can do so will depend on the nature of costs and of demand. Similarly, conspiratorial prices may not guarantee profits and their aim may be merely to cut losses.

Legality of Trade Association Activities

Sherman Act. The sugar refiners did not wait for either the permission or the invitation. The Court rejected for lack of supporting evidence the refiners' contention that price discrimination was in fact tending to lessen competition or to create a monopoly.

Courts Find Conspiracy

Students of this case may differ in their judgments on the economic and legal significance of price discrimination and on the significance to workable competition of the refiners' price-reporting program, but they are unlikely to challenge the district court's finding and the Supreme Court's confirmation that the sugar refiners had conspired to adhere to publicly announced future prices, terms, and conditions of sale, to eliminate certain consignment points and ports of entry for sugar, to maintain and police a delivered-pricing system, to determine transportation charges to be collected from customers, to eliminate quantity discounts and long-term contracts, to boycott distributors performing both brokerage and wholesaling functions, and to withhold from buyers the statistical information exchanged among themselves, and that the dominant aim of the institute was to preserve uniform, high prices. Activities such as these could not have been designed to insure open and free competition among business rivals, but rather to protect sugar refiners from the harassing and disturbing consequences of price competition in an industry suffering from surplus capacity and shrinking markets. Few economists are likely to regard the Sugar Institute's program in its entirety as consistent with the principle of workable competition; at least, none of the expositors of the concept have suggested that conspiracy to restrain competition is an attribute of workability.

Even the institute's open price-reporting plan considered separately has serious defects. The agreement among members to adhere to their publicly announced prices, terms, and conditions of sale until they announced a change inevitably tended to check general price reductions. By eliminating all concessions the plan deprived individual buyers of an opportunity to negotiate on prices, a useful practice in markets of imperfect competition. By withholding from buyers market information which it supplied to sellers, the institute also made it difficult for buyers to plan their buying programs as soundly as sellers could plan their production programs. On the whole the system tended to prevent effective competition, not to make competition more workable, and both the lower court and the Supreme

Court found most of the institute's activities to be unreasonable restraints of trade.[174]

FEDERAL TRADE COMMISSION CASES

The Antitrust Division of the Department of Justice has not been alone in challenging the legality of trade association activities. The Federal Trade Commission has conducted many proceedings against trade associations under Section 5 of the Federal Trade Commission Act.[175] The more important of these include the *Salt Producers Association*,[176] the *United States Maltsters Association*,[177] the *Milk and Ice Cream Can Institute*,[178] the *National Crepe Paper Association of America*,[179] and the *Tag Manufacturers Institute* [180] cases.

The *Salt Producers* and the *Maltsters* cases have a great deal in common. In each of the industries involved, a relatively small number of sellers accounted for most of the business, each of the associations had eighteen members, each was managed by industrial consultants specializing in trade association activities, and each association carried on a program which apparently was designed to promote the individual welfare of trade rivals by promoting their welfare as a group. In more technical terms, each program apparently was designed so to inform oligopolists about market conditions that they would be persuaded, without agreeing to do so, to

---

174. The district court refused to order the dissolution of the institute but enjoined so many of its activities that shortly after the Supreme Court's opinion the sugar refiners disbanded it. Pearce, *op. cit. supra* note 159, at 142.

175. Section 5 prohibits "unfair methods of competition in commerce." 38 Stat. 719 (1914), as amended, 15 U.S.C. § 45(a) (1958). The Supreme Court has held that a combination to eliminate competition, unlawful under the Sherman Act, may be prosecuted as an unfair method of competition. Federal Trade Commission v. Cement Institute, 333 U.S. 683 (1948), *rehearing denied*, 334 U.S. 839 (1948). In fact, "it was the object of the Federal Trade Commission Act to reach not merely in their fruition but also in their incipiency combinations which could lead to these [price-fixing arrangements] and other trade restraints and practices. . . ." Fashion Originators' Guild v. Federal Trade Commission, 312 U.S. 457, 466 (1941). Between the end of NRA and December 1, 1939, the Commission issued cease and desist orders in thirty-five price conspiracy proceedings, most of them against trade associations. Guthrie, "Federal Trade Commission Price Conspiracy Cases, 1935–1939," 8 Geo. Wash. L. Rev. 620 (1940).

176. 34 F.T.C. 38 (1941), *modified and aff'd*, 134 F.2d 354 (7th Cir. 1943).

177. 35 F.T.C. 797 (1942), *order modified*, 37 F.T.C. 342 (1943), *aff'd*, 152 F.2d 161 (7th Cir. 1945).

178. 37 F.T.C. 419 (1943), *aff'd*, 152 F.2d 478 (7th Cir. 1946).

179. 38 F.T.C. 282 (1944), *aff'd sub nom.* Fort Howard Paper Co. v. Federal Trade Commission, 156 F.2d 899 (7th Cir. 1946).

180. 43 F.T.C. 499 (1947), *rev'd*, 174 F.2d 452 (1st Cir. 1949).

Legality of Trade Association Activities

behave as oligopolists of the theoretical model are supposed to behave— i.e., like monopolists.

These cases can be disposed of briefly. They lend little support to those who contend that the principle of workable competition has been violated in applying the antitrust statutes to trade association activities. Both the salt producers' and the maltsters' associations were organized and operated under the guidance of Stevenson, Jordan & Harrison, trade association consultants, who had earlier expressed unequivocally their belief that competition and free enterprise were "idols of brass and stone into whose fiery maws are being thrown the peace, security, and happiness of all our people." [181] They had boldly advocated a change in federal statutes to provide for a system of industrial self-government, to be applicable to the whole of an industry on a decision by representatives of two-thirds of the industry's capital, which would include the regulation and allocation of output among plants and territories and a determination of the price at which an industry would offer its product to the public.[182]

Salt Producers Association

In the Salt Producers Association, Stevenson, Jordan & Harrison apparently tried to put its notions into operation on a voluntary basis without benefit of legislation. At any rate, six months after the Supreme Court had invalidated the National Industrial Recovery Act [183] this firm conducted a survey covering the production, sales, plant capacity, marketing expense, average yield f.o.b. plant in delivered price zones, etc., of the leading salt producers during the previous four years and ten months. The firm calculated composite figures on these data for the industry and supplied each association member with the several composites and with similar figures calculated for each firm separately. At a meeting of the association members in Chicago in April 1936 representatives of Stevenson, Jordan & Harrison pointed out that salt producers had a large excess of capacity, that their sales expense was inordinately high, and their rate of earnings distressingly low. These unhappy conditions resulted from the unremitting efforts of the several producers to get a larger share of the salt business without proper regard to the cost of getting it. For thirty days

---

181. See Wilcox, *Competition and Monopoly in American Industry* (TNEC Monograph No. 21, 1941), p. 253.
182. *Id.* at 253–54.
183. Act of June 16, 1933, c. 90, 48 Stat. 195, invalidated May 27, 1935, in A.L.A. Schechter Poultry Corp. v. United States, 295 U.S. 495 (1935).

77

after the Chicago meeting Stevenson, Jordan & Harrison conducted a personal educational campaign among the several salt producers, explaining to each the "fundamental economic truths" developed by the survey, namely, that unrestrained trade rivalry in selling salt predestined salt producers to high costs and low returns. The association consultants then held a second meeting with the salt producers, at which the producers commissioned them to collect monthly statistics on production, sales, and marketing expense and to calculate a composite figure for each producer. To insure the accuracy of these figures the salt producers agreed that Stevenson, Jordan & Harrison should audit their books from time to time.

The Salt Producers Association held monthly meetings at which its consultants explained and interpreted the monthly statistics on current production and yield, at times giving their opinion on the trend in demand. From time to time when conducting audits of members' books, representatives of Stevenson, Jordan & Harrison emphasized to company managers the probable consequences of an overzealous effort to get business at the expense of fellow members. Apparently familiar with the theories of oligopolistic pricing, they pointed out that in selling a homogeneous product any seller could get business at the expense of his rival only by lowering his price; that other sellers would promptly meet a price cut; and that each seller would continue to sell approximately the same amount at the lower price.[184] When their educational campaign proved inadequate to restrain the competitive practices of salt producers, representatives of Stevenson, Jordan & Harrison urged them to consider the unhappy consequences to themselves of trying to get more than their customary share of the market.

The Federal Trade Commission found that the salt producers' program as formulated under the guidance of Stevenson, Jordan & Harrison was "carried out in every particular," and it concluded that the "normal conflict of contending competitive forces engendered by an honest desire for gain was thereby restrained and suppressed."[185] In the proceedings before the Commission the respondents admitted the facts as alleged,[186] and on

---

184. This argument apparently rests on what might be termed the ideal oligopolistic solution as expounded by Chamberlin in his *Theory of Monopolistic Competition*. See p. 27 *supra*. Chamberlin's theory was based on carefully stated assumptions, and he recognized that uncertainties might lead to prices ranging between monopoly prices and those established by pure competition. *Id.* at 51–53.

185. Salt Producers Association, 34 F.T.C. 38, 53 (1941).

186. The court of appeals noted that initially the respondents filed individual answers to the Commission's complaint, denying the Commission's allegations, then withdrew their original answers and substituted answers wherein "they admit(ted)

Legality of Trade Association Activities

appeal they challenged only certain provisions of the Commission's cease and desist order.[187]

Obviously, here was no trade association designed to enable buyers and sellers of salt independently to make informed decisions and thereby facilitate the operation of market forces. Here was no program to free markets from imperfections imposed by ignorance, but a program to subject it to rigidities created by one-sided knowledge. It was a collective endeavor to circumvent competition and to enhance the security of salt producers at the expense of salt buyers. It was an interesting attempt to persuade real oligopolists in business markets to behave like the ideal oligopolists of the theorists' models—a conscious effort to pluck the fruits of conspiracy without paying its legal penalties. It is not surprising that it failed.

United States Maltsters Association

Stevenson, Jordan & Harrison also managed the United States Maltsters Association, for which they devised a simpler program. This was on its face a price-reporting plan designed to inform maltsters of the state of the market. Under the plan each member furnished the association and the association compiled and sent all members daily reports on all malt sales, showing the name of the seller, the date of sale, quantity, grade, and price received. Each member reported weekly and monthly his total malt shipped, clean barley steeped, unfilled malt orders, unfilled commitments, malt stocks on hand, total barley on hand, in process and to arrive, barley purchases for the week, orders and commitments booked and cancelled, and malt shipped to or for another maltster.[188] The information is obviously of the sort essential for wise decisions by trade rivals. The association was not content, however, merely to supply its members with aggre-

---

all of the material allegations of fact set forth in said complaint and waive[d] all intervening procedure and further hearing as to the said facts." Salt Producers Ass'n v. Federal Trade Commission, 134 F.2d 354, 356 (7th Cir. 1943).

187. The salt producers objected to the Commission's use of the phrase "any common course of action" to supplement its prohibition of conspiracy to fix or maintain the prices of salt or regulate its production, arguing that competition or even coincidence might produce a common course of action. The court of appeals substituted the phrase "any planned common course of action," "so that only illegal *contractual* arrangements will be subject to contempt proceedings." *Id.* at 357. The court also limited the Commission's prohibition of delivered-price zones to those established by agreements, and its prohibition of the exchange of price information to situations in which such exchange is part of a scheme to restrict competition. *Id.* at 358, 359.

188. United States Maltsters Ass'n v. Federal Trade Commission, 152 F.2d 161, 162–63 (7th Cir. 1945).

Workable Competition and Antitrust Policy

gate figures. Each member got precise data on all other members. The buyers got none of the information.

Other features make the plan look less like a plan for removing market imperfections by banning ignorance than a plan for insuring uniform pricing by educating trade rivals. Each member supplied all other members with his price list. Each reported by wire any deviation from list price and the association manager immediately relayed the information by wire to all members. All members promptly conformed their prices. All members reported prices f.o.b. Chicago, although only three had their principal place of business there.[189] All members sold only on a delivered-price basis, quoting a delivered price equal to the Chicago price plus a standard freight rate from Chicago to the point of delivery. Each member quoted identical terms of sale. The Commission found that association members had agreed on several price-affecting practices which they followed. They had agreed to adopt grading standards, to quote only delivered prices f.o.b. final destination, and to adopt the grading specifications recommended by the association's executive committee in all instances where a guaranty of specifications was required. They had agreed on a standard form of contract, not to sell malt for resale, not to permit sales agents handling domestic malt to sell imported malt, to adopt a uniform discount of one-half cent a bushel, and that the association managers should audit their books to insure the accuracy of their reporting.[190]

The Commission found this arrangement a price-fixing conspiracy, although it found no evidence of a specific agreement to fix prices. The record revealed, however, that for two years and four months all maltsters in the association had sold at identical prices. While revealing 100 per cent uniformity in the members' price for malt, the record revealed great diversity in their cost of producing malt. The most important element in the cost of producing malt is the cost of barley, representing as it does from 80 to 85 per cent of the total cost. Maltsters bought their barley by sample at terminal markets. No doubt maltsters paid about the same price for barley at any particular time, but barley prices fluctuated greatly. Transportation costs from terminal markets or country elevators to malting plants and from malting plants to customers' breweries varied greatly among different producers. The Commission found that manufacturing costs among the association members varied by as much as 30 per cent. With such diversified and fluctuating costs the fact that the maltsters

189. United States Maltsters Ass'n, 35 F.T.C. 797, 799–800, 809 (1942). Most of the plants were located in Wisconsin.
190. *Id.* at 807, 808, 810.

Legality of Trade Association Activities

sold at identical prices over a period of two years and four months would seem to justify the Commission's conclusion that the maltsters' program represented a conspiracy to restrain competition. The court of appeals agreed.

By the standard which this study sets up the maltsters' price-reporting program had not contributed to workable competition in their industry.[191] It did not provide both buyers and sellers with basic information essential for intelligent decisions. On the contrary, it apparently provided sellers with a mechanism whereby they could be assured that price competition among themselves would be eliminated.

Milk and Ice Cream Can Institute

Eight firms making about 95 per cent of the metal milk and ice-cream cans sold in the United States organized the Milk and Ice Cream Can Institute in 1930.[192] In doing this they had the advice of D. S. Hunter, a professional promoter and manager of trade associations, doing business as D. S. Hunter & Associates. Hunter, serving the institute as "commissioner," its sole officer, supervised its meetings, recommended its activities, and collected and disseminated certain market information on milk and ice-cream cans. Under the institute's program each member reported daily on forms approved by the institute all orders received and all contracts entered into or fulfilled. The daily reports showed the date of the order, the name, address and business of the purchaser, quantity, capacity, and description of the cans, unit price with extras or deductions, discounts and terms, and freight rate added or "allowed to equalize" with a given basing point. Hunter mailed to each member a consolidated daily report

---

191. Not all economists would agree. One economist testified for the maltsters that the price uniformity that prevailed under the association's program was "consistent with and a necessary consequence of the normal functioning of competition in such an industry." United States Maltsters Ass'n v. Federal Trade Commission, 152 F.2d 162, 165 (7th Cir. 1945). The court conceded that this line of testimony furnished "the basis for a good argument" but insisted that it could not stand up against the Commission's findings. As for the maltsters' complaint that the Commission ignored the economic forces in their industry that made for price uniformity, the court said: "It is true that the Commission made no findings upon petitioners' theory in this respect. It does not follow, however, that such factors were ignored. It merely indicates, so we think, that the Commission, after considering all the evidence, came to the conclusion, and we think correctly, that it was more reasonable to believe that petitioners' price structure resulted from an agreement rather than economic factors." *Ibid.*

192. The description of the industry is taken from the Federal Trade Commission proceedings, Milk and Ice Cream Can Institute, 37 F.T.C. 419 (1943).

giving similar information on all sales or contracts but omitting the name of the reporting member and the name and address of the customer. Each member reported monthly on forms approved by the institute the quantity, capacity, and description of cans shipped into each state and for export, unfilled orders, volume of business for the month, average daily productive capacity, and percentage of capacity utilized during the month.

Institute members when quoting prices had followed the practice of equalizing freight with the nearest competitor's point of shipment before they organized the institute. By agreement they continued the practice and through the institute contracted for a freight rate reporting service which, although showing rates between members' shipping points and various destinations specified by Hunter, gave no information as to routing and was useful primarily in quoting delivered prices and invoicing customers. Upon evidence or suspicion from the daily reports that members quoted or sold at nonidentical delivered prices Hunter would "call such deviation or possible deviation to the attention of the members as a whole, and from time to time requested . . . members to review their data to determine if the discrepancies were due to errors in compilation." [193]

Hunter's task of checking errors was facilitated by a classification of cans of different types (which were sold under various trade names) and by the use of symbols to identify a can's classification. The Commission found that the institute had carried its standardization program beyond government requirements or the requirements of customers and that it had done so the more easily to standardize prices.[194] It found that the in-

---

193. *Id.* at 433.
194. A commentator has criticized the Commission's complaint in this proceeding as attacking the institute's efforts to standardize milk and ice-cream cans, even though trade association standardization programs have been generally recognized as beneficial and the Department of Commerce since 1921 has sponsored the standardization of products through its program for Simplified Practice Recommendations. He says: "[A] reading of this complaint and order cannot help but lead to the conclusion that the Federal Trade Commission is looking askance at standardization programs even when not connected with price fixing, *if it feels that the purpose or effect is to eliminate competition* among the products of the members engaging in the standardization program." Timberlake, "Standardization and Simplification under the Anti-Trust Laws," 29 Cornell L. Q. 301, 314 (1944). Emphasis supplied. The logic of Timberlake's position is obscured by the fact, which he himself points out before quoting the paragraphs in the complaint to which he objects, that the *Milk and Ice Cream Can Institute* complaint is directed against agreements on product standardization as *one of the means and methods* used by institute members to carry out an unlawful combination to suppress competition. This would seem to be a far cry from attacking standardization in and of itself.

The complaint also charges that the institute's standardization program was used to discourage quality competition, in a list of specific means and methods adopted

Legality of Trade Association Activities

stitute for similar purposes had defined and classified customers and for a short period before 1932 had agreed on discounts to be allowed so-called "five-car or more" buyers. On a basis of these and other findings the Commission concluded that the institute's program had a dangerous tendency to restrain competition in the sale of milk and ice-cream cans and had actually done so.

On petition by institute members for review of the Commission's order, the court of appeals saw as the essential question before it "whether the members of the Institute acted in combination or by agreement for the purpose of fixing prices, or their activities contributed to such result. . . ." [195] The court rejected the petitioners' argument that there must be direct proof of an agreement and declared that circumstantial evidence was enough and that the Commission, like "any other fact finding body, is entitled to draw any reasonable inference from the circumstances of the situation." [196] The court was impressed by the record evidence that (1) for more than four years before the Commission issued its complaint, the prices charged by the milk and ice-cream canmakers had been identical for buyers at any point regardless of the location of the seller; (2) uniform delivered prices were made possible by the canmakers' freight-equalization plan; (3) the purpose of the freight-equalization plan as revealed in the minutes of institute meetings and other evidence was to fix the delivered price of milk and ice-cream cans, and its effect was seriously to impair price competition; (4) the institute's system of receiving daily reports from members permitted Hunter to supervise their price activities, and its purpose was to enable a member to determine whether his competitors were adhering to the price list; (5) the institute established a classification of buyers and determined the discount allowable to each class; (6) the manufacturers exerted such a meticulous effort to standard-

---

"pursuant to and in furtherance of the aforesaid combination." Timberlake suggests that the Commission *may* have only intended to charge that standardization was used as a means of effectuating a price-fixing conspiracy. At first blush it would seem either that Timberlake is unwilling to accept the possibility that a trade association's standardization program may be used to eliminate quality competition or that he believes the elimination of such competition inevitably accompanies standardization but is offset by the savings effected through standardization. He fails to clarify the ambiguity of his interpretation of the *Milk and Ice Cream Can Institute* case, but the conclusion of his study seems to be that a trade association may safely set up product standards (definitions) and formulate standard product lines (classifications) as long as members do not agree to make only standard products or to eliminate nonstandard items.

195. Milk and Ice Cream Can Institute v. Federal Trade Commission, 152 F.2d 478, 480 (7th Cir. 1946).
196. *Ibid.*

ize their products as to indicate an agreement; and (7) the institute took steps revealed in its minutes to place restrictions on the sale of "seconds" and to widen the price difference between them and "firsts." [197] The court of appeals concluded from its study of the record:

> No good purpose would be served in a [more] detailed discussion of the various activities of the Institute and its members, relied upon by the Commission in support of its finding that they acted in concert and by agreement. A study of the record is convincing not only that the finding is substantially supported but that it would be difficult to reach any other conclusion.[198]

The court's treatment of the case appears to rest on a fair appraisal of all the significant elements in the factual situation before it. Its conclusion meets the standard of workable competition set up in this study. Nothing in the plan followed by the Milk and Ice Cream Can Institute suggests that it was designed to facilitate the operation of a free market by giving buyers and sellers alike information essential to informed but independent decisions. It looks more like a scheme to insure identical pricing by closely knit oligopolists selling to isolated consumers over a wide market.

National Crepe Paper Association of America

On October 7, 1941, the Federal Trade Commission issued a complaint against the National Crepe Paper Association of America and the eight companies accounting for all the crepe paper made in the United States.[199] The complaint charged the respondents with having conspired to restrain competition in the sale of crepe paper. This case grew out of association activities inaugurated during the NRA, when the association was first organized. The Commission found that association members had entered into numerous agreements during the NRA period which restrained competition among themselves. These included agreements to standardize trade practices and products, file current and future prices with the association, classify customers for pricing purposes, fix prices and terms of sale, and establish a zone pricing system with standard price differentials between the several zones. The Commission found that association members had continued these agreements after the expiration of the NRA, except that some of them ceased to file their price lists and invoices with the association. In making this finding the Commission relied largely on evi-

---

197. *Id.* at 481-83.
198. *Id.* at 481.
199. National Crepe Paper Ass'n of America, 38 F.T.C. 282 (1944).

dence contained in numerous minutes of association meetings extending from June 11, 1935, through May 3, 1939.

The Commission ordered respondents to "cease and desist from entering into, continuing, cooperating in, or carrying out any planned common course of action, agreement, understanding, combination, or conspiracy"[200] to do any of the specific acts it enumerated, which constituted the elements of the alleged conspiracy.

Three of the crepe-paper makers appealed, including two who had withdrawn from the association almost two years before the Commission issued its complaint.[201] The Court of Appeals for the Seventh Circuit sustained the Commission.[202] With only three appellants before it, two of whom were no longer members of the association, the court attached less weight than did the Commission to the documentary evidence of a conspiracy. In upholding the Commission the court said:

> It is the agreement to fix prices in concert that renders the conspiracy illegal. No formal agreement, however, is necessary to constitute an unlawful conspiracy. The essential combination or conspiracy may be found in a course of dealings or other circumstances as well as in any exchange of words.[203]

The principal course of dealings about which the court spoke at some length was the industry's zone pricing system, which resulted in identical delivered prices by trade rivals to all points within a particular zone and in arbitrarily standardized price differentials between zones.[204] The court concluded that "[t]he existence of substantial similarity in delivered prices to zoned territories having identical zone price differentials, by six manufacturers located at different places, was not a happenstance."[205] The reference to six manufacturers seems to be a mistake, since the court found that the two nonmembers continued to adhere to the zone system of pricing.[206]

---

200. *Id.* at 293.
201. Dennison Manufacturing Co. and The Reyburn Manufacturing Co. withdrew from membership in November 1939.
202. Fort Howard Paper Co. v. Federal Trade Commission, 156 F.2d 899 (7th Cir. 1946).
203. *Id.* at 905.
204. The United States was divided into three zones for pricing bulk crepe paper and into two zones for pricing packaged crepe paper. Six manufacturers were located in the northeastern section of the country and the other two in Wisconsin, but Zone 1 included nineteen states and all eight manufacturers. The system did away with the use of freight rate books but permitted identical prices to all customers within a zone regardless of the location of either buyer or seller.
205. Fort Howard Paper Co. v. Federal Trade Commission, 156 F.2d 899, 906 (7th Cir. 1946).
206. *Id.* at 908.

Workable Competition and Antitrust Policy

This is one of the decisions cited by Oppenheim in support of his statement, "A series of civil cases instituted by both the Department of Justice and the Federal Trade Commission produced judicial opinions that countenanced in decision or dicta a deep thrust of the implied conspiracy doctrine." [207] The court's failure to deal explicitly with the specific differences in price policies and practices which the three appellant crepe-paper makers claimed to exist among themselves and in contrast with practices recommended by the trade association may be disturbing, but the court's reliance on circumstantial evidence of conspiracy in this case should not be. To discuss the implied conspiracy doctrine in any thoroughgoing way would lead beyond the scope of this study.[208] But it may be of interest to point out again that eight firms made all the crepe paper produced in this country, they all had belonged to the association, they had standardized their practices under the NRA, and they maintained their zone pricing system—the "artificiality and arbitrariness" of which the court of appeals found "so apparent [that] it can not withstand the inference of agreement." [209]

Concerted action among few sellers may well lead to common pricing policies without any overt agreement.[210] The fewer the sellers and the more nearly identical the conditions under which they operate, the greater the likelihood it will do this. In an old industry like the manufacture of crepe paper, selling a standardized product under well-established trade practices with only eight producing companies, the tendency to uniformity of pricing policies would be strong. The experience in collective discipline acquired under the NRA would accentuate this and would seem likely to carry over into the manufacturers' attitude toward their trade association. Continuing concerted action under these circumstances constitutes a heavy threat to effective competition. The evidence of concerted action

---

207. Oppenheim, *supra* note 2, at 1167.

208. For discussions of the implied conspiracy doctrine from several points of view see Sumner S. Kittelle and George P. Lamb, "The Implied Conspiracy Doctrine and Delivered Pricing," 15 Law and Contemp. Prob. 227 (1950); Stocking, "The Economics of Basing Point Pricing," 15 Law and Contemp. Prob. 159 (1950); Stocking, "The Law on Basing Point Pricing: Confusion or Competition," 2 J. Pub. Law 1 (1953); Joseph S. Wright, "Collusion and Parallel Action in Delivered Price Systems," 37 Georgetown L. J. 201 (1949).

209. Fort Howard Paper Co. v. Federal Trade Commission, 156 F.2d 899, 907 (7th Cir. 1946).

210. See discussion of Chamberlinian theory, p. 27 *supra*. A corollary of this theory is that the mutual dissemination of market data among oligopolists may afford the basis for a common interpretation of the market and common pricing policies without conspiracy. See Stocking and Watkins, *Monopoly and Free Enterprise*, at 252–55.

Legality of Trade Association Activities

in the crepe-paper industry seems convincing and the propriety of striking it down scarcely debatable. Economists who emphasize the importance of industrial structure to price behavior may find a mere prohibition of conspiracy an inadequate remedy, but they are unlikely to challenge it as interfering with workable competition.[211]

Tag Manufacturers Institute

Under the NRA the manufacturers of tags operated under a code of fair competition, a major feature of which was an open price-filing system. Under this system tag makers filed tag prices with the code authority and sold their tags at such prices until seven days after they had filed a new price list.[212] For a tag maker to sell for less than his list prices as filed with the code authority was to violate the law. After the Supreme Court invalidated the National Industrial Recovery Act in the *Schechter* decision of May 27, 1935,[213] the tag makers entered into a contract with Frank H. Baxter Associates entitled "Voluntary Code Agreement Between Tag Manufacturers and Frank H. Baxter," dated June 5, 1935, effective August 14, 1935.[214]

New agreements were substituted for the old from time to time—on September 22, 1936,[215] on January 15, 1938,[216] and on November 25, 1940.[217] Thirty-one manufacturers accounting for 95 per cent of the industry's output—four of them for 55 per cent—subscribed to the last two agreements. These agreements differed in important details, some of which will be noted later, but their basic characteristics remained unchanged.

---

211. Those who believe that market forces can be trusted as the best regulators of economic behavior may find some comfort in the fact that despite concerted action among crepe-paper manufacturers, price competition was not entirely eliminated. See Stocking and Watkins, *Monopoly and Free Enterprise*, at 247–49.

212. Code of Fair Competition for the Tag Industry as approved on February 1, 1934, Commission's Exhibit 194B, Tag Manufacturers Institute, 43 F.T.C. 499 (1947).

213. A.L.A. Schechter Poultry Corp. v. United States, 295 U.S. 495 (1935).

214. Commission's Exhibit 74, Tag Manufacturers Institute, 43 F.T.C. 499 (1947). Before the parties signed this agreement Baxter wrote a general letter to the tag makers under date of June 13, 1935, which read in part as follows: "Please understand the Tag Code Open Price Policy is not in force as such. Individual price reporting is still permissible however and we expect it will take organized form very shortly under the Liquidated Damages Agreement." Commission's Exhibit 825, *ibid.*

215. Commission's Exhibit 75, *ibid.*

216. Commission's Exhibit 1, *ibid.*

217. Commission's Exhibit 76, *ibid.*

Workable Competition and Antitrust Policy

The 1935 agreement declared one of its basic purposes to be to promote "a free and open market among both buyers and sellers" of tags and to "reduce the uneconomic results which flow from the spread of misinformation and unfair and unfounded rumor." [218] Apparently the tag makers never abandoned this agreement's professed objective. Baxter in a circular letter to the subscribers said of the 1940 agreement: "[O]ur aim has in fact been to make the entire new Agreement shorter and simpler without taking away any of the rights and obligations of subscribers which are necessary to the successful accomplishment of the endeavor which is now well understood by all." [219]

Willard Thorp, now a professor of economics at Amherst College, testifying on behalf of the tag makers, expressed the opinion that such a plan "will improve the open, competitive character of the industry." [220] In short, the tag makers professed to be interested in making the tag industry more workably competitive by supplying interested parties with market information essential for rational decision-making.

How the Plan Operated

How did this work out? Under the 1940 agreement the tag makers sent Baxter, on the day they became effective, comprehensive price lists and detailed statements covering all terms and conditions of sale for every classification of tag or tag component that they sold. They also filed complete specifications of their products. From these individual reports Baxter prepared and distributed to his subscribers a loose-leaf compilation of list prices, arranged alphabetically in schedules according to various types of tags and showing each manufacturer's list prices for the myriad of tags which the industry produced. The schedules were set up in such a way that each seller could determine at a glance how his list price for any particular stock tag or component of a made-to-order tag compared with the last list price reported by Baxter for any rival seller.[221] Made-to-order tags

218. Commission's Exhibit 74, p. 1, *ibid*.
219. Letter dated May 14, 1940, Commission's Exhibit 4-Z-260, *ibid*. The 1940 agreement was not adopted until November 25 of that year.
220. Report of Proceeding before the Commission, April 1, 1943, p. 2140, *ibid*.
221. Tags were grouped under such schedules as A, Stock Shipping Tags; B, Made-to-Order Shipping Tags; C, Large Tags, etc. Within a schedule, prices for tags of a particular specification or the components thereof were set up as a table showing prices for varying quantities and sizes. Such a table, which might contain as many as a hundred prices, was identified as an "item." Price information not in tabular form might also appear on the compilation sheets as an item. A page might contain as many as eight items. On the opposite page tag manufacturers were listed

comprised about 80 per cent of all tag sales by value.[222] Price compilations on these tags covered prices for the several standard components that might go into a custom-made tag.[223] The possible combinations of components are almost infinite in making the thousands of different kinds of tags that enter into everyday use.[224]

Compilations of every manufacturer's terms and conditions of sale, showing which tag makers followed certain policies or practices and in what respects other tag makers followed different ones, plus detailed definitions and specifications for each quality of tag product sold, supplemented the schedules of list prices.

Whenever a tag maker revised his price list or issued a new one to the trade, under the agreement he filed the revision or the new list with Baxter within twenty-four hours. Baxter thereafter made the necessary changes in his compilation and forwarded the new list prices on loose-leaf "blue sheets" to all subscribers. Tag makers making any sales at off-list prices were obligated to report them to Baxter within twenty-four hours and Baxter was obligated to report them daily to all his subscribers, which he did on "pink sheets." Any variation in price, however small, or in terms of sale, however trivial, was to be promptly reported.[225] To make certain that their reports were reliable and complete, tag makers were obligated

in a vertical column with eight adjoining columns, each headed with an item number. In the appropriate item column an "x" was noted opposite each manufacturer using a particular list price. A quick perusal of a page would indicate the extent of uniformity among the several price lists. Commission's Exhibit 2-Z-34, *ibid*.

222. Brief for Petitioners, at 21, Tag Manufacturers Institute v. Federal Trade Commission, 174 F.2d 452 (1st Cir. 1949).

223. The standard components were (1) the paper board or cloth stock; (2) strings, wires, and fasteners; (3) punches, patches, slots, and eyelets; (4) inspection and ganging; (5) stapling, gumming, paraffining, pasting, lacquering, or other special treatment; (6) printing composition and changes; (7) numbering; and (8) original plates and art work. Brief for Petitioners, at 11, *ibid*.

224. There are eight standard sizes of shipping tags alone, sixty-four grades, weights, or qualities of tag stock, and thirty-six different kinds of printing. *Ibid*.

225. The thoroughness of the report is indicated by its description in the 1935 agreement. It called for a "complete statement of prices, terms, and conditions of sale affecting each and every executed contract for sale of, . . . order for, and invoice or other memorandum of shipment or delivery of both printed and unprinted tags, both stock and special, and all others for the sale thereof." The statement was to be prepared in accordance with a form specified by Baxter and "shall show the quantity, grade or quality, price, and terms and conditions of sale of such tags, or component elements thereof and shall be accompanied by a full statement of all pertinent information covering quantity tolerances, free goods, replacements and samples, and concessions of every nature." Commission's Exhibit 74, §§ 1a–f, Tag Manufacturers Institute, 43 F.T.C. 499 (1947).

Workable Competition and Antitrust Policy

to send Baxter duplicates of all invoices by the close of the next business day after mailing them to customers.

For failure to make prompt and accurate reports tag makers were subject to a penalty, characterized in the agreement as "liquidated damages."[226] To insure compliance with this obligation each subscriber contributed from $200 to $500 annually, depending on sales volume, to a "revolving fund" against which "liquidated damages" were charged. Baxter investigated complaints of noncompliance and two or three times

---

226. Counsel for the tag makers objected strenuously to the Commission's use of the word "penalty" to describe the forfeitures specified in their Liquidated Damages Agreement. Brief for Petitioners, at 76–77, Tag Manufacturers Institute v. Federal Trade Commission, 174 F.2d 452 (1st Cir. 1949). As one interested in preciseness in the use of language, I see no grounds for their objection. *Webster's New International Dictionary* (2d. ed. unabridged) defines "penalty" as "the sum to be forfeited to which a person subjects himself by covenant or agreement in case of nonfulfillment of stipulations; forfeiture; fine." Counsel for the tag makers described the agreement as providing for "stipulated liquidated damages applicable in cases of failure to comply with the undertakings set forth" in it and said, *"This was done because actual damage is impossible accurately to be determined."* Brief for Petitioners, at 27, *supra.* Emphasis supplied. This candid admission suggests that the purpose of the assessments was to enforce compliance, not to compensate for noncompliance.

Before publication I submitted my discussion of the *Tag* case to counsel for the Tag Institute and counsel for the Federal Trade Commission for criticism. Counsel for the Tag Institute characterized my analysis as prejudiced. Among other passages, he specifically objected to the sentence in the text above in which I refer to liquidated damages as penalties. He suggested that a more accurate and judicious statement would be, "For failure to make prompt and accurate reports tag makers were subjected to liquidated damages for failure to comply with their contractual agreements, characterized by the Commission as penalties." Counsel also objected to my use of the foregoing definition of "penalty." About this he stated: "You do not indicate . . . what is the fact—that the definition you quote is a secondary definition, not the usual and specific meaning of the word given first by Webster. I also am interested in preciseness of the use of language, and because I am it was the primary meaning of the word as defined by Webster that I was talking about in my brief."

Webster gives four groups of definitions of "penalty," each group marked by a heavy black numeral, 1 to 4. On page xciv, paragraphs 44 and 47, the publishers make the following comments on the significance of number groupings:

44. Heavy-faced Arabic numerals (1., 2., 3., etc.) are used to number definitions when the meanings are numerous or are quite divergent from one another.

47. Arrangement of definitions in the *historical order of development* should not be taken to imply that each sense has developed from the immediately preceding sense. Sometimes sense 1 gives rise to sense 2, sense 2 to sense 3, and sense 3 is the source of sense 4. Sometimes, however, each of the several senses derived in independent lines from sense 1 has served as the source of a number of other meanings. [Emphasis supplied]

The sense 1 of "penalty," which I presume is "primary," is given as "pain," a meaning designated as rare. Sense 2 refers to "punishment for crime" and is obviously not relevant to the "liquidated damages" of the tag makers' contract. I chose sense 3, which seems to me relevant and appropriate.

a year made unannounced audits of the books of subscribers to determine whether or not they were fully complying with their obligations under the contract. Where an investigation revealed noncompliance Baxter assessed "liquidated damages" in conformity with a schedule provided in the agreement.[227] From Baxter's decision an offender could appeal to a Board of Arbitration consisting of three members outside the industry.

The theoretical basis for assessing "liquidated damages" was that tag makers were paying Baxter for accurate information on market factors essential to intelligent and informed business decisions and that all were hurt by inaccurate or incomplete market information.[228] Liquidated damages were distributed among all subscribers on a basis of their relative sales volume. Information supplied by Baxter included data on the total sales of tags, from which any subscriber could determine his relative position in the market.

Baxter and the tag makers regarded this arrangement as an innocent effort to make a market of imperfect competition more workably competitive. The Federal Trade Commission looked at it differently.

Commission Challenges Plan

On May 2, 1941, the Commission issued a complaint against the Tag Manufacturers Institute, Frank H. Baxter individually and as secretary-treasurer and executive director of the institute, and thirty-one tag manufacturers, charging them with having conspired to restrain and eliminate price competition in the sale and distribution of tags by fixing and maintaining their price.[229] After a hearing covering 2,500 pages of testimony and including the presentation of approximately 1,500 exhibits, the Commission's trial examiner issued his report on the evidence. He found that

227. Article IV of the 1940 agreement specified liquidated damages for noncompliance as follows: $5 per day for delay in filing any report on prices, terms or conditions of sale, up to 10 per cent of the value of the transaction; 10 per cent of the aggregate value of all of the subscriber's transactions on which he failed to file copies of invoices within ten days after mailing the invoices to customers, up to $100 per day; and $25 per day for delay or refusal in answering inquiries by Baxter or in submitting books and records for audit. Commission's Exhibit 76, pp. 9–10, Tag Manufacturers Institute, 43 F.T.C. 499 (1947).

228. The 1940 agreement expressed it this way: "[I]naccurate, incomplete or tardy dissemination of market information which is the essential aim hereof will, it is agreed, cause pecuniary damage to every other Subscriber in proportion to the extent of his interest in the marketing of the products." Commission's Exhibit 76, p. 10, *ibid.*

229. Tag Manufacturers Institute, 43 F.T.C. 499 (1947).

Workable Competition and Antitrust Policy

the respondents had "combined, agreed, and conspired . . . to adopt and . . . carry out" a program "reasonably supposed and intended by them to lessen competition and restrain trade, and which through their mutual understandings and cooperation did lessen, injure, and restrain price competition in the tag industry." [230] The Commissioners examined the record and heard arguments of counsel and on May 19, 1947, found the respondents guilty of an unfair method of competition within the meaning of Section 5 of the Federal Trade Commission Act.[231] The respondents appealed, and on May 12, 1949, Chief Judge Magruder of the United States Court of Appeals for the First Circuit handed down a decision reversing the Commission.[232] The Commission did not seek review by the Supreme Court.

These several proceedings engendered a stark heat but a hazy light. In a bold, brash brief, counsel for the tag makers challenged the integrity and competence of the Commission, heaped ridicule on its counsel, and charged them with deliberately making "utterly false and grossly unfair" claims "without supporting evidence and in the face of clear and convincing" contrary proof.[233]

Cooperation Originates Under NRA

This is an important case—not merely because it involves a reversal of the Commission, but because it liberalizes the doctrines laid down by the

---

230. Trial Examiner's Report on the Evidence, filed December 2, 1943, p. 44, *id.*
231. Tag Manufacturers Institute, 43 F.T.C. 499 (1947).
232. Tag Manufacturers Institute v. Federal Trade Commission, 174 F.2d 452 (1st Cir. 1949).
233. This language appeared in the tag makers' brief as respondents before the Commission and was quoted in their brief as petitioners before the court of appeals. Brief for Petitioners, at 58, Tag Manufacturers Institute v. Federal Trade Commission, 174 F.2d 452 (1st Cir. 1949). Similar language was indulged in throughout this brief: the Commission was accused of a "lack of desire . . . accurately to find the facts" (*id.* at 25); of demonstrating that the court "may not rely upon the accuracy of its findings" (*id.* at 40); of showing "total" or "utter disregard for the truth" (*id.* at 40, 41); of deliberate misrepresentation or . . . complete lack of interest in factual accuracy" (*id.* at 72); of slipping into "a fallacy of fantastic magnitude" (*id.* at 99); and of having "peculiar ideas of proof" (*id.* at 107). The validity of the Commission's study of uniformity in price lists was denounced with "Anyone who has progressed beyond the one plus one stage of mathematics knows that figures produced on the basis outlined above are utterly meaningless" (*id.* at 46). The Commission's finding that competition had been eliminated and prevented was characterized as "sheer nonsense" and its finding that competition had been lessened, as "equally nonsensical" (*id.* at 47). The Commission's cease and desist order was interpreted to say "perfectly ridiculous" things (*id.* at 104).

Legality of Trade Association Activities

courts in earlier cases covering the use of price statistics [234] and because it gives approval to a scheme which, whatever its consequences, apparently has as its objective the discouragement of competition among business rivals.[235] The several tag makers' agreements were an outgrowth of their cooperative activities under NRA. The National Industrial Recovery Act, despite its statutory rejection of codes designed to promote monopoly, represented a sharp departure from traditional antitrust policy.[236] It was

234. To recapitulate, the earlier cases seem to stand for the following doctrines; genuine competitors do not contract to submit their books and records to audit by their rivals; where price reports go only to sellers, they cannot be justified as comparable to published reports available to all [American Column & Lumber Co. v. United States, 257 U.S. 377, 410, 411 (1921)]; where competitors enter an agreement requiring them to reveal to each other the intimate details of their business, under penalty for failure to report any deviation from their published price lists, the situation is wholly unlike an exchange where dealers assemble and buy and sell openly [United States v. American Linseed Oil Co., 262 U.S. 371, 390 (1923)]; a trade association whose members take no concerted action with respect to prices or production or restraining competition and in which the names of *sellers* and buyers *in individual transactions are not revealed* may "openly and fairly" gather and disseminate information on prices received in past transactions [Maple Flooring Manufacturers Ass'n v. United States, 268 U.S. 563, 586 (1925)]; competitors may take concerted action to exchange information for the purpose of correcting fraudulent practices in their industry [Cement Manufacturers Protective Ass'n v. United States, 268 U.S. 588 (1925)]; but corrective measures which in themselves become restraints on competition will not be allowed [Sugar Institute v. United States, 297 U.S. 553 (1936)]. A legal comment sums up the "rules" for a trade association statistical program as follows: "(1) the information must be fully available to all interested parties; (2) the identity of particular contributors must not be disclosed; (3) supervisory powers of the association must not be excessive; and (4) the data must be released without comment, analysis, or subsequent discussion at association meetings." "Trade Association Statistics and the Anti-Trust Laws," 18 Univ. Chi. L. Rev. 380, 384–85 (1951). This valiant attempt at certainty is quite properly qualified: "Nevertheless, complete compliance does not guarantee a plan's legality any more than does occasional departure from the rules assure the government's success." *Ibid.* The record indicates that the Tag Manufacturers Institute violated the first two of these rules and in my judgment supports the inference that it violated the third.

235. Counsel for trade associations may persuade a court that attempts to create conditions which encourage uniformity of pricing are not unlawful when they fall short of complete success, and many economists would discount such attempts as not a serious handicap on the economy. But what useful purpose do they serve? Do they suggest a principle for public policy—to substitute controlled decision-making by groups of sellers for the operation of the free market so long as this does not show measurably harmful effects? What effect does this policy have on buyers' and sellers' spirit of enterprise?

236. Title I, § 3(a) of the act authorized "trade or industrial associations or groups" to submit to the President of the United States codes of fair competition for their respective industries, to be approved if the President found, among other things, that the codes were not "designed to promote monopolies" and did not permit monopolistic practices. But § 1 of the same title announced the public policy of

Workable Competition and Antitrust Policy

enacted during an economic crisis when man's faith in a free-enterprise economy had almost vanished. As businessmen witnessed a sharp decline in the aggregate demand for their goods and services, as their plants idled and their earnings shrank, they found the customary restraints on price-cutting wholly inadequate. Faced with an intensity of competition that threatened their solvency, businessmen sought security in collective action. The NRA provided the mechanism by which competition was tempered and cooperation stimulated. The tag code made it unlawful for tag makers to price tags below cost or depart from the prices which they filed with the code authority.[237] By providing for a waiting period during which an announced price revision was made inoperative it discouraged price-cutting. By calling attention to price discrepancies among rival sellers it encouraged identical pricing. When the code expired, the industry sought security in industrial self-government. The president of the largest corporate producer of tags was a few years later to set forth his philosophy of business cooperation in a book entitled *Modern Competition and Business Policy*, written jointly with a well-known economist.[238] In this book the authors question the self-regulatory character of modern business rivalry,[239] lament industry experiences with cut-throat competition,[240] reject the notion that modern corporate enterprise rewards socially desirable and penalizes socially undesirable behavior,[241] encourage publicizing trade statistics so that businessmen may know more about the affairs of each other,[242] and advocate the inauguration of a program of industrial self-government, voluntarily if industry will respond but otherwise at the initiative of the government and in any event under its supervision.[243]

The NRA tag code provided an experiment in business cooperation in an industry whose security had been undermined by the Great Depression

---

promoting the organization of industry for the purpose of cooperative action among trade groups, and § 5 provided that any code approved under title I and any action complying with its provisions while it was in effect should be exempt from the provisions of the federal antitrust laws. 48 Stat. 195, 196, 198 (1933).

237. Code of Fair Competition for the Tag Industry as approved on February 1, 1934, Commission's Exhibit 194-B, Tag Manufacturers Institute, 43 F.T.C. 499 (1947).

238. H. S. Dennison and J. K. Galbraith, *Modern Competition and Business Policy* (New York: Oxford University Press, 1938).

239. *Id.* at 33.
240. *Id.* at 35 *et seq.*
241. *Id.* at 77.
242. *Id.* at 96.
243. *Id.* at 106 *et seq.*

Legality of Trade Association Activities

and whose organization was such that competition inevitably worked imperfectly. The cooperative experiment was carried on in the successive tag agreements, with important modifications from time to time.[244] All provided for open price-filing, but without a waiting period. None prohibited below-cost selling. All made clear a seller's right to depart at will from his prices as filed with Baxter, and all disavowed any desire to restrict competition. The plan was ostensibly designed to make competition open and informed but free.

Filed Prices: Future or Past

A study of the several tag agreements suggests, despite their nominal disavowal of it, that their objective was to discourage price competition. Counsel for the tag makers argued vigorously that prices as filed with Baxter were neither current nor future but merely a record of past transactions;[245] but the 1936 agreement provided that "a general offer to the

---

244. The Commission found that "[t]he purpose of these agreements was to keep in force and effect the open price-reporting plan originally adopted under the National Industrial Recovery Act." Tag Manufacturers Institute, 43 F.T.C. 499, 515 (1947). The court of appeals characterized "this crucial finding" as "a pure assumption, not a rational inference from the evidence." Tag Manufacturers Institute v. Federal Trade Commission, 174 F.2d 452, 458 (1st Cir. 1949). But the Supreme Court has held that it is an "established judicial rule of evidence that testimony of prior or subsequent transactions, which for some reason are barred from forming the basis for a suit, may nevertheless be introduced if it tends reasonably to show the purpose and character of the particular transactions under scrutiny." Federal Trade Commission v. Cement Institute, 333 U.S. 683, 705 (1948).

245. The argument was as follows: each manufacturer issued to the trade a list of the prices at which he was selling his products and then furnished Baxter with a copy of it. Baxter's compilation could in the nature of things be no more than a book of reference with respect to past market conditions since it merely gave wider circulation to facts already published. At any given moment a subscriber might have one or more different list prices in effect from those shown in the compilation, since his obligation was only to report changes after they had gone into effect. The court of appeals described this state of facts and then observed: "[I]t is obvious that the Compilation in the hands of the Subscribers is more than an object of academic historical interest and is designed for a practical business purpose. Manufacturers do not change their price lists every day. A price list may remain in effect for weeks, often for months, without change. While at any given moment it is possible that the most recently revised price list of one or two manufacturers might not yet have been reflected in the Compilation, there is every assurance that for the most part the Compilation discloses current price list information. Examination of the Compilation, together with the more recent 'pink sheets' showing off-list sales, will give a quite accurate picture of the current price structure in the industry. Also, the 'pink sheets' for several weeks past and recent revisions of price lists noted in the Compilation may disclose trends indicative of future market conditions." Tag Manufacturers Institute v. Federal Trade Commission, 174 F.2d 452, 458 (1st Cir. 1949).

Workable Competition and Antitrust Policy

trade to sell tags and tag products at specified prices, terms, and conditions of sale shall constitute a past or effective price when said general offer has in fact been circulated through the customary channels of the trade, and is available to all buyers for immediate acceptance, and not before." [246] This seems to transform a current or future price into a past price by so defining it. Although the record makes it clear that tag makers retained their right to depart at their discretion from their prices as filed with Baxter, the record also contains specific evidence that some tag makers regarded their filed prices as representing current and, until a new filing was made, future prices. For example, C. H. Barber, president of the Keystone Tag Company, in a letter dated May 19, 1938, expressed annoyance with Baxter's having reminded him in a letter dated May 18, 1938,[247] that Baxter had not received Keystone's new general offer as required under the agreement. Barber wrote:

What you inform my competitors is up to you, but I am not going to sacrifice my health nor put on additional office force in order to get these out any quicker than we are doing. . . . *We are, however, cooperating 100% with our competitors by using prices to the trade as reflected in our price book which you now have.*[248]

Again, this colloquy appears in the record on the cross-examination of Arthur H. Swett, Jr., vice-president of the American Tag Company, by counsel for the tag makers:

Q. In referring to your operations under the price reporting agreement, you stated that you attempted to observe something which was not entirely clear in my mind just what it was which you attempted to observe, with reference to the contract.
A. Attempted to observe.
Q. You observed the prices?
A. We observe our prices.
Q. Do I understand your answer to be that you observe prices?
A. We observe our file prices. I don't know just what you mean.
Q. You don't understand my question?
A. No.
Q. Let me repeat it. You stated that you observed the contract. By that you mean what?
A. Our file prices.

246. Commission's Exhibit 75, § 1-(A), pp. 1–2, Tag Manufacturers Institute, 43 F.T.C. 499 (1947).
247. Commission's Exhibit 1011, *ibid.*
248. Commission's Exhibit 1010-A, B, *ibid.* Emphasis supplied.

This answer was apparently not satisfactory to counsel for respondent; and so he continued:

Q. Do you mean to say that the contract calls upon you to observe file prices?
A. No, it does not. It definitely does not.
Q. What does the contract call upon you to observe?
A. That we must file restricted offers, if we quote other than our file prices.[249]

Off-list Prices Discriminatory

The 1936 agreement characterized any departure from a firm's general-offer price list as a "discriminatory price."[250] It also characterized as discriminatory a general-offer price decrease if followed within twelve days by a price increase.[251] It was such departures from their list prices, together with all revisions in their list prices or terms and conditions of sale, that tag makers were required under penalty of "liquidated damages" to report to Baxter in detail within twenty-four hours and to verify by filing duplicates of invoices with Baxter within five days after mailing them to customers.

Characterizing such price-cutting as discriminatory would, I should think, in and of itself tend to discourage price competition. But the agreement went further. It implied that such off-list pricing might be unlawful as well as "discriminatory." A firm's report of a "discriminatory" price was to be followed by an affidavit "setting forth all facts essential to the establishment of said transaction as a lawful exception to the statutory prohibitions against price discrimination . . . not later than noon of the succeeding business day."[252] Presumably reference is intended to Section 2 (a) of the Clayton Act as modified by the Robinson-Patman Act, which outlaws price discrimination whose effect may be substantially to lessen competition.[253] I think it farfetched indeed to assume that if a tag maker

249. Report of Proceedings before the Commission, November 28, 1941, p. 811, *ibid*.
250. "Sec. 1-(B) A price, term or condition of sale made to a specific customer, or restricted to a specific locality, and not made available to all customers or localities under like circumstances, shall constitute a discriminatory price." Commission's Exhibit 75, p. 2, *ibid*.
251. Sec. 1-(E), *id*. at 7.
252. Sec. 1-(D), *id*. at 7.
253. The words of the statute are: "That it shall be unlawful for any person engaged in commerce, . . . either directly or indirectly, to discriminate in price between different purchasers of commodities of like grade and quality, . . . [in interstate commerce] where the effect of such discrimination may be substantially to lessen competition or . . . to injure, destroy, or prevent competition with any person

97

Workable Competition and Antitrust Policy

cuts prices to get any particular order he may thereby be lessening competition. Certainly he is not diminishing the vigor of his competition with his rivals. And since the buyers of tags for the most part are ultimate consumers engaged in different lines of business activity, such price cuts can have little or no effect at the secondary level. Eventually the tag makers seemed to have reached this conclusion. At any rate, the 1937 agreement abandoned the term "discriminatory," but it did not abandon the practice of setting apart as special those prices to isolated buyers which were more favorable than those quoted in the tag makers' filed price lists. These were called "restricted offers" and, as in previous agreements, required to be reported within twenty-four hours to Baxter under penalty of "liquidated damages."[254] The 1940 agreement discontinued the term "restricted offer," but not the practice of reporting off-list sales nor the penalty for failing to report them.

Price Filing or Price Maintenance?

Counsel for the Commission argued that this practice tended to discourage making such off-list prices and thereby to restrain competition. They characterized the whole agreement as designed for this end. The Commission so found. I believe the Commission was correct. Not only does the logic of the arrangement warrant this conclusion, but tag makers themselves have expressed attitudes consistent with this interpretation. In reporting to Baxter two orders at off-list prices, A. H. Swett, Jr., vice-president of the American Tag Company, reviewed all orders which his company had executed during the life of the several agreements from 1935 to March 1938 to determine how many had been made at price concessions. He found his company's record was good. Under date of March 15, 1938, he wrote in part:

who either grants or knowingly receives the benefit of such discrimination, or with customers of either of them." 38 Stat. 730 (1914), as amended, 49 Stat. 1526 (1936), 15 U.S.C. § 13(a) (1958).

254. Commission's Exhibit 1, § II-B, pp. 11–12, Tag Manufacturers Institute, 43 F.T.C. 499 (1947). Tag makers were obligated to report to Baxter within twenty-four hours all prices and terms on all sales that differed in any respect from their terms and prices already on file. This was true of general offers as well as restricted offers. But the requirement that restricted offers be reported promptly meant much more than the requirement that general offers be reported promptly. Firms customarily sent their general offers direct to the trade and frequently to their competitors. Special offers in the absence of an agreement to report them would ordinarily have been regarded as the private business of the firms making and receiving them and no one else's, and if they were not filed with Baxter their rivals could not easily obtain them.

Legality of Trade Association Activities

I simply want to point out to you that we have been able to maintain our regular schedule in the face of competition. We are sorry indeed that it was necessary to make a special concession for the two recent orders, but we felt that it was necessary in order to retain the account.[255]

E. L. McCusker, of the Reyburn Manufacturing Company, implied in a letter written to Baxter on July 12, 1940, that as he saw it the harm to the industry was not merely in failing to report price cuts but in making them as well. Reyburn had apparently accepted a $1,980 order for three million No. 6 tags at 66 cents a thousand, a price below its list price and so reported to Baxter. Thereafter the buyer notified Reyburn that one of Reyburn's competitors had made him an even better offer—60 cents a thousand. To keep the business Reyburn met its rival's cut. Neither Reyburn nor its rival reported the lower quotation. After Reyburn had closed the order, its rival complained to Baxter of Reyburn's failure to file its 60-cent quotation. Baxter investigated, established the failure, and assessed Reyburn 10 per cent liquidated damages. Reyburn protested Baxter's not assessing similar damages against its rival. About this McCusker wrote:

It seems to us that in the first case where we have to be liable for damages that we may do to the members of the Institute for failure to file a lower quotation, that the same thing should apply where a competitor makes a lower quotation than what we have received for the order and where he has damaged us to the extent of $180.00, therefore should be assessed 10% of the total amount of the order.

A proposition of this character is a very serious one and should be given very serious consideration by your office. After this letter has answered your purpose, which is strictly confidential, kindly return for our files.[256]

Baxter in replying to McCusker stated that with no formal complaint against Reyburn's rival Baxter's office could do nothing about the matter.[257] In writing McCusker, Baxter undertook to straighten out McCusker's thinking about the tag industry agreement. About this he wrote:

In the last three paragraphs of your letter you have reflected a brand of thinking that I am sure is not truly indicative of your understanding of what the Tag Industry Agreement proposes to accomplish. I do not want to make an

---

255. Commission's Exhibit 834, *ibid*.
256. Commission's Exhibit 776-A, B, *ibid*. The 1937 agreement, which continued in force until November 25, 1940, required subscribers to report restricted *offers* to Baxter. Commission's Exhibit 1, pp. 11–12, *ibid*.
257. McCusker's letter had not identified the offending rival. Baxter's letter stated: "Of course, you haven't made a complaint in the matter and you haven't afforded me an opportunity to make one, for there is no name on the letter. . . ." Letter of July 23, 1940, Commission's Exhibit 775, *ibid*.

issue of the situation, but I do feel that we must be so careful in this office to keep the thinking of our subscribers straight that we cannot afford to "pass one single red flag." [258]

Apparently Baxter frequently found it necessary to straighten out the tag makers' conception of the agreement. When G. M. Huey of the Denney Tag Company tried to justify failure to report a price cut by citing a rival that had cut prices, Baxter pointed out that the rival had filed his off-list prices as the agreement required, and he advised Huey: "At the risk of seeming tedious we must point out that our concern must not be with what prices are quoted by subscribers, but only with whether the prices are reported as the agreement requires." [259]

Tag Agreements Did Not Eliminate Price Concessions

Both the agreements and the way subscribers looked at them indicate to me that the object of the several agreements was to discourage competition. Waiving or granting this, did the agreements in fact lessen competition or, as counsel for the tag makers contended, did they merely permit rival sellers to obtain market data which enabled them to interpret market forces correctly and to adjust their individual operations to them? One conclusion is clear: the 1940 tag agreement did not eliminate all price concessions. Several tag manufacturers testified they were free under the contract to use their own discretion in off-list pricing [260] and equally free, of course, in announcing new general offers, and that they exercised their freedom.[261] The Commission cited 468 instances in which list prices of the several tag makers were identical but in which two or more tag makers quoted prices to a single customer. Counsel for the tag makers calculated that in 443 of these cases, representing 95 per cent of the total, customers were quoted two or more different prices. In 289 of the cases two tag makers bid and in 267 of these the prices offered were not identical. In 112 cases three tag makers bid and in 109 of these the customers had a choice of two or more prices. In 67 of these cases the customers had a choice of three prices.[262] Moreover, there was no consistency among rival

---

258. *Ibid.*
259. Letter dated February 29, 1940, Commission's Exhibit 87-D, *id.*
260. See, for example, testimony of Walter C. Bailey, Jr., of The Reyburn Manufacturing Company, Report of Proceedings before the Commission, November 26, 1941, pp. 585–87, *ibid.*
261. Approximately 25 per cent of all sales were made at off-list prices. This fact was not disputed and both the Commission and the court of appeals accepted it.
262. Brief for Petitioners, at 34, citing Commission's Exhibit 1022, Tag Manufacturers Institute v. Federal Trade Commission, 174 F.2d 452 (1st Cir. 1949).

Legality of Trade Association Activities

sellers in their off-list pricing. Percentage of total business done off list ranged from 2.1 per cent to 63.9 per cent.[263] Nor was off-list pricing confined to any one section of the country. It was both substantial and nationwide.

Most Business Done at List Prices

Nevertheless, three-fourths of the total business was done at list prices, and apparently these for the most part were identical for all tag makers. A government accountant made a study of price lists filed with Baxter at intervals over a two-year period. This study covered fourteen varieties of tags in varying sizes with varying prices for different quantity lots. According to the Commission the study was "representative of the tags sold in any appreciable volume."[264] It showed virtually 100 per cent uniformity of list prices for eleven varieties of tags on May 12, 1939, and a similar uniformity in the list prices for the same tags on August 27, 1940.[265] For three varieties of tags the uniformity of list prices ranged from 70 per cent to 86 per cent at the beginning of the test period and from 70.7 per cent to 93.7 per cent at the close of the test period.

Counsel for the tag makers appropriately criticized the Commission's trial examiner for having calculated a simple arithmetical average for all fourteen varieties of tags of 96.8 per cent as a measure of list-price identity at the beginning of the test period and 97.5 per cent at its end. With equal propriety counsel criticized the Commission's broader generalization that at the beginning of the test period "the *compilation* reflected 96.8 per cent uniformity and at the end of the period . . . 97.5 per cent uniformity of general-offer filed prices among the respondent members."[266]

In addition to challenging the Commission's use of a simple arithmetical average as a measure of price identity in the sample of tag prices, counsel for the tag makers challenged the adequacy of the sample itself, asserting that it consisted largely of stock tags, among which greater price uniformity

263. Brief for Petitioners, at 33, *ibid.*
264. Brief for Respondent, at 76–77, *ibid.*
265. *Ibid.* Just how many prices are represented in these schedules is not clear, but presumably they ran into the thousands. I sampled at random the price lists on page B-210 of the compilation, Commission's Exhibit 2-Z-100. It showed the price schedule or "item" for each of three different qualities of stock factor (the basic component for tags) for eight sizes of made-to-order shipping tags (not over 19.53 sq. in. in size) for sale in thirteen different quantity lots. The three items contained a total of 312 prices. All thirty tag makers filed identical prices for these items.
266. Tag Manufacturers Institute, 43 F.T.C. 499, 525 (1947).

101

Workable Competition and Antitrust Policy

was to be expected than among made-to-order tags. This criticism has merit on its face; but the tag makers' brief before the court of appeals indicates that made-to-order shipping tags alone accounted for just under 40 per cent of the total tag business [267] and the Commission included this kind of tag (Schedule B) in its sample, finding that 86 per cent of the filed prices for tags of this class were identical at the beginning of the test period and that 93.7 per cent of them were identical at the end of the test period.[268]

Commission Ignores Terms and Conditions of Sale

Counsel appropriately criticized the Commission's calculations because they ignored terms and conditions of sale. The Commission's accountant had undertaken the relatively simple task of calculating the percentage which identical list prices represented of total filed prices by the sampling method. As far as it goes this is an appropriate procedure. Price differences lend themselves to mathematical measurement. Concessions in terms and conditions of sale, like concessions in prices, are useful in attracting business, but they do not lend themselves so readily to mathematical treatment. To have combined variations in both prices and terms of sale in a mathematical measure of price identity would indeed have been a colossal and fruitless task. Terms and conditions of sale alone as filed with Baxter and compiled and distributed by him to each tag maker covered about fifty pages. The price schedules covered many more pages, on some of which hundreds of prices were listed. Each company made thousands of different kinds of tags representing all sorts of combinations of the separately priced components. To establish 100 per cent uniformity in both price lists and conditions of sale for all tags even between two companies would require a comparison of thousands of items. If perfect uniformity were established, change in a single item would destroy it. With the potential variation among the price lists of some thirty tag makers almost infinite, any substantial degree of uniformity would indeed be surprising in the absence of some mechanism for establishing it. And yet a high degree of uniformity is a striking fact about the schedules appearing in the compilation.

But the difficulty of determining the price significance of variations in terms and conditions of sale does not justify the Commission's ignoring

---

267. Brief for Petitioners, at 21, Tag Manufacturers Institute v. Federal Trade Commission, 174 F.2d 452 (1st Cir. 1949).
268. Brief for Respondent, at 77, *ibid*.

Legality of Trade Association Activities

them. Certainly buyers would not ignore them. The variations in terms to some classes of buyers seem very significant indeed. In sales to the federal government listed discounts granted by the different tag makers ranged from 10 to 40 per cent,[269] and this is substantial. The time over which deliveries on an order might be spread varied from four to twelve months.[270]

In dealings with private buyers apparently such discrepancies as appeared tended to balance out, for petitioners contended that no price variation was too small to be commercially significant. As they put it: "The minimum difference between items in price lists is one cent per 1,000 tags and this is enough to control the placement of orders."[271]

Price Reporting Contributed to Identical Pricing

By providing the machinery for a ready comparison of rival prices for any particular tag or tag component the price-reporting system contributed to identical pricing. It is fairly clear that it was intended to do so. The record indicates that at times both Baxter and the tag makers concerned themselves with even trivial variations in prices of terms of sale[272] and sought to avoid them. For example, on November 16, 1938, George E. Phelps, vice-president of Allen-Bailey Tag Company, notified Baxter that he had reduced by 5 per cent the price of tag stock and the charge for making and printing and composition changes on tags of a certain size.[273] After discussing the proposed changes with Baxter's office, he agreed that Baxter should withhold publication of the filing "for a couple of days" while Baxter could "ascertain exactly the condition of the market with reference to the practice of other manufacturers in applying 5% discount to large tags involving various additional specifications."[274] About this matter C. A. Adams of Baxter's office testified that Phelps wanted to ascertain whether when "you applied the 5 per cent, . . . you took 5 per

---

269. See, for example, Commission's Exhibit 2-Z-12, Tag Manufacturers Institute, 43 F.T.C. 499 (1947).

270. Commissions' Exhibit 2-Z-18, *id*. For other illustrations of departures, see Brief for Petitioners, at 32, Tag Manufacturers Institute v. Federal Trade Commission, 174 F.2d 452 (1st Cir. 1949).

271. Respondents' Brief, at 26, Tag Manufacturers Institute, 43 F.T.C. 499 (1947).

272. The 1936 agreement required each tag maker to declare a definite rule regarding fractions of a cent in the computation of prices from his price book. Commission's Exhibit 75, p. 6, *id*. The same requirement appeared in the 1937 agreement but was omitted fom the less detailed 1940 agreement.

273. Commission's Exhibit 1017, *ibid*.

274. Commission's Exhibit 1016, *ibid*.

Workable Competition and Antitrust Policy

cent of the total, or if they multiplied their total price by the factor of .95, which would give you a net result of a penny's difference. I told him we would ask the other subscribers to let us know how they applied this 5 per cent, and when we did we would publish it and that is published as a G letter."[275] Adams' investigation revealed no standard practice. Allen-Bailey Tag Company, forced to make a choice on this penny issue, chose to follow the industry's biggest tag maker. It noted on a revised filing, dated April 4, 1938: "This filing is to make our terms the same as those published by the Dennison Manufacturing Company in General Letter No. G 18."[276]

On November 22, 1938, S. B. Seaton of the Acme Tag Company wrote Baxter as follows:

We enclose a tag printed on the front in one color reverse plate, and on the reverse side a Benday cut of a bunch of bananas.

It is reported that quotations have been made to this company on which Form 7 Printing was used in figuring the price, while we believe the price should be based on Form 8 Printing. Both of these printing rates come under schedule B.

What is the opinion of the Institute office as to which of the two forms of printing is the correct one to use according to the lowest filed price?[277]

To this inquiry C. A. Adams of Baxter's office replied on November 26:

In answering your letter of November 22, relative to the printing schedule to be used in connection with the attached tag, *we must, of course, make it clear that this office has no authority to establish any rule for printing merchandise.* The most that we can do is refer to the filings of various subscribers and state their practices as so reported.

On page B 262 of the Compilation, Item 1 represents the filings of *all* subscribers to the Industry Agreement with the exception of A. Kimball Company and states that all reverse plate printing, or Benday copy, aggregating 2 sq. in. or more per side is considered as reverse plate. The tag in question has more than 2 sq. in. of reverse plate or Benday copy of both sides and, hence, according to these filings, would come under the rule stated.

That being the case, Form 8 reverse plate printing as shown on page B 262–1 would seem to apply in the case of this job.[278]

275. Report of Proceedings before the Commission, p. 2002, *ibid*.
276. Commission's Exhibit 1019, *ibid*. Apparently the date on this letter is incorrect. The year should be 1939.
277. Commission's Exhibit 187-Z-4, *ibid*.
278. Commission's Exhibit 187-Z-3, *ibid*. Emphasis supplied. Adams, after having rebuked Seaton for asking "which form of printing" is the correct one, proceeded to advise him that Form 8 "would seem to apply."

Legality of Trade Association Activities

Off-list Pricing Discouraged

Not only did the agreement provide machinery for facilitating identical price filing, as previously pointed out, but it provided machinery for discouraging departure from filed prices. The record indicates that this machinery did not work perfectly. Only 75 per cent of sales conformed to list. But that is a lot.[279]

Under the arrangement imposed by the tag makers upon themselves they sacrificed the privacy by which business decisions are ordinarily protected and by which buyers, in such a market as the market for tags, may exercise most effectively such bargaining power as they possess. Tag buyers are myriad, unorganized, and scattered. They do not buy tags in an organized, competitive market where all the forces behind demand and supply operate in an impersonal way to determine an identical price for all buyers and all sellers, and the nature of tag purchases is such that they cannot. They buy tags at list prices compiled by tag makers under customary terms of sale, or they bargain for better prices and terms. Their bargaining power is one of the market forces with which tag makers must contend. They can contend with it more effectively by presenting a united front. But by doing this they weaken a market force making for lower prices. Under the tag makers' arrangement, sellers anxious to get business even at off-list prices must report promptly all such sales that they make. It is not a characteristic of an imperfectly but effectively competitive market that sellers, anxious to get business by cutting prices, report their success to their rivals. That they agree to do so suggests that their primary concern is not with supplying full market information to their rivals that they all may make intelligent decisions about the market but with curbing their own normal impulse to sacrifice prices rather than business. And to the extent that they succeed they are blocking, not facilitating, the operation of market forces.

The Logic of "Liquidated Damages"

To evaluate the tag makers' arrangement properly, one must be more interested in logic than in language. It is no doubt proper for the tag

---

279. Antitrust prohibitions are not confined to activities which completely eliminate competition but make unlawful *"every* contract, combination in the form of trust or otherwise, or conspiracy, in restraint of trade or commerce" and every attempt "to monopolize *any part* of the trade or commerce among the several States. . . ." Sherman Antitrust Act, §§ 1 and 2, 26 Stat. 209 (1890), as amended, 50 Stat. 693 (1937), 15 U.S.C. §§ 1 and 2 (1958). Emphasis supplied.

Workable Competition and Antitrust Policy

makers, anxious to stay within the law, to characterize the penalty which they agreed to impose on themselves for failure to report an off-list sale as "liquidated damages" for preventing their rivals from getting full and accurate information about the market. But it is indeed difficult to see just how any one seller's failure to report one off-list sale hurts all other sellers on the theory advanced by the tag makers, and it is even more difficult to recognize an equivalence between such damage as a seller might conceivably suffer and his share of the "liquidated damages."[280] Tag makers are scattered all over the map—from Massachusetts in the East to San Francisco in the West, from Minnesota in the North to Texas in the South, with a tendency to concentrate in the Mid-West. How a San Francisco tag maker is hurt in any specific or measurable way by a Massachusetts tag maker's failure to report an off-list sale to a Maine tag buyer I fail to see. On another, and I believe a more plausible, theory I can see a causal relationship between the phenomena in question. Price-cutting tends to undermine the tag price structure and if generally indulged in may bring lower prices all around. Cutting without reporting encourages cutting. Failure to report therefore hurts all tag makers. This theory makes sense. That the deterrent to price-cutting was not adequate to prevent it does not undermine the theory. And it is a reasonable conclusion from the theory and consistent with the facts that the arrangement contributed to more stable and higher tag prices than would have prevailed without it. Most sales were at list prices and list prices remained unchanged over long periods.[281]

280. Baxter had some discretion in determining liquidated damages. As the Commission's trial examiner put it when describing the provisions of the 1940 agreement: "Liquidated damages are not authorized whenever counsel advises against it as possibly constituting 'an unlawful penalty or forfeiture' or where 'probable actual damages' are not found." Trial Examiner's Report on the Evidence, p. 17, Tag Manufacturers Institute, 43 F.T.C. 499 (1947). Moreover, a tag maker could appeal from Baxter's decision to the Board of Arbitration.

281. The court of appeals found that price lists might remain unchanged for weeks and even months. The Commission's trial examiner found that list prices "on numerous classes of products" indicated that "filings on a preponderant number of items remained unchanged with scattering variations from six months to one year between August 24, 1939, to August 27, 1940," and gave examples. Trial Examiner's Report on the Evidence, p. 36, *ibid.*

I am not convinced that the institute's program affected the stability of *list* prices, even though they apparently remained unchanged for long periods; but if it tended to reduce price-cutting, it thereby tended to make realized prices more stable. On the question of stability, counsel for the tag makers introduced in evidence the price lists of the largest producer of tags for a twelve-year period before the signing of the first tag agreement (Respondents' Exhibits 373-79) and contended: "These lists show that changes in price lists before the alleged conspiracy were actually

Legality of Trade Association Activities

Price-Reporting System Had Serious Defects

If in fact the object of the arrangement was to insure more intelligent decisions in market transactions, it had a serious defect. Buyers did not in fact have equal access to information which the sellers regularly received. It may serve at law to say that sellers did not try to bar them from it; but those interested in the economic, not the legal, aspect of the arrangement may appropriately point out that as a practical matter buyers' access to the details of the market facts which Baxter assembled, compiled, and distributed to tag makers was nominal, not real. For a while Baxter made his compilations available in Dun & Bradstreet's twelve regional offices. After this practice was discontinued, the tag makers on the advice of institute counsel followed Dennison's and Reyburn's practice of stamping each invoice with the following notation: "In common with most tag manufacturers, we file up-to-date records of tag prices with Frank H. Baxter Associates, 370 Lexington Avenue, New York City, where they are open for inspection." [282]

Tag buyers also had the privilege of subscribing to the service at cost, and one tag jobber did in fact subscribe. Buyers generally did not; buying in small quantities as they did, they could not afford either to subscribe or to consult the compilations in Baxter's office. To protect their interests they did not need all the information required by the sellers. All they needed to know was the price at which tags were sold both at list and off-list. For intelligent decision-making on both sides of the market buyers needed this information as much as sellers did; and if they had received it in the same detail that sellers did, I am confident that tags generally would have sold for less. I realize that tag makers are unlikely to view favorably a suggestion that each of them report to all customers every off-list sale

---

less frequent than during the period of the alleged conspiracy." Brief for Petitioners, p. 48, Tag Manufacturers Institute v. Federal Trade Commission, 174 F.2d 452 (1st Cir. 1949). The significant factor is not the stability of the price lists but the stability of realized prices. Moreover, as compared with the depressed 1930's, the prosperous 1920's are likely to have contributed to stable prices.

282. Quite obviously the court of appeals felt that buyers, who did not contribute to the compilation of the data, should be content with whatever terms and conditions the sellers might lay down for their accessibility. "We are clearly of the opinion that if the reporting agreement is otherwise unobjectionable, it cannot be said to have become illegal for failure of the Subscribers to make the information generally available. Customers are notified on each invoice that 'up-to-date records of tag prices' are open for inspection at Baxter's New York office. If a customer living outside New York City has any curiosity in the matter, he can use the mails. . . ." Tag Manufacturers Institute v. Federal Trade Commission, 174 F.452, 462–63 (1st Cir. 1949).

Workable Competition and Antitrust Policy

(i.e., price cut) that they make. If the courts were to require dissemination to buyers of information on all off-list sales, identifying the price cut—in short, supplying to all tag buyers the identical information that tag sellers get—as a condition for continuing their price-reporting activities, I suspect they would abandon them. And without the courts' requiring it, I suspect that they would regard a suggestion that they do so as a whimsical idea of an ivory-towered academician.

But the concept of workable competition is a product of the theorist just as is the concept of pure competition. And it is a part of the theory that, lacking all of the characteristics of perfect competition, a market may be more workably competitive if some imperfections which might be removed are retained.[283] Applying this doctrine to the tag market, a reasonable conclusion may be that if it is not practicable to provide buyers as well as sellers with all available information on past prices, it will restrain, not promote, competition to furnish such information to sellers. Compulsory reporting to tag makers, under penalty of "liquidated damages," of all deviations from a filed price list without reporting such information to tag buyers, may push an imperfectly competitive market toward the cartel model and away from the competitive model. I believe that it does.

The court of appeals looked at it differently, resting its approval of the institute's program on the fact that the Federal Trade Commission had not proved a price-fixing agreement, on the judicial precedents upholding the exchange of trade statistics where not a part of such an agreement, and on its characterization of the tag makers' price lists as "pretty much public property" and of their obligation to report off-list sales as "no more than the reporting of past transactions."[284] The court's reliance on precedent and its failure to consider the economic implications, pointed out above, of reporting individual seller's off-list sales, would seem to disqualify this decision as a "rule of reason" case.[285]

HAVE THE COURTS AND THE COMMISSION UNDERMINED FAITH IN THE TRADE ASSOCIATION?

One must look to other than these leading cases to justify Oppenheim's gloomy observation that "trade association executives and their legal counsel have ample ground for contending that the subtleties and refine-

283. Clark, "Toward a Concept of Workable Competition," 30 Am. Econ. Rev. (Proceedings of the American Economic Ass'n) 241, 242 (1940).
284. Tag Manufacturers Institute v. Federal Trade Commission, 174 F.2d 452, 463 (1st Cir. 1949).
285. But Oppenheim so classifies it. Oppenheim, *supra* note 2, at 1151 n. 21.

ments of the rules of evidence and burden of proof, manifested in the broadening of the implied conspiracy doctrine through per se violation rules, have shaken the foundation of trade associations to an alarming degree."[286] Fortunately Oppenheim has suggested a place to look. It is in the cases involving basing-point pricing systems [287] that the doctrine of implied conspiracy, or as the Federal Trade Commission has dubbed it, "conscious parallelism of action," has had its fullest development. What the Federal Trade Commission has found in these cases and what it has said about them may justify the inference that the Commission believes that, lacking conspiracy, basing-point pricing will not be systematically followed by an industry, and that if followed systematically it lessens competition. And some students believe that the Commission was endeavoring to develop principles and precedents under which it would eventually strike down delivered pricing per se.[288]

But it never did so, and later developments suggest that it is unlikely to do so within the foreseeable future. In its statement of policy toward geographic pricing issued for staff guidance on October 12, 1948, the Com-

286. *Id.* at 1173.
287. *Id.* at 1166.
288. In the *Rigid Steel Conduit Association* proceeding the Commission went further than in any previous case in trying to ban individual participation in industry-wide systematic basing-point pricing, charging that each respondent, by individual use of a basing-point system, which the Commission had found to restrain competition, while knowing that every other conduit maker was also using it, engaged in an unfair method of competition in violation of Section 5 of the Federal Trade Commission Act. Rigid Steel Conduit Ass'n, 38 F.T.C. 534 (1944). The court of appeals affirmed, stressing the existence in the record of "direct proof of conspiracy" but, on the strength of the Supreme Court's opinion in Federal Trade Commission v. Cement Institute, 333 U.S. 683 (1948), refusing to set aside the Commission's order directed at individual use of the basing-point pricing method as followed in the rigid steel conduit industry. Triangle Conduit & Cable Co. v. Federal Trade Commission, 168 F.2d 175, 180 (7th Cir. 1948). The Supreme Court affirmed by a four-to-four vote. Clayton Mark & Co. v. Federal Trade Commission, 336 U.S. 956 (1949). Other cases involving actual conspiracy but containing dicta which lend support to the implied conspiracy doctrine are United States Maltsters Ass'n v. Federal Trade Commission, 152 F.2d 161 (7th Cir. 1945); Milk and Ice Cream Can Institute v. Federal Trade Commission, 152 F.2d 478 (7th Cir. 1946); Fort Howard Paper Co. v. Federal Trade Commission, 156 F.2d 899 (7th Cir. 1946); and Allied Paper Mills v. Federal Trade Commission, 168 F.2d 600 (7th Cir. 1948), *cert. denied*, 336 U.S. 918 (1949). Circumstantial evidence of conspiracy was abundant but less direct and specific in Bond Crown & Cork Co. v. Federal Trade Commission, 176 F.2d 974 (4th Cir. 1949). See Bueford G. Herbert, "Delivered Pricing as Conspiracy and as Discrimination: The Legal Status," 15 Law and Contemp. Prob. 181 (1950); Kittelle and Lamb, *supra* note 208; Stocking, "The Economics of Basing Point Pricing," 15 Law and Contemp. Prob. 159 (1950); Stocking, "The Law on Basing Point Pricing: Confusion or Competition," 2 J. Pub. Law 1 (1953); Wright, *supra* note 208.

Workable Competition and Antitrust Policy

mission laid down the per se rule that *conspiracy* to use any delivered-pricing system is unlawful. While recognizing that identical pricing is not alone sufficient to establish conspiracy, it expressed the conviction that the sustained use of rigid, complex, basing-point pricing systems affords substantial but not necessarily conclusive evidence of conspiracy. However, in the *Cement Institute* hearing it received 40,000 pages of evidence and 50,000 exhibits in an effort to determine whether or not cement makers had in fact conspired to use a basing-point pricing system. It found that they had,[289] but the record does not indicate that respondents were inhibited or restricted in their effort to prove their innocence.

In settling by consent its case against the steel producers, the Commission specifically sanctioned delivered pricing even where it involved freight absorption "when innocently and independently pursued, *regularly* or otherwise, with the result of promoting competition."[290] And steel producers once more are absorbing freight to get into remote markets.[291] The Commission rejected "uniformity of prices or any element thereof of two or more sellers at any destination or destinations alone and without more as showing a violation of law."[292] This appears to be a retreat from the per se principle.[293]

Courts Apply Both Per Se Principle and Rule of Reason

The courts have applied both the rule of reason and the per se principle

---

289. Cement Institute, 37 F.T.C. 87 (1943). See note 148 *supra*. On appeal counsel for the institute argued that the Commission had not established conspiracy and the court of appeals set aside the Commission's order. Aetna Portland Cement Co. v. Federal Trade Commission, 157 F.2d 533 (7th Cir. 1946). The Supreme Court sustained the Commission. Federal Trade Commission v. Cement Institute, 333 U.S. 683 (1948).

290. American Iron and Steel Institute, 48 F.T.C. 123, 154 (1951). Emphasis supplied.

291. In 1953 United States Steel Corporation announced it would absorb freight to meet competition but would continue to quote f.o.b. prices or, when customers requested them, delivered prices that included full transportation charges. Benjamin Fairless, chairman of the corporation's board of directors, emphasized that the "revised sales policy . . . does not constitute a return to the multiple basing point" pricing system. Wall Street Journal, Oct. 1, 1953, p. 1, col. 2. The following day Jones & Laughlin, National Steel, and several smaller companies announced a similar policy. Wall Street Journal, Oct. 2, 1953, p. 1, col. 2. On November 30, 1953, Republic Steel announced a "simplified pricing system under which it will quote nothing but delivered prices" for hot rolled carbon bars. It hoped to bring its other products under this system in the future. Wall Street Journal, Nov. 30, 1953, p. 1, col. 2.

292. American Iron and Steel Institute, 48 F.T.C. 123, 154 (1951).

293. The Commission of 1951, before the 1952 elections brought a change in

Legality of Trade Association Activities

in the trade association cases, but the per se principle has been applied only to the legality of conspiracies to fix prices, while the rule of reason has permitted broad latitude in the presentation and analysis of evidence. Defendants not only have had great freedom in marshalling facts and opinions designed to show the beneficial nature of their statistical activities, but they have had the help of economists who have passed expert judgment on them. In short, they have had their day in court.[294]

It is important to note that the delivered-pricing cases were not primarily trade association cases.[295] Apparently the Commission was trying in these cases to strike down an instrument which it believed businessmen were using to make competition less effective. True, businessmen had resorted to their trade associations for help in wielding the instrument, but the legitimacy of open price-reporting was not a major issue in any of these cases and in some it was no issue at all. Nothing in the basing-point pricing cases warrants pessimism by businessmen about their right to compile and

national administration, was speaking. Statements by the new heads of the Antitrust Division and the Federal Trade Commission expressed their intention to take a "common sense" approach to the problems of competition and monopoly. On June 25, 1953, Edward F. Howrey, Chairman of the Commission, stated that under his administration the Commission would concentrate on "the prevention, rather than the cure, of diseased business conditions," and that its stress would be on "compliance, not punishment." N.Y. Times, June 25, 1953, § 1, p. 26, cols. 3, 4. Judge Stanley N. Barnes, Assistant Attorney General in charge of the Antitrust Division, declared that his bureau would not be used as "an agency for the promulgation of political or sociological doctrines or belief." N.Y. Times, Aug. 28, 1953, § 2, p. 25, col. 4.

294. The courts have persistently refrained from applying to trade association activities the rigid doctrine laid down in the Socony-Vacuum price-fixing case, where the Supreme Court said: "Any combination which *tampers* with price structures is engaged in an unlawful activity. Even though the members of the price-fixing group were in no position to control the market, to the extent that they raised, lowered, or *stabilized* prices they would be directly interfering with the free play of market forces. The Act places all such schemes beyond the pale and protects that vital part of our economy against any degree of interference." United States v. Socony-Vacuum Oil Co., 310 U.S. 150, 221 (1940). Emphasis supplied.

295. In the Glucose cases the Commission proceeded against eight respondents separately, charging among other things that the practice of selling glucose at delivered prices based on Chicago resulted in price discrimination among the respondents' customers which injured competition and violated Section 2 of the Clayton Act as amended by the Robinson-Patman Act. A. E. Staley Mfg. Co., 34 F.T.C. 1362 (1942); Clinton Co., 34 F.T.C. 879 (1942); Corn Products Refining Co., 34 F.T.C. 850 (1942); The Hubinger Co., 32 F.T.C. 1116 (1941); Union Starch & Refining Co., 32 F.T.C. 60 (1940); Penick & Ford, 31 F.T.C. 1494 (1940); Anheuser-Busch, Inc., 31 F.T.C. 986 (1940); Piel Bros. Starch Co., 30 F.T.C. 1384 (1939).

Workable Competition and Antitrust Policy

distribute trade statistics to sellers and buyers alike as an aid to informed decision-making—a prerequisite to effective competition.

Trade Association Membership Has Increased

Available statistics on the trade association movement do not justify Oppenheim's observation that "[t]rade association membership . . . has not only been discouraged, but the existing membership is so constantly confronted with the threat of antitrust that membership has become a ticket to decrees of antitrust violation."[296] The latest Department of Commerce directory on trade associations that was available in 1951 or 1952, when Oppenheim was writing, indicates that as of 1949 there were 1,500 national trade associations in the United States with paid staffs totalling 16,000 persons and with a gross membership of over 1,000,000 firms, plus 300 other national trade associations in which businessmen constituted most of the membership. Including local associations and branch chapters, there were 12,000 trade associations.[297] The rate of growth in trade association membership can be gauged by the fact that the preceding directory published by the Department of Commerce stated that as of 1941 there were 1,900 national trade associations in the country, with a gross membership of over 600,000 firms, plus 300 other national trade associations to which businessmen belonged for special purposes, and that local, interstate, and national trade associations totalled 8,000.[298] Apparently trade associations grew stronger between 1942 and 1948—the period in which most of the "implied conspiracy" cases were decided. Approximately 120 trade associations with 15 or more paid employees added a total of 1,500 employees to their staffs in those years, an increase of 27 per cent; and membership in those trade associations increased by 30 per cent to a total of over 450,000 firms. In 1949, of the 1,510 national trade associations which were active, 210 had staffs of 15 and over.[299]

Some Activities "Concededly Laudable"

The trade association cases, far from indicating that membership in

296. Oppenheim, *op. cit. supra* note 2, at 1173.
297. National Associations of the United States viii (U.S. Dep't of Commerce, 1949).
298. Trade and Professional Associations of the United States 1, 3 (U.S. Dep't of Commerce, 1942).
299. National Associations of the United States ix (U.S. Dep't of Commerce, 1949).

Legality of Trade Association Activities

trade associations is a ticket for an antitrust proceeding, should give businessmen increasing confidence in the legitimacy of the cooperative collection, compilation, and dissemination of trade statistics which contribute to enlightened competition by acquainting both buyers and sellers with the basic facts that shape market forces. The principles laid down in the *Maple Flooring* case still govern.[300] Nor should the cases arouse uneasiness about the legality of the many other socially salutary activities in which trade associations engaged. None of the practices listed as "concededly laudable" by Oppenheim—"[c]ooperative research on product innovation, production, and distribution efficiency, market and merchandising surveys, cooperative advertising, recommended product and quality standards, publication of trade journals, circulation of information concerning government activities and conduct of relations with government, representation of the industry or trade in dealing with labor and consumer groups"[301]—seem in danger.

What Businessmen Say about Trade Associations

Little evidence in what businessmen have said about trade association activities or in what they have done about them warrants Oppenheim's dismal observation about trade association membership. Earl Constantine, president of the National Association of Hosiery Manufacturers, speaking before the Trade and Industry Law Institute in New York on October 11, 1949, was more cheerful about this matter. He observed that "[d]uring the last 25 years the establishment and maintenance of industry-wide trade associations has spread with great rapidity, and there is hardly an industry or business in the United States today which does not maintain a trade association."[302]

He recognized, of course, that trade associations run the risk of court condemnation if they indulge in price-stabilization activities and about this he said:

Most trade associations abstain from conducting any statistical surveys which deal with price, or which can affect or tend to standardize the price structure of

---

300. See pp. 43–44 *supra*.
301. Oppenheim, *supra* note 2, at 1171–72. In truth, Oppenheim cites a public address by a former Assistant Attorney General in charge of the Antitrust Division in support of his characterization of these activities. Wendell Berge, "Trade Associations and the Antitrust Laws," address before the Washington Trade Association Executives, May 16, 1945.
302. Earl Constantine, "The Purpose and Nature of Trade Association Statistics," No. 4, Current Business Studies (New York: Trade and Industry Law Institute, 1949), p. 3.

113

Workable Competition and Antitrust Policy

the industry. I happen to be of those who believe in such abstention and who have found by experience that *without such activities* a trade association can still prove to be a highly useful instrument to the industry, to the market it serves and to the public.[303]

A competent lawyer with great experience in these matters has pointed out that the statistical activities of trade associations, even though designed to affect the market, have never been condemned in isolation. He observed:

Statistical data of different kinds are collected and distributed by trade associations for some purpose and their use may produce some effect on trade. We start with that proposition because we must never suppose that the collection and dissemination of data is an idle exercise. Members of a particular industry pay for a statistical service because it serves some useful commercial purpose in that industry. . . . [T]he legality of this trade association activity has never been judged in court as an activity standing apart. . . . What might appear to be squarely within the borders of legality under a Supreme Court decision may fall because it is but a part—and, standing alone, a lawful part—of an illegal whole. It is all too familiar law today that a lawful act becomes unlawful when done in furtherance of an unlawful end.[304]

Price-fixing is still per se unlawful.

Charles T. Lawson, vice-president in charge of sales of the Nash-Kelvinator Corporation, speaking before the same group, gave a forthright and illuminating account—apparently with no fear of governmental intervention—of the role which the statistical services of the National Electrical Manufacturers Association had played in his company's business planning. He averred that the statistical services of the association had developed and expanded over a twenty-year period "with increasing confidence and cooperation." [305]

The growth of trade association membership would seem to justify broadening this generalization.

Courts Have Approved Cooperative Dissemination of Market Information

The courts have indeed recognized that business judgments on production and consumption policies, on selling and buying, to be intelligent must be informed, and they have therefore placed their approval on the

303. *Id.* at 8. Emphasis supplied.
304. Breck P. McAllister, "Legal Aspects of Trade Association Statistics," *id.* at 19.
305. Charles T. Lawson, "Benefits Kelvinator Receives from Trade Association Statistics," *id.* at 13.

Legality of Trade Association Activities

cooperative dissemination of market information designed to educate buyers and sellers alike. Unfortunately, they have not always stopped here but have at times approved arrangements clearly designed to promote the interests of producers at the expense of consumers. If the standards of workable competition laid down in this study are appropriate guides for judicial policy, the courts have already gone too far in approving control schemes. What is needed in passing judgment on the legality of open price-reporting systems is not a more liberal interpretation of the rule of reason and a less rigid application of the principle of workable competition than this study sets up, but a clearer recognition of the role which price plays in a free-enterprise economy. If the aim of policy is to make competition more effective by supplying decision-makers with market information essential to an enlightened interpretation of market forces, buyers and sellers must be treated alike, and open price-reporting programs must not be used as elements in a more complex arrangement designed to restrict competition. Open price-reporting systems defective in these respects transgress the principles of effective or workable competition.

Other Notions of Workable Competition

Some of the advocates of antitrust revision have a different conception of workable competition than that expounded in this study. They are not always precise in their statement of it, but it is pretty clear from what some of them have said that they lack faith in competition as a rationer of goods, an allocator of resources, and a distributor of income. They do not propose to discard competition as a symbol, but they would let businessmen collectively control market behavior in order to make it better serve the public interest. According to this view, the workability of arrangements that involve tampering with the market should be judged not by their effect on competition, but by their effect on public welfare. As Oppenheim has expressed it, "In particular factual situations, evidence of legal, economic, and social justifications" should be "weighed under close judicial scrutiny to arrive at a determination of whether the restrictions are reasonable or unreasonable when measured against the effects upon competition." [306]

Other advocates of change in the antitrust statutes have been equally vague about the standards by which the effectiveness of competition is to

306. Oppenheim, *supra* note 2, at 1160.

Workable Competition and Antitrust Policy

be judged. Blackwell Smith has this to say about the application of the principle to trade association activities: "Public policy should be in favor of such joint or group activities in so far as they advance tendencies toward more and better goods and services for more people in proportion to human efforts, and tend to provide better tools for Effective Competition, including information." [307] No one can object to this in principle, but who is to say what it means in practice?

Conclusions

If the good in trade association activity lies in its restriction on competition, how much good should associations be encouraged to do? That is to say, how much restriction on competition is socially desirable? How much restriction on competition leaves it workable? I don't know. Nor do other economists. But if businessmen are told that concerted action *may* by restricting competition promote the general welfare, they are entitled to know the appropriate limits of such restrictions. If they are told that concerted action to restrict competition is unlawful, they proceed collectively at their own risk. Outlawing concerted action to restrict competition is a far more certain guide to business behavior than setting up the vague and debatable principle of workable competition.

The chief objection to a proposal to liberalize the law on open price-reporting activities is its ultimate, not its immediate, consequences. It is unlikely that the market-control activities of either the Maple Flooring Manufacturers Association or the Tag Manufacturers Institute, judged separately, had any serious effect on the economy as a whole. The maple-flooring association probably contributed to high prices in the short run but apparently exerted little influence on long-run prices. The tag institute's program has probably resulted in higher prices for tags than would have prevailed without it. Both arrangements probably contributed to a redistribution of income in favor of sellers as against buyers. But tag purchases, at any rate, constitute a trivial part of ultimate consumer expenditures, and the benefits of lower tag prices to consumers would have been too diffuse for measurement.

General resort throughout the whole of industry to trade association activities like those of the maple-flooring association and the tag institute would be likely to exert a significant, though not precisely measurable, influence on the economy. This influence would, I believe, be undesirable in

307. Smith, *supra* note 2, at 419.

two ways. In normal times it would retard economic readjustments necessitated by an uneconomic distribution of productive resources. In bad times, it might well retard recovery directly by adversely affecting income distribution [308] and indirectly by reducing the effectiveness of federally administered fiscal and monetary policies.

Moreover, if the nation is to rely on "free private enterprise" to guide economic processes, "workable competition" applied to concerted action is a dangerous principle. In a democracy, with authority should go responsibility. If associated activity among businessmen is to be substituted for the forces of the market in guiding economic processes, decisions on how far the principle should be carried before it clashes with the public interest should be made by commissions of experts responsible to all the people rather than by business groups answerable to the people only when they transgress the law by carrying their associated activities *too* far.[309] This might well lead to a type of control ultimately destructive of private enterprise. In short, if the aim of public policy is to perpetuate a free-enterprise economy, it should outlaw associated activity designed to restrict competition. Where this is its object, failure to achieve it is not a very good reason for permitting business rivals to work together.

This does not mean that trade associations are or ought to be per se unlawful. They may and do perform many useful activities, not the least of

308. This is a complex and debatable issue. For an exposition of my point of view on it, see Stocking and Watkins, *Cartels or Competition?* chap. 7. For a contrary view see Boulding, "In Defense of Monopoly," 59 Q. J. Econ. 524 (1945); Schumpeter, *op. cit. supra* note 2, chap. VIII, especially at 93–94. See also Abram Bergson, "Price Flexibility and the Level of Income," 25 Rev. Econ. Stat. 2 (1943); Alfred C. Neal, *Industrial Concentration and Price Inflexibility* (Washington, D.C.: American Council on Public Affairs, 1942), chap. 9.

309. The British have avoided the legal dilemmas which arise when the standard of "public interest" is substituted for the standard of free competition by creating just such a commission of experts and not requiring judicial review of its findings. The Monopolies and Restrictive Trade Practices (Inquiry and Control) Act, adopted July 30, 1948, provides that the Board of Trade may refer restrictive trade practices to a permanent commission for investigation to determine "whether any such things as are specified in the reference . . . operate or may be expected to operate against the public interest." 11 & 12 Geo. VI, c. 66, § 6 (2) (1948). The criteria set up for the commission's guidance are extremely vague and not unlike some of those suggested for determining the existence of workable competition: (a) the most efficient production and distribution of goods of the type and quality, in the volume, and at a price that will best serve home and overseas markets; (b) an organization of industry that will encourage efficiency and new enterprise; (c) full employment and economical distribution of men, materials, and industrial capacity; and (d) development of technology, expansion of existing markets, and the opening up of new markets. *Id.* § 14. But the British, unlike Americans, are not committed to a free-enterprise economy.

Workable Competition and Antitrust Policy

which is the dissemination of basic market information. The courts have done fairly well in telling them what they can lawfully do. From the decided cases and existing law, it is clear that they will not be molested so long as they do not deliberately and collectively tamper with market forces to restrict competition. If we should adopt a policy whereby concerted action among business rivals is to be judged not by its effect upon competition but by its effect on the public welfare, we will have indeed launched on a sea of doubt; and, while our ultimate destination may now be obscure, it is a good guess that we will be drifting toward the haven of a collective society where security is bought at the expense of freedom and economy.

3

The Rule of Reason, Workable Competition, and Monopoly

AGITATION FOR CHANGING THE ANTITRUST LAWS is as old as the laws themselves, but the intensity of the demand for modification, and its objectives, have varied. In 1953 the clamor for change culminated in the appointment of the Attorney General's National Committee to Study the Antitrust Laws. The most ardent proponents of revision had laid down two principles by which they would have the Sherman Act interpreted: the rule of reason and the concept of workable competition.[1] This article will

Note: Reprinted from the *Yale Law Journal*, Vol. 64, No. 8 (July 1955).

1. For an exposition of the rule of reason and the concept of workable competition as modifications of antitrust policy, see S. Chesterfield Oppenheim, "Federal Antitrust Legislation: Guideposts to a Revised National Antitrust Policy," 50 Mich. L. Rev. 1139 (1952). The effectiveness of Oppenheim's demand for change is reflected in his having been made co-chairman with Judge Stanley N. Barnes, Assistant Attorney General in charge of the Antitrust Division, of the Attorney General's National Committee to Study the Antitrust Laws. Endorsement of these principles appears in Blackwell Smith, "Effective Competition: Hypothesis for Modernizing the Antitrust Laws," 26 N.Y.U.L. Rev. 405 (1951); U.S. Dep't of Commerce, *Effective Competition: Report to the Secretary of Commerce by His Business Advisory Council* (1952). See also Morris A. Adelman, "Effective Competition and the Antitrust Laws," 61 Harv. L. Rev. 1289 (1948); Thomas E. Sunderland, "Changing Legal Concepts in the Antitrust Field," 3 Syracuse L. Rev. 60 (1951).

Although the demand for a change in the law to comply with the rule of reason and the concept of workable competition seems to have been the occasion for setting up the Attorney General's Committee, the Committee carefully avoided recommending that the law be modified to conform to the theory of workable competition, cautioning that it "does not provide a standard of legality under any of the antitrust laws." *Report of the Attorney General's National Committee to Study the Antitrust Laws* (1955), p. 316. But having shut out workable competition at the front door, the Committee brought it in by the back. It recognized that "it provides the courts with tools of analysis in making the factual inquiry into problems of competition and monopoly. . . ." *Ibid.* Blackwell Smith, a member of the Committee, acknowledges more specifically the Committee's endorsement of the concept of

Workable Competition and Antitrust Policy

sketch briefly the development of these two ideas and analyze their significance to one sector of antitrust policy, that dealing with industrial consolidation and monopoly.

WORKABLE COMPETITION

Chamberlin's *Theory of Monopolistic Competition*, published in 1933, one of the century's really significant contributions to economic thinking, greatly disturbed students of industrial structure and policy. Other economists had noted with concern the impact of two great merger movements [2] on the structure of the American economy, but few had recognized with Chamberlin's insight the significance of structure to economic behavior,[3] and none had developed a satisfactory theory of monopolistic competition. Chamberlin's analysis was disturbing in two respects. On the basis of his very rigorous assumptions [4] he concluded that (1) oligopolists, if they are rational and take account of both the direct and indirect consequences of their decisions on prices, will without conspiring behave like monopolists; and (2) although rivalry among the producers of differentiated products may eliminate monopoly profits, it will not minimize costs.

No less disturbing than Chamberlin's analysis was the intellectual re-

---

workable competition as a legal standard. He says: "The central concept of workable or effective competition is described in the Report in terms which parallel very closely the legal policy statements elsewhere in the Report as to characteristics of acceptable competition"; and that out of the report "comes the most realistic set of standards for legal and socially acceptable competition since the Business Advisory Council Report on Effective Competition published by Secretary of Commerce Sawyer. The present Report makes more official a great deal of what was then and there recommended." Trade Practice Bulletin, May 1955, p. 4.

2. Between 1898 and 1904, 239 corporate consolidations of national or regional significance, each capitalized for more than $1,000,000 and together covering practically every important manufacturing industry, took place. John Moody, *The Truth about the Trusts* (Chicago: Moody Publishing Co., 1904), pp. 453–67. The second merger movement began in 1925, when 554 mining and manufacturing firms were merged, and ended in 1929, when 1,245 such firms were merged. Willard E. Thorp, "The Merger Movement," in *The Structure of Industry* (TNEC Monograph No. 27, 1941), table 1, p. 233.

3. Joan Robinson, *The Economics of Imperfect Competition* (London: Macmillan, 1933), appeared in England about the same time. However much it differs from Chamberlin's theory in the details of its logic, it is an intellectual response to similar institutional developments and arrives at similar conclusions on the nature of pricing in markets of few sellers.

4. Chamberlin postulated an industrial structure of few sellers, a standardized product, and identical demand and cost curves known to the sellers. Edward Chamberlin, *The Theory of Monopolistic Competition* (7th ed.; Cambridge: Harvard University Press, 1957), pp. 30–31.

action to it. Arthur R. Burns, arguing that contemporary industrial structure is largely a response to modern technology and that its monopolistic character is therefore inevitable, advocated such a comprehensive program of social control [5] that one of his more severe critics characterized his study as "planning for totalitarian monopoly." [6] Edwin G. Nourse, similarly arguing that modern technology decrees business units so large and so few that market forces cannot be relied on to insure competitive pricing, sought to promote the public welfare by persuading businessmen that their long-run interests lie not in charging what the traffic will bear but in passing on to consumers in the form of lower prices the gains from technological innovation.[7] Such measures were not acceptable to the socialists, who identified the modern industrial structure with monopoly and advocated for its social control a comprehensive program of public ownership.

Other economists found solace in a new logic. The new logic drew its inspiration and designation from John Maurice Clark's paper before the American Economic Association in December 1939, "Toward a Concept of Workable Competition." [8] Clark in pioneering this concept noted what other economists had observed—that the economists' models of pure and perfect competition were abstractions to which the realities of the business world do not conform—and he sought a general concept more useful in analyzing markets and evaluating their economic significance. Recognizing that actual market arrangements are intermediate between those of pure competition and monopoly, he sought to describe those which are workably competitive. In markets of workable competition such control as a seller may exert is slight, and under certain circumstances it may do more good than harm. In any event a market arrangement, to be workably competitive in Clark's terms, must be economically more advantageous to the general public than any practically attainable alternative. Other economists have busied themselves with the concept of workable competition, and it has become a part of the profession's stock-in-trade.[9] As others have con-

5. Arthur R. Burns, *The Decline of Competition* (New York: McGraw-Hill, 1936), chaps. 11–12.
6. Frank A. Fetter, "Planning for Totalitarian Monopoly," 45 J. Pol. Econ. 95 (1937).
7. Edwin G. Nourse, *Price Making in a Democracy* (Washington, D.C.: Brookings Institution, 1944).
8. 30 Am. Econ. Rev. (Proceedings of the American Economic Ass'n) 241 (1940).
9. Corwin D. Edwards, *Maintaining Competition* (New York: McGraw-Hill, 1949), pp. 9–10; Adelman, *supra* note 1; Joe S. Bain, "Workable Competition in Oligopoly," 40 Am. Econ. Rev. (Proceedings of the American Economic Ass'n) 35 (1950); Jesse W. Markham, "An Alternative Approach to the Concept of Workable Competition," 40 Am. Econ. Rev. 349 (1950); Edward S. Mason, "Methods

tributed to it the concept has acquired greater depth and breadth but not greater precision. What it is rapidly coming to mean is not very different from what economists of an earlier period meant by the less pretentious term "competition." According to the modernized concept an industry is effectively or workably competitive if market forces—*i.e.*, the total influence of independent decisions by buyers and sellers regardless of their number—provide the drive for technological innovation, the allocation of resources, the organization of production, and the distribution of income.[10]

The architects of workable competition, despite the vagueness of the concept, have laid down certain criteria by which it may be gauged. Most would agree that in determining the effectiveness or workability of competition in any particular industry one should examine its structure, the conduct of firms within it, and the performance of the firms and of the industry as a whole. Conclusions based on any one of these criteria may be ill-founded, but together all three criteria may form a logical basis for judgment.

The Structure of an Industry

By an industry's structure economists refer to an industry's make-up, how it is put together, how its parts are interrelated. How many firms are in it? What is their relative size? Does a single firm dominate it? How difficult is the movement of resources into and out of it? What are the limits of its market? How sharply is it differentiated from other "industries" producing rival products readily substitutable for the product it makes? Economists believe that the answers to such questions will throw some light on the effectiveness or workability of competition.

Where an industry consists of only two or a few firms each producing a homogeneous product and operating under identical cost conditions, each fully informed of market conditions and each taking account of the in-

of Developing a Proper Control of Big Business," 18 Acad. Pol. Sci. Proc. 40 (1939); Mason, "The Current Status of the Monopoly Problem in the United States," 62 Harv. L. Rev. 1265 (1949); George J. Stigler, "The Extent and Bases of Monopoly," 32 Am. Econ. Rev. (No. 2 Supp., Pt. 2) 2–3 (1942); Clair Wilcox, *Competition and Monopoly in American Industry* (TNEC Monograph No. 21, 1940).

10. Contemporary critics of the theory of "pure" competition criticize that theory —which is largely of their own invention, they having supplied the qualifying "pure" and the concept it describes—on the grounds that it is concerned with equilibrium in a static economy and that it ignores the nature of, and the forces providing, technological innovation. I do not find this a shortcoming of the leading economists of the late nineteenth century, Alfred Marshall and John Bates Clark, for example.

The Rule of Reason and Monopoly

direct as well as the direct consequences of its decisions, Chamberlin argued that the firms will behave like monopolists.[11] That is to say, they will produce the same amount as a single firm would produce and sell it at the same price. To insure monopoly behavior the firms need not conspire, but the results will be the same as though they had conspired. As the number of firms increases, the likelihood of their behaving like monopolists decreases. Eventually the number of sellers may become so large that some one (and hence all) will conclude that he need not take account of the indirect consequences of his decisions. That is to say, he will behave like a competitor and the result will be pure competition. Chamberlin recognized that lack of knowledge about the market or differing interpretations of it might lead to nonmonopolistic behavior, and he was not unaware of the fact that no business situation is likely to conform exactly to his model.

While Chamberlin's analysis may have convinced some economists that a market of few sellers is less likely to be workably competitive than a market of more numerous sellers, it has certainly not convinced all. Adelman, for example, regards competition as compatible with "many small firms . . . with a few large ones . . . and with large and small ones together." [12] Adelman no doubt expresses the views of many other economists. Clark recognized that potential competition may afford an effective check on the temptation of oligopolists to exploit their markets.[13] And in any event economists generally recognize that the absence of a large number of firms is not in all cases a useful criterion, for in many industries the optimum scale of production is so large that maximum efficiency decrees a small number of sellers.

When the market for a product is ill-defined, so that the product faces competition from products so slightly differentiated that they meet almost identical needs, producers of similar products may serve as an adequate check on each other in what is loosely regarded as an industry. Whether they do in fact so check each other will depend on what economists call the cross-elasticity of demand. Cross-elasticity reflects the extent to which price changes in one product affect the amount of another product that buyers will buy. Where the cross-elasticity of demand for rival products is great, a decline in the price of one decreases the sale of the other and may lead to a decline in its price. The production of numerous similar products

11. Chamberlin, *op. cit. supra* note 4, at 49–50.
12. Adelman, "Effective Competition and the Antitrust Laws," 61 Harv. L. Rev. 1289, 1303 (1948).
13. Clark, *supra* note 8, at 246–47.

Workable Competition and Antitrust Policy

with a high cross-elasticity of demand may perform about the same economic function as does the existence of numerous sellers of the same product. Thus rival products may contribute to the workability of competition, but they do not guarantee it.

Conduct

How firms behave may be more important than structure in determining the effectiveness of competition, but behavior is a matter about which generalization is hazardous. The vigor of competitive rivalry may depend as much on the character and aspirations of the executive officers of a firm as on the industry's structure. Not all businessmen are dedicated to the principle of maximizing earnings. Some may aspire to earn only a "reasonable" profit; when they do, other firms may be forced to accept a similar goal. Business analysts may differ in their opinions as to the effects of price cuts on output and costs, and they may make different value judgments. Even though firms may eschew price competition, they do not necessarily forego competitive rivalry. They may try to improve organizational efficiency and the productive process, thus reducing costs and perhaps eventually prices as well. Or they may improve their product or the services supplied with it, thus offering better goods for the same money.

But in oligopolistic industries business conduct is not necessarily of a salutary character, and structure itself may shape conduct. Such conduct may include the sort of predatory practices that the old Standard Oil Trust made notorious—secret rebating, local price discrimination, espionage, operation of bogus independents, and the like—but it also includes business practices that are regarded as sound and ethical by the firms that pursue them. Price leadership and basing point pricing are illustrations. Although the Chamberlinian theory of oligopoly points to the conclusion that conspiracy among few sellers may be unnecessary to insure noncompetitive pricing, few economists would rely on the theory alone in reaching a conclusion about business behavior. Most economists would concede, however, that fewness of sellers may encourage the development and use of business practices—types of business conduct—not consistent with effective competition.

Conduct as the term is here used may refer to neither predatory nor ordinary business practices, but to the strategy resorted to by a firm in seeking to protect an advantage it already has. Such strategy or conduct aims at the protection of a trade secret, a patent, or a superior source of supply, or at blocking entrance to an industry or a market. Strategy is the weapon

The Rule of Reason and Monopoly

of a firm operating in an imperfectly competitive market, but resort to strategy is not necessarily inconsistent with workable competition. As suggested, it may lead to the improvement of processes and products. It may mean better goods at lower prices. On the other hand, conduct or strategy that on its face reflects a vigorous rivalry may serve to isolate a producer from the impact of competition long enough to prevent its being workable.

In short, the conduct of firms alone may be no more satisfactory for determining the effectiveness of competition than structure alone. Just as structure may reflect itself in conduct, so conduct may reflect itself in performance.

Performance

By performance economists mean the effectiveness or efficiency with which, from the economic point of view, a firm or industry acquits itself. Is it dynamic or lethargic? Is it quick to introduce new methods and improve its product? What is the course of its prices? Do they reflect reductions in cost which are rapidly passed on to consumers? What is its rate of profit? Is "progress" its "most important product"? Does it make "better things for better living" at prices within the reach of those who desire them? In measuring performance, as in evaluating conduct, an economist must be careful of his conclusions. A monopolist may be lethargic or dynamic. A mature industry may be highly competitive but not progressive. A young industry may display remarkable vitality even though few firms occupy it. Its rate of return may merely express the rapid expansion of demand for its products. Contrariwise, it may reflect monopoly elements.

While no one of these criteria—structure, conduct, performance—is wholly satisfactory, many economists believe that together they may afford a useful guide in determining the effectiveness of competition within an industry. Of course guideposts are no better than the wayfarer's interpretation of them. Nevertheless a belief in their dependability led the Secretary of Commerce's Business Advisory Council and others to propose workable or effective competition under a rule of reason as a standard of legality in antitrust cases.[14]

14. U.S. Dep't of Commerce, *Effective Competition.* Some students of antitrust have a different notion of the concept of workable competition from that expounded above. Oppenheim, *supra* note 1, at 1160, seems to imply that the workability of any particular industrial arrangement should be judged not only by its effect on competition but also by its effect on public welfare. He says: "In particular factual situations, evidence of legal, economic, and social justifications [should] . . . be weighed under close judicial scrutiny to arrive at a determination of whether the

Workable Competition and Antitrust Policy

The Rule of Reason

The proposals for modifying the antitrust statutes to require that they be interpreted and administered in accordance with "the rule of reason" justify reconsideration of the derivation of the principle, its use at common law, the intent of Congress about it, and the courts' interpretation and application of it.

The principle is old. As applied to restraints of trade it developed in common law litigation growing out of private contracts. There the term "restraint of trade" had a technical meaning.[15] It was used to characterize agreements not to compete between buyers and sellers of property, partners in a joint enterprise, apprentices and masters, and the like. For example, a buyer of a business wished to protect himself against the seller's future competition, or a seller of part of a business wished to protect the part he retained from the buyer's new competition. In consideration of the sale the buyer or the seller agreed not to compete in such a way as to detract from the value of the property retained or sold. Such contracts involved a *restraint of trade*. They also involved a *restriction on competition*,[16] but neither English nor American legislatures outlawed them by statute. Contracts in restraint of trade first came before the courts only when one of the parties violated the contract. When the injured party resorted to litigation, the courts had to decide whether the contract was enforceable. In the early history of such contracts the English courts held that all of them were void because contrary to the public interest in two ways: they deprived an individual of a means of livelihood, and they deprived the public of his talents.[17]

restrictions are reasonable or unreasonable when measured against the effects upon competition." I understand this to mean that arrangements may be economically and socially justifiable even though they restrict competition; and if they are, the restriction should be regarded as reasonable. Smith, *supra* note 1, at 419, is equally obscure. He says: "Public policy should be in favor of such joint or group activities in so far as they advance tendencies toward more and better goods and services for more people in proportion to human efforts. . . ."

15. For a somewhat similar view of the law on restraint of trade and of the development of the rule of reason, see Myron W. Watkins, *Industrial Combinations and Public Policy* (Boston: Houghton Mifflin, 1927), pp. 224–27; Milton Handler, "Restraint of Trade," 13 Encyc. Soc. Sci. 339–41 (1934).

16. They have no significance in a purely competitive market. No wheat farmer in selling a farm ever agrees as part of the bargain that he will not compete with the purchaser in raising and selling wheat. Contracts to "restrain trade" have meaning only where products are differentiated, sellers are few, or special skills or trade secrets are involved.

17. Apparently the earliest recorded case of a contract in restraint of trade is Dyer's Case, Y.B., 2 Hen. 5, f. 5, pl. 26 (1415), in which the court not only re-

The Rule of Reason and Monopoly

But as trade and industry expanded in England and the obstacles to entry became less formidable; as the customs and laws governing British economic life, especially the laws of apprenticeship, were relaxed; as workmen moved more freely from one occupation to another; as the opportunities for contractual employment expanded; as freedom under contract replaced security based on status; and as the means of communication and transportation improved and markets broadened, the courts modified the common law by distinguishing between reasonable and unreasonable restraints on trade.[18] In passing judgment on the reasonableness of restrictive contracts, they re-examined the nature of the transaction from the two points of view from which they had originally condemned them: the protection of the parties and the protection of the public.[19] In determining whether the individuals had been injured they looked to the consideration binding the contract. In determining whether the public interest had been hurt they considered the seriousness of the restrictions on competition. Where there was a legal consideration for the restraint and the re-

fused to enforce a bond conditioned on the defendant's not practicing his trade as a dyer in the plaintiff's town for six months but threatened: "[A]nd by God, if the plaintiff were here he should go to prison till he had paid a fine to the king." In Colgate v. Bacheler, Cro. Eliz. 872, 78 Eng. Rep. 1097 (K.B. 1601), the defendant's bond to pay £20 if he should use the trade of a haberdasher in certain cities was held void: "[I]t was resolved by the Court, that this condition is against law, to prohibit or restrain any to use a lawful trade at any time, or at any place; for as well as he may restrain him for one time or one place, he may restrain him for longer times and more places, which is against the benefit of the commonwealth; for being freemen, it is free for them to exercise their trade in any place."

18. A contract restraining a joiner from practicing his trade for a certain time (twenty-one years) and in a certain place (the city of London) was upheld early in the seventeenth century. Rogers v. Parrey, 2 Bulst. 136, 80 Eng. Rep. 1012 (K.B. 1614). Broad v. Jollyfe, Cro. Jac. 596, 79 Eng. Rep. 509 (K.B. 1621), held that "for a valuable consideration, and voluntary, one may agree that he will not use his trade." But Mitchel v. Reynolds, 1 P. Wms. 181, 24 Eng. Rep. 347 (Ch. 1711), is the leading case on testing the validity of a restraint of trade by its reasonableness. The seller of a bakery who had given his bond for £50 not to practice his trade within the parish for five years resumed his trade and defended himself against the buyer's action for debt on the ground that the restaint was void. It was resolved by the court: "And we are all of opinion, that a special consideration being set forth in the condition, which shews it was reasonable for the parties to enter into it, the same is good. . . ." The court also distinguished between general restraints "not to exercise a trade throughout the kingdom," which were "of no benefit to either party, and only oppressive," and those "limited to a particular place," which were good. *Id.* at 182, 24 Eng. Rep. at 348.

19. Mitchel v. Reynolds, 1 P. Wms. 181, 190, 24 Eng. Rep. 347, 350 (Ch. 1711). Chief Justice Parker pointed out another danger in restrictive contracts: "the great abuses these voluntary restraints are liable to; as for instance, from corporations, who are perpetually labouring for exclusive advantages in trade, and to reduce it into as few hands as possible. . . ." *Ibid.*

127

Workable Competition and Antitrust Policy

strictions on competition were not regarded as oppressive, the courts came to uphold such contracts.[20] This was the common law rule of reason, developed in the English courts and adopted in America.[21]

In evaluating the significance of this development it is important to keep in mind that the contracts whose reasonableness was initially in question were ancillary to transactions whose legality was not in dispute. During the latter part of the nineteenth century rival businessmen with increasing frequency contracted to restrict or eliminate competition among themselves. These arrangements were not incidental to contracts whose legality was beyond question. They were not designed to protect an individual in purchasing property or teaching a trade; they were aimed at market control. Their object was to lessen the severity of competition among business rivals or to monopolize markets. When injured parties brought suit against of-

20. Some courts in upholding contracts imposing partial restraints on trade declared that only a partial restraint supported by a consideration which the court found adequate was valid. Homer v. Ashford, 3 Bing. 322, 327, 130 Eng. Rep. 537, 539 (C.P. 1825). Others said that the court need not weigh the reasonableness of the consideration so long as it was a legal one. Hitchcock v. Coker, 6 Ad. & E. 438, 112 Eng. Rep. 167 (Ex. 1837). In 1837 the Exchequer Chamber upheld a general restraint (a carrier's agreement not to engage in his trade but to become an assistant to the defendants for the rest of his life), saying that general restraint is good if made on sufficient consideration "and the public gain some advantage." Wallis v. Day, 2 M. & W. 273, 281, 150 Eng. Rep. 759, 762 (Ex. 1837). Sometimes an unreasonably extensive restraint was held invalid while the reasonable portions of the same contract were upheld. Mallan v. May, 11 M. & W. 653, 152 Eng. Rep. 967 (Ex. 1843) (dentist's agreement not to practice in London held good, but his agreement not to practice in any towns or places in England or Scotland where plaintiff's had practiced, bad). In 1869 an agreement not to engage in the leather cloth business anywhere in Europe was upheld, the court saying that public policy enables a man "to enter into any stipulation however restrictive it is, provided that restriction in the judgment of the Court is not unreasonable, having regard to the subject matter of the contract." Leather Cloth Co. v. Lorsont, L.R. 9 Eq. 345, 354 (1869). And in Rousillon v. Rousillon, 14 Ch.D. 351 (1880), the court upheld a champagne salesman's general contract not to deal in champagne for ten years, saying that the invalidity of all general restraints of trade had never been the law of England.

21. E.g., Pike v. Thomas, 7 Ky. (4 Bibb) 486 (1817); Alger v. Thacher, 36 Mass. (19 Pick.) 51 (1837); Hubbard v. Miller, 27 Mich. 15, 19–20 (1873). In 1873 the Supreme Court upheld a buyer's contract not to use a certain steamer in California waters or on the Columbia River and its tributaries for ten years, saying: "In order that it may not be unreasonable, the restraint imposed must not be larger than is required for the necessary potection of the party with whom the contract is made." Oregon Steam Navigation Co. v. Winsor, 87 U.S. (20 Wall.) 64, 67 (1873). And in Diamond Match Co. v. Roeber, 106 N.Y. 473, 482, 13 N.E. 419 (1887), the court upheld a ninety-nine year contract not to manufacture or sell friction matches in the United States except in Nevada and Montana, saying: "If [a man's] . . . business extends over a continent, does public policy forbid his accompanying the sale with a stipulation for restraint co-extensive with the business which he sells?"

The Rule of Reason and Monopoly

fenders who violated such contracts, the courts, confronted with a different kind of restraint on trade, sought refuge in the old doctrine.[22] But in resorting to the rule of reason they did not always apply it in the same way.

Courts and commentators have disagreed about the way the common law rule of reason was applied to contracts whose purpose was market control. Judge Taft (later Chief Justice), in his review of the common law on restraint of trade in the *Addyston Pipe and Steel Company* case,[23] concluded that the courts had generally held void all contracts having the sole object of restraining competition. Courts that had held otherwise, he contended, by assuming "the power to say . . . how much restraint of competition is in the public interest, and how much is not" had "set sail on a sea of doubt."[24] Five years earlier Judge Sanborn, in deciding the *Trans-Missouri Freight Association* case in the district court,[25] had reviewed the common law and reached a contrary conclusion. He found that at common law only pooling contracts among competing common carriers, or contracts or combinations to restrict or monopolize supply or to raise prices or pool profits among producers or dealers in "staple commodities of prime necessity to the people," were illegal restraints of trade;[26] but contracts "between common carriers which imposed some restrictions upon competition have been frequently sustained by our highest courts, and the rule has been often applied that the test of their validity was not the existence, but the reasonableness, of the restriction imposed."[27] Handler, after reviewing the

---

22. While ostensibly applying the principles of Mitchel v. Reynolds, 1 P. Wms. 181, 24 Eng. Rep. 347 (Ch. 1711), or other ancillary contract cases, some English and American courts sustained contracts designed only to divide territories, raise prices, control markets, or prevent competition. Wickens v. Evans, 3 Y. & J. 318, 148 Eng. Rep. 1201 (Ex. 1829) (agreement between three competing trunk and box manufacturers to assign markets in England and Wales, not to pay in Oxford more than 6d. or 8d. for any tea chest, and to meet for mutual assistance if outside competition arose); Collins v. Lock, 4 App. Cas. 674 (1879) (agreement by four stevedoring firms to divide the business at the port of Melbourne); Kellogg v. Larkin, 3 Pin. 123 (Wis. 1851) (an exclusive dealing contract between a grain dealer and a warehouseman, one of a series by which grain dealers were seeking full control of the Milwaukee wheat market); Leslie v. Lorillard, 110 N.Y. 519, 18 N.E. 363 (1888) (steamship corporation's contract to pay another not to compete).

23. United States v. Addyston Pipe & Steel Co., 85 Fed. 271 (6th Cir. 1898), *modified and aff'd*, 175 U.S. 211 (1899).

24. *Id.* at 85 Fed. 271, 284 (6th Cir. 1898).

25. United States v. Trans-Missouri Freight Ass'n, 58 Fed. 58 (8th Cir. 1893), *rev'd*, 166 U.S. 290 (1897).

26. *Id.* at 58 Fed. 58, 69 (8th Cir. 1893).

27. *Id.* at 74. Judge Sanborn said that the *reason* contracts of the kinds he described were held void was that their "main purpose . . . is to suppress, not simply to regulate, competition. . . ." *Id.* at 69. John C. Peppin, "Price-Fixing Agreements

cases and the commentators, recognizes three trends in the authorities before 1890: (1) The prevailing view was that contracts among business rivals that restrained or eliminated competition were unlawful per se. (2) Some jurisdictions, finding the contracts before them so limited in scope as to be ineffective, reached the somewhat anomalous conclusion that they were therefore enforceable. (3) Other courts, seemingly lacking faith in competition as a regulator of economic activity, found price-fixing agreements valid when the prices were designed not to exploit the public but to rectify "intolerable industrial conditions."[28] Thorelli[29] suggests that the conflicts in common law decisions may have been due in part to a divergence in English and American public policy toward restrictive arrangements, which developed in the nineteenth century:

> In the course of the 19th century the doctrine of restraint of trade was extended to cover, ultimately, restrictions on trade in general. It is in this broad sense that it has been of such great significance in the development of American antimonopoly policies. Whereas the extension of the restraint of trade concept in England marked the beginning of a continuous relaxation of public policy, American courts moulded the broadened doctrine into a useful, if imperfect, general antimonopoly instrument. And whereas the "rule of reason," adopted from the "narrow" restraint of trade doctrine, was used to implement the gradual weakening of the extended doctrine in England, there was relatively little use of it in this new field in the United States.[30]

With the courts and the commentators thus in disagreement a layman may reasonably conclude that the common law on restrictions of competition was inconsistent and confused.

---

under the Sherman Anti-Trust Law," 28 Calif. L. Rev. 297, 667 (1940), supports Judge Sanborn's interpretation. His thesis is that the common law always upheld agreements directly affecting prices without directly fixing them, and that beginning early in the nineteenth century nonancillary agreements eliminating price and all other competition between the parties were upheld if reasonable. He says that while the early cases invalidating price-fixing agreements did not refer to them as restraints of trade, "it would seem clear that such was the real objection. . . ." *Id.* at 324.

28. Milton Handler, *A Study of the Construction and Enforcement of the Federal Antitrust Laws* (TNEC Monograph No. 38, 1941), pp. 4–5.

29. Hans B. Thorelli, *The Federal Antitrust Policy* (Baltimore: Johns Hopkins Press, 1955), came off the press as this article was being completed. Although written by a Swedish scholar, this work gives the most comprehensive, detailed, and penetrating analysis yet to appear of the legal, economic, social, and political background of the Sherman Act and its administration through 1903. Of the significance of the common law he says: "It was the *belief,* common in the 17th and quite general in the 18th and 19th centuries, *that the common law 'always' had been opposed to monopolies,* or even actively favored competition, *rather than an inherently antimonopolistic quality in its relevant doctrines* that proved important." *Id.* at 51.

30. *Id.* at 52–53.

The Rule of Reason and Monopoly

The Sherman Act

The Sherman Act, many commentators unwittingly imply, was designed to perpetuate this confusion. The record reads differently. To understand the purpose of the Sherman Act one must understand the temper of the times that gave it birth. The decade of the 1880's was the heyday of the trusts. The Standard Oil Trust, the Cottonseed Oil Trust, the Linseed Oil Trust, the National Lead Trust, the Whisky Trust, the Sugar Trust were all of this era. The power of these great combines and the predatory practices by which they achieved or perpetuated their power greatly disturbed consumers who bought their products, businessmen who confronted them as rivals in the market, politicians elected to promote the public welfare, and students of industrial structure and business behavior. This anxiety was reflected in contemporary professional and popular literature [31] and in political convention halls. Both the Democratic and the Republican parties in their 1888 platforms scathingly condemned combinations that controlled markets and exploited consumers; [32] and the Democrats, more specific than their political rivals, declared their faith in Adam Smith's "obvious and simple system of natural liberty"—or as they called it, "natural competition." [33]

Senator Sherman, although he wrote not a word of the act that bears his name,[34] appropriately has been regarded as its father. It is Senate Bill

---

31. *E.g.*, William Barry, "The Moloch of Monopoly," 7 The Forum 436 (1889); James F. Hudson, "Modern Feudalism," 144 The North American Review 277 (1887); Henry Wood, "The Bugbear of Trusts," 5 The Forum 584 (1888); Editorial, "Trusts and Confidences," 44 The Nation 380 (1887). In the professional journals appeared such articles as George Gunton, "The Economic and Social Aspect of Trusts," 3 Pol. Sci. Q. 385 (1888), and Arthur T. Hadley, "Private Monopolies and Public Rights," 1 Q. J. Econ. 28 (1886).

32. The Republicans declared their "opposition to all combinations of capital, organized in trusts or otherwise, to control arbitrarily the condition of trade among our citizens; and . . . all schemes to oppress the people by undue charges." Thomas H. McKee, *The National Conventions and Platforms of All Political Parties 1789 to 1905* (6th ed.; Baltimore: Friedenwald, 1906), p. 241. The Democrats asserted: "[T]he interests of the people are betrayed when, by unnecessary taxation, trusts and combinations are permitted to exist, which, while unduly enriching the few that combine, rob the body of our citizens by depriving them of the benefits of natural competition." *Id.* at 235.

33. *Ibid.*

34. See Albert H. Walker, *History of the Sherman Law* (New York: Equity Press, 1910), p. 2; Hornblower, " 'Antitrust' Legislation and Litigation," 11 Col. L. Rev. 701 (1911). See also Edward Berman, *Labor and the Sherman Act* (New York: Harper, 1930), chap. 3; James A. McLaughlin, ed., *Cases on the Federal Antitrust Laws of the United States* (Cambridge: published by the editor, 1933), pp. 7, 18–25; and especially Thorelli, *op. cit. supra* note 29, at 210–14.

Workable Competition and Antitrust Policy

No. 1, introduced by Sherman in the first session of the Fifty-first Congress on December 4, 1889, and the congressional debates on it, that reveal what Senator Sherman and Congress were aiming at. Sherman apparently wanted Congress to go as far as it could in outlawing arrangements that restricted competition. But a ban by Congress on contracts to restrain competition had to be brought within its constitutional power to regulate commerce among the states and with foreign countries. Section 1 of the Sherman bill indicated its twofold purpose: to outlaw as far as it could all arrangements that limited competition and at the same time to keep the ban within the jurisdiction of Congress.[35]

Two substitute bills offered in the Senate grappled with these twin problems of comprehensiveness and constitutionality.[36] The debates on these several measures reflected continuing doubt on both scores, and Senator Sherman made it clear that he did not believe that the proposed bills presented a new principle of law, but rather that they banned by federal statute what the states had banned by statute or at common law.[37] Sherman's statements on this issue may raise some question about his

---

35. Section 1 provided:
That all arrangements, contracts, agreements, trusts, or combinations between persons or corporations made with a view or which tend to prevent full and free competition in the importation, transportation, or sale of articles imported into the United States, or in the production, manufacture, or sale of articles of domestic growth or production, or domestic raw material that competes with any similar article upon which a duty is levied by the United States, or which shall be transported from one State or Territory to another, . . . are hereby declared to be against public policy, unlawful, and void.
21 Cong. Rec. 1765 (1890). The antitrust bills introduced in the 50th Congress on August 14, 1888, by Senator Sherman, S. 3445, 19 Cong. Rec. 7513, and Senator Reagan, S. 3440, 19 Cong. Rec. 7512, had shown similar purposes. Despite the circumlocutions of S. 1, 51st Cong., 1st Sess. (1889), Senator George of Mississippi challenged its constitutionality on the ground, among others, that it proposed to regulate manufacture and production within a state. 21 Cong. Rec. 1768 (1890).

36. A substitute bill presented by the Senate Finance Committee on March 21, 1890, limited its scope to contracts, etc., between parties in different states or with foreigners, but banned all arrangements made with "a view or which tend to prevent full and free competition." 21 Cong. Rec. 2455 (1890). Senator Reagan of Texas offered a substitute for the substitute which defined trusts comprehensively, including any arrangement that prevented competition or restricted trade. 21 *id.* at 2455–56.

37. "It does not announce a new principle of law, but applies old and well recognized principles of the common law to the complicated jurisdiction of our State and Federal Government. Similar contracts in any State in the Union are now, by common or statute law, null and void." 21 Cong. Rec. 2456 (1890). Sherman reviewed at length a number of recent state cases holding combinations to prevent competition illegal and of no effect and said he might add "innumerable" others. 21 *id.* at 2458–59.

The Rule of Reason and Monopoly

knowledge of the common law,[38] but they raise no doubt about his intentions and in no way restrict the meaning of the language by which he proposed to outlaw arrangements that substituted collusion for competition in the market place.[39]

On March 27, 1890, the Senate referred the antitrust bill to the Committee on the Judiciary.[40] Instructed to report within twenty days, the committee did so within a week. It offered as a substitute for the original Sherman bill a bill which passed the Senate with only one dissenting vote,[41] which passed the House with no dissent,[42] and which with Presi-

38. See Handler's classification of common law principles, pp. 129-30 *supra; cf.* Peppin's views, note 27 *supra.*

39. Senator Sherman stated to the Senate: "Mr. President, the object of this bill, as shown by the title, is 'to declare unlawful trusts and combinations in restraint of trade and production.' It declares that certain contracts are against public policy, null and void." 21 Cong. Rec. 2456 (1890). Sherman also described his bill as "a remedial statute to enforce by civil process in the courts of the United States the common law against monopolies." 21 *id.* at 2461. Thorelli, *op. cit. supra* note 29, at 228, concludes that "there is ample evidence that not only the bills reported by Sherman in the 51st Congress but also the bill finally passed were intended by their sponsors primarily to be federal codifications of the common law of England and the several states." But it is apparently the common law as applied by courts to hold unlawful contracts to restrict competition and block the operation of market forces that Thorelli has in mind, for he asserts and reiterates, "Congress believed in competition." *Id.* at 226. "There can be no doubt," he says, "that Sherman's views were typical in the sense that the vast majority of congressmen were sincere proponents of a private enterprise system founded on the principle of 'full and free competition.' " *Ibid.*

40. 21 Cong. Rec. 2731 (1890).

41. 21 *id.* at 3153.

42. 21 *id.* at 6314. Despite the unanimity with which Congress acted, some scholars contend that it was not seriously concerned with the monopoly problem. John Davidson Clark, *The Federal Trust Policy* (Baltimore: Johns Hopkins Press, 1931), p. 30, states that the "brief consideration of the bill in the Senate and the cavalier handling of it in the House are cogent proofs that the legislators themselves were not greatly aroused by any 'trust peril.'" Merle Fainsod and Lincoln Gordon, *Government and the American Economy* (New York: Norton, 1941), p. 450, say: "While hindsight justly views it as one of the most important measures ever passed by Congress, it is doubtful if any member of the 51st Congress so thought of it." An examination of the Congressional Record creates a different impression. The persistence with which the legislators considered it and the language they used in discussing it indicate grave concern about the trust problem. In the first session of the 50th Congress, Senators introduced four bills designed to deal with the trust problem and in the House twelve similar bills were introduced. 19 Cong. Rec. *passim* (1888). Senator Sherman's bill, S. 3445, was debated on three occasions in the second session of the 50th Congress. 20 Cong. Rec. 1120, 1167, 1457-62 (1889). In the first session of the 51st Congress, Senators Sherman, George, and Reagan introduced three antitrust bills (including S. 1, later rewritten into the Sherman Act); Senator Turpie introduced a resolution to include in the proposed penal enactments against trusts a provision for the seizure of "trust goods," 21

Workable Competition and Antitrust Policy

dent Harrison's signature on the second of July became the Sherman Act.[43] The language of the Sherman Act was wholly different from the language of the initial Sherman bill, but nothing in the Congressional Record indicates that its purpose was not the same.[44] It apparently aimed, as had its predecessors, to go as far as the jurisdiction of Congress permitted in banning every restriction on competition.[45] As Congressman Stewart of Vermont put it, "The provisions of this trust bill are just as broad, sweeping, and explicit as the English language can make them to express the power of Congress over this subject under the Constitution of the United States."[46] The new language eliminated all doubt about jurisdiction, but despite Mr. Stewart's characterization it started a debate about scope that has continued until today.

The Rule of Reason and Monopoly

The debate was precipitated in the *Trans-Missouri Freight Association* case,[47] when Justice Peckham and a majority of the Supreme Court held

Cong. Rec. 125 (1890); and Senator George introduced a joint resolution to amend the Constitution to enable Congress to prohibit combinations in restraint of trade, S.R. 67, 51st Cong., 1st Sess. (1890). Its counterpart, H. Res. 30, 51st Cong., 1st Sess. (1890), was introduced in the House of Representatives, where members also introduced eighteen bills to outlaw trusts as variously defined or trusts in specific industries, such as cattle. 21 Cong. Rec. *passim* (1890). In debating these measures many Congressmen expressed with fervor their condemnation of monopolies and trusts.

43. 26 Stat. 209 (1890), as amended, 15 U.S.C. § 1 (1958).

44. Senator Hoar explained the bill's purpose as follows:

The complaint which has come from all parts and all classes of the country of these great monopolies, which are becoming not only in some cases an actual injury to the comfort of ordinary life, but are a menace to republican institutions themselves, has induced Congress to take the matter up.... Now, the Judiciary Committee has carefully and as thoroughly as it could agreed upon what we believe will be a very efficient measure, under which one long forward step will be taken in suppressing this evil. We have affirmed the old doctrine of the common law in regard to all interstate and international commercial transactions, and have clothed the United States courts with authority to enforce that doctrine by injunction.

21 Cong. Rec. 3146 (1890).

45. Section 1 outlaws "*Every* contract, combination in the form of trust or otherwise, or conspiracy, in restraint of trade or commerce among the several States, or with foreign nations"; and § 2 makes guilty of a misdemeanor "*Every* person who shall monopolize, or attempt to monopolize, or combine or conspire with any other person or persons, to monopolize *any part* of the trade or commerce among the several States, or with foreign nations." Emphasis supplied. 26 Stat. 209 (1890), as amended, 15 U.S.C. § 1 (1958).

46. 21 Cong. Rec. 6314 (1890).

47. United States v. Trans-Missouri Freight Ass'n, 166 U.S. 290 (1897). "When

The Rule of Reason and Monopoly

that the language of the Sherman Act meant what it said—that the law banned every contract that restrained trade, regardless of form, and every conspiracy to achieve this end. Justice White and three other Justices dissented, and in doing so reviewed the common law rule of reason.[48] Fourteen years later Chief Justice White, writing for a majority in the 1911 *Standard Oil* decision, concluded that Congress had not outlawed all contracts that restrained trade but only those that *unreasonably* restrained it;[49] despite the fact that two years earlier, with the issue before it, Congress had refused to modify the statute,[50] and despite the fact that

> ... the body of an act pronounces as illegal every contract or combination in restraint of trade or commerce among the several States, etc., the plain and ordinary meaning of such language is not limited to that kind of contract alone which is in unreasonable restraint of trade, but all contracts are included in such language, and no exception or limitation can be added without placing in the act that which has been omitted by Congress." *Id.* at 328.

48. White noted the law's progression from Dyer's Case, Y.B., 2 Hen. 5, f. 5, pl. 26 (1415), through Mitchel v. Reynolds, 1 P. Wms. 181, 24 Eng. Rep. 347 (Ch. 1711), to Nordenfelt v. Maxim Nordenfelt Guns & Ammunition Co., [1894] A.C. 535, in which the House of Lords ruled that the old distinction between partial and general restraint was an incorrect criterion and that the true test was whether, considering all the circumstances, the contract was reasonable or unreasonable. "If reasonable, it was not a contract in restraint of trade, and if unreasonable, it was." United States v. Trans-Missouri Freight Ass'n, 166 U.S. 290, 347 (1897).

49. Standard Oil Co. v. United States, 221 U.S. 1 (1911). White reasoned that (1) the context of the Sherman Act "manifests that [it] ... was drawn in the light of the existing practical conception of the law of restraint of trade," since it ignores the early precise meaning of contracts in restraint of trade and includes under that term contracts or acts designed to monopolize as well; and (2) because many new forms of contract and combination were evolving from changing economic conditions, Congress "by an all-embracing enumeration" had sought "to make sure that no form of contract or combination by which an undue restraint of interstate or foreign commerce was brought about could save such restraint from condemnation. The statute under this view evidenced the intent not to restrain the right to make and enforce contracts, whether resulting from combination or otherwise, which did not unduly restrain interstate or foreign commerce, but to protect that commerce from being restrained by methods, whether old or new, which would constitute an interference that is an undue restraint." *Id.* at 59–60.

50. S. 6440, 60th Cong., 2d Sess. (1909), would have amended the Sherman Act to provide, among other things, that no prosecutions under its first six sections should be maintained for past offenses unless the contract or combination was in unreasonable restraint of trade. The Senate Committee on the Judiciary rejected this proposal, saying that to make "civil and criminal prosecution hinge on the question of reasonableness or unreasonableness ... destroys ... the provisions of the act as to criminal prosecutions, and renders them nugatory, and opens the door wide to doubt and uncertainty as to civil prosecutions. ... The defense of reasonable restraint would be made in every case and there would be as many different rules of reasonableness as cases, courts, and juries." S. Rep. No. 848, 60th Cong., 2d Sess. 9–11 (1909).

Workable Competition and Antitrust Policy

White identified restraint of trade with restriction of competition,[51] as Congress had done. Thus, recognizing that Congress intended to give a broad new meaning to the term "restraint of trade," White nevertheless read into it the rule of reason which had qualified the original common law use of the term.

If Congress had used "restraint of trade" in its narrow technical meaning as a contractual limitation on the right of a seller of property, a participant in a partnership, or an apprentice to exercise his trade, and if it had been guided by either common sense or precedent, it must certainly have distinguished between reasonable and unreasonable restraint. But seeking as it was to preserve a competitive society, Congress was under no obligation to make such a distinction. In truth, in outlawing every restriction on competition it did all that it could do but no more than was necessary to achieve its objective.[52]

Many students of the law and economics of monopoly argue that the courts have been forced to adopt a rule of reason in applying the Sherman Act. If by this they mean that courts must exercise discretion and judgment, after considering all the relevant facts, in determining whether a contract restrains or promotes competition,[53] they are right. If they mean

---

51. White described the purpose and nature of the law on restraint of trade as follows:

> [T]he dread of enhancement of prices and of other wrongs which it was thought flow from the undue limitation on competitive conditions caused by contracts or other acts of individuals or corporations, led, as a matter of public policy, to the prohibition or treating as illegal all contracts or acts which were unreasonably restrictive of competitive conditions. . . .

Standard Oil Co. v. United States, 221 U.S. 1, 58 (1911).

52. The first Sherman Act case before the Supreme Court seemed to indicate that Congress had not done enough. The Court construed the statute as applicable only to combinations to monopolize interstate commerce, not to combinations within one state to monopolize the manufacture of a product sold in interstate commerce. United States v. E. C. Knight Co., 156 U.S. 1, 17 (1895). This drastic limitation of the law's scope, together with the Court's assertion that "Congress did not attempt . . . to assert the power to deal with monopoly directly as such; or to limit and restrict the rights of corporations created by the States . . . or to make criminal the acts of persons in the acquisition and control of property which the States of their residence or creation sanctioned," *id.* at 16, apparently gave the Great Combination Movement approved legal status just as it was getting under way. Beginning with Northern Securities Co. v. United States, 193 U.S. 197 (1904), however, the Supreme Court receded from its narrow conception of Congress' power over interstate commerce.

53. Certain passages in the 1911 *Standard Oil* opinion read as if this is what Chief Justice White meant. In answering the government's contention that the Sherman Act embraces every contract, etc., in restraint of trade and "imposes the plain duty of applying its prohibitions to every case within its literal language," White declared that this interpretation erred in assuming the matter to be decided,

The Rule of Reason and Monopoly

that it is a proper judicial function to determine to what extent competition may be impaired by contract without harming the public interest,[54] I believe they are wrong. More important, they would impose on the courts, which must undertake the unavoidable task of determining whether a contract does in fact impair competition, the additional burden of determining whether contracts that impair competition do so unreasonably. To determine how much restriction on competition by private enterprise can be justified on economic grounds is an almost insuperable task, even for economists.

In the *Standard Oil* case it was important that Chief Justice White find an easy way to answer an insoluble problem. To determine whether the Standard Oil Company's officers and subsidiaries had combined or conspired to restrain trade, the Supreme Court looked to their motives. To determine motives the Court examined their conduct. As this discussion has indicated, an appraisal of conduct broadly conceived is not irrelevant to economic considerations, but it is not a substitute for them, particularly where conduct is judged primarily by ethical standards. But since the task which the Court had set itself was beyond its capacities, this standard was almost the only one open to it. The Court found that Standard Oil had relentlessly absorbed its rivals or ruthlessly driven them out of business. In shipping oil it had obtained discriminatory rebates; in selling oil it had resorted to discriminatory pricing; in combating rivals it had engaged in espionage; in selling petroleum products it had practiced deceit.[55] The Court concluded that

since *judgment must be exercised* to determine whether a particular act falls within the statutory classes and if it does whether its nature or effect makes it "a restraint of trade within the intendment of the act." Standard Oil Co. v. United States, 221 U.S. 1, 63 (1911). Oppenheim, *supra* note 1, at 1176–77, at times seems to have a similar conception of the rule of reason. He says: "When all relevant economic and factual data are considered, the Rule of Reason enables a judgment to be made regarding the effects of any arrangement in resolving the question whether it promotes more competition than it restrains, or the reverse." At other times he seems to mean something quite different. See note 54 *infra*.

54. Oppenheim's most elaborate exposition of the significance of the rule of reason implies this. He would have proof of "a restrictive agreement alleged to be in violation of the antitrust laws" constitute a prima facie case of illegality which the respondent might answer by showing "justification within the allowable limits of the antitrust statutory standards," whereupon the court would "apply the Rule of Reason to the entire record"; that is, it would exercise discretion in evaluating the evidence "to arrive at a *value judgment*" which apparently could include toleration of "restrictions of joint conduct" "in individualized situations where there are overriding legal, economic and social justifications" for them. Oppenheim, *supra* note 1, at 1159, 1161. Emphasis added.

55. The government's description of Standard Oil's allegedly unlawful practices

no disinterested mind can survey the period in question without being irresistibly driven to the conclusion that the very genius for commercial development and organization which it would seem manifested from the beginning soon begot an intent and purpose to exclude others which was frequently manifested by acts and dealings wholly inconsistent with the theory that they were made with the single conception of advancing the development of business power by usual methods, but which on the contrary necessarily involved the intent to drive others from the field and to exclude them from their right to trade and thus accomplish the mastery which was the end in view.[56]

In applying the rule of reason in the *American Tobacco* case [57] the Court again looked to motives, and to determine motives it examined conduct. In finding American Tobacco's behavior reprehensible the Court was even more explicit in making illegality synonymous with bad conduct. The Court reasoned that in view of "the undisputed facts . . . , it remains only to determine whether they establish that the acts, contracts, agreements, combinations, etc., which were assailed were of such an *unusual* and *wrongful* character as to bring them within the prohibitions of the law." [58] The Court found that they were. In truth it found an "ever-present manifestation . . . of a conscious wrongdoing." [59] Such were the primary grounds on which it concluded that the Standard Oil and American Tobacco Companies had violated the Sherman Act.

The 1911 *American Tobacco* and *Standard Oil* decisions are important not merely because of the importance of the particular industrial combinations involved but because the suits were initiated as a challenge to the most significant combination movement this country has ever experienced. Between 1898 and 1904 the great merger movement had transformed the structure of American industry. It had changed markets of many sellers into markets of few sellers and markets of few sellers into markets of fewer sellers. It had created few if any outright monopolies, but the changes it had wrought in the pattern of industry undoubtedly had affected market behavior.

Although the Supreme Court found that the Standard Oil and American Tobacco Companies had violated the Sherman Act and ordered their dissolution, the decisions reflected a judicial attitude friendly to industrial consolidation and a complacency about market power not evidenced

covered fifty-seven pages of the printed record. Standard Oil Co. v. United States, 221 U.S. 1, 42 (1911).
56. *Id.* at 76.
57. United States v. American Tobacco Co., 221 U.S. 106 (1911).
58. *Id.* at 181. Emphasis added.
59. *Id.* at 182.

The Rule of Reason and Monopoly

by the Congress that enacted the statute. The Court's enunciation of the rule of reason and its emphasis on intent and conduct laid the basis for a series of decisions that left undisturbed some of the greatest of the industrial combines.[60] It is scarcely an exaggeration to say that it validated the new industrial structure.

The 1920 *Steel* case [61] illustrates this generalization. Here was a suit to dissolve the greatest combination that had come out of the country's greatest combination movement. The United States Steel Corporation, America's first billion-dollar concern, was a combination of combinations into the making of which some 180 independent firms had gone. But the Supreme Court in the *Standard Oil* and *American Tobacco* cases by its rule of reason put such combinations beyond the reach of Section 1 of the Sherman Act unless they had a long history of predatory practices showing a continuing intent to suppress competition. That left Section 2, of course, as an instrument for striking down combinations that had monopolized their markets. But unfortunately monopoly is a no more precise term than restraint of trade. By the time the *Steel* case reached the courts the corporation's percentage of steel ingot output had shrunk from its original two-thirds to about one-half, and its relative share of the output of finished steel products had similarly lessened.[62] The Supreme Court found the corporation large, but it concluded that the Act did not condemn mere size. The corporation in the Court's judgment lacked monopoly power and had not abused such power as it may have had.[63]

---

60. United States v. Winslow, 195 Fed. 578 (D. Mass. 1912), *aff'd*, 227 U.S. 202 (1913) (United Shoe Machinery Co.); United States v. American Can Co., 230 Fed. 859 (D. Md. 1916); United States v. United States Steel Corp., 251 U.S. 417 (1920); United States v. International Harvester Co., 274 U.S. 693 (1927).

61. United States v. United States Steel Corp., 251 U.S. 417 (1920).

62. U.S. Bureau of Corporations, *Report on the Steel Industry* (1911), Pt. I, p. 56.

63. Students of antitrust have commonly concluded from a study of the *American Tobacco* and *Standard Oil* cases and the 1920 *Steel* case that the Supreme Court distinguished between the existence of monopoly power and its abuse. The Attorney General's Committee on the antitrust laws rejected this conclusion. In its brief analysis of the *Steel* case it found: "Technically . . . the decision does not depend upon the so-called 'abuse' theory of Section 2." *Report of the Attorney General's National Committee to Study the Antitrust Laws* (1955), pp. 50–51. But the dissenters in the *Steel* case, fresh from their contact and discussions with the majority, thought differently. Justice Day said: "That the exercise of the power may be withheld, or exerted with forbearing benevolence, does not place such combinations beyond the authority of the statute which was intended to prohibit their formation. . . ." United States v. United States Steel Corp., 251 U.S. 417, 464 (1920). Did the dissenters misconstrue the majority opinion? If in rejecting the nonexercise of market power as an answer to § 2 charges they were only knocking down

Workable Competition and Antitrust Policy

The extent to which this interpretation emasculated the Sherman Act as an instrument for preserving a competitive industrial structure in the American economy is, I believe, not generally understood. As previously indicated, the Great Combination Movement created few if any complete monopolies, but it considerably changed the pattern of industry by reducing the number of sellers in many national markets. In so doing it created the modern problem of oligopoly, where structure may influence conduct and conduct may influence performance. But unless their conduct is predatory, combinations falling short of monopoly under the rule of reason as originally enunciated are beyond the statute's reach.[64]

The majority of the Attorney General's Antitrust Committee apparently failed to see this significance in the Supreme Court's decision in the *Steel* case, or having seen it were silent. The dissenters in the case were more discerning. Unequipped with the modern tools of economic analysis and unfamiliar with professional jargon, the minority of the Court made a direct and uncomplicated, though certainly oversimplified, finding that the Steel Corporation, "fortified and equipped," as it was, "could if it saw fit dominate the trade and control competition. . . ."[65] Some members of the Attorney General's Committee were equally discerning. They pointed out, as the dissenting opinion had done, that "it was erroneous in a case dealing with a combination or conspiracy which suppressed free competition, to require 'complete monopolization.'"[66] I believe they are correct.

Later Decisions Disturb Business Leaders

But it is not against these applications of the rule of reason that the contemporary advocates of change have complained. Clearly big business would have much to gain by a return to the rule of reason as applied in the cases heretofore considered. Certain later decisions disturb them. They allege that big business as such is now under attack. The implica-

---

a straw man they had set up, Judge Hand in United States v. Aluminum Co. of America, 148 F.2d 416 (2d Cir. 1945), was doing the same thing twenty-five years later.

64. The Supreme Court's decision in American Tobacco Co. v. United States, 328 U.S. 781 (1946), of course condemned conspiracy among oligopolists and recognized that circumstantial evidence might be adequate to convict; but this was a criminal case and left the structure of the industry undisturbed.

65. United States v. United States Steel Corp., 251 U.S. 417, 464 (1920).

66. *Report of the Attorney General's National Committee to Study the Antitrust Laws* at 51.

The Rule of Reason and Monopoly

tions of the 1945 and 1950 decisions in the *Aluminum* case[67] and of the minority opinion in the *Columbia Steel* case[68] are their chief source of worry.

In the 1945 *Aluminum* opinion the Court of Appeals for the Second Circuit, sitting as a court of final review, was concerned primarily with the meaning and application of Section 2 of the Sherman Act. The specific questions it posed were: (1) Did the Aluminum Company of America have a monopoly of the manufacture and sale of aluminum ingots? (2) If it did, had it violated the Sherman Act in obtaining it? In answering the first question Judge Learned Hand, speaking for the court, adopted an economic criterion. He found that for the five years 1934–1938 inclusive Alcoa had supplied over 90 per cent of the virgin aluminum bought by domestic consumers in ingots or fabricated products, and he ruled that this percentage "is enough to constitute a monopoly."[69] In rejecting the lower court's finding that between 1929 and 1938 Alcoa had controlled only 33 per cent of the domestic market—which the lower court had delineated as including secondary aluminum[70] but not Alcoa's fabricated products—Judge Hand acknowledged that control of so small a percentage certainly did not constitute monopoly; and he said that control of 64 per cent (the proportion of Alcoa's total production, including the aluminum it fabricated, to total secondary and imported virgin aluminum) was "doubtful."[71]

Having determined that Alcoa had a monopoly of the domestic market in aluminum ingots, the court turned to the second question: Had Alcoa violated the Sherman Act in achieving monopoly? To establish this, the court stated, it is unnecessary to show bad conduct or specific intent. A monopolist is not a sleepwalker;[72] it knows where it is going. In so reasoning the court discarded intent as a test of illegality where monopoly

---

67. United States v. Aluminum Co. of America, 148 F.2d 416 (2d Cir. 1945), *new petitions considered,* 91 F. Supp. 333 (S.D.N.Y. 1950).

68. United States v. Columbia Steel Co., 334 U.S. 495, 534 (1948).

69. United States v. Aluminum Co. of America, 148 F.2d 416, 423–24 (2d Cir. 1945).

70. Economists have criticized Judge Hand's exclusion of secondary aluminum as a component of the market Alcoa faced in selling ingots, contending that it is doubtful that Alcoa's production policies actually took account of the fact that eventually, five to twenty-five years later, some ingot aluminum came on the market again as secondary aluminum and competed for certain uses.

71. United States v. Aluminum Co. of America, 148 F.2d 416, 424 (2d Cir. 1945).

72. See Eugene V. Rostow, "The New Sherman Act: A Positive Instrument of Progress," 14 U. Chi. L. Rev. 567, 579–80 (1947).

Workable Competition and Antitrust Policy

power has been achieved [73] and held that Alcoa's having acquired monopoly was enough to condemn it, unless perhaps monopoly had been thrust upon it. Thus the court recognized that not all monopolies fall within the meaning of the statute. Apparently if the optimum size of a firm precludes competition, a firm that becomes a monopoly in the quest for efficiency does not violate the law.[74] But for a firm to maintain a monopoly deliberately, seizing every opportunity for growth by forecasting demand and expanding to provide for it and in this way precluding the entry of rivals, is to monopolize in violation of the law. The court found that Alcoa had so monopolized. In reaching this conclusion the court rejected the distinction made by earlier courts between possessing power and using or abusing it. The court reasoned that every transaction by a monopolist involves the exercise of power. As the court put it, "The power and its exercise must needs coalesce." [75] It is against power over the market that the statute is directed, the power to exclude rivals and the power to control prices.

Businessmen and some students of antitrust see in these doctrines a threat to bigness. Certain pronouncements in the 1950 decision of the district court in the same case have added to their anxiety. Although the district court tempered somewhat the appellate court's condemnation of monopoly maintained through foresight,[76] it retained jurisdiction over

---

73. Specific intent—"an intent which goes beyond the mere intent to do the act"—the court explained, is an essential element in establishing the crime of attempting to monopolize; but where, as in Alcoa's case, the possession of monopoly power has been established, it is enough that Alcoa "meant to keep, and did keep, that complete and exclusive hold upon the ingot market with which it started. That was to 'monopolize' that market, however innocently it otherwise proceeded." United States v. Aluminum Co. of America, 148 F.2d 416, 432 (2d Cir. 1945).

74. Judge Wyzanski illuminated this principle in deciding the *Shoe Machinery* case, saying:
> [T]he defendant may escape statutory liability if it bears the burden of proving that it owes its monopoly solely to superior skill, superior products, natural advantages (including accessibility to raw materials or markets), economic or technological efficiency (including scientific research), low margins of profit maintained permanently and without discrimination, or licenses conferred by, and used within, the limits of law (including patents on one's own inventions, or franchises granted directly to the enterprise by a public authority).

United States v. United Shoe Machinery Corp., 110 F. Supp. 295, 342 (D. Mass. 1953).

75. United States v. Aluminum Co. of America, 148 F.2d 416, 428 (2d Cir. 1945).

76. The district court took as a guide the Supreme Court's pronouncement in United States v. Columbia Steel Co., 334 U.S. 495, 526 (1948), that "no direction has appeared of a public policy that forbids, *per se,* an expansion of facilities of an existing company to meet the needs of new markets of a community, whether that

The Rule of Reason and Monopoly

the case for five years and warned Alcoa that "if, for any reason, it should appear that [the competition of Reynolds Metals Company and Kaiser Aluminum and Chemical Corporation] . . . is feeble, uncertain and ineffective," [77] the court would take additional appropriate action. Whether this was an invitation to Alcoa to hold an umbrella over its weaker rivals or merely an admonition to check its own growth deliberately by refusing to utilize such competitive advantages as it might have, business leaders have interpreted the court's warning as a threat to bigness as such.

They see in the minority opinion of Justice Douglas in the *Columbia Steel* case [78] an even more certain manifestation of hostility. United States Steel Corporation's acquisition of Consolidated Steel Corporation, said the minority,

> gives it unquestioned domination [of the Pacific Coast steel industry] . . . and protects it against growth of the independents in that developing region. That alone is sufficient to condemn the purchase. Its serious impact on competition and the economy is emphasized when it is recalled that United States Steel has one-third of the rolled steel production of the entire country. The least I can say is that a company that has that tremendous leverage on our economy is big enough.[79]

Such decisions represent to business leaders and their spokesmen a drift toward a condemnation of size per se.[80]

From such hostility big business understandably seeks security in a return to the old rule of reason. But some advocates of change have expounded the rule quite differently from the exposition hereinbefore given, and they have coupled with it the principle of workable competition. What they seem to want is a rule of reason that will place an obligation on the courts to consider all relevant economic facts and in the light of them to reach a judgment on the question, is the arrangement

---

community is nation-wide or county-wide." United States v. Aluminum Co. of America, 91 F. Supp. 333, 346 (S.D.N.Y. 1950).

77. *Id.* at 418.
78. United States v. Columbia Steel Co., 334 U.S. 495, 534 (1948).
79. *Id.* at 540.
80. Thomas E. Sunderland, general counsel, Standard Oil Co. of Indiana, voiced a typical reaction in a speech at the University of Chicago, Feb. 7, 1951:
    Underlying these trends in the law seems to be a deep-seated suspicion of big business, a suspicion which has been taken advantage of by those who want to redesign the business and industrial setup in this country. For them, and the politician as well, the attack on big business is as safe politically as a crusade against sin. As a consequence, it has not always been necessary to be entirely objective.
Sunderland, "Changing Legal Concepts in the Antitrust Field," 3 Syracuse L. Rev. 60, 76 (1951).

complained of consistent with the principle of workable or effective competition? [81] That, as I understand it, is pretty close to what the Sherman Act, unamended and uncorrupted by doubtful and confusing judicial interpretations, aimed at. Unfamiliar with a professional jargon not yet created, and undisciplined in the intricacies of economic theory, Congress apparently sought to outlaw those arrangements that hindered competition—the unimpeded operation of market forces—and to encourage those that promoted it.

Such an interpretation of the rule of reason would purge it of the element of value judgment on the over-all reasonableness of a restriction on competition, and would simply condemn all market arrangements that tend to make competition less effective or workable. This standard has not yet been applied; if it had been, the results in some major cases might have been different. This study will examine three industries in which the Department of Justice has at one time or another charged a dominant firm with having violated the Sherman Act—steel, cellophane and tin cans—and will try to answer the question how each industry would have fared if tested in terms of a rule of reason embodying the standard of workable competition.

THE STEEL COMBINATION

Structure

The merger movement in the steel industry, which culminated in the organization of the United States Steel Corporation, transformed a market of many sellers into a market of a few sellers. As previously indicated, the Steel Corporation controlled about two-thirds of the country's production of crude steel and from one-half to four-fifths of the principal rolled steel

---

81. In its 1952 report on Effective Competition, the Secretary of Commerce's Business Advisory Council declared that "to install a modernized Rule of Reason it is also necessary to find an acceptable standard for judging competition." It offered as such a standard "effective competition," under which "there should be unhampered business incentives and freedom of choice, with reasonable alternatives for buyers and sellers." U.S. Dep't of Commerce, *Effective Competition*, at 8. Italics omitted. Oppenheim, *supra* note 1, at 1145, ties the concept of workable competition to the rule of reason more tightly: "[T]he Rule of Reason would provide the central artery of a procedural device for considering all relevant legal and economic factors in any given factual situation. Thereby the concept of Workable Competition can be given . . . substance. . . ." And he recommends a "congressional declaration of national antitrust policy" which will "expressly state that the competition which the antitrust laws seek to foster and maintain is Workable Competition." *Id.* at 1144.

The Rule of Reason and Monopoly

products. In the intervening years, although it has increased its assets enormously, it has grown less rapidly than its major rivals. Yet today it accounts for approximately one-third of the country's steel ingot capacity. It is more than twice as large as its nearest rival, together with which it accounts for almost half the country's ingot output. With eight rivals it accounts for about four-fifths.[82]

The steel industry's structure is oligopolistic, and it is likely to remain that way. Entrance is so difficult that no fully integrated steel company has developed to challenge the position of the leading producers except by merger.[83] Two obstacles block entry. First, steel production is a large-scale enterprise.[84] Benjamin Fairless while chairman of United States Steel Corporation's board testified before the Senate Committee on Currency and Banking on March 21, 1955, that to build a steel plant from the ground up would cost $300 per ton of crude steel capacity.[85] Thus a medium-sized plant of 1,000,000-ton capacity would cost $300,000,000. Second, new ventures with the attendant risks offer little inducement to top managerial talent. Why should well-paid steel executives managing but not owning successful corporations surrender reasonable security in a going concern to accept managerial responsibility without ownership in new enterprises whose future is uncertain?

The large optimum size of a steel company influences its costs. Fixed costs—that is, costs the aggregate of which do not change with changes in output—constitute a large part of total costs. Average variable costs, the aggregate of which changes with changes in output, tend to remain constant over a wide range of output. Many of the costs encountered in

---

82. Calculated from reported capacities of United States Steel Corp. and of Bethlehem, Republic, Jones & Laughlin, National, Youngstown, Armco, Inland, and Wheeling Steel Cos. (*Moody's Industrials, 1954, passim*), and from total United States capacity as reported by the American Iron and Steel Institute, Steel Facts, vol. 127, August 1954 Supp., p. 4.

83. National Steel Corporation is the most recent challenger of the majors. It was created in 1929 by merging three independent firms, including an iron ore producer. *Moody's Industrials, 1930*, pp. 3091–92. At the outset it ranked eighth among the largest steel companies; by 1935 it ranked fifth.

84. Charles F. Ramseyer, consulting engineer to the steel industry, testified before the Celler Committee that to provide the necessary facilities to convert iron ore into finished steel on an economical scale required an investment at 1948 prices of about $250,000,000. *Hearings before the Subcommittee on Study of Monopoly Power of the House Committee on the Judiciary*, 81st Cong., 2d Sess., ser. 14, pt. 4A, at 417 (1950). Ernest T. Weir, chairman of the National Steel Corporation's board of directors, testified that to duplicate the facilities of National—the nation's fifth largest producer but also the fifth smallest of the big nine—would cost $1,100,000,000. *Id.* at 817.

85. Wall Street Journal, March 22, 1955, p. 2, col. 3.

making finished steel products are joint. It is difficult to allocate accurately a proper proportion of total cost to any specific product. And finally, continuous operation of a steel plant is necessary to keep average costs down. It is expensive to stop and start blast furnaces, coke ovens, and steel furnaces.[86]

Steelmakers believe that the demand for steel is price-inelastic; at any particular time a change in price of any given percentage will bring a smaller change in purchases. Moreover, demand is cyclical. The demand for steel is a derived demand, stemming from the demand for things made wholly or in part from steel—buildings, roads, bridges, automobiles, refrigerators, stoves and the like. Steel products are durable, and in a business recession demand for them falls off sharply. Much unused steel capacity results. In the forty years before World War II the production of steel ingots declined in periods of business recession by more than 20 per cent six times, by more than 30 per cent four times, and by more than 50 per cent twice. At the depth of the 1929–1933 depression steel companies produced less than one-fourth the tonnage of steel ingots they had produced in 1929.[87]

Finally, steel is a homogeneous product. Steel bought from stock is standardized. Special steels are bought on specifications with which any producer can comply. One man's steel is as good as another's.

Conduct

The conduct of the industry stems from and reflects its structure. The nature of cost and the nature of demand paradoxically both stimulate and inhibit competition. Because a large part of his aggregate costs are fixed, a producer's temptation to cut prices with a decline in aggregate demand is great, and the difficulty of allocating costs precisely aggravates the temptation. With demand inelastic, price cuts may increase total industry sales but little. They will, however, shift business from one supplier to another. If one producer cuts, all must sooner or later meet the lower price or lose business. Believing that a price cut may result in approximately the same volume and distribution of business, producers are reluctant to cut. Self-restraint tends to prevent price cutting. But it is generally not enough. To avoid it, steel producers have resorted to three practices: they have

---

86. For a more complete discussion of the economic characteristics of the iron and steel industry see George W. Stocking, *Basing Point Pricing and Regional Development* (Chapel Hill: University of North Carolina Press, 1954), chap. 2.

87. Id. at 27.

The Rule of Reason and Monopoly

followed the price leadership of the Steel Corporation;[88] they have sold steel under a basing point pricing system;[89] and they have collectively determined the average cost of producing extras and used this as a basis in pricing them.[90]

The combination that in 1901 reduced the number of steel sellers and made the Steel Corporation the dominant producer facilitated these practices. The Steel Corporation from the outset busied itself with the problem of stabilizing prices. This was both Judge Elbert H. Gary's policy and his practice. As chairman of the board of the Steel Corporation he testified at a congressional hearing in 1911 that he believed competition in the steel industry inevitably tended to be ruinous and that cooperation—under government supervision if necessary—should replace competition.[91] Participation by the corporation's subsidiaries in various pooling arrangements during its early history, the Gary dinners, and "Pittsburgh Plus" implemented the corporation's stabilization policy. Despite Clark's contention that in an industry with the characteristics of steel, basing point pricing tends to develop spontaneously,[92] the record indicates that the industry deliberately adopted it as a device to insure identical delivered prices by rival sellers.[93] Coupled with the industry's acceptance of the Steel Cor-

---

88. In 1936 the president of United States Steel testified, "I would say we generally make the prices." *Hearings before the Senate Committee on Interstate Commerce on S. 4055*, 74th Cong., 2d Sess. 595 (1936). Eugene Grace when president of Bethlehem Steel testified before the Temporary National Economic Committee in 1939 that he could not recall Bethlehem's ever having initiated a price decrease and that his company "would normally await the schedules as published by the Steel Corporation." "As a general practice," he said, the "pace is set . . . by the Steel Corporation." *Hearings before the Temporary National Economic Committee on Investigation of the Concentration of Economic Power*, 75th Cong., 3d Sess. (hereinafter TNEC Hearings), pt. 19, at 10601–02 (1939).

89. On July 21, 1924, the Federal Trade Commission ordered the United States Steel Corp. to cease selling steel under the "Pittsburgh Plus" system of pricing. United States Steel Corp., 8 F.T.C. 1 (1924). On October 5, 1948, the Third Circuit entered a consent decree affirming the Commission's 1924 order. United States Steel Corp. v. Federal Trade Commission, 4 *Statutes and Decisions*, Federal Trade Commission (1944-1948), 789 (1948). On August 10, 1951, the Federal Trade Commission again ordered respondents representing over 85% of total domestic steel production to cease quoting prices calculated according to any system or formula which produces identical price quotations. American Iron and Steel Institute, 48 F.T.C. 123 (1951).

90. The Federal Trade Commission persistently forbade the uniform pricing of extras in each of the proceedings described in note 89 *supra*.

91. *Hearings before the House Committee on Investigation of the United States Steel Corporation*, 62d Cong., 2d Sess. 61–297 (1911).

92. John Maurice Clark, "Basing Point Methods of Price Quoting," 4 Can. J. Econ. Pol. Sci. 477 (1938).

93. As usual, Judge Gary, the Steel Corporation's first president and later chair-

poration's price leadership and its use of common freight rate books, basing point pricing provided a means of fortifying the natural reluctance of oligopolists to engage in competitive pricing.

The industry's practice in pricing extras contributed to the same end. Under the basing point system of pricing, the published base prices covered products of specified standards. Buyers frequently wanted steel of different specifications. Differences in quality, dimensions, weight, finish, chemical content, known to the trade as "extras," all called for different prices. The possible combinations of extras varied, and costs were myriad. Without some common guide for determining their price, competitive pricing was inevitable. The industry's method of solving this problem changed from time to time. For a decade after the Steel Corporation's organization, steel companies apparently collaborated in making and distributing price lists.[94] Thereafter technical committees of the American Iron and Steel Institute made cost studies for determining the average cost of making extras.[95] The Steel Corporation used these as a basis for pricing extras, and other companies followed suit.

These practices—uniform pricing of extras and basing point pricing—reflect the Steel Corporation's continuing live-and-let-live policy which in 1920 apparently won Supreme Court approval.[96]

man of its board, was quite candid in describing the purpose of basing point pricing: "It was deemed necessary for the orderly conduct of the business to have one basing price, and that was not alone for the benefit of the producer, but for the benefit of the purchaser, . . . so that every user of steel all over the country bought and used his steel on a certain basis, knowing in advance that everyone else who bought steel had to pay exactly as he did, with the addition of the increased freight depending upon where he wanted to use the steel." Brief for States of Illinois, Iowa, Minnesota and Wisconsin as Amici Curiae, p. 884, United States Steel Corp., 8 F.T.C. 1 (1924). H. P. Bope, who was with Carnegie Steel Company from 1879 to 1918, testified: "I should say that the Pittsburgh Plus system was a man-made proposition necessitated by chaotic conditions in the steel market, which seemed to render it the only available means of stabilizing the industry." Id. at 876.

94. United States v. United States Steel Corp., 251 U.S. 417, 440 (1920).

95. Benjamin Fairless when president of the Steel Corporation testified: "[S]ince our motive is only to charge cost for services rendered, then obviously it is our duty to develop the best cost that exists, not only within our own company but within this industry." TNEC Hearings, pt. 19, at 10560 (1939). The Department of Justice after examining the extras books of twenty-five steel companies found that each quoted identical prices for all extras covering sixteen major steel products. Id. at 10724–25. In its 1951 cease and desist order against the American Iron and Steel Institute and ninety steel companies the Federal Trade Commission forbade "any planned common course of action" to fix prices or any element thereof or to collect, compile, or exchange price lists or extra charges or deductions, or to use such lists as a factor in computing price quotations. American Iron and Steel Institute, 48 F.T.C. 123, 152 (1951).

96. The policy, not the practices, was approved. Said the Court, "The Corporation

The Rule of Reason and Monopoly

Performance

Has the Steel Corporation's and the industry's performance been compatible with the principle of workable competition? What has been the course of steel prices? Has the Steel Corporation been an efficient producer of steel? Has it contributed to technical and industrial progress? Has it discovered new and better ways of producing steel and put them into use? Has it discovered new and better steel products and offered them to the public on increasingly attractive terms?

The corporation's efforts to stabilize prices did not always succeed. At times when demand was slack, basing point pricing weakened. At other times steelmakers sold below their quoted prices and discriminated among buyers. The Great Depression weakened steel prices as it did other prices. But the movement of steel prices brings into clear focus the influence of structure on price behavior. Between 1926 and their depression low points (1931–1934) the price indexes of steel products whose production was least concentrated showed the largest decline. Concentration was greatest in the production of steel rails, shapes, plates, bars and tin plate; it was least in the production of wire nails, hot and cold rolled strip, and hot and cold rolled sheets. With the Steel Corporation and three other companies accounting for 100 per cent of the domestic production of steel rails, their average annual base price declined only 15.4 per cent from 1926 to their depression low. With the corporation and four other companies accounting for 90.5 per cent of total capacity for making steel shapes, their average annual price declined 19.4 per cent. With the corporation and four other companies accounting for 73.3 per cent of domestic capacity for making steel plates (and ten companies accounting for 91 per cent), the average annual price declined 16.5 per cent. With the corporation and four other companies accounting for about 80 per cent of tin plate capacity, tin plate prices declined only 19.5 per cent. With the corporation and four other companies accounting for 73 per cent of domestic capacity for making steel bars, their price declined

was formed in 1901, no act of aggression upon its competitors is charged against it. . . ." United States v. United States Steel Corp., 251 U.S. 417, 451 (1920). Again, "[C]ompetitors, dealers and customers of the Corporation testify in multitude that no adventitious interference was employed to either fix or maintain prices and that they were constant or varied according to natural conditions. . . . [W]e may . . . wonder that the despotism of the Corporation, so baneful to the world in the representation of the Government, did not produce protesting victims." *Id.* at 449. Inasmuch as business rivals profited from these practices mutually indulged in, the wonder is after all not so great.

Workable Competition and Antitrust Policy

only 21.5 per cent.[97] During approximately the same period wholesale prices of all manufactured commodities declined by almost 30 per cent.[98]

In contrast to the relatively stable prices of steel rails, plates, shapes, bars, and tin plate, the prices of wire nails, hot and cold rolled strip, and hot and cold rolled sheets were very flexible indeed. With five leading companies accounting for only 68.2 per cent of nailmaking capacity, prices declined by 29 per cent; with five leading producers accounting for 65.7 per cent of hot rolled strip capacity, prices declined 37.9 per cent. With five leading companies accounting for only 64.6 per cent of the hot rolled sheet capacity, prices declined 31.6 per cent; with the five leading companies accounting for only 43 per cent of the cold rolled strip capacity, prices declined 45.2 per cent; and with the five leading companies accounting for 61.1 per cent of the cold rolled sheet capacity, prices declined 42.3 per cent.[99]

While quoted prices do not always reflect realized prices, a more recent study by the United States Bureau of Labor Statistics [100] reveals both the relative stability of quoted prices of eight major steel products (despite major fluctuations in output) and only minor departures of actual delivered prices from quoted prices. For example, with steel ingot production only 51 per cent of capacity in the second quarter of 1939, realized prices for steel plates were 97 per cent of quoted prices. With steel ingot production at 98 per cent of capacity in the second quarter of 1941, actual prices for steel plates were 100 per cent of quoted prices. Quoted prices for steel plates remained unchanged despite an almost 100 per cent increase in steel ingot output. The variations in quoted prices between these two periods and the departures from quoted prices were somewhat greater for hot and cold rolled sheets and hot and cold rolled strip, but about the same for

97. For data on concentration of production see American Iron and Steel Institute, *Directory of Iron and Steel Works of the United States and Canada* (23d ed.; New York: American Iron and Steel Institute, 1938); *TNEC Hearings*, pt. 18, Appendix, Exhibit No. 1349, Table XVII, at 10409. For data on price movements, see United States Steel Corp., *TNEC Papers* (New York [?] United States Steel Corp., 1940), Vol. II, at 76; Iron Age, Jan. 4, 1940, p. 172.

98. Index of Manufactured Products (U.S. Bureau of Labor Statistics data), reproduced in *Report of the Joint Committee on the Economic Report*, "December 1949 Steel Price Increases," Rep. No. 1373, 81st Cong., 2d Sess. 22 (1950).

99. See note 97 *supra*.

100. The Bureau's study, made in 1943, is not available in published form, but its findings were reproduced in a trade journal article, "Labor Department Examines Consumers' Prices of Steel Products," Iron Age, April 25, 1946, pp. 118–145H. Data on production in percentages of capacity for certain quarters of the years 1939 and 1941 appear in Iron Age, Jan. 7, 1943, p. 204.

The Rule of Reason and Monopoly

merchant bars and structural shapes.[101] In all instances the course of prices was impressive evidence of the effectiveness of the industry's price stabilization policy.

Apparently the corporation's preoccupation with stabilizing prices was bought at a high cost, both to consumers and to the corporation itself. In the period for which data are available, steel prices were not only relatively stable, they were relatively high. High costs made them high. The steel industry's practices described under *Conduct,* above, increased the average cost of shipping steel by increasing the average distance shipped and by discouraging the use of low-cost production and transportation facilities; they increased the cost of selling steel by substituting sales effort for price competition; and they increased the average cost of producing steel by encouraging inefficiency and protecting high-cost producers. The first two points should be fairly obvious.[102] The third requires brief comment.

The Steel Corporation while concerning itself with stabilizing prices neglected the problem of efficiency. Apparently it was more concerned with selling steel at high prices than with making it at low cost. In its effort to keep the whole industry orderly it failed to keep its own house in order. The corporation has itself presented the supporting evidence for these generalizations. After Judge Gary's death in the late 1920's a new management, troubled by the corporation's loss of relative position in the industry, subjected it to a severe and penetrating self-analysis. When its own engineers concluded that its operation was shot through with waste and inefficiency and proposed radical measures to overcome these deficiencies, the corporation employed a firm of industrial engineers to investigate its organization and operations in order to disprove or corroborate its own engineers' findings. In a 240-volume report the outsiders confirmed the findings of the insiders. Myron Taylor, retiring chairman

---

101. These findings are based on data compiled by the U.S. Bureau of Labor Statistics, reproduced in Iron Age, April 25, 1946, p. 118.

102. Basing point pricing results in persistent crosshauling and encourages the use of rail transportation even when cheaper water or truck transportation is available. The Ford, Bacon & Davis 1935–1938 survey of the Steel Corporation's operations, described in the next paragraph of the text, reportedly found that the corporation's practice of supplying Texas and its southwestern and even its Pacific Coast markets from its northern and eastern plants, instead of from its low-cost Birmingham facilities, was costing the corporation $1,000,000 annually. The literature on the economics of basing point pricing is voluminous, including Fritz Machlup, *The Basing-point System* (1949); John Maurice Clark, *supra* note 92: Carl Kaysen, "Basing Point Pricing and Public Policy," 63 Q. J. Econ. 289 (1949); Vernon A. Mund, "The 'Freight Allowed' Method of Price Quotation," 54 Q. J. Econ. 232 (1940); George J. Stigler, "A Theory of Delivered Price Systems," 39 Am. Econ. Rev. 1143 (1949).

Workable Competition and Antitrust Policy

of the corporation's board of directors, on his own initiative told the story in a series of articles in *Iron Age* in 1938;[103] and in 1950 Benjamin Fairless while president of the corporation somewhat reluctantly brought out the details under a relentless examination by the chief counsel of the Celler Committee.[104] The report as revealed by Fairless indicated that the Steel Corporation was a big, sprawling, inert giant, whose production operations were improperly coordinated; suffering from the lack of a long-run planning agency; relying on an antiquated system of cost accounting; with an inadequate knowledge of the cost or the relative profitability of the many thousands of items it sold; with production and cost standards generally below those considered everyday practice in other industries; with inadequate knowledge of its domestic markets and no clear appreciation of its opportunities in foreign markets; with less efficient production facilities than those of its rivals; and slow in introducing new processes and new products. Specifically, the report revealed that the corporation was slow in introducing the continuous rolling mill; slow in getting into the production of cold rolled steel products; slow in recognizing the potentialities of the wire business; slow to adopt the heat-treating process for the production of steel sheets; slow in getting into stainless steel products; slow in producing cold rolled sheets; slow in tin plate development; slow in utilizing waste gases; slow in utilizing low-cost water transportation because of its consideration for the railroads; in short, slow to grasp the remarkable business opportunities that a dynamic America offered it. The corporation was pictured as a follower, not a leader, in industrial efficiency.

Conclusions

This brief analysis of the steel industry's structure and conduct and of the Steel Corporation's performance warrants the conclusion that under the corporation's lead the industry did not conform to the standard of workable competition. Its structure contributed to conduct incompatible with an effective interplay of market forces, and its structure and conduct

---

103. Myron C. Taylor, "Ten Years of Steel," Iron Age, April 7, 1938, pp. 70-A–71; April 14, 1938, pp. 50–53, 92–94; April 28, 1938, pp. 36–38; May 5, 1938, pp. 47, 73-75. The "outsiders'" report is the Ford, Bacon & Davis report referred to in note 102 *supra*.

104. *Hearings before the Subcommittee on Study of Monopoly Power of the House Committee on the Judiciary*, 81st Cong., 2d Sess., ser. 14, pt. 4A, at 465–673 *passim*, especially 627 (1950).

The Rule of Reason and Monopoly

resulted in unacceptable performance.[105] It seems not unlikely that in an antitrust proceeding based on the rule of reason and the principle of workable competition as herein expounded, the corporation would have fared badly.[106]

THE CELLOPHANE INDUSTRY

An analysis of the district court's opinion in the *Cellophane* case [107] suggests that those who agitate to incorporate the principle of workable competition into the antitrust laws so that existing oligopolistic structures may be preserved have won their campaign without a battle. It also suggests that the principle may be a treacherous guide to courts not schooled in the intricacies of economic analysis. In formulating his opinion Judge Leahy stated that the case raised two questions: (1) Does Du Pont possess monopoly power in making and selling cellophane? (2) If so, has it been guilty of monopolizing within the meaning of the Sherman Act as interpreted in the *Aluminum* case? [108] The court reasoned that if it answered

---

105. More detailed studies have led to similar conclusions. See Louis Marengo, *Basing Point Pricing in the Steel Industry* (unpublished Ph.D. dissertation, Harvard University, June 1950); Stocking, *op. cit. supra* note 86, chap. 6.

106. It should be noted that the Steel Corporation of the 1930's is not the Steel Corporation of today. According to Fairless' testimony before the Celler Committee, *Hearings before the Subcommittee on Study of Monopoly Power of the House Committee on the Judiciary, supra* note 104, the corporation adopted such of the engineers' suggestions as it felt warranted. The corporation has reorganized, modernized, and expanded its facilities and operations at a cost of hundreds of millions of dollars, and Fairless' modest contention that the corporation was then as efficient as any of its rivals, *id.* at 631, seems reasonable. But that the industry's structure still impedes competitive price adjustments with changes in demand is indicated by later price movements. Between July 1953 and July 1954, when production of ingots and steel for castings declined from 93.1% of capacity to 68.1%, the price of cold rolled and hot rolled strip, cold rolled and hot rolled sheets, and steel plates remained unchanged. Iron Age, Jan. 6, 1955, p. 340. In July 1954, when production dropped to 62.9% of capacity, United States Steel raised steel prices. The Steel Corporation's explanation of this anomaly was an increase in labor costs. Wall Street Journal, July 2, 1954, p. 1, col. 2. Other companies followed the lead. Iron Age, July 8, 1954, pp. 146–48; July 15, 1954, pp. 106–68.

107. United States v. E. I. du Pont de Nemours & Co., 118 F. Supp. 41 (D. Del. 1953). The discussion that follows in the text is based on the record in this case. Government exhibits contained in the record will be designated GX and defendant's exhibits DX. The title of the case will be repeated only for references to the opinion. For a more comprehensive analysis of the economic issues involved in the case, see Stocking and Willard F. Mueller, "The Cellophane Case and the New Competition," 45 Am. Econ. Rev. 29 (1955).

108. United States v. E. I. du Pont de Nemours & Co., 118 F. Supp. 41, 54 (D. Del. 1953).

Workable Competition and Antitrust Policy

"no" to the first question, it need not consider the second. It was quite positive in its conclusion, for it stated: "Facts, in large part uncontested, demonstrate duPont cellophane is sold under such intense competitive conditions acquisition of market control or monopoly power is a practical impossibility." [109] This study challenges the validity of the court's conclusion that Du Pont had no monopoly in selling cellophane, though it leaves to the Supreme Court the question whether such monopoly power as Du Pont may have had violates the statute.[110] In challenging the district court's conclusions the analysis will consider Du Pont's stategy (conduct) in protecting cellophane from the competition of rival products; analyze the structure of the cellophane industry and its market; and evaluate Du Pont's performance in making and selling cellophane.

Conduct

In 1923 Du Pont entered into contracts with the world's sole producer of cellophane, Comptoir des Textiles Artificiels, a French corporation, which granted to a jointly owned company, Du Pont Cellophane Company, Inc., the exclusive right to the Comptoir's patents and know-how in making and selling cellophane in the North and Central American market.[111] Du Pont at this time recognized that the patents might not guarantee it complete protection from rival producers but considered that the patents together with the trade skills and technical knowledge accompanying them justified an investment of some $2,000,000, on which it anticipated annual earnings of over $600,000, or earnings at an annual rate on investment of over 31 per cent.[112] Believing that it had a highly differentiated if not a unique flexible wrapping material for which a large and expanding market could be readily developed, it sought to protect itself from the competition of other producers of cellophane. To do this it proceeded on both domestic and foreign fronts. To curb imports of cellophane it both sought a tariff increase [113] and made agreements

109. *Id.* at 197–98.
110. On October 14, 1954, the Supreme Court noted probable jurisdiction. United States v. E. I. du Pont de Nemours & Co., 348 U.S. 806 (1954). For an analysis of the Supreme Court's opinion see chap. 8 *infra*.
111. Option contract of Jan. 6, 1923, GX 1458, pp. 5999–6008; organizational agreement of June 9, 1923, GX 1001, pp. 989–997; license agreement of Dec. 26, 1923, GX 1002, pp. 998–1001.
112. Report of Dr. Fin Sparre, head of Du Pont's development department, April 14, 1923, GX 392, p. 5451.
113. About Du Pont's effort to get higher duties on cellophane L. A. Yerkes, president of Du Pont Cellophane Co., Inc., wrote W. C. Spruance, Du Pont vice presi-

The Rule of Reason and Monopoly

with foreign producers providing for a division of markets. While it did not succeed immediately in getting a direct tariff increase, it obtained a reclassification of cellophane which on February 24, 1929, raised the duty from 25 to 60 per cent ad valorem. The higher duty soon reduced annual foreign sales in the American market from more than 20 per cent of the total domestic business to less than 9 per cent.[114] The Tariff Act of 1930 fixed the duty on imported cellophane at 45 per cent ad valorem—a smaller duty than the reclassification had brought but still enough to keep foreign cellophane out of the United States market. From 1930 to 1947 annual cellophane imports accounted for less than 1 per cent of domestic consumption.[115]

On May 7, 1929, Du Pont entered a patent exchange agreement with Kalle & Company, Germany's exclusive cellophane producer under the Comptoir patents, by which the parties agreed to exchange without charge except for patent fees all patent rights and technological data that they then had or might later acquire on cellophane.[116] The agreement, according to C. M. Albright, Du Pont Cellophane's vice president, did not "for obvious reasons" designate the countries within which Kalle got exclusive rights, but Albright listed them in a letter for the benefit of Du Pont's Buffalo office.[117] Later Du Pont assigned Kalle exclusive patent rights on moistureproof cellophane in the countries of Kalle's territory.[118]

---

dent, on July 25, 1925: "In order that you shall be entirely familiar with the Cellophane status, I want to let you know that we are endeavoring to have the duty on Cellophane raised from 25% to 45%, and Curie, Lane and Wallace are of the opinion that we have a fair chance of getting this through." GX 1068, p. 1142.

114. Du Pont Cellophane's quarterly competitive report, first quarter 1929, reported that importers had had 21% of domestic business in 1927 and 24% in 1928. GX 431, p. 5677. Its report for the fourth quarter 1929 showed that Du Pont had 91.6% of domestic business. GX 434, p. 5714. The increased tariff and decreased imports apparently contributed to the stability of cellophane prices. Du Pont Cellophane's competitive report, second quarter 1929, said:

The present tariff rate (.40 per pound) as fixed by the United States Customs Court, has increased the cost of importing Transparent Cellulose Sheeting to such an extent that the competitors are adhering more rigidly to their published price list. Their selling policy in the past has been to obtain preference with the manufacturer by offering special price concessions.

GX 432, p. 5690.

115. GX 182A, p. 515A; GX 182, p. 515.
116. GX 1087, pp. 1183–86.
117. Letter of Oct. 30, 1929, GX 1091, p. 1195.
118. Du Pont Cellophane memorandum dated March 17, 1933, GX 1098, p. 1205; Letter to Kalle dated March 20, 1933, GX 1099, p. 1206; memorandum dated April 27, 1934, review of the Du Pont-Kalle relations, prepared by Du Pont's patent service, GX 1102, pp. 1210–12.

Workable Competition and Antitrust Policy

In 1935 Du Pont and British Cellophane Limited entered into a similar patent exchange agreement which specifically designated the areas within which each party would confine its operations.[119] Meanwhile, on February 12, 1930, all the world's leading cellophane producers except Du Pont had entered into a cartel agreement assigning markets and fixing quotas.[120] Du Pont representatives attended the first day of the conference as guests but did not sign the agreement. The trial court found that they were not authorized to make any commitment and did not.[121] Nevertheless, the agreement, which did not cover moistureproof or photographic cellophane, recognized the North American market as belonging to Du Pont and Sylvania Industrial Corporation of America.[122] The subsequent course of the cartel is not clear, but apparently it broke down under the strain of the Great Depression and World War II. In 1940 Du Pont disavowed all formal territorial limitations,[123] although its agreements with Kalle and British Cellophane were to have run for twenty years.

On the domestic front, in 1930 Du Pont found itself confronted by a rival producer, Sylvania Industrial Corporation of America. To improve cellophane's usefulness as a wrapping material and to fortify it against domestic competition, Du Pont had already developed and patented a

119. Agreement of May 3, 1935, GX 1109, pp. 1229–34.
120. "Official report," signed by producers, GX 1414, pp. 1841–44.
121. United States v. E. I. du Pont de Nemours & Co., 118 F. Supp. 41, 221 (D. Del. 1953).
122. Sylvania had come into the American market by the back door. Société Industrielle de la Cellulose (SIDAC) had built a cellophane plant in Belgium using the Comptoir's patented processes and secret know-how, which it had obtained from two former employees of the Comptoir's French affiliate, La Cellophane, Société Anonyme. Memorandum of Feb. 17, 1944, on the history of Du Pont cellophane, prepared in Du Pont's cellophane division, GX 1, p. 12. SIDAC at first exported to the American market and later established Sylvania as its American subsidiary. Du Pont Cellophane Company's quarterly competitive report, third quarter 1929, GX 433, p. 5702. When La Cellophane sued SIDAC for patent infringement and in settlement took stock in SIDAC, this brought La Cellophane indirectly through Sylvania into competition with Du Pont in the American market in violation of its 1923 contract. After prolonged negotiations for a settlement with La Cellophane, during which Du Pont pondered how to "accept reparations and at the same time protect its future position without contravening American statutes," memorandum of a Nov. 14, 1929, discussion by DuPont officials, GX 1410, p. 1831, La Cellophane waived the 1923 restrictions confining Du Pont to the North and Central American markets and granted it equal rights with itself in Japan and South America. Letter of March 6, 1930, from Du Pont to La Cellophane, GX 1013, pp. 1027–29; excerpt from minutes of May 8, 1930, meeting of Du Pont's board of directors, GX 1015, p. 1031.
123. Identical letters dated Oct. 17, 1940, to Kalle, British Cellophane, Canadian Industries Limited, and La Cellophane, GX 1273, p. 1602; GX 1274, p. 1603; GX 1275, p. 1604; GX 1276, p. 1605.

The Rule of Reason and Monopoly

moistureproof product. The initial moistureproof cellophane product patent, issued in 1929, was broad in scope and comprehensive in its claims.[124] Having improved its patent position, Du Pont notified Sylvania, which meanwhile had developed a moistureproof cellophane of its own, that it was infringing Du Pont's patents. Eventually Du Pont sued Sylvania but settled the suit by a patent exchange and licensing agreement, under which Sylvania agreed to pay Du Pont a 2 per cent royalty on its net sales of moistureproof cellophane in return for the use of Du Pont's patents. For sales in excess of 20 per cent of total domestic sales, Sylvania agreed to pay a royalty of 20 cents a pound or 30 per cent of net sales, whichever was higher. Its penalty-free share of the market was to be graduated upward at intervals of 1 per cent per annum until by 1942 it was scheduled to reach 29 per cent.[125] For such use if any as it should make of Sylvania's patents, Du Pont agreed to a similar penalty for exceeding its basic quotas, but it never used Sylvania's patents.

This settlement apparently was based on a mutual recognition that if Du Pont won the suit Sylvania would be foreclosed from producing cellophane except on such terms as Du Pont might impose, and if Sylvania won both parties would lose to an intensification of competition.[126] Whatever the purpose of the penalty royalty, it in effect geared Sylvania's output to Du Pont's and gave Du Pont as the dominant firm the power to

---

124. About its research program to improve cellophane, L. A. Yerkes, president of Du Pont Cellophane, later said:

> This work was undertaken as a defensive program in connection with protecting broadly by patents the field of moistureproofing agents other than waxes which was the only class of material disclosed in our original Cellophane moistureproofing patents. The investigations on this subject did, in fact, lead to the discovery of a number of classes of materials which could serve equally well for moistureproofing agents. . . . Each of these classes has been made the subject of a patent. . . . Altogether, 13 patent applications are being written as a result of the work done under this project, all in view of strengthening our Moistureproof Cellophane patent situation.

December 1933 report to Du Pont Cellophane's board of directors, Jan. 22, 1934, GX 488, p. 6478.

125. Agreement dated April 26, 1933, GX 2487, pp. 3212–33.

126. Du Pont's patent attorney, after a conference with Sylvania's general counsel, summed up the situation as follows:

> During the conference Mr. Menken stated that in his opinion the case should be settled. He said that they were very fearful of what the result would be to their company in the event they succeeded in having the claims of the patents which are involved in the litigation held invalid. He seemed to realize the old adage that the defendant can never win. . . . If the Du Pont Cellophane Company succeeds and the patents are held to be infringed, Sylvania Industrial Corporation will be under injunction and will be obliged to stop manufacturing moistureproof wrapping tissue. On the other hand, if they succeed in having the broad claims of the

Workable Competition and Antitrust Policy

determine how much moistureproof cellophane would come on the market.[127]

Du Pont's efforts to protect itself from the competition of rival cellophane producers was the strategy of a monopolist. Its conduct is consistent only with the belief that in cellophane Du Pont had a highly differentiated if not a unique product in exploiting which it had something to gain by being the single seller.

Structure

Any innovator has a temporary monopoly. The questions crucial to the economic significance of his monopoly—to its becoming workably competitive—are whether rival producers of the identical product appear and whether substitute rival products with a sufficiently high cross-elasticity of demand exist or appear.

An examination of the structure of the cellophane industry and of changes in it over the years throws light on these questions. In truth, the analysis of conduct has already answered the first question. Du Pont's strategy succeeded in keeping rival cellophane producers except Sylvania out of the domestic market, and the way in which the two companies settled their patent infringement suit geared Sylvania's production of cellophane to Du Pont's. No other rival producer of cellophane had appeared when the government instituted its antitrust proceedings.[128]

The second question—whether there was a high cross-elasticity of demand—involves an analysis of the market for flexible wrapping materials. The court concluded that no separate identifiable market for cellophane existed; the market for cellophane was identical with that for flexible wrapping materials.[129] It was largely on this finding that the judge based

patents held invalid they will throw the art open, so far as the broad claims are concerned, to anyone and therefore will have additional competition.
Letter dated Aug. 4, 1932, from W. S. Pritchard to B. M. May, Du Pont Cellophane vice president, GX 2811, pp. 6073–74.

127. In 1945, as the court pointed out, the parties agreed to smaller royalties and abandoned the penalties. United States v. E. I. du Pont de Nemours & Co., 118 F. Supp. 41, 158 (D. Del. 1953).

128. The government filed its suit December 13, 1947, but the case was not decided until December 14, 1953; and a third producer, Olin Industries, Inc., began the production of cellophane in June 1951, while the case was being tried. Testimony of Fred Olsen, Olin vice president, Transcript of Testimony, p. 6829, United States v. E. I. du Pont de Nemours & Co., 118 F. Supp. 41 (D. Del. 1953).

129. Judge Leahy said: "The relevant market for determining the extent of duPont's market control is the market for flexible packaging materials. . . ." United States v. E. I. du Pont de Nemours & Co., 118 F. Supp. 41, 60 (D. Del. 1953).

The Rule of Reason and Monopoly

his conclusion as to the effectiveness of the competition Du Pont encountered in selling cellophane.

A characteristic of a competitive market is that the prices of identical products tend to be identical. Where the products are nonidentical, their prices will reflect the comparative evaluation that marginal buyers (those just induced to buy at the prevailing prices) make of their want-satisfying qualities. For a product that a consumer regards as better satisfying a particular requirement he will be willing to pay more. The higher price that he pays will result in higher profits to the producer of the preferred article, unless perchance it costs more to make it. If obstacles to entry do not exist, the higher profits will attract additional producers, and price must eventually decline until it equals average cost. If differentiated but competitive products are selling at competitive even though nonidentical prices, a change in the price of one will affect the amount of the other that can be sold at prevailing prices. A price decline in one will decrease the other's sales and hence tend to lower its price. If the initial price decline reflects a reduction in cost, unless the seller of the rival product can lower his cost, eventually he must go out of business. Before he does so he no doubt will lower his price. Thus a decline in the price of one differentiated product tends to bring a decline in the price of a rival product. Contrariwise an increase in the demand for products of the same general class which brings an increase in the price of one of several differentiated products will tend to raise the price of all. In short, although price differences may exist which reflect differences in cost among differentiated products and differences in the importance that consumers attach to them, the prices of the differentiated products tend to move in unison. Cost-price relationships may thus be helpful in determining whether differentiated products do in fact meet in a common market.

Does cellophane compete with all other flexible wrapping materials in a single market? Flexible wrapping materials fall into four major categories: opaque nonmoistureproof wrapping paper, moistureproof films, nonmoistureproof films, and moistureproof materials other than films. Cellophane by reason of its qualities and its price is apparently excluded entirely from the market of the principal opaque nonmoistureproof wrapping paper—kraft. Kraft paper is used primarily for convenience and protection in handling packages. The housewife brings her groceries home in it. It sells for less than cellophane costs, and for general wrapping it meets consumers' needs better. Clearly its market is not cellophane's.

Cellophane is a film of regenerated cellulose—thin, transparent, nonfibrous. It is sold in both moistureproof and nonmoistureproof form. Its

Workable Competition and Antitrust Policy

leading moistureproof film rivals include Saran, cellulose acetate, polyethylene, and pliofilm. In 1949 their prices ranged from over 40 per cent to over 160 per cent higher than the price of moistureproof cellophane,[130] and they were less satisfactory for most uses to which cellophane was put. Data are not available to compare the trend of the prices of these films with the prices of cellophane—except for cellulose acetate, which Du Pont itself made—but a Du Pont market analysis report for 1948 makes it clear that Du Pont did not regard the rival films as competitive:

> The principal markets for non-viscose films have been competitive with Cellophane only to a very minor degree up to this time. Some are used very little or not at all in the packaging field—others are employed principally for specialty uses where Cellophane is not well adapted—none have been successfully introduced into any of Cellophane's main markets due to their inherent shortcomings.[131]

The combination of cellophane's qualities is such that in one important segment of the flexible packaging material market it has captured the market completely. In recent years, save during temporary periods of shortage, cigarette makers have used no other overwrap.[132] But in the food packaging industry, which in 1949 accounted for 80 per cent of Du Pont's cellophane sales, cellophane encounters several lusty rivals—vegetable parchment, greaseproof paper, glassine, waxed paper, and aluminum foil. In 1949 cellophane accounted for 6.8 per cent of the total quantity of selected flexible wrapping materials (in millions of square inches) sold by nineteen major converters for wrapping bakery products, 24.4 per cent of that used in wrapping candy, 31.9 per cent of that used in wrapping snacks, 34.9 per cent of that used in wrapping meat and

---

130. This comparison, in terms of prices per thousand square inches, rests on data appearing in a price survey made for Du Pont by Robert Heller & Associates, management consultants. DX 995, reproduced in part in United States v. E. I. du Pont de Nemours & Co., 118 F. Supp. 41, 83 (D. Del. 1953).

131. DX 595, p. 1147. Olin Industries, Inc., later to become the country's third producer of cellophane, concluded similarly:

> There are no films currently marketed which are potentially competitive to any substantial degree in Cellophane's major markets.... Other transparent films will find their place for those low volume uses which can absorb the additional cost of the film and which necessitate certain physical properties not possessed by Cellophane.

Report on "the evidence in support of entry by Olin Industries into the Cellophane business, based on the purchase of patent license and 'know-how' from du Pont," Dec. 15, 1948, GX 566, p. 7575.

132. Judge Leahy referred to cellophane's temporary "displacement" by other cigarette overwraps in the mid-forties, when cellophane was in short supply. United States v. E. I. du Pont de Nemours & Co., 118 F. Supp. 41, 108 (D. Del. 1953).

The Rule of Reason and Monopoly

poultry, 26.6 per cent of that used in wrapping crackers and biscuits, 47.2 per cent of that used in wrapping fresh produce, and 33.6 per cent of that used in wrapping frozen foods excluding dairy products.[133]

Certainly on their face these figures do not indicate that cellophane monopolized the market for flexible wrapping materials. Moreover, the court found that "shifts of business between duPont cellophane and other flexible packaging materials have been frequent, continuing and contested."[134] In the face of these facts and this judgment, how can economists justify the conclusion that Du Pont exercised monopoly power in selling cellophane? First, note that a monopolist's pricing policy does not guarantee that he will get all the business he would like to have at any particular moment. His pricing policy is designed to maximize earnings over some period of time. He may revise prices from time to time in response to changing cost and demand functions. But having determined the price at which he will sell for a period of time, he foregoes business that he might have had at a lower price. If he could isolate his markets, it would pay him to discriminate among customers and get both the low-price and the high-price business; but if he cannot, by cutting prices he will realize less on what he might have sold at the higher price. To compensate for this, after deciding on a price policy at any particular time he may rely more on sales effort than on price competition. H. O. Ladd, director of Du Pont's trade analysis division, put it this way:

> The main competitive materials . . . against which Cellophane competes are waxed paper, glassine, greaseproof and vegetable parchment paper, all of which are lower in price than Cellophane. We do not meet this price competition. Rather we compete with these materials on the basis of establishing the value of our own as a factor in better packaging and cheaper distribution costs and classify as our logical markets those fields where the properties of Cellophane in relationship to its price can do a better job for the user.[135]

A more reliable test of monopoly power than the percentage of a broad, ill-defined market that a particular seller holds is the one set up here—the relative price movements of the single seller's product and of "competing" products. Stated in technical terms the question becomes: Is the cross-elasticity of demand so low that Du Pont can price cellophane independently and still make monopoly profits in selling it?[136]

133. *Id.* at 111–13. A detailed comparison appears in the opinion.
134. *Id.* at 91.
135. GX 589, p. 7530.
136. The Supreme Court recognized the significance of cross-elasticity of demand in Times-Picayune Publishing Co. v. United States, 345 U.S. 594, 612 n. 31 (1953). It said:

Workable Competition and Antitrust Policy

The course of moistureproof cellophane prices shows that Du Pont has followed a farsighted policy in pricing cellophane. While at any particular time it has apparently foregone price competition to get business, it has deliberately adopted a long-range pricing policy designed to expand sales continuously. From an average price of $2.508 a pound in 1924, Du Pont reduced cellophane prices every year until 1936, when its prices averaged 41.3 cents a pound.[137] By 1940 further reductions had brought the annual average price down to 38 cents a pound. In the inflation of the war and postwar periods Du Pont reversed cellophane's price trend. By 1950 it was charging an average of 49 cents a pound. But despite this long downward trend in prices, the principal type of moistureproof cellophane (300 MST-51) sold continuously at from two to seven times the price of 25# bleached glassine and from two to four and a half times the price of 30# waxed paper, its most important rivals.[138]

What is more important, Du Pont cellophane prices moved independently of rival products' prices, which remained relatively stable or moved slightly upward [139] while cellophane prices were dropping sharply. When wartime and postwar inflation brought higher prices for these wrapping materials, Du Pont cellophane, which had continually sold at higher prices, moved up with the rest, but less rapidly. Thus it continued its relative decline in price. Such independent price movements suggest noncompetitive pricing as between cellophane and the rival products. That the sellers of the other wrapping materials did not reduce their prices as cellophane prices were moving downward indicates a low cross-elasticity

> For every product, substitutes exist. But a relevant market cannot meaningfully encompass that infinite range. The circle must be drawn narrowly to exclude any other product to which, within reasonable variations in price, only a limited number of buyers will turn; in technical terms, products whose "cross-elasticities of demand" are small.

137. United States v. E. I. du Pont de Nemours & Co., 118 F. Supp. 41, 82 (D. Del. 1953) (table of annual average prices from 1924 to 1950).

138. Brief for Defendant, Appendix A (graph based on prices per thousand square inches), United States v. E. I. du Pont de Nemours & Co., 118 F. Supp. 41 (D. Del. 1953).

139. Bleached glassine prices were unchanged from 1924 to 1933 and again from 1934 to 1938. They rose in 1939 and again in 1940. Waxed paper prices were virtually unchanged from 1933 to 1940, fluctuating between .5c. and .52c. per thousand square inches. They increased to .62c. in 1940. Between 1924 and 1928 vegetable parchment prices declined slightly from 1.3c. to 1.0c. per thousand square inches and thereafter remained relatively stable, moving between .95c. and 1.05c. Bleached greaseproof prices rose from .45c. per thousand square inches in 1933 to .55c. in 1940. These price comparisons rest on data collected for Du Pont by Robert Heller & Associates, management consultants. DX 994-A. The price of one principal standard type of each material was used.

The Rule of Reason and Monopoly

of demand between the products. It suggests, although it does not prove, that the rival products were selling too close to average cost at the time when cellophane, which was continuously higher in price despite its down trend, was selling above its average cost. Apparently rival products were not sufficiently close substitutes to constitute effective competition with cellophane.[140]

Performance

Some economists would regard the cellophane industry's record of performance as good when measured by the course of prices. Certainly Du Pont's long-run pricing policy was farsighted; however, it was not inconsistent with that of a monopolist. A monopolist interested in maximizing earnings must not only take account of the short-run effect on profits of price changes but must also consider their long-run effects on costs and sales. He may find, as Du Pont apparently did, that lower prices eventually increase sales and thereby lower costs and increase earnings. In determining its long-run pricing policy Du Pont sought larger earnings through increased volume.[141] Whether its pricing policy maximized its earnings is not clear, but that it kept them at a high level is beyond dispute. From 1924 to 1950 Du Pont's rate of operative earnings (before taxes) on investment in cellophane ranged from 62.4 per cent in 1928 to

140. The judgment of a Du Pont division manager supports the above conclusion. During the war and early postwar years increased taxes brought a lower rate of net earnings on Du Pont's cellophane investment, reducing it from 20.4% in 1940 to 11.2% in 1947. 1947 profit and loss statement of Du Pont's cellophane division, GX 591, p. 7539. To reverse this trend Du Pont raised cellophane prices from an average of 41.9c. a pound in 1947 to 46c. in 1948. By May 1948, Du Pont's rate of earnings on its cellophane investment had increased to 31%. At this time Du Pont's cellophane division manager announced that "if operative earnings [before taxes] . . . of 31 per cent is [sic] considered inadequate, then an upward revision in prices will be necessary to improve the return." The manager proposed a schedule of prices to earn about 40%. Du Pont put this into effect in August 1948. Operative earnings for that year averaged only 27.2% (calculated from 1948 profit and loss statement, GX 577, p. 7323), but by 1949 they had increased to 35.2% and by 1950 to 45.3%. The latter figure represented net earnings of 20% on Du Pont's 1950 investment in cellophane facilities. GX 573 (I), p. 8. (This exhibit was impounded by the court but was cited in the government's Proposed Findings of Fact, p. 48, and Brief for the United States, pp. 144–45, United States v. E. I. du Pont de Nemours & Co., 118 F. Supp. 41 (D. Del. 1953).)

141. President Yerkes of Du Pont Cellophane had concluded as early as 1924 that the company should lower cellophane prices. "[I] think it will undoubtedly increase sales and widen distribution. . . . Our price I think is too high based purely on manufacturing cost and too high in comparison with other wrapping papers. . . ." Memorandum of some remarks made at a meeting of the board of directors, Du Pont

163

Workable Competition and Antitrust Policy

19.1 per cent in 1947. In 1950 it reached a postwar high of 45.3 per cent. Over a twenty-six year period it averaged 34.4 per cent. The rate of net earnings (after taxes) ranged from 51.5 per cent in 1928 to 8.4 per cent in 1942. In 1950 it reached a postwar high of 20 per cent. Over the twenty-six-year period it averaged 24.2 per cent.[142]

On their face these look like noncompetitive earning rates. But many factors besides the intensity of competition affect earnings, and a sustained high rate of earnings in a particular product does not prove that earnings are monopolistic. Cellophane has met a rapidly expanding demand, as have other wrapping materials. Unfortunately data are not available for comparing cellophane's earning rates with those of rival materials. However, Du Pont's rate of earnings on cellophane—of which for half a dozen years Du Pont was the sole domestic producer and thereafter until 1951, with Sylvania, one of two producers—can be compared with Du Pont's earnings on its rayon investment before World War II. Many similarities in the two industries justify the comparison. Du Pont produced both products. They stem from the same raw materials. They were initially both produced under noncompetitive conditions. Both enjoyed tariff protection. Both have close substitutes. Both have been characterized by rapid expansion in consumption, rapid reduction in cost, and a rapid decline in price. The single relevant difference is the structure of the two industries. Rayon production began as a monopoly, with American Viscose Corporation the sole producer until after World War I, when Du Pont entered the field; by 1930 eighteen rivals confronted the two leaders.[143] In 1920, when Du Pont first engaged in rayon production, American Viscose made 64.2 per cent on its investment before taxes.[144] Entry was relatively free, however, and the high rate of earnings attracted newcomers. By 1929 earnings for the industry averaged 18.1 per cent before taxes; Du Pont made 19 per cent.[145] With six more firms entering the industry in 1930,

Cellophane Co., Inc., Dec. 11, 1924, DX 337, p. 643. Walter S. Carpenter, Jr., chairman of Du Pont's board of directors, testified that "the purpose of reducing our price and also improving our quality was to broaden our market. . . ." Transcript of Testimony, p. 6728, United States v. E. I. du Pont de Nemours & Co., 118 F. Supp. 41 (D. Del. 1953).

142. Stocking and Mueller, "The Cellophane Case and the New Competition," 45 Am. Econ. Rev. 29, 57 n. 107, 59 (1955). This article is reprinted in *Readings in Industrial Organization and Control*, ed. Richard B. Heflebower and George W. Stocking (Homewood, Ill.: Irwin, 1958), p. 118.

143. Jesse W. Markham, *Competition in the Rayon Industry* (Cambridge: Harvard University Press, 1952), p. 46.

144. *TNEC Hearings*, pt. 31, *Investments, Profits, and Rates of Return for Selected Industries* (a study by the Federal Trade Commission), at 17985.

145. *Id.* at 17988, 17990, 17998.

The Rule of Reason and Monopoly

the average return for the industry was only 15 per cent, and Du Pont lost money, its losses equaling 0.9 per cent of its investment. During the next eight years Du Pont averaged 7.5 per cent on its rayon investment.[146] On cellophane it averaged over 25 per cent. This significant difference in earnings probably reflects the relative intensity of competition.

Conclusions

The foregoing analysis indicates that cellophane production has not conformed to the conception of workable competition developed herein. Du Pont's conduct (strategy) was that of a monopolist. The industry's structure has been oligopolistic; and the market for cellophane, while not clearly defined, is scarcely identical with that for flexible wrapping materials. If entry had been free and genuine rivals had confronted Du Pont in selling cellophane,[147] Du Pont would have been forced to sell it for less and would have made a lower rate of return.

But the fact that cellophane has not been sold under conditions of workable competition does not mean that the industry's performance has been wholly bad. Far from it. Du Pont has continuously improved the product, developed new types, found new uses for them, lowered its price, helped converters and packagers in developing new markets, and developed and improved packaging machinery. It has been a most progressive rival wherever flexible wrapping materials are sold. The district court would have been on sounder ground had it concluded that cellophane has been sold under conditions of workable monopoly, and it is this confusion between workable monopoly and workable competition that makes this decision a bad precedent. Rarely does a monopolist sell in a completely isolated market. In one sense every want-satisfying product must compete with all others for the consumer's dollar, and the rivalry among the sellers of rival products may be intelligent and vigorous. But it is a

146. *Ibid.*
147. Correspondence between Lammot du Pont and L. A. Yerkes, president of Du Pont's Cellophane, reveals the attitude of potential rivals toward competing with Du Pont (and incidentally Du Pont's attitude toward the competition of rivals). Written at a time when the Union Carbide & Carbon Corp. had considered entering the field, Du Pont's letter of December 2, 1931, which was based on an hour's conversation with representatives of Union Carbide & Carbon, stated: "They assured me repeatedly they did not wish to rush into anything, most of all a competitive situation with du Pont. Their whole tone was most agreeable. . . . In the course of the conversation, various efforts at co-operation between Carbide and du Pont were referred to, and in every case assurances of their desire to work together, given." GX 4381, p. 4300.

Workable Competition and Antitrust Policy

deceptive rivalry, which if accepted by the courts as a substitute for competition will narrow greatly the applicability and probably the usefulness of the Sherman Act.

THE TIN CAN INDUSTRY

The district court's decision in the 1916 *American Can Company* case [148] affords a striking illustration of the unfortunate implications of the rule of reason as laid down in *Standard Oil* and *American Tobacco*. The organizers of the American Can Company with a single exception were promoters, not canmakers. They set out to monopolize canmaking [149] and to make money in the manipulation of securities. Immediately they succeeded in both endeavors. American Can acquired over a hundred canmaking plants, for most of which it paid exorbitant prices, [150] and two-thirds of which it dismantled within two years. Together these plants accounted for 90 per cent or more of the cans sold in the domestic market. [151] To make their monopoly enduring the promoters obtained agreements from most of the former plant owners not to engage in canmaking for fifteen years within three thousand miles of Chicago, and they worked out various arrangements with the manufacturers of canmaking machinery designed to prevent potential rivals from becoming canmakers. [152] Exercising its monopoly power, American Can obtained

---

148. United States v. American Can Co., 230 Fed. 859 (D. Md. 1916), *decree rendered*, 234 Fed. 1019 (D. Md.), *appeal dismissed*, 256 U.S. 706 (1921). Statements of fact in the text about the can industry in 1916 and earlier are based on the opinion in this case unless otherwise indicated.

149. Said the court, "What has been proved is . . . that the defendant was organized to monopolize interstate trade in cans. . . ." United States v. American Can Co., 230 Fed. 859, 861 (D. Md. 1916). "There can be no possible explanation of such transactions, except that the defendant and its promoters wanted to extinguish competition and did not stop to inquire how much it would cost to do so." *Id.* at 877.

150. Judge Rose found that the prices paid ranged from one and a half to twenty-five times the value of the property acquired, and he said that for half or probably a third of the $25,000,000 given in cash or capital stock American could have "purchased land, erected buildings, and equipped them with machinery which would have had a greater capacity, could have operated at a smaller cost, and would have been at least as well, if not better, located. . . ." *Id.* at 870–71.

151. *Id.* at 869. In arriving at the 90% figure the court noted that one witness had testified that he believed that American Can had at the outset acquired from 95 to 98% of the country's total capacity for making cans for sale.

152. About these arrangements the court said:

The record amply justifies the assertion that for a year or two after defendant's formation it was practically impossible for any competitor to obtain the most modern, up-to-date, automatic machinery, and that the difficulties in the way of getting such machinery were not altogether removed until the expiration of the

The Rule of Reason and Monopoly

secret rebates from the American Sheet and Tin Plate Company, a United States Steel subsidiary, amounting over a twelve-year period to $9,000,000. As had the Standard Oil and American Tobacco Companies, American Can operated bogus independents.

Despite its having achieved at the outset a virtual monopoly of canmaking and despite its early "bad" conduct, the court found American's contemporary performance good. The company made good cans and sold them at prices against which customers did not complain. The company claimed (as the court put it, "with much reason") that it was the first to study can industry problems systematically and scientifically, and it spared no effort to meet its customers' needs. It had a more varied line of equipment than its rivals and "having great facilities habitually used them to give intelligent, courteous, and kindly aid [to its customers]. It is unmistakably popular in the trade." [153] With its plants widely dispersed it could make prompt deliveries, which the court regarded as perhaps "its most valuable service to the trade." [154]

Not only did the court find its performance good, but it found that American Can had reformed its conduct: "[T]he testimony has disclosed nothing in the recent conduct of defendant, other than that which the government particularizes, to which any serious exception, or indeed any exception at all, can be taken." [155]

And finally the industry's structure had changed somewhat. The court found that American Can by 1913 was selling only about half the cans sold in the United States. Continental Can Company sold approximately one-fourth of the cans not sold by American, and numerous smaller concerns accounted for the balance. Although he recognized that the American Can Company had power over the market, Judge Rose was "frankly reluctant to destroy so finely adjusted an industrial machine as the record shows defendant to be." [156] In considering the legal principals involved he asserted that

> one of the designs of the framers of the Anti-Trust Act was to prevent the concentration in a few hands of control over great industries. They preferred a social and industrial state in which there should be many independent pro-

---

six years for which the defendant had bound up the leading manufacturers of such machinery.
Id. at 875.
153. Id. at 897.
154. Id. at 896.
155. Id. at 881. "The competitors of the defendant are satisfied. . . . As has sometimes been suggested, it seems to hold an umbrella over them." Id. at 898.
156. Id. at 903.

Workable Competition and Antitrust Policy

ducers. Size and power are themselves facts some of whose consequences do not depend upon the way in which they were created or in which they are used. It is easy to conceive that they might be acquired honestly and used as fairly as men who are in business for the legitimate purpose of making money for themselves and their associates could be expected to use them, human nature being what it is, and for all that constitute a public danger, or at all events give rise to difficult social, industrial and political problems.[157]

Then turning his back on his own conception of the Sherman Act, the judge found the American Can's power, though great, was limited by "a large volume of actual competition and to a still greater extent by . . . potential competition. . . ."[158] In a decree that left American Can's structure undisturbed, Judge Rose expressed the hope that "all potential restraints upon free competition . . . will pass away as speedily without as with dissolution." "Dissolution," he said, "will cause far more loss and business disturbance than will attend the gradual re-establishment of competitive conditions by the play of economic forces."[159] Still somewhat uneasy, the court retained the bill and reserved the right to decree dissolution should "the size and power of the defendant" ever be "used to the injury of the public" or should American Can's size and power, "without being intentionally so used," give it "a dominance or control over the industry, or some portion of it, so great as to make dissolution or other restraining decree of the court expedient."[160] When the Supreme Court refused to dissolve the United States Steel Corporation in 1920, the government abandoned its appeal in the *Can* case.[161]

Did later developments in the industry warrant the court's optimism about the power of existing competition and the development of potential competition? Did the industry become workably competitive? To answer these questions an analysis of the industry's structure, conduct, and performance since the 1916 decision is necessary.

Structure

The American Can Company today is a far larger concern than it was when the court refused to dissolve it. In 1913 its total sales were

157. *Id.* at 901.
158. *Id.* at 903.
159. United States v. American Can Co., 234 Fed. 1019, 1021 (D. Md. 1916) (decree).
160. *Ibid.*
161. Commerce Clearing House, *The Federal Antitrust Laws with Summary of Cases,* 1890–1951 (1952), p. 104.

The Rule of Reason and Monopoly

$39,000,000;[162] in 1954 they were $652,000,000,[163] an increase of 1,572 per cent. Its share of total domestic production increased from about one-third in 1913 to over 40 per cent in 1946, and in that year it sold 46.4 per cent of all the cans sold in the United States.[164] Its total assets grew from $30,500,000 in 1901 [165] to $432,000,000 in 1953.[166] Except for the sale of $69,000,000 in debentures and $25,000,000 of common stock, since 1939 American has financed its expansion by the investment of retained earnings.[167]

But the can industry has grown tremendously since 1913, and some companies have expanded more rapidly than American Can. First among its rivals is the Continental Can Company. In 1904 one of the organizers of American took the initiative in organizing Continental, when he "and several others decided to break away from the combine" and bought the patents of one of the few canmaking machinery companies not controlled by American.[168] In 1913 Continental produced approximately one-eighth of the cans produced for sale in the United States—one-fourth as many as American. Its sales totalled $7,185,000.[169] By 1954 they totalled $616,-000,000,[170] an increase of 8,700 per cent, and they equalled 92.9 per cent of American's total sales. Together these two companies in 1946 accounted for 80 per cent of all cans made for sale in the United States;[171] in 1954 they accounted for 71 per cent of the industry's nearly $1,400,000,000 sales.[172]

American and Continental have in recent years met the rivalry of four medium-sized companies, National Can Corporation, Pacific Can Com-

---

162. Charles H. Hession, *Competition in the Metal Food Container Industry 1916–1946* (Columbia University thesis, Brooklyn, 1948), p. 39.

163. *Standard & Poor's Industry Surveys*, "Containers," C4–10 (April 21, 1955).

164. United States v. American Can Co., 87 F. Supp. 18, 21–22 (N.D. Cal. 1949).

165. American Can paid about $23,500,000 for the ninety-five plants turned over to it "on the day after it was organized." United States v. American Can Co., 230 Fed. 859, 870 (D. Md. 1916). "The promoters were to furnish $7,000,000 cash, or, in all, in stock and money they were to lay out $30,500,000 for which they received $39,000,000 preferred and $39,000,000 of common stock." *Id.* at 873. Most of the new company's cash went into the purchase of stocks of merchandise in the plants it took over, and "it really began life without a free dollar to its name, . . ." *Id.* at 874.

166. *Moody's Industrials*, 1954, pp. 1733–36.

167. *Ibid.*

168. Robert Sheehan, "Continental Can's Big Push," *Fortune*, April 1955, p. 121.

169. Hession, *Competition in the Metal Food Container Industry 1916–1946*, at 39.

170. *Standard & Poor's Industry Surveys*, "Containers," C4–11 (April 21, 1955).

171. United States v. American Can Co., 87 F. Supp. 18, 22 (N.D. Cal. 1949).

172. *Standard & Poor's Industry Surveys*, "Containers," C4–5 (April 21, 1955).

Workable Competition and Antitrust Policy

pany (which merged with National in December 1954),[173] Crown Cork and Seal Company (which in December 1953 merged with its wholly owned subsidiary, Crown Can Company), and Heekin Can Company, all producing both packers' and general line cans.[174] In 1946 National, Pacific, Crown, and Heekin together accounted for only 13.6 per cent of the total can sales in the United States;[175] with American and Continental they accounted for 93.6 per cent. Threescore or more minor companies, most of them producing only general line cans, accounted for the remaining 6.4 per cent.[176] Those that produce packers' cans frequently do so for a single canning company, to which they are a sort of satellite.

That two companies accounted for approximately 80 per cent of the cans sold in the United States in 1946 and four others for most of the remainder, does not reveal adequately the significance of structure to competition in the sale of cans. Because cans are bulky and transportation costs relatively heavy, they are generally sold in local or regional markets from plants located close to their customers. American, with fifty-eight widely scattered can factories,[177] sells in all United States markets and in Canadian markets as well. Continental—and only Continental—with forty-one can factories,[178] challenges American's leadership in most of these markets. American has supplied virtually the entire sardine canning in-

---

173. National Can Corporation purchased the capital stock of Pacific Can Company at $28.57 a share. The merger combined twelve plants expected to have a total annual sales volume of more than $80,000,000. N.Y. Times, Dec. 24, 1954, p. 20, col. 2.

174. Packers' cans, sometimes called sanitary cans, are closed by machines and are used in the packing of fruits and vegetables. General line cans embrace a large number of specialized cans, the most important being those used in canning coffee, shortening, beer, motor oil, and chemicals. Although American is the major manufacturer of cans for beer, coffee, shortening, and meat, conditions of entry and economies of scale in the making of general line cans permit small manufacturers to get into this sector of the industry more easily than into the making of packers' cans.

175. United States v. American Can Co., 87 F. Supp. 18, 22 (N.D. Cal. 1949).

176. *Id.* at 22 n. 9. Sheehan, *supra* note 168, at 122, places the number of small, regional canmakers operating today at "eighty-odd." Standard & Poor's say there are approximately 100 active companies in the metal can field, "about one-third of which are packers operating captive plants." *Standard & Poor's Industry Surveys,* "Containers," C4–5 (April 21, 1955).

177. In addition to its metal container plants American operates three fiber can and package plants and eight factories for the manufacture and repair of canmaking machinery. *Moody's Industrials, 1954,* p. 1734.

178. Continental also has fourteen fiber and paper container plants, nine bag and flexible package material plants, three crown cap plants, two defense plants, one plastic plant, and eight factories for the manufacture and repair of canmaking machinery. *Id.* at 2159.

The Rule of Reason and Monopoly

dustry in Maine from its plant at Lubec.[179] In Utah and Hawaii American has a complete monopoly, and in Alaska it has 80 per cent of the business.[180] In California the National-Pacific combine is the only substantial rival of American and Continental, and in the Pacific Northwest, American and Continental meet no effective competition.[181]

Canmaking is highly concentrated, but canmakers meet no similar concentration on the buying side of the market. They sell packers' cans to thousands of food canners. These are widely distributed thoughout the country, with a tendency to cluster around the production center of the crop they pack. Few are large enough to exert any influence on the price of cans, but some large buyers have been able to get cans on better terms than their smaller rivals. In 1941 American's fifteen largest purchasers bought only about one-third (in dollar value) of all the cans it sold; six companies bought about 42 per cent of the packers' cans American sold.[182] Continental's selling was probably less concentrated. Three of the country's four largest canners packed only 13 per cent of the country's canned vegetables and 30 per cent of its canned fruit in 1937.[183] Thousands of other canners accounted for the balance. Decentralization in food canning suggests that countervailing power affords inadequate protection against such power as the two big canmakers may have.

But entry into canmaking is relatively easy. Canmaking on an economical scale requires a relatively small amount of capital.[184] Control of neither patents nor canmaking machinery affords a serious obstacle to entry.[185]

179. Hession, "The Tin Can Industry," in *The Structure of American Industry*, ed. Walter Adams (rev. ed.; New York: Macmillan, 1954), p. 409.
180. United States v. American Can Co., 87 F. Supp. 18, 23 (N.D. Cal. 1949).
181. Hession, "The Tin Can Industry," in *The Structure of American Industry*, at 409.
182. These calculations are based on data appearing in Professor James W. McKie's study of the metal container industry which has been published since the first appearance of this paper. See *Tin Cans and Tin Plate* (Cambridge: Harvard University Press, 1959), tables 20 and 21, p. 107. The data are from Exhibits 63 and 3124, United States v. American Can Co., 87 F. Supp. 18 (N.D. Cal. 1949).
183. Hession, "The Tin Can Industry," in *The Structure of American Industry*, at 410.
184. According to McKie's study, *supra* note 182, a general line can plant with eight production lines and an annual capacity of 500,000,000 cans would cost about $7,000,000, including land, buildings, machinery, and lithographing equipment. A packers' can plant not requiring lithographing equipment would no doubt cost less but because of seasonal variation in demand would probably produce only half as many cans.
185. No basic patents block entry, but the leading producers have many improvement patents—American's and Continental's running into the hundreds. Crown Can Company apparently had little difficulty in getting the necessary machinery when it went into business in 1936. Hession credited an executive of American

Workable Competition and Antitrust Policy

On the other hand, while the technological optimum is relatively small, a firm with several plants so located that cross-shipments are not exorbitant can more readily meet the seasonal demands of its customers than can single-plant firms. Moreover, the firm large enough to engage in research in canmaking and can using has a distinct advantage over the smaller firm. Service to canners and the development of cans for new uses are important functions of the larger canmakers. But the principal obstacle to the growth of smaller firms has been the conduct of the large ones.

Conduct

In 1916 the district court found that the American Can Company had discontinued such of its conduct as reflected an intent to monopolize. As the court put it, "[N]obody in the trade feels that defendant is hurting anybody, or for a number of years past has hurt anybody, or has tried to." [186]

Yet as previously stated, American Can's superior bargaining power had enabled it to get secret rebates from the American Sheet and Tin Plate Company in buying tin plate.[187] The cost of tin plate is the largest single item of expense in making cans, constituting approximately 65 per cent of the total cost. American Can's secret rebate amounted to around 64 cents on the tin plate required to make 1,000 3-pound packers' cans. This, as the court put, was "far from negligible" and in the competitive struggle "might well have proved a decisive factor." [188] But the court found that "the preferential ended in April, 1913, some seven months before this suit was brought." [189] Despite the court's finding, two decades later negotiations on the Steel Code under the National Recovery Administration revealed that American Can was again receiving a secret concession—7½ per cent—in buying tin plate from Carnegie-Illinois Steel Corporation (American Sheet and Tin Plate's successor and a United States Steel Corporation subsidiary).[190]

Can with saying that no other can manufacturer really needs American's patents. They have their own. Hession, *Competition in the Metal Food Container Industry 1916–1946*, at 169.

186. United States v. American Can Co., 230 Fed. 859, 897 (D. Md. 1916).
187. American's top executives had taken great pains to conceal its favored treatment not only from the trade but from other company executives as well. Only two of them were in on it. *TNEC Hearings*, pt. 20, at 10789.
188. United States v. American Can Co., 230 Fed. 859, 875 (D. Md. 1916).
189. *Id.* at 885.
190. *TNEC Hearings*, pt. 20, at 10777–78. When the code of fair competition for the steel industry made this discount applicable to the trade generally, American Can insisted that under its contract with Carnegie-Illinois it was entitled to a further

The Rule of Reason and Monopoly

While American Can was receiving confidential discounts from the "official" price of tin plate, it was tying its can prices to published tin plate prices.[191] Each year Carnegie-Illinois and American Can negotiated the official price, which became the price at which Carnegie-Illinois and other tin plate companies offered tin plate to all other buyers. Other large canmakers followed American Can's lead in tying tin can prices to tin plate prices. American Can in this way for many years was the price leader. The smaller canmaking companies, whose service to canners is far less adequate, customarily sold at slightly lower prices. Continental, though generally selling at prices identical with those of American, did not always rely on its independent discretion in doing so. In truth, at times it has conspired with American in fixing prices, allocating customers, dividing markets, and assigning fields of production. On June 26, 1946, a federal grand jury indicted both American and Continental and seven of their officers on a charge of criminal conspiracy.[192] All the defendants pleaded *nolo contendere* and on January 28, 1947, paid maximum fines under the Sherman Act.

Two years later a district court in civil proceedings against American and Continental concluded:

> The pattern of evidence herein suggests more than a following on the part of Continental of the prices fixed and established by American. . . . American and Continental, through their officers, agents, and servants, did directly agree to fix prices. This is manifest from the evidence, as well as the pattern of the price lists which appeared in the exhibits.[193]

In reaching this conclusion the court quoted Justice Douglas' characterization of such arrangements as "monopoly competition"—"a regime of friendly alliances, of quick and easy accommodation of prices even without the benefit of trade associations, of what Brandeis said was euphemistically called 'cooperation.' "[194]

---

discount of 7½%. When the steel company rejected this interpretation, American Can filed suit. In an out-of-court settlement Carnegie-Illinois paid American $2,250,000. *Id.* at 10778–79.

191. Before 1939, in contracts with its customers American Can stated the price for each standard size of packers' cans and established a scale of differentials for increasing or decreasing can prices with each 10c. change in Carnegie-Illinois' official price per base box of 100-pound coke plate, 14" x 20", 112 sheets to the box, f.o.b. mill, Pittsburgh, Pa. *TNEC Hearings*, pt. 20, at 10763.

192. United States v. American Can Co., Cr. No. 30323-S (N.D. Cal. June 26, 1946).

193. United States v. American Can Co., 87 F. Supp. 18, 33–34 (N.D. Cal. 1949).

194. Standard Oil Co. v. United States, 337 U.S. 293, 318 (1949), quoted in United States v. American Can Co., *supra* note 193, at 33.

Workable Competition and Antitrust Policy

While serving as a price leader in the industry, American Can engaged in other practices inconsistent with workable competition. Fifteen months after the court had refused to destroy "so finely adjusted" an industrial machine, a Federal Trade Commission investigation revealed that American Can was requiring the lessees of its closing machines (which it leased but would not sell) to buy cans exclusively from it.[195] American Can agreed to eliminate the tying clause, and on April 29, 1924, the Federal Trade Commission dismissed its complaint.[196] A quarter of a century later a federal district court found that American Can was accomplishing indirectly what it had previously achieved directly by contract.[197] In leasing its closing machines American timed the lease to any customer to run concurrently with the customer's contract for the purchase of cans. In selling cans it generally contracted to supply a customer's total requirements for long periods of time (three to twenty years throughout much of American Can's existence, and a standard five years shortly before the 1949 antitrust case), and it leased closing machines only to its own customers. American Can's executives coached its salesmen to include no tying clause in a lease but to make certain that the terminable dates for a customer's lease and for its requirements contract should be the same. If a customer did not renew its purchase contract, American Can did not renew its lease. Most of American Can's closing machines were not protected by patents, and with a slight adjustment could be used to close cans made by other manufacturers; and so American charged below-cost rentals for its machines, in order to foreclose competition from other machinery makers and to keep its lessees content with its system of tying the leases to its long-term requirements contracts.[198] In this way American Can continued to be the sole

195. Apparently the FTC did not publish a report on its 1917 investigation of American Can. The district court described its outcome in United States v. American Can Co., 87 F. Supp. 18, 25 (N.D. Cal. 1949).

196. The complaint, issued May 1, 1918, had also charged American Can with discriminating in price and using long-term contracts to stifle competition. The Commission did not assign reasons for dismissing it. The American Can Co., 7 F.T.C. 541 (1924).

197. United States v. American Can Co., 87 F. Supp. 18 (N.D. Cal. 1949). Statements of fact in the rest of the paragraph are based on this opinion.

198. The court found that this practice "has tended to restrict the market for closing machine manufacturers and has limited the number of concerns engaged in this business." United States v. American Can Co., 87 F. Supp. 18, 24 (N.D. Cal. 1949). The court quoted the government's brief for the point that of the thirty-four canmakers named as "competitors" of American Can in the trial examiner's report on the facts in the Federal Trade Commission's 1924 proceedings, see note 196 *supra*, only six "are now in existence, a mortality rate of 82%." United States v. American Can Co., *supra* at 22 n. 9.

The Rule of Reason and Monopoly

supplier of most of its customers, and in addition made it difficult for new canmakers to get into business and for those already in it to grow.[199]

The conduct of the leading firms has made it difficult for other can sellers to grow. Have can buyers fared better? Lawsuits against American Can reveal that by discriminating among its customers in pricing and servicing cans it has placed small canners at a disadvantage. It has favored large buyers by secret discounts, has loaned them its closing machines without charge, and has granted them bonuses and special allowances. The courts have found that its preferential prices were not justified by differences in costs nor made in good faith to meet competition.[200] Such practices reflect in part the greater buying power of the large canners, who continuously hold over their suppliers the threat of making their own cans [201] and who with Continental's growth have been able to play Continental against American Can. After court proceedings exposed American's discriminatory practices and some of the injured parties collected treble damages, American tried to bring its practices within the law. At any rate, it established quantity discounts and made them available to any buyer who qualified; but by basing its discounts on annual cumulative purchases it placed them beyond the reach of small buyers, and in 1949 the district court held this practice unlawful.

On the whole, American Can's conduct since the 1916 decision has scarcely justified the court's optimism about the restoration of a free market. What about its performance?

Performance

By negotiating the price of tin plate annually and tying the price of tin cans to it, American Can made the price of tin cans relatively stable: tin

---

199. The court concluded that "the five year requirements contracts and closing machine leases unreasonably restrain trade in violation of the Sherman Act. The evidence discloses that competitors have been foreclosed from a substantial market by the contracts and leases." *Id.* at 29.

200. George Van Camp & Sons Co. v. American Can Co., 278 U.S. 245 (1929); American Can Co. v. Ladoga Canning Co., 44 F.2d 763 (7th Cir. 1930); Bruce's Juices, Inc. v. American Can Co., 87 F. Supp. 985 (S.D. Fla. 1949), *aff'd*, 187 F.2d 919 (5th Cir.), *cert. dismissed*, 342 U.S. 875 (1951); Russellville Canning Co. v. American Can Co., 87 F. Supp. 484 (W.D. Ark. 1949), *rev'd*, 191 F.2d 38 (8th Cir. 1951) (plaintiff failed to establish ascertainable damage proximately resulting from discriminations).

201. Among the large packers who now make their cans are Campbell Soup, the country's third largest canmaker, Heinz, Pet Milk, Carnation Co., Sherwin-Williams, and Texas Co. *Standard & Poor's Industry Surveys*, "Containers," C4–5 (April 21, 1955).

can prices have customarily remained unchanged throughout the calendar year and sometimes for considerably longer periods.[202]

Stability in can prices throughout the canning season eliminates risk and speculation in buying cans and contributes to a more orderly marketing of tin cans and of canned foods, but cyclical and secular stability in can prices has no such virtue. Stable prices in the face of long-run changes in demand and cost functions interfere with the effectiveness of the pricing mechanism. They tend to place the burden of readjustments to changing demand-supply relationships largely on the canners, to the benefit of the canmakers. Tin cans cost almost as much as the food they contain: in 1918, for example, canners paid 33 cents for a dozen No. 2 cans, but they paid only 34 cents for the corn to fill them and 36 cents for the same amount of string beans.[203] Between 1929 and their depression lows the wholesale prices of canned vegetables and fruits fell 25 per cent and 40 per cent respectively, while between 1929 and 1933 American Can's published prices for No. 2 cans declined less than 13 per cent. By 1934 canned vegetable prices had risen about 6 per cent above their 1932 level and canned fruit prices about 22 per cent; the price of No. 2 cans had risen to within less than half of 1 per cent of the 1929 level. The prices of canned fruits and vegetables fell sharply in 1935 and 1937 and reached their low points in 1938; in 1938 American's published price of No. 2 cans rose slightly.[204] Competition among food growers and food canners has traditionally been very effective, and in the absence of governmental controls neither group has had a mechanism for shielding itself from the impact of market forces. Such price behavior not only placed canners at a sharp economic disadvantage; it no doubt contributed to the high mortality rate in the canning industry.[205]

202. They were stable throughout 1924 and 1925 and at a slightly lower level throughout 1926 and 1927; they dropped again in 1928 but showed little change through 1929, 1930, and 1931; they were lower in 1932 and reached their depression low point in 1933. They were sharply higher by 1934 and remained unchanged until the end of 1936. In 1937 they fell to their 1933 level, at which level after minor fluctuations they were stabilized by wartime controls. Hession, "The Tin Can Industry," in *The Structure of American Industry*, at 423.

203. Federal Trade Commission, *Report on Canned Foods* (1918), tables 4, 8, pp. 26, 30.

204. Hession, *Competition in the Metal Food Container Industry 1916–1946*, charts VI, VII, at 222, 227. Apparently embarrassed by the disparity between their earnings and those of their customers, see note 205 *infra*, canmakers granted their customers "rebates equivalent to 25 cents a box on tin plate purchases for 1938." *Poor's Industry and Investment Surveys*, "Container Manufacturing," C3–8 (Dec. 19, 1940).

205. While some canners had prospered, a survey by the National Canners As-

The Rule of Reason and Monopoly

But the canners were not the only ones to suffer from the failure of can prices to respond more promptly to market forces. Between 1934 and 1939 out of every dollar spent at wholesale for canned tomatoes, corn, and peas in No. 2 cans, from 22.5 to 40.6 cents went to can manufacturers.[206] Assuming that on the average the cost of cans represents 30 per cent of the total cost of canned foods, and taking 1939 consumption as a normal year, a 3 per cent reduction in the price of cans if passed on to consumers would have reduced their living costs by $6,000,000 a year.[207] Plagued as the country was by unemployment and low national income during the 1930's, such a price reduction would without doubt have contributed to the general welfare.

While canners and consumers were adversely affected by the conduct of American Can, the company fared relatively well. During the ten years from 1930 through 1939 its net revenue averaged 9.7 per cent on its capitalization; and although between 1929 and 1932 American's rate of earnings declined by more than 50 per cent, it earned over 6 per cent on its capitalization.[208] During the same period the net income of 728 industrial companies declined 94 per cent, and many of them suffered severe losses.[209] During the generally more prosperous years 1922–1928 inclusive

sociation reveals that by 1938 more than half the canners in business at the beginning of 1929 had disappeared. The study recognized that not all disappearances represented liquidation. Some were due to changes of name, death of owners, mergers, and the like. But it concluded that the actual annual mortality rate in the years covered was about 7%. National Canners Association, Some Phases of the Canning Industry, Supplement to the Information Letter, Jan. 3, 1942, quoted in Hession, *Competition in the Metal Food Container Industry 1916–1946*, at 254 n. 69. *Fortune* in 1934 in commenting on the divergence of price behavior had the following to say:

American and Continental make cans, but they *never* fill them. That is the canner's job. And the canner is at present an extremely depressed individual. Van Camp's is in bankruptcy. Hawaiian Pineapple has been reorganized. . . . Libby, McNeil & Libby, operating sixty-three canneries, lost $6,248,000 for the year ending March 4, 1933. Hundreds of small canners have gone out of business. But the can maker is still prosperous. . . . [T]he two big container corporations . . . are embarrassed because they are so much more prosperous than their customers and none release sales figures for fear that the customers might want them to reduce their prices.

"Profits in Cans," Fortune, April 1934, pp. 77–78.

206. *TNEC Hearings*, pt. 20, exhibit No. 1402, at 10989.

207. Computed from data in U.S. Dep't of Commerce, *Statistical Abstract of the United States* (1943), pp. 648, 695. The wholesale value of canned food produced in 1939 amounted to roughly $700,000,000.

208. These calculations are based on Hession, *Competition in the Metal Food Container Industry 1916–1946*, table 26, at 245.

209. *Id.* at 160.

Workable Competition and Antitrust Policy

American earned at a slightly higher rate, 10.1 per cent. This compared with an average return of 9.7 per cent for 2,046 manufacturing corporations.[210]

An examination of American's contribution to the advance of technology reveals a better picture. It has taken its research opportunities seriously and has improved both the making and the use of cans. It opened its first laboratory in 1906 with a research staff of 35 persons. In 1926 it launched its central laboratory at Maywood, Illinois, operating on a far larger scale. By developing the Johnson double-seamer and the so-called inverted type of lock and lap seam it made the manufacture of cans almost wholly automatic.[211] By substituting the "roll form" body-maker for the "wing form," American increased can output per machine from 150 cans a minute to 200, later to 300, and still later to 400.[212] Cooperating with steel companies, its research staff has greatly improved the quality of tin plate. It has encouraged its employees to perfect new ideas: in 1943 alone they obtained more than 100 patents, to that date an all-time record.[213] Its service to canners has been a distinctive feature of its sales technique. Its sales engineering division has assisted in installing the company's machines in customers' plants and in designing the most efficient plant layout. In short, American has been a pacemaker in technology.[214] Only Continental has rivaled it in this field.

But in evaluating its conduct and over-all performance it is difficult to see how economists could characterize the industry as having been workably competitive. Those who know it best have not done so.[215] Nor did a federal

---

210. *Id.* at 159; Ralph C. Epstein, *Industrial Profits in the United States* (New York: National Bureau of Economic Research, 1934), p. 56.

211. Hession, *Competition in the Metal Food Container Industry 1916–1946*, at 277.

212. *Id.* at 261.

213. *Id.* at 171.

214. It still is. When the Korean hostilities and the government's stockpiling led to shortages of tin, American Can developed special coatings which permanently replaced tin in some applications. In 1954 it reported that the motor oil industry was using almost exclusively cans containing no tin or solder. *Standard & Poor's Industry Surveys*, "Containers," C4–2 (April 21, 1955).

215. Hession in discussing "the record in retrospect" in 1954 stated: "Our study discloses that Continental Can has grown, but American Can has not declined relatively, so that a condition of near-duopoly has been created. . . . [P]rice leadership and price stabilization . . . has [sic] denied canners and consumers most of the savings made possible by technological progress." Hession, "The Tin Can Industry," in *The Structure of American Industry*, at 432. Hession recognized obstacles to entry as having been one of the principal obstacles to workable competition and characterized the 1950 antitrust decrees as "a major effort to correct this condition." *Id.* at 441. About the prospects he expressed a wait-and-see attitude.

court in 1949. The court recognized that American as price leader dominated the can market and that the preferential treatment given big buyers—together with American's long-term requirements contracts and its practice of coordinating and timing its closing machine leases with its purchase contracts—had served as an effective obstacle to entry and had blocked expansion by small companies.[216]

The 1950 Antitrust Decrees

The consequences of the 1950 decrees against both Continental and American [217] seem to have demonstrated the validity of the district court's findings. The decrees prohibited American and Continental from offering buyers annual cumulative volume discounts or discriminating among buyers except on a basis of actual cost savings; from entering into requirements contracts extending beyond a year; and from conditioning the sale or lease of closing machines on the use of the lessor's cans directly or by any subterfuge. The court also ordered each defendant to sell such closing machines as it then had, giving preference to existing lessees, and any it might build within ten years. According to McKie the industry has promptly taken advantage of the opportunities that the decrees have opened to it, and the industry's performance reflects its greater freedom. He finds that by the middle of 1954 canners had bought more than 75 per cent of the closing machines they held under lease from American and Continental in 1950; that the abandonment of leasing will broaden markets for the independent closing machine manufacturers; that exclusive supplier-customer relations are breaking down; that open-order purchasing has greatly increased; that small firms are now getting a part of the business previously done by the large suppliers and their market position has thereby been greatly strengthened; that tin plate prices are becoming more flexible and open-order purchasing of tin plate has increased; that rivalry between American and Continental has intensified; that American's price

---

McKie's analysis of developments since the decree is more optimistic. He concludes, "A forecast of workable competition appears to be justified." McKie, "The Decline of Monopoly in the Metal Container Industry," 45 Am. Econ. Rev. 499, 508 (1955).

216. United States v. American Can Co., 87 F. Supp. 18 (N.D. Cal. 1949).

217. Continental on June 26, 1950, agreed to a consent decree imposing substantially the same prohibitions on it as those imposed on American. United States v. Continental Can Co., 1950–1951 Trade Cas. ¶ 62680 (N.D. Cal. 1950). The decree against American was filed June 22, 1950. United States v. American Can Co., 1950–1951 Trade Cas. ¶ 62679 (N. D. Cal. 1950).

Workable Competition and Antitrust Policy

leadership has become wholly barometric; and that the inability of the dominant firms to give large canners preferential treatment is making the threat of integration a more effective check against their exploiting the market.[218]

All economists may not share McKie's optimism,[219] but few are likely to challenge the implication of his analysis—that until the relief afforded by the court in 1950 the industry had not been workably competitive. Whatever its future, canmaking as judged by the criteria applied in this article —structure, conduct, performance—had not met the requirements of workable competition. The industry's oligopolistic structure contributed to practices that led to economically unacceptable performance.[220]

Conclusions

If the foregoing analysis is sound, application of the principle of workable competition under the rule of reason would obligate the courts to examine all facts relevant to determining whether a combination hinders the operation of market forces or whether a firm is monopolizing a market; but having found either to be the case, the courts would have no discretion in assessing the social desirability of such hindrances or in passing on

---

218. McKie, *supra* note 215, at 506–07.

219. Hession, writing about a year earlier than McKie, was more restrained in his evaluation of the significance of the decree. Hession, "The Tin Can Industry," in *The Structure of American Industry*, at 437–41. So was *Standard & Poor's Industry Surveys*, "Containers," C4–5 (April 21, 1955):

> The possibility that newcomers may make important inroads into the business of large can companies is small. On the one hand, a large part of the business is done on the basis of contracts, and, on the other, capping and sealing machinery are leased by the companies which supply the cans, with users having the right of purchase since June, 1950. In addition, plants of existing concerns generally are strategically located in important consuming areas.

McKie of course did not base his optimism on the probable entry of newcomers other than through backward integration of canners.

220. Whether the public interest would be better served by dissolution of American and Continental, both of which might be brought within the prohibitions of the Sherman Act should Congress see fit to incorporate the rule of reason and the principle of workable competition in it, is a matter of conjecture, and one's conjecture about it is apt to be greatly influenced by his preconceptions. I believe that dissolution would re-establish an industrial structure more consistent with the objectives of the Sherman Act. McKie, although recognizing that "several firms could have been fashioned out of either of the leaders without an appreciable loss of efficiency," and that thereafter "the market would in time have enforced a high degree of competition," perhaps correctly concludes that under existing law a monopoly charge could not be sustained; and as indicated above, he believes the 1950 decrees will provide adequate remedies. McKie, *supra* note 215, at 507.

The Rule of Reason and Monopoly

the reasonableness of arrangements designed to control markets. Such an obligation, so restricted, *might* have resulted in decisions adverse to the corporations here considered. It *might* have led to a more, not a less, vigorous antitrust policy. It *might* have brought within the purview of the Sherman Act combinations that the 1911 decisions placed beyond its reach.

But might not even the application of these principles still leave beyond the law's reach market structures that are dominated by neither a combination nor a monopoly but that when judged by the number and relative size of firms and their conduct and performance do not meet the tests of workable competition? Some firms operating within an oligopolistic market structure might not be regarded as combinations, except perhaps in an "archeological" sense; nor as monopolies within the meaning of Section 2 of the Sherman Act as interpreted by Judge Hand in the *Aluminum* case. They may have been created originally by combining rival firms, but their growth in recent years may have been primarily by internal expansion. How can such firms in an industry that does not meet the tests of workable competition as herein developed be brought within the scope of the Act?

The courts, tending to look to conduct alone, have sometimes been reluctant to disturb restrictive structures and arrangements because their origins are "archeological." But this analysis has suggested that oligopolistic structure, as a continuously operative fact, may be conducive to conduct and performance that are inconsistent with the objectives of the Sherman Act. For example, the outstanding contemporary feature of the steel industry's structure—the existence of the United States Steel Corporation—came into being many years ago, when the Steel Corporation was formed by the combination of numerous originally independent firms. The Steel Corporation's overtowering size in relation to other companies in the industry, and the relative fewness of its rivals, have contributed to its leadership in pricing steel and to its rivals' acceptance of that leadership; to the collective and systematic use of basing point pricing; to collaboration in determining the average costs of extras and in pricing them. Not only has the structure of the industry facilitated these practices, but the practices have contributed to unacceptable industry performance. A consideration of all the circumstances at work in an industry—as the rule of reason would require—should lead the courts to attach great significance to the continuing interaction of structure and conduct in determining the legality of the practices pursued and in shaping remedies for an industry found not to be workably competitive. That the structure rests on old combina-

Workable Competition and Antitrust Policy

tions should not hallow it in the light of a law designed to assure competitive conditions here and now.

A more realistic interpretation of the Sherman Act's prohibition of conspiracies in restraint of trade and of attempts to monopolize provides yet another way of bringing oligopolistic structures that do not meet the tests of workable competition within the Act's reach. What business firms are up to is relevant in determining whether they violate the law. If the sellers in a market of few firms adopt a strategy designed to preserve the market's oligopolistic character by blocking entry and handicapping rivals, or to substitute collective patterns of behavior for independent decision-making, clearly they should be found to violate Section 1 of the Sherman Act, as engaging in a conspiracy in restraint of trade. The courts might properly find a conspiracy from the total configuration of the contracts and practices employed even though no one of them was illegal per se. Likewise if a dominant firm pursues a course of conduct as a result of which imports of competing products are restricted; if patent infringement suits are used to bring would-be competitors to terms; and if patent license agreements become the means of dividing markets, the courts might properly find in such acts an attempt to monopolize within Section 2 of the Sherman Act. In doing so, of course, they must apply a less rigid conception of monopoly than that advanced in *Aluminum*—the firm's control of any given percentage of the relevant market. Oligopoly is not necessarily incompatible with workable competition; but when the facts establish that it is, it should be treated like monopoly.

Where structure exerts a continuing pernicious influence on conduct, fines and injunctions against law violators may prove inadequate to insure workable competition. A change in structure may be called for. Dissolution proceedings might pave the way to more acceptable industry performance. Such proceedings should be aimed at creating not an atomistic industrial structure, but the sort of structure that would have arisen had the firms in the industry not resorted to competition-suppressing tactics. Penalizing bad conduct is unlikely to reform it where an industry's structure makes it both effective and profitable. In such situations the courts should help establish a new architecture in which restrictive practices are unlikely to be inevitable or even to flourish.

It may be difficult to attain an interpretation and application of the concept of workable competition as it has been expounded here. Amendment of the law is unlikely to be the solution: many of the advocates of change apparently hope for a gentler, not a more rigorous, application of the statutes to big business. The concept of workable competition is vague,

The Rule of Reason and Monopoly

and differences among experts as to its meaning are inevitable. As Mason has suggested, the preconceptions of the analyst as well as the facts may influence his judgment on the competitive workability of any particular arrangement.[221]

If amendment of the Sherman Act is an inadequate solution, judicial broadening of the Act to include the concept of workable competition, however desirable it may seem in theory, may not prove in fact a more promising remedy. As has been pointed out, without any change in the statute the doctrine of workable competition is creeping into the decisions. This is strikingly evident in Judge Leahy's decision in the *Cellophane* case, which reveals how a superficial understanding of the concept and its application to a particular set of facts may defeat the objectives of the Sherman Act. If this decision becomes a precedent, it will be difficult to establish the existence of monopoly in any industry confronted by rival products that for some uses may be substitutable and among which a vigorous rivalry appears to exist.

Judges no less than economists may be influenced as much by the totality of their experience and by the institutional matrix in which they formulate their ideas as they are by the logic of a particular situation. Judges and economists live in an economy of big business units, and most of them have learned to like it. Any proposal to disturb these "finely adjusted industrial machines" would encounter serious institutional obstacles. The American private enterprise system in the past decade and a half has earned the admiration and envy of the civilized world, and many Americans have accepted the easy explanation that giant industrial units are responsible for the gigantic achievements of the American economy. This belief is rapidly becoming a part of the American folklore. But in truth, the causes of the striking technological progress in this country and of the high standards of living it has brought are complex. The spirit of enterprise, the bold initiative of business leaders in a general atmosphere of freedom, a technology enriched by the unhampered achievements of scientists and engineers throughout a half-century or more, and the expansive force of deficit financing occasioned by hot wars and a continuing cold war, have all contributed to it. In short, the recent achievement of American capitalism is a phenomenon larger than the firms that have played a role in it. The contemporary bigness of firms is perhaps as much an effect as a cause of this achievement.

221. "It seems probable that individual judgments will always be influenced to some extent by ideological considerations." Mason, "The Current Status of the Monopoly Problem in the United States," 62 Harv. L. Rev. 1265, 1283 (1949).

Workable Competition and Antitrust Policy

I believe, although I cannot prove, that the economic achievements of the last fifteen years would have been in no way impaired and that economic opportunities would have broadened and multiplied had business units been somewhat smaller and more numerous—if the economy had boasted more big firms but fewer industrial giants. And I believe that applying the concept of workable competition as herein expounded in enforcing the antitrust laws would have contributed to such a development. Many people will reject the thesis that giantism in business is not the essential element in America's economic progress—it will be least acceptable to representatives of the industrial giants themselves. "What a dust we raise," said the fly on the chariot wheel.

4

The Attorney General's Committee's Report: The Businessman's Guide through Antitrust

THE PRESERVATION OF A COMPETITIVE ECONOMY

SEVENTY YEARS HAVE ELAPSED since Congress enacted the Sherman Antitrust Act with only a single senator dissenting.[1] Throughout this period neither Congress nor the courts have abandoned the law's central objective—the preservation of a competitive economy. Time has brought vast changes in the size and texture of the American population, the structure of industry and the pattern of its ownership, the complexity of technology and the productivity of machines, the theory of competition and the behavior of business rivals. But through it all— with only occasional aberrations—policymakers and business leaders have proclaimed their desire to preserve a free private enterprise economy. Not all those who have clung steadfastly to this ideal have recognized the Sherman Act as a proper instrument for its realization. A prominent corporation lawyer prophesied soon after its adoption that the restrictive provisions of the Sherman Act would drive capital from the country.[2] Many policymakers and students of law after brief experience with the

Note: Reprinted from the *Georgetown Law Journal,* Vol. 44, No. 1 (November 1955).

1. Senator Blodgett of New Jersey voted against the Sherman Act. 21 Cong. Rec. 3153 (1890). Although he did not state his reasons, he may have felt the inconsistency between its objectives and New Jersey's 1889 legislation permitting corporations organized in that state to hold stock in other corporations. Laws of the State of New Jersey, 1889, c. 265, § 4, p. 414. Mead said of this legislation: "[T]he little state of New Jersey . . . by simple act of amending its corporation law, nullified the antitrust laws of every State which had passed them." Edward S. Mead, *Trust Finance* (New York: Appleton, 1903), p. 39.

2. William D. Guthrie, "Constitutionality of the Sherman Anti-Trust Act of 1890," 11 Harv. L. Rev. 80 (1897).

Workable Competition and Antitrust Policy

law thought it inadequate to prevent monopoly,[3] and business leaders later complained to Congress that the vagueness of the Sherman Act exposed them to punishment for activities innocent in intent.[4] Dissatisfaction with the Act and its administration have at times built up such pressure that government officials could scarcely ignore it. Congress as early as 1898 established the Industrial Commission to investigate the contemporary combination movement and to recommend legislation about it.[5] In 1903 Congress created the Bureau of Corporations in the Department of Commerce and Labor to investigate "the organization, conduct, and management" of corporations and combinations in interstate commerce and to recommend legislation for the regulation of such commerce.[6] A decade later the Republican, Democratic, and Progressive parties all pledged themselves to a modification of the antitrust statutes[7] and the Democrats,

---

3. Former President Taft writing in 1914 said of the Supreme Court's decision in United States v. E. C. Knight Co., 156 U.S. 1 (1895): "The effect of the decision . . . upon the popular mind, and indeed upon Congress as well, was to discourage hope that the statute could be used to accomplish its manifest purpose and curb the great industrial trusts. . . . So strong was the impression . . . that both Mr. Olney and Mr. Cleveland concluded that the evil must be controlled through State legislation, and not through a national statute, and they said so in their communications to Congress." William H. Taft, *The Anti-Trust Act and the Supreme Court* (New York: Harper, 1914), p. 60.

4. *Hearings before the Senate Committee on Interstate Commerce Pursuant to Sen. Res. 98*, 62d Cong., 2d Sess. *passim*, especially pp. 696, 704–05, 1092–95, 1294 (1911–12).

5. The Industrial Commission's final secretary said of its purpose: "The rise of the trusts was probably the chief ground which led to its establishment. . . ." E. Dana Durand, "The United States Industrial Commission: Methods of Government Investigation," 16 Q. J. Econ. 564 (1902). The act creating the Commission was less specific; it said that the Commission was to explore means and suggest laws "in order to harmonize conflicting interests and to be equitable to the laborer, the employer, the producer, and the consumer." Act of June 18, 1898, c. 466, § 3, 30 Stat. 476.

6. Act of Feb. 14, 1903, c. 552, § 6, 32 Stat. 827.

7. The Republicans promised legislation to set up a federal trade commission and to outlaw "those specific acts that uniformly mark attempts to restrain and monopolize trade, to the end that those who honestly intend to obey the law may have a guide to their action and that those who aim to violate the law may the more surely be punished." *Republican Campaign Text Book* (1912) p. 272, quoted by Gerard C. Henderson, *The Federal Trade Commission* (New Haven: Yale University Press, 1925), p. 16. The Democrats wished to correct such evils as holding companies, interlocking directorates, stock watering, price discrimination, and "the control by any one corporation of so large a proportion of any industry as to make it a menace to competitive conditions." *Republican Campaign Text Book*, at 279, quoted by Henderson, *op. cit. supra*, at 17. The Progressives advocated establishment of a federal trade commission and the prohibition of certain "unfair trade practices." Theodore Roosevelt, *Progressive Principles*, Appendix, p. 319, quoted by Henderson, *op. cit. supra*, at 20.

The Attorney General's Committee's Report

having won the 1912 election, carried out their campaign promises by enacting the Clayton and Federal Trade Commission Acts. After the Great Depression and the disillusioning experience of the National Recovery Administration, Congress at the request of the President established the Temporary National Economic Committee to study the whole problem of industrial concentration and what should be done about it.[8] TNEC hearings and monographs filled eighty volumes; they cost the country over a million dollars.[9] Before the TNEC had made its modest recommendations for strengthening the antitrust statutes,[10] World War II necessitated a degree of cooperation among business rivals and between business and government scarcely compatible with the ideology of the statutes.

Postwar Move to Modify Antitrust Laws

The postwar period has revealed little disposition by any influential group to abandon the principles of the antitrust laws. It has, however, sparked a movement for their modification. This movement, which culminated in the Attorney General's National Committee to Study the Antitrust Laws,[11] has its origin in two developments, the one in economic thinking, the other in the interpretation and administration of the antitrust statutes. Until the early 1930's price theory, which was the core of neoclassical economics, was concerned primarily with competitive pricing. American economists had regarded monopoly as an industrial aberration, which brought an uneconomic allocation of resources and exploitation of the consumer and should be outlawed by statute or regulated by commissions. The Great Combination Movement at the turn of the century and the less spectacular merger movement of the 1920's changed the structure of American industry and eventually the thinking of economists about it. A change in the manifestation of business rivalry accompanied the change in industrial structure. In the twentieth century American businessmen have not generally sold undifferentiated products in competition with many rivals, but highly advertised products for which they

---

8. Pub. Res. No. 113, 52 Stat. 705 (1938).
9. *Final Report and Recommendations of the Temporary National Economic Committee*, Sen. Doc. No. 35, 77th Cong., 1st Sess. 730 (1941).
10. *Id.* at 35–40.
11. See *Report of the Attorney General's National Committee to Study the Antitrust Laws* (March 31, 1955); S. Chesterfield Oppenheim, "Highlights of the Final Report of the Attorney General's National Committee to Study the Antitrust Laws," 1 Antitrust Bulletin 6 (1955).

Workable Competition and Antitrust Policy

have built up consumer preference, frequently at great cost. The old theory of competition did not fit the facts of contemporary society, and economists became discontented with traditional doctrines. Edward Chamberlin's *The Theory of Monopolistic Competition,* published in 1933, and Joan Robinson's *The Economics of Imperfect Competition,* published the same year, were the American and the British responses to the incompatibility between neoclassical theory of economic behavior and the facts of economic life. Chamberlin created a theoretical model[12] which led him to conclude that where a few sellers of an undifferentiated product dominated a market, if rational and informed they would without collusion behave like monopolists. Where sellers, many or few, sold differentiated products, they also had some power over the market. If entry were free, business rivals would lose their power to exploit a market and eventually would be forced to sell at the average cost of production; but production costs would be above competitive levels.

The Chamberlinian doctrines, which eventually got into the textbooks —unfortunately without the rigorous qualifications to which Chamberlin had subjected them[13]—disturbed students of antitrust policy. They observed that the antitrust laws as interpreted by the courts were woefully inadequate to cope with oligopoly. Later, when certain decisions read as though the Chamberlinian doctrines were affecting the thinking of judges, they greatly disturbed business leaders. Conscious parallelism of action,[14] unabused power,[15] and general rather than specific intent[16] were disquieting concepts that seemed to constitute a threat to bigness

---

12. Chamberlin postulated a market of few sellers, a standardized product, and identical demand and cost curves known to the sellers, who seek to maximize their profits and who take account of their total influence upon price, indirect as well as direct. Chamberlin, *The Theory of Monopolistic Competition* (7th ed.; Cambridge: Harvard University Press, 1957), chap. 3.

13. Not only was Chamberlin's model a distinctly theoretical one—witness the assumptions listed in note 12 *supra*—but he sharply qualified his conclusions by pointing out the effect of each seller's uncertainty as to how and when his competitors would react to any move he might make. For example, he declared that since a seller is uncertain how soon a rival would meet a price cut, "no assumption as to the intelligence which the sellers apply to the pursuit of their maximum gain, short of omniscience, would render the outcome determinate." *Id.* at 53.

14. Triangle Conduit & Cable Co. v. Federal Trade Com'n, 168 F. 2d 175 (7th Cir. 1948), *aff'd by an equally divided court sub nom.* Clayton Mark & Co. v. Federal Trade Commission, 336 U.S. 956 (1949); *Statement of Federal Trade Commission Policy Toward Geographic Pricing Practices, for Staff Information and Guidance,* Oct. 12, 1948, corrected Oct. 21, 1948, CCH Trade Reg. Rep. ¶ 3601.

15. United States v. Aluminum Co. of America, 148 F.2d 416 (2d Cir. 1945); American Tobacco Co. v. United States, 328 U.S. 781 (1946).

16. United States v. Aluminum Co. of America, 148 F.2d 416 (2d Cir. 1945).

The Attorney General's Committee's Report

per se. Moreover, while the courts were revealing a hostile attitude toward big business, the Federal Trade Commission in administering the Robinson-Patman Act was not merely reflecting a similar attitude but was allegedly interpreting the statute to protect little businessmen rather than competitive markets.[17] The courts and the Commission appeared to be drifting away from the rule of reason [18] and to be condemning specific practices in and of themselves regardless of their effect on competition.

Workable Competition

Eventually a reaction set in against the idea that big business was synonymous with monopoly, and the economists played an important role in it. Recognizing that pure competition was an abstraction, a theoretical model of their own making designed to aid clarity in thinking and precision in exposition, they acknowledged that the theory of monopolistic competition was equally unsuited to describe actual business behavior, and they substituted a more realistic but less precise concept, that of workable competition.[19] Workable competition describes market structure and business

---

17. Thomas E. Sunderland, "Save the Sherman Act from Its 'Friends,'" *1950 Institute on Antitrust Laws and Price Regulations* (Dallas: Southwestern Legal Foundation), p. 211.

18. In 1911 a majority of the Supreme Court first incorporated in the Sherman Act the rule of reason, which it said meant, among other things, that the Act forbade only contracts and combinations that *unreasonably* restrained interstate commerce. Standard Oil Co. v. United States, 221 U.S. 1 (1911); United States v. American Tobacco Co., 221 U.S. 106 (1911). Some critics of certain court and Federal Trade Commission decisions in recent years have urged a revision of the antitrust laws to incorporate a "modernized" rule of reason. U.S. Dep't of Commerce, *Effective Competition: Report to the Secretary of Commerce by His Business Advisory Council* (1952); Oppenheim, "Federal Antitrust Legislation: Guideposts to a Revised National Antitrust Policy," 50 Mich. L. Rev. 1139 (1952); Blackwell Smith, "Effective Competition: Hypothesis for Modernizing the Antitrust Laws," 26 N.Y.U.L. Rev. 405 (1951). Under a modernized rule of reason the trier of facts would weigh the respondent's legal, economic, and social justifications for restrictions on competition in each case and arrive at a value judgment as to "whether the restrictions are reasonable or unreasonable when measured against the effects upon competition." Oppenheim, *supra* at 1160. For a fuller exposition and criticism of the modernized rule of reason, see George W. Stocking, "The Rule of Reason, Workable Competition, and Monopoly," 64 Yale L. J. 1107 (1955); Stocking, "The Rule of Reason, Workable Competition, and the Legality of Trade Association Activities," 21 U. Chi. L. Rev. 527 (1954).

19. John M. Clark, "Towards a Concept of Workable Competition," 30 Am. Econ. Rev. 241 (1940), is the pioneer work. Other expositions include Corwin D. Edwards, *Maintaining Competition* (New York: McGraw-Hill, 1949), pp. 9–10; Clair Wilcox, *Competition and Monopoly in American Industry* (TNEC Monograph No. 21, 1940); Morris A. Adelman, "Effective Competition and the Antitrust

Workable Competition and Antitrust Policy

behavior intermediate between pure competition and pure monopoly. It takes account of the facts that pure competition is not generally attainable and that pure monopoly rarely exists; and that in an industrial society unavoidably characterized by some market imperfections, not all departures from pure competition are economically unsound. Some departures that lend themselves to social control may merely compensate for others that do not. A workably competitive market is the best market situation attainable under private enterprise, and it is good enough. To determine whether any particular industry is workably competitive necessitates careful economic analysis of its structure, the behavior of the firms that comprise it, and its performance. If an industry is dynamic, if business firms are efficient, if prices respond quickly to changes in the conditions of demand and supply, if entrepreneurs pass on to consumers promptly the cost reductions that follow technological innovation, and if profits are reasonable, an industry is workably competitive regardless of the number and size of the firms that comprise it. Such in brief is the concept of workable competition.

Many economists believed that in workable competition they had found a standard by which to evaluate departures from the competitive ideal. Businessmen and their legal and economic advisors saw in workable competition, coupled with a modernized rule of reason,[20] practical criteria for judging the legality of alleged violations of the antitrust laws. The Secretary of Commerce's Business Advisory Council endorsed the concepts; Professor S. Chesterfield Oppenheim expounded them elaborately and approvingly; and Blackwell Smith and others concerned with antitrust problems urged their adoption by statutory amendment.[21]

THE ATTORNEY GENERAL'S COMMITTEE

The Attorney General's National Committee to Study the Antitrust Laws was an outgrowth of these developments. The Committee repre-

Laws," 61 Harv. L. Rev. 1289 (1948); Joe S. Bain, "Workable Competition in Oligopoly," 40 Am. Econ. Rev. (Proceedings of the American Economic Ass'n) 35 (1950); Jesse W. Markham, "An Alternative Approach to Workable Competition," 40 Am. Econ. Rev. 349 (1950); Edward S. Mason, "Methods of Developing a Proper Control of Big Business," 18 Acad. Pol. Sci. Proc. (No. 2) 40 (1939); Mason, "The Current Status of the Monopoly Problem in the United States," 62 Harv. L. Rev. 1265 (1949); George J. Stigler, "The Extent and Bases of Monopoly," 32 Am. Econ. Rev. (Supp. Pt. 2) 2, 3 (1942).
  20. See note 18 *supra*.
  21. See note 18 *supra*.

The Attorney General's Committee's Report

sented a novel if not a unique instrument for evaluating and recommending changes in federal antitrust policy. It was established by the head of the chief agency for enforcing the antitrust laws. It was a committee of experts, for the most part specialists in antitrust law, drawn from private life to serve without compensation. The Attorney General recognized that experts in antitrust were likely to have something to do with its enforcement. Most of those selected were familiar with the significance of antitrust policy from experience as well as study. Almost half were practicing lawyers who at one time or another had represented defendants in antitrust proceedings, and some of these had previously served with the Department of Justice; many were the counsel in cases pending when the Committee was established.[22] But the Committee had on its membership professors of law and of economics, as well as practicing attorneys, and the Committee's co-chairmen were careful to select men "representative of interacting viewpoints on controversial aspects of antitrust policy."[23] The Attorney General demanded only that the Committee members "be guided by the broadest viewpoint of what is best for American economy rather than what benefits may accrue to any particular industry, any specific business, or any individual reputation."[24] The Committee was chairmaned by Professor Oppenheim, a distinguished professor of law and a recognized expert in the field, and by Judge Stanley N. Barnes, a distinguished public servant who, despite a relatively brief acquaintance with antitrust problems, had won the confidence of the Antitrust Division's staff and made a creditable record in enforcing the statutes. The Committee co-chairmen saw in the affiliation of its members no hindrance to objectivity. "'Objectivity,'" they said, "requires only that they act fairly in keeping their minds open to persuasion in reaching conclusions in friendly interchange of views and in considering antitrust policy through reason-

---

22. Congressman Wright Patman listed some of the pending antitrust proceedings in which twenty-three of the forty-five practicing lawyers on the Attorney General's Committee were representing respondents, either directly or through their firms, and some of the past antitrust cases in which twenty-seven of them had represented respondents, either directly or through their firms. Statement of Congressman Wright Patman before a subcommittee of the House Committee on the Judiciary, 84th Cong., 1st Sess. Appendix A (May 10, 1955).
23. U.S. Dep't of Justice Release (mimeographed), Aug. 27, 1953, Barnes and Oppenheim, "Organization of the Attorney General's National Committee to Study the Antitrust Laws" 15, Statement prepared for delivery before American Bar Ass'n, Section on Antitrust Law, Boston, Mass.
24. U.S. Dep't of Justice Release (mimeographed), June 26, 1953, "Our Antitrust Policy" 7, Address by the Attorney General of the United States before the Judicial Conference of the Fourth Circuit, White Sulphur Springs, W. Va.

Workable Competition and Antitrust Policy

ing processes applied to antitrust objectives and ascertainable facts." [25] Nor did they find in the conflicting views of the Committee members a serious obstacle to unanimity. The final report should reflect the thinking of the Committee as a whole. By noting individual differences of opinion which the study might develop, the "analysis, conclusions and recommendations in the Final Report will . . . crystallize an evaluation of antitrust policy to which all members of the Committee have contributed." [26]

The Committee's task was "to evaluate the antitrust laws in their *fundamental aspects*" [27]—that is, to make a systematic appraisal of their effectiveness as instruments for preserving competition. The Committee was a study group, not a fact-finding body. It was not to engage in basic research but to review and analyze the materials that research had already made available in convenient form or that lay untapped in the "archives of antitrust"—"administrative and judicial records and decisions of the federal agencies." [28] From the study and thought of experts, generously performing a public service, was to flow a wisdom to guide congressmen and the courts in making the antitrust laws a more effective instrument "to preserve American free enterprise against monopoly and unfair competition." [29]

The Committee assumed its task promptly and pursued it expeditiously. The Committee took only a year and a half to analyze virtually every aspect of the antitrust statutes and to report its analysis, conclusions, and recommendations in a 393-page monograph.[30] The eight chapter headings indicate the scope of the Committee's inquiry. Chapter 1 deals with "A Policy Against 'Undue Limitations on Competitive Conditions'—Sections 1 and 2 of the Sherman Act Generally"; chapter 2 with "'Trade or Commerce . . . with Foreign Nations'"; chapter 3 with "Mergers"; chapter 4 with "Antitrust Policy in Distribution (*Principally under Sections 2 and 3 of the Clayton Act*)"; chapter 5 with "Patent-Antitrust Problems"; chapter 6 with "Exemptions from Antitrust Coverage"; chapter 7 with "Economic Indicia of Competition and Monopoly"; and chapter 8 with "Antitrust Administration and Enforcement." To have dealt with such a

25. U.S. Dep't of Justice Release (mimeographed), Aug. 27, 1953, p. 7.
26. *Id.* at 12.
27. *Id.* at 3. Emphasis added.
28. *Id.* at 3–4.
29. Statement by President Eisenhower on the importance of the Attorney General's Committee, quoted by Attorney General Brownell, U.S. Dep't of Justice Release (mimeographed), June 26, 1953, p. 11.
30. *Report of the Attorney General's National Committee to Study the Antitrust Laws* (March 31, 1955) (hereinafter *Antitrust Report*).

The Attorney General's Committee's Report

variety of complex problems in as detailed a manner as did the Committee within a time so short reflects the thoroughness with which the Committee's work must have been organized and the persistence and industry with which it must have been pursued. Expressing as it does the opinions of the country's leading experts on a dynamic problem of tremendous social, political, and economic significance, the report is entitled to the careful consideration of all those concerned with antitrust.

Major Shortcomings of the Report

To me the report is a disappointing document—primarily for three reasons. First, it never really comes to grips with the "fundamental aspects" of antitrust problems. In truth, it never quite sees them. It deals with fragments and it deals with them in a piecemeal manner. It is so concerned with the trees that it never sees the forest. In the dissenting words of Rostow, the report "is largely a review and restatement of the substantive doctrines of antitrust law, together with an analysis of the procedures through which the laws are enforced."[31] Having lost sight of its main assignment, the Committee fixed its eyes on one of its own choosing. "The scope of this entire Report," the Committee stated, "indeed reflects our concern with marking out, so far as possible, the bounds between legal and proscribed conduct."[32] The report is likely to prove more useful as a guide to businessmen anxious to avoid violating the statutes[33] than to lawmakers seeking to improve them.

Second, although the report displays sweet reasonableness and gentle tolerance in commenting on controversial antitrust issues that have come before the courts and the Federal Trade Commission, the Committee's recommendations if carried out would, I believe, weaken, not strengthen the statutes. If this judgment is correct, the President's hope that the Committee would "provide an important instrument to prepare the way for modernizing and strengthening our laws to preserve American free enterprise against monopoly and unfair competition"[34] has not been realized.

31. *Id.* at 388.
32. *Id.* at 368. References to the Committee throughout this article are to the majority. In some instances not noted in the text a minority dissented from the position accredited to the Committee.
33. Of the significance of the report Blackwell Smith, a Committee member, has said: "More remains to do to show how a businessman can behave so as to be *entitled* to a clean bill of health, but this Report is a great step forward." Trade Practice Bulletin, May 1955, p. 8. Emphasis in the original.
34. See note 29 *supra*.

Workable Competition and Antitrust Policy

Finally, the Committee strove so desperately for unanimity that both its recommendations and the minority dissents lost force and meaning. Frequently the report presents its recommendations so casually and the dissents so perfunctorily that the reader cannot be sure that a recommendation has been made or a dissent registered. Were it not for the stubborn persistence of a few of its dissenters, Walter Adams, John M. Clark, Alfred E. Kahn, Eugene V. Rostow, and especially Louis B. Schwartz—all academicians—the reader might get the impression that those who know most about antitrust problems see them with a single eye. In truth, without reading Schwartz's separately printed dissent [35] a reader is scarcely aware of the significant differences of opinion the Committee's counsels generated.

Fundamental Aspects of Antitrust

The Attorney General in establishing the Committee asked it to study the antitrust laws in their fundamental aspects. What are they? Although differing in the means of attaining it, the several antitrust laws have as a basic objective the preservation of a competitive economy. The lawmakers who enacted the Sherman Act, and the plain folk they represented, were not schooled in the intricacies of economic theory. But they were not blind to the realities of economic life, and they held common-sense ideas that were the counterpart of the esoteric theories. They favored an economy in which economic activity was controlled by the market. They were skeptical of the concentration of economic power, and they were troubled

---

35. Schwartz's dissenting opinion states in the preface to the privately published edition that it was printed independently "because the Co-Chairmen of the Committee refused to publish it as submitted . . . on the ground that other committee members were content to have their differences noted at particular points in the Report. [The Report] does not fairly present the views of those who differ with its basic philosophy." Adams, Clark, Kahn, and Stigler, four of the eight economists on the Committee, and Rostow and Robinson, lawyers, expressed concurrence with either major segments of Schwartz's dissent or its central thesis: "that the Report inadequately deals with the problem of Bigness and that most of the specific recommendations tend to weaken rather than strengthen the antitrust laws." Ibid. In addition to the private printing, Schwartz's dissent appears at 1 Antitrust Bulletin 37 (1955).

Rostow also objected to the co-chairmen's decision to paraphrase and leave unidentified many dissents from majority opinions. On March 23, 1955, he wired the Attorney General: "I must vehemently protest recent attempts . . . to interfere with the right of members of the Attorney General's Anti-trust Committee to express dissent in their own language and form. I regard this policy as not only unprecedented in the procedure of public bodies and unwise in itself but a breach of faith so far as the Committee is concerned." *Hearings before Antitrust Subcommittee of House Committee on the Judiciary*, 84th Cong., 1st Sess. 1873 (1955).

The Attorney General's Committee's Report

by the means used by the trusts of their day in achieving it. Schooled in the realities of an egalitarian society, they feared that vast aggregations of capital circumscribed individual opportunity, and they saw something of the political implications of an economic order dominated by a few large concerns. What the plain people saw then not all economists are blind to now. While economists now look to effective or workable rather than pure competition to regulate economic activity, most of them would recognize as effective only that kind of competition in which resources are allocated in response to independent decisions of rival business firms, none of whom has any considerable power over the market. Most economists today would recognize, as did their professional predecessors, that a competitive society tends to maximize individual liberty and that liberty in political affairs is a counterpart of liberty in economic affairs. In favoring regulation of economic activity by the market rather than by men, they recognize that an ever-increasing concentration of economic power leads to the coalescence of economic and political power and to the loss of individual liberty in both spheres.

Most economists would subscribe to these ideas, and they are relevant to the study of the antitrust laws in their fundamental aspects. I have said that the Committee never got around to them. What is the evidence? It did not consider the vast changes in industrial structure that have occurred since the enactment of the Sherman Act—and the significance of these changes to the functioning of markets—nor did it consider the relationship of the law and its interpretation to these changes. The majority apparently were oblivious of the Great Combination Movement of the turn of the century, the less spectacular merger movement of the 1920's, and the mid-century merger movement. In truth, the majority nowhere used the term merger movement nor discussed the phenomenon.

The Rule of Reason

One result of this omission is a failure to appreciate the significance of the rule of reason as laid down in the 1911 *Standard Oil* and *American Tobacco* cases [36] and as applied for three decades thereafter. The Sherman Act was designed to maintain an industrial structure consistent with competition by two means: it outlawed all combinations that restrain trade and it outlawed all efforts to monopolize any part of the domestic or

36. Standard Oil Co. v. United States, 221 U.S. 1 (1911); United States v. American Tobacco Co., 221 U.S. 106 (1911).

foreign commerce. The all-encompassing language of Section 1 apparently reflects an intent by Congress to go as far as it could, within its jurisdiction over interstate commerce, to outlaw all combinations that restrict competition.[37] Nothing in the congressional debates suggests that congressmen considered a partial monopoly less reprehensible than a complete one or wished to distinguish between a combination that restrains competition and one that restrains it unduly. The statute struck down all combinations that restrict competition. The term combination is an all-inclusive one aimed at industrial consolidations and mergers of business rivals whether in the form of trusts or otherwise. But nothing in the law nor in the debates that shaped it indicates any congressional intent to prohibit business firms from consolidating in the interests of efficiency or to avoid bankruptcy, unless they thereby obtain power over the market. In short, the Sherman Act sanctions an industrial structure in which the market controls business decisions, rather than one in which business decisions control the market.

Sherman Act Fails to Prevent Industrial Concentration

Most students of the antitrust laws and their administration recognize that the Supreme Court's ruling in the E. C. Knight case[38] sparked the Combination Movement of 1897–1904; and although economists still are debating the motives and precise consequences of this movement,[39] few would argue that it did not increase industrial concentration or create an industrial structure less compatible with effective competition than the structure it replaced. Few would deny that it was the sort of movement the Sherman Act had been designed to forestall. Certainly those close to it recognized it as such.[40] Students of industrial history will probably agree that the Act aimed to forestall such mergers as the American Sugar Refining Company, a consolidation of business rivals that in 1895 accounted for 98 per cent of the refined sugar capacity of the country; the Standard Oil Company of New Jersey, with its virtually complete control of pipelines, refineries, and market outlets; the American Can Company, a consolidation of more than 100 business rivals controlling 90 per cent or

---

37. For a fuller exposition of this thesis and the ideas that follow in the paragraph, see chap. 3, pp. 131–34 *supra*.
38. United States v. E. C. Knight Co., 156 U.S. 1 (1895).
39. Markham, "Survey of the Evidence and Findings on Mergers," in *Business Concentration and Price Policy* (National Bureau of Economic Research report, Princeton: Princeton University Press, 1955), pp. 141, 154–67.
40. See note 3 *supra*.

The Attorney General's Committee's Report

more of the industry; United States Steel Corporation; International Harvester Company; United Shoe Machinery Corporation; and American Tobacco Company. No economic historian can easily escape the conclusion that by 1911 the Sherman Act had largely failed in its purpose.

The Attorney General's Committee ignored these fundamental aspects of the antitrust problem. It failed to see that the rule of reason in effect validated the Great Combination Movement and laid a legal basis for the merger movement of the 1920's. The rule of reason placed outside the reach of the Sherman Act any combination that falls short of monopoly within the meaning of Section 2 unless it has been persistently guilty of predatory acts.[41] Section 2 does not define monopolizing, it merely prohibits it, but from the 1920 *Steel* case [42] to *Aluminum* [43] the courts have emphasized the fact that mere size is no offense. In the *Steel* case the Supreme Court put it this way: "[T]he law does not make mere size an offense or the existence of unexerted power an offense. It ... requires overt acts...."[44] The Steel Corporation had combined some 180 independent steelmaking firms, and two of the four district court judges found that it had been organized to monopolize the making and selling of steel.[45] The district court estimated that at the outset the Steel Corporation accounted for from 80 to 95 per cent of the country's major steel products,[46] but this the court found not enough to give the corporation control of the market—a conclusion for which the court found support in the corporation's participation at times in various pooling arrangements designed to eliminate competition in the sale of certain

---

41. For an exposition of this thesis see chap. 3, pp. 134–40 *supra*.
42. United States v. U.S. Steel Corp., 251 U.S. 417 (1920).
43. United States v. Aluminum Co. of America, 148 F.2d 416 (2d Cir. 1945).
44. United States v. U.S. Steel Corp., 251 U.S. 417, 451 (1920).
45. Judge Woolley, with whose opinion Judge Hunt concurred, said: "I am of opinion that the circumstances which led up to and surrounded the organization of the Steel Corporation show that those who organized the Steel Corporation intended it to monopolize and unduly restrain trade." United States v. U.S. Steel Corp., 223 Fed. 55, 171 (D.N.J. 1915). Judge Buffington, with whose opinion Judge McPherson concurred, found that the corporation was a natural consummation of the tendencies of the industry arising from "the metallurgical method of making steel and the physical method of handling it." 223 Fed. at 117. The Supreme Court after paraphrasing both opinions said: "The opinions indicate that the evidence admits of different deductions as to the genesis of the Corporation and the purpose of its organizers ... and we concur in the main with that of Judges Woolley and Hunt." United States v. U.S. Steel Corp., 251 U.S. 417, 442 (1920).
46. United States v. U.S. Steel Corp., 223 Fed. 55, 167 (D.N.J. 1915). Handler says this figure seems much too high and that most writers put it at about 60 or 70 per cent. Handler, "Industrial Mergers and the Anti-Trust Laws," 32 Col. L. Rev. 179, 220 (1932).

steel products. Since the Steel Corporation had discontinued these conspiratorial arrangements and had not resorted to predatory practices of the sort made notorious by the Standard Oil and American Tobacco Companies, the court ruled and the Supreme Court affirmed that, despite its size, it had violated neither Section 1 nor Section 2 of the Sherman Act. In accepting the Supreme Court's interpretation of Section 1 the Attorney General's Committee placed its blessing on a rule of reason that gives legal status to any combination that falls short of monopoly's undefined boundary. The Committee has not been helpful in drawing the boundary. Delimiting monopoly is not easy, and Judge Hand in the *Aluminum* case has not helped. He said that ninety per cent of output "is enough to constitute a monopoly; it is doubtful whether sixty or sixty-four per cent would be enough; and certainly thirty-three per cent is not." [47] As the Committee noted, the Supreme Court has qualified Judge Hand's rule of thumb. In the *Columbia Steel* case it said: "We do not undertake to prescribe any set of percentage figures by which to measure the reasonableness of a corporation's enlargement of its activities by the purchase of the assets of a competitor. The relative effect of percentage command of a market varies with the setting *in which that factor is placed.*" [48]

"These guides, while necessarily indefinite," the Committee found "nonetheless helpful." [49] I find them, when coupled with the rule of reason, an invitation to merger, and apparently businessmen have seen in them a similar invitation. They have contributed to the creation and maintenance of an industrial structure in which effective competition becomes less certain and more difficult; for industrial structure may condition business conduct and business conduct may condition industrial performance. It was the structure of the canmaking industry that made it possible for American Can Company over more than a quarter of a century to obtain secret rebates in the purchase of tin plate and to tie the price of tin cans to the published price of tin plate, to become the industry's price leader, and to discriminate among its customers in selling cans.[50] It was the structure of the steel industry—with one firm

47. United States v. Aluminum Co. of America, 148 F.2d 416, 424 (2d Cir. 1945).
48. United States v. Columbia Steel Co., 334 U.S. 495, 527–28 (1948). Emphasis added by the Committee, *Antitrust Report*, at 49.
49. *Antitrust Report*, at 49.
50. See chap. 3, pp. 166-79 *supra*, especially 167, 172–73. For an economic analysis of the can industry, see Charles H. Hession, *Competition in the Metal Food Container Industry 1916-1946* (Columbia University thesis, Brooklyn, 1948),

The Attorney General's Committee's Report

accounting for from one-third to two-thirds of the country's steel ingot capacity and a half-dozen firms for from 80 to 90 per cent of it throughout the last fifty years [51]—that made basing point pricing, price leadership, and the uniform pricing of "extras" reasonably effective devices for stabilizing steel prices and lessening the rigor of competition.[52] Industrial structure may transform "conscious parallelism of action" from an elusive abstraction to a sound business practice.[53]

SECTION 7 OF THE CLAYTON ACT

Congress has recognized what the Committee ignored: the significance of industrial concentration to the growth of monopoly. Congress concluded as early as 1914 that something more than the Sherman Act was necessary "to prevent monopolies and unwarranted mergers which would substantially lessen competition."[54] The failure of the Sherman Act to forestall the Great Combination Movement prompted enactment of Section 7 of the Clayton Act. Congressmen believed that the holding company, first legalized by New Jersey, was the instrument that made the combination movement feasible. The House Committee on the Judiciary, in reporting on the proposal to outlaw the acquisition by one company of stock in another company where such acquisition might substantially lessen competition between the two companies or tend to create a monopoly, aimed at limiting the power of this instrument. Conceding the *primary* purpose of a holding company to be the holding of stock in another company, the Judiciary Committee regarded it as

> an abomination and . . . a mere incorporated form of the old-fashioned trust.
> . . . .
> . . . . [E]xperience has taught us that the "holding company" . . . no longer serves any purpose that is helpful to either business or the community at large

---

passim; Hession, "The Tin Can Industry," in *The Structure of American Industry*, ed. Walter Adams (rev. ed.; New York: Macmillan, 1954), pp. 411–28. Calling attention to the significance of structure is not to deny that business practices may contribute to the shaping of structure. As Hession pointed out, price stabilization and price leadership after 1916 contributed to the development of a duopolistic structure in canmaking. *Id.* at 427–28.

51. Stocking, *Basing Point Pricing and Regional Development* (Chapel Hill: University of North Carolina Press, 1954), pp. 20–22; chap. 3, pp. 139, 145 *supra*.

52. *Ibid.*

53. "Conscious parallelism" the Committee regarded as a phrase of "uncertain meaning and legal significance." *Antitrust Report*, at 36.

54. H.R. Rep. No. 1191, 81st Cong., 1st Sess. 3 (1949). The House Committee on the Judiciary, in reporting on H.R. 2734 (which became the Celler-Kefauver Anti-Merger Act of 1950), reviewed the economic background of § 7 of the Clayton Act.

when it is operated purely as a "holding company." Section 8 [later to become Section 7] is intended to eliminate this evil. . . ."[55]

Section 7's Objective

The Attorney General's Committee recognized what all students of antitrust know, that Section 7 failed to achieve its objective. Court interpretations,[56] "many felt, frustrated apparent Congressional design and, as a result, Section 7 fell short of its intended purpose to stop in its incipiency undue concentration of economic power or monopoly."[57] Awareness of the failure of Section 7 led to the 1950 Celler-Kefauver amendment.[58] The Committee approved its objectives.[59] But in analyzing its provisions and discussing the proper standards for administering it, the Committee failed to consider amended Section 7 in its "fundamental aspects." Both Senate and House committee reports on the proposed amendment to Section 7 make it clear that the objective of the amendment was to prevent further concentration in industry. The Senate Committee on the Judiciary put it this way: "The purpose of the proposed bill, H.R. 2734, is to limit future increases in the level of economic concentration resulting from corporate mergers and acquisitions."[60] The House Committee on the Judiciary considered the problem in greater detail. It recognized that the "level of economic concentration in the American economy is high."[61] It alleged that "the long-term trend of concentration has been steadily upward. . . . This long-term rise in concentration is due in considerable part to the external expansion of business through mergers, acquisitions, and consolidations."[62] Although

55. H.R. Rep. No. 627, 63d Cong., 2d Sess. 17 (1914).
56. *E.g.*, Arrow-Hart & H. Co. v. Federal Trade Commission, 291 U.S. 587 (1934); Internat. Shoe Co. v. Federal Trade Commission, 280 U.S. 291 (1930); Federal Trade Commission v. Western Meat Co., 272 U.S. 554 (1926); United States v. Republic Steel Corporation, 11 F. Supp. 117 (N.D. Ohio 1935).
57. *Antitrust Report*, at 117.
58. 64 Stat. 1125 (1950), 15 U.S.C. § 18 (1958).
59. In commenting on the courts' role in narrowing the application of § 7 and on the limitations of Sherman Act § 1 as interpreted in *Columbia Steel* in curbing mergers, the Committee said: "This background immediately preceding amended Section 7 discloses the apparent Congressional objective of establishing more effective rules against mergers. The Committee believes that this intention provides the main guide to the administrative and judicial construction of that provision." *Antitrust Report*, at 117.
60. Sen. Rep. No. 1775, 81st Cong., 2d Sess. 3 (1950).
61. H.R. Rep. No. 1191, 81st Cong., 1st Sess. 2 (1949).
62. *Ibid.*

The Attorney General's Committee's Report

the Attorney General's Committee did not concern itself with the extent or direction of industrial concentration or its causes, I doubt that any of its members would challenge the House Judiciary Committee's conclusion that industrial concentration is high. Morris A. Adelman, a member of the Attorney General's Committee, demonstrated the truth of this generalization in his study of the measurement of industrial concentration. He estimated that in 1947 the two hundred largest nonfinancial corporations, constituting less than one-twentieth of 1 per cent of all corporations, held approximately 40 per cent of all corporate assets and approximately 24 per cent of all national income-producing wealth.[63]

Is Industrial Concentration Increasing?

The Attorney General's Committee might have challenged the House Judiciary Committee's finding that industrial concentration had steadily increased. Adelman, who recognized that the Great Combination Movement at the turn of the century and the lesser movement of the 1920's increased industrial concentration, after carefully analyzing developments between 1931 and 1947 cautiously concluded that a "strong and continuing tendency since 1931 to greater concentration in manufacturing . . . probably does not exist."[64] A more recent Federal Trade Commission study indicated that since 1949 "the pace of important mergers and acquisitions has been rising; in 1954 the number reported in financial manuals was three times that of 1949, and just slightly less than the number reported for each of the years 1946 and 1947 when merger activity reached a postwar peak."[65] And even Adelman, who alleged that the merger movement of 1940–47 existed only "in some people's fertile imagination," in 1955 was imaginative enough to concede that we are "probably" in the midst of "a real, not a fictitious merger movement . . . *right now.*"[66] In 1954 the Federal Trade Commission reported that industrial concentration as measured by changes in the total value of shipments of all manufacturing industries accounted for by the two hundred largest manufacturing firms had increased from 37.7 per cent to 40.5 per

---

63. Adelman, "The Measurement of Industrial Concentration," 33 Rev. Econ. Stat. 269, 277 (1951).
64. *Id.* at 290.
65. Federal Trade Commission, *Report on Corporate Mergers and Acquisitions* (May 1955), p. 2.
66. Adelman, "General Comment on the Schwartz Dissent," 1 Antitrust Bulletin 71, 74 (1955). Emphasis added. Adelman defines a merger movement as one in which mergers increase the degree of concentration in the economy. *Id.* at 73.

cent, or by 2.8 per cent, between 1935 and 1950.[67] The evidence clearly indicated that a merger movement was taking place.

Influence of Mergers on Industrial Structure

On the influence of mergers on contemporary industrial structure, opinions differ. J. Fred Weston, after analyzing the growth of 74 large firms in 22 industries from date of organization to 1948, each with a high concentration ratio, concluded:

> Approximately one-fourth of the growth of the 74 firms studied was directly accounted for by mergers. . . . At least 70 per cent of the firms studied grew by internal expansion to the extent of more than half of their total growth. . . . For only a small proportion of the firms does external growth represent a high percentage of total growth. The direct effect of mergers on the absolute size of large firms appears to have been small.[68]

Although Weston's calculations reveal that mergers have played a substantial role [69] in the growth of contemporary industrial giants, for two reasons they understate rather than overstate the influence of mergers. In the first place, Weston's analysis does not take account of the indirect effects a merger may have on the rate of a firm's growth. The power of a combination to grow is made up of the power of each previously independent unit to grow, plus or minus such accelerating or retarding influence as the combination exerts on the rate of growth. Although a large part of the absolute size of many contemporary oligopolies is directly ascribable to internal growth, if the mergers that compose them had not taken place the assets of the separate companies might conceivably have shown a rate of growth comparable to that of the combinations. Assets as large as those today under the control of a single firm might have been under the control of as many companies as went into a particular merger. More important, in the absence of

---

67. Federal Trade Commission, *Report on Changes in Concentration in Manufacturing, 1935 to 1947 and 1950* (1954), p. 17.
  In its study of corporate mergers and acquisitions, *supra* note 65, at 2, 6, the *Federal Trade Commission* found that during the 1948-54 period companies with assets of $10,000,000 or more accounted for nearly two-thirds of the acquisitions recorded; and that between January 1951 and July 1954 one-fifth of the acquisitions recorded were made by companies with assets of $50,000,000 or more.

68. Weston, *The Role of Mergers in the Growth of Large Firms* (Berkeley: University of California Press, 1953), p. 30.

69. Weston's own figures in my judgment belie his conclusion that "the direct effect of mergers on the absolute size of large firms appears to have been small." *Id.* One-fourth of total growth is a substantial proportion.

The Attorney General's Committee's Report

an oligopolistic industrial structure created by mergers, entry into an industry might have been easier and its growth might have been shared by a larger number of firms.

In the second place, Weston's analysis overlooks the influence that World War II has exerted on the internal growth of large firms. The significance of mergers in explaining the size of the modern industrial giants is obscured by Weston's having made his calculations between only two dates—the date of the firm's origin (or the first year for which data were available) and 1948. Had he made similar calculations to determine the role of mergers in the size of his 74 firms as of 1940, before a government spending program and inflation had swollen both the physical assets and the capitalization of nearly all firms, he would have found that external growth (growth by acquisition) constituted a much larger percentage of his firms' total growth. Such a calculation based on data obtained from Weston's work sheets [70] has revealed that external growth represented 54.9 per cent of the total growth of 73 of the firms he studied. In some instances the figures were strikingly higher. The United States Steel Corporation's assets acquired by mergers through 1940 represented approximately 100 per cent of its total 1940 assets.[71] The Republic Steel Corporation's assets acquired by merger through 1940 represented 92.6 per cent of its total 1940 assets. Corn Products Refining Company's assets as of 1940 acquired by merger represented 82.5 per cent of its total assets. National Distillers Product Corporation's assets acquired by merger represented 80 per cent of its total 1940 assets; American Tobacco's represented 78.5 per cent; Jones & Laughlin Steel Corporation's, 74.4 per cent; Chrysler Corporation's, 71.6 per cent; Standard Oil

---

70. Weston has made his work sheets available to all students who request them. James Mack Folsom, a graduate student at Vanderbilt, in 1954 made the calculations referred to in the text.

71. Weston used three methods for calculating external growth: (1) He treated initial assets as representing wholly external growth. These plus assets subsequently acquired by mergers represented a firm's total external growth. Assets of the terminal year represented total growth. (2) He treated initial assets as a base from which to calculate internal and external growth, the difference between total assets at the end of the period and initial assets constituting total growth. Acquisitions subsequent to the initial year constituted external growth. (3) He treated initial assets as a separate component of growth, neither internal nor external. Subsequent acquisitions constituted external growth; assets of the terminal year constituted total growth. With the external growth derived by each method he calculated the percentage of total growth it represented. The percentages given in the text are derived by Weston's first method (but, as explained, with 1940 instead of 1948 as the terminal year) because most of the firms discussed originated through mergers.

of Indiana's, 65.6 per cent; and Bethlehem Steel Corporation's, 60.2 per cent.

These calculations support the generalization, which a broader study of industrial history justifies, that mergers have played a vital and substantial role in creating industry's oligopolistic structure. Contemporary mergers, though less dramatic than those of half a century ago, are no doubt helping to preserve it.

Apparently the House Committee on the Judiciary was correct in two of the assumptions it made in concluding that Section 7 needed amending: industrial concentration is high; mergers have made it high. Whether or not it was correct in finding that concentration was on the increase at the time it made its report, that observation was appropriate to the decade that followed.

Committee Overlooks Fundamentals

In dealing with Section 7 as amended, what did the Attorney General's Committee have to say about these matters? Not much. The Committee recognized, of course, that Congress intended through amended Section 7 "to strike down some mergers beyond the reach of the Sherman Act";[72] or, as the Senate committee report put it, "to cope with monopolistic tendencies in their incipiency and well before they have attained such effects as would justify a Sherman Act proceeding."[73] From a consideration of similar remarks by the House committee the Attorney General's Committee concluded that Section 7 "requires findings and conclusions, not of *actual* anticompetitive effects, but merely of a *reasonable probability* of a substantial lessening of competition or tendency toward monopoly."[74] The Committee's concern was not with the several merger movements that have characterized American industry during the last half-century or so or with where they may be heading, but with the statutory tests the Federal Trade Commission and the courts should apply in determining the legality of any particular merger. It concluded that the statutory standards require findings on two questions: (1) What is the relevant market in which the merged firms sell their products? (2) What prospective anticompetitive effects must be shown in order to justify finding the substantial lessening of competition or tendency toward monopoly prohibited by Section 7? In considering these questions

72. *Antitrust Report*, at 117.
73. Sen. Rep. No. 1775, 81st Cong., 2d Sess. 4–5 (1950).
74. *Antitrust Report*, at 118. Emphasis by the Committee.

The Attorney General's Committee's Report

the Committee examined what the courts have said in the *Transamerica* and *Benrus* cases [75] and what the Federal Trade Commission has said in the *Pillsbury* case.[76] Noting with approval the courts' and the Commission's findings in these cases, the Attorney General's Committee summed up as follows:

[M]ergers are a common form of growth; they may lessen, increase, or have no effect upon competition. A merger as such involves no necessary connotations of coercion, dominance, or lack of effective competitive pressures. In addition, mergers may ease from the market companies which have failed in the competitive struggle and thus prevent potential bankruptcies.[77] Finally they may

---

75. Transamerica Corp. v. Board of Governors, 206 F.2d 163 (3rd Cir.), *cert. denied*, 346 U.S. 901 (1953); Hamilton Watch Co. v. Benrus Watch Co., 114 F. Supp. 307 (D. Conn.), *aff'd*, 206 F.2d 738 (2d Cir. 1953).

76. Pillsbury Mills, Inc., 50 F.T.C. 555 (1953). The Commission charged that Pillsbury had violated § 7 as amended by acquiring the assets of Ballard and Ballard Co. and Duff's Baking Mix Division of the American Home Products Corp. The record showed that these acquisitions increased its share of the Southeast market for bakery mixes from 22.7 per cent to 44.9 per cent and gave it first place in the national market, with 23 instead of 16 per cent of the industry. *Id.* at 561. After a hearing the Commission's trial examiner dismissed the complaint, ruling that the evidence did not support its allegations. The Commission reversed and remanded for further consideration, in an opinion that stated for the first time its conception of the economic analysis required to establish a § 7 case.

77. In interpreting § 7 neither the Supreme Court, nor Congress, nor the Attorney General's Committee accepted the cruel logic of the competitive process. In International Shoe Co. v. Federal Trade Commission, 280 U.S. 291 (1930), the Supreme Court reversed both the Federal Trade Commission and the court of appeals to rule that International Shoe's acquisition of another shoe company did not violate old § 7 for two reasons: the markets reached by the two companies were not the same, and the acquired company faced probable bankruptcy. The House and Senate committee reports on H.R. 2734, which became the Celler-Kefauver Anti-Merger Act of 1950, ignored the Supreme Court's basic finding of no substantial competition between the acquiring and acquired companies and interpreted *International Shoe* as disposing of the objection "that a corporation in bankrupt or failing condition might not be allowed to sell to a competitor. . . . It is well settled that the Clayton Act does not apply in bankruptcy or receivership cases." Sen. Rep. No. 1775, 81st Cong., 2d Sess. 7 (1950). See H.R. Rep. No. 1191, 81st Cong., 1st Sess. 6 (1949). The Attorney General's Committee accepted this distortion of *International Shoe* and pointed out that proof of an acquired firm's probable business failure may be "the only rebuttal to the basic market facts" and is a defense "preserved by explicit references in the legislative history." *Antitrust Report*, at 123.

Competition involves risk-taking, and neither the theory nor the practice of competition promises that no firms will fall by the wayside. In truth, the economic allocation of resources in response to constantly changing consumer demands, new sources of supply, or advancing technology can scarcely be effected without some bankruptcies. The obligation of a society committed to competition is to create an environment favorable to the shift of resources, not to legalize mergers that may retard the shift and make competition less effective. This is not to argue that when a profitable firm acquires one near bankruptcy, competition is necessarily adversely

spur operating economies by spreading overhead costs or enabling improved technology or management.[78]

That not all mergers affect competition adversely will seem a reasonable conclusion to most students of industrial concentration. Separating the sheep from the goats under the Clayton Act, which is no easy task, falls to the Commission and the courts. They do it on a case-by-case basis. The Attorney General's Committee made some helpful suggestions as to how these agencies may determine the probable economic consequences of a merger. They should study

(1) the character of the acquiring and the acquired company, (2) the characteristics of the markets affected, (3) immediate changes in the size and competitive range of the acquiring company and in the adjustments of other companies operating in the markets directly affected, and (4) probable *long-range* differences that the acquisitions may make for companies actually or potentially operating in these markets.[79]

In short, the task calls for thorough economic analysis, broad in scope and comprehensive in detail, and, according to the Committee, as the *Pillsbury* case suggests, "no one pattern of proof can meet the requirements of all cases." [80] Each is a separate problem. Both the chairman of the Federal Trade Commission and the former acting director of its Bureau of Economics had already declared that the Commission proposed to make just this workmanlike approach in grappling with Section 7.[81]

Recommended Procedure May Defeat Purposes of Amended Section 7

That the Federal Trade Commission is applying the rule of reason and the principle of workable competition in its approach to the merg-

affected; it is to argue that if competition is adversely affected, saving a firm from bankruptcy may be a high price to pay.
78. *Antitrust Report,* at 124–25.
79. *Id.* at 125. Emphasis by the Committee.
80. *Id.* at 123.
81. Chairman Howrey said: "[E]xcept where the Supreme Court or Congress has directed otherwise, the Commission should determine competitive effects by examination, analysis and evaluation of relevant market facts." Only by such a procedure can "the forward march of the per se doctrine . . . be halted." Trade Practice Bulletin, July 1954, p. 1. Markham, the Commission's acting chief economist in 1954, in pointing out that some mergers are designed to influence the market and eliminate competition while others may be due to "a host of other business motives" and have "scarcely any observable effect on competition," declared: "Only a serious economic analysis that considers all the relevant facts is likely to separate the former from the latter." Trade Practice Bulletin, August 1954, p. 7.

The Attorney General's Committee's Report

er problem, a procedure that the Attorney General's Committee recommended, will be gratifying to some economists. This procedure not only makes for thoroughness in inquiry and reasonableness in judgment, but it will enlist the services of more economists in Government. As Chairman Howrey said, "FTC needs specialists to gather facts and . . . it needs economic as well as legal experts to analyze and evaluate those facts." [82] But it will also need time, and a lot of it. When the job is done for any one merger, it will have to be done again for any other.

Moreover, Section 7 of the Clayton Act carries no effective penalty for noncompliance. For example, the Federal Trade Commission on December 16, 1960—nine years after Pillsbury Mills, Inc., now the Pillsbury Company, had acquired the assets of Ballard and Ballard Company and Duff's Baking Mix Division of the American Home Products Corporation and seven years after the filing of the Commission's complaint—gave its decision finding that the acquisitions violated Section 7 and directing that an order be entered requiring Pillsbury to divest itself of the acquired firms so as to restore them as "going concerns" and to restore competitive conditions as they existed before the acquisitions.[83] If before the expiration of sixty days from the date of the order Pillsbury should appeal to the courts, months if not years may elapse before the courts render a decision. If Pillsbury does not appeal or if the Supreme Court sustains the Federal Trade Commission, Pillsbury must take steps to comply with the Commission's order. Even if Pillsbury is forbidden to sell "to anyone it controls or is connected with, directly or indirectly," [84] the community of interest built up in nine years of union with the two firms may continue to have the effect of tending to lessen competition. The worst penalty a company that violates the statute is likely to suffer is the inconvenience of disposing of the acquired properties. Meanwhile it will have been enriched by whatever valuable experience or know-how or profit-earning capacity the acquired companies may have brought with them; and—as in Pillsbury's case, where the Commission refused to order divestiture of subsequent acquisitions—it may be permanently enlarged by assets that it may have acquired as a result of controlling the forbidden acquisitions.

82. Edward F. Howrey, Speech before Texas Bar Association, quoted in Trade Practice Bulletin, August 1954, p. 3.
83. Pillsbury Mills, Inc., F.T.C. Dkt. 6000, decision of Dec. 16, 1960, Trade Reg. Rep. ¶ 29,277.
84. From an account of the initial order dated March 11, 1959, in Trade Practice Bulletin, April 1959, p. 7.

Workable Competition and Antitrust Policy

Clearly, administering amended Section 7 in accordance with the rule of reason and the principle of workable competition is unlikely to achieve the goal that Congress set for it: the prevention of further concentration. Since the amendment of Section 7 mergers have greatly accelerated, and the Federal Trade Commission's deliberate action is not likely to halt the movement. The horse seems likely to have been stolen long before the stable door is locked. And under the statute there seems no way of locking stable doors generally.

This analysis suggests that the Attorney General's Committee looked at relatively insignificant aspects of Section 7 while overlooking fundamentals and recommended a procedure that will defeat the intent of the law. It may be that Congress erred in assuming that industrial concentration is a problem, but if so the Committee had an obligation to say as much. It may be, granting it is a problem, that the Federal Trade Commission and the courts are doing all they reasonably might be expected to do under the law. That is to say, it may be that the law is inadequate to cope with the problem. If so, the Committee had an obligation to say so. But on these matters the Committee is silent. Only Schwartz and his companion dissenters seemed to recognize industrial concentration as a problem.

TRADE ASSOCIATION ACTIVITIES

In discussing trade association activities the Committee was no more discerning or helpful than in discussing mergers. It endorsed the rule of reason in dealing with them: "Antitrust requires distinguishing constructive trade association activities operating to promote competition from those which *unduly* limit competition among members or with outsiders,"[85] but it offered no standard for judging effects on competition other than a noncommittal comment on the leading Supreme Court trade association cases: "These cases present the issue of whether the defendants' plan, its purpose or effect, limits price competition *and whether the defendants have enough market power to achieve this result.*"[86] The Committee then gave a brief statement of the decisions in the *Hardwood Lumber*,[87] *Linseed Oil*,[88] *Maple Flooring*,[89] *Cement Manufacturers*,[90]

---

85. *Antitrust Report*, at 17. Emphasis added.
86. *Id.* at 18. Emphasis added.
87. American Column Co. v. United States, 257 U.S. 377 (1921).
88. United States v. American Linseed Oil Co., 262 U.S. 371 (1923).
89. Maple Flooring Ass'n v. United States, 268 U.S. 563 (1925).
90. Cement Mfrs. Ass'n v. United States, 268 U.S. 588 (1925).

The Attorney General's Committee's Report

Sugar Institute,[91] and *Cement Institute* [92] cases, accepting without question the Supreme Court's view of each case.[93]

The Committee's concern with the legality of specific practices—with distinguishing between "the permissible limits and the prohibited features of statistical activities" [94]—led it to neglect the historical background and economic significance of trade association market-reporting activities. It seemed unaware of the doctrines promulgated in 1912 by Arthur Jerome Eddy in his *The New Competition* and of the role they played in uniting business rivals in cooperative associations designed to bring market forces under collective control. It ignored the NRA experiment in industrial self-government, which encouraged and legalized associated activities to lessen the rigor of competition, and the aftermath of restrictive trade association activities that permeated the economy in the late 1930's.[95] It disregarded the TNEC study,[96] which admirably analyzes the

91. Sugar Institute v. United States, 297 U.S. 553 (1936).
92. Federal Trade Commission v. Cement Institute, 333 U.S. 683 (1948).
93. For an analysis of these highly incongruous opinions when measured by a uniform economic standard, see chap. 2.
94. *Antitrust Report*, at 18.
95. Salt Producers Ass'n, 34 F.T.C. 38 (1941), *modified and aff'd*, 134 F.2d 354 (7th Cir. 1943); United States Maltsters Ass'n, 35 F.T.C. 797 (1942), *order modified*, 37 F.T.C. 342 (1943), *aff'd*, 152 F.2d 161 (7th Cir. 1945); Milk and Ice Cream Can Institute, 37 F.T.C. 419 (1943), *aff'd*, 152 F.2d 478 (7th Cir. 1946); National Crepe Paper Ass'n of America, 38 F.T.C. 282 (1944), *aff'd sub nom.* Fort Howard Paper Co. v. Federal Trade Commission, 156 F.2d 899 (7th Cir. 1946); Tag Manufacturers Institute, 43 F.T.C. 499 (1947), *rev'd*, 174 F.2d 452 (1st Cir. 1949). The court of appeals reversed the Commission's decision in *Tag Manufacturers Institute* and the Commission did not seek review by the Supreme Court, but a thorough analysis of the evidence has convinced me that the trade association's program was designed not to permit business rivals to make independent informed decisions in pricing their products, but to insure that informed collaborators would price alike. See pp. 77–87 *supra*.
96. Charles A. Pearce, *Trade Association Survey* (TNEC Monograph No. 18, 1941). On the aims of trade associations Pearce let some executives speak for themselves in "materials submitted by several associations":

> The principal achievement of the association has been the preservation of competition in its original sense of "to strive together for common interests."
> The association has . . . helped to eliminate to a great extent competitive antagonism. . . .
> . . . .
> While prices are not discussed, the fact that the members know one another and are friendly has had a stabilizing influence on the prices of . . . machinery during the life of the association.
> Definite price fixing, as such, is not necessary nor wanted in this industry. Price stability is very essential and will be encouraged.
> It is part of the function of the trade association—and this Association has tried to specialize on this particular activity—to bring its members into a clear appraisal

Workable Competition and Antitrust Policy

scope and aims of trade association activities, and it took no account of the role management engineering firms have played in organizing and directing the efforts of some trade associations to achieve a common pattern of business behavior.[97]

The Committee's discussion of the leading Supreme Court trade association cases throws no new light on their legal and economic significance, but its approval of the appellate court's construction of Section 5 of the Federal Trade Commission Act in the *Tag Manufacturers Institute* case [98] illuminates its view of the statute. The Committee said: "Without going into the details of the Institute's price reporting plan, it is worth noting that the court, in sustaining the plan, emphasized that Section 5 required proof of an illegal agreement which 'in purpose and effect unduly restrained and suppressed competition.'" [99] Under the Committee's twin standards of Sherman Act proof for trade association activities—purpose or effect of limiting price competition and "enough" market power to achieve that effect—and with Section 5 cases held to a rule-of-reason Sherman Act test of illegality, the trade association that cannot enjoy the fruits of conspiracy while avoiding its penalties will have to be very clumsy indeed.

Monopoly in International Markets

In the two decades before World War II, thought and practice on international cartels underwent a revolution. England, at one time the home of free trade and economic liberalism, abandoned its traditional policies toward competition, and British business leaders joined with German in planning the cartelization of world trade. The Düsseldorf Agreement [100] was the instrument through which they were to achieve

---

of the industry. . . . All too often business, and the business activities connected with industry, are conceived as a fight over the division of wealth. When concentration on the production of wealth is abandoned for a fight over the division of wealth, then the devices of a low order of cunning are likely to be more effective than the high order of intelligence.

Pearce, *op. cit. supra*, at 47–48.

97. For a description of that role see George W. Stocking and Myron W. Watkins, *Monopoly and Free Enterprise* (New York: Twentieth Century Fund, 1951), pp. 236–42.

98. Tag Mfrs. Institute v. Federal Trade Commission, 174 F.2d 452 (1st Cir. 1949).

99. *Antitrust Report*, at 22 n. 77.

100. *Industry and Politics*, published in England in 1928, written by Sir Alfred Mond, the organizer of Imperial Chemical Industries, Ltd., set forth his beliefs that competition was outmoded and that only the rationalization of industry through

The Attorney General's Committee's Report

co-operative exploitation of world markets. The war brought a temporary end to such machinations, but there is little evidence that it changed the attitudes or broke the spirit of international business collaborators. During the same period American businessmen manifested scarcely more concern for the preservation of free markets than did the British. Through direct negotiation, export associations organized under the Webb-Pomerene Act,[101] and patent interchanges, they had frequently abandoned competition for cooperation in world markets.[102] National governments, interested in protecting domestic producer groups and export industries in a world committed to restrictive trade agreements, sponsored or encouraged international cartels covering a wide range of products. In short, there was and is a monopoly problem that transcends national boundaries.

Only a minority of the Attorney General's Committee recognized such developments as basic to a consideration of appropriate antitrust policy in international markets. Only a minority acknowledged that foreign monopolies and cartels burden the American economy and directly or indirectly raise domestic prices by checking imports, restricting exports, limiting investment opportunities abroad, and preventing the free use of

---

mergers and cartel arrangements, not merely within national industries but on a world basis, could overcome the wastefulness of plant duplication, excessive inventories, etc. By the end of the 1930's these ideas had gained considerable acceptance by British businessmen and economists. In 1938 British and German government officials, including Dr. Hjalmar Schacht, president of the German Reichsbank, and Oliver Stanley, president of the British Board of Trade, explored the avenues of closer co-operation between British and German industry. Out of a conference held at Dusseldorf March 15–16, 1939, between a British delegation headed by Sir William Laske, chairman of the Federation of British Industries, and a German delegation headed by Herr Ernst Poensgen, president of Vereinigte Stahlwerke, came a "joint declaration" stating in part:

> [I]t is agreed that it is essential to replace destructive competition wherever it may be found by constructive cooperation, designed to foster the expansion of world trade, to the mutual benefit of Great Britain, Germany and all other countries.
> The two organizations realize that agreements upon prices or other factors between Germany and Great Britain are only a step, although a most important step, towards a more ordered system of world trade. They would welcome the participation of other nations in such agreements.

Stocking and Watkins, *Cartels or Competition?* (New York: Twentieth Century Fund, 1948), p. 62.

101. 40 Stat. 516 (1918), 15 U.S.C. §§ 62, 63, 65 (1958).

102. Examples are the international arrangements in explosives, steel, aluminum, magnesium, incandescent electric lamps, alkalies, nitrogen, and other chemicals, described in Stocking and Watkins, *Cartels in Action* (New York: Twentieth Century Fund, 1946).

Workable Competition and Antitrust Policy

technology.[103] Recognizing the scope and significance of the international cartel movement,[104] a minority of the Committee concluded that the United States should "move, with other governments, by means of procedures of international cooperation, towards an agreed solution of the problems which restrictive arrangements pose for the American economy."[105] Contending that the Sherman Act "can deal at best with few of the restraints which international cartels impose upon the American economy,"[106] the minority specifically supported a proposal that the Committee "recommend that the government support, negotiate and sign, and the Congress by appropriate procedures ratify, an international treaty or convention against restraints of trade and monopolies of international concern. . . ."[107] The majority were content with denying that "consideration of international means for curbing undue restraint of trade and monopolistic practices" came within the scope of the Committee's report.[108]

Having made "no independent factual study to provide any basis for determining whether our antitrust laws have helped or hindered the foreign commerce of the United States or for generalizing about the effect of antitrust on any related governmental policy,"[109] the Committee rejected any proposal for blanket exemption of foreign commerce from the antitrust laws. It also rejected the proposal that the Webb-Pomerene

---

103. The minority observed that "in the last thirty years, governmental reports alone have reviewed cartel plans with respect to more than 120 commodities or services of significance in world trade, including aluminum, diamonds, wood pulp, nickel, copper, rubber, various chemical and electrical products, dyes, cocoa, shipping, magnesium and machinery of many types." *Antitrust Report*, at 99.

104. Rostow, with Wendell Berge's specific concurrence, spoke for the minority as follows: "Years of effort by committees, governments, foundations and individual scholars have fully documented the significant role of cartels in the world economy. The importance of foreign cartels to our own economy has long been generally understood." *Id.* Yet the Committee, "by a narrowly divided vote, refused to comment on the possibility of action by means of international agreement to protect the American economy against exploitation by foreign cartels. *Our deliberate silence on this question constitutes the most serious single defect in our Report.*" Ibid. Emphasis added.

105. *Id.* at 101.
106. *Id.* at 98.
107. *Id.* at 102.
108. *Id.* at 98. Gilbert H. Montague, a Committee member, vigorously rejected the notion that the Sherman Act was inadequate to deal with the restraints international cartels impose on the American economy, and especially the proposal that the United States approve and participate in the program recommended by the United Nations Economic and Social Council. For his ably presented position see *id.* at 105–08.

109. *Id.* at 66.

The Attorney General's Committee's Report

Act, which has served as an instrument for numerous antitrust violations,[110] be repealed. Since it did this without making any factual study—and apparently without consulting such factual studies as have been made [111]—its judgment can represent little more than an expression of preconceptions.

Disavowing consideration of the broader and more fundamental aspects of international cartels, the Committee devoted its talents to procedural details—"clarification and improvement of the criteria for interpreting existing statutory standards." [112] In doing so the Committee manifested greater solicitude for the rights of business firms whose international operations may run afoul of the antitrust laws than for freedom in international trade. One statutory standard the Committee considered involves the jurisdiction of the antitrust laws over persons or conduct beyond the territorial limits of the United States. The Committee sought from a review of cases arising under the Sherman Act's foreign commerce clause [113] guides "to assure that the Sherman Act remains within its Congressionally intended application to persons and activities abroad"—that is, limited to arrangements having such "substantial anticompetitive effects"

110. E.g., United States v. United States Alkali Export Ass'n, 86 F. Supp. 59 (S.D.N.Y. 1949); Carbon Black Export, Inc., 46 F.T.C. 1245 (1949); Pipe Fittings & Valve Export Ass'n, 45 F.T.C. 917 (1948); Export Screw Ass'n, 43 F.T.C. 980 (1947); Sulphur Export Corp., 43 F.T.C. 820 (1947); Phosphate Export Association, 42 F.T.C. 555 (1946); Florida Hard Rock Phosphate Export Ass'n, 40 F.T.C. 843 (1945).

111. The Committee neither accepted nor rejected the findings of numerous studies of international cartels that have been made; it ignored them. One such study by the Twentieth Century Fund found that in 1939, 86.9 per cent by value of the mineral products sold in the United States, of a character that made cartelization feasible, were products in the sale of which international cartels of varying degrees of effectiveness had been organized. For agricultural products the corresponding figure was 47.4 per cent; for manufactured products, 42.7 per cent. Stocking and Watkins, *Cartels or Competition?* at 93–94, Appendix B. On the significance of cartels to the world economy the literature is voluminous. Edwards, *Economic and Political Aspects of International Cartels*, Monograph No. 1 of Subcommittee on War Mobilization of Senate Committee on Military Affairs, 78th Cong., 2d Sess. (1944); Ervin Hexner and Adelaide Walters, *International Cartels* (Chapel Hill: University of North Carolina Press, 1945); Edward S. Mason, *Controlling World Trade: Cartels and Commodity Agreements* (research study for Committee for Economic Development, New York: McGraw Hill, 1946); Stocking and Watkins, *Cartels in Action*.

112. *Antitrust Report*, at 66.

113. United States v. Aluminum Co. of America, 148 F.2d 416 (2d Cir. 1945); United States v. Imperial Chemical Industries, 100 F. Supp. 504 (S.D.N.Y. 1951), decree, 105 F. Supp. 215 (S.D.N.Y. 1952); United States v. Timken Roller Bearing Co., 83 F. Supp. 284 (N.D. Ohio 1949), aff'd, 341 U.S. 593 (1951); United States v. General Electric Co., 82 F. Supp. 753 (D.N.J. 1949); United States v. National Lead Co., 63 F. Supp. 513 (S.D.N.Y. 1945).

on this country's foreign commerce as to amount to "unreasonable restraints" [114] and enforced by decrees so worded as to protect business firms from being caught between their prohibitions and the operation of foreign laws. Determining jurisdiction requires an interpretation of "the scope and content in the Sherman Act of 'trade and commerce . . . with foreign nations.'" [115] The Committee recommended that these words be construed "to include not only the import and export flow of finished products, their component parts and adjunct services, but also, as in domestic commerce, capital investment and financing." [116] The Committee went to great lengths to dispel certain doubtful constructions of dicta in the *Timken* and *Minnesota Mining* cases [117] and to insure that "taken out of context, [they] should not develop into a mercantilistic policy of discouraging American investment abroad in the name of protecting American manufacturing." [118] Since the dicta when read in context are most unlikely to have such an effect,[119] a greater danger may lie in the Committee's disapproval of isolated phrases in proper judicial condemnations of American companies' restrictive combinations—combinations that the companies de-

114. *Antitrust Report,* at 76.
115. *Id.* at 77.
116. *Id.* at 80.
117. *Id.* at 78–79. The sentences in Timken Co. v. United States, 341 U.S. 593, 599 (1951), that the Committee objected to are the following, as quoted by the Committee: "[T]he provisions in the Sherman Act against restraints of foreign trade are based on the assumption, and reflect the policy, that export and import trade in commodities is both possible and desirable. These provisions of the Act are wholly inconsistent with appellant's argument that American business must be left free to participate in international cartels, that the free foreign commerce in goods must be sacrificed in order to foster export of American dollars for investment in foreign factories which sell abroad." The dicta in United States v. Minnesota Mining & Mfg. Co., 92 F. Supp. 947, 962 (D. Mass. 1950), that the Committee objected to are as follows: "It is no excuse for the violations of the Sherman Act that supplying foreign customers from foreign factories is more profitable and in that sense is, as defendants argue, 'In the interest of American enterprise' (Def. Rep. Br. 31). Financial advantage is a legitimate consideration for an individual nonmonopolistic enterprise. It is irrelevant where the action is taken by a combination and the effect, while it may redound to the advantage of American finance, restricts American commerce. For Congress in the Sherman Act has condemned whatever unreasonably restrains American commerce regardless of how it fattens profits of certain stockholders. Congress has preferred to protect American competitors, consumers and workmen."
118. *Antitrust Report,* at 79.
119. See note 117 *supra.* For an example of the Committee's own misleading emphasis compare page 79 of its report, where, in expressing fear that American investment abroad may be discouraged, it said that the court in *Minnesota Mining* "said that any factory established abroad by a single American company would 'be a restraint upon American commerce with foreign nations,' although not accom-

fended as good investments abroad. Without saying so directly, the Committee seemed to endorse a judicial weighing of the adverse effects that collaborative activities by domestic concerns in foreign markets might have on competition at home or in foreign commerce against the beneficial effects that their foreign investments might have on their financial profits, the balance of payments, foreign exchange, and an economical allocation of resources and division of labor in international markets. This is a difficult task, probably beyond the courts' competence and certainly beyond the scope of "trade and commerce . . . with foreign nations" as written in the Sherman Act.

The Committee asked itself what judicial inquiries would be "relevant to determining 'undue limitations on competitive conditions' in foreign commerce." [120] On this issue the Committee heartily endorsed the application of the rule of reason, insisting that the nature and effect of the challenged conduct should be determined in the context of a particular market and suggesting that in foreign commerce cases this may require "consideration of market factors not operative in domestic commerce." [121] Such factors may include tariff policies, export-import controls, dollar shortages, foreign exchange restrictions, price control measures, and the like. A basic issue that the courts may have to decide in cases of collaborative action by American firms operating in foreign markets is whether the activities had as their purpose the fixing of prices and regulating of markets or merely represented an effort by a business firm to adjust its operations to the requirements of the foreign market.

Within the framework of the rule of reason as thus expounded the Committee reviewed recent cases involving patent interchanges to control markets, the relationship between a parent company and its foreign subsidiary, and activities carried on abroad jointly by American firms alone or combined with foreign competitors. Although the Committee did not take exception to the court rulings in the several international patent cartel cases it considered—*National Lead*,[122] *Imperial Chemical Industries*,[123] and the *General Electric* cases [124]—it emphasized that

plished by combination or conspiracy, and hence not in violation of Section 1," with page 91 of its report, where it cited the *Minnesota Mining* case for "assurance for legitimate individual operation of foreign facilities" and quoted the passage which follows the quotation given earlier.

120. *Antitrust Report*, at 80.
121. *Id.* at 81.
122. United States v. National Lead Co., 63 F. Supp. 513 (S.D.N.Y. 1945).
123. United States v. Imperial Chemical Industries, 100 F. Supp. 504 (S.D.N.Y. 1951).
124. United States v. General Electric Co., 82 F. Supp. 753 (D.N.J. 1949)

Workable Competition and Antitrust Policy

"valid patent rights may provide a lawful main purpose to which restrictions may be ancillary and therefore legal," [125] and it warned that international cartel arrangements of the National Lead, GE, and ICI sort "must be distinguished from cases where further inquiry is needed to determine when restraints, within the scope of the claims of valid patented inventions, are reasonably ancillary to a lawful main purpose." [126] It cited no such cases. With respect to foreign subsidiaries the Committee took the common-sense view that a corporation cannot conspire with its wholly owned subsidiary to fix prices or divide markets, and it saw in the *Timken* case, properly read, no threat to this doctrine. This seems to be a logical position. If monopolization or lessening of competition results from relations between a parent and its wholly owned subsidiary, certainly resort to the law of conspiracy is an unrealistic way of handling the problem. Divestiture would be more logical. The Committee did not consider this alternative. On the problems involved in joint activity of business rivals in foreign markets, the Committee repeated its position: "Manufacturing or distribution activities carried on abroad jointly by American firms alone, or combined with foreign competitors, should be upheld unless they create unreasonable restraints on the commerce of the United States." [127] Surprisingly, in view of its concern over certain dicta in *Minnesota Mining* already discussed,[128] it found no threat to this position in that case or in *Imperial Chemical Industries*.

As indicated, the Committee did not challenge the courts' position in the several cases it reviewed. Its apparent purpose in reviewing them was to furnish a guide to businessmen anxious to stay within the law as now interpreted, and to the courts in their future interpretation of the statute in its application to the foreign operations of domestic firms. Its analysis is marked by a spirit of reasonableness, but it reflects greater concern for freedom of firms than for freedom of markets.

PATENT-ANTITRUST POLICY

The Committee did not dig deep in considering the antitrust problems that patent practices have created. It was concerned with the range of

(incandescent lamp); United States v. General Electric Co., 80 F. Supp. 989 (S.D.N.Y. 1948) (Carboloy).
125. *Antitrust Report*, at 84.
126. *Id.* at 85–86.
127. *Id.* at 90.
128. See p. 214 and n. 117 *supra*.

The Attorney General's Committee's Report

patent practices that may run afoul of the antitrust laws rather than with the basic conflict that has developed between the legalization of limited monopolies through patents and a program designed to maintain competition generally throughout the economy.[129]

The conflict stems from changes in the inventive process on the one hand and in the institutions of ownership and management on the other. It reflects a shift from an individualistic to an organizational economy. The Founding Fathers who wrote the Constitution had witnessed a war of revolution that aimed not merely at political freedom but at freedom in economic affairs. The restrictive practices of a mercantilistic state committed to subordinating the economic development of the colonies to the broader interests of the Empire had occasioned the revolution. The colonists sought political freedom not merely as an end in itself but as a means to economic freedom. They wanted the right to make their own iron, to build and man their own ships, to export what they pleased where they pleased, when they pleased, free of taxes imposed by a distant and alien Parliament. Self-government was necessary to insure economic development of the sort the colonists wanted. But their economy was dependent on agriculture and handicrafts. Many of the colonial statesmen saw the need of encouraging domestic manufacturing, and all recognized the role that invention might play in an economy short of tools and capital equipment. Invention was then the province of the individual craftsman working part-time with mechanical devices of his own contrivance. The Constitution laid the basis for a patent system designed to "promote the Progress of Science and useful Arts, by securing for limited Times to . . . Inventors the exclusive Right to their . . . Discoveries." [130] The inventor by receiving a patent on a mechanical contrivance for a limited period could scarcely hope to monopolize an entire industry.

Science and the modern corporation have changed all this. Inventions and discoveries are expected to come not so much from solitary men of genius as from men of science working as teams with expensive equipment in research laboratories—laboratories that the large corporation is best able to support. The modern corporation has become not merely an agency for performing the traditional entrepreneurial functions in competitive markets but an instrument by which markets may be controlled and com-

---

129. The Committee stated the scope of its inquiry as follows: "Virtually all of the patent-antitrust matters we consider stem from the impact of the antitrust laws upon the utilization and transfer of patent rights which in their inception fall squarely within the patent law." *Antitrust Report,* at 225.
130. U.S. Const. Art. I, § 8.

merce regulated. The patent has become a tool of the corporation in its struggle for power. Hamilton described how this may come about:

> The inventor assigns his rights to a corporation; the corporation licenses various concerns to manufacture. Into the license agreements, as circumstances and profit-making may decree, are written restrictions in respect to territory, output, market channel, price. . . .
>
> . . . .
>
> . . . [If the patent] is valid, the patent owner becomes sovereign to an industry. The sole condition of his feudal tenure is that he keep alive a few patents essential to production. He must shape invention and discovery, not to an advance of the technical arts, but as a defense against public policy. If he can do so, his czar-like power extends to quality, grades, brands, capacity, output, price, channels of trade, allocation of wares, division of territory, terms of sale. His authority has, in fact, banished the market from the control over the conduct of the industry.[131]

The giant corporation with its research laboratories and its extensive facilities for acquiring and commercializing patented products and processes has become a depository of technology, without general access to which enterprise can scarcely be free or competition unrestricted. I hazard the judgment, although I cannot establish it empirically, that next to war and mergers control of patents has been the biggest factor in the development of corporate giants with power over markets.

The Attorney General's Committee was not concerned with such fundamental issues. Rather, it was interested in drawing the line between the lawful and unlawful use of patents under the antitrust statutes. As the Committee put it, "In this section, we consider the special problems which arise in applying the antitrust laws to patent practices."[132] Specifically, the Committee suggested factors relevant to determining (1) when a corporation's purchase of patents from a competitor is improper; (2) the legality of grant-back covenants; (3) when the nonuse of patented inventions reflects reasonable justification or a design to restrain trade; and (4) the permissible scope of patent license limitations. The Committee recommended that where the plaintiff's antitrust violation is offered as a defense to a contributory infringement suit, the courts should order "separate trials of the antitrust issues and the patent issues,"[133] giving precedence to the trial of the infringement issue. The majority was concerned lest the doctrine of patent misuse (*i.e.*, that the courts will not grant patent relief

---

131. Walton Hamilton and Irene Till, *Antitrust in Action* (TNEC Monograph No. 16, 1940), pp. 16–17.
132. *Antitrust Report*, at 223.
133. *Id.* at 249.

to a patentee who sues for infringement at the same time he is using his patent to restrain competition with his sale of an unpatented product [134]) become a bar to a patentee's right to sue for contributory infringement. Finally, the majority of the Committee considered compulsory royalty-free licensing of patents used in an antitrust violation an inappropriate remedy, "penal rather than remedial in character, and hence beyond the Sherman Act's authority to 'prevent and restrain' violations." [135]

In discussing these problems the Committee recognized the difficulty of distinguishing between the exercise of a legitimate patent right and the illegitimate extension of a monopoly privilege, but the Committee's fear of the latter was generally outweighed by its jealous defense of the former. In general, the Committee's solution of the dilemma was an application of the rule of reason to patent practices challenged as antitrust violations. For example, on the issue of nonuse the Committee believed "that an improper purpose *unduly* to restrain trade, to monopolize or attempt to monopolize . . . should give rise to antitrust liability. On the other hand where there is no affirmative showing that the purpose or effect of nonuse is *unreasonably* to restrain trade, to monopolize or attempt to monopolize, the patentee's conduct does not transgress the antitrust laws." [136] In approving the Supreme Court's position in the 1926 *General Electric* case [137] on the issue of price fixing the Committee majority concluded that "in the absence of horizontal agreement among licensees, or any plan aimed at or resulting in industry-wide price fixing, licenses with price fixing provisions fall within the orbit of the patent and need not run afoul of the antitrust laws." [138] Disapproving the trend in Supreme Court opinions to condemn all tying clauses that require licensees to purchase from the patentee unpatented or patented articles not within the scope of the licensed patent,[139] the Committee "feels . . . that in determining whether a tying clause may substantially lessen competition under the Clayton Act, or is unreasonable under the Sherman Act, the fact that

134. This is a paraphrase of the doctrine as stated in Morton Salt Co. v. Suppiger Co., 314 U.S. 488, 492–93 (1942), quoted in *Antitrust Report*, at 250.
135. *Antitrust Report*, at 256.
136. *Id.* at 231. Emphasis added.
137. United States v. General Electric Co., 272 U.S. 476, 490 (1926).
138. *Antitrust Report*, at 235.
139. The Committee said: "On a number of occasions the Court has regarded the patent itself as involving sufficient market power to make any tying clause a violation of the antitrust law. See United States v. Columbia Steel Co., 334 U.S. 495, 522 (1948); Times-Picayune Pub. Co. v. United States, 345 U.S. 594, 601 (1953); International Salt Co., Inc., v. United States, 332 U.S. 392, 396 (1947)." *Antitrust Report*, at 238 n. 57.

the tying product is patented need not be decisive of illegality.... [T]he patentee should be permitted to show that in the entire factual setting... the patent does not create the market power requisite to illegality of the tying clause." [140] Thus for the majority of the Committee a patent, although recognized as a "grant of monopoly," [141] does not necessarily imply "the wielding of monopolistic leverage" [142] in patent license tying clauses—the Committee's approved test of illegality when discussing tying clauses in general.[143] And in suggesting factors relevant to the antitrust significance of patent interchanges, the Committee would have the courts weigh the business advantages of settling patent conflicts expeditiously against the likelihood of restrictive patent pool practices: "In all instances, the sound resolution of the antitrust status of the interchange demands recognition, on the one hand, of the necessity of the interchange to resolve patent problems and, on the other, of the opportunity it may bring to engage in anticompetitive conduct." [144]

In thus indicating the scope and focus of the Committee's concern with "patent-antitrust problems" I do not mean to imply that the Committee is necessarily wrong in the positions it has taken on specific aspects of the law, or unjudicious or inaccurate in its analysis. I merely mean to show that the Committee never really came to grips with the basic problem of the relation between patent policy and the prevalence of monopoly and the preservation of competition. Nor do I mean to suggest that the national patent policy is wholly bad. What I lament is the Committee's failure to aid Congress in considering the question whether it can modify the patent laws to strengthen the incentive to innovation and at the same time weaken the incentive to monopoly.

ANTITRUST POLICY IN DISTRIBUTION

"Antitrust policy in distribution" is expressed primarily in the Clayton Act as amended by the Robinson-Patman Act,[145] in the Sherman Act as amended by the Miller-Tydings Act,[146] and in the Federal Trade Com-

140. *Id.* at 238.
141. *Id.* at 225.
142. "[T]he essence of illegality in tying agreements is the wielding of monopolistic leverage...." Times-Picayune v. United States, 345 U.S. 594, 611 (1953).
143. See p. 232 *infra.*
144. *Antitrust Report,* at 247.
145. 38 Stat. 730 (1914), as amended, 49 Stat. 1526 (1936), 15 U.S.C. §§ 13, 13a, b, 21a (1958).
146. 26 Stat. 209 (1890), as amended, 50 Stat. 693 (1937), 15 U.S.C. §§ 1–7 (1958).

The Attorney General's Committee's Report

mission Act as amended by the McGuire Act.[147] The Clayton Act was a response to the inadequacy of the Sherman Act to prevent industrial concentration and practices that business firms had used in monopolizing markets. It was primarily a preventive measure designed to nip monopoly in the bud. Section 2 of the Act made it unlawful for a seller to discriminate among buyers in pricing commodities where the effect might be to lessen competition substantially or to tend to create monopoly in any line of commerce. But the ban was not absolute. If a seller justified his price differences by differences in grade, quality or quantity of the commodity sold, or in selling or transportation costs, or if he made the lower prices in good faith to meet competition, they were beyond the prohibition of the law even though they might lessen competition or tend to create a monopoly.

Court Interpretations of the Clayton Act

Such was the statutory prohibition on price discrimination until the Robinson-Patman amendment in 1936. To understand the significance of the Robinson-Patman Act and its interpretation it is necessary to understand the forces behind it. Section 2 of the Clayton Act was aimed primarily at local price cutting when practiced by firms operating in national or regional markets as a means of bankrupting their local rivals and strengthening or creating a monopoly; nevertheless, it prohibited price discrimination that might lessen competition or create a monopoly *in any line of commerce*. This all-encompassing language would seem to have made the law applicable to discriminatory pricing whether it tended to eliminate competition among the purchasers of a product or among the sellers. But the courts decided differently. In the *Mennen* and *National Biscuit Company* cases [148] the Court of Appeals for the Second Circuit overruled Federal Trade Commission findings that discriminations in favor of wholesalers, or chain stores that pooled the purchases of all their units, against groups of independent merchants who wished to pool their purchases, violated Section 2. The Supreme Court denied certiorari. A half-dozen years later in two privately litigated cases, *Van Camp* and

147. 38 Stat. 717 (1914), as amended, 66 Stat. 632 (1952), 15 U.S.C. §§ 41-58 (1958).
148. Mennen Co. v. Federal Trade Commission, 288 Fed. 774 (2d Cir.), *cert. denied*, 262 U.S. 759 (1923); National Biscuit Co. v. Federal Trade Commission, 299 Fed. 733 (2d Cir.), *cert. denied*, 266 U.S. 613 (1924).

Workable Competition and Antitrust Policy

Ladoga,[149] the courts reversed the position they had taken in the two earlier cases and recognized that the Act was applicable to price discriminations that tended to lessen competition among buyers. But in these cases the practices of the parties complained against were surrounded by deceit and fraud, and the decisions scarcely warranted the expectation that Section 2 might become an effective instrument generally in preventing price discrimination from injuring competition among the buyers as well as the sellers of a product.

Encouraged by the courts' decisions in the *Van Camp* and *Ladoga* cases, the Federal Trade Commission proceeded against the Goodyear Tire and Rubber Company.[150] Goodyear had agreed with Sears, Roebuck & Company to fill its tire requirements at cost plus 6 per cent. To get the contract it had paid bonuses in cash and Goodyear stock. The Commission found that Goodyear's price to Sears could not be wholly justified by differences in costs. After making allowance for cost differences, including savings in selling expenses, the Commission found that Goodyear's discrimination in favor of Sears represented between 11 and 22 per cent of the prices charged other distributors on eight popular sizes of tires and ordered Goodyear to stop discriminating. The Commission had interpreted the "due allowance for differences in cost" proviso of the Clayton Act as limiting allowable quantity discounts. Goodyear appealed, and the Court of Appeals for the Sixth Circuit reversed the Commission.[151] The Supreme Court by denying certiorari [152] some three years after the passage of the Robinson-Patman Act made it clear that the Clayton Act could not prevent price discrimination based on quantity discounts. The Federal Trade Commission in its final report on the chain store investigation in 1934 concluded that Section 2 was inadequate to curb excessive concessions to mass buyers.[153]

Chain Stores and the Robinson-Patman Act

This sketch of the courts' interpretation of Section 2 of the Clayton Act throws some light on the agitation that culminated in the passage of the

149. George Van Camp & Sons v. American Can Co., 278 U.S. 245 (1929); American Can Co. v. Ladoga Canning Co., 44 F.2d 763 (7th Cir. 1930).
150. Goodyear Tire and Rubber Co., 22 F.T.C. 232 (1936).
151. Goodyear Tire and Rubber Co. v. Federal Trade Commission, 101 F.2d 620 (6th Cir. 1939).
152. Federal Trade Commission v. Goodyear Tire and Rubber Co., 308 U.S. 557 (1939).
153. Federal Trade Commission, *Final Report on Chain Store Investigation*, Sen. Doc. No. 4, 74th Cong., 1st Sess. 51, 96–97 (1935).

The Attorney General's Committee's Report

Robinson-Patman Act. The immediate factor behind the demand for a change in the law was the growing power of chain stores. The chain store represented an organizational innovation. Chains had expanded their business rapidly by selling for less. They could afford to sell for less because they were more efficient than small local stores. Chains bought in large amounts, and they frequently integrated manufacturing, wholesaling, brokerage, and warehousing. As manufacturers making goods for an assured market, they could stabilize operations at the optimum scale. As retailers selling tremendous amounts on a self-service, cash-and-carry basis, they could operate profitably on a small mark-up. The consumers were the chief beneficiaries of chain store economies; wholesalers, brokers, and independent retailers, the chief sufferers. Organized, articulate, and with their livelihood threatened, they turned to Congress for relief. Fortunately for them the Federal Trade Commission's investigation of the chains had revealed that the chains were not only more efficient, they were more powerful, and their power brought them preferential treatment that their weaker rivals could not command.[154] In buying they customarily obtained quantity discounts and promotional, advertising, and brokerage allowances. While these were in part bona fide allowances for services rendered, the evidence does not indicate that the discounts were always commensurate with the services. At any rate the concessions did not represent the independent judgment of businessmen as to the cost advantages of doing business with the chains. The Federal Trade Commission found that of 129 grocery manufacturers interviewed, 76 granted preferential treatment to large buyers. Of these 33 alleged that the chain stores had resorted to threats and coercion to obtain preferential treatment.[155]

Major Changes in the Clayton Act

The Robinson-Patman Act was a response to inroads the chains were making in the business of independent grocers; but Congress also designed it to remedy defects the courts had injected into the Clayton Act. Congress subjected the bills that eventually became the Act to hearing, debate, and amendment, made the Act applicable to the whole of industry, and more nearly reconciled it with the general purposes of traditional antitrust policy—more nearly, but not perfectly.[156] It broadened the price

---

154. See *id.* at 24–25.
155. *Id.* at 24.
156. Correctly or incorrectly, some congressional leaders believed or professed to believe that price discrimination was the chief cause of the growth of the chains and

Workable Competition and Antitrust Policy

discrimination prohibitions of Section 2, making price discrimination unlawful where it might "injure, destroy, or prevent competition with any person who either grants or knowingly receives the benefit of such discrimination, or with customers of either of them." It provided as an absolute justification for price "discrimination," even though it might lessen competition or tend to create a monopoly, price differentials that make *"only* due allowance for differences in the cost of manufacture, sale, or delivery resulting from the differing methods or quantities in which such commodities are . . . sold or delivered." (Emphasis supplied.) It authorized the Federal Trade Commission to fix quantity limits beyond which discounts could not be made, regardless of cost differences, where "available purchasers in greater quantities are so few as to render differentials on account thereof unjustly discriminatory or promotive of monopoly in any line of commerce." It placed the burden of rebutting a prima facie case of price discrimination on the person charged with the violation, and it provided that "nothing herein contained shall prevent a seller rebutting the prima-facie case thus made by showing that his lower price or the furnishing of services or facilities to any purchaser or purchasers was made in good faith to meet an equally low price of a competitor. . . ."

In language prolix and obscure it prohibited the payment of brokerage except for services rendered "either to the party to such transaction or to an agent, representative, or other intermediary therein where such intermediary is acting in fact for or in behalf, or is subject to the direct or indirect control, of any party to such transaction other than the person by whom such compensation is so granted or paid." Section 2(d) forbade paying for, and Section 2(e) forbade furnishing, advertising or promotional services or facilities except on proportionally equal terms to all buyers.

The Meaning of Amended Section 2

In extending the Clayton Act's prohibitions against price discrimination to price differentials that may "insure, destroy, or prevent com-

that they threatened to monopolize grocery retailing. Commenting on the probable consequences of the disappearance of the independent grocery, Congressman Patman said, "[W]e would have a monopoly and along with that monopoly would come higher prices and oppression. . . ." *Hearings before Committee on the Judiciary on* H.R. 8442, H.R. 4995, and H.R. 5062, 74th Cong., 1st Sess., ser. 10, pt. 2, at 6 (1936). Other congressmen voiced similar fears. They also viewed the chain stores as limiting economic opportunities for men of small capital, as destructive of individualism and democracy, and the preferential treatment they received from sellers as violating basic rules of fair play.

The Attorney General's Committee's Report

petition with any person who either grants or knowingly receives the benefit of such discrimination," the Robinson-Patman Act resolved the uncertainty the courts had created in the *Mennen* and *National Biscuit* cases. It also broadened the purposes of the Clayton Act. How it broadened them has been a moot question. Those who framed the language made it clear what they intended the Act to do. The original Patman Bill had prohibited price discrimination per se regardless of its effects on competition.[157] The language of the law as enacted is that recommended by the Senate Judiciary Committee after hearings on S. 3154 (the counterpart of the Patman Bill, introduced by Senator Joseph Robinson of Arkansas). About the purpose of Section 2 as amended the Senate Judiciary Committee said:

> It tends to exclude from the bill otherwise harmless violations of its letter, but accomplishes a substantial broadening of a similar clause now contained in section 2 of the Clayton Act. The latter has in practice been too restrictive, in requiring a showing of general injury to competitive conditions in the line of commerce concerned; whereas the more immediately important concern is in injury to the competitor victimized by the discrimination. Only through such injuries, in fact, can the larger injury result, and to catch the weed in the seed will keep it from coming to flower.[158]

The Federal Trade Commission's administration of the "competition with" provision in keeping with the above congressional purpose is partially responsible for the charge that the Act encourages a soft rather than a hard competition and that it conflicts with the philosophy of the Sherman Act. This criticism has merit. Much, of course, can be said on sociological and political grounds for a law designed to give special protection to small business regardless of its significance to competition, but it is not the special province of the economist to say it. I shall stick to my last.

Although the Attorney General's Committee recognized a disposition on the part of the Commission in its earlier decisions to identify an injury to a competitor with "injury to competition," the Committee did not recommend a change in the statute. The Committee believed that the " 'competitive injury' terminology of Section 2(a) in its present form can

---

157. A copy of H.R. 8442, 74th Cong., 1st Sess. (1935), as originally introduced, shows the "effect on competition" clause of § 2 of the Clayton Act enclosed in black brackets to indicate its proposed omission. H. R. Rep. No. 2287, 74th Cong., 2d Sess. 18 (1936).

158. Sen. Rep. No. 1502, 74th Cong., 2d Sess. 4 (1936). The House Judiciary Report contained almost identical language. H.R. Rep. No. 2287, 74th Cong., 2d Sess. 8 (1936).

Workable Competition and Antitrust Policy

be administered to conform with overall antitrust policy."[159] The Committee found that

courts have tended to abandon prior *misinterpretations* of the Act, in favor of the workable principles exemplified by the *Minneapolis-Honeywell* case. Hence, all tribunals are free to construe Section 2(a) in accord with the Sherman Act's policy of free competition, and guided by the *Automatic Canteen* decision's declaration of a "duty to reconcile" Section 2(a), insofar as the text of the Act permits, "with the broader antitrust policies that have been laid down by Congress."[160]

The Attorney General's Committee found in the Federal Trade Commission as constituted in 1955 a gratifying determination to "vindicate [its] expert status" by making a thorough economic analysis of market data in adjudicating complaints of price discrimination. The Committee recommended that "analysis of the statutory 'injury' center on the vigor of competition in the market rather than hardship to individual businessmen. For the essence of competition is a contest for trade among business rivals in which some must gain while others lose, to the ultimate benefit of the consuming public."[161] With this principle few economists will disagree, but I find it difficult to reconcile with the solicitude that the Committee, in approving the *International Shoe* opinion discussed earlier,[162] manifested over the plight of bankrupt or near-bankrupt firms in defending the right of business rivals to absorb them, even though the consequence may be the lessening of competition. And some students of political processes may be disturbed by the Committee's approval of changing the law by judicial and administrative reinterpretation instead of legislation.

Robinson-Patman's Internal Conflicts

The Robinson-Patman Act is not only somewhat out of harmony with the principles of the Sherman Act, but it contains conflicting principles within itself. While designed to preserve competition by prohibiting price discriminations that may destroy it, it legalizes discriminations where they can be justified by differences in cost [163] even though they may lead

---

159. *Antitrust Report*, at 163.
160. *Id.* at 164. Emphasis added. See Minneapolis-Honeywell Reg. Co. v. Federal Trade Commission, 191 F.2d 786, 789, 790 (7th Cir. 1951), *cert. dismissed*, 344 U.S. 206 (1952); Automatic Canteen Co. v. Federal Trade Commission, 346 U.S. 61, 74 (1953).
161. *Antitrust Report*, at 164.
162. See note 77 *supra*.
163. The language of the act is loose and inaccurate. Price differences that can be justified by differences in cost are not in an economic sense discriminatory. As

The Attorney General's Committee's Report

to monopoly. The Act also legalizes discriminatory pricing where it involves a good faith meeting of a rival's price even though such discrimination may destroy competition or create monopoly.

The Attorney General's Committee failed to come to grips with the issue this conflict raises, and it was critical of the manner in which the Federal Trade Commission met the good faith issue by holding that it tic efficiency versus competitive pricing. Price differences that merely reflect cost differences are not in fact discriminatory. They merely pass on to the more efficient firm the pecuniary equivalent of his superiority. But if such efficiency leads to monopoly, do we want it? That is the issue. The good faith defense presents a similar issue. Meeting a rival's price is the essence of the competitive process, but if meeting it tends to enhance the imperfections of the market—which the very fact of discrimination reflects—that is, if it tends to destroy competition or create monopoly, do we want it? That is the issue raised by the good faith defense. The Federal Trade Commission reconciled the conflict. The issue is monopolis- was a procedural, not a substantive defense; if discriminatory pricing, even though made in good faith to meet the equally low price of a competitor, had the effect prohibited by the statute, it was unlawful.[164] The Supreme Court in the *Standard Oil of Indiana* case [165] overruled the Federal Trade Commission, making the good faith proviso an absolute defense. The Attorney General's Committee approved the Court's having done so.

Where the Federal Trade Commission found discriminatory pricing tended to lessen or destroy competition, it solved the problem of the cost justification provision by setting up such rigorous and ill-defined standards of justification that few sellers could meet them. As the Attorney General's Committee pointed out, after a single successful cost defense in 1937, "not until the *B. F. Goodrich* case seventeen years later did an accused seller in a fully contested proceeding succeed in establishing a complete cost defense to defeat every element in a discrimination

---

Adelman has pointed out, the Federal Trade Commission in administering the act never challenges as discriminatory identical prices for transactions that involve substantial cost differences. Adelman, "The Consistency of the Robinson-Patman Act," 6 Stanford L. Rev. 3, 7–8 (1953). Moreover, the Commission has held certain price differences that do not take full account of differences in cost to be justified under the act. *Id.* at 10, citing Kraft-Phoenix Cheese Corp., 25 F.T.C. 537 (1937).

164. Standard Oil Co. of Indiana, 41 F.T.C. 263 (1945), *modified*, 43 F.T.C. 56 (1946), *modified and aff'd*, 173 F.2d 210 (7th Cir. 1949), *rev'd and remanded*, 340 U.S. 231 (1951), *new order by Commission*, 49 F.T.C. 923 (1953), *order vacated*, 233 F.2d 649 (7th Cir. 1956), *aff'd*, 355 U.S. 396 (1958).

165. See note 164 *supra*.

227

charge."[166] While in two other proceedings "a cost defense partially prevailed, the Federal Trade Commission in seven other recorded instances rejected attempted cost justifications out of hand."[167] Moreover, past adjudications have evolved no "workable criteria by which the cost defense can attain its intended role."[168] According to the Committee, the result is that "businessmen and consumers have largely been deprived to date of the cost proviso's intended benefits."[169] While the difficulty is partly that of an obscure and perplexing statutory text, according to the Committee, the remedy lies not in a revision of the text but in a change in its interpretation. As the Committee put it:

[T]he statutory language is complex and obscure. Yet sufficient flexibility inheres in the "due allowance" concept and a broad view of cognizable "methods" of sale or delivery for enabling a responsive tribunal to accommodate the Robinson-Patman cost defense to the realities of business and broader antitrust objectives, while at the same time implementing the legislative design to preserve for the consumer the economies of efficient distribution processes.[170]

Significance of Committee's Recommendations

What do these several changes the Committee would make through administrative and court interpretation do to the Robinson-Patman Act, and more important, what do they promise to do to the economy? They appropriately direct the Act to the prohibition of discrimination that weakens competition. Most economists would approve this end. Having thus narrowed the application of the Act, the Committee would make it easier to justify what would otherwise be unlawful price discrimination by cost differences and would make the good faith defense and the cost defense absolute. Under what circumstances, then, does price discrimination become unlawful? To answer this question it is necessary to realize that businessmen do not resort to discriminatory price cutting just for the fun of it. Four circumstances may lead them to do so: (1) in a predatory price war, they hope to drive a weaker rival out of existence and ultimately to monopolize the market; (2) they believe that a larger quantity or a particular method of dealing justifies a lower price to one buyer than to another; (3) they want to meet the equally low price of a rival; or (4) they may be

166. *Antitrust Report*, at 171, citing B. F. Goodrich Co., F.T.C. Dkt. 5677 (1954); Sylvania Electric Products Co., F.T.C. Dkt. 5728 (1954).
167. *Antitrust Report*, at 171.
168. *Ibid.*
169. *Id.* at 172.
170. *Id.* at 175.

The Attorney General's Committee's Report

coerced into cutting by the pressure of an oligopolistic buyer. It was against predatory price cutting that the Clayton Act was primarily directed, and neither the Federal Trade Commission nor the courts have been disposed to approve of it. It is unlikely that such price cutting would be held lawful even by the somewhat less vigorous cost standards that the Attorney General's Committee proposed, and there is no reason to believe the Committee wanted it to be.

But the Committee's recommendations would make it impossible to bring within the prohibition of the statute such price cuts as were made in good faith to meet equally low prices, regardless of their effect on competition, and they would make it difficult if not impossible to bring within the prohibition of the statute such price cuts as reflect a businessman's judgment of the relative profitability of two different transactions even though such price cutting may destroy competition. Finally, what does the Act as the Committee would have the courts interpret it do to price cuts forced upon a businessman by the pressure to which buyers can subject him? The Committee apparently intended to leave them beyond the reach of the law, for in discussing the buyer's liability under the Robinson-Patman Act and in approving the Supreme Court's opinion in the *Automatic Canteen* case [171] it stated:

Especially significant was the Court's recognition of the *imperative necessity* for preserving the legal freedom of buyers to engage in aggressive bargaining over price as basic to effectively competitive distribution. In markets characterized by sellers enjoying a significant degree of control over price, the exertion of offsetting force by some large and aggressive buyers bargaining for concessions can contribute materially to lower prices for all. Not only is one reduction likely to spread; but each entering wedge enhances the negotiating position of other traders who can insist on equal concessions from the supplier with the ancient gambit of buying elsewhere unless he accedes. And unless competition on the buyers' level is wholly defunct, the ultimate consumer stands to benefit by lower prices. Legalistic impediments to this normal bargaining process, we think, might well deprive the public of gains that under effective competition it has a right to expect.[172]

This reads like sound economics, but the principle does not call for the sort of law that the Committee would make of the Robinson-Patman Act. The fault lies in the Committee's failure to resolve the issue of monopolistic efficiency versus competitive pricing. To determine whether price cuts not made available to all buyers will tend to lessen competition or create monopoly, on the one hand, or make competition more effective, on the

---

171. Automatic Canteen Co. v. F.T.C., 346 U.S. 61 (1953).
172. *Antitrust Report*, at 196. Emphasis added.

other, is not easy; and neither the Act nor the Federal Trade Commission may have solved the problem; but if under a properly devised statute, a competent administrative agency has determined that price cuts not available to all buyers may destroy competition and create monopoly, do we want any kind of cost or good faith justification? If the results of price discrimination are to create or preserve monopoly, there is no reason to expect that such lower costs as might be thereby realized will be passed on to the consumer. An illustration previously mentioned will clarify this point. For roughly a quarter of a century the American Can Company obtained substantial price concessions in buying tin plate from the United States Steel Corporation. Under an oligopolistic industrial structure it was able to tie the price of tin cans to the quoted price of tin plate and pocket its cost savings. Selling tin plate to the American Can Company in larger amounts than any other buyer, the Steel Corporation might have been able to justify the price differences on a basis of cost difference, but competition would not have been preserved by permitting it to do so.

If this analysis is correct, the interpretations of Section 2(a) of the Robinson-Patman Act that the Committee recommended would virtually emasculate it. If the Committee wanted that, it would have done better to recommend the Act's repeal, a possibility that, as one member noted, the Committee did not even consider.[173]

Indirect Discounts, Brokerage Fees, and Service Allowances

The Committee was on sounder ground in its analysis of other sections of the Robinson-Patman and Clayton Acts. The Committee pointed out that as the Federal Trade Commission has administered and the courts have interpreted Section 2(c), "the payment of middleman's commissions to any but pure 'brokers' becomes *per se* illegal, even though valuable distributive services are performed, even when no adverse competitive effect results, and even where the challenged concession reflects actual savings in the seller's distribution costs." [174] The Committee found that the Federal Trade Commission "has evolved a rule of thumb for testing the requisite proportional equality [Sections 2(d) and 2(e)] in allowances or services by comparing the promotional benefit with the dollar volume of purchases by various customers," [175] but it pointed out that "the Act as currently construed forbids any 'proportionally *unequal*' promotional allowance or

173. *Id.* at 220.
174. *Id.* at 189.
175. *Ibid.*

The Attorney General's Committee's Report

service, though no actual or probable lessening of competition is shown to exist."[176] The Committee recommended legislation to "restore the original vigor of the exception 'for services rendered' in Section 2(c)" and interpretative reform to reconcile Sections 2(d) and 2(e) with "'broader antitrust objectives.'"[177]

Tying Contracts and Exclusive Dealing

Section 3 of the Clayton Act prohibits tying contracts and exclusive dealing arrangements where they may lessen competition substantially or tend to create a monopoly in any line of commerce. The Attorney General's Committee recognized the validity of the principle incorporated into Section 3. As the Committee put it, "By restricting access to the market by the seller's rivals . . . some 'tying' agreements obviously may impair competition in the distribution of the 'tied' product."[178] Under the typical tying arrangement the owner of a machine conditions its sale or lease on an agreement by the buyer or lessee that he will use only supplies or services furnished by the seller or lessor. Full-line forcing binds the distributor of one item on which the supplier generally holds a patent or goodwill monopoly to accept nonmonopolized items as a condition of obtaining the monopolized product. In short, a seller or lessor uses a monopoly as a lever by which to expand the sale of nonmonopolized products or services. The Supreme Court, which had held that such practices were beyond the reach of the Sherman Act,[179] invalidated them under the Clayton Act.[180] In *International Salt*,[181] even though the record did not indicate that the International Salt Company dominated the salt market, the Court condemned the tying arrangement as embracing a "not insignificant or insubstantial" volume of commerce in the tied supplies. In *Times-Picayune*[182] the Court laid down the principle that if a supplier enjoys "a monopolistic position in the market for the 'tying' product, *or* if a substantial volume of commerce in the 'tied' product is restrained, a tying arrangement violates the narrower standards expressed in § 3 of the Clayton Act because from either factor the requisite potential lessening of competition

---

176. *Id.* at 190.
177. *Id.* at 192–93.
178. *Id.* at 138.
179. Henry v. A. B. Dick Co., 224 U.S. 1 (1912).
180. International Machines Corp. v. United States, 298 U.S. 131 (1936); United Shoe Mach. Co. v. United States, 258 U.S. 451 (1922).
181. International Salt Co. v. United States, 332 U.S. 392 (1947).
182. Times-Picayune v. United States, 345 U.S. 594, 608–09 (1953).

is inferred." The Attorney General's Committee found no fault with these interpretations, concluding that "a relatively narrow inquiry for testing the validity of tying arrangements that 'wield monopolistic leverage' is fully compatible with economic realities and business facts." [183]

The Committee found the law on exclusive dealing less satisfactory. The disturbing issue was whether exclusive dealing contracts involving a substantial share of any market are unlawful per se under Section 3, as the Supreme Court seems to have held in the *Standard Stations* case,[184] or whether they should be held unlawful only on evidence that competitors have in fact been foreclosed from a market. The Committee believed that the illegality of such arrangements should be determined only after an analysis of significant market data and a determination, in Sherman Act cases, whether competitors have in fact been denied access to the market or, in Clayton Act cases, whether there is a reasonable probability that they will be. In brief, it favored a rule of reason rather than a per se approach to the problem.

Resale Price Maintenance

While recognizing that fair trade laws reflect some legitimate commercial aims, *e.g.*, the prevention of loss-leader sales and debasement of quality items in consumers' minds, the Committee regarded them as inappropriate instruments for achieving such ends. Believing that the Miller-Tydings and McGuire amendments conflict with the elementary principles of a dynamic free enterprise system, the Committee recommended their repeal, a recommendation likely to meet with the approval of economists generally and one in which I heartily concur.

Functional Discounts

The Committee in its analysis of the economics of functional discounts concluded that where a distributor performs the function of wholesaling

---

183. *Antitrust Report*, at 145. As indicated in this article, the Attorney General's Committee considered the economic and legal significance of tying arrangements at two points, in its discussion of patents and in its discussion of distribution. The two discussions appear to be somewhat in conflict. The Committee approved "a relatively narrow inquiry" for testing the validity of tying arrangements that "wield monopolistic leverage" in distribution, but it insisted on an inquiry into "the entire factual setting" for tying clauses in patent licenses (see p. 220 *supra*). The difference in approach is so striking as to suggest that different authors wrote the two sections and that the Committee never reconciled their positions.

184. Standard Oil Co. of California v. United States, 337 U.S. 293 (1949).

The Attorney General's Committee's Report

by relieving his supplier of risk, storage, transportation, administration, and the like, he should be entitled to discounts to compensate him for these functions even though he may also engage in retailing. A legal rule that disqualifies the wholesaler-retailer from receiving discounts for his wholesaling function forces him to perform the function free of charge or discontinue it. It subjects him to a handicap that the integrated producer does not encounter, and in so doing it prevents the free play of competitive forces. The Committee therefore recommended that

> suppliers granting functional discounts either to single-function or to integrated buyers should not be held responsible for any consequences of their customers' pricing tactics. Price cutting at the resale level is not in fact, and should not be held in law, "the effect of" a differential that merely accords due recognition and reimbursement for actual marketing functions.[185]

These are principles that an economist can accept—without, however, passing judgment on whether the Committee's analysis does justice to all the issues in the *Standard Oil of Indiana* case, to which it applied its principles.

Delivered Pricing

The Committee recognized that basing point pricing may be systematically and collusively used as a device for lessening competition. It also correctly believed that delivered pricing may be used by a firm in one location to compete with a more distant rival. The Federal Trade Commission's attack on basing point pricing through the Robinson-Patman Act and Section 5 of the Federal Trade Commission Act made the Committee uneasy. It was also concerned over court dicta and Commission findings that suggest that any departure from f.o.b. pricing may involve discrimination. The Committee's concern is not without justification. The Federal Trade Commission, impressed with the difficulty in conspiracy cases of banning collective behavior that stifled competition, found in the Robinson-Patman Act a new weapon. In using it in the *Glucose* cases [186]

---

185. *Antitrust Report*, at 208.
186. A. E. Staley Manufacturing Co., 34 F.T.C. 1362 (1942), *remanded*, 135 F.2d 453 (7th Cir.), *modified*, 4 Statutes and Decisions, Federal Trade Commission (1944–1948), 795 (1943), *rev'd*, 144 F.2d 221 (7th Cir. 1944), *rev'd*, 324 U.S. 746 (1945); Clinton Co., 34 F.T.C. 879 (1942); Corn Products Refining Co., 34 F.T.C. 850 (1942), *aff'd*, 324 U.S. 726 (1945); Hubinger Co., 32 F.T.C. 1116 (1941); American Maize-Products Co., 32 F.T.C. 901 (1941); Union Starch & Refining Co., 32 F.T.C. 60 (1940); Penick & Ford, Ltd., Inc., 31 F.T.C. 1494 (1940); Anheuser-Busch, Inc., 31 F.T.C. 986 (1940); Piel Brothers Starch Co., 30

the Commission ruled that differences in delivered prices occasioned by either phantom freight or freight absorption that had lessened competition were unlawful price discriminations, and it banned both. To have complied with the Commission's orders literally a firm would have had to sell only f.o.b. The industry did not interpret them as requiring this.[187]

The *Rigid Steel Conduit* proceeding,[188] a Federal Trade Commission Act Section 5 case, similarly reflected the Commission's conviction that industry-wide basing point pricing inevitably lessens competition. The first count of the complaint charged that the manufacturers of rigid steel conduit had conspired to use a basing point pricing system; the second count, that each respondent had used it knowing that its rivals did so. The Commission's findings sustained both counts, and it ordered the respondents to quit conspiring and individually to cease quoting or selling rigid steel conduit at prices calculated on a basing point system "for the purpose or with the effect of systematically matching delivered-price quotations."[189] The findings and order on the second count especially disturbed the Committee. It believed that basing point pricing, conspiratorially contrived and administered, will reveal itself through "persistent standardization and surveillance of freight charges, delivery methods, service extras and discounts" and that "the disciplined maintenance of a 'delivered' pricing system over a period of time as an instrument of collusion will disclose some overt index of agreement among participating sellers."[190] The Committee recommended that the government proceed against basing point pricing exclusively under the Sherman Act.

In condemning the Commission's findings on the second count of the *Rigid Steel Conduit* complaint, the Committee overlooked an important part of the findings—that the "purpose and effect" of each respondent's using delivered pricing, under the circumstances of this case, was to restrict competition. Moreover, the Committee was only half right in its

F.T.C. 1384 (1939). Although the Commission proceeded against each of these companies separately, it was evidently trying to break down an industry-wide practice that restricted competition.

187. A Federal Trade Commission staff member has challenged the above interpretation, indicating that in fact compliance did not result in f.o.b. prices. For a complete development of this point see Stocking, *Basing Point Pricing and Regional Development*, at 165–70.

188. Rigid Steel Conduit Ass'n, 38 F.T.C. 534 (1944), *aff'd sub nom.* Triangle Conduit & Cable Co. v. Federal Trade Commission, 168 F.2d 175 (7th Cir. 1948), *aff'd by an equally divided court sub nom.* Clayton Mark & Co. v. Federal Trade Commission, 333 U.S. 956 (1949).

189. 38 F.T.C. 534, 595.

190. *Antitrust Report*, at 216.

The Attorney General's Committee's Report

conclusion that where delivered pricing is continuously and systematically used, supplementary pricing practices that bulwark it are likely to reveal conspiracy. Where sellers are few and disciplined, this is not necessarily true. In another connection the Committee acknowledged as much in recognizing that where sellers are few, "the possibility of successful collusion is greater, to detect it is harder, and its rewards may be more immediate and tempting." [191] Under such circumstances a finding like that in *Rigid Steel Conduit* may serve the cause of competition. Much, of course, can be said for proceeding against basing point pricing under the Sherman Act, but the Committee did not say all that it might have said. The chief objection to proceeding under Section 5 of the Federal Trade Commission Act is the inadequacy of available remedies; the Commission can order respondents to stop conspiring but it cannot change the structure of an industry. As long as an industry is dominated by a few large firms that are well disciplined and habituated to restrictive pricing practices, Federal Trade Commission orders to quit conspiring are unlikely to change industrial behavior. Where an industry's behavior is rooted in its structure, a change in structure may be the only remedy for pricing practices that restrain competition. When this is called for, it can be achieved if at all only through court action under the Sherman Act.

Three circumstances would seem to justify Robinson-Patman proceedings against basing point pricing: when it results in phantom freight (whether obvious or concealed in price differentials); when a firm refuses to sell f.o.b. mill and to permit the customer to choose the means of transportation; and when a multiplant firm engages in local price discrimination by absorbing freight with the long-run effect of lessening competition by putting a local rival out of business.

EXEMPTIONS FROM ANTITRUST COVERAGE

Just as, in considering antitrust prohibitions on noncompetitive behavior, the Committee never really came to grips with the fundamental aspects of the problem of maintaining competition, so in considering legislative exemptions designed to protect certain groups and industries from the rigors of competition, the Committee carefully refrained from passing judgment on their economic validity. It put policy questions beyond the scope of its inquiry, except for a repeated but vague endorsement of "competition as the major rule in our private enterprise economy." [192] Instead,

191. *Id.* at 326.
192. *Id.* at 269.

Workable Competition and Antitrust Policy

the Committee chose to mark out "the precise limits of each exemption" and appraise the extent to which regulatory agencies and courts "give effect to whatever Congressional standards relating to competition appear in any given statute." [193] The Committee proceeded to do this for mergers and rate agreements among rival firms in the transportation field, but it carefully avoided judgment on the significance of congressional standards for competition—and their application in administering regulatory statutes—to the preservation of a private enterprise economy. On the necessity of rate agreements by shipping conferences, railway bureaus, or airlines the Committee expressly passed "no judgment." [194]

The Committee did not even consider two important sectors of the economy in which state and federal action has placed cartelization beyond the reach of the antitrust laws—insurance and oil production. It had nothing to say about the adequacy of state regulation as a substitute for competition in keeping insurance rates down nor about the competitive significance of the skillfully devised program by which oil producing states, while protecting oil resources from wasteful exploitation, have controlled the price of oil by regulating its flow into the domestic market.

Since the Committee avoided considering the significance of an oligopolistic industrial structure to the preservation of a competitive economy, it was scarcely in a position to consider the significance to a free market of powerful labor unions collectively selling their services to business giants. It avoided all reference to industry-wide collective bargaining, privately negotiated and corporate-financed social insurance programs, and the whole range of fringe benefits that unions are seeking, in their impact on the flexibility of costs and the fluidity and mobility of the labor force. It was concerned exclusively with the conspiratorial aspects and legal status of labor-management agreements and union-imposed restrictions that directly affect competition in the sale of goods or services. The Committee's discussion of the legal steps by which many trade union activities have been placed beyond the reach of the antitrust laws and its delimitation of the boundary between what unions can and cannot lawfully do in interfering with competition, are meticulous and discerning. The discussion should be useful to businessmen and union leaders anxious to avoid clashing with the law; it also should be of interest to Congress, for the Committee with only two dissenters recommended that unions be prohibited by statute from engaging in "activities which have as their direct object direct control of the market, such as fixing the kind or amount of

193. *Id.* at 261.
194. *Id.* at 277.

The Attorney General's Committee's Report

products which may be used, produced or sold, their market price, the geographical area in which they may be sold, or the number of firms which may engage in their production or distribution." [195]

The Committee traced with equal skill and clarity the line that the statutes, administrative agencies, and courts have drawn between lawful and unlawful market-control activities by agricultural cooperatives. It urged that the statutory exemptions in this area "should not reduce antitrust prohibitions to a ghostly residuum." [196] Although the Committee did not believe that agricultural cooperatives have offered any serious threat to effective competition in the sale of agricultural commodities, it recommended that "where cooperatives attempt to or actually obtain monopoly power by means not sanctioned by Section 1 of Capper-Volstead, the Sherman Act should apply *even though the monopolized product's price is not unduly enhanced.*" [197]

On the whole, it seems to me that the Committee's dedication to competition stands out more clearly in its discussion of labor practices and the activities of agricultural cooperatives than it does in its discussion of business behavior.

ECONOMIC INDICIA OF COMPETITION AND MONOPOLY

As previously indicated, except for the persistency of a few dissenters a reader of the Committee's report might get the impression that the antitrust experts see the problems alike; but there is evidence that the Committee's deliberations engendered considerable controversy. It centered about the significance of industrial structure to economic behavior, and the alignment on the issue was the academicians versus the "real-life practitioners." [198] In contrast to the other sections of the report, apparently the academicians spoke for the Committee in chapter 7, "Economic Indicia of Competition and Monopoly."

The academicians recognized that the prospect for competition improves with an increase in the number of sellers in any market. As they expressed it,

195. *Id.* at 304.
196. *Id.* at 311.
197. *Ibid.* Emphasis added.
198. The reassuring phrase is Blackwell Smith's, a Committee member, who described the controversy. Smith, "Antitrust Report to Narrow Gap Between Law and Economics," Trade Practice Bulletin, May 1955, p. 4.

Workable Competition and Antitrust Policy

[A]s the number of independent sellers reaches unity, the market obviously reaches monopoly. . . .

. . . .

When sellers are few, each producing a significant share of total market supply, each seller is aware of the fact that any substantial change in his price or his production will have an appreciable effect upon total market supply and market price, and will tend to elicit responsive changes in the prices and outputs of his rivals. Hence there is a mutual awareness rather than an impersonal market relationship. . . . [It follows that] when sellers are few, even in the absence of conspiracy, the market itself may not show many of the characteristics of effective competition, and in fact may not be effectively competitive in the economic sense.[199]

According to Blackwell Smith, a nonacademic member of the Committee, the nonacademic members were at one stage afraid of endorsing such ideas.[200] But the general give and take of the larger meetings, "with real-life practitioners wearing away at abstract theoreticians and vice versa did much to reduce the disparity among groups." [201]

Despite the compromise that the report's discussion of "economic indicia of competition and monopoly" reflects, it is on the whole a sensible, coherent, and logical analysis of the conditions essential to effective competition in industrial markets. If the influence of the "real-life practitioners," who constituted a majority of the Committee,[202] had not been so great, other sections of the report might have reflected more accurately the logic of this discussion.

Antitrust Administration and Enforcement

An analysis of the Committee's recommendations on administration and enforcement is more properly the task of the lawyer than the economist, and I shall not undertake it. I must confess, however, that I find the recommendations disturbing.[203] On a basis of two years' experience

199. *Antitrust Report,* at 326.
200. Smith, *supra* note 198.
201. *Ibid.*
202. See note 22 *supra.*
203. An example is the Committee's recommendation on increasing the penalty for antitrust violation. Many students of antitrust have long recognized the inadequacy of the financial penalties imposed—frequently trivial in comparison with the gains of monopoly—to curb violations. The Committee was more impressed with the decline in the value of the dollar since 1890 than with the need for stiffer penalties; it recommended that, "to take some account for inflation, the present $5,000 ceiling should be increased to $10,000." *Antitrust Report,* at 352. Yet in January 1955 the President's Economic Report had recommended that Congress, without waiting for the Attorney General's Committee's report, raise the maximum fine "substantially,"

The Attorney General's Committee's Report

with antitrust administration I find merit in the conclusions reached by Schwartz in his dissent that "added together the total effect of the recommendations is clear: to restrict the Antitrust Division's power of investigation, to curtail use of criminal prosecutions, to slow up the filing of complaints, to encumber the exercise of prosecutor's discretion with novel internal administrative reviews on request of a defendant, to expand the use of the consent decree in a manner calculated to remove the last possibility of public scrutiny of this useful but dangerous practice which, among other things, shields the defendants from damage suits by private parties, to water down the threat of treble damage recovery, etc." [204] If Schwartz is correct and the Committee's views prevail, the administration of antitrust laws will lose its vigor.

Conclusion

The Committee was not a fact-finding body but a study group. As a study group it made surprisingly little use of available studies relevant to preserving free enterprise, and it manifested no curiosity about the inadequately explored areas of business behavior and structural relationships that, if illuminated, might aid greatly in shaping sound policy toward business. What are the basic factors in the national economy making for bigness? Does bigness bring business advantages to a firm without corresponding benefits for society? What is the relationship between size and efficiency? What is the significance of bigness to research and of research to bigness? What is the role of the individual inventor in a corporate economy? What are the economic advantages of diversification and what is its significance to firm size? What are the relationships between small suppliers and the larger manufacturers and between large manufacturers and their distributors? Do suppliers and distributors function as independent business firms or as satellites? How important are advertising and selling outlays to cost? What is their significance to freedom of entry? The

---

"to strengthen the deterrent to violation of the Sherman Antitrust Act." *Economic Report of the President,* Jan. 20, 1955, p. 50. Subsequently, the Attorney General, stating that the deterrent effect of a $5,000 fine against a large corporation is "almost negligible except for the stigma of conviction," asked Congress to increase the maximum fine from $5,000 to $50,000. Trade Practice Bulletin, February 1955, p. 3. Following these recommendations, Congress passed and the President approved an amendment to the Sherman Act increasing the maximum fine to $50,000. 69 Stat. 282 (1955), 15 U.S.C. §§ 1 and 2 (1958). Congress' action indicates the modesty of the Attorney General's Committee's recommendation.

204. *Antitrust Report,* at 388.

Workable Competition and Antitrust Policy

Committee could not have been expected to answer such questions, but it would have performed a public service by recognizing the need for answers and by suggesting studies and investigations for obtaining them; for the answers to such questions would provide a basis for sound public policy toward business, little and big. They would get at the antitrust problem in its fundamental aspects.

It is exceedingly difficult to deal with questions of economic policy with complete objectivity, and experts on policy questions are not necessarily "open-minded." They bring to the problem on which they are experts minds filled with facts, and experience and understanding that give them a point of view about it. The point of view of the Attorney General's Committee is clear. It is not so much reflected in any particular thread of bias running through the Committee's discussion of particular problems— in truth the Committee has woven with deft and delicate hands—rather it is revealed in the general pattern of the fabric. The Committee views the contemporary industrial structure with equanimity. It has faith in an economy of big business, and its recommendations reflect this faith. Its solicitude for big business outweighs its fear of monopoly. Wesley Mitchell used to tell his Columbia University students that the problems with which economists concern themselves and how they look at them are determined by the institutional matrix in which they find themselves. The Committee's report reflects this principle. The report is not a study of the fundamental aspects of the antitrust problem but a profession of faith in the industrial status quo—a confessional of a group of dedicated men who have made peace with their environment.

5
On the Concept of Workable Competition as an Antitrust Guide

DIRLAM AND STELZER'S ARTICLE, "The Cellophane Labyrinth,"[1] combined a rejection of workable competition standards as measures of antitrust violation with a misstatement of what Mueller and I were doing in our analysis of du Pont's position in the manufacture and sale of cellophane.[2] They stated, "Without enquiring into the consequences of relying on exclusively economic tests in antitrust cases, nor exhibiting awareness of the dangers that had been pointed out of the employment of this particular concept, two economists proceeded to attack the *Cellophane* decision simply on grounds that competition in cellophane was not workable."[3] This is not what we did at all. What we did was to challenge Judge Leahy's conclusion that Du Pont had no monopoly in making and selling cellophane.[4] This is an economic problem and we resorted to economic analysis to answer it.

Since, as my published work on the subject shows,[5] I am among those

Note: Reprinted from the *Antitrust Bulletin*, Vol. II (September 1956).

1. Joel B. Dirlam and Irwin M. Stelzer, "The Cellophane Labyrinth," 1 Antitrust Bulletin 633 (1956).
2. George W. Stocking and Willard F. Mueller, "The Cellophane Case and the New Competition," 45 Am. Econ. Rev. 29 (1955), reprinted in American Economic Ass'n, *Readings in Industrial Organization and Control*, ed. Richard B. Heflebower and George W. Stocking (Homewood, Ill.: Irwin, 1958), p. 118.
3. Dirlam and Stelzer, *supra* note 1, at 641.
4. In the antitrust case brought by the Department of Justice Judge Leahy of the federal district court for Delaware ruled that Du Pont had no monopoly power over cellophane and that if it did it was not unlawful. United States v. E. I. du Pont de Nemours & Co., 118 F. Supp. 41 (D. Del. 1953). The Supreme Court affirmed, 351 U.S. 377 (1956).
5. George W. Stocking and Myron W. Watkins, *Monopoly and Free Enterprise* (New York: Twentieth Century Fund, 1951), pp. 92–109; articles now presented as chaps. 2, 3, and 4 of this book. Later in this chapter I discuss the position I took in these earlier writings.

Workable Competition and Antitrust Policy

economists who reject workable competition as an antitrust guide, my present endeavor is to trace the development of the proposal that the concept be adopted in antitrust proceedings, show my position with respect to it, and attempt to clear up any misunderstanding that my two published discussions of cellophane [6] may have created.

At the outset it may be helpful to restate as succinctly as I can the concept of workable competition. Both pure competition and pure monopoly are neoclassical conceptions. They are both abstractions. Pure competition reflects the absence of all monopoly power; pure monopoly, the absence of all competition except competition for the consumer's dollar. Pure competition contemplates a market in which sellers and buyers are so numerous and so small—and products are so standardized—that none can exert any influence over the market by the decisions he makes. Price is a datum. It influences the decisions of every entrepreneur as to how much he produces, but the decision of each has no effect on it. Under pure monopoly a single seller's product has an isolated market. It has no rival products. The contemporary business world obviously cannot conform to the economists' models of either pure competition or pure monopoly. In many industrial sectors the number of producers is necessarily small, and many businessmen have through advertising and innovation so differentiated their product that they can set its price. In few if any markets does a "monopolized" product fail to meet the competition of distant substitutes. Some degree or characteristic of monopoly pervades nearly all sectors of business. Since neither pure competition nor pure monopoly is desirable or attainable, a private enterprise economy must get along with an acceptable compromise. Workable competition is a term economists give to that rather ill-defined market situation that is socially acceptable. It is the best available and it is good enough. Personal judgments obviously enter into the evaluation of any competitive arrangement when judged by the standard of workable competition. But economists have indicated what to look for in making judgments. They regard industrial structure, business conduct, and business performance as relevant. Industrial structure is significant in judging the degree of monopoly power. Business conduct indicates whether businessmen are engaging in practices detrimental to competition. Industrial performance is ill-defined, but some economists believe it is useful in determining the social acceptability of market arrangements. Economists differ in the emphasis they would give to these three criteria, but most would acknowledge the relevance of each.

6. Stocking and Mueller, *supra* note 2, and chap. 3, pp. 153–66 *supra*.

Workable Competition as an Antitrust Guide

Origins of the Proposal to Use Workable Competition in Antitrust

Efforts to revise the antitrust laws to insure their administration in accordance with economic principles rather than legalistic standards, although greatly intensified in recent years, originated some two decades ago. Edward S. Mason in a 1937 article on "Monopoly in Law and Economics" [7] lamented the difference between the legal and the economic concepts. Mason found that the term monopoly was being used in the law as a standard of evaluation, and that the courts determined its status by examining business practices. Contracts that restricted competition unreasonably were unlawful, and the use of predatory business practices was evidence of the intent to monopolize. Economists, on the other hand, regarded monopoly as a tool of economic analysis and looked on market control as evidence of monopoly. Thus Mason apparently recognized the significance of structure to competition. "The antithesis of the legal conception of monopoly," he said, "is *free* competition. . . . [T]he antithesis of the economic conception of monopoly is not *free* but *pure competition*. . . ." [8]

Mason recognized that in using the monopoly concept as a tool of analysis economists will find no clear-cut dichotomy of monopoly and competition. He pointed out that nearly all market situations contain elements of both competition and monopoly; nevertheless, they should not be condemned wholesale. While Mason apparently recognized the significance of structure to competition, he also regarded performance as an important test of the social acceptability of market arrangements.

It is not enough to find evidence of the existence of market controls, nor is it sufficient to conduct purely analytical and descriptive studies of various types of control situations. While this is important, the formulation of public policy requires a distinction between situations and practices which are in the public interest and those that are not.[9]

For the courts to inquire into the actual or probable results of restrictive agreements "would be to give up the traditional tests of monopolizing and

---

7. 47 Yale L. J. 34.
8. *Id.* at 36. Emphasis in the original.
9. *Id.* at 49. Dirlam and Alfred E. Kahn have incorrectly interpreted Mason as concerned solely with market structure, and not market performance as well, as evidence of monopoly. *Fair Competition: The Law and Economics of Antitrust Policy* (Ithaca: Cornell University Press, 1954), p. 29.

to grapple with the problem of what is an unreasonable control of the market." [10]

Mason did not regard the courts as alone responsible for the inadequacy of antimonopoly law. The blame also rests with Congress. The shortcomings of public policy "can only be corrected by legislation which will redefine the monopoly and trade practice problem and provide tests by means of which market situations and business practices considered to be favorable to the public interest can be separated from those that are not." [11] Price leadership, price rigidity, advertising expenditures and the like may be sufficient evidence of monopoly, but they are not "sufficient evidence of . . . market controls adverse to the public interest." [12]

This is surely the forerunner of the demand that antitrust laws be formulated and administered in accordance with the concept of workable competition under a rule of reason.

Three years later, John M. Clark gave a name and a more specific content to the concept of workable competition.[13] Recognizing that pure competition is unattainable, Clark argued that the public interest may best be promoted by accepting some departures from it that might be corrected by regulation, because some other departures are ineradicable and to achieve some of the characteristics of pure competition without achieving all may do more harm than good. Workable competition is the best of market arrangements practically achievable under a private enterprise system, and it is good enough. Although he never clearly differentiated between the two, Clark like Mason would apparently use both structure and performance as tests of workable competition. His workable competition called for a sufficient number of sellers (structure) selling substantially the same product to serve as a check on monopolistic exploitation (performance).[14] Clark argued that in the short run oligopolistic controls may perform a positive public service; in the long run potential competition and the competition of substitutes are likely to insure cost-price relationships and an allocation of resources consistent with pure competition. Moreover, Clark argued, technical progress may be expected to curb monopolistic power by bringing about "still closer and more general sub-

10. 47 Yale L. J. 34, 48.
11. *Id.* at 46.
12. *Id.* at 49.
13. "Toward a Concept of Workable Competition," 30 Am. Econ. Rev. (Proceedings of the American Economic Ass'n) 241 (1940).
14. *Id.* at 243. See also the quotation in the text at note 21, *infra*, for evidence of Clark's recognition of the performance test.

stitution."[15] This, together with the increased use of specifications in buying and more knowledge about them, will "increase the number of industries which, despite large-scale production, have the characteristics of fairly healthy and workable imperfect competition, rather than those of slightly-qualified monopoly."[16] As to the policy implications of his analysis, Clark expressed the hope "that government need not assume the burden of doing something about every departure from the model of perfect competition."[17]

In his several articles on basing point pricing,[18] Clark denied the conspiratorial character of this practice, arguing that in oligopolistic industries with certain specific characteristics it was of spontaneous origin,[19] and he regarded it as not inconsistent with workable competition. Writing in 1950 after the Supreme Court had upheld the Federal Trade Commission in its condemnation of systematic basing point pricing,[20] Clark argued that

> where impairment of competition is an issue, there should be a showing of how competition is impaired, by comparison with an identifiable concept of what would constitute unimpaired competition in an industry having the unavoidable physical and economic characteristics of the one whose practices are being adjudicated. Accepting the necessity of flexibility and Commission discretion and some resulting uncertainty, it seems that the evils of this situation are aggravated by present procedure, and could be mitigated by introducing, as an integral and arguable part of the case, a comparison of the economic results of existing practice and those which competition could be expected to produce in the industry in question—also, if at all possible, the probable results of the order the Commission proposes to issue. Such a comparative study is the heart of the economics of the case, and should logically be the heart of the law.[21]

On the proper relation between law and economics, Clark further stated his position as follows: "In general, the writer accepts the idea that legality

---

15. *Id.* at 256.
16. *Ibid.*
17. *Ibid.*
18. "Basing-Point Methods of Price Quoting," 4 Can. J. Econ. and Pol. Sci. 477 (1938); "Imperfect Competition Theory and Basing-Point Problems," 33 Am. Econ. Rev. 283 (1943); "Rejoinder to Professor Mund," 33 Am. Econ. Rev. 616 (1943); "The Law and Economics of Basing Points: Appraisal and Proposals," 39 Am. Econ. Rev. 430 (1949); "Machlup on the Basing-Point System," 63 Q. J. Econ. 315 (1949).
19. "Imperfect Competition Theory and Basing-Point Problems," 33 Am. Econ. Rev. 283, 288 ff. (1943). See Stocking, "The Economics of Basing Point Pricing," 15 Law and Contemp. Prob. 159, 163 (1950).
20. Federal Trade Commission v. Cement Institute, 333 U.S. 683 (1948).
21. "The Orientation of Antitrust Policy," 40 Am. Econ. Rev. (Proceedings of the American Economic Ass'n) 93, 98 (1950).

should depend on the economic effects of practices, and that this should be judged by a specialized commission." [22]

While Clark was apparently growing friendlier to a specific modification of the statutes to bring them into conformity with the concept of workable competition, Mason was becoming less certain of the validity of the distinction he had earlier drawn between monopoly in an economic sense and illegality,[23] and he recognized that the problem of determining the workability of any concrete industrial situation was not simple. Writing in 1949, he weighed the usefulness of an industry's structural characteristics against its performance in determining its competitive workability and concluded that the one test should supplement the other. But he recognized the limitations of both. About them he said,

> The relative importance to be assigned to the objective of establishing appropriate market limitations on the scope of action of firms as against the objective of encouraging efficient performance in the use of economic resources no doubt presents serious difficulties. It seems probable that individual judgments will always be influenced to some extent by ideological considerations."[24]

Despite the problems it presented, Mason was unwilling to abandon the concept of workable competition as a criterion for administering antitrust, although he thought it more appropriate at some levels of public action than at others: "[T]he most important level within the framework of traditional antitrust policy, at which the question of appropriate standards and objectives can be discussed, is at the level of the enforcement agencies."[25] In selecting cases the enforcement agencies should not ask whether they can win the case but what difference it will make. This "clearly involves a consideration of whether a different structure of the market and set of business practices . . . will be better . . . than the existing structure and practices."[26] This is the essence of the economists' concept of workability.

Jesse W. Markham developed this idea further in his 1950 article, "An Alternative Approach to the Concept of Workable Competition," where he concluded: "An industry may be judged to be workably competitive when, after the structural characteristics of its market and the dynamic forces that shaped them have been thoroughly examined, there is no

---

22. *Id.* at 99.
23. "The Current Status of the Monopoly Problem in the United States," 62 Harv. L. Rev. 1265 (1949). See especially p. 1272.
24. *Id.* at 1283.
25. *Id.* at 1284.
26. *Id.* at 1284–85.

clearly indicated change that can be effected through public policy measures that would result in greater social gains than social losses."[27] While apparently accepting the principle of workable competition as a policy guide,[28] Markham recognized its limitations. "It seems hardly necessary to point out, however," he said, "that definitions of workable competition which follow the above suggested pattern, like all others, will not be divorced from value judgments."[29] A few years later Markham's skepticism was even sharper. In 1954 he stated,

> Both its advocates and critics would agree that the concept of workable competition, or its necessary equivalent, has not yet been formally developed to the point where it can usefully be incorporated into the law itself. That is to say, indicia of monopoly that can be unswervingly and uniformly applied to all industries, irrespective of their market environment and stage of development, have not yet been clearly identified.[30]

Clare E. Griffin perhaps more than any other economist has emphasized performance as a test of workable competition. Specifically, he recognized five criteria for judging performance:

> (1) Is the industry (or company) efficient? (2) Is it progressive? (3) Does it show a reasonable and socially useful profit pattern? (4) Does it have as high a degree of freedom of entry as the nature of the industry permits? (5) Is it well suited to serve national defense needs?[31]

Although Griffin recognized the vagueness of these tests and the part judgment would play in administering them, he thought they might be useful to enforcement agencies in determining whether to prosecute, to courts and administrative agencies in formulating remedies, to legislatures in amending the statutes or in passing new laws, and in a more limited way to courts in deciding cases.

---

27. 40 Am. Econ. Rev. 349, 361 (1950).

28. Markham did not specifically advocate a change in the antitrust laws to make them conform to the principles he enunciated, but he clearly contemplated that the principles would be of use in shaping public policy. In defending his concept of workable competition he said, "[I]t would ascribe paramount importance to that which should be uppermost in the minds of those who formulate public policy —the possibility of prescribing appropriate remedial action. For, unless the concept of workable competition is to be an instrument of public policy, there is little reason for differentiating between workable and pure competition." *Id.*

29. *Ibid.*

30. "The Per Se Doctrine and the New Rule of Reason," paper delivered before the Southern Economic Ass'n, 24th annual conference, Biloxi, Miss., Nov. 20, 1954, 22 Southern Econ. J. 22, 29 (1955).

31. *An Economic Approach to Antitrust Problems* (New York: American Enterprise Ass'n, 1951), p. xiii.

Workable Competition and Antitrust Policy

Other economists, notably Morris A. Adelman, Joe S. Bain, Richard B. Heflebower, A. D. H. Kaplan, and Ross M. Robertson, have made significant contributions to the concept of workable competition and in doing so have implied, without indicating just how, that it should be of some use in public policy.[32]

RIGOROUS ANTITRUST DECISIONS ALARM BUSINESSMEN

While economists were thus viewing with commendable skepticism their own suggestions as to the usefulness of the concept of workable competition as a standard for antitrust policy, court decisions actually bringing the legal concept of monopoly more nearly into conformity with the economic concept were arousing grave concern among businessmen. For example, Judge Learned Hand's application in the *Aluminum* case[33] of the market control concept in defining monopoly; his recognition that power over the market, not its abuse, was the essence of the monopoly problem; his distinction between a firm's achieving monopoly and having monopoly thrust upon it; his denial of the doctrine of specific intent—all made big business uneasy about its legal status. The Supreme Court's decision in the 1946 *Tobacco* case[34] further disturbed business leaders. The Court's acceptance of circumstantial evidence as proof of conspiracy; its acknowledgment of the relevance to monopoly power of the combined percentage of the cigarette market supplied by the "big three"; its recognition of the significance of advertising expenditures and warehousing costs as obstacles to entry; its refusal to distinguish between actual exclusion and the power to exclude—these looked like threats to big enterprise per se. The Court's initial decision in the *Yellow Cab* case,[35] which seemed

---

32. Adelman, "Effective Competition and the Antitrust Laws," 61 Harv. L. Rev. 1289 (1948); Adelman, "Integration and Antitrust Policy," 63 Harv. L. Rev. 27 (1949); Bain, "Workable Competition in Oligopoly: Theoretical Considerations and Some Empirical Evidence," 40 Am. Econ. Rev. (Proceedings of the American Economic Ass'n) 35 (1950); Heflebower, "Economics of Size," 24 J. of Bus. of U. Chi. 253 (1951); Kaplan, *Big Enterprise in a Competitive System* (Washington, D.C.: Brookings Institution, 1954); Robertson, "On the Changing Apparatus of Competition," 44 Am. Econ. Rev. (Proceedings of the American Economic Ass'n) 51 (1954). Also Joseph A. Schumpeter, *Capitalism, Socialism, and Democracy* (New York: Harper, 1942), although not concerned specifically with the concept of workable competition, has influenced considerably those who have been; in particular, his discussion of "the perennial gale of creative destruction" has influenced those who emphasize performance as a test of workability.
33. United States v. Aluminum Co. of America, 148 F.2d 416 (2d Cir. 1945).
34. American Tobacco Co. v. United States, 328 U.S. 781.
35. United States v. Yellow Cab Co., 332 U.S. 218 (1947).

Workable Competition as an Antitrust Guide

to bring vertical integration and restrictions on competition affecting merely an "appreciable part" of commerce within the ban of the Sherman Act, contributed to the anxiety of business leaders and their legal advisers.

Academicians' interpretation of the significance of these decisions did not calm the businessmen. William H. Nicholls, in commenting on the *Tobacco* decision before the 1948 meeting of the American Economic Association, characterized it as a milestone in the social control of oligopoly and concluded: "By permitting the inference of illegal conspiracy from detailed similarity of behavior and by shifting attention from the abuse of power to its mere existence . . . the courts have at last brought oligopolistic industries within reach of successful prosecution under the antitrust laws." [36] Eugene V. Rostow saw even greater significance in these decisions. Where a few sellers dominate a market and behave alike with respect to it, proof of conspiracy, he concluded, was unnecessary. About the *Tobacco* decision he said:

When three companies produce so large a percentage [68 per cent] of market supply, that fact alone is almost sufficient evidence that the statute is violated. Ruthless and predatory behavior need not be shown. The actual elimination of small competitors is unnecessary. . . . Parallel action, price leadership, a reliance on advertising rather than price competition as a means of inducing changes in each seller's share of the market, and, above all, size—the market advantage of a small number of large sellers or buyers—these are now key points to be proved in a case of monopoly, or of combination in restraint of trade. . . . Painstaking search for scraps of evidence with a conspiratorial atmosphere are no longer necessary. . . . decisive elements are the power to assert a degree of control over price and output in the market as a whole. . . . [37]

To businessmen the extension of the doctrine of per se antitrust violation was equally disturbing. This took place along a number of fronts. In its long struggle to outlaw industry-wide basing point pricing systems, the Federal Trade Commission developed its doctrine of "conscious parallelism of action," and in the *Cement Institute* case [38] it prohibited respondents from following "a planned common course of action" in selling cement on a delivered price basis. In the *Rigid Steel Conduit* case,[39] find-

---

36. "The Tobacco Case of 1946," 39 Am. Econ. Rev. (Proceedings of the American Economic Ass'n) 284, 296 (1949).

37. "The New Sherman Act: A Positive Instrument of Progress," 14 U. Chi. L. Rev. 567, 585 (1947).

38. Cement Institute, 37 F.T.C. 87 (1943), *aff'd*, 333 U.S. 683 (1948).

39. Rigid Steel Conduit Ass'n, 38 F.T.C. 534 (1944), *aff'd sub nom.* Triangle Conduit & Cable Co. v. Federal Trade Commission, 168 F.2d 175 (7th Cir. 1948), *aff'd by an equally divided court sub nom.* Clayton Mark & Co. v. Federal Trade Commission, 336 U.S. 956 (1949).

ing that each respondent had used the basing point system knowing that its rivals did so, thereby preventing competition, the Commission not only banned conspiracy but prohibited respondents individually from selling rigid steel conduit at prices calculated on a basing point system for the purpose or with the effect of systematically matching delivered prices. In the *Glucose* cases [40] the Commission's orders against individual respondents had prohibited price discrimination through either collecting phantom freight or absorbing freight.[41] In each case the Supreme Court sustained the Commission. In its several basing point pricing cases the Commission seemed to be driving toward an outlawing of basing point pricing per se. Irving S. Olds, chairman of the board of directors of the United States Steel Corporation, reflected the businessman's response to these several decisions when he concluded that the *Cement Institute* decision promised to disrupt industry and that business should either get the law changed or "educate the Supreme Court." [42] Businessmen professed to believe that to follow customary industrial practices would be dangerous since the Federal Trade Commission might see implied conspiracy in them and hold them illegal per se, regardless of the economic conditions that gave rise to them or their effects on the industry in question.

Like the implied conspiracy doctrine, the *Socony-Vacuum* opinion's pronouncement that "[a]ny combination which tampers with price structures is engaged in an unlawful activity" [43] was capable of being used to strike at the exchange of statistical information on costs and prices by a trade association. Although in the *Socony-Vacuum* case the Supreme Court undertook to distinguish the *Appalachian Coals* case [44] by concluding that the coal producers' common selling agency was not designed to fix market price, the similarities between the two cases are more obvious than their differences. The rule of reason had saved the earlier effort to deal with

---

40. Corn Products Refining Co., 34 F.T.C. 850 (1942), aff'd, 324 U.S. 726 (1945); A. E. Staley Mfg. Co., 34 F.T.C. 1362 (1942), aff'd, 324 U.S. 746 (1945).

41. I base this interpretation of the Commission's orders on their prohibiting the Corn Products Refining Co. from discriminating "in the manner and degree set forth in paragraphs 4 and 5 of the findings as to the facts herein...." 34 F.T.C. 850, 877. Subparagraph (d) of paragraph 4 of the findings recognized freight absorption on sales from the company's Kansas City plant alike with phantom freight as resulting in price discrimination. The *Staley* findings and order were similar. See Stocking, *Basing Point Pricing and Regional Development* (Chapel Hill: University of North Carolina Press, 1954), pp. 165–67.

42. New York Journal of Commerce, April 28, 1948, p. 1.

43. United States v. Socony-Vacuum Oil Co., 310 U.S. 150, 221 (1940). Emphasis added.

44. Appalachian Coals, Inc. v. United States, 288 U.S. 344 (1933).

"distress" coal; the per se violation doctrine outlawed a similar effort to deal with "distress" gasoline.

In certain Clayton Act cases the Supreme Court, without analyzing the actual or probable effects of a challenged practice on competition in the industry affected, concluded that the effect of proscribed practices might be substantially to lessen competition or tend to create a monopoly. In the *Morton Salt* case it simplified proof in price discrimination cases by holding that a "reasonable *possibility*" [45] of injury to competition was sufficient to convict. In the *Standard Stations* case [46] the Court declared that exclusive dealing contracts become illegal on proof that "competition has been foreclosed in a substantial share of the line of commerce affected." [47] Since competition is foreclosed by the existence of a requirements contract, illegality per se follows a showing that the requirements contracts affect a substantial share of the commerce involved. In the *Standard Stations* case 6.7 per cent of the petroleum products sold in a seven-state area was "a substantial share."

The Supreme Court's attempts to deal with restrictive arrangements between firms linked by common stock ownership brought forth two decisions that found conspiracy where some students of antitrust saw only a parent-subsidiary relationship.[48]

The Lawyers' Adaptation of Workable Competition

Articulate and influential lawyers, whether they saw in the doctrine of workable competition a crude tool for blunting the impact of the antitrust statutes or a delicate instrument for separating socially desirable from anti-social business practices, and good market structures from bad, clamored for a change in the antitrust statutes. Chief among these were Blackwell Smith, long a skeptic of antitrust policy and exponent of industrial self-government along NRA lines,[49] and S. Chesterfield Oppenheim, dis-

---

45. Federal Trade Commission v. Morton Salt Co. 334 U.S. 37, 46 (1948). Emphasis added. See also Corn Products Refining Co. v. Federal Trade Commission, 324 U.S. 726, 742 (1945).
46. Standard Oil Co. of California v. United States, 337 U.S. 293 (1949).
47. *Id.* at 314.
48. Kiefer-Stewart Co. v. Joseph E. Seagram & Sons, 340 U.S. 211 (1951); Timken Roller Bearing Co. v. United States, 341 U.S. 593 (1951).
49. Smith was associate counsel for the National Recovery Administration and defended its constitutionality and purposes in a speech delivered to the Federal Bar Ass'n Nov. 15, 1933, "Legal Problems Confronting the National Recovery Administration," 2 Fed. Bar Ass'n J. 3 (1934). In 1938, reviewing Walton Hamilton's *Price and Price Policies* (New York: McGraw-Hill, 1938), Smith quoted with

Workable Competition and Antitrust Policy

tinguished professor of law and expert in the antitrust field. Smith set forth his views at length in an article, "Effective Competition: Hypothesis for Modernizing the Antitrust Laws." [50] Smith, like the well-known economists from whom he borrowed, recognized that pure competition and pure monopoly are abstractions remote from the realities of industrial life. It is in the middle ground between perfect competition and complete monopoly that public policy must contend with business behavior. According to Smith, public policy should be directed towards maintenance of effective, not pure, competition. Not all competition is good; not all is bad. Big business is not to be confused with monopoly. But in separating the sheep from the goats he would rely primarily on performance. Competition, whether among industrial pygmies or industrial giants or between the two groups, is effective when it performs well. "It should be presumed that competition is of the good kind when actual performance shows that there is a healthy condition, judged by actual creation of adequate alternatives in goods, services and markets for both buyers and sellers." [51]

Despite the vagueness of effective competition's performance test, Smith would incorporate the standard of effective competition into an antitrust statute to be enforced under a "new Rule of Reason." [52] Smith's concept did not gain in precision as he translated it into a statement of policy, but the translation made it clear that Smith is no slavish devotee of competition and is willing to substitute the public welfare as the goal of antitrust policy: "The object of such policy would be stated to be to encourage such competitive performance as would tend to serve the public interest in providing more and better relative values in goods and services for more people in proportion to human effort." [53] Smith listed the following "relevant circumstances" his new rule of reason would require courts and administrators to consider "[i]n determining whether any commercial prac-

---

approval Hamilton's views on the necessity for collective action in industry: " 'The state, with the club of the criminal law, can never beat the behavior that attends the pursuit of gain into accord with rigid norms. The quick staccato of industry cannot be timed to the decorous processes of a legal procedure developed in the days of petty trade. . . . A proper freedom of collective action, within the strict limits of the public interest, must be accorded agencies of business.' Of course, this means authority and control, both public and private." Book Reviews, 48 Yale L. J. 359, 363 (1938).

50. 26 N.Y.U.L. Rev. 405 (1951). The article was a revision of sections of a report Smith submitted to the Business Advisory Council of the Department of Commerce in 1950.

51. *Id.* at 412.
52. *Id.* at 429.
53. *Ibid.*

tices or courses of conduct promote Effective Competition or are *unreasonably* injurious thereto":

such actual or probable results of the conduct, under like circumstances in the market, as the increase or decrease of: (1) alternatives available to customers or sellers; (2) volume of production or services; (3) quality of the services or goods; (4) number of people benefited; (5) incentives to entrepreneurs; (6) efficiency and economy in manufacturing or distribution; (7) the welfare of employees; (8) the tendency to progress in technical developments; (9) prices to customers; (10) conditions favorable to the public interest in defending the country from aggression; (11) the tendency to conserve the country's natural resources; (12) benefits to the public interest assuming the relief requested by the government in the proceedings.[54]

The Business Advisory Council of the Department of Commerce adopted Smith's ideas with little modification, and in its report to the Secretary of Commerce in 1952 it recommended drastic changes in administrative standards and procedures under the antitrust statutes.[55] Like Smith, the Council would set up effective competition as a standard of business performance and administer it under a rule of reason. The Council recognized inconsistencies in the antitrust statutes vexing to businessmen; it regarded bigness as a relative concept and contended that a big economy requires big enterprise, and it lamented a growing tendency to confuse bigness and monopoly. It proposed the creation of a Review Board, consisting of competent businessmen, engineers, economists, and non-prosecuting lawyers, "to insure that government commencement of Antitrust cases conforms to national policy," [56] and that no government agency begin a major investigation or proceeding until the Board had made its recommendations. In these and other ways the Council would have modified antitrust laws and their administration to make them conform better to the structure and functioning of the contemporary economy. The Council's recommendations aimed at making the laws consistent with market structure and business practices rather than making structure and practice conform to the law.

Oppenheim's role in the struggle to inject the concept of workable competition and the rule of reason into the antitrust laws is too well known to require much comment. His 1952 article, "Federal Antitrust Legislation: Guideposts to a Revised National Antitrust Policy," [57] engendered

54. *Id.* at 441. Emphasis added.
55. U.S. Dep't of Commerce, *Effective Competition: Report to the Secretary of Commerce by His Business Advisory Council* (1952).
56. *Id.* at 3. Emphasis in the original omitted.
57. 50 Mich. L. Rev. 1139.

the creation of the Attorney General's National Committee to Study the Antitrust Laws and furnished a blueprint for its deliberations. The Attorney General appropriately appointed Oppenheim to serve as co-chairman of the committee with Assistant Attorney General Barnes, head of the Antitrust Division of the Department of Justice. Oppenheim in his article deplored the tendency of administrative agencies and the courts to broaden the scope of the per se violation doctrine and to "dilute the Rule of Reason . . . approach"; [58] he was disturbed by the alleged inconsistencies between the Robinson-Patman Act and its administration and the Sherman Act; and he pointed out contradictions in judicial interpretation of Section 2 of the Sherman Act. Like Smith and the Business Advisory Council he found present antitrust laws incompatible with the effective operation of a virile, dynamic, private enterprise economy in which big business has come to play an increasingly important role. Like Smith and the Council he saw in the principle of workable competition administered under a rule of reason a standard by which the performance of American industry could be gauged and by means of which the antitrust statutes might be made sufficiently flexible to meet the needs of dynamic capitalism. Oppenheim's discussion of the need for change in the antitrust statutes was broader in scope and more penetrating in analysis than Smith's, but it also was vague and at times confusing.

In applying the rule of reason to and determining the workability of any particular industrial arrangement, Oppenheim would have the administrative agencies and the courts "consider all of the relevant economic factors bearing upon the interaction of structure, behavior, and accomplishments." [59] But he did not always make clear whether judgment of workability is to rest on the effects of the arrangements on competition or on the public welfare. Proponents of competition have generally assumed that its promotion is identical with promotion of the public welfare, and the neoclassical economists have built a substantial foundation for this belief. It is by no means clear that either Oppenheim or Smith subscribes to it. Oppenheim believed that "[i]n particular factual situations, evidence of legal, economic, and social justifications" should be "weighed under close judicial scrutiny to arrive at a determination of whether the restrictions are reasonable or unreasonable when measured against the effects upon competition." [60] I take this to mean that promotion of the public welfare might involve some sacrifice of competition and that under the antitrust

58. *Id.* at 1156.
59. *Id.* at 1190.
60. *Id.* at 1160.

Workable Competition as an Antitrust Guide

laws as Oppenheim would shape them the courts and administrative agencies should have discretion to choose between such alternatives.[61] At any rate, while I am not always sure that I understand exactly what Oppenheim is saying, I have no trouble in reaching the conclusion that under his rule of reason and concept of workable competition the antitrust laws would be less vigorously enforced than I should like to see them.

The Attorney General's Antitrust Committee

Oppenheim's article bore fruit. A year after its publication the Attorney General announced his intention to establish a National Committee to Study the Antitrust Laws. Except for the way in which it was financed, the Attorney General's Committee conformed closely to the Oppenheim model in its objectives, its composition, its procedures, and the scope of its analysis. Within less than two years after its appointment (the maximum time Oppenheim had allowed for the work of his committee), it made its report.[62]

The Committee's report may prove to be a significant document in the interpretation and administration of the antitrust statutes. What the Committee refrained from doing directly, it may have achieved by indirection. Despite the fact that demand for amendment of the law to incorporate the concept of workable competition and the rule of reason occasioned the Committee's creation, the Committee not only did not recommend such a change, it specifically rejected the "theory," cautioning that it "does not provide a standard of legality under any of the antitrust laws."[63] It is not clear whether this position is due to the inability of a majority of the 52 lawyers on the Committee to persuade a minority of their group, the single labor leader, and the eight economists to recommend the change, or to their recognition of the almost insuperable task of persuading the Congress to legislate it. But the victory of those who oppose such recommendations is more apparent than real. Having shut out workable competition at the front door, the Committee brought it in by the back. It recognized that the concept "provides the courts with tools of analysis in

---

61. Specifically, Oppenheim proposed the substitution of a prima facie case of illegality for the per se violation rule in the field of restrictive agreements. "When all of the evidence is introduced, the trier of fact would then apply the Rule of Reason to the entire record. He would exercise discretion in evaluation of this evidence to arrive at a value judgment...." *Id.* at 1159.

62. *Report of the Attorney General's National Committee to Study the Antitrust Laws* (March 31, 1955) (hereinafter *Antitrust Report*).

63. *Id.* at 316.

making the factual inquiry into problems of competition and monopoly. . . ."⁶⁴

The Committee's recommendations for change in the antitrust statutes were with few exceptions relatively minor, but its advice to the courts and administrative agencies was of profound significance. Despite having been established "to evaluate the antitrust laws in their fundamental aspects," ⁶⁵ the Committee undertook the simpler and perhaps more congenial tasks of analyzing "the main course of . . . antitrust policy, its interpretation and decisions," evaluating these developments, and reaching conclusions that will serve "as future guides to enforcement agencies, Congress, and the courts." ⁶⁶ The Committee expressed the hope that from its clarification of the statutes and decisions "will emerge more practical guides for business seeking to comply with the antitrust laws and for Government officials charged with enforcing their prohibitions." ⁶⁷ In its analysis of trends in the application of the statutes, the Committee commended the courts when they examined all of the relevant economic factors to determine their significance to public welfare, and it looked with skepticism on decisions applying the doctrine of per se violation. About the significance of this, Blackwell Smith, a Committee member, has said: "Out of it all comes the most realistic set of standards for legal and socially acceptable competition since the Business Advisory Council Report on Effective Competition published by Secretary of Commerce Sawyer." ⁶⁸ The report, said Smith, "should be a bench mark for a long time to come against which to make comparisons of decisions, administrative actions, and legislation to see how far they drift from true readings." ⁶⁹

To help keep the courts on the narrow path of truth, Oppenheim arranged for copies of the report to be supplied to all federal judges.⁷⁰ How influential the document may prove remains to be seen, but Oppenheim has written, "[I]n my opinion the report is commanding the respect

64. *Ibid.*
65. Barnes and Oppenheim, "Organization of the Attorney General's National Committee to Study the Antitrust Laws" 3, Statement prepared for delivery before American Bar Ass'n, Section on Antitrust Law, Boston, Mass., U.S. Dep't of Justice Release (mimeographed), Aug. 27, 1953.
66. *Antitrust Report,* at 3.
67. *Id.* at 4.
68. Smith, "Antitrust Report to Narrow Gap between Law and Economics," Trade Practice Bulletin, May 1955, p. 4.
69. *Id.* at 1.
70. Testimony of S. Chesterfield Oppenheim, *Hearings on Price Discrimination before House Select Committee on Small Business,* 84th Cong., 1st Sess. 194–95 (1955).

Workable Competition as an Antitrust Guide

and serious consideration of the bar and Government officials."[71] A former Assistant Attorney General in charge of antitrust has corroborated this opinion, saying:

[T]he effect of the report is unquestionably very significant when you are arguing a case in court.... After all, a large committee of supposedly expert people will inevitably have an effect upon the courts.[72]

ECONOMISTS QUESTION CONCEPTS AS AN ANTITRUST STANDARD

The foregoing account traces the more important steps in the effort to inject the principle of workable competition into the administration of antitrust statutes. Economic theory gave impetus to the effort, but economists generally have not given it their wholehearted support, and some have viewed it with great skepticism. They have seen in it an effort to temper the vigor of antitrust enforcement—to provide a legal environment within which contemporary business practices are secure. Most articulate among the skeptics are Corwin D. Edwards, George J. Stigler, Ben W. Lewis, Walter Adams, Alfred E. Kahn, and Joel B. Dirlam.

Edwards in a discussion of "Public Policy and Business Size"[73] criticized vigorously the use of the performance test in antitrust proceedings. He pointed out that

we accept competitive policy because we believe that the performance of business under competition is generally better than otherwise. Competition is properly regarded as the means and good economic performance as the end."[74]

To judge the social acceptability of a monopoly on a basis of its performance would be as unworkable "as to decide whether a driver is permitted to run a red light in traffic by determining whether, on balance, he is a good or bad citizen."[75]

Stigler in condemning workable competition as a criterion in antitrust proceedings quoted with approval the opinion expressed by unidentified minority members of the Attorney General's Committee on Antitrust who said:

[We] stress that the "doctrine" of workable competition is only a rough and ready judgment by some economists, each for himself, that a particular industry

71. Letter dated Aug. 1, 1955, to unidentified addressee, *id.* at 194.
72. Testimony of Thurman Arnold, head of Antitrust Division of U.S. Dep't of Justice from 1938 to 1943, *id.* at 5, 6.
73. 24 J. of Bus. of U. Chi. 280 (1951).
74. *Id.* at 285.
75. *Ibid.*

Workable Competition and Antitrust Policy

is performing reasonably well—presumably relative to alternative industrial arrangements which are practically attainable. There are no objective criteria of workable competition, and such criteria as are proffered are at best intuitively reasonable modifications of the rigorous and abstract criteria of perfect competition.[76]

Lewis in criticizing the performance test showed commendable insight when he said:

> I am willing to accept considerable leeway and tolerance in the operation of competition (or any other regulatory force, for that matter), but I am not willing to judge its effectiveness or to decide whether or not it is workable and working solely or even largely on the basis of "results." . . . Results alone throw no light on the really significant question: have these results been *compelled* by the system—by *competition*—or do they represent simply the dispensations of managements which, with a wide latitude of policy choices at their disposal, happened for the moment to be benevolent or "smart"? This points up the real issue.[77]

Adams in a discerning article published in 1954, "The 'Rule of Reason': Workable Competition or Workable Monopoly?,"[78] took sharp issue with Oppenheim and the Business Advisory Council on the usefulness of the concept of workable competition under a rule of reason as an antitrust standard. He exposed the flimsy nature of the argument that the antitrust laws are an uncertain guide to business behavior, showed how the proposed revisions when applied to price-fixing agreements would lead to a cartelization of American industry, pointed out the logical relationship between industrial structure and business behavior, and indicated the treacherous character of industrial performance as a standard for judging the legality of oligopolistic market arrangements. Recognizing that "there are unresolved problems in applying the per se doctrine of Section 1 and the market structure test of Section 2," Adams rightly concluded that the twin approach of workable competition and the rule of reason was not "well calculated to resolve these problems in a manner consistent with traditional antitrust objectives."[79]

Dirlam and Kahn jointly presented their views on the pitfalls in testing the legality of antitrust violations by the concept of workable competition

---

76. Stigler, "Report of the Attorney General's Committee on Antitrust Policy: Discussion," 46 Am. Econ. Rev. (Proceedings of the American Economic Ass'n) 504, 505 (1956), quoting *Antitrust Report*, at 339.
77. Lewis, "The Effectiveness of the Federal Antitrust Laws: A Symposium," ed. Dexter M. Keezer, 39 Am. Econ. Rev. 689, 706, 707 (1949). Emphasis in the original.
78. 63 Yale L. J. 348 (1954).
79. *Id.* at 370.

Workable Competition as an Antitrust Guide

in a penetrating analysis, *Fair Competition: The Law and Economics of Antitrust Policy* (1954). Kahn had done so separately in an article, "Standards for Antitrust Policy." [80] Like other economists, Dirlam and Kahn recognized that pure competition is an abstraction and that a realistic antitrust policy will have to content itself with "workable competition." They apparently regarded neither monopoly nor oligopoly as inconsistent with workable competition but believed that the traditional antitrust approach provides a more effective method of "preserving workable competition" than "the policy implications of the new economic criticism." [81] They specifically rejected market structure and industrial performance as tests of the workability of competition. In rejecting the former they stated:

If monopoly elements inevitably pervade the economy, and are in some measure essential to a good performance, it would clearly be quixotic to attack monopoly as such. If the courts were really prepared now to outlaw "the power to raise prices," . . . few industries would be exempt. The economy would have to be "purified" right out of the twentieth . . . century.[82]

And, they concluded, "there exists no generally accepted economic yardstick *appropriate for incorporation into law* with which objectively to measure monopoly power or to determine what degree is compatible with workable competition." [83] They recognized that the adoption of the vague market performance test would weaken the legal safeguards of competition and provide defendants in antitrust cases with innumerable loopholes. They were unreservedly against it.

But although Dirlam and Kahn rejected structure and performance as tests of acceptable competition, they by no means despaired of effective antitrust enforcement in a society shot through with monopoly. What the antitrust laws should do is to insure fair play among firms, big or little. As they viewed it, workable competition is more or less synonymous with fair competition. Courts must look to the way business firms play the game to determine violations of the antitrust statutes. Conduct and intent are the only acceptable criteria for determining violations of antitrust. In many cases "intent alone 'fills the bill' for a sensible antitrust policy." [84] In other cases conduct is more indicative.

The quest for an explanatory intent does not involve psychoanalysis. The ques-

80. 67 Harv. L. Rev. 28 (1953).
81. *Op. cit. supra* note 9, at 31.
82. *Ibid.*
83. *Id.* Emphasis in the original.
84. *Id.* at 51.

tion is not: "Why did A really do what he did?" but simply: "What was A really doing? Was he competing or was he suppressing competition?" [85]

In short, to Dirlam and Kahn "[t]he function of antitrust can only be to see to it that no one attempts to stifle or pervert the process of competition by collusion, by unreasonable financial agglomeration, or by exclusion. Illegality must inhere in the act, not in the result." [86]

My Position on Workable Competition

Although not always agreeing in detail with the economists who have specifically rejected the concept of workable competition as a criterion for gauging antitrust violations, I too—Dirlam and Stelzer to the contrary notwithstanding—have viewed with oft-repeated skepticism proposals to incorporate the principle into either the administration or the interpretation of antitrust statutes. In analyzing the implications for public policy of Clark's concept of workable competition and Schumpeter's "perennial gale of creative destruction," Myron W. Watkins and I in 1951 stated:

The public policy implications of this line of reasoning are fairly obvious. It leads readily to acquiescence in the status quo and to a low estimate of the value of remedial action designed to increase the number of sellers and reduce the monopoly elements in industrial markets.[87]

We specifically rejected Clark's contention that oligopolistic pricing serves as sound economic purpose in preventing prices from falling to marginal costs in the short run. We emphasized the function competitive pricing performs in the allocation of resources and in economic progress and challenged the notion that price rigidities are consistent with effective competition. We concluded, "If society wants to preserve a private enterprise economy, public policy must keep the market free from monopolistic controls, whether they rest on size alone or on conspiracy." [88]

When in 1952 Oppenheim asked me to serve on the Attorney General's Committee to Study Antitrust, I declined the invitation because I was then engaged in testing Oppenheim's hypothesis that the concept of workable competition administered under a rule of reason provided an acceptable standard in antitrust procedures, and I wished to carry on this research unhampered by whatever restrictions service on a public body

---

85. *Id.* at 50.
86. *Id.* at 49.
87. *Monopoly and Free Enterprise*, at 99.
88. *Id.* at 109.

Workable Competition as an Antitrust Guide

of this character might impose. The first results of this research were published by the *University of Chicago Law Review* in an article, "The Rule of Reason, Workable Competition, and the Legality of Trade Association Activities."[89] In this article I first analyzed the concept of workable competition and the rule of reason and reached the general conclusion that the vagueness of both made them unacceptable as standards in antitrust enforcement. I then examined at length, in the light of the rule of reason and the concept of workable competition, the development of antitrust law and its application to the activities of trade associations, demonstrating how deceptive the standards were likely to prove. In commenting specifically on Smith's public welfare test I raised the following question:

> If the good in trade association activity lies in its restriction on competition, how much good should associations be encouraged to do? That is to say, how much restriction on competition is socially desirable? How much restriction on competition leaves it workable?[90]

I indicated that neither I nor other economists had satisfactory answers to these questions, but I observed,

> [I]f businessmen are told that concerted action *may* by restricting competition promote the general welfare, they are entitled to know the appropriate limits of such restrictions. If they are told that concerted action to restrict competition is unlawful, they proceed collectively at their own risk. Outlawing concerted action to restrict competition is a far more certain guide to business behavior than setting up the vague and debatable principle of workable competition.[91]

And I concluded, "[I]f the nation is to rely on 'free private enterprise' to guide economic processes, 'workable competition' applied to concerted action is a dangerous principle."[92] I have not since changed my opinion.

The *Yale Law Journal* published the second of my studies dealing with workable competition, "The Rule of Reason, Workable Competition, and Monopoly."[93] In this study, to which Dirlam and Stelzer refer, I developed in a more precise and rigorous manner criteria for determining the workability of competition, indicating the significance of structure, conduct, and performance. I pointed out that, although many economists believe that together these criteria may afford a useful guide in determining the effectiveness of competition in an industry, "guideposts are no

---

89. 21 U. Chi. L. Rev. 527 (1954), reprinted as chap. 2 *supra*.
90. *Id.* at 617, p. 116 *supra*.
91. *Ibid.* Emphasis in the original.
92. *Id.* at 618, p. 117 *supra*.
93. 64 Yale L. J. 1107 (1955), reprinted as chap. 3 *supra*.

better than the wayfarer's interpretation of them." [94] I also tried to make it clear that the object of an appropriate performance test should be merely to determine whether the arrangement is consistent with competition. I then traced the historical development of the rule of reason as applied to antitrust. I observed that the extent to which the 1911 Supreme Court's distinction between reasonable and unreasonable restrictions on competition had "emasculated the Sherman Act as an instrument for preserving a competitive industrial structure in the American economy is . . . not generally understood." [95] Although rejecting the traditional rule of reason, I recognized that "courts must exercise discretion and judgment, after considering all the relevant facts, in determining whether a contract restrains or promotes competition." [96]

Having developed the standards by which I would apply the rule of reason and the principle of workable competition, I then analyzed three industries, steel, tin cans, and cellophane, in each of which the courts in proceedings against the leading producers had found no violation of the antitrust laws.[97a] I examined their structure, the conduct of the alleged law violators, and the industry's performance, to determine whether or not the arrangements were consistent with workable competition as I had developed the standard. In each case I concluded, despite the court's finding that none of the defendants had transgressed the law, that the industry did not conform to "the conception of workable competition developed herein." [97b] But in reaching this conclusion I called attention to the danger of a general reliance on the concept in administering antitrust statutes. About this I said:

It may be difficult to attain an interpretation and application of the concept of workable competition as it has been expounded here. Amendment of the law is unlikely to be the solution: many of the advocates of change apparently hope for a gentler, not a more rigorous, application of the statutes to big business. The concept of workable competition is vague, and differences among experts as to its meaning are inevitable. As Mason has suggested, the preconceptions of the analyst as well as the facts may influence his judgment on the competitive workability of any particular arrangement.

If amendment of the Sherman Act is an inadequate solution, judicial broad-

---

94. *Id.* at 1112, p. 125 *supra.*
95. *Id.* at 1125, p. 140 *supra.*
96. *Id.* at 1122, p. 136 *supra.*
97a. United States v. United States Steel Corp., 251 U.S. 417 (1920); United States v. American Can Co., 230 Fed. 859 (D. Md. 1916); United States v. E. I. du Pont de Nemours & Co., 118 F. Supp. 41 (D. Del. 1953), *aff'd* 351 U.S. 377 (1956).
97b. P. 165 *supra.* See also pp. 153 and 180 *supra.*

ening of the act to include the concept of workable competition, however desirable it may seem in theory, may not prove in fact a more promising remedy. As has been pointed out, without any change in the statute the doctrine of workable competition is creeping into the decisions. This is strikingly evident in Judge Leahy's decision in the *Cellophane* case, which reveals how a superficial understanding of the concept and its application to a particular set of facts may defeat the objectives of the Sherman Act. If this decision becomes a precedent, it will be difficult to establish the existence of monopoly in any industry confronted by rival products that for some uses may be substitutable and among which a vigorous rivalry appears to exist.[98]

Dirlam and Stelzer's Criticisms

In criticizing the Mueller-Stocking analysis of the *Cellophane* case Dirlam and Stelzer started with a basic error that led to much discussion that would otherwise be irrelevant. They objected to our alleged use of the concept of workable competition in judging the legality of Du Pont's alleged cellophane monopoly. But this is a straw man of their own contriving. That they set him up is not difficult to understand, but it is hard to justify. It may be that I have unwittingly contributed to their confusion. At any rate they failed to distinguish between what I was doing in the *Yale Law Journal* article and what Mueller and I were doing in the *American Economic Review* article. In the former, as I have just indicated, I undertook to test the usefulness of the concept of workable competition under a simplified rule of reason in determining the economic significance of alleged violations of the antitrust statutes; and despite the findings my analyses led me to in judging the workability of competition in the steel, tin can, and cellophane industries, I concluded that the concept was not very useful: a conclusion that Dirlam and Stelzer ignored. In the *American Economic Review* article Mueller and I were testing the court's findings that Du Pont had no monopoly power in making and selling cellophane, not the usefulness of the concept of workable competition.

In the Mueller-Stocking article our analysis was shaped by the major

98. *Id.* at 1161–62. In another, later study, an appraisal of the Report of the Attorney General's Committee, in discussing the Committee's recommendations on Section 7 of the Clayton Act, I again made clear my skepticism of the usefulness of the concept of workable competition. I stated: "Clearly, administering amended Section 7 in accordance with the rule of reason and the principle of workable competition is unlikely to achieve the goal that Congress set for it: the prevention of further concentration." "The Attorney General's Committee's Report: The Businessman's Guide through Antitrust," 44 Georgetown L. J. 1, 24–25 (1955), reprinted as chap. 4 *supra*, p. 208.

issues in the *Cellophane* case and by the court's findings about them. The government brought its suit under Section 2 of the Sherman Act, charging Du Pont with having attempted to monopolize and having conspired to monopolize the manufacture and sale of cellophane and cellulosic caps and bands. Judge Leahy in his decision pointed out that the charge of having monopolized involved two questions: "1. does duPont possess monopoly powers; and 2., if so, has it achieved such powers by 'monopolizing' within the meaning of the Act and under United States v. Aluminum Company of America[?] . . . Unless the first is decided against defendant, the second is not reached." [99] Judge Leahy need not have reached the second question because he concluded that Du Pont did not possess monopoly power in cellophane. Since Dirlam (in his work with Kahn) has indicated that he does not believe the question, Does a firm have monopoly power? is the definitive one in antitrust proceedings, he might well have criticized the court for undertaking to answer the question. But it is difficult to understand why he should challenge economists for doing so, since the *Cellophane* case in fact turned on this issue and such questions are the stock-in-trade of economists. In directing our analysis to the question we tried to make it clear that we were concerned with economics, not with the law.[100] In answering the question we used the tools our profession has given us, but did not suggest their usefulness in answering the second question that Judge Leahy raised, namely, has Du Pont monopolized within the meaning of the Sherman Act? This is Dirlam and Stelzer's straw man.

To answer the question, Does Du Pont have monopoly power in making and selling cellophane? we tried to set up tests relevant to the evidence the trial developed.[101] We found three: (1) What role has business strategy

99. United States v. E. I. du Pont de Nemours & Co., 118 F. Supp. 41, 54 (D. Del. 1953).

100. In "The Cellophane Case and the New Competition," 45 Am. Econ. Rev. 29 (1955), at page 32 we stated explicitly, "[W]e do not mean to suggest that its strategy was immoral or *unlawful*." Emphasis added. We reiterated on page 34 that we were not concerned with the legality of Du Pont's control of cellophane. In the light of these statements I find it difficult to understand how Dirlam and Stelzer can say, "Professors Stocking and Mueller conclude that duPont had a (presumably illegal) [sic] monopoly." "The Cellophane Labyrinth," 1 Antitrust Bulletin 633, 642 (1956). We reached no such conclusion.

101. Whatever the defects of the government's development of its case (and I am inclined to agree with Dirlam and Stelzer that a simpler analysis might have been more effective), the defendants introduced all economic data relevant to determining the effectiveness of competition. In fact, Judge Leahy's decision seems to be based on a concept of workable competition and the rule of reason. Dirlam and Stelzer, identifying the concept of workable competition almost exclusively with

Workable Competition as an Antitrust Guide

played in Du Pont's production and sales policies? (2) Is cellophane a sufficiently differentiated product to have a distinct market, or is its market that of all flexible wrapping papers? (3) Do the trend and level of earnings reflect monopoly power or competition? It is important in evaluating our application of these tests to keep in mind what we were testing, namely, Has Du Pont had monopoly power in making and selling cellophane? In most of Dirlam and Stelzer's criticisms of our use of these tests they had in mind their own question, Is the concept of workable competition useful in determining the legality of monopoly? Thus, in evaluating our analysis of Du Pont's business strategy in protecting its domestic market from the competition of foreign cellophane producers, Dirlam and Stelzer saw in it a test of the industry's performance to determine the monopoly's legality. They similarly judged the significance of Du Pont's participation in market-dividing schemes and its quota arrangements under its patent exchange with Sylvania—to prove their point that performance (which they confuse with conduct)[102] is not a useful standard in determining the social acceptability of monopolistic arrangements. In trying to prove their case they found it convenient to agree with Judge Leahy's evaluation of these practices.[103]

the performance test, would disagree. They said, "The Judge's consideration of duPont's market performance (an integral part of the measurement of workable competition) was subsidiary to his conclusion that it was pointless to discuss the monopolization of cellophane because the cellophane market was so narrow that the product could not in any meaningful sense be said to be monopolized." *Op. cit. supra* note 100, at 635. But those who have set up the criteria of workable competition have not limited them to market performance. They have looked to the structure of the industry and to the power of substitutes as means of lessening such monopoly power as a monopolist or as oligopolists might have. This is what Judge Leahy did.

102. Why Dirlam and Stelzer should criticize our use of Du Pont's strategy in protecting its domestic market—that is, its business conduct, not the industry's performance—as evidence of its having a monopoly it wanted to protect, is particularly difficult to understand since Dirlam and Kahn, *op. cit. supra* note 9, would make conduct—what a firm is up to—the primary test of antitrust violation.

103. Dirlam and Stelzer's willingness to defend Judge Leahy's findings is pretty good evidence that they were relying on his 381-page opinion (unofficial print), most of which was lifted bodily from the defendant's proposed statement of facts, rather than on the 7,500 pages of testimony and 7,000 exhibits introduced in the case. For example, Dirlam and Stelzer stated, "According to the court, the foreign cellophane was of such poor quality it could not have been successfully imported even without the tariff." *Op. cit. supra* note 100, at 643. The facts are that in 1927 importers had 21 per cent of domestic cellophane sales and in 1928, 24 per cent. Du Pont Cellophane Co.'s quarterly competitive report, first quarter 1929, Government's Exhibit 431, p. 5677, United States v. E. I. du Pont de Nemours & Co., 118 F. Supp. 41 (D. Del. 1953). After the reclassification of cellophane in 1929 with the consequent rise in import duties, importers supplied less than 9 per cent

Workable Competition and Antitrust Policy

In criticizing our analysis of the market for flexible wrapping paper to determine whether Du Pont has monopoly power in cellophane, Dirlam and Stelzer attacked both our conclusion and that of their own straw man. In attacking our conclusion they distorted our arguments. They said we conceded "that food packaging business shifts back and forth from one wrapping material to another with *slight changes in product prices*"; [104] and they said this argues, contrary to our findings, for "a very high cross-elasticity of demand between cellophane and its substitutes in some areas." [105] We made no such concession, nor does the record warrant one. What we said was that

some buyers of packaging materials changed from one kind to another in *trying to get their money's worth*. Some candymakers and some bread bakers, for example, operating on narrow margins in the mid-thirties switched from cellophane to a less costly wrapper when their other production costs mounted.[106]

So far as the record indicates, the shift was not occasioned by price changes in either cellophane or substitute wrapping materials customarily selling for less than cellophane. The buyers of cellophane, like the buyers of other products, no doubt tried to get their money's worth and to do so compared qualities of cellophane (some of which were unequalled in any other wrapping material) and its price with the qualities and prices of substitutes. No doubt there were marginal buyers who switched from one to the other in response to price changes, just as some did with changes in other costs. But apparently most cellophane buyers were so wedded to the product that Du Pont could and did price it independently of the prices of its rivals. It did so in both lowering and raising prices, and by its own assertion it did so to increase its profits. In 1948, for example, when its division manager concluded that "if operative earnings of 31 per cent is [sic] considered inadequate, then an upward revision in prices will be necessary," [107] Du Pont issued a revised price schedule designed to yield 40 per cent. Operative earnings responded promptly, moving from 27.2 per cent in 1948 to 35.2 per cent in 1949, and to 45.3 per cent in 1950.

of the domestic market. *Id.*, fourth quarter 1929, GX 434, p. 5714. After a change in the tariff rate under the Tariff Act of 1930, imports did not amount to as much as 1 per cent in any year up until 1947. GX 182, p. 515; GX 182A, p. 515A.
104. Dirlam and Stelzer, *supra* note 100, at 644. Emphasis added.
105. *Ibid.*
106. Stocking and Mueller, *supra* note 100, at 52-53. Emphasis added.
107. Government's Exhibit 591, p. 7539, United States v. E. I. du Pont de Nemours & Co., 118 F. Supp. 41 (D. Del. 1953).

Workable Competition as an Antitrust Guide

The nub of the problem of cross-elasticity as Dirlam and Stelzer conceived it in determining the legality of Du Pont's cellophane monopoly—their problem, not ours—is to prove that cellophane enjoys *"as much immunity from competition as aluminum ingot, the only morning newspaper in New Orleans, or first-run movie theaters."* [108] Such proof is obviously irrelevant to our problem, Does Du Pont have a monopoly in selling cellophane? Even if it were relevant, a quantitative comparison of immunities is beyond the competence of either judges or economists.

So also with their criticism of the Mueller-Stocking conclusion that Du Pont's rate of earnings in cellophane (ranging from 18 per cent to 62.4 per cent over a thirteen-year period, and averaging 35.6 per cent) reflects monopoly power: most of their objections stemmed from their preoccupation with the concept of workable competition. But while most of their criticisms are beside the point, Dirlam and Stelzer interestingly enough came to the same conclusion that I had earlier reached about the usefulness of the concept of workable competition as a standard for determining illegality in antitrust cases. They don't think it will work. As they put it,

> Proof that will demonstrate to an economist the existence of monopoly power [the task Mueller and I assayed] . . . is far from showing illegal monopoly power. But a proof that some (unquantified) degree of monopoly power has been economically misused [the task they credited to us] . . . is something that [can] rarely be relied upon to convince anyone but its author, let alone a court of law.[109]

The Role of Economic Analysis in Antitrust

In denying the usefulness of the concept of workable competition in determining antitrust violations, Dirlam and Stelzer recognized that they had not disposed of the question of the proper role of economic analysis in antitrust proceedings. Their discussion of this contains some useful suggestions; it also leaves something to be desired. They said that economic analysis may be useful in selecting cases for action and in fashioning decrees. And that is all. Although they indicated clearly their skepticism of economic analysis as a basis for determining the legality of alleged antitrust violations, they stated the principle on which they would apply the Sherman Act only in general terms: "Guilt or innocence in Sherman Act cases must inevitably be determined by the courts from an application

---

108. Dirlam and Stelzer, *supra* note 100, at 644. Emphasis added.
109. *Id.* at 648.

of the traditional legal appraisal of the character of conduct, and its associated intent."[110] Dirlam and Kahn have elsewhere expounded the principle in more detail. As indicated earlier in this article, they look to the traditional application of the rule of reason to insure the sort of competition the antitrust statutes contemplate. In elucidating this principle they quoted with approval Chief Justice White's finding in the *Standard Oil* decision that the antitrust laws condemn

> all contracts or acts . . . *unreasonably* restrictive of competitive conditions, either from the nature . . . of the contract or act or where the surrounding circumstances were such as . . . to give rise to the inference or presumption that they had been entered into or done with the intent to do wrong to the general public and to limit the right of individuals, thus restraining the free flow of commerce. . . .[111]

Throughout *Fair Competition* they reiterated that only through the traditional approach can a reasonable and a reasonably effective administration of the antitrust laws be expected. I have discussed elsewhere the history and significance of the rule of reason in antitrust cases. It was the rule of reason that identified intent with bad conduct and led to a distinction between good and bad monopolistic combinations; it was the rule of reason that allowed the courts to ignore structure and the relationship between structure and business behavior; and it was the rule of reason as set forth in the *Standard Oil* and *Tobacco* cases of 1911 and as subsequently applied in the *American Can, United Shoe Machinery, United States Steel, International Harvester,*[112] and other leading cases growing out of the Great Combination Movement that validated an industrial structure inconsistent with the objectives of the Sherman Act.

Although intent as evidenced by conduct may be useful in passing on the validity of arrangements that may injure competition, unfortunately there is no simple formula for determining good conduct. More important, the motives for business behavior and the behavior itself may by any reasonable legal standard be wholly exemplary, yet the conduct may tend to lessen the vigor of competition. The motives behind the business de-

110. *Id.* at 634.
111. Dirlam and Kahn, *op. cit. supra* note 9, at 49–50. Emphasis in the original omitted; emphasis added.
112. Standard Oil Co. v. United States, 221 U.S. 1 (1911); United States v. American Tobacco Co., 221 U.S. 106 (1911); United States v. American Can Co., 230 Fed. 859 (D. Md. 1916); United States v. Winslow, 227 U.S. 202 (1913); United States v. United Shoe Machinery Co., 247 U.S. 32 (1918); United States v. United States Steel Corp., 251 U.S. 417 (1920); United States v. International Harvester Co., 274 U.S. 693 (1927).

Workable Competition as an Antitrust Guide

cisions that led to the Great Combination Movement were diverse and obscure. Promoters sought speculative profits; bankers sought the stabilization of security values; businessmen sought relief from the vigor of competition; industrial engineers sought economies of management and integration. But the result of these mixed motives was an industrial structure shot through with monopolistic restraint—for which the Sherman Act under the 1911 rule of reason was no remedy. Moreover, the application of the rule in subsequent cases accelerated and accentuated the merger movement of the 1920's. The motives behind the latest merger movement are perhaps more mixed than those that characterized the earlier movements. Tax savings, security through diversification and integration, a sure supply of raw materials, economical entrance into new fields and new geographic areas, economical expansion of plant—these are among the major motives of the contemporary merger movement. Clearly the traditional antitrust approach is inadequate to grapple with such a movement.[113] The courts and the Congress cannot ignore consequences if the country is to preserve an industrial structure consistent with effective competition. There is no evidence that when General Motors bought out a little diesel engine company and a small locomotive manufacturer in the 1930's it sought to monopolize the locomotive field. Quite the contrary. It did battle with a quasi-decadent monopoly in steam locomotives. Today General Motors makes about 70 per cent of all locomotives sold in this country. It probably has not sought monopoly, but its power as one of the biggest buyers of railway services is a distinct asset in selling diesel locomotives. No purchaser of railway equipment can overlook the fact that in buying from General Motors he is dealing with a powerful customer, and he would be somewhat less than human if he were not influenced by it. General Motors no doubt is one of the country's most efficient producers of automobiles, but its chief advantage over smaller rivals may be that it gets better deals in buying, not because it is more efficient but because it has power in the market. What is true of General Motors is more or less true of other large concerns. The point is that refusing to examine economic consequences means failing to grapple effec-

---

113. Although Dirlam and Kahn stated as a general principle that neither structure nor performance is of significance in determining violation of the antitrust laws (*op. cit. supra* note 9, at 44), at times they conceded that the courts and the Federal Trade Commission must consider economic consequences in enforcing the Clayton Act. Despite noting specific exceptions (*e.g.*, p. 231 n. 42), however, they never abandoned their main thesis. They concluded their analysis with the declaration, "We are unsympathetic to proposals for reorganizing market structures to make them more purely competitive. . . ." *Op. cit. supra* note 9, at 284.

269

Workable Competition and Antitrust Policy

tively with the problem of structure. This, of course, does not imply undertaking to "purify the economy out of the twentieth century," but it does mean that believers in free enterprise cannot shut their eyes to the relationship between structure and competition.[114]

Certain antitrust prohibitions obviously require the examination of economic consequences. Section 7 of the Clayton Act prohibits mergers that may lessen substantially competition in any market. Section 2 prohibits price discrimination where the effect may be to lessen substantially or to injure competition. Motives may be pure, conduct immaculate, yet mergers and price discrimination may wipe out competition. To recognize this is not to justify an economic analysis that makes enforcement impossible. The Federal Trade Commission's thoroughgoing inquiry into all the economic ramifications of Pillsbury's acquisition of Ballard and Ballard and Duff may comfort those who believe in the utilization of the standard of workable competition in antitrust administration, but such a procedure in the enforcement of amended Section 7 promises to emasculate it.[115] As Mason has indicated, pushing economic inquiry very far

---

114. Dirlam and Kahn's own failure to recognize the full significance of this relationship led them to accept the court's remedies in the *National Lead* case. The conduct of the National Lead and Du Pont Companies clearly indicated an intent to monopolize titanium in the domestic market. They participated in a cartel so tight that in the words of the district court, "It was more difficult for the independent outsider to enter this business than for the camel to make its proverbial passage through the eye of a needle." United States v. National Lead Co., 63 F. Supp. 513, 521 (S.D.N.Y. 1945), aff'd, 332 U.S. 319 (1947). Yet the district court and the Supreme Court, ignoring structure and its relationship to conduct, were content with a mere injunction against the unlawful acts, as apparently are Dirlam and Kahn.

115. Although the *Pillsbury Mills* opinion rejected the "quantitative substantiality" test and found prima facie evidence of Section 7 violation in Pillsbury's acquisition of Ballard and Ballard and Duff, the Commission recognized that its obligation under the statute was to determine the probable effects of these acquisitions on competition. To do this in merger cases, it declared, "[t]here must be a case-by-case examination of all relevant factors in order to ascertain the probable economic consequences." Pillsbury Mills, Inc., 50 F.T.C. 555, 565 (1953). Commissioner Mead, concurring, objected to the all-embracing character of the economic inquiry contemplated, saying, "The facts to be determined may be so apparent that a reasonable man could fairly decide the issues without the benefit of extensive data." *Id.* at 575. The significance of Chairman Howrey's requirement, on behalf of the Commission, of an extensive economic inquiry can only be fully understood by reference to what Howrey has said elsewhere on the importance of economic evidence in antitrust cases. While recognizing that the tests in a merger case under amended Section 7 of the Clayton Act might be "quite different from those in a restraint of trade case brought under Section 5 of the Federal Trade Commission Act," he discussed the tests which should be applied in antitrust cases arising under these statutes without distinguishing between them. "Economic Evidence in Antitrust

is "an invitation to nonenforcement";[116] but so is reliance solely upon intent and conduct. In some cases per se rules may afford the best method of preserving competition. In other cases economic inquiry must be carried to the point where a reasonable inference may be reached as to whether the business arrangements promote or hinder competition. That is far enough.

Dirlam and Kahn, although overemphasizing the adequacy of intent and conduct in judging the legality of business procedures, recognized that economic analysis cannot be dispensed with entirely in the administration of the antitrust laws. In criticizing the Federal Trade Commission's findings in certain price discrimination cases they found:

> The trouble is that the Commission itself provided precious little evidence in the latter cases that it had made even the necessary appraisal of offsetting benefits and costs of its decisions and orders.... [B]y failing ... to consider seriously the economic consequences of its orders or the possibility of achieving the desired results at less economic cost by a different kind of order, in short, by being more legalistic than the courts, the Commission was apparently intent on destroying its own *raison d'etre* as an expert, flexible administrative agency.[117]

Dirlam and Stelzer might well concede what Dirlam and Kahn affirmed. In truth it may be that they contemplated such when they stated: "That the anti-trust implications of behavior and intent must of course be interpreted against a background of analysis of economic power of the firm and structure of the industry goes without saying."[118] But whether or not Dirlam and Stelzer agree with Dirlam and Kahn, they can scarcely

---

Cases," 19 J. of Marketing 119, 120–21 (1954). In doing so he stated, "It is recognized that the public policy of the antitrust laws is governed by the reality that imperfect competition exists in most competitive markets. This concept, particularly when accompanied by a rule of reason approach, is sometimes referred to as 'workable' or 'effective' competition." *Id.* at 121. He then laid down sixteen tests relevant to determining "whether or not competitive conditions in a particular market comply with the requirements of the antitrust laws." *Ibid.* These tests included consideration of business conduct, market structure, and performance. Howrey made it pretty clear that he would apply the principle of workable competition under the rule of reason in the administration of the antitrust laws. In the light of this it is surprising that Dirlam and Kahn, who reject structure as evidence of the unworkability of competition, commended the Commission for its use of structure in finding a prima facie case against Pillsbury and saw in the Commission's remand calling for a painstaking and thorough economic inquiry no application of the principle of workable competition and no threat to a vigorous enforcement of Section 7. *Op. cit. supra* note 9, at 282-83.

116. Mason, "Market Power and Business Conduct: Some Comments" (Report of the Attorney General's Committee on Antitrust Policy), 46 Am. Econ. Rev. (Proceedings of the American Economic Ass'n) 471, 475 (1956).

117. Dirlam and Kahn, *op. cit. supra* note 9, at 254.

118. Dirlam and Stelzer, *supra* note 100, at 634.

Workable Competition and Antitrust Policy

challenge the professional propriety of economists' utilizing the vast resources of economic data that antitrust cases develop to determine whether competition or monopoly characterizes an industry.

Although Dirlam and Stelzer understated the role of economic analysis in antitrust proceedings and incorrectly alleged Mueller's and my acceptance of the concept of workable competition as a guide, they did not overemphasize the threat that utilization of the concept—particularly when identified with industrial performance—represents to effective antitrust enforcement. But they failed to recognize what the Supreme Court minority opinion in the *Cellophane* case clearly discerned, that structure may be evidence of the unworkability of competition. In the language of Chief Justice Warren's dissent, in which Justices Black and Douglas joined:

> This case, like many under the Sherman Act, turns upon the proper definition of the market. In defining the market in which du Pont's economic power is to be measured, the majority virtually emasculate § 2 of the Sherman Act.
> . . . .
> The conduct of du Pont and Sylvania illustrates that a few sellers tend to act like one and that an industry which does not have a competitive structure will not have competitive behavior. The public should not be left to rely upon the dispensations of management in order to obtain the benefits which normally accompany competition. . . . Only actual competition can assure long-run enjoyment of the goals of a free economy.[119]

---

119. United States v. E. I. du Pont de Nemours & Co., 351 U.S. 377, 414, 426 (1956).

6

Economic Tests of Monopoly and the Concept of the Relevant Market

SECTION 2 OF THE Sherman Act prohibits monopolizing, attempting to monopolize, or conspiring to monopolize. Monopolizing involves acquiring a monopoly and is basically an economic concept. Trying to monopolize involves motives and is basically a psychological concept. Conspiring is a matter of the law. A balanced interpretation of the Sherman Act would seem to embrace three disciplines—economics, psychology, and the law. Fortunately judges, versatile by training and experience and self-reliant by disposition, have not felt the need of psychologists in applying the Sherman Act. Since motives have economic significance only as they reveal themselves in business conduct, there is indeed little reason for the courts to call in the psychologists in administering Section 2. Only recently have they felt the need of economists. Economists perhaps can do double duty. Surely they know something about monopoly, and they should have special competence in determining whether business conduct—that is, business practices—is competitive or monopolistic in character. In short, the economists' function with reference to Section 2 should be to determine whether a defendant has really obtained a monopoly. It is for the courts to decide whether he has monopolized within the meaning of the Sherman Act, because the law bans only monopolies that have been unlawfully acquired or maintained.

Even for economists, determining the existence of monopoly is difficult. It was perhaps simpler when we knew less about it. In the good old days before we had learned of the purity and perfection of competition, when monopoly was merely an ugly, blood-thirsty Moloch, it was easier to recognize. Today we know that pure monopoly is no less an abstraction than is pure competition and is rarely found in real markets. No market

Note: Reprinted from the *Antitrust Bulletin*, Vol. II (March 1957).

Workable Competition and Antitrust Policy

situation is apt to be entirely free from monopolistic restraints, and no monopolist can ignore the rivalry of substitutes.

Technical progress and mechanical ingenuity have so broadened markets and dimmed boundaries that among firms and products with previously isolated markets a vigorous rivalry has broken out. Aluminum was for many years a classic example of domestic monopoly. Today other materials are available for the uses it serves: copper for electrical cables and conductors, lead for tubes and cables, zinc, brass, and magnesium for alloys, steel for trucks, vans, and trailers, and wood, steel, and copper for construction. For the manufacture of cooking utensils aluminum meets the rivalry of glass, tin ware, stainless steel, cast iron, enamel ware, and copper. As uses for aluminum have multiplied, its exclusive domain has so diminished that today it has few markets in which it does not meet the rivalry of alternative materials. The same is true of most other products throughout industry. As firms have diversified their operations and broadened their product mix, they not only have intensified rivalry with each other but have created a rivalry within themselves by producing different products that serve the same general function.

These developments raise a challenging question for antitrust lawyers, economists, and the courts. Does rivalry among substitutes provide the protection to consumers contemplated by the antitrust statutes? Many people believe it does. Businessmen have noted these developments with pride; economists, with optimism. Businessmen have pointed to them as evidence not only of the virility of private enterprise but of the rejuvenation and intensification of competition. Economists in loftier language, more technical and abstruse, have seen in them a waning of oligopolistic power. Demand functions for any firm, we are told, have lost their dependable stability [1] and have acquired a commendable consumer-protecting cross-elasticity.

But the optimism of the economists has not been matched by their ability to agree on the extent of monopoly power in particular situations or on the weight that should be given to various factors in identifying and measuring it. Economists like judges cannot free themselves of all preconceptions. Depending on their point of view, they have been willing to use their tools either for defendants or for the government in antitrust cases. And in independent analysis of antitrust proceedings, when they must select significant facts from the multitude of data spread over thou-

---

1. Ross M. Robertson, "On the Changing Apparatus of Competition," 44 Am. Econ. Rev. 51, 52 *et seq.* (1954).

Economic Tests of Monopoly

sands of pages of testimony and exhibits, what they find may unwittingly be influenced by what they are looking for.

With this acknowledgment of the frailties that affect us, I shall endeavor to indicate as objectively as I can what I regard as proper criteria for determining monopoly and to show their significance to the *Cellophane* case.[2]

THE CONCEPT OF WORKABLE COMPETITION

Economists, recognizing the imperfections of competition in the market place and the many and unique patterns into which it falls, have sought to differentiate the socially acceptable situation from the unacceptable by developing the concept of workable competition.[3] According to this concept, a market structure is workably competitive if it yields acceptable performance that cannot be improved without abandoning the market entirely as a regulator of economic activity. In determining workability economists look to three factors: industrial structure, business conduct, and economic performance. As my published work indicates,[4] I do not believe that the standard of workability is an appropriate one by which to determine the legality of business arrangements under the antitrust statutes. The least acceptable of these criteria is performance. Bad per-

---

2. United States v. E. I. du Pont de Nemours & Co., 118 F. Supp. 41 (D. Del. 1953), aff'd, 351 U.S. 377 (1956).

3. John M. Clark, "Toward a Concept of Workable Competition," 30 Am. Econ. Rev. (Proceedings of the American Economic Ass'n) 241 (1940); Clair Wilcox, *Competition and Monopoly in American Industry* (TNEC Monograph No. 21, 1940), pp. 8–9; George J. Stigler, "The Extent and Bases of Monopoly," 32 Am. Econ. Rev. (No. 2 Supp., Pt. 2) 2–3 (1942); Morris A. Adelman, "Effective Competition and the Antitrust Laws," 61 Harv. L. Rev. 1289 (1948); Corwin D. Edwards, *Maintaining Competition* (New York: McGraw-Hill, 1949), pp. 9–10; Edward S. Mason, "The Current Status of the Monopoly Problem in the United States," 62 Harv. L. Rev. 1265 (1949); Joe S. Bain, "Workable Competition in Oligopoly," 40 Am. Econ. Rev. 35 (Supp. 1950); Jesse W. Markham, "An Alternative Approach to the Concept of Workable Competition," 40 Am. Econ. Rev. 349 (1950).

4. George W. Stocking and Myron W. Watkins, *Monopoly and Free Enterprise* (New York: Twentieth Century Fund, 1951); Stocking, "The Rule of Reason, Workable Competition, and the Legality of Trade Association Activities," 21 U. Chi. L. Rev. 527, 617–19 (1954); Stocking, "The Rule of Reason, Workable Competition, and Monopoly," 64 Yale L. J. 1107, 1161–62 (1955); Stocking, "The Attorney General's Committee's Report: The Businessman's Guide through Antitrust," 44 Georgetown L. J. 1, 23–24 (1955); Stocking, "On the Concept of Workable Competition as an Antitrust Guide," 2 Antitrust Bulletin 3 (1956). The four articles appear as chaps. 2, 3, 4, and 5 of this book.

Workable Competition and Antitrust Policy

formance may be an appropriate criterion for determining public policy towards a competitive industry,[5] but good performance can scarcely justify private monopolies in a society dedicated to free enterprise. As Ben W. Lewis has expressed it,

> Results alone throw no light on the really significant question: have these results been *compelled* by the system—by *competition*—or do they represent simply the dispensations of managements which, with a wide latitude of policy choices at their disposal, happened for the moment to be benevolent or "smart"? This points up the real issue.[6]

Although I do not regard the principle of workability as an acceptable guide in antitrust cases, I do believe that the criteria that economists have developed for determining workability—structure, conduct, and performance—can serve a useful, perhaps indispensable, function in determining the existence of monopoly.

Industrial Structure and the Relevant Market

In examining industrial structure one looks to the the number of firms in an industry, their relative size, the extent to which a few dominate it, ease of entry, availability of substitutes, and similar characteristics that have relevance to economic behavior. Some economists have contended that structure does not have a definitive relationship to behavior. M. A. Adelman, for example, has argued that competition can be effective with only a few large firms in an industry, with many small firms, or with a mixture of large and small firms.[7] This may be true, but most economists would probably admit that the fewer the firms in an industry the greater the likelihood of their following common pricing policies and common business practices calculated to maximize their earnings; in short, the greater the likelihood of their behaving like monopolists. In truth, structure may dictate behavior. Despite the vogue that the Chamberlinian theory of oligopolistic pricing[8] attained shortly after its enunciation,[9] economists

---

5. For example, the waste that accompanies unrestricted competition in producing oil justifies regulation to assure its production in a manner consistent with the geological units in which it occurs.

6. "The Effectiveness of the Federal Antitrust Laws: A Symposium," ed. Dexter M. Keezer, 39 Am. Econ. Rev. 689, 707 (1949). Emphasis in the original.

7. "Effective Competition and the Antitrust Laws," 61 Harv. L. Rev. 1289, 1303 (1948).

8. Edward Chamberlin, *The Theory of Monopolistic Competition* (Cambridge: Harvard University Press, 1933).

9. "For the historian of economic thought, the most revolutionary feature of monopolistic competition theories will probably be the unprecedented pace at which

generally would probably now accept the proposition that without tacit agreement oligopolists are as likely to behave like competitors as like monopolists. Uncertainties, as Chamberlin pointed out, may make the outcome indeterminate.[10] What is certain is that some structural patterns are more conducive to tacit agreement than others. When only a few sellers dominate a market they need no formal agreement to insure their acting in a way to promote their mutual interests. And they can readily find pricing devices—basing point pricing, price leadership and the like —that will insure their doing so.

Students of industrial structure who emphasize the role that substitutes play in determining the effectiveness of competition believe that the relevant market for any product may be broader than that of the firms producing it. Ross M. Robertson, an able exponent of this view, has declared,

> To assess the competitive situation of a firm we must still resort to counting. . . . Yet counting only those firms which are within the "industry" tells us very little. We must do our counting by taking categories of uses for the output of an industry, considering what products of other industries directly compete within these categories.[11]

But if counting substitutes is to have any real significance, some method of calculating the substitutability of the so-called substitutes is required. All products compete with each other for the consumer's dollar, and in this sense each product is a substitute for any other. Substitutes regarded in this light have no significance to the monopoly problem. To have meaning they must be close enough to insure an economical allocation of resources and to protect consumers from exploitation. Economists have developed the concept of cross-elasticity to measure substitutability, and the courts have borrowed it in trying to determine a product's relevant market. For reasons I shall make clear later, I believe this concept alone cannot be of much use in antitrust cases and that its use by those not trained in economics will lessen the effectiveness of Section 2 of the Sherman Act.

they conquered their audience. . . . five years had not elapsed before textbooks were revised, one after another, in order to insert one or two chapters on the new theory." Robert Triffin, *Monopolistic Competition and General Equilibrium Theory* (Cambridge: Harvard University Press, 1940), p. 17.

10. Chamberlin, *op. cit. supra* note 8, 7th ed. (1957) at 51–53.
11. Robertson, *supra* note 1, at 53–54.

Workable Competition and Antitrust Policy

Business Conduct and the Relevant Market

Conduct or business strategy may be not only designed to insure common policies among business rivals but may be used by a single firm to protect some advantage—that is, some monopoly power—that it possesses. Some economists, notably Joseph A. Schumpeter, have argued that temporary monopolistic advantages are essential to economic progress.[12] Every innovation represents a monopoly and if it meets with popular acceptance is likely to bring to the innovator, for a time at least, monopoly profits. Without the promise of such profits, Schumpeter argues, innovations would cease and progress would be stifled. But while Schumpeter would apply a performance test to the acceptability of monopoly, he would not deny that the innovator possesses monopoly power.

This country's patent policy was based on the Schumpeterian theory long before Schumpeter advanced it. That business firms acquire patents is indicative of their belief that the patented process or product has unique qualities that so differentiate it from rival processes or products as to enable the possessor to make gains greater than he could make if everyone were free to use it. Patents may legalize monopoly power, but that they create it can scarcely be denied. Other forms of business strategy designed to give a business firm power in the market do not enjoy legal status, but they similarly reflect an effort to isolate firms from the unrestrained competition of their rivals. Dividing territories, setting market quotas, and the like are devices of the monopolist or of the would-be monopolist. That businessmen resort to such devices makes them suspect under both Section 1 and Section 2 of the Sherman Act. When they do, both the economists and the courts may find their task simplified.

Where monopolistic strategies are entirely lacking, it may be necessary to determine the precise boundary of a seller's market as a step in determining whether he has monopoly power. But when business strategy provides the answer to the question whether a firm has monopoly power, the difficult task of determining the boundaries of the relevant market may be avoided. Businessmen do not try to protect a position that has no value. When they act with respect to their position as though they believe it possesses elements of monopoly, this is persuasive evidence that it does. Business conduct, in short, can be a significant factor in determining the existence of monopoly.

12. Joseph A. Schumpeter, *Capitalism, Socialism, and Democracy* (New York: Harper, 1942), pp. 89–90.

Economic Tests of Monopoly

Business Performance

Judges may regard business conduct as a slender reed on which to hang the determination of antitrust violation. But rarely will they have to rely on it alone. Business performance may so reinforce a judgment on structure and conduct as to leave little doubt that a firm in fact has power over the market. The economist's interest here is not whether a firm with monopoly power serves society well, but whether a firm has monopoly power. The aspects of performance most relevant to determining whether a firm possesses monopoly power are its pricing policy and its profits record. The courts have defined monopoly power as the power to exclude competitors and the power to control price.[13] In doing so they doubtless have been influenced by economists. At any rate, economists will not take exception to their definition although they might suggest a narrowing of it to the single concept, the power to control price, since the power to exclude competitors will reflect itself in the power to control price.

To distinguish competitive pricing from monopolistic pricing is not always easy. In a perfectly competitive market rivals will sell at identical prices at any moment of time, but prices will change frequently in response to changing consumer wants and consumer evaluations of the relative importance of different products and in response to changing conditions of supply. In a market of pure monopoly, prices will similarly change in response to changes in consumer evaluations and in response to changes in cost. The difference is that in competitive markets the average cost of production (including a normal rate of return on investment) sets the limit to long-run price, while in a monopolized market the monopolist continuously re-evaluates demand and cost functions and tries to so adjust output as to maximize earnings by keeping price above cost. The greater the power of a monopolist the greater the likelihood that his prices will be flexible. The limitations on monopoly power in most industrial markets are such that noncompetitive or quasi-monopolistic pricing is apt to result in identical pricing by business rivals, with prices stable over a long period. In short, the closer markets are to perfect competition or to perfect monopoly the greater the similarity in their price behavior.

The characteristics that distinguish monopolistic from competitive markets where both have flexible prices are their cost-price ratios and their rate of earnings. In competitive markets prices tend to equal costs—

---

13. United States v. Paramount Pictures, Inc., 334 U.S. 131 (1948); United States v. Griffith, 334 U.S. 100 (1948); American Tobacco Co. v. United States, 328 U.S. 781 (1946).

Workable Competition and Antitrust Policy

marginal in the short run, average in the long run. In monopolistic markets prices tend to exceed marginal costs in the short run and average costs in the long run. The excess shows up in abnormal, that is, noncompetitive profits. Because economists rarely have access to cost data they may be forced to rely on profits data in determining the existence of monopoly. Pure profits of course are not confined to monopolistic markets. Competitors who respond to a rapidly expanding demand may realize earnings in excess of normal competitive rates. That they do so reflects the frictions that retard shifts in the use of resources. But such earning rates are apt to be short-lived. Long-term profits rates may be an aid in determining the existence of monopoly.

ECONOMIC TESTS OF MONOPOLY AND THE CELLOPHANE CASE [14]

Let us now examine the *Cellophane* case in the light of the several criteria for determining the existence of monopoly outlined above—structure, conduct, and performance. My task is to answer the first of the two questions [15] set by Judge Leahy in the district court: Does Du Pont have a monopoly in making and selling cellophane? The second question, whether Du Pont has monopolized within the meaning of Section 2 of the Sherman Act, is a proper one for the courts to have determined.

Structure

Only two domestic firms made and sold cellophane in the domestic market when the government filed its antitrust case in 1947—Sylvania Industrial Corporation of America and the Du Pont Company—and Du Pont accounted for over three-fourths of domestic sales. The structure of the industry was clearly not conducive to effective competition in selling cellophane if cellophane be considered a differentiated product. But is not cellophane's relevant market determined by the products that serve

---

14. For a more complete discussion of this topic see Stocking and Willard F. Mueller, "The Cellophane Case and the New Competition," 45 Am. Econ. Rev. 29 (1955), which documents fully the statements of fact given here in abbreviated form.

15. "The charge here is duPont monopolizes cellophane. The charge involves two questions: 1. does duPont possess monopoly powers; and 2., if so, has it achieved such powers by 'monopolizing' within the meaning of the Act and under United States v. Aluminum Company of America, 2 Cir., 148 F.2d 416, 429. Unless the first is decided against defendant, the second is not reached." United States v. E. I. du Pont de Nemours & Co., 118 F. Supp. 41, 54 (D. Del. 1953).

a similar function? Judge Leahy concluded that it was. In doing so he decided, and the Supreme Court sustained him, that cellophane was not a unique product, that in most of its end uses it met the competition of other wrapping papers, and hence that its relevant market was that for flexible wrapping materials. Of this broader market Du Pont obviously had no monopoly. In food packaging, for which Du Pont sold 80 per cent of its cellophane output, its percentage of all of the cellophane, aluminum foil, glassine, films, and waxed and other specialty wrapping papers sold by nineteen major converters in 1949 varied from 6.8 per cent in bakery products to 47.2 per cent for wrapping fresh produce. Foil, glassine, and waxed and other speciality papers outsold cellophane for every important food except fresh produce.[16] In finding that these several flexible wrapping materials gave vigorous competition to cellophane Judge Leahy noted that shifts in business between cellophane and other materials were "frequent, continuing and contested."[17] From this the district court and the Supreme Court concluded that cross-elasticity was high. By delimiting cellophane's market according to the areas in which it met the rivalry of substitute products and by applying the concept of cross-elasticity, this decision brings the law into harmony with recent concepts of competition. Nevertheless I find the courts' analysis and their conclusions unsound. As I have indicated, I do not believe the concept of cross-elasticity is of much use in determining whether a firm has a monopoly. In the first place, it calls for more precise information than antitrust cases can be expected to provide. Cross-elasticity defines the extent to which a change in the price of one commodity, for example, A, affects the sales of another commodity, B. If a decrease in the price of A diminishes the sales of B, cross-elasticity is positive. All that this tells us is that one product can be substituted for another, and that some consumers will make the substitution if their evaluation of the two products warrants it. If a given percentage change in the price of one product causes a relatively large change in the sales of the other product, cross-elasticity is high. On this question the record in the *Cellophane* case is necessarily silent; to answer it would involve disclosure of confidential information by business rivals. In the second place, even if the data were available, positive cross-elasticity alone may not warrant the conclusion that the seller of neither product can be a monopolist. To determine the existence of monopoly power economists and the courts must examine both the price response of the firms

16. See tables, *id.* at 113 (reproduced in United States v. E. I. du Pont de Nemours & Co., 351 U.S. 377, 407–9 (1956)).
17. *Id.* at 91.

losing business and the cost-price relationships of firms selling both products. If a price decrease by a firm selling product A shifts business from B to A, firms selling B must reconsider their pricing policies. To recapture lost business or, where cross-elasticity is high, to prevent the loss of what they have, they must lower their prices. If price changes by producers of one commodity are unaccompanied by price changes in the rival commodity, this indicates a lack of competition between the two commodities. Either the loss of business is too slight to matter—the cross-elasticity is low—or the firm cutting prices has a monopoly advantage not possessed by those not cutting prices. The firms not cutting prices must already be selling their product at a price equal to their marginal cost, while the firm that cut may have been getting a price in excess of its marginal cost.

So much for the principles. What are the facts? Between 1924 and 1938 Du Pont through a series of price cuts reduced the average price of cellophane by over 80 per cent. During this same period the average prices of glassine and waxed paper remained virtually constant. Between 1938 and 1940 Du Pont decreased the price of cellophane a further 8.6 per cent, while the prices of glassine and waxed paper actually increased.[18] Obviously the cross-elasticity of demand was very low. In selling cellophane Du Pont was able to ignore the prices of rival wrapping papers. Between 1924 and 1950, as Du Pont dropped its average price of cellophane from $2.51 to 49 cents a pound, prices for the principal type of moistureproof cellophane were from two to seven times the price of 25# bleached glassine and from two to four and one-half times the price of 30# waxed paper.[19] That Du Pont could continuously sell cellophane in so-called competition with glassine and waxed paper, never charging less than twice as much, is sufficient evidence that cellophane was a unique product. As the Supreme Court dissenting opinion put it,

We cannot believe that . . . practical businessmen would have bought cellophane in increasing amounts over a quarter of a century if close substitutes were available at from one-seventh to one-half cellophane's price. That they did so is testimony to cellophane's distinctiveness.[20]

18. Table of annual average cellophane prices from 1924 to 1950, *id.* at 82. Price comparisons between cellophane and other wrapping materials appear in Defendant's Exhibit 994-A.
19. Defendant's Brief on the Facts and the Law, Appendix A (graph based on prices per 1,000 sq. in.), United States v. E. I. du Pont de Nemours & Co., 118 F. Supp. 41 (D. Del. 1953).
20. United States v. E. I. du Pont de Nemours & Co., 351 U.S. 377, 417 (1956).

Economic Tests of Monopoly

That marginal buyers, candymakers, for example, shifted their purchases from one product to another from time to time does not indicate that Du Pont had no monopoly in selling cellophane. No monopolized product is completely isolated from rival products, and consumers anxious to get their money's worth are constantly comparing values and shifting purchases. They are not dissuaded from doing so merely because one of the products they desire is sold by a monopolist and another by competitors.

Conduct

Du Pont officials themselves are on record as believing that they had in cellophane a unique product for which there was no effective substitute,[21] and they adopted a strategy to protect Du Pont's monopoly. Du Pont entered the business in 1923 by joining with La Cellophane, a French company that owned the original patents, to form the Du Pont Cellophane Company, which acquired the exclusive right to exploit the patents in the American market. In 1929 Du Pont Cellophane Company

---

21. In 1923, when Du Pont was considering entry into cellophane production, its development department made a comparative survey of glassine, sheet gelatin, and tin foil, cellophane's closest rival products, and concluded that they offered no serious competition because of price or quality differences. Government's Exhibit 392, pp. 5437–38, United States v. E. I. du Pont de Nemours & Co., 118 F. Supp. 41 (D. Del. 1953). Twenty-five years later Du Pont still believed that serious rivals had not appeared. Its 1948 market analysis of cellophane concluded: "The principal markets for non-viscose films have been competitive with Cellophane only to a very minor degree up to this time. Some are used very little or not at all in the packaging field—others are employed principally for specialty uses where Cellophane is not well adapted—none have been successfully introduced into any of Cellophane's main markets due to their inherent shortcomings." Defendant's Exhibit 595, p. 1147, *ibid*. Olin Industries, Inc., a company that Du Pont in 1948 decided to encourage to enter cellophane production (and that did so in 1951), after investigation reported: "According to Du Pont, Cellophane is considered the only all purpose film, and any product to be truly competitive with Cellophane must have the following attributes: (1) low cost, (2) transparency, (3) operate with a high efficiency on mechanical equipment, (4) print well both as to speed and appearance. There are no films currently marketed which are potentially competitive to any substantial degree in Cellophane's major markets when measured by the above attributes necessary for wide usage. Other transparent films will find their place for those low volume uses which can absorb the additional cost of the film and which necessitate certain physical properties not possessed by Cellophane." Report on "the evidence in support of entry by Olin Industries into the Cellophane business, based on the purchase of patent license and 'know-how' from Du Pont," December 15, 1948, Government's Exhibit 566, p. 7575, *ibid*. A Du Pont survey of competitive conditions in 1950 made no reference to glassine, waxed paper, or sulphite paper but said, "Competition for du Pont cellophane will come from competitive cellophane and from non-cellophane films made by us or by others." Record, p. 4070, *ibid*.

Workable Competition and Antitrust Policy

entered into a patent exchange agreement with Kalle & Company of Germany, and in 1935 it entered into one with British Cellophane, Ltd. In effect these agreements were also divisions of territory. While not signers of the 1930 cartel agreement dividing world markets, Du Pont representatives attended the Paris cartel conference, and Du Pont Cellophane Company later relied on the cartel agreement to protect its claim to the West Indies market. It took steps to obtain tariff protection that eventually excluded virtually all imports of cellophane. It settled its patent-infringement suit against Sylvania by a patent-exchange and cross-licensing agreement that geared Sylvania's production to its own. It launched a research and patent-accumulation program that, according to President Yerkes, was designed as a defense measure to protect "the field of moistureproofing agents other than waxes."[22] By these steps it forestalled genuine competition in selling cellophane in the American market. Its strategy was that of a monopolist.

Performance

The district court found Du Pont to be an aggressive and progressive competitor of all flexible packaging material producers, quick to improve its product and processes, quick to lower its prices, and quick to promote its sales by acquainting potential users with cellophane's superior qualities. In the broad market for flexible wrapping materials Judge Leahy found a vigorous and healthy competition, and for its farsighted, aggressive management in meeting this competition he thought Du Pont deserved praise, not censure. From the same record I find that Du Pont behaved as any intelligent monopolist might have behaved. Through research and experience it improved the quality of its product and the processes for making it. It was continuously alert to the market potentialities of cellophane, and it took aggressive steps to acquaint potential users with its peculiar qualities. Its management periodically re-examined its costs and sales, actual and potential, and shaped its price and production program to improve its earnings. In doing so, as I have indicated, it was able to ignore the pricing policies of producers of rival wrapping materials. Du Pont officials recognized that they had control over cellophane prices, and the record shows they used it to achieve specified profit goals. In May 1948, with earnings on investment in cellophane averaging 31 per cent before taxes, a division

22. December 1933 report to Du Pont Cellophane's board of directors, Jan. 22, 1934, Government's Exhibit 488, p. 6478, *ibid.*

manager suggested that if such earnings were considered inadequate Du Pont should raise its prices; and he proposed a schedule of prices calculated to yield 40 per cent.[23] After adoption of the schedule Du Pont's earnings rate increased to 35.2 per cent in 1949 and to 45.3 per cent in 1950.[24] An intracompany memorandum indicates that in considering a price increase during the postwar inflation Du Pont was more concerned about its effect on public relations than on rivals or customers. Du Pont's pricing policies were clearly those of a monopolist.

Du Pont's earnings were likewise monopolistic. Its annual rate of earnings on investment, before taxes, in cellophane ranged from 18.0 per cent to 62.4 per cent and averaged 35.6 per cent during the period 1925 to 1938. Du Pont's earnings on its investment in rayon during the same period ranged from –0.9 per cent to 34.2 per cent and averaged only 12.9 per cent. During the nine years from 1930 to 1938 inclusive, when competition had become vigorous, earnings on rayon averaged only 6.6 per cent.[25] This comparison has unique significance. Cellophane and rayon stem from the same basic raw materials. Both were innovations appearing about the same time. Both were initially manufactured under noncompetitive conditions and both enjoyed substantial tariff protection. Du Pont produced both. Both have reasonably close substitutes. As output increased both were the beneficiaries of continuing improvements in production, a rapid reduction in costs, and a rapid decline in price. The significant difference in making and selling the two products is the structure of the two industries. Both began as monopolies, but in rayon rival producers quickly appeared. By 1930 American Viscose Corporation, the country's first producer, and Du Pont, its second, met the rivalry of eighteen other rayon makers. This intensification of competition eventually resulted in competitive pricing and the disappearance of monopoly earnings.

The basic issue in the *Cellophane* case really boils down to this: Would freedom of entry have brought in a larger number of cellophane producers and ultimately lower prices and earnings than have prevailed? I believe it would have. Moreover, if the rivalry of substitute packaging materials, particularly glassine and waxed paper, had in fact forced competitive pricing on Du Pont, as the court concluded, Du Pont should have been indifferent to the entry of rival cellophane producers. Competition from

23. Government's Exhibit 591, p. 7539, *ibid.*
24. Calculated from annual profit and loss statements of the cellophane division of the Du Pont Company. See Stocking and Mueller, *supra* note 14, at 59.
25. Calculated from table prepared by Stocking and Mueller, *id.* at 62.

Workable Competition and Antitrust Policy

either cellophane or waxed paper would have resulted in precisely the same cost-price ratios in selling cellophane. As judged by structure, conduct, and performance, Judge Leahy erred in giving a negative answer to his first question: Does Du Pont have a monopoly in making and selling cellophane?

What can be said about the broader significance of the Supreme Court's opinion affirming Judge Leahy's decision? If it becomes a precedent, the Supreme Court minority is right in declaring that the Court has emasculated Section 2 of the Sherman Act. If cellophane is merely a flexible wrapping material, then airlines, railways, bus lines, and river steamers are merely transportation facilities; aluminum, copper, brass, and steel are merely metals; and cotton rugs, linen rugs, nylon rugs, woolen rugs, linoleum, and similar substitutes are merely floor coverings. Under the Supreme Court's *Cellophane* ruling a monopoly in any one of them need not violate Section 2 of the Sherman Act, and in denying the existence of monopoly the courts need only ascertain that people choose among alternative products serving similar functions in trying to get their money's worth.

This conclusion on the significance of the decision is unlikely to disturb the exponents of the new competition, because they believe that neither the courts nor Congress need worry about monopoly. They need not worry because, according to this view, "there is probably not much of it." [26] Despite the dramatic changes in industrial structure that the last seventy years have seen, the exponents of the new competition by a resort to loose counting have brought us back to the neoclassical economics of large numbers. This return to a pseudo-nineteenth-century economics should bring comfort to business executives anxious not to transgress the vague and shifting boundary that in antitrust decisions separates a public service from a criminal offense. Although the invisible hand now guides through a more complicated industrial maze, we are told that it still guides to promote the public welfare. Indeed, all things work together for good to them that love God.

26. Robertson, *supra* note 1, at 61.

7
Business Reciprocity and the Size of Firms

ACCORDING TO THE THEORY of pure competition, the growth of a firm involves frictionless adjustment in response to various profit-affecting functions. Since in a purely competitive model the individual firm has no control over supply-and-demand functions, internal technical factors determine firm size. Each firm strives for the optimum and in a given state of the industrial arts and with known cost functions presumably achieves it. With change in any variable a new adjustment is automatic; but theories of pure competition are concerned primarily with static equilibrium, not with economic change. In the simplest model progress has no place. However, economists acknowledge the gulf between the theory of pure competition and the sort of business rivalry that characterizes the contemporary economy.

In actual markets where sellers are few, knowledge is imperfect, and change is continuous, firms do not accept their supply-and-demand functions as given. To control them, they have resorted to numerous strategies conditioned by the nature of their product and its market, the character of their costs, and the ingenuity of management. They have differentiated their products in substantial or trivial ways and have spent large sums to convince customers of the importance of this differentiation.[1] They

Note: Written jointly by George W. Stocking and Willard F. Mueller, associate professor of agricultural economics at the University of Wisconsin. Reprinted from the *Journal of Business of the University of Chicago*, Vol. 30, No. 2 (April 1957).

1. The cigarette industry affords an example of the role advertising may play in the growth of a firm. The fortunes of the major cigarette manufacturers are so closely allied to advertising that "[t]he principal managerial skill needed in the cigarette industry has been the ability to originate and direct advertising campaigns and to adjust to dynamic changes in tastes, demand, and costs. If the scale of the major firms has enabled them . . . to hire more able and costly executives, the principal advantages gained thereby have been on the side of advertising and salesmanship." William H. Nicholls, *Price Policies in the Cigarette Industry* (Nashville: Vanderbilt University Press, 1951), p. 200.

Workable Competition and Antitrust Policy

have resorted to secret rebates and tie-in sales. They have engaged in price wars to expand demand at the expense of their less hardy rivals. They have increased their share of the market by buying out competitors. In these and other ways firms have sought to control the factors conditioning their size and rate of growth.[2] And when they have not encountered serious diseconomies of scale as they have expanded their output, they have frequently succeeded.

Economists are acquainted with the use by business firms of such growth-fostering techniques, but they have for the most part ignored one method of influencing sales that we believe is both significant and more frequently resorted to than is generally recognized—business reciprocity.[3] The silence of economists on this practice no doubt reflects lack of information about it. When firms resort to reciprocity in business dealings, they do not advertise the fact.[4] Since the government has not often challenged the legality of the practice,[5] governmental investigations throw

---

[2]. Paradoxically, much of the dynamic nature of the American economy can be explained only by the use of such practices. In many industries price competition is dormant if not dead, and few economists and businessmen have mourned its passing. In such industries competition can remain virile only if businessmen engage in rigorous non-price competition. While we make no distinction here between those non-price practices that intensify competition and those that stifle it, or between those that result in socially desirable performance and those having socially undesirable results, such a distinction obviously can be made. We have merely listed a few of the most common forms of non-price competition that are important to firm growth.

[3]. Students of marketing have given more attention to reciprocal dealing than have economists generally, but they have been primarily concerned with its significance to a firm rather than its significance to the economy. For example, Howard T. Lewis, who probably has written more about the practice than any other student of marketing, takes the businessman's approach to the problem: "Under what circumstances, if at all, shall reciprocity be practiced?" *Procurement: Principles and Cases* (Homewood, Ill., Irwin, 1952), p. 404.

[4]. After receiving responses from 251 firms to a questionnaire on the practice of reciprocal buying, the most common type of business reciprocity, Lewis concluded: "One of the most interesting things about this whole problem is the extreme reticence with which many businessmen talk about reciprocity. Some deny that their companies practice it, even in the face of a common knowledge to the contrary. Others deny it publicly, but will occasionally admit in confidence that they do follow it, and even describe in considerable detail their method of handling the problem. Still others, although they state quite frankly that they have such a policy, refuse to discuss even the general organization and procedure for handling the problem." "The Present Status of Reciprocity as a Sales Policy," 16 Harv. Bus. Rev. 299, 312 (1938).

[5]. The administrative agencies that have challenged reciprocal buying have held it illegal. Only one Interstate Commerce Commission report and three Federal Trade Commission cases dealing primarily with reciprocal purchasing agreements appear in the reported cases. They are discussed later in the text at notes 12–14, 15,

Business Reciprocity and the Size of Firms

little light on it; but evidence recently made available suggests that reciprocal dealing is of sufficient importance to justify analysis of it.

What Is Business Reciprocity?

"Business reciprocity" as we shall use the term describes business dealings between independent firms whereby they make mutual concessions designed to promote the business interests of each. The practice is somewhat analogous in principle to the old-fashioned bilateral reciprocal agreements in international trade. Hadley more than seventy years ago defined reciprocal trade agreements as "a relation between two independent powers such that the citizens of each are guaranteed certain commerical privileges at the hands of the other." [6] In making such agreements, negotiators no doubt believe that they promote their country's interests. So it is with business reciprocity, except that one of the parties may be confronted with a choice of the lesser of two evils rather than the better of two attractive propositions.

The best-known form of business reciprocity is reciprocal buying. Reciprocal buying involves the use by a firm of its buying power to promote its sales. Nearly all business and professional men are familiar with the phenomenon.[7] "You patronize me, I'll patronize you," is an attitude char-

and 18. In United States v. E. I. du Pont de Nemours & Co., 126 F. Supp. 235 (N.D. Ill., 1954), the government's charge of conspiracy alleged that reciprocal dealing was one of the means used to effectuate the conspiracy. The record in the *Du Pont* case furnishes the most detailed information currently available about the nature and operation of reciprocal dealings between large firms. In United States v. National City Lines, 186 F.2d 562 (7th Cir.), *cert. denied*, 341 U.S. 916 (1951), public transportation companies serving forty-five cities reciprocated General Motors' and other suppliers' purchases of their stock by entering requirements contracts with them. The court held this was a conspiracy to monopolize trade.

Corwin D. Edwards has said that "reciprocal buying is illegal when it contravenes the general prohibitions of the Sherman Act against unreasonably restrictive agreements and efforts to create monopolies." *Maintaining Competition* (New York: McGraw-Hill, 1949), p. 179. The same could be said of any business practice, and Edwards cites no cases. He would approve of legislation outlawing reciprocal buying "that has the effect of substantially lessening competition or that tends to create or support a monopolistic position," since this would indicate that "Congress believed the practice capable of jeopardizing the broad purposes" of antitrust law. *Id.*

6. "Reciprocity," *Cyclopedia of Political Science*, ed. Lalor, III (1888), 537.

7. The practice is old. Adam Smith, in lamenting British restraints on the wine trade, particularly the preference given to Portuguese exporters because they bought more British manufactures than the French, had this to say about it: "As they give us their custom, it is pretended, we should give them ours. The sneaking arts of underling tradesmen are thus erected into political maxims for the conduct of an empire; for it is the most underling tradesmen only who make it a rule to employ

289

Workable Competition and Antitrust Policy

acteristic of little as well as big business. This study is concerned with reciprocity in national, not local, markets, with big rather than little business.

Conditions Conducive to Reciprocal Buying

Reciprocal buying is economically significant when a firm can make sales in this way that it could not otherwise make or could make only at greater costs. It is a characteristic of imperfectly competitive markets. In a purely competitive market such as that for agricultural products, producers have no pecuniary incentive to seek out particular buyers, nor buyers to seek out particular producers. Any farmer can sell all he produces at prevailing prices, and any buyer can obtain at prevailing prices as much of any farm product as he wishes to buy. But when a few sellers provide the entire supply of any commodity, they may find it advantageous to resort to non-price competition to increase sales. Reciprocal buying is essentially a selling technique in markets of imperfect competition. Although reciprocal buying is a characteristic only of imperfectly competitive markets, it is not equally well adapted to all markets of imperfect competition or to all firms in such markets. For it to be effective one or more of several conditions must be met.

First, the suppliers or potential suppliers of a firm must be its potential customers. Unless they buy goods of the sort made by the firm wishing to practice business reciprocity, suppliers do not lend themselves readily to such arrangements. But reciprocity may be practiced on a multilateral basis. If firm A, a potential supplier of firm B, is buying materials from firm C, which uses materials of the type produced by firm B, firm A may obtain B's business if it can persuade C to buy from B. Firm A may be able to do this by threatening to withdraw its patronage from C unless C submits to the arrangement. Firms selling direct to consumers or to distributors of consumers' goods cannot use reciprocal buying effectively. Their suppliers are at best only small potential customers, and their customers may have nothing to sell to them. In the early 1920's when General Motors made nothing but automobiles, trucks, and automobile accessories, it had little use for reciprocal buying, because through its distributors it sold its output largely to the final consumer. Although it was a heavy

---

chiefly their own customers. A great trader purchases his goods always where they are cheapest and best, without regard to any little interest of this kind." *The Wealth of Nations*, ed. Edwin Cannan (New York: Putnam, 1937), p. 460.

Business Reciprocity and the Size of Firms

buyer of raw materials, automobile parts, shipping services, and labor,[8] its suppliers bought relatively few cars. It could not readily use its purchasing power to coerce or persuade its suppliers to buy heavily from it. In short, reciprocal buying is most likely to be practiced among business firms that make products for sale to industry.

Second, a sloping demand curve facing an individual firm in an industry where marginal costs are constant over a wide range of output invites the use of reciprocal buying. An oligopolist's own demand curve may determine its long-run growth. Over the long run aggressive firms are unlikely to accept their demand curves as uncontrollable external factors; they frequently resort to strategy to control them. To resort to advertising may be unattractive, because in industrial markets a firm's product is generally standardized or sold on specification to informed buyers. But reciprocal buying, by shifting a firm's demand curve to the right, may enable a firm to expand its sales and, if it can work out long-term reciprocal arrangements, to grow at the expense of rivals.

Third, the existence of unused capacity in the short run, although not essential to reciprocal buying, is conducive to it. When demand slackens or an industry is overbuilt, a firm may be tempted to get business by cutting prices. But since rival firms are likely to meet such price cuts promptly, to yield to such temptation may aggravate a firm's difficulties. A firm that can increase its sales through the use of its buying power may force less fortunate firms to bear the main burden of declining demand.

A fourth condition conducive to the effective use of reciprocal buying is some lack of symmetry in the market. If all firms in an industry were of the same size, sold identical products, and bought identical inputs, reciprocal buying would give none an advantage over any other. Each firm could use its buying power as effectively as any rival. If all used it with equal effectiveness, none could expand its sales at the expense of others. When firms differ in size, the results may be different. For example, assume that one large firm in industry A buys 50 per cent of some essential product sold by industry B to industry A and then ten smaller firms in industry A buy the remainder, each taking 5 per cent of

---

8. Of course in buying its labor it might have insisted on reciprocal dealing. "I'll not hire you unless you buy your car from me." There is no evidence that General Motors has done so. Instead of coercing its employees to buy its products, General Motors apparently makes it attractive for them to do so by granting them substantial discounts, much to the discomfort of its dealers. See testimony of Lee C. Anderson, former General Motors dealer in Lake Orion, Michigan. *Hearings before the Subcommittee on Antitrust and Monopoly of the Senate Committee on the Judiciary*, 84th Cong., 1st Sess. 3323–24 (1955).

industry B's total sales to A. Assume further that industry B is composed of four firms, each buying 25 per cent of industry A's sales to B. Given such structural asymmetry, the large firm in A through reciprocal buying might capture the entire industry B market. It might do so by distributing its patronage equally among the four firms in return for their promise to buy all their industry A requirements from it. Any one of the small firms in industry A would be at a disadvantage in trying to protect its market by threatening to retaliate. None could take more than 5 per cent of industry A's total needs or more than one-fifth of any industry B firm's output. The large firm in industry A could with no change in its operations buy from each industry B firm 12½ per cent of industry A's requirements, or one-half of each industry B firm's output. By taking over the business previously done by the smaller firms in industry A, the large firm could provide a market for all of industry B's sales to A. The large firm in industry A clearly gains by the transaction, while the firms in industry B may lose nothing.

A fifth factor conducive to reciprocal buying is diversification. The large diversified firm has better opportunities for using reciprocal buying than the single-line producer. As previously pointed out, to use its buying power readily to increase sales, a firm must find a potential buyer of the goods it sells that is also a potential supplier of the goods it buys. Single-line producers may not always find one. Where they cannot, they may resort to triangular arrangements, but these are awkward. A firm that makes many products can more readily find a supplier that is also a potential buyer of what it makes. And, if it is a large purchaser, it may readily persuade its suppliers to buy from it. If a mere suggestion is not adequate, a threat to withhold patronage may do the trick. A diversified firm may use its purchases in making one product to push its sales of others; and if, as is not infrequent, a diversified firm has a near-monopoly of some product (in the sale of which it need not resort to reciprocal buying), it can use its purchases of raw materials for this product to increase its sales of products encountering more nearly competitive markets.

Diversification not only increases the number of opportunities for reciprocal buying; it increases their magnitude. A single-line producer, even though a near-monopolist, may buy so little of some material that reciprocal buying has little influence on suppliers as potential customers. But by diversifying—making other products requiring the same input—a firm may so enlarge its buying as to give it the power to increase its sales. Practically all of a giant diversified firm's purchases of goods and services may achieve importance as a means of increasing sales. Even advertising

Business Reciprocity and the Size of Firms

accounts, which are likely to be relatively small for a firm selling to industrial consumers, may aggregate such large sums as to give the advertiser a leverage in obtaining business. For example, Du Pont, long a large advertiser, spending $18,000,000, or about 1 per cent of its sales, for advertising in 1954,[9] was able as early as 1935 to bring pressure on the Curtis Publishing Company to get business from a supplier of its affiliate.[10]

Such then are the conditions conducive to effective use of reciprocal buying—production for sales to industry, a sloping demand curve with marginal costs constant over a wide range of output, surplus capacity, lack of symmetry in industrial structure, and diversification of output. The large diversified firm producing for sale to other industries has an advantage in the strategy of reciprocal dealing.

Reciprocal Buying by Railroads

An examination of reciprocal buying in practice will throw some light on the above principles. Until recently, detailed information on this practice was confined largely to its use by railroads and various industries doing business with them. Although railroads have nothing to sell but transportation, they are heavy buyers of steel rails and coal, and steel companies and coal producers are among the most important buyers of railroad transportation. In 1929, when railroads were systematically engaging in reciprocal dealing, Class I railroads bought almost $300,000,000 of coal and over $338,000,000 of steel rails and related products.[11] Together coal and steel accounted for almost 48 per cent of total Class I railroad expenditures for fuel, materials, and supplies. Except at the peak of the business cycle the railroads have chronically operated at less than capacity. That is to say, they customarily can supply additional services with no increase in fixed costs. Because railway rates are established by the Interstate Commerce Commission, the railroads must resort to non-price competition to get business. The Interstate Commerce Commission's 1932 report on "Reciprocity in Purchasing and Routing" [12] reveals that during the 1920's and early 1930's the railroads generally resorted to reciprocal dealing. They customarily allocated the purchase of steel rails and coal in proportion to the freight traffic given them by the different steel mills. They made similar arrangements with other suppliers—lumber mills, ice com-

9. Du Pont, *Annual Report*, 1954, p. 9.
10. For an account of this episode see pp. 302–3 *infra*.
11. "Reciprocity in Purchasing and Routing," 188 I.C.C. 417, 418–19 (1932).
12. 188 I.C.C. 417 (1932).

293

panies, and makers of railway equipment. The record indicates that many railroads tried systematically to increase business through reciprocal buying. Their purchasing departments notified their traffic departments of the firms from which they bought, and the traffic departments used this information in soliciting traffic.[13]

RECIPROCAL BUYING BY PACKERS

Two Federal Trade Commission proceedings reveal significant cases of reciprocal buying during the 1920's by two of the country's largest meat packers, Armour & Company[14] and Swift & Company.[15] As packers, neither company had anything to sell to the railroads, although both were large buyers of railroad services; but the officials of each found a way of utilizing their company's tremendous buying power to promote their business interests. Their doing so illustrates the roles asymmetry in industrial structure and diversification in a firm's output may play in making reciprocal buying effective and also the influence reciprocal buying may exert on firm size and industrial capacity.

Two traffic officials of Armour & Company, in acquiring stock in the Waugh Equipment Company, a relatively unknown maker of draft gears, agreed to use Armour's huge purchases of railway freight services to persuade the railroad companies to buy draft gears and other railway equipment from Waugh. When they began the arrangement in 1924, Waugh sold less than 1 per cent of all draft gears sold for new equipment and was the smallest of six companies producing draft gears. Linked with Armour, it became in effect a large diversified firm, able to use Armour's huge purchasing power to increase its sales. In 1928, with railroad companies ordering fewer freight cars (each of which required two draft gears) than in any year except two in twenty-eight years, Waugh rose to fourth place in the industry. By 1930, with railroad companies ordering fewer freight cars than in any year except two in thirty years, Waugh had become the country's largest producer of draft gears.[16]

---

13. The Commission's report does not indicate that any railway used reciprocal buying more effectively than any other, and it concludes that the practice resulted in "a shifting rather than an increase in traffic." *Id.* at 433–34. Since the shippers were sometimes persuaded to ship by a particular line when it was not economical to do so, the practice made "the handling of existing traffic more expensive." *Id.* at 434.
14. Waugh Equipment Co., 15 F.T.C. 232 (1931).
15. Mechanical Mfg. Co., 16 F.T.C. 67 (1932).
16. Waugh Equipment Co., 15 F.T.C. 232, 242–45 (1931). The Federal Trade Commission ruled that the respondents' use of reciprocal buying "gives to the

Business Reciprocity and the Size of Firms

The second case is less spectacular but illustrates the same principle. Certain traffic managers of Swift & Company, together with the Swift Estate and members of the Swift family, were stockholders in the Mechanical Manufacturing Company, which made meat-packing machinery and equipment and also bumping posts, draft gears, and other railway equipment. Armed with Swift's power as a large buyer of railroad transportation, Swift's traffic managers used it to persuade railroads to buy equipment from Mechanical. The Federal Trade Commission does not recount the details of its success, but it indicates that the managers of Swift & Company's traffic department successfully solicited business for Mechanical by letters and personal interviews, urging railroad companies to reciprocate for the services Swift bought of them. To achieve their goal, the traffic managers at times threatened to and actually did divert traffic.[17] Here again, what was in effect a huge diversified firm was able to use its purchases of service to promote the growth of its affiliated manufacturer of railway equipment at the expense of the manufacturer's rivals.

A few years later another diversified packing company used its purchasing power obversely from the meat packers' use of it—to increase a subsidiary's sales of freight services by promising to increase its purchases of packing-house supplies if the suppliers routed their shipments through its subsidiary's terminal—and threatening to withdraw its business if the supplier did not.[18] In 1936 the California Packing Corporation was the world's largest packer and distributor of dried fruits and vegetables and an important factor in the Hawaiian pineapple, sardine, and tuna industries, owning more than a hundred canning factories in ten states and Alaska and Hawaii. It owned most of the stock in a large salmon-packing company that in turn owned a shipping terminal on San Francisco Bay. As large purchasers of boxes, containers, cartons, tin, steel, copper, etc., the two companies were able to induce their suppliers to route shipments through their terminal instead of through other, less expensive terminals.[19]

---

concern that controls the largest volume of freight traffic an unfair advantage that will more than offset the higher efficiency in the production and sales methods of competing concerns which control no such traffic" and violated Section 5 of the Federal Trade Commission Act. *Id.* at 247.

17. Mechanical Mfg. Co., 16 F.T.C. 67, 73 (1932). The Commission ruled that the practices in question tended to hinder and restrain "the freedom of competition in the natural customary channels of trade in the draft gear industry" and were unfair methods of competition under Section 5 of the Federal Trade Commission Act. *Id.* at 75.

18. California Packing Corp., 25 F.T.C. 379 (1937).

19. The Commission ruled that the respondents' practices, "by requiring that the principal consideration for the purchase of said products be the volume of

Workable Competition and Antitrust Policy

Extent and Systematic Use of Reciprocity

Reciprocal buying has not been confined to products sold to and services bought from railroad companies. Lewis' 1938 study revealed that

> to a greater or less degree reciprocity is found in nearly every type of manufacturing business as well as in banking institutions and insurance, public utility, transportation, and construction companies. . . . It is among manufacturers of industrial goods, however, that the practice is most common. It appears to be particularly prominent among manufacturers of machinery and other iron and steel products, electrical supplies, paper and printing, chemicals (including paints) and non-ferrous metals, petroleum, and rubber.[20]

The Great Depression accelerated the practice of reciprocal buying. Operating on a part-time basis with their markets demoralized by price-cutting, many firms turned to reciprocal buying to get business. The *New York Times* of November 6, 1932, noted:

> Growing recognition of the importance of reciprocity in the buying and selling of products . . . has led in recent months to the establishment of special departments by large companies to handle such matters. . . . The number of such [reciprocal] compacts is steadily growing.[21]

The special departments differed in their organization and responsibilities, but they were designed to centralize control over buying and selling and to so co-ordinate activities in both areas that a company's buying power would enhance its sales.[22]

A major antitrust suit [23] provided further examples of the successful

tonnage routed by said industrial concerns through the said Encinal Terminals . . . instead of the usual and normal competitive considerations such as quality, service, and price," constituted an unfair method of competition. Id. at 398–99.

20. Lewis, "The Present Status of Reciprocity as a Sales Policy," 16 Harv. Bus. Rev. 299 and 300 (1938).

21. § F. p. 8, col. 6.

22. Lewis' study reveals that over 50 of the 176 firms whose purchasing agents responded to a questionnaire had set up definite procedures for handling reciprocal purchases and sales. The purchasing officer was usually responsible for final decisions on reciprocity, or the purchasing officer and the sales manager were jointly responsible. Some companies designated their departments for handling reciprocity problems as "trade relations departments." Lewis, "The Present Status of Reciprocity as a Sales Policy," 16 Harv. Bus. Rev. 299, 305, 311 (1938).

23. United States v. E. I. du Pont de Nemours & Co., 126 F. Supp. 235 (N.D. Ill., 1954). In the discussion that follows references are to the exhibits and testimony in this case, with the government's exhibits designated "GX," Du Pont exhibits "DP," General Motors exhibits "GM," U.S. Rubber exhibits "USR," and transcript of testimony "Tr."

The government charged that the Du Pont Co. had acquired a controlling interest

Business Reciprocity and the Size of Firms

use of reciprocity by large diversified industrial firms. It indicates that E. I. du Pont de Nemours & Company and United States Rubber Company, the country's largest producer of chemicals and its third largest producer of rubber goods, respectively, adopted the policy of reciprocal buying and put it on a systematic basis more than thirty years ago.

Du Pont's Practice of Reciprocity

E. I. du Pont de Nemours & Company recognized almost forty years ago that it might use its extensive purchases to expand its sales. It was at that time not only the country's largest maker of explosives but one of its most important chemical manufacturers, producing a wide range of products for sale to industry.[24] Possessing a large fund of liquid capital obtained primarily from its war sales of explosives, the Du Pont Company had carried on an aggressive program of diversification and expansion.[25]

in General Motors Corp. and that members of the Du Pont family had acquired a controlling interest in U.S. Rubber Co., which control they used "to enhance the size, power, and market control of each" of the three companies "at the expense of its competitors" (complaint filed June 30, 1949, p. 15 [mimeographed]). The Du Ponts allegedly accomplished this purpose by making General Motors and U.S. Rubber closed markets for their companies' requirements of products manufactured by Du Pont; granting General Motors and U.S. Rubber secret rebates and preferential prices; agreeing that the three companies should exchange patents, technical data, and trade information; dividing fields of production to keep General Motors from manufacturing chemicals and tires and to keep U.S. Rubber from expanding into chemicals and related fields; and "inducing suppliers of each defendant manufacturer to purchase products on a basis of reciprocity from one or more of the other defendant manufacturers." *Id.* at 17. The government also charged that Du Pont used its control of General Motors to add General Motors' purchasing power to its own in selling Du Pont's products to other concerns on a basis of reciprocity. *Id.* at 40. The district court dismissed the complaint, and the government appealed to the Supreme Court, which on June 3, 1957, reversed the decision. 353 U.S. 586. For a discussion of this case see chap. 8 *infra*.

24. By 1922 Du Pont was selling explosives, celluloid (Pyralin), lacquers, coated fabrics (Fabrikoid), acids and other heavy chemicals, solvents, nitrates, synthetic indigo, synthetic camphor, pigments, and dyestuffs. Du Pont, *Annual Reports*, 1907–22.

25. During the five years from 1914 to 1918 Du Pont's munitions sales totaled $1,245,000,000. *Hearings before Senate Special Committee Investigating the Munitions Industry*, 73d Cong., pt. 5, at 1023 (1934). This was twice its total sales over a life of more than a hundred years. Its net profits for 1915–18 aggregated $232,000,000, of which $128,000,000 was distributed in dividends leaving over $100,000,000 for expansion. *Moody's Industrials*, 1915–19. Du Pont promptly used its undistributed earnings to acquire several paint, varnish, and chemical companies, a celluloid company, an artificial leather company, and a rubber-coated-fabrics company, all of which made it an important supplier of products bought by General Motors Corp., and in December 1917 Du Pont began to purchase com-

Workable Competition and Antitrust Policy

George H. Kerr of Du Pont's explosives department, which had successfully experimented with reciprocal buying as early as 1922, was so impressed with its potentialities by 1924 that he wrote Pierre S. du Pont, then chairman of both the Du Pont and the General Motors boards of directors, urging that Du Pont seek General Motors' co-operation in using it. In doing so, Kerr described as follows the elaborate administrative machinery already in use in the explosives department:

> Having secured the co-operation of the Purchasing Department, who agreed to send us copies of all their orders and contracts . . . we devised a system to take care of this data, carding up all the names and indicating by signals important information. In addition, we advise our Sales executives and branch offices of purchases not only daily, but also by means of statements monthly and a general summary semiannually, showing the status of all the concerns from whom we buy, as of those dates, i.e. if they have been purchasing from competitors, are they continuing to purchase from them,—and various other details of interest to the Purchasing Department.[26]

Kerr said that the plan had paid off. As he put it, the department had used it "most diligently and intelligently" and had "secured a great deal of business by doing so." While the practice was novel to Du Pont, it was not unique to industry. Kerr alleged that it was being generally practiced by other companies. "We are confronted with it," he said, "wherever we go, and it seems to me that we are overlooking a valuable adjunct to our business if we do not take full advantage of our purchasing power."[27] Aware of Du Pont's close affiliation with General Motors, Kerr proposed that Du Pont explore the possibility of linking General Motors' vast purchasing power to its own, and he predicted that General Motors' power added to Du Pont's "would be irresistible, and if intelligently used, would doubtless result in securing a large amount of business for us."[28] In

mon stock in General Motors. Post-trial Brief for the United States, pp. 67–85, United States v. E. I. du Pont de Nemours & Co., 126 F. Supp. 235 (N.D. Ill., 1954). The General Motors investment, today representing about 23 per cent of that company's outstanding stock, proved highly significant in Du Pont's growth. Besides providing a market for its products, General Motors between 1920 and 1953 paid Du Pont $1,060,600,000 in dividends, or $997,500,000 after taxes, representing about 36 per cent of Du Pont's income from all sources; and at the end of 1952 the market value of Du Pont's General Motors stock was $1,360,000,000, or about seventeen times its market value at the time of purchase (calculations from data in *Moody's Industrials*, 1920–52, and Du Pont's annual reports, 1920–52).

26. Letter from G. H. Kerr to P. S. du Pont, March 31, 1924, GX 530, p. 1.
27. *Id.* at 3.
28. *Id.* at 1. Although Kerr did not mention it to Pierre du Pont in his letter of March 31, 1924, the Du Pont Co. already had asked General Motors for this kind of assistance. In a letter dated January 19, 1924, to J. N. Main, of General Motors'

Business Reciprocity and the Size of Firms

expressing this judgment, Kerr was not relying solely on logic. He noted that the Bethlehem Steel Company had already classified Du Pont and General Motors as a single buyer in its own reciprocity file [29] and that this had led Bethlehem to give Du Pont's acid and heavy chemical division "special consideration." [30] Apparently, Pierre du Pont approved of Kerr's proposal. At any rate, Du Pont wrote Alfred P. Sloan, Jr., who had been recently made president of General Motors, requesting that Kerr be given an opportunity to explain the plan to General Motors officials.[31] Sloan agreed, and Kerr promptly conferred with General Motors' general purchasing committee. On April 18, in reporting the conference's outcome, he stated that Lynah, secretary of General Motors' general purchasing committee, had agreed with him that it would be desirable to combine the purchasing power of General Motors and the Du Pont Company, "if it is possible" and "if it is used intelligently and diplomatically." [32] Kerr said Lynah had emphasized the importance of its being used systematically, if at all, and had pointed out that "some other units are using it . . . in a haphazard manner, which he felt was apt to be dangerous and unsatisfactory." [33]

Kerr's optimism about linking General Motors' and Du Pont's purchasing power was not wholly warranted. General Motors' general purchasing committee took the position that General Motors ordinarily could not practice reciprocity to advantage, because it sold cars largely to individ-

purchasing staff, L. R. Beardslee, of General Motors, stated that H. G. Haskell, of Du Pont, had requested "the names of the companies from whom we are buying coal and steel." GX 529. Beardslee explained: "You know the Du Pont Company has a very large business with the Steel Corporation and other kindred lines and I presume such information might be helpful in acquiring orders for explosives." He could see no objection to giving Du Pont information but told Main it was "entirely within your discretion." *Ibid.*

29. According to Kerr, Bethlehem considered reciprocal buying so important a means of getting business that it had established a reciprocity board consisting of five executives. Letter to P. S. du Pont, March 31, 1924, GX 530, p. 2.

30. *Ibid.* Kerr described the special considerations in a letter to Alfred P. Sloan, Jr., president of General Motors. Kerr said that Du Pont was "anxious to have an opportunity to get the approval of [Bethlehem's] purchasing agent to try one of our products. It developed in consultation with the Bethlehem Steel officers that they have a reciprocity file and . . . they consider the purchases of the Du Pont Company and the General Motors Corporation as one. The volume of our purchases on their reciprocity card was sufficient to influence the Bethlehem Steel Company's purchasing agent to not only try out the product . . . but it finally resulted in a large trial order, and there is every prospect of our securing their entire business for that particular product." Letter of April 30, 1924, GX 535.

31. Letter of April 7, 1924, GX 531.

32. Letter from Kerr to P. S. Du Pont, April 8, 1924, GX 534, p. 3.

33. *Ibid.*

Workable Competition and Antitrust Policy

uals.[34] However, General Motors did not reject Du Pont's proposals outright. On September 5, 1924, its general purchasing committee decided that, although General Motors could not undertake to supply the Du Pont Company regularly with information showing the volume of business done with its suppliers, "in special cases, upon request by the President of the Du Pont Company to the President of General Motors, the situation would be properly dealt with."[35] Specifically, General Motors indicated that, if Du Pont were to "furnish to General Motors a list of suppliers whom it is desired to favor with inquiries, our divisions would endeavor to meet their wishes in this regard."[36]

Du Pont apparently found General Motors' disposition of its request satisfactory[37] and from time to time took advantage of General Motors' willingness to lend its purchasing power on special occasions to Du Pont to help it get business.[38] As early as August 13, 1924, Sloan had informed Lynah that Du Pont had requested General Motors' help in contacting the Fisk Rubber Company and that, after a meeting in a General Motors executive's office between Du Pont and Fisk representatives, "a very valuable business has been given to the Du Pont interest by the Fisk people."[39] A month later, when Du Pont was trying to sell Bethlehem Steel Company certain acid chemicals, Hunter Grubb of the Du Pont paint department, wrote a "personal and confidential" letter to John Lee Pratt, General Motors vice-president and general purchasing committee

34. According to Kerr, Lynah had said, however, that "the General Motors Truck Co. are using it with good results." Ibid.
35. Excerpts from minutes of meeting No. 16 of Interdivisional Relations Committee, General Purchasing Committee, General Motors Corp., Sept. 5, 1924, GX 537.
36. Ibid.
37. In acquiescing in General Motors' decision, Irenee du Pont, president of Du Pont, recognized, as had Lynah, the dangers of handling reciprocal buying in an unsystematic manner and the administrative difficulties in a large concern's using reciprocity without carefully co-ordinating its buying and selling. He noted that "letting both sales and purchases stand on their own bottoms . . . avoided the endless complications resulting from an endeavor to carry out reciprocity, especially as the little fellow can work it better than can a big corporation." However, Du Pont, after adopting "a new form of organization definitely segregating its management by industries," had found that "reciprocity yielded very excellent results." Letter from Irenee du Pont to James Lynah, Sept. 8, 1924, GX 540.
38. In advising Du Pont of General Motors' willingness to cooperate on occasion in Du Pont's effort to get business, Lynah had warned Du Pont that it should avoid leaving "the impression that the Du Pont Company could influence General Motors purchases." Letter from James Lynah to Irenee du Pont, Sept. 6, 1924, GX 539. Just how it could do this and at the same time achieve its goal is not clear.
39. Memorandum from Sloan to Lynah, Aug. 13, 1924, GX 536.

Business Reciprocity and the Size of Firms

chairman, requesting information on General Motors' purchases from the Bethlehem Steel Company. Pratt replied that one of General Motors' subsidiaries had been buying "quite extensively" from Bethlehem during the first six months of the year and would continue to do so "if the Bethlehem's price and quality continue to be favorable in comparison with other companies." And he added: "The above is about all the information I can give you on this subject." [40]

Official information on the extent to which Du Pont used General Motors' purchasing power to augment its own sales is fragmentary. In 1928, when Du Pont faced the prospect of losing sales of explosives to Jones & Laughlin Steel Company and to the Inland Steel Company, Lammot du Pont, president of Du Pont, appealed to Sloan, president of General Motors, for help. Lammot du Pont wrote Sloan that a competitor was taking customers away "in what is generally known as the 'reciprocity' argument" and declared:

[W]e desire to put before the Jones & Laughlin Steel Company interests and the Inland Steel Company interests the facts as to what of their products the du Pont Company and its affiliated companies buy from them. For this purpose, could you have someone send me a statement of the 1927 purchases by General Motors Corporation and its subsidiaries from the Jones & Laughlin interests . . . [and] . . . from the Inland Steel Company. . . .

It is, of course, understood that in presenting these figures to our customer it will be for the purpose of retaining trade now enjoyed. There will be no promise or assurance that these purchases will continue or that the du Pont Company's efforts in the past have caused G. M. to place this business. We simply want to be in a position to place before the steel companies the actual facts as they have existed. This is a very important trade to us and I would greatly appreciate the assistance you can render. . . . [41]

40. Letter of Sept. 22, 1924, GX 542. Apparently one reason General Motors' general purchasing committee was reluctant to permit Du Pont to use General Motors' purchasing power to get business was that, although General Motors could not practice reciprocity extensively in selling cars, it could use its large purchases to get price concessions from suppliers. In 1921 or 1922 Sloan urged that General Motors adopt "a more definite form of administration in order to capitalize on the perfectly enormous advantages of consolidating our purchasing power." Testimony of Alfred P. Sloan, Jr., operating vice-president of General Motors from 1921 to 1923 and president from 1923 to 1937, Tr. 2519. General Motors adopted Sloan's recommendations and established a general purchasing committee. Ibid., Tr. 2534. In 1926 the committee estimated that savings from consolidated purchasing amounted to about $3,000,000. Testimony of James Lynah, general purchasing committee secretary from 1922 to 1931, Tr. 2615–16.

41. Letter of Jan. 18, 1928, GX 543.

Workable Competition and Antitrust Policy

General Motors' purchasing committee assembled the requested information and sent it, although begrudgingly, to Lammot du Pont.[42]

Although Du Pont never fully realized Kerr's hope to make its purchasing power "irresistible" by wedding it to General Motors',[43] Du Pont continued to use its own purchasing power in this way whenever and wherever it could. Its widespread use of reciprocal buying during the 1930's was common knowledge in the business world. *Fortune* in a 1934 feature article on Du Pont stated that Du Pont "made a fetish of reciprocity."[44] As *Fortune* viewed it, Du Pont was in an especially favorable position to use this sales strategy, "since nearly everybody can use *some* Du Pont product—if only paint." Therefore, "the principle of you-buy-from-me-and-I'll-buy-from-you has a very wide application."[45]

A 1935 incident dramatically highlights the circuitous route an influential firm may follow in using its purchasing power to augment its sales. In that year Charles Warner, a director of the Atlas Powder Company, Du Pont's second largest explosives rival, sent a veiled warning to Lammot du Pont and to H. Fletcher Brown, Du Pont vice-president, about Atlas' loss of business to Du Pont because of the latter's use of reciprocal selling.[46] Warner told the following story. Du Pont was seeking to

---

42. In doing so, John L. Pratt, general purchasing committee chairman, protested to Sloan that Du Pont had no more right to such information than other stockholders and argued: "If there was anything to be gotten [from reciprocity] our position should be to see that it is gotten for General Motors Corporation, rather than the Du Pont Company." Letter from Pratt to Sloan, Jan. 21, 1928 (GM 201), read by counsel for defense during Pratt's direct testimony. Tr. 3292.

43. Du Pont's last two presidents, Walter S. Carpenter and Crawford H. Greenewalt, testified that until the government started its suit they were unaware of the 1924 resolution providing that in "special cases" General Motors' purchasing power could be used to further Du Pont sales. Testimony of Carpenter and Greenewalt, Tr. 6617–18 and 6735–36.

44. "Du Pont II: A Management and Its Philosophy," Fortune, December 1934, p. 190.

45. *Ibid*. Skeptical of the benefits reciprocity might bring, *Fortune* pointed out that the best customer may not be the best supplier and that reciprocity is "rather an old-style policy for what is presumably a new-style company." *Ibid*.

46. Atlas' executive committee had apparently already protested to Du Pont, and Warner assured Brown that he was not making a further protest. Instead, he said, he was writing to him as an individual because of his "very broad interest in the Du Pont Company." He was prompted to write Brown about the "danger of extreme reciprocity" because he was concerned over what "may eventually reflect on the Du Pont Company thru public investigations which might be started at any time by some small disgruntled competitor." Letter of June 27, 1935, from Warner to Brown. GX 549. On July 29, 1935, Warner sent Lammot du Pont a copy of his letter to Brown, speaking of Atlas' concern to see Du Pont "avoid complications at Washington or elsewhere in these troublesome times." *Ibid*.

Business Reciprocity and the Size of Firms

get a bigger share of the explosives business of the Rochester and Pittsburgh Coal Company of Indiana, Pennsylvania . . . [which] sells largely to the Castonia Paper Company, which in turn is owned largely by the Curtis Publishing Company. . . . du Ponts [sic] put the pressure on the Curtis Publishing Company, based on their own and (by inference) General Motors' advertising account, to have the coal company increase its purchase of explosives from them.

Atlas had enjoyed for years a large part of this explosives business, averaging around 80%. It appeared at one time as tho this pressure would force a large part, if not all, of the coal company's explosives orders to du Pont. Atlas naturally retaliated and developed an alliance with Chrysler Corporation to buy all of its trucks from Dodge. Advertising pressure from Chrysler to Curtis helped to reduce the effect of the du Pont pressure. However, Atlas's proportion of this business came down to about 49% in 1934.[47]

Warner commented as follows on the intensive use of reciprocity by Du Pont and other companies:

I also understand thru other channels, that the du Pont reciprocity department, or whatever it is called, reviews and participates in directing over 50% of the du Pont purchases, in order to utilize all lines of influence and trading reciprocity that may be applied to assist the sale of du Pont products. I am fully alive to the fact that this is done by a great many corporations, such as the U.S. Steel Company, and others, on probably as extensive a basis.[48]

Atlas was not the only explosives company placed at a sales disadvantage because of Du Pont's use of reciprocal buying. Even Du Pont's largest rival, the Hercules Powder Company, suffered. *Fortune* alluded to this in a 1935 article on Hercules.

It is particularly to the point that Hercules men be smart and sure with advice [to its customers] because competitively Du Pont has an enormous advantage over Hercules in the size and range of its activities. The chemical industry is notably addicted to reciprocity, but Du Pont, which devotes an entire department to the mere task of recording purchases and checking them against sales for the immediate reference of any of its salesmen, has exalted reciprocity to the level of a fine art or exact science. And any one of the dynamite-using companies from which Du Pont buys its chemical raw materials is pretty well sewed up in the Du Pont bag.[49]

Du Pont's advantage over Hercules and Atlas resulted from its greater size and diversification. Atlas and Hercules were primarily explosives-makers with sales of only $12,000,000 and $25,000,000, respectively, in

47. Letter from Warner to Brown, June 27, 1935. Id. The Rochester and Pittsburgh Coal Co. was evidently a substantial consumer of explosives, having produced 4,563,508 tons of coal in 1934. *Moody's Industrials, 1935*, p. 1889.
48. Letter from Warner to Brown, June 27, 1935, GX 549.
49. "Hercules Powder," Fortune, September 1935, p. 62.

Workable Competition and Antitrust Policy

1934. Du Pont, long a diversified firm, had sales of $179,000,000. By 1934 it had further diversified into tetraethyl lead, ethyl alcohol, seed disinfectants, inorganic heavy chemicals, zinc, viscose and acetate rayon, cellophane, plastics, synthetic ammonia, motion-picture film, titanium oxide, carbon bisulfide, and fluorine compounds for use as refrigerants and for other purposes, in addition to its 1922 range of products.[50] Whereas Atlas and Hercules could for the most part use reciprocity only with suppliers providing raw materials for explosives, Du Pont with its broader range of activities could open sales doors closed to Hercules, Atlas, and lesser companies.[51]

Information is not available on the extent of Du Pont's use of reciprocity today. Defense spending and inflation through World War II and the prolonged cold war following it made it much easier for both little and big firms to get business, but with Du Pont annually buying in the neighborhood of half a billion dollars of supplies from some thirty thousand firms and selling a wide range of products to some sixty-five thousand customers, fifteen thousand of whom are also its suppliers,[52] it would be surprising indeed if Du Pont had conducted its postwar expansion without using its power in buying to increase its ability to sell.[53]

50. *Moody's Industrials, 1935*, pp. 1683–84. For a list of Du Pont products as of 1922 see note 24 *supra*.

51. It is impossible, of course, to estimate accurately what part of Du Pont's total expenditures could be used in trying to get the patronage of potential customers. In 1934 its sales totaled $175,400,000. It spent $58,900,000 in wages and salaries; its operating income was $25,500,000. The difference between the sum of these two figures and total sales, $91,000,000, represented depreciation, expenditures on raw materials, advertising, and other expenses. Most of this represented buying power that might be used in influencing sales. If Atlas is correct in stating that Du Pont's "reciprocity department" reviewed the placing of 50 per cent of the Du Pont purchases (see p. 303 *supra*), expenditures that influenced sales may have aggregated approximately $45,000,000.

52. According to President Crawford H. Greenewalt, in 1948 Du Pont purchased $450,000,000 of supplies from 30,000 companies and sold about $970,000,000 of goods to 65,000 customers, and Greenewalt commented: "[A]fter duplication between customers and suppliers, we are dealing with perhaps 80,000 business concerns." U.S. News and World Report, Sept. 16, 1949, p. 36.

53. That Du Pont did not abandon reciprocal dealing during the postwar expansion of demand is suggested by the statement in 1950 of a vice-president of the Pittsburgh Consolidation Coal Co., of which Du Pont was the largest explosives supplier, that three factors guided his company's purchases: price, quality, and the amount of coal business given it by potential suppliers. Earlier evidence comes from the executive of a small powder company, who reported in 1942 that over 80 per cent of the explosives sold in Pennsylvania and neighboring states involved reciprocity. Edward W. Proctor, "Antitrust Policy and the Industrial Explosives Industry" (unpublished Ph.D. dissertation, Harvard University, 1951), p. 407. As

Business Reciprocity and the Size of Firms

United States Rubber's Use of Reciprocal Buying

Evidence recently made available indicates that the United States Rubber Company has for a long time resorted systematically and persistently to reciprocal buying. Whether it was influenced by the Du Ponts [54] in doing so is not clear, but in any event by the late 1920's it was following the practice. Initially certain departments had introduced the practice independently; [55] but as General Motors and Du Pont executives had earlier recognized, United States Rubber officials came to realize that reciprocal buying cannot be practiced in a haphazard manner if it is to be exploited effectively. On September 11, 1930, company officials met to develop a program to place "reciprocity on a sound basis from a company as well as departmental standpoint." [56] The more specific objective of the program was, in the words of Tisdale, to permit the company to take "advantage of the volume of our purchases in such a way as to produce the best feeling with our possible customers . . . and to increase as far as possible our sales of rubber goods." [57] The committee formulated a "Proposed Plan for Handling the Question of Reciprocal Business." [58] Because the plan stated so explicitly the objectives and methods of United States Rubber's reciprocal buying program, we quote it at length. The first section set forth a need

---

noted in the section following the next one, Du Pont has regularly practiced reciprocity with U.S. Rubber.

54. As of June 1949, members of the Du Pont family owned 18 per cent of U.S. Rubber's common stock and 11.5 per cent of its preferred. Chart showing stockholding relationships of the Du Pont family and the Delaware Realty & Investment, the Christiana Securities, the Du Pont, the General Motors, and the U. S. Rubber Companies, June 1949, GX 1303. Most of the Du Ponts' holdings in U.S. Rubber date from June 21, 1927. Brief for Defendants E. I. du Pont de Nemours & Company, Christiana Securities Company, Delaware Realty & Investment Company, Pierre S. du Pont, Irenee du Pont, pp. 402–7, United States v. E. I. du Pont de Nemours & Co., 126 F. Supp. 235 (N.D. Ill., 1954).

55. The earliest evidence of U.S. Rubber's use of reciprocal buying appears in an intracompany communication dated March 22, 1929, from George M. Tisdale, then U.S. Rubber's assistant general purchasing agent, to E. C. Burkman, assistant to the president. USR 85. Burkman had requested information on U.S. Rubber's purchases from U.S. Steel Corp.'s subsidiaries, and Tisdale informed him that the company had bought $503,456 of goods from U.S. Steel subsidiaries in 1928. Burkman's request followed a luncheon meeting between President F. B. Davis of U.S. Rubber and the chairman of U.S. Steel's purchasing agents' committee. Letter from Burkman to L. D. Tompkins, U.S. Rubber's vice-president in charge of sales (USR 83), read by counsel for defense during Tisdale's direct testimony, Tr. 6088.

56. Letter from G. M. Tisdale, director of purchases, to H. E. Smith, a company vice-president, Sept. 17, 1930, USR 75.

57. *Ibid.*

58. USR 76 (undated).

for a co-ordinated plan if the company's over-all interests were to be adequately protected.

To properly control and handle the subject of reciprocity all activities in connection therewith should be centralized so as to permit co-ordinated effort amongst or between interested Operating Departments and Service Departments and, at the same time, *keep to the fore the fact that the interests of the United States Rubber Company are in the final analysis the primary consideration.*[59]

The plan was designed to bring virtually all the company's purchases, including the purchase of transportation,[60] under its scope and to so co-ordinate them that the company could present a united front in trying to get business. As the plan expressed it:

No operating Department and/or Service Department is to make purchases involving any great amount ($1000) or any recurring amount of $250 or more per month without first clearing thoroughly with the Purchasing Department in New York to obtain the Company viewpoint and Company situation in order that we may be assured at all times a united front being presented to the outside. This is considered necessary as some departments are placing orders involving such amounts without clearing with the Purchasing Department for such study.[61]

The plan, designed to promote the company's over-all interests in accordance with profit-maximization principles, recognized that a conflict of interest might arise between the sales department, anxious to increase sales, and the purchasing department, wishing to get supplies at the lowest cost. To reconcile these interests, the plan provided that "no department is to be penalized by purchases because of a possible advantage to itself or some other department from a sales angle without the departments involved first having the opportunity to review the situation and decide what they feel is to the best interests of all concerned." [62] If in applying the "we'll-buy-from-you-if-you-buy-from-us" principle the company encountered higher prices from a particular supplier-customer than it met elsewhere and the supplier-customer could not be persuaded to reduce his price to meet competition, then the sales department was to be given an opportunity "to absorb the excess purchase value in order to maintain their sales

---

59. *Id.* at 1. Emphasis added.
60. The plan applied to purchases of services as well as of goods. It provided: "Wherever the word purchases is mentioned it is understood to include our tonnage movements for transportation both inbound and out-bound." *Ibid.*
61. *Ibid.*
62. *Id.* at 1–2.

Business Reciprocity and the Size of Firms

situation."[63] The report cited the following example drawn from the company's experience to show how this would work out:

> For several years we have purchased in the neighborhood of $400,000 to $700,000 in merchandise from the U.S. Steel Corporation and subsidiaries. During the same time the United States Rubber Company and subsidiaries (primarily the Mechanical Department) have sold merchandise to the extent of about $300,000 annually. One of the large items in money value purchased by us from the Steel Corporation is sulphate of ammonia for use as fertilizer on our Plantations in the Far East. A situation has arisen this year where the best quotation obtainable for our requirements from the Steel Corp'n is $6,478 in excess of a quotation for a satisfactory fertilizer of German production. . . . Knowing the valuable account Mr. Gussenhoven's Department has with the Steel Corp'n and the close relations he has maintained with them, the Purchasing Department felt that before giving our fertilizer business to a foreign competitor, it was better for the Company to ask Mr. Gussenhoven to consider this question from two angles: first, whether or not he could get the Steel Corp'n to meet the foreign offer and, second, in case he were unsuccessful, Mr. Gussenhoven to decide if the value of his sales account was sufficiently important to warrant his agreeing to absorb the $6,478 difference so as not to penalize the Plantations Company. The so-called machinery to carry this particular example out is now being used, although a definite decision has not been reached. Many other similar situations will arise, in fact, there are several now reported as needing such handling by the Purchasing Department.[64]

To insure the widest possible application of the program, the plan called for an immediate study by industries of all company purchases exceeding $500 annually and of all sales and for making the information available quarterly to all interested departments. The plan specifically provided that "no department is to be excluded from the operation of this plan merely because it has no interest from a selling angle . . . with or without interest they are to be brought into the picture because of the value of their purchases in a sales way to some other one of the company's departments."[65]

63. *Id.* at 2.
64. *Id.* at 2–3. A conflict between purchases and sales may be a characteristic of any reciprocal buying program. The *New York Times,* in recounting the development of reciprocal buying in the early 1930's, pointed out: "As the scheme developed in importance and size and necessitated higher costs . . . it became expedient to turn it over to the purchasing departments. The plan worked smoothly for a while . . . but here again the higher prices paid for goods in reciprocal agreements became a troublesome subject. Recently it was decided by the majority of companies to charge the difference in the cost of products to sales expense when reciprocity was involved. In this manner the extra expense is definitely charged to one department and the added cost brings to sales divisions a realization of their responsibility in making reciprocal agreements." N.Y. Times, Nov. 6, 1932, § F, p. 8, col. 6.
65. USR 76, at 4.

Workable Competition and Antitrust Policy

On September 22, 1930, United States Rubber's executive committee officially approved the reciprocity plan.[66] The purchasing department's administration of it apparently proved unsatisfactory. Two years later, on September 27, 1932, United States Rubber appointed a reciprocity committee made up of leading company officials: Herbert E. Smith, vice-president and member of the executive committee and the board; J. O'Shaughnessy, general manager of the tire department; L. M. Simpson, general sales manager of the tire department; and G. M. Tisdale, director of purchases.[67] This committee assumed responsibility for making reciprocity work. The record of the plan's operation is fragmentary, but the minutes of several meetings of the sales and executive committees indicate the company's continuing interest in utilizing its purchasing power to promote its sales.[68] The testimony of company officials indicates that as late as 1953 the company had not abandoned its program. L. D. Tompkins, vice-president in charge of tire sales from 1928 to March, 1944, testified to United States Rubber's continuous use of reciprocity,[69] and Tisdale named United States Steel Corporation, Bethlehem Steel Company, Allen Creek Coal Company, Consolidation Coal Company, and International Paper as among the companies with which United States Rubber had made reciprocity deals.[70]

RECIPROCAL DEALINGS BETWEEN UNITED STATES RUBBER AND DU PONT

Ownership by members of the Du Pont family of a substantial block of United States Rubber stock [71] obscures somewhat the nature of the commercial relations between the two companies. Whether the reciprocal dealings between them reflect a program imposed by the Du Ponts on

---

66. Extract from minutes of meeting of executive committee of U.S. Rubber Co., Sept. 22, 1930, "V. Reciprocity Procedure," USR 77. Indicative of its concern that its purchasing power be fully exploited in influencing sales, the executive committee suggested that "payments for electric power be included in the report of purchases." *Ibid.*

67. Extract from minutes of joint meeting of executive committee and operating committee of U.S. Rubber Co., Sept. 27, 1932, USR 78.

68. Extracts from minutes of meetings of sale committee, March 3, 1936 (USR 79), May 12, 1936 (USR 221), and April 12, 1938 (USR 222); extracts from minutes of meetings of executive committee, May 14, 1940 (USR 223), and Aug. 20, 1940 (USR 224).

69. Tr. 5829-30.

70. Tr. 6087. Tisdale testified that U.S. Rubber's reciprocity arrangements included railroad and steamship lines and that, "to a greater or lesser extent, it is still an active subject." Tr. 6071.

71. See note 54 *supra.*

Business Reciprocity and the Size of Firms

United States Rubber or represent the independent judgment of the respective company executives how best to promote their separate interests is not clear. What is clear is that each company has accorded the other preferential treatment in buying and selling. When they inaugurated the policy in the early 1930's, neither was a large customer of the other.[72] In 1931 Du Pont's sales to United States Rubber amounted to $737,000 and its purchases from United States Rubber to $204,000.[73] Although United States Rubber's sales to Du Pont were relatively small, it got most of the business Du Pont had to give. In eleven months of 1931 Du Pont bought only $48,000 of goods from eight competitors of United States Rubber, while selling them $542,000 of goods.[74] As Du Pont developed first rayon tire yarn and later nylon, the disparity between its sales and purchases from United States Rubber grew. In 1946 Du Pont sold United States Rubber over $10,000,000 of goods [75] while buying only $669,000 worth,[76] but this represented over one-half of Du Pont's industrial rubber requirements.[77]

72. As early as 1926, when Irenee du Pont held only 10,000 shares of U.S. Rubber common stock, he hinted that three-way reciprocal dealing without price discrimination among U.S. Rubber, General Motors, and Du Pont might be desirable. On June 26 of that year he wrote President Charles B. Seger of U.S. Rubber in part as follows: "Our Paint and Pigment Division are particularly anxious to get the lithopone business of the U.S. Rubber Company and as I, personally, am a considerable stockholder (in the name of the Granogue Investment Co.) in the Rubber Company and a firm believer in its future, I feel that I am not presumptuous in writing you very frankly." GX 1058. In soliciting this business, Irenee du Pont made it clear that the Du Pont Co. did not ask for any benefits in price or terms. "To do so would be impudent and unbusinesslike, but it [Du Pont Co.] does feel that the great corporations of the country, especially those who are leaders in business ethics and in service to the economic structure, should stand together without fear of veiled threats from companies which are more predatory. I am, therefore, writing to suggest that you ask your lieutenant in charge of purchases to award the lithopone contract purely on the merits of price, quality and service of that particular article and not to be swayed by fears of an increased price in some other commodity on the one hand, nor expected favors in tire sales to *our interests* on the other. In other words, 'let each tub rest on its own bottom.'" *Ibid.* Emphasis added.

73. Report to Lammot du Pont, president of Du Pont, from Du Pont's purchasing department, Feb. 15, 1932, GX 1059.

74. *Ibid.*

75. U.S. Rubber Co., "Total Requirements and Sources of Supply of Products of the Type Offered by Du Pont Co., 1946–48," compiled by U.S. Rubber's Treasurer's Department, USR 217.

76. This figure includes Du Pont's purchases of $111,000 of diphenyl methane, aniline, and certain latex products from a U.S. Rubber subsidiary. Memorandum to Lammot du Pont from L. D. Reed, director of Du Pont's trade analysis division, February 26, 1947, GX 1062.

77. Du Pont bought $1,264,348 worth of industrial rubber in 1946. *Id.* Relatively,

Workable Competition and Antitrust Policy

The director of Du Pont's trade analysis division gave two reasons why Du Pont did not buy more products from United States Rubber: Du Pont's inability to get from United States Rubber all types of rubber needed [78] and Du Pont's desire to give some business to its other customers. But while Du Pont's sales to United States Rubber far exceeded United States Rubber's sales to Du Pont, each was the other's leading customer for certain types of products. A letter from President Davis, of United States Rubber, to President Lammot du Pont, of the Du Pont Company, dated January 13, 1932, reflects the zeal with which Du Pont and United States Rubber pursued their reciprocity program.

I am happy to be able to report that a check as to the paint used on our building here verifies my understanding that only du Pont products were used. While the painters may have been using a Pratt & Lambert can, the can contained du Pont paint from a larger container, because we told him he could not have the contract unless he used du Pont paints. He told us that on this basis he would not be able to maintain the price he quoted on the contract, so we bought the paint through our own Purchasing Department to be sure none but your products were used.

Knowing of the genuine interest of our people in using and recommending du Pont products wherever possible, I did not believe we could have missed this opportunity.[79]

General Motors and Reciprocal Dealing

As long as General Motors was primarily a producer of automobiles, it had little incentive or opportunity to resort to reciprocal buying. As it has broadened the scope of its operations, more particularly as it has engaged in the production of goods used by other industries, its opportunities to utilize its purchasing power to increase its sales have multiplied. By 1954 General Motors was doing business with over twenty-one thousand suppliers, many of whom used some General Motors products. One of the most important groups of suppliers was the railroads. Shipping as it

---

Du Pont was doing better by U.S. Rubber than U.S. Rubber by Du Pont. In 1946 U.S. Rubber bought from Du Pont only 36.5 per cent of its total purchases of goods of the type produced by Du Pont; in 1948, only 28.8 per cent. USR 217.

78. He offered as an illustration Du Pont's purchase of $218,000 worth of a trade-named chemisal, "Hycar," sold only by B. F. Goodrich. GX 1062. Lammot du Pont explained the discrepancy in trade between the two companies this way: "U.S. Rubber buys from Du Pont a number of products which are raw materials for U.S. Rubber; whereas Du Pont buys from U.S. Rubber substantially nothing, except products that are used as supplies or small items in construction of machinery and equipment." Memorandum from Lammot du Pont to Reed, GX 1060 (undated).

79. GX 1063.

Business Reciprocity and the Size of Firms

did thousands of tons of finished products to numerous customers and transporting a similarly heavy tonnage of raw and semifinished materials from its many suppliers, General Motors' annual expeditures on railway services, direct and indirect, must have run into the millions. General Motors is not only a large buyer of railway services but sells many products essential to railroads. Its Hyatt Bearings Division is one of the country's leading makers of railway journal boxes and bearings for diesel locomotives and for passenger and freight cars. Its Frigidaire Division produces complete air-conditioning equipment for railway cars. Its Allison Division makes transmissions for railway cars and parts for diesel locomotives. Its Delco Products Division makes motors and generators for heating, cooling, and power, all of which are required by diesel locomotives. Its Electro-Motive Division makes diesel locomotives.

General Motors' expansion in the manufacture of diesel locomotives has been little short of spectacular. In 1930 through an exchange of stock it acquired the Winton Engine Company and the Electro-Motive Engineering Company. The Winton Company, organized in 1912, had built the first all-American diesel engine in 1913 and soon became an important maker of both diesel and gasoline engines. The Electro-Motive Company, an important Winton customer, made gasoline-engine-driven railroad cars and in 1930, when General Motors acquired it, had plans under way for making diesel locomotives.[80] From these simple beginnings General Mo-

---

80. Harold L. Hamilton, a former General Motors vice-president, testified recently that, when General Motors acquired these companies, Winton's business was "pretty badly shot" and that Electro-Motive's business was "very, very slow," although the latter's financial reserves were "in a very healthy position." *Hearings before the Subcommittee on Antitrust and Monopoly of the Senate Committee on the Judiciary*, 84th Cong., 1st Sess. 2422, 2432, 2429 (1955). Available information does not corroborate this testimony about Winton. The Winton Company's gross profits on sales increased from $585,675 in 1927 to $1,462,498 in 1929; its net income increased from $305,579 to $925,035 during the same period. *Moody's Industrials, 1930*, p. 2427. Its cash position, its total assets, its current assets, and its working capital all increased substantially. Winton's last financial report, issued just before its merger with General Motors and covering the first four months of 1930, showed a net profit of $220,732 after federal taxes, equivalent to $2.32 a share on its combined no par preferred and common stocks. N.Y. Times, May 13, 1930, p. 49, col. 3. This compares with net earnings of $241,939, or $2.54 a share, for the corresponding 1929 period. *Ibid*. Considering that the Great Depression was on, this is a remarkable showing. General Motors apparently recognized Winton's strong financial position and its promising future, for it exchanged for Winton's assets, carried on Winton's books at $4,047,262 (*Moody's Industrials, 1930*, p. 2427), 126,667 shares of its own common stock with a market value on May 15, 1930, of $6,000,000. N.Y. Times, May 16, 1930, p. 34, col. 3. Similar details are not available on Electro-Motive, but, if its business and financial position were no worse than Winton's, it was in very good shape indeed.

Workable Competition and Antitrust Policy

tors had become by 1955 the country's largest maker of diesel locomotives, accounting for more than three-fourths of all domestic sales.[81] Many factors no doubt contributed to this dramatic growth—the failure of the Baldwin Locomotive Works and the American Locomotive Company, the country's leading steam-locomotive builders, to see the future of the diesel; [82] General Motors' imaginative grasp of the diesel's prospects when produced on a mass-production basis; [83] its experience in the mass production of automobiles; its program to educate customers in the use and maintenance of diesels; [84] and its generally aggressive policy of finding new markets for new products.

81. Table appearing in testimony of V. H. Peterson, vice-president of Fairbanks, Morse & Co. *Hearings before the Subcommittee on Antitrust and Monopoly of the Senate Committee on the Judiciary,* 84th Cong., 1st Sess. 2358 (1955). See also tables appearing in testimony of O. DeGray Vanderbilt III, Baldwin-Lima-Hamilton Corp. vice-president. *Id.* at 2377–80.

82. Baldwin (since 1950 Baldwin-Lima-Hamilton Corp.) and American (renamed Alco Products, Inc., in April 1955) together produced about 80 per cent of the country's steam locomotives for more than a century—until the close of World War II, when the diesel locomotive captured most of the market. Their monopolistic practices helped kill their market. Baldwin and American divided markets so consistently that "railroads were identified as accounts of specific locomotive suppliers. For example, the Union Pacific was recognized as an Alco account and the Pennsylvania Railroad as a Baldwin account." Statement by C. R. Osborn, General Motors vice-president in charge of the engine group, *id.* at 3953. Baldwin and American not only divided markets; they shared the business. Osborn cited an incident supporting this statement. In 1939, after one of the companies had built and sold to one of its "historical customers" a demonstration unit of a new locomotive type it had designed, it turned over the design drawings and patterns to its rival, "who delivered . . . eleven locomotives to the historical customer of the design builder." *Ibid.* Unchallenged in their dominance of the field, Baldwin and American continued to make steam locomotives, in the words of William F. Lewis, Alco Products vice-president, "by strong backs and blood, sweat, and tears . . . a handmade product. We were not keyed up for what we would term today as mass production." Testimony of Lewis, *id.* at 2385. With heavy capital investments and "captive" markets for their steam locomotives, Baldwin, American, and Lima Locomotive Works, the country's third supplier, ignored the full technological significance of the diesel and throughout the 1930's defended steam against the diesel in speeches and advertising. As late as 1945 and 1948 the Lima Locomotive Works (later Lima Hamilton Corp., merged into Baldwin-Lima-Hamilton Corp. in 1950) was still advertising, "Steam Is Still Supreme" and "She, too, is truly MODERN." Exhibits H and I, *id.* at 3990–91.

83. "[A]ctually the greatest competitive advantage the Electro-Motive division of General Motors enjoyed was the attitude of its competitors. When Mr. Kettering was being questioned by Senator O'Mahoney . . . in a hearing some years ago regarding General Motors' percentage of the diesel market, he replied that our greatest competitive advantage is our competitor's belief that we are crazy." Statement by C. R. Osborn, *id.* at 3954.

84. General Motors, in determining to standardize the diesel locomotive for sale to all railroads, had to overcome the industry's long-established custom of building

Business Reciprocity and the Size of Firms

But, despite the testimony of a General Motors official that General Motors deliberately renounced the use of "traffic reciprocity" in selling diesel locomotives,[85] it would be strange indeed if General Motors' heavy purchases of transportation services were not also an important factor in General Motors' outstripping all rivals in selling diesels. Its competitors believe that this has been a factor in General Motors' rapid expansion in this field. One of them testified: "I think we would be naive to assume that General Motors' tremendous volume of traffic over the railroads does not have a profound influence on railroad purchasing."[86] Witnesses supporting this point of view included William F. Lewis, vice-president of Alco Products, Inc., and V. H. Peterson, vice-president of Fairbanks, Morse & Company.[87]

Charles W. Perelle, former president of the ACF Brill Company in Philadelphia, a large manufacturer of trolley coaches and busses, was somewhat more explicit in his testimony regarding the role of reciprocity in selling equipment to the railroads. He recognized the long-standing practice of railroads to give preference in buying to their large shippers:

> That is historical. I think it is the pattern of the railroad industry for many years. I don't think anybody has to write letters about it or influence anybody. I think it is just a pattern that has developed and has been given a great deal of consideration and a great deal of weight and influence.[88]

On questioning, Perelle was more specific. He testified to a particular instance in which ACF Brill in 1950 or 1951 lost to General Motors a sale of six busses to the New York, New Haven & Hartford Railroad because General Motors was a heavy shipper. Perelle put it this way:

> I was told by our people who were handling that job that the purchasing department of the New York, New Haven & Hartford Railroad told them that there were *so many* freight cars a week involved in this order, and that he, as

steam locomotives to each railroad's specifications. To soften customer resistance, General Motors agreed that the railroad might return the locomotive if it did not meet certain operating guaranties; it initiated and developed a new sales method, the economic study, which projects the economies and return on investment of substituting diesel locomotion for steam throughout a railroad's line; and, before making its first diesel freight locomotive sale in 1940, it demonstrated the diesel on twenty-six railroads, operating in heavy freight service for 86,000 miles. *Id.* at 3957, 3950, and 3954.

85. *Id.* at 3957–59.
86. Testimony of O. DeGray Vanderbilt III, Baldwin-Lima-Hamilton Corp. vice-president, *id.* at 2370.
87. *Id.* at 2391 and 2350.
88. Testimony of C. W. Perelle, president of American Bosch Arma Co., Garden City, Long Island, New York, *id.* at 2652–53.

an individual, wasn't going to take the responsibility of crossing that up. I just recite that as a statement of fact, and I don't think anybody had to put any pressure on anybody to have him realize that there is a reciprocity problem in this freight picture.[89]

Perelle, whose broad industrial experience should give special weight to his testimony, further testified that the people who were responsible for selecting a new president of the American Locomotive Company approached him about the job but that he "decided definitely against going ahead with" the matter after looking "into the history of the background of the locomotive industry."[90] He concluded that General Motors' dominant position in the sale of diesel locomotives was largely due to the preference given it by the railroads as a large freight shipper. Believing that this practice would limit American's capacity for growth—or, as he put it, that the volume of business was "pretty well controlled"[91]—he did not care to assume responsibility for managing American's business.

General Motors has not confined reciprocal dealings to reciprocal buying. In the fall of 1950, when its cash and government bond holdings totaled $1.3 billion [92] and it faced an acute steel shortage, General Motors went into the money-lending business to assure itself a supply of steel. Along with insurance companies and commercial banks, General Motors agreed to finance a steel-expansion program by Jones & Laughlin Steel Corporation; General Motors' loan was $28 million at 3 per cent, repayable in instalments through 1966.[93] Subject to government controls,[94] General Motors agreed that, when operating at capacity, it would continue to buy as much steel annually as it had been buying before the loan and would take an additional 290,000 tons from Jones & Laughlin's new capacity.[95] In return for its banking services, General Motors was to get first call on a stipulated but undisclosed amount of Jones & Laughlin steel. When not operating at capacity, General Motors could at its option reduce the amount of steel it bought. Within less than a year General Motors agreed

89. *Id.* at 2653. Emphasis added.
90. *Ibid.*
91. *Ibid.*
92. "GM Turns Lender," Business Week, Dec. 16, 1950, p. 112.
93. *Id.* at 111–12.
94. "The amount of steel that GM can actually get depends to a considerable extent on government priorities, the Controlled Materials Plan, etc. But GM figures that, with . . . more steel, it is sure to get more for itself," "GM's in Steel," Business Week, May 19, 1951, p. 26.
95. *Ibid.*

Business Reciprocity and the Size of Firms

to help finance a similar expansion program by Republic Steel Corporation, lending it $40 million.[96]

Such reciprocal arrangements assure General Motors preferential treatment in getting steel in times of shortage without obliging it to take surplus steel when business shrinks. They also enable General Motors to put some of its huge cash reserves to work at 3 per cent. On the other hand, the steel companies get needed funds without recourse to the usual money market and are assured a continued share of General Motors' business.

Economic Significance of Reciprocal Dealing

This study indicates that many firms have resorted to reciprocal dealing in trying to advance their business interests. Some large firms have practiced it deliberately, systematically, and continuously. How many we do not know but doubtless enough to justify the question, "What is its significance to industrial structure and performance?" Reciprocal dealing, as we have indicated, is a manifestation of imperfect competition. It both derives from and contributes to imperfections in the market. It can be used most effectively by large diversified firms selling their products to other industrial producers. Such firms may use reciprocal dealing for a variety of purposes. Among the more important are these: (1) to divide their fields of operation and thereby lessen the severity of competition; (2) to insure themselves an adequate supply of an essential raw material in times of shortage; and (3) to expand sales without resorting to price competition. As shown below, dye manufacture illustrates the first; General Motors' excursion into banking, the second; and General Motors' sale of railway equipment, Waugh, Du Pont, and United States Rubber, the third.

Charles D. Pack, a Department of Justice attorney, in testifying before the Senate Committee on Patents, indicated how dyemakers have used reciprocity to divide fields. He stated that in the 1930's this kind of reciprocity was "so widespread . . . that we find the rather unique situation wherein the largest customer of any one major dyestuff concern is a competing company."[97] Apparently no manufacturer made a complete

---

96. "It's no coincidence that GM's entry into the steel picture involves Republic and J & L. These two, and National Steel, are the only firms that turn out the wide sheets used in the auto industry." *Id.* See also N.Y. Times, May 10, 1951, p. 47, col. 5.

97. Testimony of Charles D. Pack, attorney, Antitrust Division, *Hearings before Committee on Patents on S. 2303 and S. 2491*, 77th Cong., 2d Sess., pt. 5, at 2126 (1942). In his testimony Pack presented a Du Pont intracompany memorandum (Pack Exhibit No. 117, p. 2492) indicating that in eleven months of 1939 Du Pont

Workable Competition and Antitrust Policy

line of finished dyes for all purposes or a full line of intermediates. Each specialized in a relatively few lines, buying from and selling to its rivals. An obvious advantage of such reciprocal arrangements among dyemakers is that they may lower production costs. For each company to provide itself with a full line of colors and shades for every purpose might, by keeping average fixed costs high, cause an inefficient use of resources. There are less obvious and less socially salutary advantages. Such interchanges bring representatives of rival companies into continuing close contact with each other and permit an exchange of information concerning prices, products, and other market data, which may greatly facilitate the stabilization of prices.[98] But, while such reciprocal dealings promote the interests of those practicing them, they hurt the little firm. As Pack put it, "The small fellow, who wants to engage in the business of manufacturing dyestuff, is generally completely shut off from supplies of intermediates or must pay exceedingly high prices for those which he is able to obtain."[99]

General Motors, with its large financial resources, by acting as an investment banker, guaranteed itself preferential treatment in obtaining steel during periods of shortage. Similarly, Bethlehem and other steel companies have used reciprocal dealings in the postwar period to provide themselves adequate iron and steel scrap.[100] With steel users clamoring for steel, and scrap in short supply, steel companies demanded preference in buying it from their customers whose operations yielded scrap. Although this is a practice small companies can resort to, it is one in which large diversified companies are likely to have an advantage, and apparently they have not hesitated to exploit it. During 1948 at least one

---

sold dyestuffs to General Dyestuff Corp. in the amount of $1,449,804, while buying dyestuffs from General in the amount of $756,024. Omitting patented products, intercompany purchases were: Du Pont from General, $640,593; General from Du Pont, $814,611. Du Pont calculated its net return per dollar of sales to General at 27.7 per cent.

98. Pack testified that "[t]he sales managers of the several companies are in almost constant touch with each other." *Id.* at 2126–27. A. R. Chantler, director of sales of Du Pont's dyestuff division, in an intracompany memorandum stated, "We usually talk to General [Dyestuff Corp.] two or three times every afternoon." Memorandum of Oct. 29, 1935, Pack Exhibit No. 118, *id.* at 243.

99. *Id.* at 2126.

100. Bethlehem has apparently not confined its use of reciprocal dealings to assuring itself a supply of scrap. It has for a long time been known as an aggressive marketer, combining a "judicious mixture of carrot and stick" in getting business. As a *Fortune* reporter has expressed it, "Indeed, it is significant that Bethlehem . . . led the way in using the power of 'reciprocity,' a method of ensuring that dealings with a supplier bear a direct relationship with the supplier's purchases of Bethlehem steel." "Bethlehem Steel and the Intruder," Fortune, March 1953, p. 201.

Business Reciprocity and the Size of Firms

of the large mills put "the scrap return arrangement on an official basis."[101] George F. Sullivan has described this as follows:

> Steel companies with experience in this line keep records of every ton of scrap shipped back to them by every customer. From these records the sales departments are instructed to work. . . . The steel company knows his operations and has figured what percentage of scrap he should be sending back to the mill each month. If the consumer falls down an explanation is called for.[102]

But it is the power of reciprocal buying to increase a firm's sales that is most significant to industrial structure. A large diversified firm, by integrating its buying and selling, may shift its demand function to the right and thereby grow. Such growth may be at the expense of smaller firms. With a general decline in business activity, the large diversified firm can, more clearly than the small firm, stabilize its operations through reciprocal buying and keep both output and prices comparatively undisturbed by the decline in demand. Armour & Company's use of its buying power to persuade railroads to buy equipment made by the Waugh Equipment Company illustrates dramatically how reciprocal dealings may help a firm to grow. Within only six years after Armour officials acquired Waugh, it had risen from sixth place in the industry to first, while total industry sales were declining.

Data are not available to show the influence of reciprocal buying on the size and rate of growth of such large firms as General Motors and Du Pont; but, if our analysis of the theory and practice of reciprocal dealing is valid, its use by such firms may have played a significant role in shaping contemporary industrial structure. Bigness and diversification contribute to the effective use of reciprocal dealing, and reciprocal dealing contributes to bigness and diversification. Bigness may feed bigness and accelerate growth. While the technical, managerial, marketing, and financial optimums analyzed by E. A. G. Robinson[103] are likely to be achieved in a quest for efficiency, attaining the security optimum necessitates a quest for power. Monopoly is its logical goal. Reciprocity contributes to bigness, and bigness brings security. Reciprocity, most effectively practiced by a large firm, not only contributes to internal growth but encourages growth through merger. Bethlehem Steel Corporation's wish to acquire Youngstown Sheet and Tube Company perhaps reflected chiefly the desire to obtain economical access to midwestern markets and to re-

---

101. George F. Sullivan, "Confusion Rules the Scrap Market as Old Doctrines Disappear," Iron Age, Jan. 29, 1948, p. 107.
102. Ibid.
103. *The Structure of Competitive Industry* (rev. ed.; London: Nisbet, 1935).

Workable Competition and Antitrust Policy

duce the cost of assembling raw materials. But inasmuch as Youngstown does not produce steel rails, an incidental but not insignificant gain from such a merger might have been an increase in Bethlehem's sale of rails and other steel products to railroads, which have regularly allotted their business on a basis of the steel tonnage shipped by suppliers.[104]

Conclusion

It would be easy to overemphasize the influence reciprocal dealing has exerted on industrial structure and economic performance. It is but one of a variety of devices firms have resorted to in their effort to make more secure their position in the economy. Its importance is probably less in good times than in bad, but there is no evidence that business firms that have resorted to it in bad times have abandoned it in good. Although it may bring security to a firm, it does not necessarily promote the welfare of the economy. It is more likely to contribute to the imperfections of competition that impede the economical use of resources. Size and diversification become more important than efficiency in resource allocation.

Whether judged by industrial structure or economic performance, reciprocal dealing tends to make competition less workable. It affects adversely "the nature of the option actually open to buyers," [105] the heart of Clark's performance test. It is equally inconsistent with Edwards' structural tests that "new traders must have opportunity to enter the market without handicap other than that which is automatically created by the fact that others are already well established there" and that "access by traders on one side of the market to those on the other side of the market must be unimpaired except by obstacles not deliberately introduced." [106] It is one of several tools in the oligopolist's kit designed to increase sales without resorting to price-cutting.

---

104. On Nov. 20, 1958, a federal district court ruled that the proposed merger was likely to violate Section 7 of the Clayton Act. United States v. Bethlehem Steel Corp., 168 F. Supp. 576 (S.D.N.Y.). For a detailed discussion of the desire of Bethlehem to merge with Youngstown see statement of Arthur B. Homer, president of Bethlehem Steel Corp., *Hearings before the Subcommittee on Antitrust and Monopoly of the Senate Committee on the Judiciary*, 84th Cong., 1st Sess. 482 ff. (1955). As early as 1930 Bethlehem planned to merge with Youngstown. Youngstown does not produce certain key products that railroads buy—structural rails and freight cars—but the two companies' combined shipments of steel might enable Bethlehem to increase its sales of rails and freight cars. See C. E. Fraser and G. F. Doriot, *Analyzing Our Industries* (New York: McGraw-Hill, 1932), p. 257.

105. John M. Clark, "Toward a Concept of Workable Competition," 30 Am. Econ. Rev. (Proceedings of the American Economic Ass'n) 241, 243 (1940).

106. Edwards, *op. cit. supra* note 5, at 9–10.

8
The Du Pont-General Motors Case And the Sherman Act

ON JUNE 30, 1949, the Antitrust Division of the Department of Justice filed a complaint against the Du Pont Company, General Motors Corporation, United States Rubber Company, and allied defendants, alleging that since 1915 they had engaged in a combination to restrain trade in the products of the manufacturing companies and to monopolize a substantial part of that trade, in violation of Sections 1 and 2 of the Sherman Act. The complaint also alleged that Du Pont by acquiring a controlling interest in General Motors had violated Section 7 of the Clayton Act. On December 3, 1954, Judge Walter J. LaBuy of the District Court for the Northern District of Illinois decided that the defendants were not guilty.[1] The government appealed, and on June 3, 1957, Justice Brennan, speaking for the Supreme Court in a four-to-two decision (Justices Clark, Harlan, and Whittaker did not participate), reversed the lower court and referred the case back to it for determining the necessary remedies.[2]

This is one of the most important antitrust cases ever to have been heard. It is important for three reasons: First, it challenged a stock acquisition ostensibly made as an investment by what had become the world's largest chemical company in what had become the world's largest manufacturing company. Second, although Du Pont had acquired its General Motors stock more than a quarter of a century before the suit was instituted, the Supreme Court decided the issue under old Section 7 of the Clayton Act, which prohibited the acquisition by one corporation of stock in another corporation where the effect of such acquisition might be to substantially lessen competition between the two corporations or to

Note: Reprinted from the *Virginia Law Review*, Vol. 44, No. 1 (January 1958).

1. United States v. E. I. du Pont de Nemours & Co., 126 F. Supp. 235 (N.D. Ill. 1954).
2. United States v. E. I. du Pont de Nemours & Co., 353 U.S. 586 (1957).

Workable Competition and Antitrust Policy

restrain commerce in any section or community, or tend to create a monopoly of any line of commerce. The Court did not bring its decision within Sections 1 and 2 of the Sherman Act, under which not potential but actual restraint of trade and monopolization must be established to justify a finding of illegality. Third, by finding the relevant market at issue to be that for automotive finishes and fabrics—a narrower market than flexible wrapping materials—the Supreme Court in effect reversed its position of only a year earlier in the *Cellophane* case.[3] By using the Clayton Act and by narrowing its conception of the relevant market, it ostensibly opened the way for what was heralded as a general attack on big business. One eminent legal scholar[4] characterized the decision as the making of a new law, and *Fortune,* fearful of a widespread application of the principles enunciated, looked for a wholesale attack on mergers.[5]

Background of the Stock Acquisitions

A brief excursion into industrial history may help in understanding the case and the importance of the issues raised. Du Pont for nearly half a century before 1911 had engaged in one program after another to restrict competition in the sale of gunpowder, an effort that culminated in Du Pont's acquiring virtually a monopoly of the nation's commerce in that product.[6] In June 1911 the federal district court in Delaware held

3. United States v. E. I. du Pont de Nemours & Co., 351 U.S. 377 (1956).
4. Adolf A. Berle, Jr., quoted in Fortune, July 1957, p. 91.
5. Editorial, "Brennan on Bigneess," *id.* at 91–92.
6. Du Pont responded to the decline in demand for gunpowder following the Civil War—between 1859 and 1869 its eastern plants expanded capacity by 300 per cent but by the end of the period its sales had expanded by only 30 per cent—by joining with six other companies to organize the Gunpowder Trade Association (GTA) in 1872, "for the purpose of ensuring an equitable adjustment of prices and terms for sales of powder throughout the United States," the association to comprise "all manufacturers of Gunpowder in the United States, who now or hereafter may be admitted thereto." Confidential Minutes of April 29, 1872, Meeting of the Manufacturers of Gunpowder, Government's Exhibit 96-B, pp. 476–77, United States v. E. I. du Pont de Nemours & Co., 188 Fed. 127 (D. Del. 1911). Prices rose substantially, and only the competition of three outsiders threatened the "stabilization" program. Du Pont ended this by acquiring large stock interests in them in 1873 and 1877 and by persuading them to observe GTA prices. Willard F. Mueller, *Du Pont: A Study in Firm Growth* (unpublished Ph.D. dissertation, Vanderbilt University, 1955), pp. 58–61. Between 1871 and 1879 Du Pont alone or in combination with GTA associates acquired twelve Pennsylvania "soft powder" firms selling to coal mines. When the high prices enjoyed by GTA members encouraged two new firms in Ohio and a new firm in New York to enter production 1878 and 1881, GTA conducted a price war which in 1886 compelled two of them to sell out to GTA members and brought the third into GTA. United States v. E. I. du Pont

Du Pont-General Motors and the Sherman Act

that Du Pont by bringing the country's leading gunpowder makers under a single control had been guilty of conspiring to restrain and of monopolizing the trade in gunpowder.[7] To remedy this situation the court ordered Du Pont to dispose of certain of its assets and place them under the control of two separate corporations, Hercules Powder Company and Atlas Powder Company.[8] The dissolution left Du Pont in control of about 30 per cent of the country's black blasting powder, 42 per cent of the dynamite, and 100 per cent of the country's privately produced military smokeless powder.[9] Before the final decree in 1912, however, Du Pont had already begun a program of product diversification designed to give it greater security and to utilize its knowledge and experience in manipulat-

de Nemours & Co., *supra* at 131. In 1884 or shortly thereafter Du Pont and Laflin & Rand Powder Co. produced over 80 per cent of the country's black powder. Testimony of Alfred I. du Pont, Defendant's Testimony 460, United States v. E. I. du Pont de Nemours & Co., *supra*. Two years later the twelve members of GTA inaugurated a quota system which required nine of them to buy from Du Pont, Laflin & Rand, and Hazard Powder Co. an amount equal to that by which their sales exceeded their allotments at any time that the "three companies" were observing their own allotments. Government's Exhibit 7, pp. 110–22, *ibid*. Du Pont since 1876 had owned a controlling interest in Hazard Powder Co., and the "three companies" of the agreement were really only two. Arthur P. van Gelder and Hugo Schlatter, *History of the Explosives Industry in America* (New York: Columbia University Press, 1927), p. 261. High prices again brought in five new black powder companies, but by 1896 Du Pont and Laflin & Rand had acquired a controlling interest in all of them. Mueller, *op. cit. supra* at 69. Du Pont acquired seven black powder firms between 1897 and 1902. *Id.* at 71. The Indiana Powder Co., which a group of coal operators had formed in 1897 to protect themselves from the high prices exacted by the "Powder Trust," sold out to Du Pont in 1902, after GTA had organized a new company to undersell it locally. *Id.* at 72–73. In the same year Du Pont through the Delaware Securities Co. and the Delaware Investment Co. bought a controlling interest in Laflin & Rand and another company at an excessively high price. Of Du Pont's *modus operandi* the district court said: "Before 1902 the plan was to destroy competition and obtain a monopoly by the enforcement of drastic provisions in trade agreements, and from 1902 to 1907 it was to achieve the same ends by substituting corporate forms and powers for trade agreements." United States v. E. I. du Pont de Nemours & Co., *supra* at 147. GTA was dissolved in 1904, and between that year and 1907 Du Pont and the Eastern Dynamite Co., in which Du Pont owned stock, dissolved sixty-four explosives companies. *Id.* at 146–47. Du Pont in 1907 controlled 64 per cent of the country's black blasting and smokeless sporting powders, 72 per cent of its saltpeter blasting powder and dynamite, 73 per cent of its black sporting powder, and all its smokeless military powder except that made by the government. *Id.* at 145.

7. United States v. E. I. du Pont de Nemours & Co., *supra* note 6.
8. United States v. E. I. du Pont de Nemours & Co., D. C. Del., Equity No. 280, Final Decree, June 13, 1912, 1 Decrees and Judgments in Civil Federal Antitrust Cases, July 2, 1890–Jan. 1, 1949, at 194; Decree, Feb. 18, 1913, *id.* at 206.
9. Mueller, *op. cit. supra* note 6, at 107.

Workable Competition and Antitrust Policy

ing nitrocellulose, the basic raw material in the manufacture of gunpowder.[10]

Du Pont as the country's leading maker of gunpowder profited enormously by World War I. It was the only American company equipped to handle expeditiously the allied countries' demand for explosives. Its war sales totaled nearly a billion dollars, which a Du Pont vice-president estimated to represent "276 years of business,"[11] and in the four years from 1914 to 1917 it earned $232,000,000.[12] With a capacity for making explosives far in excess of the country's peacetime requirements and possessed of ample funds, Du Pont carried out systematically and on a great scale the diversification program it had earlier initiated.[13] On December 21, 1917, Du Pont's executive and finance committees approved the acquisition of $25,000,000 of common stock in General Motors Corporation, a rapidly growing company in which Pierre S. du Pont, president of the Du Pont Company, and Irenee du Pont had already made substantial investments on the recommendation of John J. Raskob, at that time treasurer of the Du Pont Company.[14] Pierre S. du Pont had become chairman of General Motors' board in 1915 and in 1917 a member of its finance committee, as had Raskob. Irenee du Pont became a member of the General Motors finance committee in 1918. By March 8, 1918, General Industries, Inc., organized by Du Pont for the purpose, had purchased about 23 per cent of the common stock of General Motors and Chevrolet Motor Company (the latter was acquired by General Motors in 1918 and 1919). By 1921 Du Pont had increased its investment in General Motors to $79,500,000, representing 38 per cent of the company's outstanding stock, and Pierre S. du Pont was its president. In 1923 Du Pont transferred the equivalent of these additional purchases to the Managers Securities Company, a corporation it had set up to effectuate

---

10. Du Pont's 1904 acquisition of the International Smokeless Powder and Chemical Co. not only gave it a monopoly of military smokeless powder but introduced it to a nonexplosives enterprise, the production of soluble cotton and lacquers. *Id.* at 96–97. In 1910, after finding that nonexplosives uses for nitrocellulose included lacquers, celluloid, artificial silk, and artificial leather, Du Pont bought the Fabrikoid Co., the country's largest manufacturer of artificial leather. United States v. E. I. du Pont de Nemours & Co., 353 U.S. 586, 599 (1957).
11. "Du Pont I: The Family," Fortune, November 1934, p. 206.
12. United States v. E. I. du Pont de Nemours & Co., 353 U.S. 586, 599 (1957).
13. For the highlights of this program, for which Du Pont allocated $90,000,000, see pp. 331–32, *infra*.
14. United States v. E. I. du Pont de Nemours & Co., 126 F. Supp. 235, 240 (N.D. Ill. 1954). Statements of fact in the remainder of the paragraph in the text are based on the district court's opinion, pp. 241–44.

Du Pont-General Motors and the Sherman Act

Pierre S. du Pont's stock bonus plan for selected executives of General Motors, and after 1930 gradually released the voting rights that the stock carried. By 1938 Du Pont's holdings in General Motors again approximated 23 per cent of its outstanding stock, where it has since remained.

On June 30, 1927, and again on September 2, 1927, certain members of the Du Pont family and certain stockholders of the Christiana Securities Company and the Delaware Realty & Investment Corporation joined with three outsiders (there were eighteen members in all) to form syndicates to buy stock in the United States Rubber Company in "quantities sufficient to give practical control, or at least a voice in the management."[15] The syndicate operation was closed in December 1927 because, Irenee du Pont testified, they already had the ear of management. The syndicate's original voting trust was superseded by the Rubber Securities Company in 1929, to take advantage taxwise of a decline in the value of the stock, and that company, which had voted 17 per cent of United States Rubber's stock as a unit, was dissolved in 1938 to enable its stockholders to borrow on their underlying United States Rubber stock. Members of the Du Pont family have continued to hold their United States Rubber stock, which on June 30, 1949, represented 18 per cent of the company's preferred and 11 per cent of its common.

The District Court's Decision

These acquisitions in General Motors and United States Rubber were the basis of a "network of interrelationships"[16] that the government alleged constituted a conspiracy to restrain trade and to monopolize a part of the commerce in products of the kind made by Du Pont. The complaint is equivalent to a charge that Du Pont obtained control of these companies and used it to insure a protected market for such of its products and those of United States Rubber as were necessary to the business of General Motors, while reserving to itself the exclusive production of certain other products. Judge LaBuy found no evidence to support these allegations. What the record discloses with respect to these charges depends as much on the preconceptions of those examining the facts as on the facts themselves. A chunk of wood to a practical-minded person is apt to be regarded as a material which on the application of a

---

15. Syndicate agreement of June 30, 1927, quoted *id.* at 256. Statements of fact about the acquisition of United States Rubber stock are based on the district court's opinion, pp. 256–57.
16. *Id.* at 237.

Workable Competition and Antitrust Policy

flame combines with oxygen to create a fire. An artist may see in it a madonna that takes shape as he skillfully and tenderly carves it. After reviewing the relevant evidence Judge LaBuy concluded that facts did

> not establish that du Pont has been the controlling force in the direction of General Motors affairs, or has been in a position to act as if it owned a majority of General Motors stock. The record shows consultation and conference, but not domination.[17]

He reached a similar conclusion with regard to Du Pont's ownership of stock in United States Rubber. The government did not appeal from this part of his decision, and this study will not consider it further.

After analyzing the trade between Du Pont and General Motors and the exchange of trade data bearing on General Motors' suppliers, Judge LaBuy concluded that

> the du Pont Company was interested in selling its products to General Motors and made efforts to do so; a fact which is not denied by the defendants. The evidence, both oral and documentary, does not establish, however, that there was any agreement between the two companies that required General Motors to buy all or any part of its requirements from du Pont. Nor does the evidence establish that du Pont dictated or controlled the purchasing policies and practices of General Motors or sought to dictate or control those policies and practices. In fact, the evidence shows that General Motors exercised complete freedom in determining where it would purchase its requirements of products of the kind that du Pont manufactured.[18]

Reviewing the same evidence I come to different conclusions, on a basis of the following facts and reasoning.

MINORITY CONTROL OF A CORPORATION

It is a well-recognized principle of corporate economics that the larger the number of shareholders and the smaller their holdings the easier it is for a group with a substantial block of stock to control the corporation. When the group has a will to do so, it can hardly be stopped. The Rockefeller group remained in practical control of the several Standard Oil companies long after the dissolution of the parent company in 1911. It did so because its members continued to hold for a time the same proportion of stock in each of the constituent companies that they had held in the parent company. Eventually they relinquished a part of their

17. *Id.* at 250–51.
18. *Id.* at 276.

Du Pont-General Motors and the Sherman Act

holdings, and in some companies they apparently were not interested in continuing control, but in others they remained the group ultimately responsible for major policy decisions. The directors realized this and in general followed policies acceptable to Rockefeller. When Colonel R. W. Stewart, chairman of the board of Standard Oil Company of Indiana, in 1929 challenged the original group's control, a proxy fight ensued. John D. Rockefeller, Jr.'s influence was such that despite ownership of only 14.9 per cent of the shares [19] he was able to oust Stewart from the board of directors and to put in a management more acceptable to his interests.

The courts on numerous occasions have recognized the ability of a minority group to control a corporation.[20] They have also recognized that control may take the form of intangible influence but be none the less effective by reason of that. "Domination may spring as readily from subtle or unexercised power as from arbitrary imposition of command."[21]

Du Pont's Evaluation of the Acquisition

So much for the legal and economic principles involved. What are the realities? Between 1918 and 1938 Du Pont owned from 23 to 38 per cent of General Motors' common stock. In 1938 and continuously since that time Du Pont has owned 23 per cent. In 1947 this was represented by 10,000,000 shares, which in 1950 were split to 20,000,000 [22] and by 1957 had increased to 63,000,000.[23] In 1947, 436,510 stockholders

---

19. Berle and Gardiner C. Means, *The Modern Corporation and Private Property* (New York: Macmillan, 1932), pp. 82–83.

20. In Morgan Stanley & Co. v. SEC, 126 F.2d 325, 328, 333 (2d Cir. 1942), the court said: "Furthermore, the 20% holding of United is the largest block of voting securities; and there is supporting evidence in the record showing various connections between United and Columbia. We are not unaware that much less than a majority of stock is frequently sufficient for purposes of control, and we see no reason to contest the legislative view that 10% may be sufficient. . . . I think we can take judicial notice of the fact that the ownership of twenty per cent of the voting power of a company makes the owner 'liable' to have practical control."

In Gratz v. Claughton, 187 F.2d 46, 49–50 (2d Cir.), *cert. denied*, 341 U.S. 920 (1951), the court said: "We take judicial notice that an effective control over the affairs of a corporation often does not require anything approaching a majority of the shares; and this is particularly true in the case of those corporations whose shares are dealt in upon national exchanges."

21. North American Co. v. SEC, 327 U.S. 686, 693 (1946).

22. United States v. E. I. du Pont de Nemours & Co., 126 F. Supp. 235, 244 (N.D. Ill. 1954).

23. Wall Street Journal, June 4, 1957, p. 2, col. 2. The *Journal* placed the market value of the stock at $2,500,000,000.

held the remaining shares.[24] Of these, 92 per cent owned no more than 100 shares each, and 60 per cent owned no more than 25 each.[25] At stockholders' meetings in the years 1928–1949 Du Pont voted from 30 to over 52 per cent of the stock voted.[26] A proxy committee set up by a management friendly to Du Pont presumably voted much of the remainder.

When Du Pont acquired its first shares in 1918, William C. Durant was president of General Motors and through the Chevrolet Motor Company owned 450,000 shares of the 825,000 outstanding. He encouraged Du Pont's original purchase and agreed to joint control of the company. Raskob in urging Du Pont to make a substantial investment in General Motors and Chevrolet Motor Company described the terms of the agreement as follows:

With Mr. Durant we will have joint control of the companies.

. . . .

Perhaps it is not made clear that the directorates of the motor companies will be chosen by Du Pont and Durant. Mr. Durant should be continued as President of the Company. Mr. P. S. du Pont will be continued as Chairman of the Board, the Finance Committee will be ours and we will have such representation on the Executive Committee as we desire . . . .[27]

In March 1918 Raskob reported to the Du Pont finance committee: "The financial management of General Motors Corporation is thrown very largely up to us and plans are under way to bring us into intimate contact with that end of the business."[28] In 1920, when Durant got into financial difficulties, Du Pont bought out his interest in General Motors. About the significance of this Du Pont in its annual report for 1920 stated, "During the latter part of November last, Mr. W. C. Durant, then President of the General Motors Corporation, requested that we take over the management and control of that corporation, advising that he desired to resign and sell his interest in the corporation

---

24. United States v. E. I. du Pont de Nemours & Co., 126 F. Supp. 235, 244 (N.D. Ill. 1954).

25. *Id.*

26. Government's Exhibit (hereinafter GTX) 1307, R. 664, 5230, United States v. E. I. Du Pont de Nemours & Co., 353 U.S. 586 (1957), The references to exhibits in succeeding footnotes are to this case unless otherwise indicated. In this study the analysis of this case is based on the documentary evidence in the record rather than the testimony.

27. GTX 124, R. 479, 3208, 3221–22. See also the district court's opinion, 126 F. Supp. at 241–42.

28. GTX 128, R. 481, 3239.

Du Pont-General Motors and the Sherman Act

in order to liquidate his personal indebtedness, which was very large and pressing."[29]

Raskob in 1923 summarized the entire transaction in which Du Pont acquired a controlling interest in General Motors as follows:

In the year 1917 the Directors of the du Pont Company after very careful consideration accepted the invitation of Mr. W. C. Durant to become interested with him as partners in the control and management of General Motors Corporation. This involved our investing a substantial sum of money and taking over the direction of the financial management of the General Motors Corporation. Mr. Durant in turn agreed to assume responsibility for the Executive Management of the company.

The management of the General Motors Corporation was carried along under this arrangement until the latter part of 1920 when Mr. Durant became so seriously involved financially that the du Pont Company much against its will was forced to take over Mr. Durant's personal common stock holdings in the General Motors Corporation, involving a net increase in the du Pont Company's investment in this security of upwards of 2,500,000 shares at a cost of upwards of $25,000,000.00, with the result that today we own 7,519,000 shares of General Motors Corporation common stock valued on our books at $_____[sic]. This gave the du Pont Company approximately 38% of the total common stock of the General Motors Corporation which is practical control and made it necessary to assume complete responsibility for the management. To properly assume this responsibility our Finance Committee called upon Mr. Pierre S. du Pont, Chairman of our Board, to take the presidency of the General Motors Corporation which he consented to do with the clear understanding that he was to occupy the position temporarily only, pending the time when a man capable of assuming the presidency permanently could be found or developed.[30]

In 1921 Raskob in computing Du Pont's voting strength at 10,907,925 shares of the 20,477,734 outstanding had stated: "As the Directors know we are now in control of the company and are completely responsible for its politics [sic] and management . . . ."[31]

Du Pont Takes Charge of Management[32]

In 1920 Pierre S. du Pont, chairman of Du Pont's board and a member of its finance committee, replaced Durant as president of General Motors. In the two and a half years of his presidency he revamped its manage-

---

29. Du Pont, *Annual Report*, 1920, p. 4.
30. GTX 235, p. 3, R. 483, 3496.
31. GTX 1345, R. 2813, 5347.
32. Statements of fact in this section are based on the district court's opinion, 126 F. Supp. at 244–46, unless otherwise indicated.

Workable Competition and Antitrust Policy

ment significantly, placing Du Pont officials in key positions in General Motors. The two most important committees in the management of General Motors, the executive and the finance committees, were reorganized. Of these the finance committee was the more important, for it was this committee that had control of the purse strings and made decisions on expansion and investment policies. In 1921 the ten-man executive committee was reduced to four members, three of whom were officers or directors of Du Pont; in 1922 two General Motors directors were added.

In May 1923, the last month of Pierre S. du Pont's presidency, the General Motors finance committee consisted of seven Du Pont men (members of its board or officials of the company) and four others, one of whom was Alfred P. Sloan, Jr., who upon Pierre S. du Pont's resignation as president of General Motors succeeded him. Sloan was selected on Pierre's recommendation and eleven days later became a member of Du Pont's board of directors.[33] Sloan, in a letter to Irenee du Pont in 1926, professed loyalty to the Du Pont organization in these words: "You must recognize that I am essentially, or at least believe and hope I am, a member of the du Pont family." [34] Concerning Sloan's election to the presidency of General Motors, Raskob, treasurer of Du Pont, had said: "We have done a splendid job in electing Alfred president of General Motors Corporation." [35] The General Motors finance committee was increased to twelve members in 1924 and eventually to fourteen. If one takes Sloan's Du Pont directorship and profession of membership in the Du Pont family at their face value (and I for one do), Du Pont men constituted a majority of the finance committee from Du Pont's original investment until 1937.[36] At that time the executive and finance committees were combined into a nine-man policy committee of which four members, including Sloan, were Du Pont directors, four were General Motors men (members of the former executive committee and not Du Pont directors), and one was an outsider.[37] Not until 1946, three years before the government filed its complaint, was the financial policy of General Motors turned over to a committee a majority of whose member-

33. GTX 184, R. 486, 3416; GTX 186, R. 486, 3421.
34. GTX 704, R. 624, 4505.
35. GTX 185, R. 486, 3418, 3419.
36. General Motors Corp. Finance Committee, May 10, 1923–May 3, 1937, General Motors Exhibit (hereinafter GM) 22, R. 6609.
37. General Motors Corp. Policy Committee, May 3, 1937–June 3, 1946, GM 23, R. 6610. George Whitney of J. P. Morgan & Co. was the outsider.

Du Pont-General Motors and the Sherman Act

ship even ostensibly represented General Motors. At that time the financial policy committee, one of two committees superseding the policy committee, consisted of Walter S. Carpenter, Jr., Donaldson Brown, and Sloan (all members of the boards of both Du Pont and General Motors), and Albert Bradley, Frederic G. Donner, John L. Pratt, Charles E. Wilson, and George Whitney (the last a member of J. P. Morgan & Company).[38] Sloan, as president of General Motors and a professed member of the Du Pont family, no doubt wielded more influence than the others.

Du Pont from the beginning took steps to gain the loyalty of all key men in General Motors. In 1923, when Pierre S. du Pont was retiring as president of General Motors, he initiated a managers' securities plan by which selected management officials became "substantial stockholders or partners"[39] in General Motors without immediately lessening Du Pont's control of the company. About this Raskob and Donaldson Brown (both men served on the finance and executive committees of both Du Pont and General Motors) said: "[The plan] will definitely tie up with us in the management and control of this huge investment the men in the General Motors Corporation who are definitely charged with the responsibility and success of the corporation."[40] They commented on the significance of the managers' securities plan as follows:

> Mr. du Pont feels that the best manner in which to attain the greatest success possible in the conduct of the affairs of the General Motors Corporation is for that Corporation to interest its principal men in the corporation as substantial stockholders or partners. He not only feels this very keenly, but feels too that the du Pont Company with its large and controlling interest in the General Motors Corporation has now a splendid opportunity to enhance the value of its own investment in the General Motors Corporation through giving to the General Motors Corporation an opportunity to interest its important employes as managing partners in this great enterprise.[41]

38. A business periodical has described Bradley and Donner as probably "Du Pont oriented." Business Week, June 8, 1957, p. 43. For Pratt's connections with both Du Pont and General Motors and for the role he played in their relationship between 1922 and 1934, see note 41 and pp. 334–35 *infra*.

39. Report of June 20, 1923 to the Du Pont finance committee by John J. Raskob, GTX 235, p. 4, R. 483, 3497.

40. *Id.*

41. *Id.* The above description of the extent to which Du Pont executives occupied key positions in General Motors does not reflect the magnitude of Du Pont's influence on General Motors so vividly as the more detailed account that follows, which is based on GTX 1309, R. 664, 5232–39 (compiled from ten other exhibits and *Moody's Industrials, 1952*), and GTX 177, R. 3397. J. A. Haskell, who became a director and vice president of Du Pont in 1915, also became a director of General Motors in 1917 and a vice president and member of General Motors' executive and finance committees in 1918. He retained all these positions until his death in 1923.

Workable Competition and Antitrust Policy

In view of Du Pont's ownership of 23 to 38 per cent of General Motors' stock with the remaining shares widely disseminated; of Du Pont's voting from 30 to over 52 per cent of the stock voted in the period for which information on this is available; of Du Pont officials' holding key positions in the company for most of the period under review; and of the managers' securities plan which was calculated to win the loyalty of important General Motors executives to Du Pont—I conclude that Du Pont in fact controlled General Motors. This is not to say that it was an unlawful control. The courts have the last word on that. Nor is it to say that Du Pont might not have lost control if it had patently managed General Motors only for its own benefit.[42]

Donaldson Brown, who became a director of Du Pont in 1918 and a member of its finance committee in 1920, became a director of General Motors in 1920 and a member of its finance committee—later renamed its financial policy committee—in 1921. He was chairman of its finance committee from 1929 to 1937, vice-chairman of its financial policy committee from 1937 to 1946, and a member of the General Motors administration committee from 1942 to 1945, of the policy committee from 1937 to 1946, and of the executive committee from 1924 to 1937. John L. Pratt, who had been a Du Pont employee during most of the period from 1905 to 1919, went to work for General Motors shortly after Du Pont acquired an interest in it. He was made vice president in 1922, a position he continued to hold until 1937. He served on the General Motors executive committee from 1924 to 1937. He became a director of General Motors in 1923 and a member of its financial policy committee in 1946. H. M. Barksdale was a vice president of Du Pont from 1915 to 1918 and a director and member of the Du Pont finance committee from 1916 to 1918. He was also a General Motors director and member of its finance committee from June to November 1918. Walter S. Carpenter, Jr., Lammot du Pont Copeland, Henry Belin du Pont, H. F. du Pont, Irenee du Pont, Lammot du Pont, Pierre S. du Pont, Angus B. Echols, John J. Raskob, all Du Pont men, and Alfred P. Sloan, Jr., who avowedly considered himself a Du Pont man, served simultaneously as directors of both companies at various periods between 1915 and 1957. Carpenter, H. F. du Pont, Irenee du Pont, Lammot du Pont, and Pierre S. du Pont were members of both Du Pont's and General Motors' finance committees. Most of them held additional posts in both companies. Carpenter was president of Du Pont from 1940 to 1948 and a member of its executive committee from 1919 to 1948, at the same time serving as a member of first General Motors' finance committee, then its policy committee, and then its financial policy committee. As of 1957 he was still a member of both companies' finance committees. Pierre S. du Pont was president and chairman of the boards of both companies, occupying the latter positions simultaneously between 1919 and 1929. Lammot du Pont served first as president then as chairman of Du Pont between 1926 and 1948 and held the chairmanship of General Motors between 1929 and 1937.

42. The district court's and Sloan's comments on the insignificance of Du Pont's having voted 52 per cent of the stock voted at certain General Motors stockholders' meetings reflect their failure to distinguish between having control and losing it. The court said: "Sloan testified that at no time had there been a contest over the selection of directors. He said that while it was true that the Du Pont block of stock represented over 51% [sic] of the stock at certain of the meetings he emphasized

Du Pont-General Motors and the Sherman Act

Control for Whose Benefit?

Du Pont might have exercised control for the benefit of General Motors as a corporate entity, each policy decision Du Pont made or influenced being designed to promote the welfare of General Motors. Or it might have used it to subordinate the business interests of General Motors to those of Du Pont. Judge LaBuy in determining the facts of control analyzed the evidence bearing on the way it was exercised. He did not think the evidence established the allegation of the complaint that Du Pont controlled General Motors in Du Pont's own business interests. Hence he denied the fact of control.

The case affords considerable evidence that Du Pont intended to exercise its control of General Motors for the benefit of Du Pont. As previously indicated, even before its acquisition of a substantial stock interest in General Motors it had carried through a program of expansion in other directions. As early as 1910 it had gone into the artificial leather business by buying the Fabrikoid Company, the country's largest manufacturer of artificial leather.[43] In 1915, while Pierre S. du Pont was chairman of the board of General Motors, Du Pont went into the celluloid business by buying the Arlington Company, one of the country's two largest celluloid manufacturers. In 1916 it entered the rubber-coated fabrics business by buying the Fairfield Rubber Company, whose product went into automobile and carriage tops. In 1917 it went into the paint and varnish business by buying Harrison Brothers & Company.[44] In purchasing stock in General Motors and Chevrolet Motor Company, Raskob of Du Pont predicted: "Our interest in the General Motors Company will undoubtedly secure for us the entire Fabrikoid, Pyralin [plastic sheeting], paint and varnish business of those companies, which is a

---

that it was not 51% of *all* the stock entitled to vote. In this connection he said: 'In case of conflict you immediately—the interest you arouse and all that, and the issues that are put before the stockholders, would mean that a much larger percentage of the stockholders would come into the meeting, and that would dilute in a way the Du Pont interest. So I can't just say what would happen. . . . It would depend, as I say, upon a lot of circumstances that I can't evaluate.'" 126 F. Supp. at 254.

43. Statements of fact in this section are based on the district court's opinion, 126 F. Supp. at 266–67, unless otherwise indicated.

44. Harrison Brothers & Co., Inc., owned 52 per cent of the capital stock of the Beckton Chemical Co., the other 48 per cent being owned by Cawley Clark & Co., which made colors. In 1917 Harrison bought Cawley Clark & Co., including its interest in Beckton, and also acquired the Bridgeport Wood Finishing Co., a varnish manufacturer.

Workable Competition and Antitrust Policy

substantial factor." [45] Du Pont's competitors for General Motors' business were equally certain of this result. In 1918 W. W. Mountain, president of Flint Varnish & Chemical Works, General Motors' principal paint supplier, asked Durant about consolidating Flint with Harrison, since, in the district court's words, "Mountain knew Du Pont had bought a substantial interest in General Motors and was interested in the paint industry . . . [and he] felt he would lose a valuable customer, General Motors." [46] Du Pont bought the Flint Works and a few months later also bought certain assets of the New England Oil Paint & Varnish Company. In 1920, when the facilities at Flint were insufficient to meet the demands of General Motors and the Du Pont sales department anticipated increased orders from it and other automobile companies, Du Pont acquired certain assets of The Chicago Varnish Company. In 1934 it acquired the assets of the Mountain Varnish and Color Works. It also made many other acquisitions and investments designed to increase its capacity to sell to the automotive industry.

The evidence indicates that Du Pont tried to increase its sales by influencing General Motors in three respects: (1) to buy specific Du Pont products; (2) to formulate a general policy governing the distribution of General Motors' business between Du Pont and competitors; and (3) to recommend Du Pont products to its customers.

Attempts to Influence Purchase of Specific Products

There was frequent and continuing correspondence between Du Pont and General Motors and within each company in the years 1918–1934 with regard to the sale of specific products.[47] In 1918 J. S. O'Rourke of

---

45. Treasurer's report to Du Pont executive committee, Dec. 19, 1917, GTX 124, R. 479, 3208, 3221. See also 126 F. Supp. at 241.

46. 126 F. Supp. at 267.

47. Letter of April 15, 1918 from J. A. Haskell, former Du Pont sales manager and vice president and in 1918 a General Motors vice president and member of the General Motors executive committee, to William Coyne, vice president of Du Pont in charge of sales, GTX 290, R. 501, 3782–83; Du Pont Co. memorandum, "Sales to General Motors Company," May 22, 1918, GTX 293, R. 502, 3786; reports to Haskell from General Motors manufacturing units on their purchases from Du Pont and its competitors, GTX 296, 298, 299, 300, R. 502–03, 3790, 3795–801; letters from Du Pont Fabrikoid Co. to Haskell, July 1918, GTX 297, R. 503, 3791–94, and GTX 302, R. 504, 3803–4; report by A. Felix du Pont, vice president of Du Pont, to Du Pont executive committee, June 1921, GTX 417, R. 526, 3992, 3998; memorandum from Du Pont's general director of sales to Lammot du Pont, Aug. 12, 1921, GTX 419, R. 528, 4009; letter from Lammot du Pont, Du Pont vice president, to Pierre S. du Pont, General Motors president

Du Pont-General Motors and the Sherman Act

the General Motors Oakland division stated in a letter to its manager that Oakland was buying artificial leather from both Du Pont Fabrikoid and the L. C. Chase Company, despite the fact that Du Pont's product was inferior to that of Chase.[48] In 1921 Pierre S. du Pont, president and chairman of the board of General Motors, inquired of Lammot du Pont, vice-president of Du Pont, whether General Motors was getting from Du Pont all its requirements of products of the kinds made by Du Pont. Lammot replied that it was not, and he listed the purchases by seven General Motors divisions of paint, varnish, fabrikoid, rubber cloth, and transparent pyralin, indicating where Du Pont had all the business, where there was "no reason" for its not having certain business, and where there was "good reason" for its not having certain business. Pierre then wrote that Du Pont's paint, varnish, and fabrikoid were doing pretty well with General Motors and that "with the change in management at Cadillac, Oakland and Olds"[49] Du Pont should be able to sell substantially all the company's requirements of those products. A. Felix du Pont, vice-president

and board chairman, Aug. 10, 1921, GTX 420, R. 528, 4010–11; letter of Aug. 23, 1921, from Pierre S. du Pont to Lammot du Pont, GTX 421, R. 529, 4012; letter of Oct. 7, 1921, from R. R. M. Carpenter of Du Pont to Pierre S. du Pont, GTX 403, R. 526, 3958–60; 1923 correspondence between Lammot du Pont and Cadillac on Cadillac's failure to use certain Du Pont paints, GTX 442–49, R. 534–36, 4066–77; proposal by Du Pont of a requirements contract on a cost-plus basis for General Motors' purchases of fabrikoid and rubber-coated fabrics, Oct. 6, 1923, GM 413, R. 528, 3987–88; 1922–1923 correspondence between Lammot du Pont and Fisher Body Corp., GTX 434, R. 532, 4054, GTX 437–41, R. 533, 4059–65, GTX 443, R. 534, 4067, and GTX 451–52, R. 536, 4079–81; 1924 and 1926 correspondence on General Motors' ethyl alcohol requirements, GTX 315–18, R. 506–7, 3827–31, and GTX 328–29, R. 509, 3845–46; June 1925 report to Du Pont executive committee on Du Pont's special discount to General Motors designed to lessen competition for Fisher Body's business, GTX 454, R. 537, 4084, 4087; Jan. 1926 correspondence by John L. Pratt, former Du Pont employee and in 1926 a General Motors vice president, with Biechler, general manager of General Motors' Delco-Light Co., and Elms of Du Pont's paint and varnish division, GTX 338–41, R. 511, 3863–67; Jan. 1927 report by Lammot du Pont to Pierre S. du Pont and John J. Raskob, chairman and vice-president of General Motors respectively, on General Motors' purchases from Du Pont's competitors, GTX 460, R. 537, 4100–3; Dec. 7, 1934, letter from Pratt to general manager of General Motors' New Departure Mfg. Co. seeking to recover business with Du Pont lost to a competitor of Du Pont, and subsequent correspondence, GM 371–74, R. 521–22, 3912–16.

48. O'Rourke referred to "two very serious complaints" about Du Pont imitation leather but said that after a letter to Du Pont about one complaint, "they immediately sent their representative to investigate . . . and I will advise you further as to whether or not this trouble has been eliminated." GTX 300, R. 503, 3798, 3800–1. See also 126 F. Supp. at 270.

49. Letter of Aug. 23, 1921, GTX 421, R. 529, 4012. See also 126 F. Supp. at 270.

Workable Competition and Antitrust Policy

of the Du Pont cellulose products department, in 1921 reported to its executive committee that "both Sales and Production departments have concentrated upon our standing with General Motors . . . and . . . today Fairfield [Du Pont's rubber-coated fabrics division] is 'solid' with General Motors." He thought that with the "community of interests" which existed between Du Pont and General Motors, "some plan should be worked out" to make this a permanent arrangement so that the profits from manufacture could be "retained within our organizations." He observed that Du Pont had overcome "the latent resentment which we experienced at the outset against the partial obligation under which the General Motors units felt themselves to be with respect to using our goods" since Du Pont had started "a fixed program of giving the best product," and that the General Motors units in general considered Du Pont products "equal or superior to those of competitors." [50]

Some General Motors executives thought Du Pont products were not so good as those of its rivals, but they indicated their readiness to give Du Pont the business whenever its products were equally satisfactory in price and quality. In 1923 in response to a letter from Lammot du Pont asking H. H. Rice, manager of Cadillac, to buy its varnish requirements from Du Pont provided Du Pont could furnish a varnish as good as or better than that being used by Cadillac, Rice replied that Cadillac was already using Flint's primer and color and finish varnish on Cadillac chassis but that he was "not satisfied to make a change" to Flint's enamel because it had not yet "passed our test." [51] Later, in response to a second letter from Du Pont, Rice stated that Cadillac was "anxious to use Flint products but was cautious in changing paints . . . and felt that as Flint material proved itself it was expected to be adopted by Cadillac." [52]

All General Motors managers were not equally determined to put the company's interest in quality above Du Pont's interest in obtaining a market for its products. John Lee Pratt, long an employee of Du Pont before holding important managerial positions for General Motors,[53] was described by the district court as "inclined to do favors for his friends [i.e., Du Pont] when as he testified, it involved no injury to General Motors." [54] In October 1922 MacGregor of Du Pont's paint department requested

50. GTX 417, R. 526, 3992, 3998, 3999. See also 126 F. Supp. at 272.
51. GTX 444, R. 534, 4068–69. See also 126 F. Supp. at 272.
52. GTX 448, R. 535, 4075–76.
53. For Pratt's positions with General Motors see note 41 *supra*. In addition to the positions already mentioned he was chairman of the general purchasing committee from 1924 to 1929. 126 F. Supp. at 272–73.
54. *Id.* at 272.

Du Pont-General Motors and the Sherman Act

Pratt's assistance in getting a share of the Hyatt Roller Bearing Company's paint business. Pratt instructed Hyatt's general manager to look into the situation and then asked MacGregor whether the quality of Du Pont's paint had been improved until it was equal to that of other manufacturers in quality, price, and service. Hyatt's general manager sent Pratt a report indicating that Hyatt was using Du Pont paints except the undercoat, which several years earlier had proved unsatisfactory; but that Hyatt's purchasing agent had again investigated the matter and "regardless of the wishes of the Paint Department" would purchase the Du Pont product, which he felt "will serve our purpose equally as good."[55]

When in 1926 the Du Pont paint and varnish department complained to Pratt that the Delco Light Company, a General Motors subsidiary, was favoring a competitor, Pratt wrote the manager of Delco Light that in view of

the sacrifice that the du Pont Company made in 1920 and 1921 . . .—the du Pont Company going to the extent of borrowing $35,000,000 . . . to prevent a large amount of General Motors stock being thrown on the open market— they should give weight to this which in my mind more than over-balances consideration of local conditions. In other words, I feel that where conditions are equal from the standpoint of quality, service and price the du Pont Company should have the major share of General Motors divisions' business on those items that the du Pont Company can take on the basis of quality, service and price.[56]

In April 1926 General Motors' AC Spark Plug division complained in a memorandum to Curtice of General Motors that Du Pont had been giving very poor service and recommended a change in suppliers. Thereafter Albert Champion, president of AC Spark Plug, personally wrote Pratt about the matter and expressed a desire to continue to do business with Du Pont. After correspondence between Pratt and Moosmann of Du Pont the matter was settled by Du Pont's improving its service.[57]

55. GTX 313, R. 506, 3823. See also 126 F. Supp. at 273.
56. GTX 340, R. 512, 3865, quoted by the Supreme Court in 353 U.S. at 605 n. 35. The Court characterized Du Pont's policy toward General Motors as "well epitomized" by this letter. Pratt's letter went on to say that he did not wish his personal sentiments to influence the general manager's "own good judgment" and that "above all the prime consideration is to do the best thing for Delco-Light Company, and . . . considerations in regard to the duPont Company or other concerns are secondary. . . ." Id.
57. See 126 F. Supp. at 275. Du Pont at times also tried to use its influence with General Motors to get business for its friends, an effort in which it was apparently not successful. Unsuccessful tries included Lammot du Pont's effort to direct General Motors' purchases of fire bricks to the General Refractories Company, a non-Du Pont concern in which the son of the governor of Pennsylvania was in-

335

Workable Competition and Antitrust Policy

ATTEMPTS TO INFLUENCE GENERAL POLICY ON PURCHASES

In 1923 at Sloan's suggestion General Motors created a general purchasing committee with James Lynah as secretary. This committee, which functioned for eight years, supervised the pooling of purchases whenever several General Motors divisions used a common product, in an effort to concentrate General Motors' buying power. Du Pont sought to enlist it in a reciprocal buying program whereby General Motors' buying power could be utilized in securing business for Du Pont from third parties.[58] Although evidence regarding the activities of the general purchasing committee is not always clear and is sometimes conflicting, apparently the committee thought it a sound policy for General Motors to have two sources of supply for every important product,[59] specifically to divide its purchases of leather substitutes and top material between Du Pont and competitors in the ratio of about four to one, provided Du Pont quoted competitive prices.[60] Although some divisions favored Du Pont in buying

terested, and Lammot's effort to persuade General Motors to stay out of the manufacture of oil burners because certain anthracite coal producers had protested to Du Pont at its going into the production of them.

58. For an analysis of the evidence in the record on Du Pont's use of reciprocal buying and General Motors' role in it see chap. 7, pp. 297-305 *supra*.

59. GTX 406, R. 527, 3966, 3979. Pierre S. du Pont, chairman of the boards of Du Pont and General Motors, in commenting on this policy in relation to Du Pont's loss of 25 per cent of the Chevrolet top material business after having had 100 per cent of it, stated that he thought the "two sources of supply" idea was foolish but that he could not "refuse permission" to Chevrolet to follow it. GTX 407–08, R. 527–28, 3982–83. In a letter to Knudsen of Chevrolet he expressed his disapproval and urged that one source of supply properly maintained was more reliable than two sources, but added, "I have no fault to find with the principle which would apply as well to other manufacturers as to the Du Pont Company." GTX 410, R. 528, 3984. See also 126 F. Supp. at 277.

60. Allen, general manager of Du Pont's cellulose department, in February 1923 reported to his executive committee that at a meeting with the purchasing agents of Cadillac and Chevrolet, and Main, Lynah, and Pratt, members of the General Motors general purchasing committee, the question of two sources of supply was discussed and the conclusion reached that General Motors should purchase 20 per cent of its leather substitute and top materials from one of Du Pont's competitors and 80 per cent from Du Pont at competitive prices. GTX 406, R. 527, 3966, 3979. From other documentary evidence and from Lynah's testimony at the trial the district court concluded, however, that Allen and the General Motors officials made no agreement to this effect. Further evidence on the matter appears in the minutes of the general purchasing committee for Sept. 27, 1923, which were sent to all division purchasing agents and provided: "It was agreed that on an equal competitive basis at least 25% of the business should be placed with sources other than the Du Pont Company. That the Du Pont Company be notified that they should make their best price in their initial offer and not count upon having the opportunity to meet competitive prices, and that on the basis of competitive prices the Divisions

Du Pont-General Motors and the Sherman Act

whether or not its prices were competitive,[61] General Motors managers for the most part insisted that quality, service, and price take precedence over favoritism in buying supplies. Du Pont strove to gain General Motors' business by improving the quality of its product and making necessary price concessions, and eventually some if not all of the operational managers became convinced of the superiority of certain Du Pont products.

Attempts to Influence Recommendations to Customers

In 1925, when Du Pont together with the Kentucky Alcohol Corporation had formed the Eastern Alcohol Corporation to make industrial alcohol, antifreeze was an important market for the product. When a newspaper story appeared stating that glycerin was more satisfactory than alcohol as an antifreeze, H. Fletcher Brown, vice-president of Du Pont, wrote Sloan asking whether General Motors was giving official approval to such publicity and if so "that their attention be called to . . . the interest which the Du Pont Company will have in the future"[62] in making and selling alcohol. Sloan replied that General Motors had discovered that alcohol had a bad effect on Duco finish and therefore General Motors must favor glycerin as an antifreeze.[63] Later Pratt wrote F. LaMotte, director of purchases at Du Pont, that General Motors had concluded after study that Union Carbide's Prestone was the most satisfactory antifreeze

---

were free to place their business to the best advantage." GTX 412, R. 528, 3986. See also 126 F. Supp. at 278. The committee's independence weakened when Du Pont agreed to give General Motors a secret "super discount" for purchases totaling a certain dollar volume. In July 1928 the general purchasing committee advised the purchasing agents of General Motors divisions that although healthy competition could be maintained if Du Pont were given 80 per cent of their purchases of its products on an even basis, utilization of Du Pont's super discount plan would materially increase earnings; and it urged the purchasing agents to "cooperate to this end." GTX 494, R. 541, 4155. See also 126 F. Supp. at 286. General Motors' purchases declined during the depression, and Du Pont terminated its super discount plan in 1932.

61. The Du Pont paint, lacquer, and chemicals department reported to the Du Pont executive committee in November 1926 that Du Pont had succeeded in selling Buick its fabrikoid requirements for the first half of 1927 "notwithstanding competition from Federal Leather Co. at a differential of 11¢ per yard under our quotations." GTX 467, R. 540-41, 4121. See also 126 F. Supp. at 286. A report for December 1926 stated that the Oakland Motor Co. had placed orders for its requirements of fabric for the first six months of 1927 "notwithstanding lower prices being quoted by Federal Leather and Cotex." GTX 468, R. 541, 4122. See also 126 F. Supp. at 286.

62. GTX 319, R. 507, 3832. See also 126 F. Supp. at 273.
63. GTX 320, R. 507, 3833. See also 126 F. Supp. at 273.

on the market and was recommending its use.⁶⁴ But Pratt himself was not satisfied with such a categorical position on the superiority of Prestone and requested the General Motors research laboratory to prepare a statement showing the distinctive advantages of both glycerin and alcohol. The laboratory report favored glycerin in several respects. Thereafter Sloan suggested that the Chevrolet instruction book omit an expression of preference for glycerin and content itself with a statement of the qualities of each. In October 1926, when Du Pont began the production of ethyl alcohol, Du Pont officials explored the possibility of selling antifreeze to General Motors and requested Pratt to find out whether the General Motors laboratory could verify glycerin's shortcomings as reported by Du Pont. In November 1926 James Lynah, executive secretary of the General Motors laboratory, reported to Pratt that alcohol-water solutions were recommended as antifreezes for any class of service and that General Motors divisions would largely use them. Phelps of the Du Pont development department later protested to Pratt that some General Motors divisions, notably Cadillac, continued to recommend glycerin instead of alcohol. Cadillac thereafter recommended that only alcohol be used.⁶⁵ Meanwhile glycerin manufacturers were also seeking General Motors' endorsement. The matter was finally closed by Sloan's advising Pratt that the general technical committee of General Motors had decided on the policy of pointing out that there were two antifreeze materials, glycerin and alcohol, that alcohol's sole disadvantage was that when spilled it would disfigure paint, and that glycerin was satisfactory if used in strict accordance with the manufacturers' recommendations. Accordingly the new instruction books were to contain a statement setting forth the advantages and disadvantages of each.

Despite General Motors' desire to placate Du Pont by letting the customers choose, General Motors technicians apparently continued to favor glycerin. At any rate Du Pont's efforts to sell ethyl alcohol to General Motors were unavailing throughout 1926, 1927, and 1928.

Du Pont's Share of General Motors' Purchases

On a basis of all the evidence the lower court concluded that there was no agreement between Du Pont and General Motors requiring General Motors to buy all or any part of its requirements from Du Pont; that

---

64. GTX 321, R. 508, 3835. See also 126 F. Supp. at 273.
65. GTX 322, 323, 326, 328, 330–35, R. 508–11, 3836, 3837, 3842, 3845, 3847–60. See also 126 F. Supp. at 274.

Du Pont-General Motors and the Sherman Act

the general purchasing committee dealt with Du Pont only in the same manner as it did with other suppliers; and that Du Pont did not seek to dictate General Motors' purchasing policies or practices. The court was no doubt correct in a narrow technical sense. The issue correctly stated would appear to be not whether there was a specific agreement that gave Du Pont preference in supplying General Motors with the things it bought but whether Du Pont by reason of its stock ownership in General Motors and its managerial influence on General Motors' affairs had an advantage over competitors in getting General Motors' business. Whatever the explanation, the fact is that Du Pont got most of General Motors' business for the more important products which it could supply. In 1947 General Motors bought Du Pont products at a total cost of $26,628,274. Of this amount $18,938,229, or 71 per cent, represented purchases from Du Pont's finishes division. Purchases of Du Pont fabrics in 1948 totaled $3,700,000. Expressed in percentages, Du Pont supplied 67 per cent of General Motors' requirements of finishes in 1946 and 68 per cent in 1947. It supplied 52.3 per cent of its requirements for fabrics in 1946 and 38.5 per cent in 1947.[66] I for one believe that both the evidence and common sense justify the conclusion that Du Pont's ownership and management relation with General Motors was an important factor in getting its business.[67]

Benefits from General Motors' Chemical Discoveries

Du Pont's stock interest in General Motors may have had a far more important effect on competition than the advantage it gave Du Pont in

---

66. United States v. E. I. du Pont de Nemours & Co., 353 U.S. 586, 596 (1957).

67. Justice Burton and Justice Frankfurter in dissenting from the majority opinion of the Supreme Court took a different view of the same evidence. They found that a supplier is not "selling to General Motors" as such but that each of its thirty operating divisions has one or more purchasing agents and represents one or more separate selling jobs for a supplier. They found that although General Motors divisions in 1947 purchased 68.4 per cent of their finishes and 38.5 per cent of their fabrics from Du Pont, they purchased much smaller percentages of other products which Du Pont might have supplied. They found that Du Pont's sales of finishes to General Motors represented a relatively small part of Du Pont's total sales of finishes to all customers. They found that the several General Motors divisions did not adopt Duco paint simultaneously and that some of them, after adopting it, later switched to competitive products. They found that for certain products General Motors used a raw material supplied by competitors of Du Pont, whereas General Motors' own competitors used a raw material supplied by Du Pont. The dissenters concluded that *"all* of the evidence after 1926 affirmatively establishes without essential contradiction that Du Pont did not use its stock interest to receive any preferential treatment from General Motors." *Id.* at 645.

Workable Competition and Antitrust Policy

the sale of automobile finishes and fabrics. The government argued that Du Pont's ownership of stock in General Motors enabled it to exploit profitable chemical discoveries made by General Motors' staff which it otherwise could not have done. The district court found that the evidence did not support this contention. The Supreme Court did not pass on the issue. Attorneys for the government argued that Du Pont's influence on General Motors' chemical developments is disclosed particularly in negotiations regarding a general chemical agreement between Du Pont and General Motors, in the arrangements regarding the manufacture and sale of tetraethyl lead, and in the agreement resulting from the development of Freon 12 as a refrigerant. The documentary evidence on these matters is not always clear and is subject to such interpretation as the interests and preconceptions of the interpreter may dictate. General Motors officials on the witness stand insisted that all these transactions were at arm's length uninfluenced by Du Pont's ownership or managerial interest in General Motors, and the lower court agreed. I shall not try to reproduce all the relevant documents or the testimony regarding them but shall try to give a brief historical summary of the significant facts relative to each.

Negotiations for General Chemical Agreement

As previously indicated, Du Pont in acquiring a stock interest in General Motors intended to make General Motors an outlet for its chemical products. It is not surprising therefore that Du Pont early took steps designed to insure its exploitation of such chemicals as General Motors might discover. The Du Pont proposal for a general agreement covering chemicals discovered by General Motors took shape in the course of negotiations regarding the production of an antiknock for motor fuels. Charles F. Kettering, president of the Delco Company, had been interested in this project as early as 1912 or 1913. It was not until 1916 or 1917 that serious research was begun, however, and the project had been transferred to Dayton Metal Products Company when in 1918 General Motors acquired United Motors, of which Delco was then a division. The precise relationship of General Motors to the Dayton project is not clear, but in 1919 General Motors took over the Dayton laboratory and with it the project. Kettering combined the talents of the scientist with those of the businessman. As a result of a talk which he made before a Cleveland audience Kurtz of the Du Pont Company contacted him in 1916; Kettering sent him a copy of a paper he was about to deliver and wrote, "[A]ny time we get anything of interest we will be glad to give you the benefit of it." [68] Several members of the Du Pont family had at that time acquired stock in General Motors, and Pierre S. du Pont was chairman of its board, but Kettering had not yet become associated with General Motors. He met some of the Du Pont chemists through the American Chemical Society, and after he became associated with General Motors he invited Du Pont representatives to visit his laboratory to see what he was doing.

By late 1919, when General Motors finally acquired the Dayton laboratory, a general understanding apparently had been reached as to the relation of the work of the laboratory to Du Pont, although its details had not been worked out. In August 1919 Dr. Midgley or Dr. Clements of the General Motors research organization reported to the manager of the Du Pont laboratory on their work.[69] The writer stated that in connection with their work on antiknock materials a study was to be made of the "homologues of aniline," and he listed the specific materials they planned to experiment with and requested that Du Pont furnish them with any information it had on the best methods of preparing compounds which Du Pont could not supply. The letter closed with the declaration, "We are anxious to cooperate with you in every possible way." [70] Two months later K. W. Zimmerschied, assistant to the president of General Motors, wrote C. M. Stine, assistant director of chemical research at Du Pont, setting forth in broad terms his conception of a working arrangement between the Dayton laboratory and the Du Pont Company. In the words of the district court, the Du Pont chemical director replied that he "had no funds available for such work and that in any case the ultimate expense of the research should be borne by whichever company derived the greatest benefit from the work." [71]

While General Motors' work in the use of aniline as an antiknock material was progressing, representatives of General Motors and Du Pont conducted a number of conferences on the problem of cooperation between General Motors and the Du Pont Company in chemical development. Apparently Du Pont was more interested in an agreement covering general chemical research and exploitation than in one cover-

---

68. Quoted by the district court, 126 F. Supp. at 302.
69. GM 243, R. 1526, 7317. Kettering testified that the letter was probably signed by Midgley but might have been signed by Clements. Kettering, R. 1526. See also 126 F. Supp. at 302.
70. GM 243, R. 1526, 7317.
71. 126 F. Supp. at 302. Identical language appears in Brief for the Defendants 260, citing Du Pont Exhibit (hereinafter DP) 154. See also *id.* at 257, where it is categorically stated that "Du Pont refused" to push its research on aniline for Kettering.

ing aniline. On April 22, 1920, a conference on the subject was held at Wilmington. Irenee du Pont, Lammot du Pont, Raskob, certain members of the Du Pont chemical department, and Kettering, director of research at General Motors, attended. Stine of Du Pont reported that "at this conference various phases of the proposal to use the Chemical Department of the Du Pont Company in a consultant capacity and for research work for the General Motors were discussed."[72] Out of this grew a specific proposal, the basis of which was suggested by Raskob, who was both chairman of the General Motors finance committee and vice-president of Du Pont. Du Pont's executive committee approved it on June 22, 1920. The proposed agreement provided that General Motors create a committee, including a Du Pont member who would be paid for his committee work by General Motors, to determine the chemical research projects to be turned over to Du Pont. The proposed agreement also set up standards for the classification of research products, designated the property rights which General Motors would have in such products, provided that Du Pont need not do experimental work at General Motors' request if it would involve modification or improvement of any Du Pont product, and made General Motors responsible for all Du Pont's expenses incurred in connection with the research, including overhead and a proportionate share of its chemical department's maintenance and operating expenses.[73] General Motors never approved the agreement; both Kettering[74] and Sloan opposed it. The two companies operated on an informal understanding (namely, that Du Pont would take up the commercial exploitation of aniline if it appeared "sufficiently attractive from the profit standpoint"[75]) until December 1921, when the General Motors research laboratory demonstrated that tetraethyl lead was a more effective antiknock than aniline.

Lammot du Pont, a Du Pont vice president and executive committee member and a member of the finance committees of both General Motors

72. GTX 579, R. 609, 4261.
73. GTX 580, R. 609, 4265–71.
74. Although Kettering opposed the specific agreement, during the negotiations he avowed his interest in cooperating with Du Pont and his belief that Du Pont could be of great value to General Motors. In 1922 he wrote Lammot du Pont, in reply to one of numerous letters urging General Motors' acceptance of the general chemical agreement: "There has never been any question in my mind but that the Du Pont organization could supplement the work of our laboratory to a tremendous degree and it has always been my desire that this should be done. . . ." GTX 592, R. 611, 4285, 4286.
75. Letter from Lammot du Pont to Kettering, Aug. 14, 1920, GTX 602, R. 612, 4300.

Du Pont-General Motors and the Sherman Act

and Du Pont, continued to press Kettering for a general contract. Finally Kettering indicated that the matter would have to be decided by General Motors' president, who at that time was Pierre S. du Pont. A file memorandum by Lammot du Pont on November 6, 1922, reveals the two Du Ponts' final disposition of the matter. Lammot du Pont wrote: "In conversation with Mr. P. S. du Pont he advised that it does not seem possible at this time to institute any plan for co-operation on chemical research between General Motors Corporation, his feeling being that, as problems come up, special arrangements with reference to each should be made between the two Companies, rather than attempt now to make a general arrangement to cover prospective cases."[76]

TETRAETHYL LEAD

General Motors' research staff had independently discovered the antiknock qualities of tetraethyl lead and developed a method of producing it commercially before they suggested that Du Pont take over its production. At that time presumably they knew more about tetraethyl lead and the hazards involved in making it than any other group of men in the country. In March 1922 Pierre S. du Pont, president of General Motors and chairman of Du Pont's board of directors, sent a memorandum to his brother, Irenee du Pont, president of Du Pont, advising him that "Kettering would like to take up the question of manufacture with the Du Pont company representatives," that a plant of 100 gallons daily capacity should be erected, and that if introduced as a commercial article "it would require about 4,500,000 gallons per annum to dope the entire gasoline supply."[77] After several conferences between Irenee du Pont and members of Du Pont's chemical staff, and Kettering and members of his staff, Du Pont began the construction of a plant to produce tetraethyl lead. On September 5, 1922, the General Motors research department reported to the General Motors executive committee that in view of the satisfactory progress of Du Pont's production program General Motors would discontinue both production and research on production.[78] On October 6, 1922, the arrangement was formalized by a contract[79] providing for the construction by Du Pont of a plant of 100 gallons daily capacity and setting a price to General Motors of $26 a gallon. The contract was to

76. GTX 598, R. 611, 4295.
77. GTX 610, R. 612, 4302, 4303.
78. GTX 615, R. 613, 4308, 4309.
79. GTX 618, R. 613, 4312–18.

Workable Competition and Antitrust Policy

be a "continuing one" but gave General Motors the right to manufacture tetraethyl lead or have it manufactured by others if Du Pont's price should not be the lowest.

It may be argued, and the defense argued it so effectively as to convince the lower court, that it was perfectly natural for General Motors to turn to a well-established chemical company with which its technicians had for some time had contact for the manufacture of a dangerous chemical in which special skills and techniques were required. Whether or not one accepts this hypothesis, it seems practically inevitable that General Motors should have done so in view of the ownership and managerial relations existing between Du Pont and it.

Gas stations in Dayton, Hamilton, and Cincinnati, Ohio, sold the first antiknock gasoline to consumers in 1923. By the middle of the year public acceptance, as characterized by the district court, was "tremendous."[80] In January 1924 General Motors made a contract with the Standard Oil Company of New Jersey for the distribution of tetraethyl lead in New York, New Jersey, Massachusetts, nine other states, and the District of Columbia. General Motors gave Standard exclusive distribution rights in this territory for three years and Standard agreed to use only antiknock mixtures supplied by General Motors.[81] General Motors had earlier made similar contracts with Standard of Indiana covering eleven midwestern states, with Standard of Louisiana covering eight southern states, and with the Gulf Refining Company covering Texas, Pennsylvania, and Delaware.[82]

Standard's Cheaper Process

The Standard Oil Company of New Jersey had become interested in the development of an antiknock fuel as early as 1919, when Frank Howard of Standard contacted Kettering.[83] Thereafter Standard started independent research on the problem. Its research was successful, and at a conference in April 1923 Howard revealed to Midgley of General Motors that Standard had developed a new and cheaper process for making tetraethyl lead than the General Motors ethyl bromide process. Bromine

---

80. 126 F. Supp. at 305.
81. GTX 620, R. 613, 4319–32.
82. GM 76, R. 1561, 6761; GM 78, R. 1564, 6779; GM 80, R. 1565, 6800.
83. Statements of fact in this discussion of Du Pont–General Motors relations with respect to tetraethyl lead are based on the district court's opinion, 126 F. Supp. at 304–13, unless otherwise indicated.

Du Pont-General Motors and the Sherman Act

was in short supply and relatively expensive and, as previously indicated, Du Pont was charging General Motors $26 a gallon for tetraethyl lead. Standard claimed that by its ethyl chloride process it could produce tetraethyl lead for less than $10 a gallon.

Standard's discovery would appear on its face to constitute a serious threat to Du Pont's monopoly in supplying tetraethyl lead. General Motors had patent applications covering both the manufacture of tetraethyl lead by the ethyl bromide process and the use of tetraethyl lead as an antiknock compound. Standard had patent applications covering the ethyl chloride process. For Standard to develop its process commercially it would need a license from General Motors. For Du Pont to utilize the chloride process it would need a license from Standard. Apparently Du Pont as well as General Motors appreciated the immediate necessity of aggressive action and eventually of a three-way agreement if Du Pont was to maintain its position as a producer of tetraethyl lead.

General Motors' first move was to authorize Du Pont to increase its tetraethyl lead capacity by the ethyl bromide process some sixfold [84] and to notify Standard that it was too early to discuss the proposal that Standard be licensed to produce tetraethyl lead.[85] In a letter to Standard Sloan pointed out that making tetraethyl lead was still in a developmental stage, that the present price of tetraethyl lead had nothing to do with the ultimate price, and that large-scale production would greatly reduce costs. He declared, "[W]e have every reason to believe that we shall be able to ultimately reach a cost that will be entirely competitive."[86] Sloan expressed a desire to cooperate with Standard in these words: "We shall at all times, however, be glad to discuss with you the relative value of your process versus ours and after such analysis if it appears that your process has value, we shall be glad, in co-operation with you, to work out some plan which will be constructive and preserve all the equities in the case."[87] Meanwhile Irenee du Pont, president of Du Pont, advised Harrington of Du Pont's chemical department, with reference to the authorization for an increase in Du Pont's tetraethyl lead capacity: "It is essential that we treat this undertaking like a war order so far as making speed and producing the output, not only in order

---

84. Letter of Jan. 12, 1924 from General Motors to Du Pont, GTX 625, R. 614, 4347.
85. GTX 624, R. 614, 4342, 4345.
86. *Id.* at 4345-46.
87. *Id.* at 4346.

Workable Competition and Antitrust Policy

to fulfill the terms of the contract as to time but because every day saved means one day advantage over possible competition and bringing one day nearer the huge production which I think will come about."[88] On January 28, 1924, Sloan advised Irenee du Pont that Standard was urging that it be permitted to make tetraethyl lead, and he expressed in these words his disapproval of the idea:

> I feel, and have held right along, that in view of the fact that we are in the development stage we should not in any way discuss with these people anything to do with the manufacture of tetra ethyl lead. I question whether it will be good business from our standpoint for them to manufacture tetra ethyl lead and at the same time have such a large slice of the distribution on same. I do not say that I fear we will not get a square deal, but that naturally comes into my mind. Anyway, I do not think it is constructive. I feel that in the final analysis the du Pont Company can manufacture the material at the lowest cost plus a reasonable return and that under such a consideration there would only be a manufacturer's profit in it for the Standard Oil Company and that they could employ their capital to equal, if not better, advantage in their own business than in the manufacture of tetra ethyl lead and that our permitting them to get into that manufacture will be a disturbing influence and would throw an uncertainty on the whole situation that would not be constructive. If it develops that these people have a process which, due to the nature of same, it should be cheaper from the standpoint of manufacture, I personally would much rather obtain a license from them, pay for it and get the du Pont Company to use it in reducing the cost than I would to deal with the Standard Oil Company as a manufacturer.[89]

Despite Sloan's expressed distaste at doing business with Standard, the conflict between economy and personal preference was finally resolved by the formation of the Ethyl Gasoline Corporation, owned jointly by Standard and General Motors. Each company owned 50 per cent of the corporation's stock; each designated five of the ten members of the board of directors; and each granted to Ethyl exclusive licenses under their respective patent applications and exclusive rights under all future discoveries that might be patented, covering the field of antiknock compounds, until August 1, 1940.[90] The agreement covering the organization of the Ethyl Gasoline Corporation gave Ethyl a monopoly in the distribution of tetraethyl lead but not in its manufacture. Rather it provided that Ethyl was to buy it "in the open market at the lowest price at which it is offered." To permit competitive bidding Ethyl was authorized "to offer

88. GTX 626, R. 614, 4348.
89. GTX 622, R. 614, 4337, 4338–39.
90. GTX 668, R. 618, 4383–4426. See also 126 F. Supp. at 307.

Du Pont-General Motors and the Sherman Act

to instruct and license any bona fide probable supplier, including the Standard...."[91]

The agreement also provided, however, that "purchases shall be made from E. I. du Pont de Nemours & Company under the existing contract between it and General Motors ... until the expiration of said contract or until a substitute therefor is made direct with the Ethyl Company."[92] The agreement was reached in August 1924. Du Pont at this time was the only company making tetraethyl lead, and two months later Ethyl Gasoline Corporation made a contract with Du Pont authorizing it to erect a plant of 4,000,000 pounds capacity to make tetraethyl lead by the ethyl chloride process.[93] Meanwhile Standard had erected a 100 gallon-a-day plant at its Bayway, New Jersey, refinery to experiment in producing tetraethyl lead by the ethyl chloride process. Whether or not Standard or any other company eventually would have been authorized to produce a significant amount of tetraethyl lead under the agreement establishing Ethyl, had it not been for the Bayway disaster described below, is a matter of conjecture.[94]

THE BAYWAY DISASTER

The Bayway disaster, an epidemic of lead poisoning at Standard's small tetraethyl lead plant, occurred in October 1924. Of forty-five workmen, five died, while thirty-five others required medical aid. Widespread front-page publicity created both alarm and resentment throughout the country. The New Jersey Board of Health requested the suspension of tetraethyl lead manufacture and the temporary discontinuance of the sale of ethyl gasoline. A grand jury inquiry was begun as a basis for criminal action. The Philadelphia Health Board suspended distribution and the

---

91. GTX 668, R. 618, 4387.
92. *Id.*
93. GTX 675, R. 618, 4436–42. See also GM 87, R. 1263, 6826.
94. Howard of Standard Oil wrote that one purpose of the Bayway plant was "to afford experience basis for future construction on this process." GM 87, R. 1263, 6826, 6828. In June 1924, when Standard proposed to erect the plant, Sloan belittled the project to Irenee du Pont. He wrote, "For psychological reasons we should permit the Standard Oil Company of N. J. to expend $35,000 or $40,000 of their own money to experiment with the 100 gallon a day outfit...." GTX 661, R. 616, 4365, 4366. Irenee du Pont had given his approval to the project provided Sloan was "convinced that a check on prices by an independent plant is desirable." GTX 660, R. 616, 4363, 4364. In a letter to Irenee du Pont on July 8, 1924, Sloan explained, "Naturally, they [Standard Oil Co. of New Jersey] are looking at the situation a little differently so far as the cost of tetra-ethyl lead is concerned than we are." GTX 664, R. 617, 4371, 4372.

Workable Competition and Antitrust Policy

New York City health authorities forbade ethyl gasoline sales within their jurisdiction. Labor organizations urged prohibitive legislation, and a distinguished professor at Yale denounced the whole venture.[95] The Surgeon General of the United States appointed a committee to investigate the hazards involved in handling tetraethyl lead.[96]

Meanwhile Du Pont had not been indifferent either to the health problem in making tetraethyl lead, which the Bayway disaster had dramatized, or to the threat to commercialization which the disaster represented. Both Du Pont and General Motors had had their troubles in experimenting with tetraethyl lead. In the year before the Bayway disaster four men at Du Pont's Deepwater plant and two men at the General Motors laboratory had died from lead poisoning. Four others at Du Pont's Deepwater plant died from lead poisoning after the Bayway disaster.[97] But Du Pont had learned much about safety in handling tetraethyl lead, and apparently it never contemplated abandoning production.[98] On December 6, 1924, Irenee du Pont wrote Sloan: "After a year's operation we believe the manufacture of tetraethyl lead is far less poisonous than such an every-day commodity as anilin."[99] He urged Sloan to contact the Surgeon General of the United States and explain to him that the accident at Bayway took place in an experimental plant manned by workers unfamiliar with handling poisonous material, and that no public body had enough experience to lay down rules for the manufacture of tetraethyl lead as wise as those evolved from actual practice. He wrote Sloan again on June 8, 1925, urging that the Ethyl Gasoline Corporation push vigorously for an early report by the Surgeon General's committee.[100] In January 1926 the Surgeon General issued a report recommending that manufacturers making tetraethyl lead and blending the ethyl fluid take certain safety precautions but finding that

---

95. 1936 report by Wescott of Du Pont on the origin and development of the tetraethyl lead business, June 9, 1936, GTX 773, R. 632, 4663, 4690–91.

96. GTX 773, R. 632, 4700.

97. Exhibit "D" attached to the Wescott report, GTX 774, R. 4733, 4757.

98. The Du Pont tragedies were accompanied by far less publicity than the sudden calamity at Bayway. In the words of the Wescott report: "An outstandingly successful job appears to have been done by the Publicity Bureau of the Du Pont Company, however, in restraining the tendency toward sensationalism and exaggeration in the press accounts of the poison cases at Deepwater, especially with respect to the two deaths in February and two in March 1925, following shortly upon the heels of the great excitement attending the Standard Oil fatalities." GTX 773, *supra* note 95 at 4694n.

99. DP 99A, R. 901, 5871.

100. DP 99B, R. 901, 5873.

Du Pont-General Motors and the Sherman Act

the handling of tetraethyl lead by service station attendants and its use by automobile drivers constituted no appreciable hazard.[101] Four months later Ethyl was again selling tetraethyl lead and Du Pont was making it under a contract to supply Ethyl's entire requirements.

Du Pont emerged from these experiences with a triple prize. Ethyl reimbursed it for the cost of constructing the ethyl chloride plant (as compensation for Ethyl's inability to accept tetraethyl deliveries following the Bayway disaster) and at the same time conceded full ownership of the plant to Du Pont; Ethyl paid it $160,000 as reimbursement of all its research expense on improvements of the commercial development of the ethyl chloride process; and Ethyl did not require Du Pont under its 1926 contract to assign patent rights or give technical information on improvements to Ethyl.[102] Du Pont remained the sole producer of tetraethyl lead until the expiration of the patents on December 31, 1947.

Such are the relevant facts. From them it is difficult to conclude that Du Pont's ownership of General Motors stock and its influence in General Motors' management did not play an important role in Du Pont's twenty-five-year monopoly of tetraethyl lead production. They are not the only factors, but they are sufficient.

KINETIC CHEMICALS, INC.[103]

The commercial production of Freon as a refrigerant by the organization of Kinetic Chemicals, Inc., affords a clearer illustration of Du Pont's influence on General Motors policy regarding its chemical discoveries than does tetraethyl lead. It will be recalled that soon after Du Pont acquired a stock interest in General Motors it tried to get a formal agreement with General Motors covering relations between the two companies in the chemical field. As previously indicated, the issue was disposed of in November 1922 when Pierre S. du Pont, president of General Motors and chairman of Du Pont's board, advised Lammot du Pont, vice president of Du Pont, that it did "not seem possible" at that time to institute any general plan of cooperation in chemical research work, but that as problems came up "special arrangements with reference to each should be

---

101. GM 262, R. 7376–99.
102. Wescott report, GTX 773, *supra* note 95, at 4697, 4749. A business magazine recounting the story of Du Pont eight years later put it succinctly: "Tetraethyl lead was a present from General Motors." "Du Pont II: A Management and Its Philosophy," Fortune, December 1934, p. 87.
103. Statements of fact in this section are based on the district court's opinion, 126 F. Supp. at 313–16, unless otherwise indicated.

Workable Competition and Antitrust Policy

made between the two Companies."[104] Such a problem arose in 1929. In 1927 General Motors had assigned to Midgley of its research staff the problem of discovering a safer refrigerant than sulfur dioxide, then being used by General Motors and its competitors. By late 1928 Midgley had solved the problem by the discovery of Freon 12, an organic fluorine compound. After protecting the discovery with a patent Midgley continued work through 1929 and into 1930 on the development of a commercial process for making it. Frigidaire Division of General Motors erected a semi-commercial plant in the winter of 1929-1930.

Biechler, general manager of Frigidaire, who with Kettering and Pratt had suggested the project, recommended that General Motors proceed with production. Pratt, who had been made vice-president of General Motors under Pierre S. du Pont's presidency, opposed this and so did Sloan.[105] Thereafter Pratt suggested to Harrington of Du Pont that General Motors and Du Pont jointly form a company to make and sell Freon. Pratt soon expanded this idea to include other chemicals discovered by General Motors that such a company could manufacture.[106] The result was the organization of Kinetic Chemicals, Inc., 51 per cent of whose stock Du Pont owned and 49 per cent of which General Motors owned. The General Motors finance committee (of which Donaldson Brown, Carpenter, Pierre S. du Pont, H. F. du Pont, Irenee du Pont, Lammot du Pont, Raskob, and Sloan—all Du Pont directors—constituted a majority) approved the formal agreement of August 27, 1930, organizing Kinetic. Regarding this action the minutes of the finance committee stated:

It was felt that because of the experience of the duPont Company in the chemical field that it is to the interest of General Motors Corporation to arrange with the duPont Company for the commercial development and production of

---

104. See p. 343, *supra*.

105. In opposing Biechler Pratt stated: "It is quite a fundamental step for us to start General Motors in chemical manufacture. Up to this time we have more or less elected to confine ourselves to the mechanical side of manufacture and I do not want to depart from this until very thorough consideration has been given to all of the factors involved." Letter of March 15, 1930, GTX 839, R. 639, 4976. See also 126 F. Supp. at 313.

106. In commenting on a memorandum prepared by Du Pont on the organization and operation of the proposed company Pratt emphasized the desirability of covering all other chemical discoveries that General Motors might make. On June 12, 1930, he wrote to E. G. Robinson, general manager of the Du Pont dyestuffs department: "In addition I would like to see the charter provide that the company could manufacture any chemicals that might originate in the laboratories of General Motors Corporation, and exclude any chemicals that originated in the Du Pont developments except Du Pont developments that flowed out of General Motors de-developments." GTX 842, R. 639, 4979.

these chemicals rather than for us to undertake the organization of the necessary personnel, technical staff, etc. for their production; and in order to give the duPont Company an incentive for the most efficient development of these chemicals it was considered mutually advantageous that the duPont Company should have the right to subscribe to 51% of the stock of the Kinetic Chemicals, Inc. Under this agreement a royalty will be paid to General Motors for the right to use the inventions transferred to Kinetic Chemicals, Inc., as covered more fully in the agreement.[107]

The agreement not only authorized Kinetic Chemicals to make and sell refrigerants but provided that "future chemical developments . . . originating in the laboratories of General [Motors], or its subsidiaries, shall be offered by General [Motors] to the New Company on such terms as may be mutually agreed upon, and if after six months the New Company shall elect not to exploit such new chemical developments, the General [Motors] shall be free to dispose of the same elsewhere."[108]

In providing that General Motors should turn over to a Du Pont-controlled company all chemicals originating in General Motors laboratories the Kinetic contract went further than had the general chemical agreement which Du Pont proposed in 1920.[109] That agreement would have given General Motors full property rights in Du Pont's improvements of processes, methods, products, or materials previously used by General Motors and would have given Du Pont only a half interest in all other developments of chemicals originating in General Motors laboratories. Moreover, neither General Motors nor Du Pont could have disposed of such inventions without the consent of the other. By contrast, the 1930 agreement gave Kinetic full exploitation rights to all chemical discoveries that General Motors might make.[110]

Except for Freon 12 and Freon 114, another refrigerant also developed in General Motors' laboratory, General Motors turned no other chemical over to Kinetic for development, and the provision for future chemical discoveries was canceled by agreement in 1945 upon the advice of General Motors counsel that it was "not enforceable."[111] But in turning over the

107. GM 238, R. 1496, 7301, 7302. See also 126 F. Supp. at 314.
108. GTX 850, R. 641, 4992, 4994.
109. See p. 342, *supra*.
110. Pratt in explaining the purpose of this provision to Lammot du Pont in July 1931 wrote: "To summarize, as far as I am concerned I hope to see General Motors Corporation utilize to the fullest extent the chemical experience of the Du Pont Company in manufacturing any chemical compounds that General Motors laboratories may discover, where there is a possibility of commercialization." GTX 899, R. 652, 5129, 5133. See also 126 F. Supp. at 314.
111. GTX 883, R. 647, 5062, 5073; DP 133, R. 1814, 5945. See also 126 F. Supp. at 315.

Workable Competition and Antitrust Policy

commercial development of Freon to a company in which Du Pont owned the controlling interest General Motors opened to Du Pont the whole field of fluorine compounds for commercial development, an opportunity which Du Pont proceeded to exploit.[112] In 1945 Du Pont's development department advised the executive committee that some of Du Pont's own developments in the field of fluorine compounds might sooner or later have to be licensed to Kinetic on a royalty-free basis, and it recommended that Du Pont buy General Motors' 49 per cent stock interest in the company.[113] The development department's report stated:

> The same desire of du Pont to have unrestricted direction of developments in important fields which has led to acquiring minority interests in other jointly owned activities, is just as pertinent in this case.
>
> . . . .
>
> Amendments to clarify the du Pont-General Motors agreement might be attempted, but such amendment would not be nearly so satisfactory as 100% ownership of Kinetic by du Pont, so that it appears desirable to secure the Executive Committee's approval to approach General Motors to explore the possibility of acquiring the minority interest.[114]

Negotiations for the purchase of General Motors' interest in Kinetic began in 1948 but had not been completed when the government brought its antitrust suit, and the government's complaint asked for divestiture of Kinetic from Du Pont. In 1949, however, the Department of Justice assented to Du Pont's purchase of General Motors' interest, and on January 1, 1950, General Motors sold it for $10,000,000.

A Combination in Restraint of Trade?

Counsel for defendants contended that these several transactions—General Motors' purchase of Du Pont products, its turning over the manufacture of tetraethyl lead to Du Pont, and the organization of

---

112. In November 1944 Donaldson Brown in a report to the General Motors policy committee declared: "The field of use of fluorine compounds has apparently just been scratched." GTX 883, R. 647, 5062, 5087. Freon was the one example of a scientific discovery in one area that leads to striking developments in another that was cited by Samuel G. Baker, general manager of Du Pont's organic chemicals department, in a speech made on Oct. 24, 1957, at the Pacific Northwest Personnel Management Conference, Seattle, Wash. Dr. Midgley of General Motors might have found the following statement in that speech somewhat surprising: "Chemists *associated with* the Du Pont Company developed a safe, nontoxic, nonexplosive refrigerant called 'Freon.'" *Dimensions of Technological Change* (published by Du Pont), p. 5. Emphasis added.
113. GTX 886, R. 648, 5093–108.
114. GTX 886, R. 648, 5106.

Du Pont-General Motors and the Sherman Act

Kinetic Chemicals—were arm's-length transactions involving no element of coercion, and the district court agreed. Responsible General Motors officials in their testimony had laid a basis for this finding. In truth a careful analysis of the circumstances surrounding each of these groups of transactions warrants the conclusion that coercion was not involved. And indeed why should it have been? With Du Pont owning from 23 to 38 per cent of General Motors' stock and with Du Pont officials sitting on its board and constituting a majority of its important committees, no coercion was called for. The contracts covering the production of tetraethyl lead and the organization of Kinetic Chemicals, Inc., involved executive decisions. Du Pont officials, who were also General Motors officials, participated in making them.

Section 1 of the Sherman Act prohibits all combinations that restrain trade. It would seem that the relationship between General Motors and Du Pont was such that Du Pont had an advantage in getting business from General Motors and an advantage over potential rivals in exploiting chemicals originating in General Motors' laboratories. The documents speak for themselves on this issue, and some of them speak a different language from that of the witnesses. The witnesses had a stake in their testimony, and they would have been less than human if they had not unconsciously evaluated the influences which affected their decisions in the light of their stake. If in fact Du Pont's ownership of General Motors stock did give it an advantage over its rivals in the sale of products to General Motors and in the exploitation of General Motors' chemical discoveries, Du Pont's acquisition of General Motors stock constituted a combination in restraint of trade. This is implicit in the lower court's opinion and explicit in the Supreme Court's. The lower court analyzed the various transactions with this thought in mind: Did Du Pont's ownership of stock in General Motors give Du Pont an advantage in dealing with General Motors? The court found that it did not, all of the relevant transactions being at arm's length. I believe that it did.

Du Pont's ownership of General Motors stock also contributed to Du Pont's market position in certain respects that the case does not reveal. Some of these may be difficult to bring under the prohibitions of the Sherman Act, but they are clearly adverse to the functioning of a competitive economy. During the years 1920–1956 General Motors paid Du Pont a net total after taxes of $1,440,000,000 in dividends, an amount equal to 61 per cent of Du Pont's total 1956 assets.[115] This has enabled Du Pont

115. Reports on the Du Pont Company, *Moody's Industrials*, 1921–1957. In the same period the value of Du Pont's holdings as carried on its books rose to $762,-

to pay liberal annual dividends to its own stockholders and at the same time, without recourse to the capital market, carry forward the expansion program initiated with its World War I gains. This in turn has contributed to the relative position it occupies in the chemical markets generally and to the monopoly or near-monopoly position it occupies in the production of special products.[116] I believe the interests of a competitive society would have been better served without such concentration of production.

As previously indicated, the Supreme Court reversed the district court by a four-to-two decision, with three judges not participating. In doing so the Court, to the surprise of everyone who had been active in the case, did not find that Du Pont's ownership of General Motors stock violated the Sherman Act, under which the case had been primarily tried, but that it violated old Section 7 of the Clayton Act, to which the prosecution had attached little importance in either the development of the testimony or the presentation of arguments.

In applying Section 7 to this case the Court laid down three new principles: (1) Section 7 is applicable to vertical as well as horizontal mergers.[117] (2) "[A] violation of [Section 7] has occurred if, as a result

100,000; hence Du Pont's total gain from its General Motors stock would amount to 93 per cent of its 1956 assets. The dividends have represented an annual average return after taxes of 68 per cent on Du Pont's investment in General Motors, which after purchases and sales (to Managers Securities Company) was about $57,000,000 in 1925 and remained at that figure throughout subsequent years. I know of no investment by Du Pont in the production of chemicals that has paid off so handsomely. Its investment in cellophane, in the production of which it had a monopoly and which it sold in a rapidly expanding market, paid it an average rate of return of 34.4 per cent on operating investment during the period 1924–1950. Stocking and Mueller, "The Cellophane Case and the New Competition," 45 Am. Econ. Rev. 29, 59 (1955).

116. In 1948, the most recent year for which figures are available from various antitrust cases, Du Pont had the following percentages of total domestic sales: nylon yarn, 100 per cent; Freon refrigerants, 90+ per cent; cellophane films, 78.4 per cent; cellulose bands, 64.1 per cent; urea, 50 per cent; methanol antifreeze, 50 per cent; cellulose sponges, 37.4 per cent; explosives, 33.4 per cent; tetraethyl lead, 33 per cent; and titanium, 32 per cent. Mueller, *op cit. supra* note 6, at 358. Where Du Pont has discovered these products in its own laboratories, as in the case of nylon yarn, the benefit to society is obvious ("Better Things for Better Living through Chemistry"). Whether and when such products would have been discovered by others had Du Pont not discovered them is a matter of conjecture, but where Du Pont has obtained them from others the net benefit to society is not so clear. Du Pont's control of capital without recourse to the capital market has probably insured Du Pont's developing the products rather than some other chemical company.

117. Hitherto the Court has held that § 7 is not applicable where the acquiring and the acquired companies are not in competition with each other. International Shoe Co. v. FTC, 280 U.S. 291, 298 (1930); Thatcher Mfg. Co. v. FTC, 272 U.S. 554, 560 (1926).

Du Pont-General Motors and the Sherman Act

of the acquisition, there was *at the time of suit* a reasonable likelihood of a monopoly of any line of commerce."[118] (3) The relevant market in determining the existence of monopoly or a tendency thereto is a narrow one. By finding that the purchases of automobile makers constituted the relevant market for the finishes and fabrics that Du Pont threatened to monopolize, the Court rejected a principle which it had accepted in the *Cellophane* case.[119]

The decision seems to its critics to threaten the legal status of stock acquisitions in one corporation by another even though made long ago and primarily for investment. It also raises once more the threat to vertical integration initially raised by the first *Yellow Cab* case [120] but since narrowed and clarified in the *Paramount* [121] and the *Columbia Steel* cases.[122] Worse than these dangers, it may seem to corporate lawyers the opening gun of a wholesale attack on mergers. I do not believe that this fear is justified. In the first place, the Court rejected the contention that Du Pont had acquired General Motors stock merely as an investment. It accepted the pronouncements of Raskob and other Du Pont officials, together with the significance of the subsequent course of dealings, as evidence that Du Pont regarded its General Motors stock as an instrument for increasing its

---

118. 353 U.S. 586, 592 (1957). Emphasis added. The Court also said: "We repeat, that the test of a violation of section 7 is whether, at the time of suit, there is a reasonable probability that the acquisition is likely to result in the condemned restraints. The conclusion upon this record is inescapable that such likelihood was proved as to this acquisition. The fire that was kindled in 1917 continues to smolder. It burned briskly to force the ties that bind the General Motors market to Du Pont, and if it has quieted down, it remains hot, and, from past performance, is likely at any time to blaze and make the fusion complete." *Id.* at 607.

119. In the *Cellophane* case, because Du Pont cellophane met the rivalry of other flexible wrapping materials in the total sales of which Du Pont cellophane constituted a relatively small part, the Court found that Du Pont had no monopoly. In short, the relevant market for cellophane was the whole market for flexible wrapping materials. In the *Du Pont-General Motors* case the Court took account of the contention of counsel for General Motors that in 1947 Du Pont's sales of finishes to General Motors represented only 3.5 per cent of all sales of finishes to industrial users, and that its fabrics sales to General Motors were only 1.6 per cent of the total sales of the same type of fabrics. About this the Court said: "Determination of the relevant market is a necessary predicate to a finding of a violation of the Clayton Act because the threatened monopoly must be one which will substantially lessen competition 'within the area of effective competition.' Substantiality can be determined only in terms of the market affected. The record shows that automotive finishes and fabrics have sufficient peculiar characteristics and uses to constitute them products sufficiently distinct from all other finishes and fabrics to make them a 'line of commerce' within the meaning of the Clayton Act." *Id.* at 593-94.

120. United States v. Yellow Cab Co., 332 U.S. 218, 227 (1947).
121. United States v. Paramount Pictures, Inc., 334 U.S. 131, 173-74 (1948).
122. United States v. Columbia Steel Co., 334 U.S. 495, 524-27 (1948).

sales of finishes and fabrics. In the second place, the Court took note of the fact that General Motors had come to occupy a dominant position in the sale of automobiles (more than 40 per cent at the opening of the suit and almost 50 per cent in 1955) and as such accounted for almost half of all purchases of automobile finishes and fabrics. In the third place, it found that Du Pont was the largest single seller of finishes and fabrics to General Motors and that it sold more of these to General Motors than to all other automobile makers. Few corporate stock ownerships are likely to duplicate these conditions.

Although I do not share the fear that the *Du Pont–General Motors* case affords a basis for wholesale onslaught against mergers, I think there is much merit in the criticism of one commentator who said, "Had the majority Justices believed the findings of the District Court to be clearly erroneous, it would seem that the appropriate remedy would have been for them to have called a 'spade' a 'spade' and thereupon to have set the facts aside." [123] In short, I believe the public interest in a competitive society would have been better served had the Supreme Court found that Du Pont's acquisition of stock in General Motors was a combination in restraint of trade, and I believe ample evidence existed for such a finding.

123. William F. Rogers, "U.S. v. Du Pont—A Judicial Revision of Section 7," 2 Antitrust Bulletin 577, 582 (1957).

9
Economic Change and the Sherman Act: Some Reflections on "Workable Competition"

In *Appalachian Coals, Inc.*,[1] Chief Justice Hughes characterized the Sherman Act as a "charter of freedom" with "a generality and adaptability comparable to that found to be desirable in constitutional provisions."[2] In making this pronouncement the Chief Justice was laying the basis for a decision more consistent with the temper of the times than with legal precedent. The Great Depression has laid low the national economy. Millions were unemployed, national income had shrunk, corporate profits had disappeared, labor unions had disintegrated, farmers were losing their farms, business firms faced bankruptcy, competition had become cutthroat, confidence in private enterprise had waned, fear and even hunger stalked the land. Businessmen, labor leaders, and politicians were insisting that competition must give way to cooperation if a business system was to be salvaged. A sick economy had aggravated the sickness of an industry. The Supreme Court in 1933 found Appalachian Coals, Inc., to be a cooperative sales agency designed to "foster fair competitive opportunities" and "thus to aid in relieving a depressed industry and in reviving commerce by placing competition upon a sounder basis."[3]

Seven years later, with the unlamented National Recovery Administration a matter of history, with New Dealers and the public losing confidence in "industrial self-government," with politicians and students of industrial structure disturbed by "the concentration of economic power," the Court condemned as unlawful a cooperative gasoline-buying program by the leading oil companies designed to raise and stabilize gasoline prices

Note: Reprinted from the *Virginia Law Review*, Vol. 44, No. 4 (May 1958).

1. Appalachian Coals, Inc. v. United States, 288 U.S. 344 (1933).
2. *Id.* at 359–60.
3. *Id.* at 374.

Workable Competition and Antitrust Policy

by insuring an orderly marketing of "distress" gasoline [4]—an experiment that had won the unofficial blessing of NRA administrators at the time it was inaugurated. While any competent law student might differentiate these two cases on the basis of their facts, the opinions reflect less the logic of the law than the temper of the times.

Judges, like other people, cannot dissociate themselves from the institutional matrix in which they have their being. This sociological principle is illustrated by a line of decisions handed down by the Supreme Court during the next decade. The climate of public opinion in which these decisions were formulated had its origin during the post-NRA and early World War II years. It was characterized by an increasing fear of industrial concentration. Berle and Means in 1932 had dramatized the extent of and trends toward industrial concentration in this country in their provocative and discerning analysis of *The Modern Corporation and Private Property*. They found that the 200 largest nonfinancial corporations, representing less than one-tenth of 1 per cent of all nonfinancial corporations, controlled approximately 50 per cent of all corporate wealth in the United States, 38 per cent of all business wealth, and 22 per cent of all national wealth.[5] They found that in the period studied the percentage of corporate wealth owned by the 200 largest corporations had increased significantly, and they estimated that by 1950, at the 1909–29 rate of increase, the 200 largest corporations would own more than 70 per cent of all corporate wealth; at the more rapid rate of increase of the six years ending in 1929, the 200 largest corporations would own 85 per cent of all corporate assets by 1950.[6]

The New Deal, which initially made economic planning a governmental responsibility, had at the same time nourished suspicion if not hostility toward big business. The New Deal's failure through political management to solve the problems of unemployment and to raise national income to satisfactory levels ultimately raised doubts among its leaders about the adequacy of centralized controls to make an economic system work. President Roosevelt, in campaigning for re-election in 1936, had noted the improved economic outlook by boasting, "We planned it that way." Only two years later, after the economic setback of 1937–1938, in recommending to Congress the authorization of the Temporary National

---

4. United States v. Socony-Vacuum Oil Co., 310 U.S. 150 (1940).
5. Adolf A. Berle, Jr., and Gardiner C. Means, *The Modern Corporation and Private Property* (New York: Macmillan, 1932), p. 32.
6. *Id.* at 40.

Economic Change and the Sherman Act

Economic Committee, Roosevelt expressed his skepticism of centralized control of industry in these words:

Private enterprise is ceasing to be free enterprise and is becoming a cluster of private collectivisms;

. . . .

No one suggests that we return to the hand loom or hand forge. . . . But modern efficient mass production is not furthered by a central control which destroys competition between industrial plants each capable of efficient mass production while operating as separate units.

. . . .

The power of a few to manage the economic life of the Nation must be diffused among the many or be transferred to the public and its democratically responsible government.[7]

But to the President governmental control was not an attractive alternative. About it he said:

Those people, in and out of the halls of government, who encourage the growing restriction of competition either by active efforts or by passive resistance to sincere attempts to change the trend are shouldering a terrific responsibility. Consciously or unconsciously they are . . . either working for control of the Government itself by business and finance or . . . a growing concentration of public power in the Government. . . .[8]

As a first step in coping with what he regarded as a dangerous concentration of economic power, the President proposed to establish a temporary national economic committee to investigate its extent and causes and to propose remedies. The TNEC, whose investigations extended over a three-year period, reflected not merely Presidential but a national concern about the decline of competition. Congress appropriated $1,070,000 for its activities and voted larger appropriations for the Antitrust Division of the Department of Justice. Under Thurman Arnold's leadership the division undertook its most aggressive campaign against conspiracies, combinations in restraint of trade, and unlawful monopolies.

Oligopoly in Theory and in Antitrust

Meanwhile economic theory had laid a logical basis for political concern about the concentration of economic power. According to the conclusions of neoclassical theory a competitive industrial structure insures an economical allocation of resources and a distribution of income in accordance

---

7. *Message from the President of the United States*, S. Doc. No. 173, 75th Cong., 3d Sess. 3, 6 (1938).
8. *Id.* at 6.

Workable Competition and Antitrust Policy

with the principle of marginal productivity. The forces of a free market—Adam Smith's "invisible hand"—economists had said would harness the selfish interests of businessmen and so guide them as to promote the public welfare. But the theory of monopolistic competition as presented in this country by Edward Chamberlin [9] and in England by Joan Robinson [10] in the early 1930's challenged the adequacy of market forces to protect the public welfare in industries where sellers are few and products standardized. Chamberlin in his discussion of oligopolistic pricing concluded on a basis of his rigid assumptions that if informed and rational oligopolists take account of the indirect as well as the direct consequences of their decisions, they will without conspiring behave like monopolists.[11] Other things equal, in oligopolistic markets consumers will pay more and get less than under competition. This disquieting conclusion and the doctrine that supported it quickly got into the textbooks and eventually had an impact on the law.

The leading cases that reflect the widespread fear of industrial concentration and monopoly during this era are *United States v. Aluminum Company of America*[12] and *American Tobacco Company v. United States*.[13] Judge Learned Hand, in deciding that Alcoa possessed an unlawful monopoly, rejected the defenses which more recent decisions have found alluring. He was unimpressed by the fact that substitutes might serve as a check on Alcoa's power to exploit the market. "There are indeed limits to [a monopolist's] power; substitutes are available for almost all commodities, and to raise the price enough is to evoke them." [14] He found unconvincing the argument that imports, actual and potential, insured adequate consumer protection.

It is entirely consistent with the evidence that it was the threat of greater foreign imports which kept "Alcoa's" prices where they were, and prevented it

9. *The Theory of Monopolistic Competition* (Cambridge: Harvard University Press, 1933).
10. *The Economics of Imperfect Competition* (London: Macmillan, 1933).
11. Chamberlin in a later article protested against the identification of oligopoly theory with "the" monopoly solution, saying this is only one among other possible solutions and that the theory "yields no certain conclusion as to what will happen, given the bare minimum of information that the number of sellers is small." "Une Formulation Nouvelle de la Théorie Concurrence Monopolistique," in Economie Appliquée, Archives de l'Institut de Science Economique Appliquée, V (1952), 192, quoted in Willard D. Arant, "Competition of the Few Among the Many," 70 Q. J. Econ. 327, 343 (1956).
12. 148 F.2d 416 (2d Cir. 1945), *new petitions considered*, 91 F. Supp. 333 (S.D.N.Y. 1950).
13. 328 U.S. 781 (1946).
14. United States v. Aluminum Co., 148 F.2d 416–26 (2d Cir. 1945).

Economic Change and the Sherman Act

from exploiting its advantage as sole domestic producer; indeed, it is hard to resist the conclusion that potential imports did put a "ceiling" upon those prices. Nevertheless, within the limits afforded by the tariff and the cost of transportation, "Alcoa" was free to raise its prices as it chose, since it was free from domestic competition, save as it drew other metals into the market as substitutes.[15]

Judge Hand rejected good performance as a justification for monopoly under the Sherman Act. As he put it, "[I]t is no excuse for 'monopolizing' a market that the monopoly has not been used to extract from the consumer more than a 'fair' profit."[16] He rejected the doctrine of specific intent as essential to a finding of monopoly. Monopolists ordinarily are not sleepwalkers; they know where they are going. Unless they have monopoly thrust upon them, they have monopolized within the meaning of Section 2 of the Sherman Act. Judge Hand brought Section 2 of the Act into harmony with Section 1 by recognizing that "the vice of the restrictive contracts and of monopoly is really one, it is the denial to commerce of the supposed protection of competition";[17] and he promulgated the doctrine that it was the existence of monopoly, when achieved by deliberate business policies, not the abuse of monopoly, that the law forbade. Rejecting the rule of reason of the 1911 *Standard Oil* and *American Tobacco* cases,[18] he declared that Congress "did not condone 'good trusts' and condemn 'bad' ones; it forbade all."[19]

The *Aluminum* decision was a vigorous affirmation of the public's distrust of the concentration of economic power as such; but it was the second *American Tobacco* decision that in addition to reflecting community hostility toward industrial concentration seemed to bring the law on monopoly into harmony with the Chamberlinian doctrine of oligopolistic pricing. A federal jury had convicted the "Big Three" cigarette makers —the American Tobacco Company, Liggett & Myers Tobacco Company, and R. J. Reynolds Tobacco Company—of having violated Sections 1 and 2 of the Sherman Act. The issue on appeal to the Supreme Court was the meaning of "monopolize" as used in Section 2 of the Act. In reviewing the evidence the Court was impressed by the combined size of the defendants. Together they had continuously accounted for more than 68 per cent and usually for more than 75 per cent of the national production

---

15. *Id.* at 426.
16. *Id.* at 427.
17. *Id.* at 428.
18. Standard Oil Co. v. United States, 221 U.S. 1 (1911); United States v. American Tobacco Co., 221 U.S. 106 (1911).
19. United States v. Aluminum Co., 148 F.2d 416, 427 (2d Cir. 1945).

of cigarettes. In the production of burley blend cigarettes their dominance was even more marked. Clearly the defendants had earned "the title of the 'Big Three.' . . . [T]he smallest of them at all times showed over twice the production of the largest outsider. . . . [C]omparative size on this great scale inevitably increased the power of these three to dominate all phases of their industry." [20] Quoting *United States v. Swift & Company* the Court said, "'Size carries with it an opportunity for abuse that is not to be ignored when the opportunity is proved to have been utilized in the past.'" [21]

Nor was the size of the Big Three reflected solely in production figures. Their combined net worth had risen from $277,000,000 in 1912 to over $551,000,000 in 1939. In each of the years 1937, 1938, and 1939 American, Liggett & Myers, and Reynolds had together spent over $40,000,000 for advertising. Tremendous expenditures for advertising and the large sums required for inventories and federal taxes tended to prevent the rise of potential competition. The power of the Big Three was reflected in buying tobacco as well as in selling cigarettes. Together they bought from 50 to 80 per cent of the domestic flue-cured tobacco, and in the burley belt of Kentucky and Tennessee their percentage of total purchases was even larger. The record produced no evidence of a written agreement among the defendants, but it indicated that in both buying tobacco and selling cigarettes they followed a common course of action. They all paid the same price for their preferred tobacco grades, and each adjusted its cigarette prices to that of the price leader's price. When, after having raised cigarette prices while the prices of raw tobacco were steadily declining, they lost ground to the so-called economy brand cigarettes, they began a tobacco-buying program that forced up the price of cheaper tobacco used in economy brands, and they cut the price of their own standard brand cigarettes. The Supreme Court concluded that the Big Three had both the power to exclude competitors and the power to control prices, and it confirmed the jury's finding of a criminal conspiracy to monopolize the sale of cigarettes.

Because the Court recognized a common course of action as sufficient evidence of conspiracy, some discriminating students of the law concluded that the Court had brought the law on monopoly into harmony with the theory of oligopolistic pricing. On the significance of the *Tobacco* decision

---

20. American Tobacco Co. v. United States, 328 U.S. 781, 796 (1946). Statements of fact about the tobacco companies are taken from the opinion.
21. 286 U.S. 106, 116 (1932), quoted *id.*

Economic Change and the Sherman Act

Eugene V. Rostow, a distinguished professor of law, trained also in economics, concluded:

When three companies produce so large a percentage of market supply, that fact alone is almost sufficient evidence that the statute is violated. Ruthless and predatory behavior need not be shown. The actual elimination of small competitors is unnecessary. . . . Parallel action, price leadership, a reliance on advertising rather than price competition as a means of inducing changes in each seller's share of the market, and, above all, size—the market advantage of a small number of large sellers or buyers—these are now key points to be proved in a case of monopoly, or of combination in restraint of trade. . . . Painstaking search for scraps of evidence with a conspiratorial atmosphere are [sic] no longer necessary. . . . [D]ecisive elements are the power to assert a degree of control over price and output *in the market as a whole*. . . .[22]

An equally discerning economist, William H. Nicholls, saw the *Tobacco* decision as

a legal milestone in the social control of oligopoly. By permitting the inference of illegal conspiracy from detailed similarity of behavior and by shifting attention from the abuse of power to its mere existence (as indicated by degree of market control), the courts have at last brought oligopolistic industries within reach of successful prosecution under the antitrust laws.[23]

THE FEDERAL TRADE COMMISSION AND OLIGOPOLY

While judges and economists, both influenced by and influencing the temper of the times, were thus beginning to conceive the monopoly problem in similar terms, administrators, too, reflected the current skepticism about the compatibility of a market of few sellers with effective competition. During the late 1930's and early 1940's the Federal Trade Commission inaugurated a number of proceedings against associated activities by trade rivals designed to lessen the severity of competition among themselves.[24] Frequently the evidence of conspiracy was circumstantial.

---

22. Rostow, "The New Sherman Act: A Positive Instrument of Progress," 14 U. Chi. L. Rev. 567, 585 (1947). Emphasis added.

23. Nicholls, "The Tobacco Case of 1946," 39 Am. Econ. Rev. 284, 296 (1949).

24. Crown Mfrs. Ass'n, 45 F.T.C. 89 (1948), aff'd, 176 F.2d 974 (4th Cir. 1949); Rigid Steel Conduit Ass'n, 38 F.T.C. 534 (1944), aff'd sub nom. Triangle Conduit & Cable Co. v. FTC, 168 F.2d 175 (7th Cir. 1948), aff'd per curiam sub nom. Clayton Mark & Co. v. FTC, 336 U.S. 956 (1949); National Crepe Paper Ass'n, 38 F.T.C. 282 (1944), aff'd sub nom. Ft. Howard Paper Co. v. FTC, 156 F.2d 899 (7th Cir. 1946); Milk and Ice Cream Can Institute, 37 F.T.C. 419 (1943), aff'd, 152 F.2d 478 (7th Cir. 1946); Cement Institute, 37 F.T.C. 87 (1943), order set aside, 157 F.2d 533 (7th Cir. 1946), rev'd, 333 U.S. 683 (1948); United States Maltsters Ass'n, 35 F.T.C. 797 (1942), modified, 37 F.T.C.

Workable Competition and Antitrust Policy

Business rivals followed common patterns of behavior without written agreements to do so and sometimes without a well-defined mechanism for insuring that they would. A common experience with the untoward consequences of price cutting where sellers were few contributed to behavior patterns calculated to insure identical pricing at stabilized levels. The Federal Trade Commission sought to ban such vaguely defined collective action among trade rivals, which it regarded as not consistent with effective competition, by broad and vaguely worded orders.

In 1941 the Commission found that the market analysis and business counselling program of the Salt Producers Association not only had a dangerous tendency to hinder competition but had prevented effective competition in selling salt.[25] It accordingly ordered association members to cease and desist from "entering into, continuing, or carrying out, or directing, instigating, or cooperating in, any *common course of action,* mutual agreement, combination, or conspiracy, to fix or maintain the prices of salt" or regulate its production.[26] On appeal by respondents and objection to the Commission's banning a "common course of action" by the salt producers, the appellate court modified the Commission's order to prohibit "any *planned* common course of action" by the defendants with respect to the matters specified in the Commission's orders.[27] Similarly in the *Cement Institute* case [28] the Commission ordered the respondents to refrain from any "planned common course of action" to sell cement according to the multiple basing point delivered-price system or to follow the practices with which the industry had implemented it. In the *Rigid Steel Conduit* case [29] the Commission developed further its doctrine of implied conspiracy or conscious parallelism of action. It charged that the makers of rigid steel conduit had conspired to use the basing point system, that each respondent had used it knowing that his rivals did so, and that such practices "have a dangerous tendency to, and have actually, hindered . . . and prevented competition in price in the sale of 'conduit.'" [30] The

342 (1943), *aff'd,* 152 F.2d 161 (7th Cir. 1945); Salt Producers Ass'n, 34 F.T.C. 38 (1941), *modified and aff'd,* 134 F.2d 354 (7th Cir. 1943).

25. Salt Producers Ass'n, 34 F.T.C. 38 (1941), *modified and aff'd,* 134 F.2d 354 (7th Cir. 1943).

26. *Id.* at 55. Emphasis added.

27. Salt Producers Ass'n v. FTC, 134 F.2d 354, 357 (7th Cir. 1943). Emphasis added.

28. Cement Institute, 37 F.T.C. 87, 260 (1943), *aff'd,* 333 U.S. 683 (1948).

29. Rigid Steel Conduit Ass'n, 38 F.T.C. 534 (1944), *aff'd sub nom.* Triangle Conduit & Cable Co. v. FTC, 168 F.2d 175 (7th Cir. 1948), *aff'd per curiam sub nom.* Clayton Mark & Co. v. FTC, 336 U.S. 956 (1949).

30. 38 F.T.C. at 550.

Economic Change and the Sherman Act

Commission not only ordered the respondents to quit conspiring or following a "planned common course of action," but ordered each respondent individually to quit quoting or selling rigid steel conduit at prices calculated on a basing point system "for the purpose or with the effect of systematically matching delivered price quotations. . . ."[31]

The Federal Trade Commission, whether deliberately or not, was thus bringing its findings and orders into closer accord with the theory of oligopolistic pricing. It aimed at banning monopolistic behavior that apparently resulted from sellers' recognition of their mutual interdependence in markets where they were few in number.

Although these decisions brought legal doctrine somewhat closer to contemporary economic logic, they did not solve the basic problem with which the judges and administrators were concerned: how to make competition effective in markets of few sellers. The decisions banned the monopolistic practices but left unmodified the industrial structure that may have shaped the practices. If the pricing practices of American Tobacco, Reynolds, and Liggett & Myers were consistent with independent non-conspiratorial decision-making in a market dominated by three companies; if a price cut by one necessarily engendered a price cut by all without any significant redistribution of or increase in the sale of cigarettes; if the business interests of each were served by following a price increase inaugurated by any one—price leadership was almost an inevitable business practice, and the finding of criminal conspiracy followed by nominal fines was mild punishment, not a basic remedy. Moreover, it left the executives of the several tobacco companies puzzled and disturbed—puzzled because they did not know just how to protect their separate business interests without following common pricing policies, disturbed by a realization that if they did so they would again run afoul of the law.[32] Conspiracy, they feared, was being identified with sound business practice. Nor was uneasiness confined to tobacco executives. When the Supreme Court sustained the Federal Trade Commission's finding that basing point pricing as practiced in the cement industry was unlawful, the chairman of the

---

31. *Id.* at 595.

32. Counsel for Liggett & Myers expressed the dilemma the "Big Three" faced: "[P]resumably, the appellants were convicted of agreement, not of the particular operations alleged to constitute agreement. Yet, on the Government's theory, continuation by more than one of the appellants of the operations alleged is evidence of a further Sherman Act agreement. . . . If this is so, how is Liggett & Myers to carry on? . . . Is everything that appellants do illegal, or evidence of illegality, if done by more than one of them?" Brief for Liggett & Myers, p. 27, American Tobacco Co. v. United States, 328 U.S. 781 (1946).

board of directors of the United States Steel Corporation announced that businessmen must educate the Court or persuade Congress to change the law.[33]

The Concept of Workable Competition

Meanwhile the economists had become concerned about the political implications of the Chamberlinian logic. If, as Arthur R. Burns[34] and other economists contended, it was the businessman's search for the economies of mass production that had shaped the structure of the contemporary economy, a rigorous enforcement of the antitrust statutes designed to insure competitive pricing could be had only at the expense of industrial efficiency. Burns believed this, but he did not believe that the nation could rely on oligopolistic markets to insure an economical allocation of resources and an equitable distribution of income; and he proposed a system of governmental controls so comprehensive that one of his critics characterized his book as "planning for totalitarian monopoly."[35] Socialists saw in industrial concentration an inevitable trend that would eventually necessitate a choice between private monopoly and the nationalization of industry.

This institutional drift was the occasion for, if not the cause of, a reexamination of the Chamberlinian logic and the implications of industrial structure to public policy. John M. Clark, a pioneer in the new thinking, in 1939 read his now famous paper on the concept of workable competition before the American Economic Association.[36] Clark, like Chamberlin, recognized that pure or perfect competition was an abstraction, a theoretical ideal realized in few if any markets. The actual markets of contemporary industry were compounded of elements of competition and monopoly, only some of which were controllable. To rid a market of some oligopolistic elements without ridding it of all might do more harm than good; and since all were not subject to control, controllable factors if left alone might

---

33. Irving S. Olds anticipated success in trying to educate the justices or to revise the statute. "I can't believe," he said, "that the country is going to let industry be disrupted by a theory that was developed many years ago by a Princeton professor." N. Y. Journal of Commerce, April 28, 1948, p. 1. The reference is to the late Professor Frank A. Fetter.
34. *The Decline of Competition* (New York: McGraw-Hill, 1936), chaps. 11–12.
35. Frank A. Fetter, "Planning for Totalitarian Monopoly," 45 J. Pol. Econ. 95 (1937).
36. "Toward a Concept of Workable Competition," 30 Am. Econ. Rev. (Proceedings of the American Economic Ass'n) 241 (1940).

Economic Change and the Sherman Act

exert a constructive influence. Clark conceived workable competition to be the best attainable functioning of markets under existing institutional arrangements, and he thought that it was good enough. Substitutes and potential competition, he argued, tended to insure consumers adequate protection from oligopolistic exploitation; rivalry among firms producing differentiated products might insure them a variety of alternatives at reasonable prices.

Clark's ideas on the significance of industrial structure to economic behavior were projected in a fertile economic and social environment, and his concept of workable competition has proved quite as revolutionary to economic thinking and economic policy as Chamberlin's earlier work. The environment that has nourished Clark's ideas is the environment with which all students of contemporary affairs are familiar. World War II inaugurated a prolonged period of deficit financing. The war was a total war, demanding the utmost endeavor of all nationals, civilian and combatant alike. It put a part-time American industry on an overtime basis. It eliminated unemployment. It raised price levels and the national income. By converting a buyers' into a sellers' market it made goods easy to sell and hard to get. It brought a business boom only temporarily interrupted by the cessation of hostilities. The postwar period found a pent-up demand for goods previously in shortage and an accumulated purchasing power with which to buy them. The cold war sustained a prosperity engendered by the hot one. It brought a prolonged expansion in gross national product and national income. It brought a level of employment earlier conceived as an admirable but remote ideal. It brought a stock market rise, lacking perhaps in the dramatic qualities of the 1928–1929 boom but equally persistent in its upward pressure on the prices of stocks of America's leading corporations. It revived the confidence of businessmen in a private enterprise economy and brought a tremendous expansion in industrial facilities financed in large part out of current earnings. It developed an entrepreneurial interest in industrial research hitherto lacking. In short, it brought to this country a level of material welfare and abundance that excited the admiration and envy of the rest of the world. And the business executives were not slow to claim credit for it. Through a spate of institutional advertising they identified corporate welfare with national welfare, economic prosperity with business efficiency, competition with private enterprise. The American economic system worked; competition must therefore have been workable.

Small wonder that businessmen, economists, administrators, and the

Workable Competition and Antitrust Policy

courts have accepted the logic of the concept of workable competition with its reassuring political and economic implications, while rejecting the Chamberlinian logic at once pessimistic and disturbing. Economists, administrators, and judges are alike in their desire to make peace with their environment. Thus the concept of workable competition is on its way to becoming a standard in antitrust proceedings.

As the concept has gained general acceptance it has undergone clarification and modification. Although economists might differ in their judgment as to the workability of any particular industrial arrangement, they are pretty well agreed on what to look for in reaching a judgment. While differing in the weight they would attach to the several criteria, they would look to an industry's structure, the conduct of the firms that comprise it, and to its performance. By structure is meant the way in which the industry is made up. Relevant questions are: How many sellers comprise it? What is their relative size? Is entry easy or difficult? Determining the boundary of an industry or the relevant market for its products is not easy because rivalry of substitutes may be so vigorous as to justify their inclusion in it. But having defined the boundaries of an industry, economists are pretty well agreed that the number of firms comprising it and their relative size may influence the effectiveness of competition. Where firms are few, in continuing close contact, and operating under similar conditions, other things equal, they may—in accordance with Chamberlinian doctrine—tend to behave like monopolists even without overtly conspiring to do so. The greater the number of firms, other things equal, the greater the likelihood of their behaving like competitors.

Conduct describes the practices and strategies which firms resort to in their dealings with each other and with the market. Trade association activities designed to lessen the severity of competition, price leadership, and basing point pricing are illustrations of the sort of practices that may reflect an absence of effective competition. Do the firms possess market advantages gained through patents or otherwise which they try to protect? Does their conduct reflect the uninhibited forces of a free market or associated activities designed to control market forces? These are relevant questions in determining the significance of conduct to the competitive workability of any industrial pattern.

By performance is meant the manner in which an industry fulfills the functions which a market economy imposes on it. Relevant questions include: What is the course of prices? of profits? of cost-price relationships? of expenditures on advertising? of technological innovation? In general, does the industry reflect the dynamic forces of competitive rivalry or the dead hand of monopoly?

Before economists had precisely defined the concept, some saw in workable competition an appropriate standard by which to judge the legality of alleged antitrust violations. Clark cautiously concluded his initial essay with the hope "that [the] government need not assume the burden of doing something about every departure from the model of perfect competition." [37] Later he urged that "where impairment of competition is an issue, there should be a showing of how competition is impaired, by comparison with an identifiable concept of what would constitute unimpaired competition in an industry having the unavoidable physical and economic characteristics of the one whose practices are being adjudicated." [38] At an earlier date Edward S. Mason [39] had indicated the usefulness of performance in drawing the line between socially acceptable and unacceptable departures from perfect competition. Jesse W. Markham [40] later defined workable competition in terms of alternatives. According to Markham, when account is taken of its structure and the forces that shaped it, an industry is workably competitive if no change "can be effected through public policy measures that would result in greater social gains than social losses." [41] Clare E. Griffin,[42] more than any other economist, has emphasized performance as a test of workable competition, and in applying the test he would take account of political as well as economic benefits.

The Lawyers and Workable Competition

Although economists have developed a logic that some think may be of use in antitrust proceedings, it is the lawyers who have been the most unrestrained in urging that the concept of workable competition be utilized as a practical standard in the adjudication of antitrust cases. The most articulate and vigorous of these are S. Chesterfield Oppenheim and Blackwell Smith. Blackwell Smith in an article on "Effective Competition:

---

37. *Id.* at 256.
38. Clark, "The Orientation of Antitrust Policy," 40 Am. Econ. Rev. (Proceedings of the American Economic Ass'n) 93, 98 (1950).
39. "Monopoly in Law and Economics," 47 Yale L. J. 34 (1937).
40. "An Alternative Approach to the Concept of Workable Competition," 40 Am. Econ. Rev. 349 (1950).
41. *Id.* at 361.
42. *An Economic Approach to Antitrust Problems* (New York: American Enterprise Ass'n, 1951), p. xiii; "Needed: A Realistic Antitrust Policy," Harv. Bus. Rev., Nov.–Dec. 1956, p. 76.

Workable Competition and Antitrust Policy

Hypothesis for Modernizing the Antitrust Laws," [43] published in 1951, proposed twelve criteria [44] for determining good industrial performance, all of them somewhat vague and difficult to apply. He advocated their application under a rule of reason in determining the legality of alleged violations of the antitrust statutes. The Business Advisory Committee of the Department of Commerce, accepting Smith's ideas virtually unchanged, in 1952 recommended drastic modifications in administrative standards and procedures under the antitrust statutes.[45] The recommended changes were designed to adjust the law to industrial structure and business practice rather than to make industrial structure and business practice conform to the law. The council identified the performance of the national economy with the performance of big firms and lamented a tendency to confuse bigness with monopoly. To temper the administration of the antitrust laws, the council recommended the creation of a review board consisting of businessmen, engineers, economists, and lawyers to pass on governmental proposals to investigate or proceed against alleged antitrust violations.

Oppenheim, in a more elaborate analysis of trends in the administration of the antitrust statutes,[46] like Smith, saw a need to bring antitrust laws into harmony with the facts of industrial life. Like Smith he vigorously advocated the utilization of the concept of workable competition under a rule of reason in administering the statutes. Like Smith he lamented tendencies in court and administrative decisions to outlaw per se certain business practices which on their face might suggest noncompetitive behavior or monopoly power, without first making a detailed analysis of their economic implications in the light of the whole industrial pattern in

---

43. 26 N.Y.U.L. Rev. 405.

44. "*Procedure Under the Rule of Reason.* In determining whether any commercial practices or courses of conduct promote Effective Competition or are unreasonably injurious thereto, all relevant circumstances shall be considered, including such actual or probable results of the conduct, under like circumstances in the market, as the increase or decrease of: (1) Alternatives available to customers or sellers; (2) Volume of production or services; (3) Quality of the services or goods; (4) Number of people benefited; (5) Incentives to entrepreneurs; (6) Efficiency and economy in manufacturing or distribution; (7) The welfare of employees; (8) The tendency to progress in technical development; (9) Prices to customers; (10) Conditions favorable to the public interest in defending the country from aggression; (11) The tendency to conserve the country's natural resources; (12) Benefits to the public interest assuming the relief requested by the government in the proceedings." *Id.* at 441.

45. U.S. Dep't of Commerce, *Effective Competition: Report to the Secretary of Commerce by His Business Advisory Council* (1952).

46. "Federal Antitrust Legislation: Guideposts to a Revised National Antitrust Policy," 50 Mich. L. Rev. 1139 (1952).

which they had developed. Like Smith he emphasized the importance of performance in determining the social acceptability of industrial patterns and structures, and like Smith he seemed to believe in a broad social rather than a narrow economic test of performance. Oppenheim's ideas also caught the attention of administrators and, largely in response to his pleas for new standards in antitrust administration, the Attorney General in 1953 created a national committee to study the antitrust laws [47] and appointed Oppenheim and Judge Barnes, Assistant Attorney General in charge of antitrust, as co-chairmen.

Although it might reasonably have been expected from the committee's make-up and from the forces that created it that the committee would recommend an amendment to the antitrust laws to provide for their administration in accordance with the concept of workable competition under a rule of reason, actually the committee specifically rejected such standards. But there is evidence that the committee tried to achieve by indirection what it did not openly advocate. Smith, a committee member, has revealed something of the committee's internal conflict on the issue of workable competition. The academic economists were skeptical, but their skepticism was matched by the determination of the "real-life practitioners." [48] The give-and-take of democratic discussion "did much to reduce the disparity among groups." [49] Smith concluded that out of the committee's deliberations has come

> the most realistic set of standards for legal and socially acceptable competition since the Business Advisory Council Report on Effective Competition published by Secretary of Commerce Sawyer. The present report makes more official a great deal of what was then and there recommended.[50]

In preference to making basic recommendations for a revision of antitrust policy and standards the committee chose to analyze the decisions of administrative agencies and the opinions of the courts in their interpretation and application of the antitrust statutes, and it sought thereby to shape policy by providing "future guides to enforcement agencies, Congress, and the courts." [51] In its analysis and evaluation the committee commended the courts and administrative agencies when they apparently

---

47. The Committee's report appeared on March 31, 1955. *Report of the Attorney General's National Committee to Study the Antitrust Laws* (1955).
48. Smith, "Antitrust Report to Narrow Gap between Law and Economics," Trade Practice Bulletin, May 1955, p. 4.
49. Ibid.
50. Ibid.
51. *Report of the Attorney General's National Committee to Study the Antitrust Laws* (1955), p. 3.

Workable Competition and Antitrust Policy

looked to all economic factors in trying to determine the significance to public welfare of the arrangements complained against, and it criticized decisions that condemned business practices in and of themselves without an examination of their full economic implications in their industrial setting. In evaluating the committee's report Smith has said:

> [The report] should be a bench mark for a long time to come against which to make comparisons of decisions, administrative actions, and legislation to see how far they drift from true readings.[52]

To insure that the courts might have at hand the committee's report as a ready guide, copies were sent to all federal judges. Oppenheim has since expressed the opinion that "the report is commanding the respect and serious consideration of the bar and Government officials." [53] Thurman Arnold, former Assistant Attorney General in charge of antitrust, has corroborated this opinion in testimony before a congressional committee, saying, "[T]he effect of the report is unquestionably very significant when you are arguing a case in court. . . . After all, a large committee of supposedly expert people will inevitably have an effect upon the courts." [54]

WORKABLE COMPETITION IN ANTITRUST DECISIONS

As previously suggested, without benefit of the committee's work the courts were already manifesting a disposition to judge alleged violations of the Sherman Act by the concept of workable competition. Smith noted this in saying,

> Legal opinions and decisions have been based progressively more and more on the concepts of effective competition. The outstanding opinion was that of Judge Knox in the Aluminum case where full play was given to the tests of effective competition, including inter-industry competition, and increasing ability of competitors to cope with the erstwhile dominant concern. Then Judge Wyzanski in the Shoe Machinery case, Mr. Justice Reed in the Columbia Steel case, and Judge Leahy in the Dupont Cellophane case have further elaborated these standards.[55]

In analyzing the effect on these or other important antitrust decisions of the economists' concept of workable competition, it is important to re-

---

52. Smith, *supra* note 48, at 1.
53. Letter dated August 1, 1955, to an unidentified addressee, *Hearings on Price Discrimination before House Select Committee on Small Business*, 84th Cong., 1st Sess. 194 (1955).
54. *Id.* at 5, 6.
55. Smith, *supra* note 48, at 4.

Economic Change and the Sherman Act

member that the concept is vague, economists are not agreed on the relative importance of structure, conduct, and performance in evaluating the workability of any particular market situation, and the judgments of both economists and jurists are influenced not only by their own preconceptions but especially by attitudes currently prevailing on the significance of big business. With such wide discretion as the application of the concept necessarily involves, decisions are likely to give approval to business arrangements acceptable to the general culture within which they have developed.

THE NATIONAL LEAD CASE

In this case the government charged that the two major producers of titanium compounds in the United States, the National Lead Company and E. I. du Pont de Nemours & Company, had conspired and combined to restrain and monopolize trade in titanium in violation of Sections 1 and 2 of the Sherman Act. The evidence established that National Lead together with Du Pont and the leading foreign producers of titanium through a series of patent exchange agreements and intercorporate arrangements had cartelized world trade in titanium. About these arrangements the district court said:

> In detail, the elapsed quarter century is crowded with negotiations, conferences, correspondence and agreements. The men who participated in these were all articulate, literate and . . . recorded what they saw, heard, said and thought with Boswellian fidelity. When the story is seen as a whole, there is no blinking the fact that there is no free commerce in titanium. Every pound of it is trammelled by privately imposed regulation. The channels of this commerce have not been formed by the winds and currents of competition. They are, in large measure, artificial canals privately constructed. The borders of the private domain in titanium are guarded by hundreds of patents, procured without opposition, and maintained without litigation. The accumulated power of this private empire, at the outbreak of World War II, was tremendous. It was more difficult for the independent outsider to enter this business than for the camel to make its proverbial passage through the eye of a needle.[56]

In the United States, Du Pont, National Lead, and two small producers, American Zirconium Corporation and Virginia Chemical Corporation, controlled titanium production—and each of the small producers was tied to National Lead or Du Pont through corporate ties and patent licensing agreements. The Supreme Court upheld the district court's find-

56. United States v. National Lead Co., 63 F. Supp. 513, 521 (S.D.N.Y. 1945).

Workable Competition and Antitrust Policy

ing that the arrangements by which titanium producers had cartelized the trade in titanium would tend to violate both Sections 1 and 2 of the Sherman Act, and it upheld the district court's injunction against a continuance or revival of such agreements.[57] But the Court denied the government's request that National Lead and Du Pont each be required to dispose of one of its two titanium plants, thereby increasing the number of firms from four to six. In rejecting divestiture the Court apparently attached greater weight to the industry's performance than to its structure in determining the effectiveness or workability of competition in the industry. The Court concluded:

There is no showing that four major competing units would be preferable to two, or, including American Zirconium and Virginia Chemical, that six would be better than four. Likewise, there is no showing of the necessity for this divestiture of plants or its practicality and fairness.[58]

The district court had found that "during the regime of the combination, the art has rapidly advanced, production has increased enormously and prices have sharply declined."[59] Fine performance of course did not justify unlawful conduct, and the Supreme Court did not hesitate to affirm an injunction against the various restrictive agreements by which titanium producers had divided world markets. It apparently believed that the industry, regardless of its structure, if rid of restrictive agreements would prove workably competitive.

THE 1950 ALUMINUM DECISION

Judge Hand in finding that the Aluminum Company of America was an unlawful monopoly decided that nothing should be done to disturb its industrial structure pending the outcome of the government's disposal of surplus aluminum plants. At the close of the war the government owned most of the capacity for producing aluminum, and it had been directed under the Surplus Property Act of 1944 [60] to dispose of its vast properties in this and other industries so as "to give maximum aid in the reestablishment of a peacetime economy of free independent private enterprise, . . . to discourage monopolistic practices and to strengthen and preserve the competitive position of small business concerns . . . [and] to foster the

57. United States v. National Lead Co., 332 U.S. 319 (1947).
58. Id. at 352.
59. 63 F. Supp. at 525.
60. 58 Stat. 765.

Economic Change and the Sherman Act

development of new independent enterprise . . . without fostering monopoly or restraint of trade. . . ." [61] From the government's disposal program Kaiser Aluminum and Chemical Corporation and Reynolds Metals Company emerged as full-fledged large-scale integrated companies with facilities acquired at only a fraction of their original cost. Thereafter, in March 1947, Alcoa petitioned the District Court for the Southern District of New York to declare that it no longer had a monopoly of the ingot market. The government filed a counterpetition alleging that competition had not been established in the aluminum industry, that Alcoa continued to dominate and control the aluminum ingot market, and that only by divestiture of certain of its plants and properties could competition be established. The government requested the establishment of an additional fully integrated producer in the industry.

On June 2, 1950, Judge Knox handed down a carefully reasoned opinion running through eighty printed pages.[62] At the outset he observed that "notwithstanding the antiquity of the action, the issues involved must be determined in accordance with the more recently established anti-trust principles, and not by those that were well recognized in an earlier day." [63] Just as the relevant legal principles had changed in the unfolding of the law, so had the relevant economic principles. Judge Knox noted that "the precise ingredients of 'effective competition' cannot be said to have been a static concept under the Sherman Act. Their applications, as well as their implications, have varied with changes in judicial thought with respect to economic and legal philosophies." [64] But Judge Knox regretted that "recent precedents . . . have fallen short of definite specifications as to the requirements of 'effective competition.'" [65] Nevertheless he was hopeful that it would be "possible to formulate a more or less concrete delineation of the standards that should be met in seeking a just decision upon the complicated facts of this case." [66]

To determine "the extent of permissible power that is consistent with the anti-trust laws in a particular industry" [67] Judge Knox applied a broad conception of the principle of workable competition, in which performance played a relatively important role. He enunciated the following factors as relevant: "the number and strength of the firms in the market;

61. *Id.* at 766.
62. United States v. Aluminum Co., 91 F. Supp. 333 (S.D.N.Y. 1950).
63. *Id.* at 339.
64. *Id.* at 340.
65. *Ibid.*
66. *Ibid.*
67. *Id.* at 347.

their effective size from the standpoint of technological development, and from the standpoint of competition with substitute materials and foreign trade; national security interests in the maintenance of strong productive facilities, and maximum scientific research and development; together with the public interest in lowered costs and uninterrupted production." [68] To Judge Knox the industry's structure, although not to be ignored, was relatively unimportant to the effectiveness of competition. "Commercial competition . . . is the independent endeavor of *two* or more persons or organizations within the realm of a chosen market place, to obtain the business patronage of others by means of various appeals, including the offer of more attractive terms or superior merchandise." [69]

Judge Knox did not find in recent precedents a precise specification for effective competition, but he did find a precise conception of monopoly. Monopoly is the power to fix prices and the power to exclude rivals from the market. Investigating these two determinants of power, Judge Knox quickly disposed of the government's contention that Alcoa's monopolistic power was manifested in its control over the price of aluminum pig and ingots. As the only producer selling these in substantial quantities to fabricators, Alcoa had "prime responsibility for prices." [70] However, the potential competition of Reynolds and Kaiser (who elected to fabricate virtually all the ingots and pig they produced) effectively limited Alcoa's power over prices. "The Government has not demonstrated that Alcoa enjoys price leadership with regard to fabricated products, a matter which would have to be included if a true representation of the industry were sought." [71] Accordingly Judge Knox held that "price domination on the part of Alcoa has not been established. . . ." [72]

Judge Knox examined more thoroughly the issue of Alcoa's power to exclude rivals from the market. He reviewed meticulously the physical resources of both Kaiser and Reynolds at the several stages of production, their comparative costs, financial resources, and control of patents. In all

---

68. *Ibid.*
69. *Id.* at 355. Emphasis added. Compare Judge Knox's conception with that of John M. Clark. Clark said: "Competition is rivalry in selling goods, in which each selling unit normally seeks maximum net revenue, under conditions such that the price or prices each seller can charge are effectively limited by free option of the buyer to buy from a rival seller or sellers of what we think of as 'the same' product, necessitating an effort by each seller to equal or exceed the attractiveness of the others' offerings to a sufficient number of buyers to accomplish the end in view." "Toward a Concept of Workable Competition," 30 Am. Econ. Rev. 241, 243 (1940).
70. United States v. Aluminum Co., 91 F. Supp. 333, 365 (S.D.N.Y. 1950).
71. *Ibid.*
72. *Ibid.*

Economic Change and the Sherman Act

respects he found that Alcoa had a substantial advantage over either of its rivals. Alcoa's financial strength enabled it to take advantage of trade opportunities and to stifle Kaiser's and Reynolds' growth whenever it wished. The evidence before it, the court said, was insufficient to assure that in the future competitive conditions of an "effective and lawful nature"[73] would prevail in the aluminum industry. But the court did not find in Alcoa's recent behavior an intent to monopolize, and it could not bring itself to disturb the organization of Alcoa's physical properties. A "strong and resourceful domestic aluminum industry" was essential to "national security" and "the peacetime welfare of the general public."[74] The development of the industry depended upon its being composed of "financially sound and well-integrated organizations."[75] Aluminum competed with other products and had not only to hold its own against them but to enlarge its acceptance as a substitute for them. This required encroaching on the fields of "strongly entrenched" competitors, and "the weakening of any aluminum producer would lessen the buoyancy of the industry as a whole."[76] Big business is "an actuality" and if it is to meet effective competition its trade rivals must be "of somewhat comparable strength."[77] The court was unwilling "to tamper unnecessarily with economic and industrial forces from which the public has reaped substantial benefits."[78]

In thus giving its blessing to Alcoa and the industry's structure the court warned that if Alcoa should use the power which its lower production costs and its financial and physical resources gave it to injure or weaken Reynolds and Kaiser, the court would have to take another look at the matter. "If, for any reason, it should appear that their competition with Alcoa is feeble, uncertain and ineffective, appropriate action . . . will be in order."[79] The court in effect, gave official sanction to Alcoa's holding an umbrella over the industry and encouragement to a pricing policy calculated to profit the industry rather than benefit the consumer of aluminum products. Because, in responding to the temper of the times, it confused a giant firm with a dynamic industry, the court lost the opportunity it had been given by the peculiar circumstances of the *Aluminum* case to "foster independent private enterprise."

73. *Id.* at 416.
74. *Ibid.*
75. *Ibid.*
76. *Ibid.*
77. *Ibid.*
78. *Ibid.*
79. *Id.* at 418.

Workable Competition and Antitrust Policy

THE UNITED SHOE MACHINERY CASE

On December 15, 1947, the government filed a complaint against the United Shoe Machinery Corporation alleging that it was monopolizing interstate commerce in the shoe machinery industry of the United States in violation of Section 2 of the Sherman Act. On February 18, 1953, Judge Wyzanski of the District Court for the District of Massachusetts handed down a decision finding the corporation guilty.[80] The defendants appealed, and on May 17, 1954, the Supreme Court upheld the lower court without writing an opinion.[81] Judge Wyzanski's opinion is important for two reasons. It clarifies the doctrine laid down by Judge Hand in the *Aluminum* case that a monopoly is guilty of monopolizing if it does not have monopoly thrust upon it, and it reflects a characteristic timidity of the courts in determining the remedies to be applied in antitrust cases.

Judge Wyzanski recognized three main sources of United's power in the shoe machinery market: (1) the original organization of the company in 1899, which combined the leading manufacturers of shoe machinery; (2) the superiority of its products and services; and (3) the business practices it had pursued, especially its system of leasing rather than selling shoe machinery. The original combination had brought under single control the two largest producers of shoe machinery, themselves the product of previous mergers, and a number of small but important producers.[82]

---

80. United States v. United Shoe Mach. Corp., 110 F. Supp. 295 (D. Mass. 1953), aff'd, 347 U.S. 521 (1954).

81. In a *per curiam* opinion the Court found the decree supported by the findings and the findings justified by the evidence. 347 U.S. 521 (1954).

82. The United Shoe Machinery Co. was the subject of both criminal and civil actions under the Sherman Act, and the several court opinions give varying accounts of the number and size of the firms that made up the original combination. Justice Clarke in dissenting from the Supreme Court's 1918 opinion holding that the combination did not violate the Sherman Act undertook to give a "plain history" of the company's formation and later acquisitions, and Justice Holmes speaking for a unanimous Court in the 1913 criminal case stated the percentages of domestic production that were controlled by the larger units that made up the combination. S. W. Winslow, the controlling spirit of the Consolidated and McKay Lasting Machine Co., with 60 per cent of the country's lasting machines, and E. P. Howe, the controlling spirit of the Goodyear Shoe Machinery Co., with 30 per cent of the country's welt-sewing machines and outsole-stitching machines—both companies being the products of earlier consolidations—organized the United Shoe Machinery Co., a New Jersey corporation, in February 1899. United by an exchange of stock acquired the Goodyear and International Goodyear Shoe Machinery Cos., and in 1900 it acquired the Seaver Co., the only lasting machine manufacturer then outside the combination. United also purchased the McKay Shoe Machinery Co., which produced 70 per cent of the country's heeling machines and 80 per cent of

Economic Change and the Sherman Act

In the language of the new corporation's president: "After the formation of the United Company it was manufacturing *every single lasting machine* that was being put out in the United States except the Seaver machine; and in 1900 we acquired the Seaver Company."[83] When Judge Wyzanski made his decision, however, the legality of the original combination was no longer in question, it having been upheld by the Supreme Court in 1918.[84]

Judge Wyzanski acknowledged the superiority of United's products and services, but he did not find that United had "achieved spectacular results at amazing rates of speed, nor has it proved that comparable research results and comparable economies of production, distribution, and service could not be achieved as well by, say, three important shoe machinery firms, as by one."[85] Moreover, the court observed,

the country's metallic fastening machines. Consolidated already owned the Davey Pegging Machine Co. Within a few weeks of its organization United acquired the only remaining strong competitor, the Eppler Welt Machine Co., and its international subsidiary. In 1901 it acquired the remaining welt machine company, the Globe. Justice Clarke quoted Winslow as saying: "Immediately after the organization of the company our welting, outsole stitching and lasting machines were doing about all the welting, outsole stitching and lasting that was being done in the United States." United States v. United Shoe Mach. Co., 247 U.S. 32, 82 (1918). On March 1, 1899, United purchased control of Goddu Co., a manufacturer of metallic fastening machines, under a contract binding the six inventors who had owned the stock to transfer to United all shoe machinery inventions they might make or acquire any interest in for a period of ten years. In 1910 United purchased for $6,000,000 the shoe machinery line that the Thomas G. Plant Co., a shoe manufacturer, had developed as a means of freeing shoe manufacturers from total dependence on United. The record showed fifty-seven purchases by United ranging from $250 for a patent application to the $6,000,000 purchase just described. Winslow and others were indicted for conspiring to restrain trade, but the Supreme Court ruled that the indictment did not charge a Sherman Act offense because the shoe machines combined were not in competition with each other (despite evidence in the record to the contrary). United States v. Winslow, 227 U.S. 202 (1913). Five years later the Supreme Court by a four-to-three vote (Justices McReynolds and Brandeis did not participate) held that the civil suit to dissolve the combination was properly dismissed for the same reason. United States v. United Shoe Mach. Co., *supra*. It also ruled that the alleged abuses of United's leasing system were but the lawful exercise of its patent rights. By 1917 the present United Shoe Machinery Corp., organized in 1905, had merged with and become the successor of the United Shoe Machinery Co.

83. Quoted by Justice Clarke in dissenting from United States v. United Shoe Mach. Co., *supra* note 82, at 81. Emphasis added.

84. United States v. United Shoe Mach. Co., *supra* note 82. The majority opinion in finding for United summed up its views in these words: "The company, indeed, has magnitude, but it is at once the result and cause of efficiency, and the charge that it has been oppressively used is not sustained." *Id.* at 56.

85. United States v. United Shoe Mach. Corp., 110 F. Supp. 295, 345 (D. Mass. 1953), aff'd, 347 U.S. 521 (1954).

Workable Competition and Antitrust Policy

United's control does not rest solely on its original constitution, its ability, its research, or its economies of scale. There are other barriers to competition, and these barriers were erected by United's own business policies. Much of United's market power is traceable to the magnetic ties inherent in its system of leasing, and not selling, its more important machines.[86]

In stating the law on monopolization Judge Wyanski elucidated the principles laid down in the *Aluminum* case, an opinion he recognized as a turning point in the interpretation of Section 2 of the Sherman Act. In doing so he referred to the Supreme Court's opinions in the *Griffith*,[87] *Schine*,[88] *Paramount*,[89] and *Columbia Steel*[90] cases and noted that in the second *American Tobacco* case the Court had "expressly approved" Judge Hand's technique and language. In these cases Judge Wyzanski saw three different but related approaches: (1) "An enterprise has monopolized in violation of section 2 of the Sherman Act if it has acquired or maintained a power to exclude others as a result of using an unreasonable 'restraint of trade' in violation of section 1 of the Sherman Act."[91] (2) It has "monopolized in violation of section 2 if it (a) has the power to exclude competition, and (b) has exercised it, or has the purpose to exercise it."[92] (3) A concern that has acquired an overwhelming share of the market "monopolizes" in violation of Section 2 whenever it does business, provided its monopoly is not solely the result of "superior skill, superior products, natural advantages, (including accessibility to raw materials or markets), economic or technological efficiency, (including scientific research), low margins of profit maintained permanently and without discrimination, or licenses conferred by, and used within, the limits of law, (including patents on one's own inventions, or franchises granted directly to the enterprise by a public authority)."[93]

Judge Wyzanski apparently thought that the facts in the case before him satisfied each of these approaches but felt precluded from adopting the first because the Supreme Court had cleared United's lease provisions under the Sherman Act in the 1918 *Shoe Machinery* case.[94] He found it unnecessary to choose between the second and the third approaches:

86. *Id.* at 344.
87. United States v. Griffith, 334 U.S. 100 (1948).
88. Schine Chain Theatres, Inc. v. United States, 334 U.S. 110 (1948).
89. United States v. Paramount Pictures, Inc., 334 U.S. 131 (1948).
90. United States v. Columbia Steel Co., 334 U.S. 495 (1948).
91. United States v. United Shoe Mach. Corp., 110 F. Supp. 295, 342 (D. Mass. 1953), *aff'd*, 347 U.S. 521 (1954).
92. *Ibid.*
93. *Ibid.*
94. See note 82 *supra*. The Court later condemned the leasing practices under

Economic Change and the Sherman Act

For, taken as a whole, the evidence satisfies the tests laid down in both *Griffith* and *Aluminum*. The facts show that (1) defendant has, and exercises, such overwhelming strength in the shoe machinery market that it controls that market, (2) this strength excludes some potential, and limits some actual, competition, and (3) this strength is not attributable solely to defendant's ability, economies of scale, research, natural advantages, and adaptation to inevitable economic laws.[95]

In short, a business firm monopolizes within the meaning of Section 2 of the Sherman Act if it achieves or maintains market power by practices which though not predatory or illegal in themselves are unnecessary to the efficient conduct of business.

Judge Wyzanski is to be congratulated for having clarified and extended the doctrine laid down by Judge Hand. His interpretation of the law (as distinguished from his application of it in formulating remedies) reflects boldness and logic and should do much to relieve the uncertainty created by Judge Hand's somewhat vague concept of monopoly's being thrust upon a firm.

When it came to remedies, Judge Wyzanski was no longer bold, although he was equally logical. He realized that the society in which he lived was satisfied with the contemporary business environment and would not tolerate judgments requiring significant changes in it. So long as the methods by which business grew big were not flagrantly predatory and even though the size achieved was larger than need be for efficiency, the public identified big business with success and would not support the necessary surgery to reconstruct it into more competitive units. As Judge Wyzanski stated the matter,

> To many champions of the anti-trust laws these cases indicate judicial timidity, economic innocence, lack of conviction, or paralysis of resolution. Yet there is another way of interpreting this judicial history. In the anti-trust field the courts have been accorded, by common consent, an authority they have in no other branch of enacted law. Indeed, the only comparable examples of the power of judges is [sic] the economic role they formerly exercised under the Fourteenth Amendment, and the role they now exercise in the area of civil liberties. They would not have been given, or allowed to keep, such authority in the anti-trust field, and they would not so freely have altered from time to time the interpretation of its substantive provisions, if courts were in the habit of proceeding with the surgical ruthlessness that might commend itself to those seeking absolute assurance that there will be workable competition, and

Section 3 of the Clayton Act, United Shoe Mach. Corp. v. United States, 258 U.S. 451 (1922), and United thereupon softened some of the more onerous provisions.

95. United States v. United Shoe Mach. Corp., 110 F. Supp. 295, 343 (D. Mass 1953), aff'd, 347 U.S. 521 (1954). Emphasis added.

to those aiming at immediate realization of the social, political, and economic advantages of dispersal of power.[96]

Thus did Judge Wyzanski adjust his decision to the temper of the times. He did not order dissolution of the United Shoe Machinery Corporation into three independent companies as asked by the government, because it was impractical to do so. He did not order United to discontinue the leasing of machines and sell them outright, a policy recommended by his economic adviser,[97] but left United with the alternative of selling or leasing them (under less restrictive terms than United had imposed) at the option of the user. He concluded that to prohibit leasing altogether would be "undesirable at least until milder remedies have been tried."[98] He did not carry divestiture as far as his economic counsellor thought desirable,[99] being content with merely ordering divestiture of United's business in nails, tacks, and eyelets—"this is the kind of dissolution which can be carried out practically"[100]—and of its distributorship of shoe factory supplies made by companies not a part of United's organization.[101] The court did not order compulsory licensing of United's patents on a royalty-free basis, but the milder remedy of compulsory licensing at reasonable royalties.[102]

96. *Id.* at 348.
97. Carl Kaysen, associate professor of economics at Harvard University, served for two years as economic assistant to Judge Wyzanski while the *Shoe Machinery* case was being tried. He completed his original memorandum for the court in October 1952 and published it with additions in book form in 1956. For his recommendations on putting an end to leasing see *United States v. United Shoe Machinery Corporation* (Cambridge: Harvard University Press, 1956), pp. 275-89.
98. United Shoe v. United Shoe Mach. Corp., 110 F. Supp. 295, 349 (D. Mass. 1953), *aff'd*, 347 U.S. 521 (1954).
99. Kaysen thought a new shoe machinery and shoe factory supply manufacturer could be created by "divesting United of B. B. Chemical Corporation, its own Cement Shoe department, its two eyelet manufacturing branches, S. O. and O. C. Co. and J. C. Rhodes, and its Eyeletting department," and setting them up with suitable administrative branches as a corporation independent of United. This would be "a step in the direction of recreating conditions similar to those which prevailed before the original mergers which created United's predecessor company." Kaysen, *op. cit. supra* note 97, at 289.
100. United States v. United Shoe Mach. Corp., 110 F. Supp. 295, 351 (D. Mass. 1953), *aff'd*, 347 U.S. 521 (1954).
101. Concerning the latter the court said, "And United ought not to be allowed to continue these distributorships because they flowed to United partly, at any rate, as an indirect consequence of United's prohibited monopolization of shoe machinery. To be sure, other advantages flowed to United from its monopolization; but the particular advantages inherent in the large scale distribution of supplies are . . . easily severable." *Ibid.* Emphasis added.
102. According to Kaysen, *op. cit. supra* note 97, at 285, the government sought royalty-free licensing, but "the reason for not requiring . . . [it] is simply that the

Economic Change and the Sherman Act

Although Judge Wyzanski rendered an opinion admirable for its logic and clarity, he refrained from such bold remedies as would satisfy those "aiming at immediate realization of the social, political, and economic advantages of dispersal of power." He chose milder ones more in keeping with the spirit of the times, with the preconceptions and prejudices of those who regard big business as one of the noblest achievements of this era. His decision is likely to find approval by all reasonable men who have made peace with their environment.

THE CELLOPHANE CASE

The doctrine of workable competition has provided an institutional basis for a lax administration of the antitrust laws. It has afforded a logical reconciliation between a law that condemns in a sweeping manner all combinations in restraint of trade and all monopolizing and attempts to monopolize, and an economic, cultural, and technological environment conducive to vast aggregations of capital in firms so large that they necessarily have power over the market. As a standard in antitrust judgments it has encouraged a rationalization of the status quo. As previously pointed

---

significance of United's patents in maintaining its market position is not so great as to warrant such a drastic remedy." Perhaps the court was guided more by legal precedent than by the patents' lack of significance to United. It found that of the 3,915 patents United held on December 15, 1947, roughly 95 per cent were the result of its own research; the remainder were acquired and served to buttress United's market power even though their economic purposes could have been fulfilled equally well by obtaining nonexclusive licenses. And "the aggregation of patents does to some extent block potential competition" by inducing inventors to offer their ideas to United and enabling it to hedge against "unforeseen competitive developments." United States v. United Shoe Mach. Corp., 110 F. Supp. 295, 339 (D. Mass. 1953), aff'd, 347 U.S. 521 (1954). The court ordered compulsory patent licensing on a reasonable royalty basis as "in effect a partial dissolution, on a non-confiscatory basis." Id. at 351.

The remedy is in line with the law's development on compulsory patent licensing in antitrust cases. Besser Mfg. Co. v. United States, 343 U.S. 444, 447 (1952); United States v. United States Gypsum Co., 340 U.S. 76, 94 (1950); United States v. National Lead Co., 332 U.S. 319, 338 (1947). The Supreme Court has refused to order royalty-free licensing on the ground that it would amount to a forfeiture of the patents, a remedy not appropriate to a Sherman Act violation having nothing to do with their validity. Hartford-Empire Co. v. United States, 323 U.S. 386, 414–15 (1945). The Court had earlier denied the right to sue for infringement to a patentee found to have used his patent to monopolize an unpatented article, Morton Salt Co. v. G. S. Suppiger Co., 314 U.S. 488 (1942); B. B. Chemical Co. v. Ellis, 314. US. 495 (1942), but it declared that denial of his property right in such circumstances was not a precedent for antitrust remedies that were confiscatory. Hartford-Empire Co. v. United States, supra, at 415.

Workable Competition and Antitrust Policy

out, the standards by which economists would judge the workability of any arrangement in which sellers vie with one another for the trade of their customers are the structure of an industry, the conduct of firms which comprise it, and their economic performance. The relative weight attached to these several criteria depends on individual judgments. Some economists and a larger number of lawyers attach little importance to structure, holding that competition may be effective with only a few firms in a market, even with only one if the market be narrowly defined.[103] Those who hold this point of view look to interindustry competition to protect the consumer from exploitation.[104] Others hold that the structure of an industry may determine the conduct of the firms that comprise it.[105] This point of view is well expressed by Chief Justice Warren in his dissent in the *Cellophane* case: "The conduct of Du Pont and Sylvania [Sylvania Industrial Corporation of America, the only other producer during the period covered by the case] illustrates that a few sellers tend to act like one and that an industry which does not have a competitive structure will not have competitive behavior." [106] Some economists, and lawyers too, who attach relatively great importance to conduct as evidence of monopoly look for discriminatory and predatory practices as the key element in antitrust violations.[107] Others examine the broad strategy of a firm, as did Judge Wyzanski in the *Shoe Machinery* case. And finally some economists and lawyers attach primary importance to an industry's performance as evidence of the workability of competition.[108] Those who do may be concerned less about the existence of power than the manner in which power is exercised. When an industry is characterized by rapid

103. Morris A. Adelman, "Effective Competition and the Antitrust Laws," 61 Harv. L. Rev. 1289 (1948); Smith, "Effective Competition: Hypothesis for Modernizing the Antitrust Laws," 26 N.Y.U.L. Rev. 405 (1951); Thomas E. Sunderland, "Changing Legal Concepts in the Antitrust Field," 3 Syracuse L. Rev. 60 (1951).
104. Ross M. Robertson, "On the Changing Apparatus of Competition," 44 Am. Econ. Rev. (Proceedings of the American Economic Ass'n) 61 (1954).
105. Walter Adams, "Dissolution, Divorcement, Divesture: The Pyrrhic Victories of Antitrust," 27 Ind. L. J. 1 (1951); Ben W. Lewis in "The Effectiveness of the Federal Antitrust Laws: A Symposium," ed. Dexter M. Keezer, 39 Am. Econ. Rev. 689, 703 (1949); Eugene V. Rostow, "The New Sherman Act: A Positive Instrument of Progress," 14 U. Chi. L. Rev. 567 (1947).
106. United States v. E. I. du Pont de Nemours & Co., 351 U.S. 377, 426 (1956). In 1946 Sylvania merged with the American Viscose Corporation.
107. E.g., Joel B. Dirlam and Alfred E. Kahn, *Fair Competition: The Law and Economics of Antitrust Policy* (Ithaca: Cornell University Press, 1954).
108. Clare E. Griffin, *An Economic Approach to Antitrust Problems* (New York: American Enterprise Ass'n, 1951); Griffin, "Needed: A Realistic Antitrust Policy," Harv. Bus. Rev., November–December 1956, p. 76; Smith, *supra* note 103.

technological advances, when cost and prices show a consistent downward trend, when the product is continuously improved—in short, when the industry's performance appears to be consistent with the general welfare—those attaching primary importance to performance may consider questions about market power merely academic. With the experts disagreeing on the relative importance of structure, conduct, and performance to the workability of competition, the judges must find standards of their own. The standards of the business community are apt to count for more with them than the standards of the academicians.

Seen in this light the district court's decision in the *Cellophane* case [109] should surprise no one. In handing down his decision (which runs through 192 printed pages and presents a detailed but superficial analysis of the evidence), Judge Leahy pointed out that the charge against Du Pont of having monopolized cellophane involved two questions: "1. does duPont possess monopoly powers; and 2., if so, has it achieved such powers by 'monopolizing' within the meaning of the Act and under United States v. Aluminum Company of America"? [110] He concluded that "unless the first is decided against defendant, the second is not reached." [111] Judge Leahy did not need to reach the second question, for he found the defendant not guilty. He concluded his opinion with these significant remarks:

The facts destroy the charges here made. There has been no monopolization or conspiracy or combination or attempt to monopolize shown. The record reflects not the dead hand of monopoly but rapidly declining prices, expanding production, intense competition stimulated by creative research, the development of new products and uses and other benefits of a free economy. [Neither] Du Pont nor any other American company similarly situated should be punished for its success. Nothing warrants intervention of this court of equity. The complaint should be dismissed.[112]

The Supreme Court by a vote of four to three affirmed this judgment.

The Relevant Market for Cellophane

Judge Leahy in reaching his decision considered many supplementary issues, but the decision rests primarily on the single question, What is the relevant market in which Du Pont sells cellophane? Is cellophane a differ-

109. United States v. E. I. du Pont de Nemours & Co., 118 F. Supp. 41 (D. Del. 1953).
110. *Id.* at 54.
111. *Ibid.*
112. *Id.* at 233.

Workable Competition and Antitrust Policy

entiated product with characteristics peculiar to itself which isolate it from the competition of other products, or is it merely one of many flexible wrapping materials that possess varied characteristics but on the whole are so much alike that one may readily substitute for another and the producers of all compete vigorously for consumers' preference? The Supreme Court accepted the issue as Judge Leahy defined it. In considering this issue Judge Leahy concluded that

cellophane is not a unique flexible packaging material in any functional or economic sense. In terms of uses for which cellophane is sold, and the qualities it brings to each use as a wrapping material, cellophane is interchangeable and *in fact* continually interchanged with many flexible packaging materials.[113]

Judge Leahy classified sixteen flexible wrapping materials according to eleven characteristics considered by industrial buyers in gauging their relative merits, and he discussed at length the characteristics of eleven—including aluminum foil, certain films, waxed and greaseproof paper, and glassine—which he regarded as interchangeable with cellophane. He noted that several hundred firms compete in their production and sale and that Du Pont in 1949 accounted for only 17.9 per cent of their total square yardage of domestic output and imports.[114]

Purchasers of flexible wrapping materials are primarily makers and distributors of the consumers' goods they package. They are cost- and profit-conscious and carefully compare the qualities and prices of available wrapping materials. They endeavor to choose the material which will win consumer preference and which, cost considered, will yield the highest profit on the goods they market.[115] Such wrapping materials fall into four main categories: (1) opaque nonmoistureproof wrapping *paper* designed primarily for convenience and protection in handling packages; (2) moistureproof *films* of varying degrees of transparency designed primarily either to protect, or to display and protect, the products they encompass; (3) nonmoistureproof transparent *films* designed primarily to display and to some extent protect, but which obviously do a poor protecting job where exclusion or retention of moisture is important; and (4) moistureproof *materials* other than films of varying degrees of transparency (foils and paper products) designed to protect and display.

113. *Id.* at 63. Emphasis in original.
114. *Id.* at 111.
115. "Manufacturer of packageable products has a choice of materials from which to choose. Purchase price, cost of application, service available, and functional qualities of each material are factors which control choice, and control volume of material that can be sold in competition with others." *Id.* at 88.

Economic Change and the Sherman Act

Kraft paper is the leading opaque nonmoistureproof wrapping paper. It is relatively cheap, strong, and pliable and gives adequate protection. It does not meet the competition of other wrapping materials for the purposes for which it is primarily designed—the convenient wrapping of packages. At less than one cent per thousand square inches, kraft paper sells for less than cellophane costs. Although Judge Leahy did not specifically recognize the fact, clearly kraft paper does not fall into the relevant market for cellophane.

In 1949, 80 per cent of Du Pont's cellophane sales were for packaging food products, and for this use cellophane encounters the vigorous rivalry of vegetable parchment, greaseproof paper, glassine, waxed paper, aluminum foil, pliofilm, Saran, and other films. Judge Leahy analyzed in some detail the nature and extent of rivalry among these materials for wrapping a large number of specific products: white bread, specialty breads, cake and sweet goods, meat, candy, crackers and biscuits, frozen foods, potato chips, popcorn and snacks, cereals, fresh produce, paper goods and textiles, butter, cheese, fish, oleomargarine, chewing gum, other food products, and cigarettes and other tobacco products. Only in the wrapping of cigarettes did cellophane supply as much as 50 per cent of the total quantity (in square inches) of wrapping materials used.[116] It sold only 6.8 per cent of the wrapping materials used for packaging bakery products. Only as a wrapper for fresh produce did it top the list, and in this field it supplied only 47.2 per cent of the total wrapping materials used. This to the district court did not look like market domination. After examining the shifts among the various materials in their several uses (particularly in the wrapping of candy), after hearing the testimony of flexible wrapping material converters and users, after receiving the results of a market survey prepared by Du Pont, after examining the reports of Du Pont salesmen, after taking judicial notice of trade publications and writings, and after a personal visit to the 1952 Annual Packaging Show in Atlantic City to see at first hand the manner in which such materials were offered for sale to the trade, Judge Leahy concluded that "duPont cellophane is sold under such intense competitive conditions [that] acquisition of market control or monopoly power is a practical impossibility." [117] By making a

---

116. In the outer wrapping of packaged cigarettes cellophane has no effective rival. Du Pont cellophane wraps 75 to 80 per cent of the cigarettes sold in the United States. *Id.* at 114. Ordinarily it is only when they can't get it that cigarette makers use any other material, e.g. during a cellophane shortage in the mid-forties. Brown and Williamson Tobacco Co. once experimented with selling Kools and Raleighs in a one-piece foil package. *Id.* at 108.

117. *Id.* at 197–98.

Workable Competition and Antitrust Policy

detailed examination of the economic factors at work in the relevant market for cellophane as he defined that market, Judge Leahy wrote an opinion that won the approval of the proponents of workable competition. But, as will be shown later, an analysis of economic factors is no better than the analyst's understanding of each factor.

Although its reasoning is more formal and technical than Judge Leahy's, the Supreme Court did not do much better. It accepted as the main issue in the case the relevant market for cellophane, and it gave the term "relevant market" a new definition: "In considering what is the relevant market for determining the control of price and competition, no more definite rule can be declared than that commodities *reasonably* interchangeable by consumers for the same purposes make up that 'part of the trade or commerce,' monopolization of which may be illegal." [118]

The Concept of Cross-Elasticity of Demand

To determine "reasonable" interchangeability the Court introduced the concept of cross-elasticity, saying:

> An element for consideration as to cross-elasticity of demand between products is the responsiveness of the sales of one product to price changes of the other. If a slight decrease in the price of cellophane causes a considerable number of customers of other flexible wrappings to switch to cellophane, it would be an indication that a high cross-elasticity of demand exists between them; that the products compete in the same market.[119]

But without testing the facts by correct application of the principle the Court accepted Judge Leahy's findings that the "'great sensitivity of customers in the flexible packaging markets to price or quality changes' prevented du Pont from possessing monopoly control over price." [120] The Court concluded that "cellophane's interchangeability with the other materials mentioned suffices to make it a part of this flexible packaging material market." [121]

Cross-elasticity is a technical economic concept. By incorporating it into its reasoning the Court ostensibly gave the law a method by which to measure more realistically the workability of competition. In the hands of experts supplied with detailed data on cost changes, price, and shifts

---

118. United States v. E. I. du Pont de Nemours & Co., 351 U.S. 377, 395 (1956). Emphasis added.
119. *Id.* at 400.
120. *Ibid.*
121. *Ibid.*

Economic Change and the Sherman Act

in demand, the concept should prove useful in determining the extent to which substitute products can prevent the exploitation of consumers by would-be monopolists. In the hands of judges in antitrust cases the concept is probably not of much use. It may prove a positive deterrent to the effective administration of the Sherman Act. The Supreme Court correctly conceived cross-elasticity as defining the extent to which a change in the price of commodity A affects the sales of commodity B. But to recognize this is to state the problem, not to solve it. If a decrease in A's price diminishes B's sales, cross-elasticity is positive. All this says is that a significant number of consumers, after considering the relative merits of the two products and their prices, have substituted a product whose price has been lowered for one whose price remains unchanged. If a given decrease in the price of one commodity results in a relatively large decrease in the sales of the other, cross-elasticity is said to be high.

On the ratio of cross-elasticity between cellophane and any other wrapping material both Judge Leahy and the Supreme Court are necessarily silent. To determine it business rivals would have had to disclose confidential information which the *Cellophane* case does not reveal. But even if the Du Pont record had disclosed the relevant confidential data on changes in sales and prices, and a high positive cross-elasticity between cellophane and a substitute wrapping paper had been shown, this would not warrant the conclusion that the seller of either product was not a monopolist. To determine whether either firm possesses monopoly power it would be necessary to examine the price response of the firm losing business and the cost-price relationships of both products. To recapture business lost or to prevent further losses to product A the firm making product B must lower its price. If price decreases in product A do not bring a decrease in the price of B, a lack of competition between them is indicated. Either the loss of business is too slight to matter—that is, cross-elasticity is low—or the producer of product A has a monopoly advantage which the producer of product B does not have. If product B was already selling at a competitive price, *i.e.*, marginal cost, its producer could not afford to reduce the price, and if it continued to lose business it would have no alternative in the long run but to cease operations. That the producer of product A could afford to reduce its price suggests that it was already getting a monopoly profit, a profit which it hopes to enlarge by selling more at lower prices.

So much for the logic. What are the facts in the *Cellophane* case? Between 1924 and 1938 Du Pont reduced the price of cellophane every

Workable Competition and Antitrust Policy

year, presumably in an effort to increase profits by increasing volume, for a total reduction of over 80 per cent.[122] During this same period the price of glassine and from 1933 the price of waxed paper (prices for earlier years are not available), the two largest selling wrapping papers, remained virtually unchanged. From 1938 to 1940 the price of cellophane declined by 8.6 per cent. During the same years the prices of waxed paper and glassine actually increased. This indicates a low cross-elasticity of demand. Apparently Du Pont could ignore the prices of rival papers in setting its own prices. From 1924 to 1950 the price of the principal type of moisture-proof cellophane was at all times for which figures are available from two to seven times that of 25# bleached glassine and from two to four and one-half times that of 30# waxed paper, despite a reduction in the average price of cellophane from $2.51 to 49 cents a pound.[123] To the economically sophisticated this is sufficient evidence that cellophane is a unique product. As the Supreme Court dissenting opinion put it:

> We cannot believe that . . . practical businessmen would have bought cellophane in increasing amounts over a quarter of a century if close substitutes were available at from one-seventh to one-half cellophane's price. That they did so is testimony to cellophane's distinctiveness.[124]

As these price changes took place, cost-conscious buyers (candy manufacturers were a conspicuous example) were constantly revising their judgment as to the relative merits of cellophane, glassine, and waxed paper at the prices at which they could be bought, and some buyers switched from one product to the other. But this is a deceptive interchangeability. Rational buyers will revise their judgment of the relative value of several products that serve roughly the same purpose whenever the price of one or the other changes, and they will not be deterred from doing so merely because the seller of one product is a monopolist. In a general sense all products compete for the consumer's dollar, and a wise monopolist will so adjust cost-price relationships as to obtain the highest return on his investment. He may do so by selling much at a low profit per unit or little at a high profit per unit. That he chooses one policy in preference to the other does not mean that he has surrendered his monopoly. He is merely exploiting it wisely.

122. Table of annual average prices from 1924 to 1950, United States v. E. I. du Pont de Nemours & Co., 118 F. Supp. 41, 82 (D. Del. 1953).

123. Defendant's Brief on the Facts and the Law, Appendix A (graph based on prices per 1,000 sq. in.), United States v. E. I. du Pont de Nemours & Co., 118 F. Supp. 41 (D. Del. 1953).

124. United States v. E. I. du Pont de Nemours & Co., 351 U.S. 377, 417 (1956).

Economic Change and the Sherman Act

Du Pont's Price Policy and Earnings on Cellophane and Rayon

Du Pont officials thought that Du Pont could make more money by reducing prices and selling more cellophane. President Yerkes of the Du Pont Cellophane Company expressed his views in this way:

> I am in favor of lowering the price. . . . [I] think it will undoubtedly increase sales and widen distribution. . . . Our price I think is too high based purely on manufacturing cost and too high in comparison with other wrapping papers on the market, and while we cannot approach the price of glassine or other oil papers, if we make a substantial reduction we will in some cases get somewhere near there.[125]

Walter S. Carpenter, Jr., Du Pont's board chairman, stated the Du Pont cellophane policy as follows:

> . . . the purpose of reducing our price and also improving our quality was to broaden our market. . . . As a general philosophy I was always in favor of the reduction of the price as we were able to do so by the reduced costs, and I think that I consistently urged that on the management.[126]

Du Pont's policy paid off. During the years from 1924 to 1950 Du Pont's cellophane earnings before taxes ranged from 18 per cent to 62.4 per cent on operating investment. They averaged 34.4 per cent.[127] Du Pont's general policy was to increase profits by lowering cost and increasing volume, but its managers did not hesitate to reverse this policy when they thought it would pay to do so. In 1947 earnings had fallen to 19.1 per cent before taxes. Not satisfied with this rate, Du Pont raised the average price of cellophane from 41.9 cents a pound to 46 cents. The result was an increase in earnings to a 31 per cent rate. At that time its division manager suggested that "if operative earnings of 31 per cent is [sic] considered inadequate, then an upward revision in prices will be necessary to improve the return." [128] He proposed a schedule of prices designed to yield about 40 per cent. This was put into effect in August 1948. Earnings

---

125. Memorandum of some remarks made at a meeting of the board of directors, Du Pont Cellophane Co., Dec. 11, 1924, Defendant's Exhibit 337, p. 643, United States v. E. I. du Pont de Nemours & Co., 118 F. Supp. 41 (D. Del. 1953). (Hereinafter the references to the exhibits and testimony in this case will not repeat the case citation.)
126. Transcript of Testimony 6278–79.
127. Du Pont's Operating Investment, Operating Earnings, and Net Earnings on Cellophane, 1925–1950, Table III, in George W. Stocking and Willard F. Mueller, "The Cellophane Case and the New Competition," 45 Am. Econ. Rev. 29, 59 (1955).
128. Government's Exhibit 591, p. 7539.

Workable Competition and Antitrust Policy

responded quickly, yielding 35.2 per cent in 1949 and 45.3 per cent in 1950. In raising prices Du Pont officials apparently were more concerned about the unfavorable publicity this might give them and the effect it might have on the case then pending before Judge Leahy than they were about the relation of cellophane prices to the prices of other wrapping materials. A Du Pont division manager put it this way:

What effect, if any, will a price increase have on our case when it is heard before the Federal Judge? I have not covered this with our Legal Department but in view of the position they took last July and August, prior to the October increase, I am inclined to think they should be brought in for a discussion on this matter.

The Du Pont Company may get some undesirable publicity from the press. A price increase on Cellophane could be looked upon as added fuel to the present recent spurt in the inflationary spiral and add to the present pressure for an increase in wages. This question is currently a live one at several of our cellophane plants. Probably it would be in order to discuss this with Mr. Brayman.[129]

Only after weighing such factors as these did Du Pont officials decide on the price increase.

That Du Pont's earnings on cellophane reflected monopoly power is indicated not only by their absolute heights but by comparison with its earnings on its rayon investment. There is a basic similarity between these two products and, up to a certain point, between the ways in which they were developed. Both are derived from the same basic raw material. Both were radical innovations. Du Pont obtained its production rights to both from French producers; both were produced under the same business management and presumably with common business aims; both products have reasonably close substitutes; both experienced a phenomenal increase in production and consumption; both were characterized by rapidly developing technology and a rapid decline in price; and both yielded a high rate of return in their early years, Du Pont's earnings on its rayon investment ranging from a high of 38.9 per cent to a low of 15.2 per cent during the period 1922–1929.[130] At the outset both were produced under

---

129. *Id.* at 7540. Mr. Brayman was the director of Du Pont's public relations department.

130. *Hearings before the Temporary National Economic Committee on Investigation of Concentration of Economic Power* (hereinafter *TNEC Hearings*), 76th Cong., 3d Sess., pt. 31, at 17988, 17990, and 17998 (1941). Comparable data on total rayon investment and earnings are not available after 1938. The district court found that Du Pont's "price policy for rayon was the same as for cellophane." 118 F. Supp. at 86.

Economic Change and the Sherman Act

conditions of monopoly or near monopoly. Here the similarity ends. Du Pont was the sole producer of cellophane until 1930 and thereafter Du Pont and Sylvania were the sole producers until 1951, when a third company with Du Pont's aid began production.[131] The American Viscose Corporation was the sole producer of rayon at the outset, soon followed by Du Pont, but by 1930 the structure of the rayon industry had markedly changed and Du Pont was meeting the rivalry of eighteen producers.[132] This intensification of competition resulted in a sharp decline in the rate of earnings. Du Pont operated its rayon division at a loss in 1930 and averaged only 7.5 per cent in the period from 1930 to 1938.[133] During this same period the rate of return on cellophane ranged from 18 to 39.9 per cent.[134]

The Strategy of a Monopolist

Not only did its rate of cellophane earnings reflect monopoly power, but Du Pont acted with respect to Sylvania as though it believed it had a valuable monopoly that it wanted to protect.[135] It originally obtained the exclusive right to make and sell cellophane in the American market under patents and with technical knowledge from La Cellophane, Société Anonyme, a French affiliate of the Comptoir des Textiles Artificiels, a French corporation from which it had previously obtained similar rights for rayon manufacture. After entering the agreement with Du Pont for the exploitation of the American market La Cellophane made a similar agreement with Kalle & Company for the exploitation of the German market—and ultimately the markets of Austria, Hungary, Czechoslovakia, Yugoslavia, Poland, Russia, Romania, China, Denmark, Sweden, Nor-

---

131. In June 1951 Olin Industries, Inc. (in 1954 this company merged with Mathieson Chemical Industries, Inc., to become Olin Mathieson Chemical Corp.) began the production of cellophane at Pisgah Forest, North Carolina. Testimony of Fred Olsen, Olin vice-president, Transcript of Testimony 6829. In 1948 Du Pont began making its technology available to Olin. Report on "the evidence in support of entry by Olin Industries into the Cellophane business, based on the purchase of patent license 'know-how' from du Pont," Dec. 15, 1948, Government's Exhibit 566, p. 7575.

132. Jesse W. Markham, *Competition in the Rayon Industry* (Cambridge: Harvard University Press, 1952), p. 47.

133. *TNEC Hearings, ibid.*

134. Stocking and Mueller, *supra* note 127, *ibid.*

135. For a more detailed discussion of the significance of strategy to monopoly see *id.* at 31–44. The statements of fact which follow in the text are based on the district court's findings unless otherwise documented.

way, and Finland [136]—and licensed British Cellophane, Ltd., for the exploitation of British markets. Du Pont thereafter entered into patent exchange agreements with Kalle and British Cellophane which had the practical effect of dividing world markets for exclusive exploitation by the several companies. Du Pont representatives attended an international cartel conference at Paris in February 1930 as guests and observers, and although they did not sign the official cartel agreement, the agreement recognized the North American market as belonging to Du Pont and Sylvania.[137] When the Belgian company Société Industrielle de la Cellulose (SIDAC), which had obtained La Cellophane's trade secrets through two former employees of La Cellophane, began to export cellophane to the American market, Du Pont sought and obtained additional tariff protection through a reclassification of cellophane. This raised the duty from 25 per cent to 60 per cent ad valorem, a rate high enough to prevent price cutting by importers.[138] A reduction of cellophane prices as Du Pont achieved quantity production and lower costs, together with a 45 per cent ad valorem tariff in the Tariff Act of 1930, was enough to virtually eliminate foreign cellophane from the American market. In no year between 1930 and 1947 did imports amount to 1 per cent of domestic cellophane consumption.

Shut out by the tariff from the rich American market, SIDAC established an American subsidiary, Sylvania Industrial Corporation of America, for the manufacture and sale of cellophane in competition with Du Pont. Du Pont inaugurated a series of negotiations with Sylvania regarding patent rights and eventually filed a patent infringement suit which was finally settled out of court.[139] The settlement involved an inter-

---

136. Letter of Oct. 30, 1929, from C. M. Albright, Du Pont Cellophane vice-president, to the company's Buffalo Office, Government's Exhibit 1091, p. 1195.

137. "Official report" of Feb. 11–12, 1930 international cellophane cartel agreement, Paris, Government's Exhibit 1414, pp. 1841–44.

138. Du Pont's quarterly competitive report, second quarter 1929, Government's Exhibit 432, p. 5690.

139. Du Pont's patent attorney gave his impressions of Sylvania's reasons for settling the infringement suit as follows: "During the conference Mr. Menken [Sylvania's general counsel] stated that in his opinion the case should be settled. He said that they were very fearful of what the result would be to their company in the event they succeeded in having the claims of the patents which are involved in the litigation held invalid. He seemed to realize the old adage that the defendant can never win.... If the Du Pont Cellophane Company succeeds and the patents are held to be infringed, Sylvania Industrial Corporation will be under injunction and will be obliged to stop manufacturing moistureproof wrapping tissue. On the other hand, if they succeed in having the broad claims of the patents held invalid they will throw the art open, as far as the broad claims are concerned, to anyone and there-

change of patent rights and a limitation of Sylvania's production. Sylvania agreed to restrict its production to 20 per cent of total sales of moistureproof cellophane in 1933, this percentage to be increased by 1 per cent annually until it reached 29 per cent in 1942 and the agreement to be enforced by prohibitive royalties for exceeding the amount specified. Sylvania not only geared its production to Du Pont's but followed Du Pont's pricing practices. Meanwhile, as a bulwark against competition from any other source, Du Pont was carrying foward a vigorous program to cover by patents all alternative methods of moistureproofing cellophane.[140]

Du Pont by these several moves clearly recognized cellophane as a unique product which it was determined to produce on a monopoly basis. Du Pont's own executives from time to time specifically acknowledged the ineffectiveness of the competition of rival products. Its development department concluded as early as 1923 that glassine, sheet gelatin, and tin foil, at that time cellophane's closest rival products, offered no serious competition because of price and quality differences. Du Pont's 1948 market analysis report evaluated the rival films that had since come on the market in these words:

The principal markets for non-viscose films have been competitive with Cellophane only to a very minor degree up to this time. Some are used very little or not at all in the packaging field—others are employed principally for specialty uses where Cellophane is not well adapted—none have been successfully introduced into any of Cellophane's main markets due to their inherent shortcomings.[141]

While Du Pont was negotiating with Olin Industries, Inc., prior to Olin's becoming the third domestic cellophane producer,[142] Olin Industries

fore will have additional competition. Sylvania . . . has plenty of ready cash but are [sic] hesitant about enlarging their plant facilities pending the litigation since, if successful, they will only invite further competition." Letter dated Aug. 4, 1932, Government's Exhibit 2811, pp. 6073-74.

140. President Yerkes of Du Pont Cellophane Co. in reporting on the success of this project in 1934 said: "This work was undertaken as a defensive program in connection with protecting broadly by patents the field of moistureproofing agents other than waxes which was the only class of material disclosed in our original Cellophane moistureproofing patents.

"The investigations of this subject did, in fact, lead to the discovery of a number of classes of materials which could serve equally well for moistureproofing agents. . . . Each of these classes has been the subject of a patent. . . . Altogether, 13 patent applications are being written as a result of the work done under this project, all in view of strengthening our Moistureproof Cellophane patent situation." Dec. 1933 report to Du Pont Cellophane's board of directors, Jan. 22, 1934, Government's Exhibit 488, p. 6478.

141. Government's Exhibit 595, p. 1147.
142. See note 131 *supra.*

Workable Competition and Antitrust Policy

reported, "According to Du Pont, Cellophane is considered the only all purpose film, and any product to be *truly competitive* with Cellophane must have the following attributes: (1) low cost, (2) transparency, (3) operate with a high efficiency on mechanical equipment, (4) print well both as to speed and appearance." [143] Olin concluded:

There are no films currently marketed which are potentially competitive to any substantial degree in Cellophane's major markets when measured by the above attributes necessary for wide usage. Other transparent films will find their place for those low volume uses which can absorb the additional cost of the film and which necessitate certain physical properties not possessed by Cellophane.[144]

Significance of the Cellophane Case

Judging by the structure of the cellophane industry between 1923 and 1951 (with only two producers and with Sylvania's output and pricing policy geared to Du Pont's), by the strategy Du Pont followed in protecting itself against the competition of rival producers, and by the industry's performance in terms of profit margins, I conclude that cellophane has been sold in American markets under the protection of private monopoly. The basic issue in the *Cellophane* case is clear. I have stated it elsewhere as follows:

The basic issue in the *Cellophane* case really boils down to this: Would freedom of entry have brought in a larger number of cellophane producers and ultimately lower prices and earnings than have prevailed? I believe it would have. Moreover, if the rivalry of substitute packaging materials, particularly glassine and waxed paper, had in fact forced competitive pricing on Du Pont, as the court concluded, Du Pont should have been indifferent to the entry of rival cellophane producers. Competition from either cellophane or waxed paper would have resulted in precisely the same cost-price ratios in selling cellophane. As judged by structure, conduct, and performance, Judge Leahy erred in giving a negative answer to his first question: Does Du Pont have a monopoly in making and selling cellophane?[145]

And the Supreme Court compounded Judge Leahy's error. If the Supreme Court's conception of cross-elasticity of demand should apply in future antitrust causes, the dissenters are probably right in declaring that the Court has emasculated Section 2 of the Sherman Act. If cellophane is merely a flexible wrapping material, the courts might as readily conclude that airlines, railways, bus lines, and river steamers are merely transporta-

---

143. Government's Exhibit 566, p. 7575.
144. *Ibid.*
145. P. 285-86 *supra*.

Economic Change and the Sherman Act

tion facilities; that aluminum, copper, brass, and steel are merely metals; and that cotton rugs, linen rugs, nylon rugs, braided rugs, linoleum, and similar substitutes are merely floor coverings. Monopolization of one such item need not violate the Sherman Act. To deny the existence of monopoly the courts need only ascertain that people choose among products serving similar functions in trying to get their money's worth.

Technological progress has increased the variety of products which will serve a particular need. Customers nearly always have a choice between rival products with different specific qualities and different prices. This is the interindustry competition which some economists and laymen think is a substitute for the competition of rival sellers selling the same product. Many believe it makes the contemporary economy workably competitive regardless of a given industry's structure. "Interindustry competition" is a concept by which "reasonable" men may judge a situation without meticulous attention to the relevant economic logic. It enables judges as well as economists to make peace with their environment. Justice Frankfurter in a concurring opinion in the *Cellophane* case put it this way:

> ... the so-called issues of fact and law that call for adjudication in this legal territory are united, and intrinsically so, with factors that entail social and economic judgment. Any consideration of "monopoly" under the Sherman law can hardly escape judgment, even if only implied, on social and economic issues.[146]

THE DU PONT–GENERAL MOTORS CASE IN THE DISTRICT COURT

On June 30, 1949, the Antitrust Division of the Department of Justice filed a complaint against Du Pont Company and the General Motors Corporation, alleging that since 1915 these companies had engaged in a combination to restrain trade in the products of the companies and to monopolize a substantial part of that trade in violation of Sections 1 and 2 of the Sherman Act. The complaint also alleged violation of Section 7 of the Clayton Act. The primary issue in the case was whether the Du Pont Company through stock acquisitions had obtained control of General Motors, and if so whether it exercised that control to insure it a protected market for such of its products as were necessary to the business of General Motors and to give it control over the chemical products and processes that General Motors might develop. The district court in finding

---

146. United States v. E. I. du Pont de Nemours and Co., 351 U.S. 377, 414 (1956).

Workable Competition and Antitrust Policy

for the defendants did not rely specifically on the doctrine of workable competition. In a hundred-page decision [147] Judge LaBuy did not even mention the concept nor did he cite a single legal precedent for his decision. He concluded that the facts did

> not establish that Du Pont has been the controlling force in the direction of General Motors affairs, or has been in a position to act as if it owned a majority of General Motors stock. The record shows consultation and conference, but not domination.[148]

Judge LaBuy may have appropriately exercised his judicial prerogative in so holding, but it is fairly clear that a district court with different preconceptions sitting in an environment less friendly to big business might just as readily have found that Du Pont controlled General Motors.

The more relevant facts on this issue may be briefly stated. Pierre S. du Pont, president of the Du Pont Company, and Irenee du Pont as individuals had bought substantial amounts of stock in the General Motors Corporation as early as 1915. In December 1917 the Du Pont executive and finance committees authorized the Du Pont Company to purchase $25,000,000 of General Motors common stock. John J. Raskob, treasurer of the Du Pont Company, in urging the company to make this purchase, said:

> With Mr. Durant we will have joint control of the companies.
>
> . . . .
>
> Perhaps it is not made clear that the directorates of the motor companies will be chosen by Du Pont and Durant. Mr. Durant should be continued as President of the Company. Mr. P. S. du Pont will be continued as Chairman of the Board, the Finance Committee will be ours and we will have such representation on the Executive Committee as we desire. . . .[149]

By 1921 the Du Pont Company had increased its investment in General Motors to $79,500,000, representing 38 per cent of the company's outstanding stock. About this transaction Raskob stated, "This gave the Du Pont Company approximately 38% of the total common stock of the General Motors Corporation which is practical control and made it necessary to assume complete responsibility for the management."[150] By 1938 Du Pont had reduced its holdings to 23 per cent by a transfer of

---

147. United States v. E. I. du Pont de Nemours & Co., 126 F. Supp. 235 (N.D. Ill. 1954), rev'd, 353 U.S. 586 (1957).
148. Id. at 250–51.
149. Government's Trial Exhibit (hereinafter GTX) 124, Record (hereinafter R.) 664, 5230, United States v. E. I. du Pont de Nemours & Co., 353 U.S. 586 (1957). See also the district court's opinion, 126 F. Supp. at 241–42.
150. GTX 235, p. 3, R. 483, 3496.

Economic Change and the Sherman Act

stock to the Managers Securities Company and through the Securities Company to select executives of General Motors under a stock bonus plan. Du Pont's holdings have since remained at 23 per cent. In 1947 this represented 10,000,000 shares, which in 1950 were split to 20,000,000 shares [151] and by 1957 had increased to 63,000,000 shares.[152] In 1947, 436,510 stockholders held the remaining shares. Of these, 92 per cent owned no more than 100 shares each and 60 per cent owned no more than 25 shares each.[153] At stockholders' meetings in the years 1928–1949 Du Pont voted from 30 to over 52 per cent of the stock voted.[154] A proxy committee set up by a management friendly to Du Pont presumably voted much of the remainder.

The record is replete with evidence that Du Pont tried to use its control to get General Motors to buy its products rather than those of its competitors, and that it was in part successful. There is an abundance of evidence indicating that Du Pont tried to get a general agreement with General Motors whereby General Motors would turn over to Du Pont for exploitation the chemical processes and products which it developed in its own research laboratories; and that Du Pont eventually obtained a monopoly in the manufacture of tetraethyl lead, first discovered in the laboratories of General Motors, and a monopoly in the exploitation of Freon (an organic fluorine compound) and its derivatives, likewise a General Motors discovery.[155]

Counsel for defendants contended that these several transactions were arm's-length transactions involving no coercion, and the district court agreed. But a different court with different preconceptions might just as readily have concluded, as an earlier court in a different case had done, that "domination may spring as readily from subtle and unexercised power as from arbitrary imposition of command."[156]

Conclusions

This study has developed the thesis that cultural environment—the economic and social milieu—determines the attitudes of the courts in

---

151. 126 F. Supp. at 244.
152. Wall Street Journal, June 4, 1957, p. 2, col. 2. The *Journal* placed the market value of the stock at $2,500,000,000.
153. 126 F. Supp. at 244.
154. GTX 1307, R. 664, 5230.
155. For a detailed analysis of the evidence supporting this view of the case see chap. 8 *supra*.
156. North American Co. v. SEC, 327 U.S. 686, 693 (1946).

Workable Competition and Antitrust Policy

antitrust decisions; and that economists who, like judges, have responded to the same influences, have afforded in the concept of workable competition a logical basis for a lax administration of the Sherman Act. The Supreme Court's reversal of the district court in the *Du Pont–General Motors* case [157] would seem to cast doubt on this thesis. Always there are some judges, doughty individualists, who do not drift with the current. That fact might offer a sufficient explanation for the Supreme Court's having overruled the district court. Justices Brennan, Black, and Douglas and Chief Justice Warren constituted the majority in this case. Many decisions of Justices Black and Douglas bear witness to their belief that a concentration of economic power constitutes a threat to the American way of life. Justice Brennan and Chief Justice Warren appeared to be like-minded. Some lawyers have expressed the opinion that had Justices Clark, Whittaker, and Harlan participated in the *Du Pont–General Motors* case the decision might have been five to four in favor of the defendants.[158] This is, of course, conjecture, though perhaps reasonable conjecture.

But the majority of the Court in reversing Judge LaBuy may not have been merely manifesting their own predilections. The flow of environmental factors has been generally in one direction, but always there have been countercurrents of varying force. Although the war-engendered prosperity gave the leaders of industry a new confidence in big business and its contribution to the social welfare ("What is good for the country is good for General Motors and vice versa"[159]), postwar developments made the going tough for many small and moderate-size firms. They frequently found it expedient to sell out to their rivals, and many that did not fell by the wayside. The survival of little business has become a national concern, expressed not only in a modification of Section 7 of the Clayton Act [160] designed to stay the forces of industrial concentration but in a program of direct federal aid to little business. It may be that the justices who constituted the Supreme Court majority in the *Du Pont–General Motors* case reflected not merely their own predilections but a countercurrent in the flow of social forces.

157. United States v. E. I. du Pont de Nemours & Co., 353 U.S. 586 (1957).
158. William F. Rogers, "U.S. v. Du Pont–A Judicial Revision of Section 7," 2 Antitrust Bulletin 577, 581 (1957).
159. Former Secretary of Defense Charles E. Wilson at his final news conference before his resignation, N. Y. Times, Oct. 3, 1957, p. 14, col. 4.
160. 64 Stat. 1125 (1950), 15 U.S.C. § 18 (1958).

10

Institutional Factors in Economic Thinking

ECONOMISTS ARE INDEBTED to Thorstein Veblen for his emphasis on the role that institutional factors play in economic thinking. To Veblen, what economists believed and had to say about the operation of economic forces in a price system was essentially a logical formulation of the preconceptions and observations of those whose daily lives were subjected to the impact of the system. As he expressed it, "The higher theoretical knowledge, that body of tenets which rises to the dignity of a philosophical or scientific system . . . is a complex of habits of thought which reflect the habits of life embodied in the institutional structure of society. . . ."[1] More specifically, about classical theory Veblen said: "In the days of the early classical writers economics had a vital interest for the layman of the time, because it formulated the commonsense metaphysics of the time in its application to a department of human life."[2]

Wesley Clair Mitchell, close friend and admirer of Veblen, expressed a similar thought throughout his brilliant lectures on types of economic theory at Columbia University. Economic doctrines, he told his students, represent intellectual responses to ever-changing economic problems. The problems economists think about and the way they think about them are determined by the institutional matrix in which they find themselves. Around this idea he built his course in the development of economic thought from Adam Smith to John R. Commons.

As a background for a similar interpretation of current economic thinking, I shall lean heavily upon what Mitchell had to say about what Adam Smith taught and why he taught it.

Note: Presidential address delivered at the seventy-first annual meeting of the American Economic Ass'n, Chicago, Illinois, Dec. 28, 1958. Reprinted from the *American Economic Review*, Vol. 44, No. 1 (March 1959).

1. *The Place of Science in Modern Civilization and Other Essays* (New York: Huebsch, 1919), p. 44.
2. *Id.* at 69.

Workable Competition and Antitrust Policy

Smith was primarily a political economist, not an economic logician. It is true that he formulated principles governing the determination of prices, the economic allocation of resources, the distribution of income, the geographic division of labor, and economic progress, and in doing so he laid the basis for late-nineteenth-century neoclassicism. But he formulated these principles as one profoundly concerned with public policy, and it is the policy implications of his principles and the persuasive manner in which he expounded them that make *The Wealth of Nations* one of the great books of all time. On public-policy issues he spoke with the knowledge of a keen observer of contemporary affairs, the wisdom of a profound philosopher, and the convictions of a great moralist. He was concerned not so much with the discovery of new truths as with the application of sound principles in determining the proper limits of governmental activity, and it was essentially a negative policy that he advocated. That negative policy was a reaction both against the teachings of the mercantilists and against the web of administrative controls in which the economic activity of the sixteenth and seventeenth centuries had been enmeshed. But when he expounded his ideas the strands of this web had already been greatly weakened by economic forces set loose by the rise of capitalism, the accelerated pace of technological innovation, and the development of the factory system.

The Classic Norm: Economic Individualism

Smith, in defending economic individualism as a means of promoting the national welfare, conceived of the national income as the aggregate of individual incomes. As he put it, "The annual revenue of every society is always precisely equal to the exchangeable value of the whole annual produce of its industry, or rather is precisely the same thing with that exchangeable value."[3] The way to maximize it is to let individuals maximize their own income in their own way. He recognized, of course, that no individual is primarily concerned with promoting the general welfare. Of this he said,

> By preferring the support of domestic to that of foreign industry, [every individual] intends only his own security; and by directing that industry in such a manner as its produce may be of the greatest value, he intends only

---

3. *The Wealth of Nations*, ed. Edwin Cannon (New York: Putnam, 1937), p. 423.

Institutional Factors in Economic Thinking

his own gain, and he is in this, as in many other cases, led by an invisible hand to promote an end which was no part of his intention.[4]

Promotion of the general welfare is a proper goal of statesmen, and they can achieve it by the abolition of all needless restrictions on economic activity. As Smith put it,

> All systems either of preference or of restraint, therefore, being thus completely taken away, the obvious and simple system of natural liberty establishes itself of its own accord. Every man, as long as he does not violate the laws of justice, is left perfectly free to pursue his own interest his own way, and to bring both his industry and capital into competition with those of any other man, or order of men.[5]

These are doctrines with which, of course, we are all familiar. What we sometimes overlook is that Smith in his exposition of economic liberalism was the spokesman of an age that needed little persuasion to accept his doctrines. Smith's was an age in which the individual had acquired an institutional significance characteristic of no previous age in English history. In the entire culture of the period the individual had acquired a new importance as innovator, initiator, and doer. Man had assumed responsibility for his own destiny and hence for society's destiny, particularly in economic affairs. The ideas Smith so brilliantly reduced to a systematic philosophy were not novel to the rapidly increasing and increasingly important entrepreneurial class of his time. Although Smith never engaged in business, during his sojourn in Glasgow he associated intimately and continuously with businessmen. Glasgow at that time was a thriving commercial and manufacturing center whose industrial progress would have been gratifying to any modern Chamber of Commerce. Nor were the businessmen, who were largely responsible for its vigorous activity, indifferent to policy questions. The more alert and public-spirited townsmen conducted a weekly discussion club expressly designed to inquire into the nature and principles of trade. Smith as a member made weekly contacts over a number of years with an informed and articulate group of businessmen who had assumed responsibility for the conduct of economic affairs. Smith's interest in economic problems may well have stemmed from these associations, and his ideas about these problems no doubt were shaped in part by them.

No society is static. As E. Lipson, the economic historian, has said:

---

4. *Ibid.*
5. *Id.* at 651. Smith, of course, was wise and humane enough to recognize the limitations of competition as a means of promoting the general welfare and to assign important functions to the state.

Workable Competition and Antitrust Policy

"Every social system contains within itself the seeds of its own decay; it is always dissolving and reforming in an infinite sequence."[6] While Smith was writing *The Wealth of Nations*, mercantilism, the folly of which Smith so lucidly and logically exposed, was already dissolving, and individualistic capitalism, the next sequence in the inexorable march of economic change, had already passed its adolescence. The restraints on the movement of labor, the restrictive rules of apprenticeship, the prohibition of exports, and the tariff on imports—the whole scheme of mercantilist controls was already obsolete and was rapidly passing into the limbo of outworn notions. Smith gave it a push, but economic forces propelled it as no philosopher, however potent his pen, could have done.

The corporate structure of mercantilist society, with its village courts, its merchant and craft guilds, and its monopolistic overseas trading companies, had already largely dissolved under the disintegrating influence of widespread and persistent individualism. Men insisted on their freedom to engage in enterprise unshackled by arbitrary controls. The rise of the spirit of individual initiative in economic affairs—a spirit embodied in the entrepreneur or "undertaker" as Smith called him—was, of course, a gradual process that had its beginning in the late Middle Ages, but it had already achieved considerable maturity by 1776. Individual entrepreneurship was the characteristic institution around which economic activity revolved, by which economic resources were allocated and production was organized, and through which the several factors of production received their rewards.

Lipson described this process with an eloquence rare in economic writings and a fidelity to the facts of English industrial development not always achieved by those who interpret broad movements in history. He showed that in industry, agriculture, and trade the "spirited pioneers of a brave new world," as he characterized the economic leaders of that era, created business opportunities that were previously nonexistent, or quickly seized them as they appeared and thereby aided in the creation of an industrial environment at once challenging and rewarding to the entrepreneur. On every score Lipson found evidence of the capitalist spirit as manifest in the conception and carrying out of speculative endeavors. Great captains of industry were relatively scarce, but the single entrepreneur who put his own and sometimes other people's money into business enterprises for profit was characteristic of the era. Individual innovators, while playing a supplementary role to entrepreneurs, aided them by dem-

6. *The Growth of English Society* (London: A. and C. Black, 1949), p. 15.

Institutional Factors in Economic Thinking

onstrating the practicality of their inventions. The men whose inventions revolutionized the textile industry in the eighteenth century are household names—James Hargreaves with his spinning jenny in 1767, Richard Arkwright with his water frame in 1768, Samuel Crompton with his cotton mule in 1775, and James Watt with his steam engine in 1782. In some instances a single individual combined the roles of entrepreneur and innovator. Arkwright, who was a barber and wigmaker, secured the services of a clockmaker, a blacksmith, and a watch-toolmaker to improve an early model of a cotton spinning machine and together with other persons invested £12,000 between 1771 and 1774 in the erection and operation of a cotton mill.[7] Abraham Darby, who was the first ironmaker to use coke instead of charcoal in iron smelting, erected 7 furnaces, which by 1756 were producing 20 to 22 tons of iron a week. The Duke of Bridgwater constructed canals to transport coal from his colliery to markets at Manchester and Liverpool.

In agriculture no less than in industry and commerce, the private individual stands out as the innovator and enterpriser. We are all familiar with the contributions to scientific farming made by Jethro Tull, Lord Townshend, and other giants of the era. What we frequently overlook is that a host of small farmers were experimenting with crop rotation and better breeding of livestock. The few names that stand out so strikingly are a reflection of a development common to all English agriculture.

But not only in economic affairs and in the advance of technology did the phenomenon of individualism manifest itself. Mitchell portrayed to his students in a striking manner the extent to which the spirit of individual enterprise and initiative permeated the whole cultural fabric of eighteenth-century England. Individuals, frequently of humble origin but always of unusual talent, imagination, and enterprise, raised the level of cultural achievement throughout its whole range. The fine arts, literature, historical writing, journalism, the law, religion, philanthropy, education—all felt the impact of individuals of great intelligence and vision who dedicated themselves to the transforming of ideas into reality. William Hogarth, son of a schoolmaster, used painting as a medium for the pointing of a moral and the telling of a tale, creating his own art by using color instead of language. Joshua Reynolds, also the son of a schoolmaster, and Thomas Gainsborough brought portraiture to new heights. In recognition of his achievement Reynolds became the first president of the

7. A. P. Usher, *The Industrial History of England* (New York: Houghton Mifflin, 1920), pp. 294–95.

Workable Competition and Antitrust Policy

Royal Academy. Daniel Defoe (1661–1731), the son of a butcher, in *Robinson Crusoe*, Samuel Richardson (1689–1761), the son of a London woodworker, in *Pamela* and *Clarissa Harlowe*, and Henry Fielding (1707–1754) in *Tom Jones* by the middle of the eighteenth century had given shape to a new form of writing, the modern English novel. James Boswell in his classic *Life of Samuel Johnson* was the creator of a new type of biography that portrayed the life of his subject in an unusually intimate and effective manner. David Hume wrote his *History of England*, William Robertson his *History of Scotland during the Reigns of Queen Mary and King James VI*, and Edward Gibbon his *Decline and Fall of the Roman Empire*, all "models of exposition concerning the past of the race" that, as Mitchell observed, carried a different appeal and suggested a different outlook on life from previous histories.

The eighteenth century witnessed the beginnings of modern journalism with the publication of newspapers combining the functions of reporting news and selling advertising. The *Morning Post* appeared in 1772, the *London Times* in 1788, and the *Morning Advertiser* in 1794. These had been preceded earlier in the century by a series of periodicals such as the *Spectator*, the *Tatler*, and the *Guardian*, influential in both politics and literature. It was in the eighteenth century that Lord Mansfield, Chief Justice of England, organized the commercial law of Great Britain and introduced important innovations in legal practice. It was in the eighteenth century that Sir William Blackstone wrote his *Commentaries*, which remained a leading legal textbook until our own century. In philanthropy James Oglethorpe promoted his scheme for colonizing Georgia with condemned criminals, confident that a wholesome environment would make of them wholesome citizens. The eighteenth century witnessed the beginnings of prison reform under the leadership of John Howard and the movement to protect children from exploitation, led by Jonas Hanway.

Stephen Hales, regarded as the father of plant physiology; John Roebuck, who introduced the use of lead condensing chambers in making sulphuric acid; Henry Cavendish, the discoverer of hydrogen as a chemical element, the first to combine hydrogen and oxygen to make water, and the first to devise an accurate method of weighing the earth; and Joseph Priestley, the first to discover the decomposition of ammonia by electricity and the first to describe the properties of ammonia, nitrous acid, sulphur dioxide, hydrogen sulphide, and carbon monoxide—all were eighteenth-century scientists. Their achievements in these various fields manifested a spirit of individualism that strongly marked the whole of eighteenth-century England. Finally, what Mitchell called government by public

Institutional Factors in Economic Thinking

discussion replaced the arbitrary and often irresponsible rule of sovereigns. In Parliament, in vestry meetings, in drawing rooms and social clubs, in coffee houses and taverns, people discussed public issues in a lively and critical manner. In these forums a public opinion crystallized, influential in both political and economic affairs. The eighteenth century in England was truly a century in which individualism was a mass phenomenon. The English historian G. M. Trevelyan has aptly characterized it as "an age of aristocracy and liberty . . . of individual initiative and institutional decay . . . of creative vigor in all the trades and arts that serve and adorn the life of man." [8]

It was in this social milieu, this institutional matrix, that the father of political economy conceived his philosophy that the way to maximize national income and promote national welfare was to leave individuals unhampered in their economic activity, free to choose their own occupations without the restrictions of a socially enforced apprenticeship, free to organize and operate business enterprise without state subsidies or state direction, and free to buy and sell in any market without interference from local and national governments.

In short, Smith's economic liberalism, "seeking to vindicate the right of the individual to shape his own destiny," was a product of his age. It reflected a mode of thinking that was manifest in politics, in religion, in the arts, in science, in commerce and industry—a spirit that had permeated the whole fabric of eighteenth-century English society.[9] It has been said that no economist has encompassed his age so thoroughly as did Adam Smith. It is perhaps equally true that no economist was so encompassed by his age as was Adam Smith.

Nothing pleases the educated mind so much as the systematic, philosophical expression of ideas with which it is familiar and which it deems good, by one whose eloquence, erudition, and profundity it can scarcely hope to achieve. *The Wealth of Nations* had a following waiting to be led. Before Smith's death it had run through five editions; by the end of the eighteenth century it had been translated into five foreign languages and had been pirated in Ireland. It was discussed in drawing rooms and quoted by parliamentarians. Many of the restrictions against which it

---

8. *English Social History* (New York: Longmans, Green, 1942), p. 339.
9. Throughout the eighteenth century individualism also found in the American colonies an environment peculiarly suited to its development. Under the leveling influence of the frontier, the Western ideals of individual freedom and equality flourished. The Declaration of Independence may appropriately be regarded as a political counterpart of *The Wealth of Nations*.

Workable Competition and Antitrust Policy

complained were embodied in laws and regulations that had largely become dead letters; nevertheless, it was not until well into the nineteenth century that Parliament wiped off the statute books the last of the mercantilistic measures and officially embraced free trade in international commerce. In doing so it responded not so much to what anybody had written as to what nearly everybody who counted thought. The success of the free-trade movement was a belated recognition of the fact that England's industry and manufacturing were the world's best and that the interests of English businessmen demanded free access to markets and raw materials.

THE ORGANIZATIONAL REVOLUTION

But economic individualism, the philosophical product of individualistic capitalism, had no sooner conquered men's minds than the great transformation was ushering in the next sequence in the inexorable flow of institutions and ideas. Corporate capitalism was soon to replace individual capitalism as the characteristic institution of a mechanized factory system, geared to mass-production methods and utilizing the sciences of chemistry and physics for utilitarian ends. The business corporation was soon to become the epicenter of an organizational revolution of earthquake proportions. Just as the individual and individualism dominated eighteenth-century society, so the organization has come to dominate twentieth-century society. In nearly all areas of twentieth-century social and intellectual life—business, sports, religion, philanthropy, civil liberties, education, communication, the arts—the organization has replaced the individual as an institution for promoting enterprise and getting things done. At the center of this organizational revolution is the business corporation.

Smith's well-known skepticism of the corporation as an entrepreneurial device for carrying on economic activity was reflected in early American attitudes. The first American work on political economy, published in 1820, regarded nongovernmental corporations as *"prima facie,* injurious to national wealth" and as institutions that should "be looked upon by those who have no money, with jealousy and suspicion." "They are," said Daniel Raymond,

and ought to be considered, as artificial engines of power, contrived by the rich, for the purpose of increasing their already too great ascendency, and calculated to destroy that natural equality among men, which God has ordained, and which no government has a right to lend its power in destroying.

Institutional Factors in Economic Thinking

The tendency of such institutions is to cause a more unequal division of property, and a greater inequality among men, than would otherwise take place. . . .[10]

In 1840 the governor of Massachusetts, where most of the existing corporations were then doing business, in a message to the Great and General Court said of them:

These societies are one of the vices of our time. They encourage speculation and fraud, mobilize landed property, overturn matrimonial arrangements, escape publicity in the transfer of real property, diminish the sense of individual responsibility, create property in mortmain, prevent all penal remedies, are lacking in moral sense, and constitute finally a grave social peril by concentrating too much power in the hands of certain of our citizens.[11]

Such ideas today sound quaint indeed. Today the corporation is regarded as the master business institution, essential to the effective utilization and progressive development of modern technology and responsible for the high standard of material welfare and prosperity that, with temporary interruptions, has characterized American society for the past half century. This change in attitude has paralleled the remarkable growth of corporate enterprise, both in the scope and magnitude of its operations and in the frequency with which it has been utilized.

The modern corporation, it should be noted, is a man-made institution, made legally possible as the states have liberalized their incorporation laws in response to the demands of businessmen, or lawyers who have spoken for them. With its perpetual existence, the almost unlimited scope of its legitimate activities, the limited liability of its legal but absentee owners, the continuity of its management, and its legal autonomy, it has afforded almost an ideal instrument for carrying on large-scale production and larger-scale business enterprise. It has made possible three great combination or merger movements that have changed the structure of American industry: the merger movement between 1897 and 1903, the merger movement of the 1920's, and the current merger movement, in progress since the close of the second world war. Economists have differed sharply as to the effect of these movements on competition, and less sharply as to their effect on industrial concentration. On the latter issue the differences of opinion that existed a few years ago now seem largely reconciled. No student of industrial history will challenge the statement that at the

---

10. *Thoughts on Political Economy* (Baltimore: F. Lucas, Jr., 1820), p. 429.
11. W. Z. Ripley, *Main Street and Wall Street* (Boston: Little, Brown, 1927), p. 22.

Workable Competition and Antitrust Policy

turn of the century the Great Combination Movement concentrated the output of many basic industries in a smaller number of firms than had previously controlled it. In truth it would seem no exaggeration to say that no other period of industrial history, in a time so brief, has experienced so great a transformation in the structure of industry. Similarly, most students accept the findings of Berle and Means that in the period from 1924 to 1929 the assets of the 200 largest business corporations increased more rapidly than the assets of all other business corporations.[12] Morris Adelman's study [13] revealed a decrease in industrial concentration from 1933 to 1947, but the merger movement of the 1950's reversed that trend.[14]

A significant characteristic of the merger movements is that each has taken place in the face of a law designed to prevent it. The Sherman Act voiced the fear of a rural and small-town citizenry that combinations threatened the opportunity and even the survival of the small businessman and endangered the welfare of the farmer. Despite its comprehensive prohibition of every combination in restraint of trade regardless of the form it took, the Sherman Act proved helpless to stay the movement inaugurated by the trusts of the 1880's and carried to completion by the corporations of the 1890's. The merger movement of the 1920's followed on the heels of a congressional effort to make good the deficiencies of the Sherman Act; Section 7 of the Clayton Act prohibited the acquisition of stock by one corporation in another where the effect would be to lessen competition between the two companies. And the merger movement of the 1950's steadily progressed in the face of the Celler-Kefauver amend-

12. Adolf A. Berle, Jr., and Gardiner C. Means, *The Modern Corporation and Private Property* (New York: Macmillan, 1932), p. 35.
13. "The Measurement of Industrial Concentration," 23 Rev. Econ. Stat. 269 (1951).
14. Census figures show a slight increase in concentration between 1947 and 1954 for 375 industries. Irving Rottenberg, "New Statistics on Companies and on Concentration in Manufacturing from the 1954 Census" (summary of paper delivered at the 117th annual meeting of the American Statistical Ass'n, Sept. 10–13, 1957), 53 Jour. Am. Stat. Ass'n 588 (1958). In 1954 the country's 200 largest companies accounted for 37 per cent of the total value added by manufacture as against 30 per cent in 1947. *Concentration in American Industry*, a report to the Subcommittee on Antitrust and Monopoly of the Senate Committee on the Judiciary, 85th Cong., 1st Sess. 11 (1957). Adelman, who in his 1951 study, *supra* note 13, was severely critical of the measurements of industrial concentration employed by the Federal Trade Commission, defends the Census statistics as "a valuable addition to our stock of basic information" and "sound in concept"; but he misreads them as showing that "concentration did not increase from 1947 to 1954." "A Current Appraisal of Concentration Statistics" (summary of paper delivered at the 117th annual meeting of the American Statistical Ass'n, Sept. 10–13, 1957), 53 Jour. Am. Stat. Ass'n 568 (1958).

ment to Section 7 of the Clayton Act, which was designed to stop it.

That the combination movement has proceeded apace while an articulate minority has tried to stem it reflects, I believe, the wholehearted acceptance of the modern corporation by contemporary society. In manufacturing, mining, wholesaling, indeed in the whole range of economic activities loosely designated by the term industry, corporate enterprise has replaced the individual entrepreneur as a characteristic business institution.[15]

The several combination movements have resulted from complex causes, but they have all represented in greater or less degree a quest by business for security. Business firms have sought through mergers to isolate themselves from the vagaries of the market. The industrial combination movement has been paralleled by the growth of powerful labor unions that, whatever their incidental benefit to individual workers, have had as their primary goal the sale of labor under noncompetitive conditions.

The use of the organization as an instrument for carrying on activity has not been confined to business and labor. To an impressive extent it has supplanted the individual in the educational and cultural areas of American life: science, creative scholarship, sports, philanthropy, religion, civil liberties, and the like.

The growth of knowledge is essentially a social process in which each generation starts with the accumulated wisdom of previous ages. Although a single generation's contribution may bulk large in comparison with that of any previous generation, at any one time it represents but a small part of society's total knowledge. While the accumulation of knowledge is a social process, traditionally it has been kept going by the discoveries of skeptical and inquiring individuals. The United States patent policy was based on this idea. To promote the progress of science and useful arts the Constitution provides that an inventor may have an exclusive right to his discoveries for a limited time under terms laid down by Congress. The Constitution, as a political instrument reflecting the influence of eighteenth-century individualism, contemplates that the rewards of technological improvement shall go to the individual inventor. It makes no

---

15. In emphasizing the role of the modern corporation as an organizational force in American industry and the extent to which it has supplanted the individual entrepreneur, I am not unmindful that the corporation has frequently been the means by which ambitious individuals have enhanced their power and influence, or of the fact that in eighteenth-century England the individual entrepreneur "organized" economic activity in the process of production. The change in the status of the individual in economic activity might be regarded as one of degree, but it is so great as to constitute a major change in institutional arrangements.

provision for teamwork or group enterprise in the inventive process. Just as the modern corporation has replaced the individual as coordinator of production and manager of business, so invention has become a group process. Research teams working in well-equipped laboratories under centralized guidance and according to well-defined plans have largely replaced the lone investigator whose research was circumscribed only by his curiosity, his intellectual ability, and his imagination. Corporations have sought to discover and foster not the individual inventor but the well-rounded scientist, loyal to the organization and willing to subordinate his personal interests to group interests and to gear his endeavors to those of like-minded colleagues, interested in discovering new ways of applying existing knowledge to the commercialization of new products and processes rather than in carrying on basic research. The following statement by an executive of a large industrial corporation illustrates the trend toward group activity: "Except in certain research assignments, few specialists in a large company ever work alone. There is little room for virtuoso performances." [16]

The federal government, which directly and indirectly through tax policy has become the chief sponsor and financier of research activities, has greatly accelerated the shift to teamwork in research directed toward practical ends. In research contracts that government agencies awarded in 1953, 1954, and 1955, 93 per cent of a $5,600,000,000 total went to applied rather than fundamental research.[17] It is a reasonable assumption that virtually all was spent on corporate or other group projects, rather than on research by individual investigators. John H. Troll, physicist and vice-president of Electronics Corporation of America, commenting on the government's subsidizing private research in defense contracts, had this to say:

This approach has debilitated all government research facilities, leaving research and development vital to our defense to be performed under contracts by private firms, under a system that leads to the selection of contractors on the basis of size and financial status rather than scientific capability. This in turn has brought about an "organization man" approach to research that destroys individual creativity in the scientist by leading to a sort of creeping collectivism more usually associated with the Soviet Union.[18]

16. William H. Whyte, Jr., *The Organization Man* (New York: Simon and Schuster, 1956), p. 214.
17. *Id.* at 218.
18. "Of Sidewinders and Dead Ends," The Reporter, Nov. 13, 1958, p. 22.

Institutional Factors in Economic Thinking

Philanthropic foundations confronted with the task of giving away hundreds of millions of dollars have generally found it convenient to support carefully designed research projects involving the joint effort of groups rather than the work of single scholars. The scholar who requests financial aid for his research lacks the glamor of a "big operation"; his only qualifications may be a talent for research, a thirst for knowledge, and an insatiable curiosity. As a former foundation administrator expressed it, "The foundations in assisting research have suffered from chronic 'projectitis.'"

Sports, religion, and philanthropy have similarly succumbed to the organizational revolution. Baseball, the great American pastime, was formerly regarded as an outlet for the play impulses of the American youth, a form of exercise and recreation useful in developing muscular coordination, manual dexterity, and mental agility. It still affords an opportunity for the display of individual prowess, but currently it has become an organized business activity in which a handful of individuals are paid to participate and millions pay to watch. Baseball teams are owned by groups of businessmen who operate them as business enterprises under franchises carrying valuable privileges. In the big leagues—around which many satellite leagues operate, primarily as feeders to the larger affiliate—the freedom of a player to pursue his career has given way to a set of rules governing the sale and purchase of all players—rules formulated in response to the business needs of the organization.

The Protestant Reformation freed the seventeenth-century individual from the supervision of an ecclesiastical hierarchy and placed upon him the responsibility of answering for himself the awesome question, "What must I do to be saved?" In contrast, twentieth-century salvation has become a group enterprise. Billy Graham is not merely a dynamic, unusually persuasive servant of God carrying Christ's message to lost and sinful souls, but he is the central figure in an organization created to carry on God's work through a series of carefully planned campaigns, locally directed by groups of religious leaders and businessmen who have been organized by an advance team of professional promoters. In the nightly battle for the Lord, Graham is assisted by a corps of ushers, advisers, and counsellors skilled in the techniques of mass salvation. In the language of a caustic commentator, Graham "operates an assembly line of faith," [19] geared to handle hundreds of souls in a single night.

19. Walter Goodman, *The Clowns of Commerce* (New York: Sagamore Press, 1954), p. 199.

Workable Competition and Antitrust Policy

Philanthropy has traditionally been an individual enterprise, a matter of the heart. People actuated by the Christian spirit have helped those who are less fortunate. Charity frequently has expressed a personal relationship between giver and recipient. Today the United Givers Fund or the Community Chest is the official organization for the dispensation of the Lord's largesse. These organizations collect contributions not as voluntary gifts individually and spontaneously given but through well-organized teams with captains, lieutenants, subordinate officers, and privates organized to collect their quotas from the groups assigned to them. The appropriate size of each contribution may be suggested by a central agency as a fixed percentage of the giver's salary. Total contributions are dispersed through intermediary organizations to the ultimate beneficiaries. The giver need never know where the gift goes, nor the beneficiary from whom it comes.

The selection of books at one time was regarded as a matter of individual choice requiring, for some readers at least, the most discriminating judgment. As an indicator of the man himself, Ben Jonson ranked a man's choice of books with his choice of friends.[20] The organizational revolution has changed all this. Beginning with the Book-of-the-Month Club in 1926,[21] by 1958 some eighty-nine commercial book clubs [22] had been organized, which, in the words of a commentator, "for yearly fees, not only relieve their subscribers of the physical exertion incidental to purchasing books, but even free them from the mental anguish of making selections." [23] Between 1954 and 1956 sales of adult trade books increased by only 4 per cent while sales of book-club books increased by 25 per cent.[24] The Business Leaders' Book Club, the Educator's Book Club, the Farmers' Book Club, the Science Book Club, the Sportman's Book Club, and the others all undertake to provide their members with books suitable to readers of a certain type; and for those who can't recognize their own type but want to buy the right book, membership can be had in Best-in-Books.

The contrast I have been illustrating between the role of the individual in eighteenth-century society and his role in twentieth-century society is sharply revealed by comparing Patrick Henry's and the American Civil

20. "When I would know thee . . . my thought looks/ Upon thy well-made choice of friends and books." Ben Jonson, *Works*, with notes critical and explanatory and a biographical memoir by W. Gifford (London: Bickers, 1875), VIII, 190.
21. Don Wharton, "Book Big-Shot," Today, Dec. 28, 1935, p. 5.
22. *American Library Annual for 1957–1958* (New York: Bowker, 1958), p. 101.
23. Wright Howes, "Major Readjustments in the Retail Book Trade, Their Causes and Significance," 23 Library Quarterly 230, 233 (1953).
24. *American Library Annual for 1957–1958*, at 87.

Institutional Factors in Economic Thinking

Liberties Union's conceptions of the nature of the fight for civil liberties. In 1775 Patrick Henry uttered his immortal words, "Is life so dear or peace so sweet as to be purchased at the price of chains and slavery? Forbid it, Almighty God! I know not what course others may take, but as for me, give me liberty or give me death." In the 1950's the American Civil Liberties Union has this to say of its own work: "The American Civil Liberties Union is the only permanent non-partisan organization defending the Bill of Rights for all—without distinction or compromise." [25]

But to recount these well-known facts on the decline of individualism is not to decry them. It is merely to indicate something of the scope and impact of the organizational revolution.

Economists and the Organizational Revolution

With the organizational revolution affecting virtually every phase of American culture and most significantly the economic sector, it would have been strange indeed had not the thinking of American economists been affected by it. As the neoclassical economists reconciled and refined the doctrines of the classical and utilitarian schools, the doctrines gained in precision and validity of logic but lost in relevance. So much so that Piero Sraffa as early as 1926 characterized current price theory as

> ... essentially a pedagogic instrument, somewhat like the study of the classics, and, unlike the study of the exact sciences and law, its purposes are exclusively those of training the mind, for which reason it is hardly apt to excite the passions of men, even academical men. . . . [26]

In 1942 Joseph A. Schumpeter, commenting in a similar vein on the proposition that under perfect competition the profit motive among businessmen tends to maximize production, remarked that "in the process of being more correctly stated and proved, the proposition lost much of its content—it does emerge from the operation, to be sure, but it emerges emaciated, barely alive." [27]

The response of American economists to the far-reaching institutional changes I have referred to was to reconstruct price theory to make it more relevant to the structure and functioning of American industry.

25. American Civil Liberties Union, Inc., *Annual Reports*, 1953–57, back covers.
26. Piero Sraffa, "The Laws of Returns under Competitive Conditions," 36 Econ. Jour. 535–36 (1926).
27. *Capitalism, Socialism, and Democracy* (3d ed.; New York: Harper, 1950), p. 77.

Workable Competition and Antitrust Policy

Edward Chamberlin [28] tried systematically to revitalize it. J. M. Clark,[29] Schumpeter, E. G. Nourse,[30] J. K. Galbraith,[31] and others have in less comprehensive but equally significant ways contributed to contemporary notions of how price is determined and how it functions when large business units by reason of their size or the differentiation of their products have power over prices and output. Except for the contribution of Chamberlin, who is interested in pure theory and approaches the price problem from a highly abstract level, the most significant aspect of these contributions to current economic thinking is that despite marked differences in the details of their logic, they all find in the industrial structure an institutional arrangement compatible with the effective functioning of the economy. And so do their many followers—the expounders of the New Competition. Just as Smith in an age of individualism regarded *laissez-faire* competition as an instrument for harmonizing man's greed with the general welfare, so these economists have discovered forces in the contemporary organization and structure of industry that if left alone will promote the public welfare.

Clark is not disturbed by the contemporary industrial structure because, despite its oligopolistic business units, he views potential competition and the competition of substitutes as checks upon their power, which, although not perfect, may result in long-run prices that will closely approach those of pure competition. He also finds that in industries of large fixed costs, short-run marginal-cost pricing would prove disastrous. He concludes his discussion of the concept of workable competition with the optimistic but guarded "hope that government need not assume the burden of doing something about *every* departure from the model of perfect competition." [32]

Nourse in his *Price Making in a Democracy* assumes that the structure of industry and the economies of mass production inevitably give to large firms power over the market; but he believes that if businessmen can be made to see their long-run interest in sustained profits and a stable economy, they will deliberately pass on to consumers in the form of lower

---

28. *The Theory of Monopolistic Competition* (Cambridge: Harvard University Press, 1933).
29. "Toward a Concept of Workable Competition," 30 Am. Econ. Rev. (Proceedings of the American Economic Ass'n) 241 (1940).
30. *Price Making in a Democracy* (Washington, D.C.: Brookings Institution, 1944).
31. *American Capitalism* (Boston: Houghton Mifflin, 1952).
32. Clark, *supra* note 29, at 256.

prices the gains made possible by advanced technology. "We can only hope," he says,

that the ultimate intellectual judgment of private businessmen will be not merely that responsibility is the best policy in the limited terms in which it has already been put in practice and validated by experience but also in that broader and more comprehensive interpretation of responsibility that requires the individual businessman to follow practices that sustain the sources of general prosperity.[33]

Despite the treacherous bypaths of monopoly and the pitfalls of short-run profits, Nourse looks to the "invisible hand" to harness the selfishness of the leaders of corporate enterprise and direct it to the general good. As he expresses it, "Adam Smith's recognition of self-interest as a perennial and dependable spring of human conduct is as true today as it was in his time." [34]

Galbraith, while in agreement with Nourse that the economies of mass production make inevitable an industrial organization that if not checked places monopoly power in the hands of businessmen, does not look to the wisdom and restraint of those who have power to insure that they will not misuse it. On the contrary he thinks that power over the market tends to breed a countervailing power that will limit the original power so that it can do no public harm. Where countervailing power does not spontaneously develop, it is the government's duty to create it. Galbraith envisages eventually a society made up wholly of power blocs arrayed against each other, and he relies on their conflicting interests to promote the public welfare.

Schumpeter believed that the essence of modern capitalism is its dynamic character. Forces inherent in it are constantly undermining any strategic advantage that a monopoly may temporarily acquire. Better processes and products are constantly replacing those that may be temporarily monopolized. Temporary monopoly itself promotes the general welfare, for it gives a security to investments which without it might not be made. The "perennial gale of creative destruction" [35] is a force before which monopoly must disintegrate, and its winds bring better products, more productive processes, more economical sources of raw materials, and more efficient forms of business organization. Schumpeter regarded the Great Combination Movement, which radically changed the structure of

33. Nourse, *op. cit. supra* note 30, at 446.
34. *Id.* at 449.
35. Schumpeter, *op. cit. supra* note 27, at 84.

Workable Competition and Antitrust Policy

industry at the close of the century, as a manifestation of this perennial gale without which the full productive potentiality of capitalism could not have been realized. Schumpeter left little place in his scheme of things for an antitrust policy; he seemed to regard it as a sort of sniping operation, which might annoy and embarrass businessmen but by itself would prove powerless to stay what he regarded as the forces of progress.

This brief résumé of the doctrines of contemporary American economists who have concerned themselves with the functioning of a price system characterized by monopolistic competition is, of course, inadequate to do justice to the details of their logic, which at times is both profound and brilliant and which has validity in its application to some industrial situations. There is something of truth in what each says, and much of truth in what some of them say. Their common ground, however, is that they all think much alike with regard to the workability of the contemporary economic system—a system whose structure is the product of an organizational revolution that has embraced virtually every aspect of American culture. That they think this way is, I believe, a reflection of the influence of the *Zeitgeist* on economic thinking.

But theorists concerned with industrial structure have a greater obligation to society than to discover that its economy works well. As political economists we should be interested in understanding the forces that have shaped our economic system and may determine its destiny; and we should know more about how it works than the proponents of workable competition have told us. On the latter point we can learn something from what corporate executives or their spokesmen have to say on the question of power and social responsibility.

Business leaders recognize what some economists are loath to see, and they acknowledge by indirection what economists often deny—that the modern corporation's relative size, the scale on which it buys and sells, and its investment policy may give it power over particular markets or over the whole economy. Having power, corporate executives are asking themselves what are their social responsibilities in using it. In answering this question they acknowledge obligations to the corporation itself, its shareholders, its employees, the consuming public, and the whole economy. Business leaders today are beginning to think of themselves as stewards in whose hands rests the economic welfare of society. The late chairman of the Johns-Manville Corporation put it this way:

In the evolution of a complex industrial society the social responsibility of management has broadened correspondingly. Management no longer represents, as it once did, merely the *single* interest of ownership; increasingly it functions on the basis of a *trusteeship* which endeavors to maintain, between four basic interlocking groups, a proper balance of equity. Today the executive head of every business is accountable not only to his shareholders, but to the members of his working organization, to his customers, and to the public.[36]

Fortune, the magazine of big business, tells us that "one of the most obvious yet least recognized facts of our time is that the large corporation is becoming one of free society's major instruments of economic justice." [37] On the question of the corporation's social responsibility, Frank W. Pierce, a director of what *Fortune* regards as America's model corporation, the Standard Oil Company (New Jersey), states that "it is becoming clear that in our modern society top management has the opportunity—in fact, I should say the duty—to act as a balance wheel in relation to three groups of interests—the interests of owners, of employees, and of the public, all of whom have a stake in the output of industry." [38]

Not only does the modern corporation recognize its obligation to the public, but it conceives that obligation broadly. It has for some time been a self-appointed guardian of private enterprise and has engaged in an educational campaign to create public opinion about itself and the traditional American way of life with which it identifies itself. In doing so it has assumed that it can sell private enterprise to the American public just as it sells soap, cosmetics, electrical appliances, or automobiles. Corporate leaders talking to each other have said, "We have a continuous selling job to do," involving the merchandising of "certain simple facts." They believe that to get the best results they should follow, as they have put it, a "down-to-earth simple approach" in which they "take people by their mental hands" [39] and lead them to the altar of free enterprise where they may find renewed faith in it. In this educational and spiritual campaign they are utilizing the usual media of mass communication—the radio, television, and the press—through which they try to shape attitudes,

---

36. Quoted by Howard R. Bowen, *Social Responsibilities of the Businessman* (New York: Harper, 1953), p. 49.
37. Gilbert Burck, "The Jersey Company," Fortune, October 1951, p. 98.
38. Quoted by Bowen, *op. cit. supra* note 36, at 51 n. 8. This point of view represents a significant contrast with Adam Smith's and suggests how far current thinking on economic matters has been affected by institutional arrangements. Smith said, "It is not from the benevolence of the butcher, the brewer, or the baker, that we expect our dinner, but from their regard to their own interest. We address ourselves, not to their humanity but to their self-love, and never talk to them of our own necessities but of their advantages. Nobody but a beggar chooses to depend chiefly upon the benevolence of his fellow-citizens." Smith, *op. cit. supra* note 3, at 14.
39. Bowen, *op. cit. supra* note 36, at 56.

Workable Competition and Antitrust Policy

curb or create prejudices, coin good will, and create habits of thought without the public's being aware that its ideas are being fabricated for it. An excellent case in point is corporate institutional advertising designed to sell not products but the corporate executives' conception of the American way of life and the corporation's place in it. The United States Steel Corporation has given vast television audiences not merely entertainment of high cultural value but a picture of itself and its numerous corporate subsidiaries as "the industrial family that serves the nation." And institutional advertising does not neglect the appeal to idealism. The American Petroleum Institute has described in eloquent language the role the American oil industry is playing in "man's quest for freedom." As an "energizer of men's thoughts and a contributor to freedom," [40] we are assured, it will continue to play an increasingly important role. General Electric, boasting that progress is its most important product, has generously identified its achievements with those of the electrical industry of which it is a part and with the growth and progress of a greater America, which it is privileged to serve.[41]

In conducting this educational campaign, spokesmen for the corporations have used the customary mass-communication media but have not relied on them alone. They have resorted to subtler and more personal means for disseminating ideas: plant tours, special programs for clergymen, and summer conferences and seminars for college professors. To the latter they have invited scores of social scientists, some of whom they have regarded as holding a warped idea of the place of big business in the American economy, and they have entertained them with a lavish generosity to which few have been accustomed. In the language of the poet, some who came to scoff remained to pray.

In recent years the corporation's educational interests have broadened, and it has assumed increasing responsibility for the financial welfare of the American system of private higher education. To meet the plight of American colleges and to forestall federal assistance, with its threat to freedom of inquiry, the corporation is stepping into the breach created by higher costs and a decline in individual giving. The courts have upheld the legal right of a corporation to bestow on educational institutions its stockholders' money without their consent, and Congress has authorized the deduction of gifts of this nature from taxable income. In 1955 corporate giving to American colleges is estimated to have totaled $100,000,-

40. Atlantic Monthly, February 1956, p. 21.
41. Atlantic Monthly, April 1956, pp. 6–7.

Institutional Factors in Economic Thinking

000, approximating from 7 to 8 cents out of every dollar spent by private schools.[42] More important, three top-flight corporate executives were instrumental in the formation of the Council for Financial Aid to Education, for whose direction a distinguished scholar and former college president was selected. With gift-hungry college presidents backing the movement and corporate executives not only recognizing, in the language of the *New York Times*, that "an increase in community-mindedness is a necessary consequence of the enormous growth in the size and power of corporations" but also identifying "the fate of the private liberal arts college with the fate of the private enterprise system,"[43] corporate giving is destined to grow both in size and in public favor.

Whither these institutional changes are leading us we do not know, and about them most economists have been little concerned. Nor have the other social scientists, who also have made peace with their environment, found them worthy of study. A noteworthy exception is Adolph Berle, who in his brilliant analysis, *The 20th Century Capitalist Revolution*,[44] recognizes the modern corporation not merely as the agency in whose power rests the economic welfare of America, but as a social and political institution whose influence extends far beyond the market it serves. In the current atmosphere of ideological warfare the great corporation, Berle tells us, has undertaken, sometimes at the behest of the federal government, sometimes voluntarily, the responsibility for policing the nation's internal security system. Berle contends that in acting as a policeman the corporation can and sometimes does violate with impunity employees' constitutional rights by arbitrarily dismissing workers whose loyalty has become suspect. He believes that not only does the modern corporation have power over the lives of tens of thousands of workers, but—having in mind the operations of a dozen large oil companies both in international trade and in exploiting the oil resources of developing countries—that it exercises a power in international affairs like that of a sovereign state.

I believe that in the task of analyzing the significance of the modern corporation to the American economy economists can play a larger role than they have thus far played. Without adequately investigating the causes of the merger movements that have restructured modern industry, they have assumed the inevitability of that structure. Because modern

---

42. A. H. Raskin, "The Corporation and the Campus," N.Y. Times Magazine, April 17, 1955, p. 12.
43. *Ibid.*
44. New York: Harcourt, Brace, 1954.

Workable Competition and Antitrust Policy

technology decrees large production units, they have assumed, without determining precisely the factors responsible for the growth of particular corporations, that giant managerial units are necessary and that their size is a reflection of their efficiency. Because corporations have identified the impressive material progress of the decades 1940–1960 with the corporate system of control, some economists have assumed that the large corporation is responsible for this progress. Because corporations have spent millions for research in well-equipped laboratories out of which have come remarkable industrial innovations, some economists have assumed that individual researchers can contribute little to the advance of technology. These I believe are conclusions that have come largely from superficial observation of the material circumstances that surround us. Instead they should be hypotheses to be tested.

There are other questions that are particularly appropriate for exploration by economists who study contemporary institutions. What is happening to the mobility of the factors of production as labor and capital become controlled by ever larger organizational units? What effect are corporate-financed social security programs and union rules governing seniority and other conditions of employment having on the mobility of labor? What effect is the corporation's interest in developing the well-rounded, loyal organization man, in preference to the nonconformist of distinction, having on the supply and mobility of managerial talent? What can we learn about prices from the recent tendency of corporations to finance expansion out of earnings without direct recourse to financial markets? What are the factors that explain the apparent anomaly of rising prices and declining production? Do the price and investment policies of big business on balance inhibit rather than promote the growth of output and investment? Do they result in a distribution of income incompatible with the fullest utilization of existing productive facilities? Finally, and most important, to what extent can the structure of industry be modified and the economy made more flexible without loss of efficiency? Can this be done through tax measures? Can it be done through more selective and vigorous administration of the antitrust laws? These are some of the questions with which students of industrial structure might well be concerned. They are becoming increasingly important to a free-enterprise economy in a world of competitive co-existence.

Oliver Wendell Holmes once remarked, "Every now and then a man's mind is stretched by a new idea . . . and never shrinks back to its former dimensions."[45] It is to be hoped that the minds of contemporary students of economic institutions that have now encompassed the corporate system may be sufficiently flexible to engender an inquiring attitude about what it means and where it is leading us.

45. O. W. Holmes, *The Autocrat of the Breakfast Table* (Boston: Houghton Mifflin, 1890), p. 226.

Table of Cases

Dates are those of the controlling court decisions, of consent decrees, of orders in Federal Trade Commission cases, and in one instance of an indictment where no trial was had. Where the United States or the Federal Trade Commission is plaintiff, the case is listed under the defendant's name. "In the matter of" is omitted from citations to FTC cases. Page numbers include citations to all stages of a case.

Addyston Pipe and Steel Co., U.S. v. (1899), 129 and n
Aetna Portland Cement Co. v. FTC (1946), 67n, 69nn, 110n. See also Cement Institute, FTC v. (1948)
Alger v. Thacher (Mass. 1837), 128n
Allied Paper Mills v. FTC (1948), 109n
Aluminum Company of America, U.S. v. (1945), 25n, 140n, 141–42 and n, 181–82, 188nn, 197n, 198n, 213n, 248, 264, 280n, 360–61
Aluminum Company of America, U.S. v. (1950), 142–43, 372, 374–77
American Can Co. v. Bruce's Juices, Inc. (1951), 175n
American Can Co., FTC (1924), 174n
American Can Co. v. Ladoga Canning Co. (1930), 175n, 222
American Can Co. v. Russellville Canning Co. (1951), 175n
American Can Co., U.S. v. (1916), 139n, 166–80 passim, 262n
American Can Co., U.S. v. (1946), 173
American Can Co., US. v. (1949), 169–74, 178
American Column and Lumber Co. v. U.S. (1921), 36–38, 46n, 93n, 208n
American Iron and Steel Institute, FTC (1951), 110nn, 147n, 148n
American Linseed Oil Co., U.S. v. (1923), 38–39, 93n, 208n
American Maize-Products Co., FTC (1941), 233n
American Sugar Refining Co., U.S. v. (1922), 71n
American Tobacco Co., U.S. v. (1911), 20n, 24n, 138–39, 166, 189n, 195n, 268, 361
American Tobacco Co. v. U.S. (1946), 25n, 138–39, 140n, 188n, 248–49, 279n, 360–63, 380
Anheuser-Busch, Inc., FTC (1940), 111n, 233n
Appalachian Coals, Inc., v. U.S. (1933), 72n, 250-51, 357n
Arrow-Hart & H. Co. v. FTC (1934), 200n
Automatic Canteen Co. v. FTC (1953), 226, 229

B. B. Chemical Co. v. Ellis (1942), 383n
Bausch & Lomb Optical Co., U.S. v. (1944), 25n
Besser Mfg. Co. v. U.S. (1952), 383n
Bond Crown & Cork Co. v. FTC (1949), 109n
Broad v. Jollyfe (K.B. 1621), 127n

California Packing Corp., FTC (1937), 295n
Cement Institute, FTC v. (1948), 66-70, 76n, 95n, 109n, 110n, 209n, 245n, 249, 363n, 364n. See also Aetna Portland Cement Co. v. FTC (1946)
Cement Manufacturers Protective Ass'n v. U.S. (1925), 61–66, 93n, 208n
Chicago Board of Trade v. U.S. (1918), 24n
Clayton Mark & Co. v. FTC (1949), 109n, 188n, 234n, 249n, 363n, 364. See also Rigid Steel Conduit Ass'n, FTC (1944)
Clinton Co., FTC (1942), 233n
Colgate v. Bacheler (K.B. 1601), 127n
Collins v. Lock (App. Cas. 1879), 129n
Columbia Steel Co., U.S. v. (1948), 141–43, 198n, 200n, 355, 372n, 380n
Continental Can Co., U.S. v. (1950), 179–80

425

Corn Products Refining Co. v. FTC (1945), 111n, 233n, 250n, 251n
Crown Mfrs Ass'n, FTC (1949), 363n

Diamond Match Co. v. Roeber (N.Y. 1887), 128n
Du Pont de Nemours, E. I., & Co., U.S. v. (1911), 24n, 320, 321
Du Pont de Nemours, E. I., & Co., U.S. v. (1956), 153–66, 183, 262n, 264-67, 272, 275, 280–86, 320, 372, 383–97
Du Pont de Nemours, E. I., & Co., U.S. v. (1957), 289n, 296–314 *passim*, 319–56, 397–99
Dyer's Case (Y.B. 1415), 126n, 135n

Ethyl Gasoline Corp. v. U.S. (1940), 25n
Export Screw Ass'n, FTC (1947), 213n

Fashion Originators' Guild v. FTC (1941), 76n
Florida Hard Rock Phosphate Export Ass'n, FTC (1945), 213n
Fort Howard Paper Co. v. FTC (1946), 85–87, 109n, 209n, 363n. *See also* National Crepe Paper Ass'n of America, FTC (1944)

General Electric Co., U.S. v. (1926), 219
General Electric Co., U.S. v. (1948), 215, 216n
General Electric Co., U.S. v. (1949), 213n, 215
Goodrich, B. F., Co., FTC (1954), 227, 228n
Goodyear Tire and Rubber Co., FTC v. (1939), 222
Gratz v. Claughton (1951), 325n
Griffith, U.S. v. (1948), 279n, 380

Hamilton Watch Co. v. Benrus Watch Co. (2d Cir. 1953), 205
Hartford-Empire Co. v. U.S. (1945), 383n
Henry v. A. B. Dick Co. (1921), 231n
Hitchcock v. Coker (Exch. 1837), 128n
Homer v. Ashford (C.P. 1825), 128n
Hubbard v. Miller (Mich. 1873), 128n
Hubinger Co., FTC (1941), 111n, 233n

Imperial Chemical Industries, U.S. v. (1951), 213n, 215–16

International Harvester Co., U.S. v. (1927), 24n, 139n, 268
International Machines Corp. v. U.S. (1936), 231n
International Salt Co. v. U.S. (1947), 25n, 231
International Shoe Co. v. FTC (1930), 200n, 205n, 226, 354n

Joint Traffic Ass'n, U.S. v. (1898), 20n

Kellogg v. Larkin (Wis. 1851), 129n
Kiefer-Stewart Co. v. Seagram & Sons, Inc. (1951), 25n, 251n
Knight, E. C., Co., U.S. v. (1895), 8–9, 19n, 70n, 136n, 186n, 196n
Kraft-Phoenix Cheese Corp., FTC (1937), 227n

Leather Cloth Co. v. Lorsont (Eq. 1869), 128n
Leslie v. Lorillard (N.Y. 1888), 129n

Mallan v. May (Exch. 1843), 128n
Maple Flooring Mfrs Ass'n v. U.S. (1925), 39–61, 93n, 208n
Masonite Corp., U.S. v. (1942), 25n
Mechanical Mfg. Co., FTC (1932), 294n, 295n
Mennen Co. v. FTC (1923), 221, 225
Milk and Ice Cream Can Institute v. FTC (1946), 81–84, 109n, 209n, 363n
Minneapolis-Honeywell Reg. Co. v. FTC (1951), 226n
Minnesota Mining & Mfg. Co., U.S. v. (1950), 214, 216
Mitchel v. Reynolds (Ch. 1711), 127nn, 129n, 135n
Morgan Stanley & Co. v. SEC (2d Cir. 1942), 325n
Morton Salt Co., FTC v. (1948), 251
Morton Salt Co. v. Suppiger Co. (1942), 219n, 383n

National Ass'n of Real Estate Boards, U.S. v. (1950), 25n
National Biscuit Co. v. FTC (1924), 221, 225
National City Lines, U.S. v. (1951), 289n
National Crepe Paper Ass'n of America, FTC (1944), 84, 209n, 363n. *See also*

Table of Cases

Fort Howard Paper Co. v. FTC (1946)
National Lead Co., U.S. v. (1947), 213n, 215, 270n, 373–74, 383n
New Wrinkle, Inc., U.S. v. (1952), 25n
Nordenfelt v. Maxim Nordenfelt Guns and Ammunition Co. (App. Cas. 1894), 135n
Northern Securities Co. v. U.S. (1904), 136n
North American Co. v. SEC (1946), 325n, 399n

Oregon Steam Navigation Co. v. Winsor (1873), 128n

Paramount Pictures, Inc., U.S. v. (1948), 279n, 355, 380
Penick & Ford, FTC (1940), 111n, 233n
Phosphate Export Ass'n, FTC (1946), 213n
Piel Bros. Starch Co., FTC (1939), 111n, 233n
Pike v. Thomas (Ky. 1817), 128n
Pillsbury Mills, Inc., FTC (1960), 205–7
Pipe Fittings & Valve Export Ass'n, FTC (1948), 213n

Republic Steel Corp., U.S. v. (1935), 200n
Rigid Steel Conduit Ass'n, FTC (1944), 109n, 234–35, 249, 363n, 364. See also Clayton Mark & Co. v. FTC (1949); Triangle Conduit and Cable Co. v. FTC (1948)
Rogers v. Parrey (K.B. 1614), 127n
Rousillon v. Rousillon (Ch.D. 1880), 128n

Salt Producers Ass'n v. FTC (1943), 77–79, 209n, 363n, 364
Schechter, A. L. A., Poultry Corp. v. U.S. (1935), 77n, 87
Schine Chain Theatres, Inc., v. U.S. (1948), 380n
Socony-Vacuum Oil Co., U.S. v. (1940), 25n, 111n, 250–51, 358n
Staley, A. E., Manufacturing Co. v. FTC (1945), 111n, 233n, 250n
Standard Oil Co. v. U.S. (1911), 20n, 24, 25n, 135–39, 166, 189n, 195n, 268, 361

Standard Oil Co. of California v. U.S. (1949), 25n, 173n, 232, 251
Standard Oil Co. (Indiana) v. FTC (1951), 227, 233
Standard Stations case. See Standard Oil Co. of California v. U.S. (1949)
Sugar Institute v. U.S. (1936), 71–73, 93n, 209n
Sulphur Export Corp., FTC (1947), 213n
Swift & Company, US. v. (1932), 362
Sylvania Electric Products Co., FTC (1954), 228n

Tag Manufacturers Institute v. FTC (1949), 87–108n, 210
Thatcher Manufacturing Co. v. FTC (1926), 354n
Times-Picayune Publishing Co. v. U.S. (1953), 161n, 220n, 231
Timken Roller Bearing Co., U.S. v. (1951), 213n, 214, 251n
Trans-Missouri Freight Ass'n, U.S. v. (1897), 20n, 25n, 129, 134–35
Transamerica Corp. v. Board of Governors (1953), 205
Trenton Potteries, U.S. v. (1927), 25n
Triangle Conduit & Cable Co. v. FTC (1948), 109n, 188n, 234n, 248n, 363n, 364n. See also Rigid Steel Conduit Ass'n, FTC (1944)

Union Starch & Refining Co., FTC (1940), 111n, 233n
Univis Lens Co., U.S. v. (1942), 25n
United Shoe Machinery Corp., U.S. v. (1918), 268, 379n, 380
United Shoe Machinery Corp., U.S. v. (1922), 23n, 231n, 381n
United Shoe Machinery Corp., U.S. v. (1953), 142n, 372n, 378–83
United States Alkali Export Ass'n, U.S. v. (1949), 213n
United States Gypsum Co., U.S. v. (1948), 25n
United States Gypsum Co., U.S. v. (1950), 383n
United States Maltsters Ass'n v. FTC (1945), 79–81, 109n, 209n, 363n
United States Steel Corp., U.S. v. (1920), 24n, 139–40, 144–53, 197n, 262n, 268

427

Workable Competition and Antitrust Policy

United States Steel Corp., FTC (1924), 66n

United States Steel Corp. v. FTC (1948), 147 n

Van Camp, George, & Sons Co. v. American Can Co. (1929), 175n, 221–22

Wallis v. Day, (Exch. 1837), 128n

Waugh Equipment Co., FTC (1931), 294n

Western Meat Co., FTC v. (1926), 200n

Wickens v. Evans (Exch. 1829), 129n

Winslow, U.S. v. (1913), 139n, 268n, 379n

Yellow Cab Co., U.S. v. (1947), 248–49, 355

Index

ACF Brill Company, 313
Acme Tag Company, 104
Adams, C. A.: quoted, 103–4
Adams, Thomas S.: cited, 66
Adams, Walter: cited, 384n; dissents from Antitrust Report, 194 and n, 208; workable competition not an antitrust guide, 258
Addyston Pipe and Steel Company case, 129
Adelman, Morris A.: on effective competition, 123, 276; on industrial concentration, 201, 410 and n; on revision of antitrust laws, 19n, 29n, 119n; on Robinson-Patman Act, 227n; on workable competition, 30, 189n, 248 and n, 275n, 384n
Agricultural co-operatives, 237
Albright, C. M., 394n; quoted, 155
Alco Products, Inc., 312 n, 313
Allen-Bailey Tag Company, 103–4
Allen Creek Coal Company, 308
Aluminum case (1945): doctrine clarified, 378–81; test of illegal monopolizing, 140n, 141–42, 153, 181–82; test of monopoly, 141, 198, 248
Aluminum case (1950), 142–43, 374–77
Aluminum Company of America, 141–43, 374–77
American Can Company: business conduct, 167, 172–75, 178; FTC 1917 investigation, 174; and Great Combination Movement, 20n, 196; industrial performance, 167, 175–80; position in can industry, 167, 169–71, 179–80 and n; pricing policy, 173; profits, 177–78; rebates in buying tin plate, 166–67, 172–73, 230
American Can Company case (1916): dissolution rejected, 168; effect of 1920 *Steel* decision, 168; held no longer trying to monopolize, 172; organizers aimed to monopolize, 166 and n; reliance on potential competition, 168; and rule of reason, 166

American Can Company decree (1950), 179–80
American Civil Liberties Union, 414–15
American Iron and Steel Institute: cost studies a basis for pricing "extras," 148; data on steel concentration, 150n; report on U.S. steel capacity, 145n
American Iron and Steel Institute case, 111
American Locomotive Company, 312, 314
American Petroleum Institute, 420
American Sheet and Tin Plate Company, 172
American Sugar Refining Company, 70–71; and Great Combination Movement, 196
American Tag Company, 96
American Tobacco Company: and Great Combination Movement, 20n, 197; role of mergers, 203
American Tobacco Company case (1911) and rule of reason, 21, 138–39, 195
American Tobacco Company case (1946): decision alarming to businessmen, 248–49; and oligopolistic pricing theory, 361–63; oligopolistic structure not changed, 140 n, 365
American Viscose Corporation, 285, 393
American Zirconium Corporation, 373
Anderson, Lee C.: cited, 291n
Antitrust administration: Antitrust Committee on, 238–39; Business Advisory Council on, 253; Dirlam and Kahn on, 259–60, 268, 271; indirect discounts, etc., per se illegal, 230–31; Oppenheim's proposals would weaken, 255; penalties will not correct structure, 182; role of economic analysis, 267–72; role of workable competition in, 245–47, 251–57; weakened by concept of workable competition, 257
Antitrust bills, purpose of, 131–32
Antitrust decisions alarming to businessmen, 140–43, 248–51
Antitrust laws: Adams on proposed re-

429

Workable Competition and Antitrust Policy

vision of, 258; Antitrust Committee recommended minor changes in, 256; attempt to violate spirit of, 54; conflict with patent policy, 216–20; and correct application of workable competition, 184; effect of New Jersey holding company law, 8; effect of war, 187; efforts to revise, 18 and *n*, 19, 26, 119 and *n*, 126, 187, 189*n*, 243, 245–46, 247, 251–53; extent of power compatible with, 375–76; fundamental aspects of, 193–220 *passim*, 226–27, 235–36, 239–40; inadequacy of traditional tests, 244; incompatible with economy of big business, 254; judicial administration tempered by current attitudes, 381–83; Mason on need to revise, 244; 1912 party platforms on, 22 and *n*; Oppenheim's proposals to revise, 26, 115, 251–55, 370–71; revision unlikely to make more rigorous, 182; and rivalry among substitutes, 274; and theory of monopolistic competition, 188–89; threat to efficiency?, 196, 366; virtual suspension of under NRA, 5, 93*n*

Antitrust literature, 131 and *n*

Antitrust policy; in international markets, 211–16; Robinson-Patman Act in conflict with, 226–27; seriousness of congressional purpose, 133*n*; Thorelli's study of, 130*n*; violation per se, 109, 248–51

Appalachian Coals case, 72, 357

Arant, Willard D.: quoted, 360*n*

Arkwright, Richard, 405

Arlington Company, 331

Armour & Company, 294, 317

Armstrong Bureau of Related Industries, 38

Arnold, Thurman, 359; quoted, 257, 372

Ashley, William James: cited, 55*n*

Atlas Powder Company, 302, 321

Attorney General's National Committee to Study the Antitrust Laws: on antitrust administration, 238; on antitrust prohibitions for labor unions and agricultural cooperatives, 236–37; on concept of workable competition, 119*n*, 255; composition of, 191*n*; on compulsory royalty-free licensing, 218; on cost justification, 227–28; on delivered pricing, 233–35; different views within, 237; dissent from report of, 194 and *n*, 208; on economic analysis, 226; and efforts to revise antitrust laws, 18*n*, 119 and *n*; evaluation of antitrust decisions, 371–72; on exclusive dealing, 232; on exemptions from antitrust coverage, 235–37; on fair trade laws, 232; faith in big business, 240; on functional discounts, 232–33; ignored antitrust exemption of insurance and oil production, 236; ignored fundamentals in antitrust problems, 193, 197, 199–201, 204–5, 208–9, 211–13, 218, 220, 227, 229–30, 234–36, 239–40; ignored oligopolistic structure, 236; on injury to competitors, 225–26; on international cartels, 210–16; on limiting scope of foreign commerce provision, 213–16; majority and minority views on 1920 *Steel* case, 139*n*, 140; on mergers, 204–6; not curious about conduct-structure relationships, 239; origins of, 187–90; and patent-antitrust problems, 216–20; on price-cutting forced by buyers, 229; purpose of, 192–93; recommendations would weaken antitrust laws and administration, 193, 229–30, 238–39; report a guide to businessmen, 216; report sent to federal judges, 372; on Robinson-Patman Act, 225–30; on rule of reason in foreign commerce cases, 215; satisfied with contemporary industrial structure, 240; on Sherman Act penalty, 238*n*; significance of advice to courts and agencies, 256; on trade association activities, 208–10; on tying clauses, 231–32 and *n*; on workable competition, 255, 371*n*

Automatic Canteen case, 226

B. B. Chemical Corporation, 382*n*

Bain, Joe S.: cited, 29*n*, 121*n*, 190*n*, 248*n*, 275*n*; on freedom of entry, 29*n*; mentioned, 248

Baker, Samuel G.: quoted, 352*n*

Baldwin-Lima-Hamilton Corporation, 312*n*

Baldwin Locomotive Works, 312

Barber, C. H.: quoted, 96

Barksdale, H. M. 330*n*

Barnes, Stanley N.: co-chairman of Anti-

Index

trust Committee, 18*n*, 119*n*, 191, 254, 371; quoted, 111*n*, 191, 256
Barry, William: cited, 131*n*
Basing point pricing: an antitrust violation per se?, 109–11, 249–50; in cement industry, 65–69; in crepe paper industry, 84–86; FTC cases, 109*n*, 233–34, 249–50; FTC position on, 109–11; *Glucose* cases, 233–34; literature on, 68*n*, 109*n*, 151*n*; in malt industry, 80; and oligopoly, 70*n*, 147, 234–35, 245, 277; *Rigid Steel Conduit* proceeding, 234–35; Robinson-Patman proceedings justified, 235; in salt industry, 77; spontaneous origin of?, 70*n*, 147, 234–35, 245; in steel industry, 147–49, 151, 181; in sugar industry, 75
Baxter, Frank H.: quoted, 99–100
Baxter, Frank H., Associates, 87–107 *passim*
Bayway disaster, 347–49
Beardslee, L. R.: quoted, 299*n*
Beckton Chemical Company, 331 *n*
Berge, Wendell: cited, 113*n*, 212*n*
Bergson, Abram: cited, 117
Berle, Adolf A., Jr.: cited, 320*n*; on significance of modern corporation, 421
Berle, Adolph A., Jr., and Gardiner C. Means: cited, 325*n*, 358 and *n*, 410*n*
Berman, Edward: cited, 131*n*
Bethlehem Steel Company: reciprocity with Du Pont and General Motors, 299–301; reciprocity a motive for merger?, 317–18 and *n*; role of mergers in growth, 203–4; use of reciprocity, 308, 316 and *n*, 317
Biechler (general manager of Frigidaire), 350
Big business: Antitrust Committee's faith in, 240; attempt to sell as essential to free enterprise, 12, 419-20; Brandeis on, 21 and *n*; cartel-like characteristics, 12; defined, 7–8; fear of and hostility toward, 18–19, 21, 131, 189, 358; identified with success, 183, 381–83, 422; judges and economists adjusted to, 139, 183, 187, 377, 381–83, 398, 416–18, 422; limiting power of, 16–17; matching with big labor, 5, 14; as much a result as a cause of American achievements, 183; new confidence in, 400; and 1950 *Aluminum* decision, 142–43, 376–77; not monopoly, 252–53; rise of, 7–13; seeks security in rule of reason, 25–26, 143; size and efficiency, 7, 9, 145, 151–52; threatened by antitrust decisions, 21–23, 140–43, 189, 248–51, 320, 360–63; and *United Shoe Machinery* decision, 381–83; views on and antitrust decisions, 139, 140–43, 168, 183, 187, 189, 248–49, 356, 361–62, 373, 376–77, 381–83, 398. *See also* Corporations; Industrial concentration; Size
Big labor: attempt to sell as essential to free enterprise, 12; a reaction to big business, 5–6, 14; rise of, 3–6, 8. *See also* Labor unions
Bigness: Antitrust Report deals inadequately with, 194*n*; Galbraith on, 13–14; penalization of may be fatal, 16; questions relevant to, 239; and reciprocal buying, 317
Black, Hugo, 400
Blackstone, Sir William, 406
Blodgett, Rufus, 185*n*
Bope, H. P.: quoted, 148*n*
Boswell, James, 406
Boulding, Kenneth E.: cited, 32 *n*, 117
Bowen, Howard R.: cited, 419*n*
Bradley, Albert, 329
Brandeis, Louis D.: quoted, 21, 173; on rule of reason, 24*n*
Brennan, William J., Jr., 319, 400
Bridgeport Wood Finishing Company, 331*n*
Bridgwater, Duke of, 405
British Cellophane Limited, 155, 284, 394
Brokerage fees: per se illegal, 230; Robinson-Patman Act provisions, 224
Brown, Donaldson, 330*n*, 350; quoted, 329, 352*n*
Brown, H. Fletcher, 302; quoted, 337
Brown Lumber Company, 41
Brownell, Herbert S.: cited, 192*n*
Burck, Gilbert: quoted, 419
Burns, Arthur R.: cited, 19*n*, 28*n*, 366; on technology and industrial structure, 121
Burton, Harold H., 339*n*
Business Advisory Council: endorsed rule of reason and workable competition, 125, 190; report on effective

competition, 18n, 119n, 125, 144n, 253, 256, 370
Business conduct: and *Aluminum* case, 141–42; of American Can Company, 166–67, 172–75; and antitrust violations by oligopolists, 182; in cellophane industry, 154–58, 283–84; Dirlam and Kahn on, 259–60; industrial structure may condition, 198, 235, 272; key element in antitrust violations, 384 and n; legal yet anticompetitive, 124, 269; may condition performance, 198; may indicate monopoly power, 58, 124, 154–58, 278, 283–84; in oligopolistic industries, 124, 287; and patents, 154–58, 278, 383n, 395; penalties on inadequate, 182; and the relevant market, 278; and rule of reason in 1911 cases, 137–39; in the steel industry, 146–48; a test for workable competition, 124–25, 242, 272, 368
Business reciprocity: Bethlehem Steel led the way in using, 316n; defined, 289; and diversification, 292–95, 303–4, 315; between Du Pont and U.S. Rubber, 308–10; by Du Pont hurt rivals, 302–3, 316; and efficiency in making dyes, 315–16; encourages mergers, 317; extent of; 296, 298; extra cost, 294n, 295, 306–7; ignored by economists, 288; and imperfect competition, 288, 315, 318; legality challenged, 288n, 294–95, 296; reticence of business men on, 288n; and size, 288, 291–92, 294–95, 303, 313, 315, 317–18. See also Reciprocal buying
Business Week: quoted, 329n

Cahill, John T.: cited, 19n
California Packing Corporation, 295
Capital District Floor Coverings Ass'n, 31n
Carnegie-Illinois Steel Corporation, 172
Carpenter, R. R. M., 333n
Carpenter, Walter S., Jr., 302n, 329, 330n, 350; quoted, 164n, 391
Cartels, 45, 236
Carter, William A.: cited, 20n
Cavendish, Henry, 406
Cawley Clark & Company, 331n
Celler Committee: cited, 145n, 152, 153n

Celler-Kefauver Anti-Merger Act, 200 and n, 204, 205n, 410–11
Cellophane: Du Pont's pricing policy, 160–64, 266, 282, 389–92; Du Pont's use of patents, 155–57, 394–95; effect of tariff on imports, 154–55 and nn, 394; monopoly of, 154, 158, 165, 264–67, 284, 383–96 *passim;* no competition from rival products, 159–63, 283, 285–86; no cross-elasticity of demand, 161–63, 266, 282–83, 388–90; performance consistent with monopoly, 163–65, 284–85, 390; price independent of rivals' prices, 161–63, 266, 282, 390; and rayon compared, 164–65, 285; relevant market for, 158–61, 272, 281, 385–93; rivalry with substitutes, 159–63, 284–85, 387; and shifts to other products, 266, 283; world cartel agreement, 156, 394; and workable competition, 165, 262
Cellophane case, 153–66 *passim,* 241, 280–86, 383–97; cross-elasticity of demand, 388–90; Dirlam and Stelzer's criticisms of Stocking and Mueller's analysis, 241, 263–67, 272; dissenting opinion, 272; *Du Pont–General Motors* decision contrasted, 320, 355 and n; and economic tests of monopoly power, 264–65, 280; findings of fact challenged, 263–67; reflects judicial use of workable competition concept, 153, 183, 263, 397; significance of, 285–86, 396–97
La Cellophane, Société Anonyme, 156n, 283, 393–94
Cement Institute case, 66–70, 110, 364
Cement Manufacturers Protective Ass'n, 61–70; basing point pricing, 65–69; cooperation the goal of, 61n; methods of reporting statistics, 64 and nn; services of, 61–62; specific job-contract information, 62–64
Chain stores, 222–23 and n
Chamberlin, Edward H.: "ideal" solution in theory of oligopoly, 78n; rejects monopoly solution in theory of oligopoly, 360n; *Theory of Monopolistic Competition,* 120, 122–24, 188 and n, 276–77, 360; theory of oligopoly, 11, 13, 27–28, 78n, 360n, 366–68 *passim;* tried to revitalize price theory, 416

Index

Champion, Albert, 335
Chantler, A. R.: quoted, 316*n*
Chase, L. C., Company, 333
Chevrolet Motor Company, 322, 331
Chicago Varnish Company, 332
Christiana Securities Company, 323
Chrysler Corporation, 203
Clark, John Bates, 122*n*
Clark, John Davidson: quoted, 133*n*
Clark, John Maurice: accepts contemporary industrial structure, 416; on basing point pricing, 68*n*, 70*n*, 147, 151*n*, 245; on caution in antitrust enforcement, 369; on concept of workable competition, 28, 108*n*, 121, 189*n*, 244–46, 275*n*, 366–67; definition of competition, 376*n*; dissents from Antitrust Report, 194 and *n*; economic effects as test of legality, 245–46; monopolist's discretion too wide, 29*n*; performance test of workable competition, 318; on potential competition, 28, 123, 244, 367; on price theory, 73*n*; on revision of antitrust laws, 19*n*, 245–46
Clark, Tom C., 319, 400
Clarke (Justice), 378–79*nn*
Clayton Act: designed to preserve competition by outlawing specific acts, 23 and *n*, 186*n*, 221; and holding companies, 199–200; and merger movements, 199–208 *passim*, 410; no effective penalty for noncompliance with § 7, 207; no help where price discrimination hurt buyers, 74*n*; predatory price-cutting, 229; price discrimination provisions, 221; Robinson-Patman amendments and background, 223–31; § 7 and *Du Pont–General Motors* case, 319–20, 354–56; § 7 objectives and administration, 199–208 *passim*; test of § 7 violation, 355*n*; tying clauses, 25*n*, 219–20; workable competition and administration of § 7, 263*n*
Collective bargaining, 2, 4, 6, 236, 422. *See also* Labor unions
Columbia Steel case, 141–43, 198
Commerce Clearing House: cited, 168*n*
Commissioner of Corporations, 20*n*
Commons, John R., 401
Competition: Antitrust Committee on economic indicia of, 237; attitude of Antitrust Division and FTC in 1953 toward, 111*n*; barriers created against by United Shoe, 380; businessmen's attitudes toward, 12, 31, 69, 115; in cellophane industry, 154–66; in cement industry, action to lessen, 67 and *n*; and concept of relevant market, 159; congressional purpose to preserve, 21–23, 133*n*; cooperation preferred by trade association, 36, 49, 61*n*; and corporation-subsidiary relations, 216; differences in views on decline of, 2, 120–22, 286; Du Pont's independence of capital market, 353–54; Du Pont's influence on General Motors' chemical development, 339–43; Du Pont's strategy, 154, 157, 284; effect of mergers on, 204, 206, 226; effects of business reciprocity on, 318; and efficient mass production, 359; extent of desirable restriction of?, 116; in flexible wrapping materials, 284; formally abandoned under NRA, 5; "full and free competition," 132*n*, 133*n*; function of price under, 32–33; and good faith defense, 227; and holding companies, 8, 199–200; identified with private enterprise, 367; and individual liberty, 195; and industrial structure, 122–24, 153*n*, 270, 272, 359-60, 365; in an inflationary economy, 31; interindustry competition, 397; *International Shoe* case, 205*n*; injury to competitors, 225; keen among canners, not canmakers, 176; and knowledge of the market, 26, 34, 79–81 *passim*, 115; labor unions and preservation of, 3–4, 6, 13; lessened under NRA, 209; lessened by systematic basing point pricing, 68, 83, 109, 111; limitations of, 31*n*, 35, 403*n*; and *Maple Flooring* decision, 44, 61; maple-flooring industry approximates model of, 39–43; Maple Flooring Manufacturers Ass'n aimed to restrain, 46, 54; modification of patent laws, 17; nature of competitive process, 205*n*; *The New Competition*, 35, 209; nonprice competition, 28, 151, 288*n*, 290; and open price reporting, 35–39 *passim*, 43–44, 67–68, 72, 75, 79–81 *passim*, 87–88, 98, 103–5, 107–8; and performance test, 257–58; and price cutting, 47, 58, 74, 229–30; versus public interest, 61, 70, 118, 126*n*, 244, 252,

433

254; pure competition defined, 242; in rayon industry, 393; reasonable and unreasonable restrictions on at common law, 126–30; restraint of trade a restriction of, 136; *Rigid Steel Conduit* proceeding, 234–35; rivalry among substitutes, 165, 274; Salt Producers Ass'n restrained, 78; Sherman Act combinations an unfair method of, 76n; Sherman Act outlawed every restriction on, 136, 192; some degree of in nearly all markets, 243; state regulation a substitute for?, 236; in sugar industry, 71; Sugar Institute not designed to insure, 75; supplanted by bilateral monopoly, 14; Tag Manufacturers Institute discouraged, 93–100 *passim*; theory of, 359–60; in tin can industry, 166n, 167n, 174–76n, 180n; trade association consultants' view of, 77; trade association standardization programs, 83n; and umbrella over rivals, 143, 149n; unfair or cut-throat, 71, 94; and United States Steel Corporation, 21, 143, 147, 153n; "workable competition" similar in meaning to, 122

Competitive markets: characteristics of, 34, 279; function of, 1–2; real markets differ from, 34

Comptoir des Textiles Artificiels, 154, 156n, 393

Concentration of economic power, 2, 357–61

Conglomerate firm, 11–12

Conscious parallelism of action: *American Tobacco* case (1946), 162–63; Antitrust Committee on, 199n; *Crepe Paper Ass'n* proceedings, 85–86; disturbing to businessmen, 188, 249-50; FTC basing point pricing cases, 109 and n, 249–50, 364–66; and industrial structure, 199; "planned common course of action," 79n, 85, 148n, 249, 364

Consolidated and McKay Lasting Machine Company, 378n

Consolidation Coal Company, 308

Constantine, Earl: quoted, 113–14

Continental Can Company, 167, 169–71, 173, 175, 179–80

Copeland, Lammot du Pont, 330n

Corn Products Refining Company, 203

Corporate capitalism, 408, 411

Corporate system: questions raised by, 422–23

Corporations: better progress if fewer giants, 184; buy labor under monopoly conditions, 13; center of organizational revolution, 408; compared with labor unions, 8; compared with sovereign, 421; conspiracy with subsidiary, 216; and constitutional rights, 421; control of wealth as of 1930, 358; credited with 1940-60 progress, 422; early distrust of, 408–9; effect on structure of American economy, 2, 8, 421–22; effects of Great Combination Movement and war, 10–11; gifts to American colleges, 420–21; instrument of industrial concentration, 8; "instrument of economic justice," 419; and the inventive process, 217–18, 412; limiting power of, 16–17; managerial responsibility, 145, 418–19; managers of one may speak for an industry, 2; mechanism for utilizing modern technology, 7; mergers and acceptance of, 411; minority control of, 324–25 and n; New Jersey holding corporation, 8; power to mold public opinion, 12, 419–20; as a social institution, 421

Cost-price relationships, 30, 38, 159, 244, 279, 282, 390

Cottonseed Oil Trust, 131

Countervailing power: Galbraith's concept, 13–16; inadequate in can industry, 171; institutional implications of, 15

Coyne, William, 332n

Creeping socialism, 15

Crompton, Samuel, 405

Cross-elasticity of demand: among cellophane and rival products, 158, 161–62, 281–82; concept of, 121, 123–24, 277, 388–90; and oligopoly, 274; significance of *Cellophane* decision, 396; uses and limitations, 281; and workable competition, 158

Curtis Publishing Company, 293, 303

Darby, Abraham, 405

Davey Pegging Machine Company, 379n

Davis, F. B.: quoted, 310

Daugherty, Carroll R.: cited, 68n

Day, William R.: quoted, 139n

Dayton Metal Products Company, 340

Index

De Chazeau, Melvin G.: cited, 68n
Defoe, Daniel, 406
Delaware Investment Company, 321n
Delaware Realty & Investment Corporation, 323
Delaware Securities Company, 321n
Delco Light Company, 333n, 335, 340
Delivered pricing: Antitrust Report on, 233–35; *Glucose* cases, 111n; in maple-flooring industry, 51n, 58; in milk and ice cream can industry, 82; in steel, 110n. *See also* Basing point pricing
Denney Tag Company, 100
Dennison, H. S., and John Kenneth Galbraith: cited, 94 and nn
Dennison Manufacturing Company, 85n, 104
Detroit Jobbers case, 227, 233
Diesel locomotives: General Motors and, 311–14
Differentiated products, 28, 159, 280, 367, 385–86
Dirlam Joel B., 261; cited, 384n; workable competition not an antitrust guide, 258–59. *See also* Dirlam and Kahn; Dirlam and Stelzer
Dirlam, Joel B., and Alfred E. Kahn: cited, 243; conduct as test of antitrust violation, 265n; on economic analysis in antitrust enforcement, 269n, 271; on monopoly power and antitrust, 264; on *National Lead* case, 270n; on 1953 *Pillsbury* decision, 271n; on traditional rule of reason, 268
Dirlam, Joel B., and Irwin M. Stelzer: on the *Cellophane* case, 241, 263–67; on conduct as test of illegality, 267–68; criticisms of Stocking-Mueller article, 241, 263–67, 272; on economic analysis in antitrust administration, 267, 271–72; performance and conduct confused, 265 and n; on proving misuse of monopoly power, 267; on workable competition and antitrust, 265, 272; mentioned, 261
Dissolution, 24, 168, 182, 382
Divestiture, 207, 216, 382 and nn, 321
Donner, Frederic G., 329
Doriot, G. F.: cited, 318n
Douglas, William O., 400; quoted, 173
Durant, William C., 326–27
Du Pont, A. Felix, 332n; quoted, 333

Du Pont Cellophane Company, 283, 284, 391n, 395n
Du Pont de Nemours, E. I., & Company: attempts to unite buying power with General Motors', 299–302, 336 and nn; attitude of potential rivals, 165n; buying power, 304n; cellophane price policy, 266, 282, 389–93; cellophane profits, 267, 391–92; cellophane sales, 280, 281; on competition with cellophane, 160, 161; diversification program, 297 and nn, 322 and n, 331; diversification and reciprocity, 304; independence of capital market, 353–54; monopoly and conduct, 154–58, 272, 320, 373, 384, 393–96; monopoly position in certain chemicals, 354n; monopoly power in cellophane?, 153, 161, 263–67, 284–85, 385–97 *passim*; munitions sales and profits, 297n, 322; *National Lead* case, 373–74; performance in cellophane industry, 163–65, 265, 284–86; "Powder Trust" case, 320 and n, 321; rayon profits and losses, 392–93; reciprocal buying and size, 317; reciprocal buying, use of, 296–304; reciprocity and Curtis Publishing Company, 293; reciprocity with General Dyestuff Corporation, 316n; reciprocity with General Motors, 298–302; reciprocity with U.S. Rubber, 309n; strategy in cellophane industry, 154–58, 283, 393–96. *See also* Cellophane; *Cellophane* case; *Du Pont–General Motors* case
Du Pont–General Motors case: antifreezes and General Motors, 337–38; advantage over competitors for General Motors' business, 332–39; attempts to unite Du Pont's and General Motors' purchases, 299–302, 336 and nn; control of General Motors, 327–32, 399; dissenting opinion, 339n; district court's decision, 323–24; dividends from General Motors, 298n, 353 and n, 354; Du Pont's evaluation of stock acquisition, 325–27, 398; Freons and General Motors, 349–52; influence on General Motors' chemical developments, 339–43; methods of influencing General Motors, 332–39; objective in buying General Motors stock, 331–32, 355–56; purchase and control of

435

General Motors stock, 322–23, 325–27, 330n, 398; reciprocity among Du Pont, General Motors, and U.S. Rubber, 297–314 *passim*; significance of decision, 319–20; "super discount" to General Motors, 337n; tetraethyl lead and General Motors, 343–49
Du Pont, H. F., 330n, 350
Du Pont, Henry Belin, 330n
Du Pont, Irenée: director of Du Pont and General Motors, 330n; investment in General Motors stock, 322, 398; on investment in U.S. Rubber stock, 322; member of committee on general chemical agreement, 342; member of Du Pont's and General Motors' finance committees, 322, 330n, 350; negotiations on tetraethyl lead, 343, 345; on reciprocal buying, 300n, 309n; on safety with tetraethyl lead, 348
Du Pont, Lammot: efforts to sway General Motors business, 332n, 333–34, 335n; member of Du Pont's and General Motors' finance committees, 330n, 350; on reciprocal dealing, 301, 310n; on Union Carbide's desire not to compete, 165n; urged general chemical agreement, 342-43
Du Pont, Pierre S.: chairman of both Du Pont and General Motors, 298, 326, 330n, 341; chairman of Du Pont and president of General Motors, 322–23, 327-29, 343, 349; on Du Pont's manufacturing tetraethyl lead, 343; on General Motors' cooperation in chemical research, 349-50; and General Motors' purchases from Du Pont, 332n, 333; on General Motors' purchasing policy, 336n; investment in General Motors stock, 322, 398; managers' securities plan, 322–23, 329
Durand, E. Dana: quoted, 186n
Düsseldorf Agreement, 210-11
Dyemakers' use of reciprocity, 315–16

Eastern Alcohol Corporation, 337
Eastern Dynamite Company, 321n
Echols, Angus B., 330n
Economic individualism, 402–3
Economists: and organizational revolution, 415; questions for study by, 422
Eddy, Arthur Jerome, 36, 209; quoted, 35

Edwards, Corwin D.: articles on basing point pricing, 68n; cited, 121n, 189n, 213n, 275n; on performance as antitrust guide, 257; on reciprocal buying, 289n; works on revision of antitrust laws cited, 19n; structural tests of workable competition, 318; study of the conglomerate firm, 11–12
Effective competition: Adelman on, 123; blocked by open pricing among sellers only, 105; conditions essential to, 238; Judge Knox on, 375–76; literature on, 119n; may be hindered by fewness of sellers, 124; none with cellophane, 163; Sugar Institute tended to prevent, 75–76; threatened by continuing concerted action, 86–87
Efficiency: and business reciprocity, 315–16; versus competitive pricing, 229–30; and dissolution of big can companies, 180n; may decree few sellers, 123
Eisenhower, Dwight D.: quoted, 192
Electro-Motive Engineering Company, 311 and n
Electronics Corporation of America, 412
Environment: effect on attitudes in antitrust decisions, 399–400; Great Depression, 5; influence of, 1; peace with, 397
Environmental factors: and *Appalachian Coals* decision, 357; fear of industrial concentration, 357-58, 360-63; and market power, 383; satisfaction with business structure, 381–83; and *Socony-Vacuum* decision, 358
Eppler Welt Machine Company, 379n
Epstein, Ralph C.: cited, 178n
Ethyl Gasoline Corporation, 346-47, 349
Exclusive dealing: "any substantial market," 25; required by American Can Company, 174, 175n; restricted in 1950 *Can* decrees, 179; rule of reason approach to, 232; *Standard Stations* case, 232, 251

Fabrikoid Company, 331
Fainsod, Merle: quoted, 133n
Fair trade laws, 232
Fairbanks, Morse & Company, 313
Fairfield Rubber Company, 331
Fairless, Benjamin: cited, 7n; cost of a steel plant, 145; delivered pricing not basing point system, 110n; U.S. Steel's

Index

inefficiency, 152, 153*n*; on uniform pricing of steel extras, 148*n*
Federal Leather Company, 337*n*
Federal Trade Commission: attack on basing point pricing, 109–110, 147*n*, 233–35; attitude toward competition and monopoly in 1953, 111*n*; conscious parallel action, 109*n*; cost justification, 227–28; on economic analysis of mergers, 206–7, 270*n*; good faith defense, 227; and oligopoly, 363-66; protection against hard competition, 23, 189, 225–26; reports cited, 164*n*, 165*n*, 176*n*, 201*n*, 222*n*; rule of reason in merger cases, 206–8
Federal Trade Commission Act: 1912 party platforms on, 22 and *n*; purpose of, 23, 186*n*; reaches Sherman Act combinations, 76*n*; § 5 remedies inadequate, 235; Sherman Act proof for § 5, 210
Fetter, Frank A.: articles on basing point pricing, 68*n*; on competitive and imperfect markets, 66*n*; criticizes Burns's program, 121; quoted, 35, 366; mentioned, 70*n*, 366*n*
Fielding, Henry, 406
Fiscal and monetary policies, 117
Fisher, Irving: cited, 56*n*
Fisher, Lloyd H.: cited, 6*n*
Fisher Body Corporation, 333*n*
Fisk Rubber Company, 300
Flint Varnish & Chemical Works, 332
Folsom, James Mack, 203*n*
Ford, Bacon & Davis report, 151*n*, 152*n*
Fortune: quoted, 177*n*, 303, 320, 322*n*, 419
Frankfurter, Felix: quoted, 339*n*, 397
Fraser, C. E.: cited, 318*n*
Free enterprise: Adam Smith on, 403; Antitrust Committee did not use studies of, 239; attempt to sell big business and big labor as essential to, 12; British not committed to, 117; desire to preserve and Sherman Act, 185; eighteenth-century flowering of, 407; endangered by workable competition concept, 117, 261; fair trade laws conflict with, 232; and governmental responsibility, 31*n*; industrial structure and, 270; invoked to fight "welfare state," 1; loss of confidence in, 5, 16, 94; and *Maple Flooring* decision, 44, 61; meaning of to economists, 1–2; meaning of to trade association consultants, 77; and private monopolies, 15, 276, 359; role of price in, 115; significance of labor unions to, 3; significance of market data exchange to, 35
Freedom of entry, 29 and *n*, 285, 396
Freight rate books: in cement industry, 65, 67*n*; in crepe paper industry, 85*n*; in maple-flooring industry, 48, 49, 51 and *n*, 58; in milk and ice cream can industry, 82
Functional discounts, 232–33

Gainsborough, Thomas, 405
Galbraith, John Kenneth: concept of countervailing power, 13–16, 416 and *n*, 417–18
Galbraith, John Kenneth, and H. S. Dennison: cited, 94 and *nn*
Gary, Elbert H., 151; on basing point pricing, 148*n*; on competition, 21, 147; federal corporation licensing bill, 22*n*
General Dyestuff Corporation, 316*n*
General Electric Company, 420
General Industries, Inc., 322
General Motors Corporation: controlled by Du Pont officials, 328–29 and *n*, 330–32; diesel locomotives, 269, 311–14; discounts to employees, 291*n*; dividends paid to Du Pont, 298*n*, 353 and *n*, 354; and Du Pont's antifreeze, 337–38; Du Pont's efforts to influence business decisions, 335*n*; Du Pont's influence on chemical developments, 339–43; Du Pont's purchase and control of stock, 322, 325–27, 330*n*; and Du Pont's reciprocity with others, 298–303, 336; Freons and Du Pont, 349–52; general purchasing committee, 336; Kinetic Chemicals, Inc., 349–52; *National City Lines* case, 289*n*; officials urged buying from Du Pont, 335; purchases from Du Pont, 332 and *n*, 333–35, 339 and *n*; reciprocal buying, 290–91, 310–15, 317; reciprocity with railroads, 313; reciprocity with steel companies, 314–15; tetraethyl lead and Du Pont, 343–49. See also *Du Pont–General Motors* case
General Refractories Company, 335*n*
George, E. B.: cited, 68*n*

437

George, James Z., 132n, 133n
Gibbon, Edward, 406
Globe Welt Machine Company, 379n
Glucose cases, 111n, 233-34, 250
Gompers, Samuel, 4
Goodman, Walter, 413n
Goodrich, B. F., case, 227
Goodyear Shoe Machinery Company, 378n
Gordon, Edward B., 56, 57
Gordon, Lincoln: quoted, 133n
Grace, Eugene: quoted, 147n
Graham, Billy, 413
Great Combination Movement, 19n, 120n; changed structure of American economy, 8–11; congressional response to, 186; created problem of oligopoly, 140; effect on economic thinking, 187; increased industrial concentration, 201, 410; given legal status by *Knight* case, 19, 136n; ignored by Antitrust Committee, 195; motives behind, 269–70; Schumpeter's view of, 417–18; Sherman Act failed to prevent, 199; validated by rule of reason, 197, 268
Great Depression, 5, 94, 149, 187
Great Western Sugar Company, 70n
Greenewalt, Crawford H.: cited, 302n; quoted, 304n
Griffin, Clare E.: cited, 19n; performance the chief test of workable competition, 247, 369, 384n
Grubb, Hunter, 300
Gulf Refining Company, 344
Gunpowder Trade Association, 320n
Gunton, George: cited, 131n
Guthrie, William D.: cited, 185n; quoted, 20

Hadley, Arthur T.: cited, 131n; quoted, 289
Hales, Stephen, 406
Hamilton, Harold L.: quoted, 311n
Hamilton, Walton: quoted, 251n
Hamilton, Walton, and Irene Till: quoted, 217n
Hand, Learned: economic criterion of monopoly, 141, 198; interpretation of Sherman Act § 2, 141–42, 181; on market power as monopoly, 140n, 248; on substitutes and potential competition, 360–61; mentioned, 374, 378, 381
Handler, Milton: cited, 19n, 197n; on common-law rules on restraints of trade, 129–30
Hanway, Jonas, 406
Hardwood Lumber Manufacturers Association, 36–38, 46
Hargreaves, James, 405
Harlan, John Marshall, 319, 400
Harrison Brothers & Company, 331 and n
Haskell, J. A., 329n, 332n
Hazard Powder Company, 321n
Heflebower, Richard B.: cited, 248 and n
Heller, Robert, & Associates, 160n, 162n
Henderson, Gerard C.: cited, 21n, 23n; quoted, 21n, 186n
Henry, Patrick, 414–15
Herbert, Bueford G.: cited, 109n
Hercules Powder Company, 303, 321
Hession, Charles H.: cited, 169n, 171–72nn, 176–78nn, 180n; quoted, 178n, 198n
Hettinger, Albert J., Jr., 57
Hexner, Ervin: cited, 213n
Hoar, George F.: quoted, 134n
Hobson, John A.: cited, 55n
Hogarth, William, 405
Holmes, O. W.: quoted, 422–23
Holmes, Oliver Wendell, Justice: cited, 378n
Homer, Arthur B.: cited, 318n
Hoover, Herbert, 55
Hornblower, William B.: cited, 131n
Howard, Frank, 344
Howard, John, 406
Howe, E. P., 378n
Howery, Edward F.: quoted, 111n, 206n, 207, 270n
Howes, Wright: quoted, 414n
Hudson, James F.: cited, 131n
Huey, G. M., 100
Hughes, Charles Evans: quoted, 357
Hume, David, 406
Hunter, D. S. & Associates, 81–82
Hurley, Edward N.: cited, 56n
Hyatt Roller Bearing Company, 335

Implied conspiracy doctrine, 86
Indiana Powder Company, 321n
Individual business conduct and conscious parallel action, 364–65
Individualism: in civil liberties, 415; decline in twentieth century, 408–15;

Index

dominated eighteenth century, 405–8; in economic affairs, 402–8; and labor unions, 2, 6; in philanthropy, 414; in religion, 413; rugged individualism, 1; in scientific research threatened, 412–13; in inventions, 217–18

Industrial concentration: Adelman's studies, 201 and *n;* Antitrust Committee ignored significance of, 195; Berle and Means study, 358, 412; in canmaking, 169–72; Clayton Act to prevent, 200, 400; differences in measurements of, 2; FTC reports, 201–2 and *n;* and Great Combination Movement, 196; hostility towards, 194, 361; and mergers, 10, 201, 204, 409–10; and political power, 195; and prices of steel, 149; significance of to monopoly, 199; socialists' view of, 366; TNEC set up to study, 187; and workable competition, 208, 263*n*

Industrial performance: and *Aluminum* decision, 361; in cellophane, 163, 165, 284–86; Dirlam and Kahn on, 259; Edwards on, 257; least acceptable test for workable competition, 257–58, 275–76; and monopoly power, 278, 279; *National Lead* decision, 374; Oppenheim and Smith on, 371; primary test for workable competition, 384–85 and *n;* and public policy, 276; and reciprocal dealing, 318; Smith on, 252; in steel industry, 149–53; test in *Cellophane* case, 264*n,* 385; test for workable competition, 30, 125, 242–43, 262, 368; in tin can industry, 175–79

Industrial structure: *Aluminum* decision (1950), 376–77; *American Can* decision, 168; "archeological" combinations, 181; in can industry, 166*n,* 167–72, 198, 199*n;* in cellophane, 158, 280; changes in, 2, 13, 138, 187, 195, 196; and conscious parallel action, 199; considered of little importance by some, 384 and *nn;* economists who accept present-day, 416; effect of in steel industry, 144–46, 153*n,* 198–99; and efficiency, 366; fewness of sellers and monopoly-like behavior, 11; inevitability of current structure assumed, 421; influence of mergers on, 138, 144, 202–4, 421; kind sanctioned by Sherman Act, 196; of maple-flooring industry, 57; may condition conduct, 120, 198, 269–70, 276–77, 365, 384 and *n;* penalizing bad conduct will not reform, 182; questions raised by 239–40, 422; and reciprocity, 317–18; and relevant market, 276, 277; and rule of reason, 24, 269; significance of to competition, 243; test for workable competition, 122, 242–43, 272, 368; transformed by institutional changes, 2, 12–13

Inland Steel Company, 301
Institutional advertising, 367, 420
Institutional changes: effect on price theory, 415–18; effect on structure of American economy, 2, 12–13
Institutional matrix and judicial decisions, 183
Interindustry competition, 372, 397
International cartels: Antitrust Committee minority's recommendation on, 212; cellophane, 284; versus free foreign commerce, 214*n;* literature on, 213*n;* and Sherman Act, 211–12; significance of, 210–16; titanium, 373–74
International Goodyear Shoe Machinery Company, 378*n*
International Harvester Company, 20*n,* 197
International Paper Company, 308
International Salt case, 231
International Salt Company, 231
International Shoe case, 226
International Smokeless Powder and Chemical Company, 322*n*
Interstate Commerce Commission, 293

Jevons, W. Stanley: cited, 66*n*
Johns-Manville Corporation, 418
Johnson, William Summers: cited, 68*n*
Jones, Franklin D.: cited, 56*n*
Jones & Laughlin Steel Corporation, 203, 301, 314
Jonson, Ben: quoted, 414*n*

Kahn, Alfred E.: cited, 384*n;* dissents from Antitrust Report, 194 and *n,* 208; workable competition not an antitrust guide, 258–59. *See also* Dirlam, Joel B., and Alfred E. Kahn
Kaiser Aluminum and Chemical Corporation, 375–77

439

Kalle & Company, 155, 284, 393–94
Kaplan, A. D. H.: cited, 248 and n
Kaysen, Carl: cited, 68n, 151n; quoted, 382nn
Keehn, George W., association secretary: cited, 49n, 55n; quoted, 44n, 46 and n, 48n, 53
Keehn, Grant, economist, 56, 61; quoted, 58
Keezer, Dexter M.: cited, 19n, 258n, 384n
Kentucky Alcohol Corporation, 337
Kerr, Clark: cited, 6n
Kerr, George H., 302; quoted, 298, 299 and n
Kettering, Charles F., 340–43; quoted, 312n, 340–41, 342n
Keystone Tag Company, 96
Kimball, A., Company, 104
Kinetic Chemicals, Inc., 349–52
Kittelle, Sumner S.: cited, 86n, 109n
Knight, E. C., case, 8–9, 18–19, 70, 136n, 186n, 196
Knight, Frank H.: cited, 32n
Knox, John C., 62, 372, 375–77
Kraemer, Robert: cited, 68n

Labor unions: accomplishments of, 3; Antitrust Committee recommendations on, 236–37; changes in membership, 4–5; coal miners' defiance of federal government, 4; compared with modern corporation, 8; effect on structure of American economy, 2; fundamental object, 3; governmental policy to increase power, 5–6; growth with combination movement, 411; limiting power a delicate task, 16; power to mold public opinion, 12; sell labor under monopoly conditions, 13; significance of to free enterprise, 3. *See also* Big labor
LaBuy, Walter J., 319, 323–24; quoted, 398
Laflin & Rand Powder Company, 321n
Lamb, George P.: cited, 86n, 109n
LaMotte, F., 337
Latham, Earl: cited, 67n
Lawson, Charles T.: quoted, 114
Leahy, Paul: Blackwell Smith on decision of, 372; on competition cellophane faced, 154, 160n, 385; decision based on a concept of workable competition, 183, 263, 264n; on Du Pont's performance, 284; findings challenged, 241, 265n, 286; on questions in *Cellophane* case, 153, 264, 280 and n; on relevant market for cellophane, 158n, 281, 386-89
Levi, Edward H.: cited, 19n
Lewis, Ben W.: cited, 384n; on performance test of competition, 258, 276
Lewis, Howard T.: quoted, 288nn, 296 and n
Lewis, John L., 3–4, 14
Lewis, William F.: cited, 313; quoted, 312n
Liggett & Myers Tobacco Company, 361–62, 365
Lilienthal, David E., 13; cited, 19n
Lima Locomotive Works, 312n
Lindahl, Martin L.: cited, 20n
Linseed Crushers Council, 38–39
Linseed Oil case, 38–39
Linseed Oil Trust, 131
Lipson, E., 403–4
Little business, 400
Loevinger, Lee, cited: 19n
Lynah, James, 336 and n, 338; cited, 301n; quoted, 300n

McAllister, Breck P.: quoted, 114
McCusker, E. L.: quoted, 99
McGuire Act, 221, 232
Machlup, Fritz: cited, 67n, 68n, 151n
McKay Shoe Machinery Company, 378n
McKee, Thomas H.: quoted, 131n
McKie, James W.: cited, 171n, 179–80; quoted, 179n, 180n
McLaughlin, James A.: cited, 131n; quoted, 23n
Managers Securities Company, 322–23, 354n, 399
Mansfield (Lord), 406
Maple Flooring Manufacturers Association: earlier associations, 44-49, 53-54; effects of activities, 55; goal of, 54, 57, 61; industry approximates competitive model, 39–43; membership, 45n; nature of information exchanged, 50–52, 59, 60n; price policy, 47n; processes in making flooring, 40; standardization of flooring, 55; statistical activities held lawful, 43–44; Supreme Court's view of, 52n
Marengo, Louis: cited, 153n

Index

Market behavior: need for information on, 34

Market power: and *Aluminum* decision (1950), 376–77; *American Tobacco* decision (1946), 361–63; deliberately achieved and Sherman Act, 142, 381; due to United Shoe's lease system, 380; environmental factors, 383; of General Motors in automobiles, 356; and monopoly, 248–49; through patents, 218; without predatory practices, 23 and n; and social responsibility, 418; tying clauses in patent licenses, 219 and n, 220

Markham, Jesse W.: quoted on workable competition, 30, 246–47, 369; study of mergers cited, 196n; study of rayon industry cited, 164n, 393n; work on workable competition cited, 29n, 121n, 190n, 275n

Marshall, Alfred, 122n

Marshall, Leon Carroll: cited, 55n

Mason, Edward S.: articles on workable competition cited, 19n, 29n, 121n, 190n, 275n; on economic inquiry in antitrust enforcement, 271 and n; on effect of preconceptions, 30, 183 and n; on industrial performance, 243, 369; on limiting the firm and efficiency, 30; on monopoly in law and economics, 243; on revision of antitrust laws, 244; on uses and limitations of workable competition, 246; work on international cartels cited, 213n; mentioned, 70, 262

Mead, Edward S.: cited, 8n; quoted, 185n

Mead, James M.: quoted, 270n

Means, Gardiner C.: *see* Berle, Adolph A., Jr., and Gardiner C. Means

Mechanical Manufacturing Company, 295

Mercantilism, 402–4

Merger movements: and corporate size, 9; effect on economic thinking, 187; ignored by Antitrust Committee, 195, 204; impact of, 120; and industrial concentration, 10; and laws designed to prevent, 196, 200, 410-11; made possible by the corporation, 409; restructured modern industry, 138, 202–4, 421; rule of reason approach inadequate, 269; in steel industry, 144

Mergers: Antitrust Committee's view of, 204–5; business reciprocity a motive for, 317; *Du Pont–General Motors* case, 320, 354–55, 397–99; economic analysis of, 206; effect on size of large firms, 202–4; FTC 1955 report, 201n; increase since 1949, 201; and industrial structure, 202–4; no effective penalty in Clayton Act, 207; objective of Celler-Kefauver amendment, 200 and n, 204; and rule of reason, 198; tests of legality, 204–8; in tin can industry, 170n; Weston's study, 9–10, 202, 203n

Michigan Sugar Company, 71n

Midgley (of General Motors), 341, 344, 350, 352n

Milk and Ice Cream Can Institute, 81–84

Miller-Tydings Act, 232

Minneapolis-Honeywell case, 226

Mitchell, Wesley Clair, 240, 401

Mond, Sir Alfred: cited, 210n

Monopolies and Restrictive Trade Practices Act, 117n

Monopolistic competition, 188, 415–18

Monopolistic markets, 280

Monopolistic practices in locomotive industry, 312n

Monopoly: absence in *Cellophane* case challenged, 154, 161, 263–67, 281–86 by American Can Company, 166; *Aluminum* decision, 141, 248, 360; *Aluminum* test modified, 198; Antitrust Committee on economic indicia of, 238; at common law, 131n; and conduct, 158, 278; confused with bigness, 253; and cross-elasticity of demand, 161–63, 388–90; curbed by technical progress, 244–45; defined as market control and power to exclude, 248–49; and deliberateness, 142; Dirlam and Kahn on, 259; economic tests of, 141, 243, 248, 273, 280; and efficiency, 142 and n, 227; element "essential to progressiveness," 14; full-line forcing, 231; good faith defense, 227; growth not prevented by enactment of Sherman Act, 21; in gunpowder by Du Pont, 320 and n, 321–22 and n; industrial performance, 361; in international markets, 210–16; judicial reluctance to disturb, 139 and n, 167–68, 377, 381–83; legal proof of,

441

142n, 243, 264, 376, 378–81; monopolistic leverage and tying clauses, 220; not workably competitive, 29; partial versus complete, 196; power versus abuse, 139n; price discrimination, 229–30; price policy in, 75n, 161, 163, 282; price policies in cellophane, 284–85, 391–93; profits, 280; profits in cellophane, 163–65, 267, 284–86, 391–93; pure monopoly defined, 242; and secret rebates, 166; and Sherman Act, 197; significance of innovator's, 158; and size, 248; some degree in nearly all markets, 242; strategy, 158, 278, 283–84, 393–96; and substitute products, 183, 263, 273–74, 283, 285–86, 360; tests of in *American Tobacco* (1946), 362–63; of tetraethyl lead by Du Pont, 349; traditional view of, 187; workable competition tests for, 276

Monopoly power: Clark on, 29; and cost-price relationships, 281, 389, 396; and definition of the market, 165–66, 265n, 272, 277–280, 285–86; of Du Pont in certain chemicals, 354n; economic tests of, 264–65; of General Motors in diesel locomotives, 269; and industrial performance, 279; and preconceptions, 274; and prices, 279; proving economic misuse of, 267

Montague, Gilbert H.: cited, 212n
Moody, John: cited, 120n
Moody's Industrials, 169n, 170n
Mountain Varnish and Color Works, 332
Mountain, W. W., 332
Mueller, Willard F.: cited, 320n; mentioned, 263. *See also* Stocking, George W., and Willard F. Mueller
Mund, Vernon A.: cited, 67n, 68n, 151n
Murray, Philip, 14

National Association of Hosiery Manufacturers, 113
National Crepe Paper Association of America, 84–87
National Distillers Product Corporation, 203
National Industrial Recovery Act, 5, 77, 87, 93–94
National Lead case, 373
National Lead Company, 373
National Lead Trust, 131
National Recovery Administration: attempt at business self-regulation, 23; competition tempered by, 94; effect on trade association activities, 84, 86, 87n, 93n, 95n, 209; experiment in business cooperation, 94–95; Steel Code and secret rebate on tin plate, 172; mentioned, 16, 187, 357

National Sugar Company, 70n
Neal, Alfred C.: cited, 117n
New Competition, 416
New Competition, The, 209; quoted, 35
New Deal, 5, 358
New Departure Manufacturing Company, 333n
New England Oil Paint & Varnish Company, 332
New Jersey holding company law, 8–9, 185n, 199
New York, New Haven & Hartford Railroad, 313
New York Times: quoted, 296
Nicholls, William H.: on advertising in cigarette industry, 287n; on *American Tobacco* decision (1946), 363; on control of oligopoly, 249
Nicols, Alfred: cited, 68n
Norris–LaGuardia Act, 5
Nourse, Edwin G.: appeal to businessmen's long-run interest, 121; on businessmen's responsibility, 416–17; cited, 70n

Oglethorpe, James, 406
Olds, Irving S.: quoted, 250, 366n
Oligopolistic pricing, 78, 361–63
Oligopolistic structure preserved, 145, 153, 165–66
Oligopoly: and *American Tobacco* case (1946), 249, 365 and n; Antitrust Committee on, 238; and basing point pricing, 70n; and business conduct, 124, 140, 181, 272, 364–65; Burns's solution, 366; in can industry, 180; Chamberlinian theory, 11, 13, 27–28, 78n, 360n, 366–68 *passim*; Clark's view of, 244; effect of uncertainties, 78n, 277; Federal Trade Commission cases, 363–66; freight rate books, 148 and n; identical pricing, 13, 84, 86; in malt industry, 76–77; and monopoly-like behavior, 120, 122–23; problem created by Great Combination Movement, 140; and reciprocal buying, 290, 318; and rivalry of substitutes,

Index

274; role of mergers, 202–4; in salt industry, 76–77; social control of, 359, 363; and trade associations, 79; and workable competition, 182, 366

Olin Industries, Inc., 158n, 283n, 393n, 395–96; quoted, 160n

Olin Mathieson Chemical Corporation, 393n

Olsen, Fred, 158n, 393n

Open price reporting: advocated by Eddy, 35; Antitrust Committee's view of, 210; and buyers, 107–8; in cement industry, 63 and n, 67–68; contributed to identical pricing of tags, 103; in crepe paper industry, 84–85; *Hardwood Lumber* decision, 38; legality of and recognition of price function, 115–16; in malt industry, 79–82; Maple Flooring Manufacturers Association, 44n; purpose of exchanging data, 36; in sugar industry, 72, 75; in tag industry, 87–108 *passim*; defects of tag makers' system of, 107

Oppenheim, S. Chesterfield: article proposing revision of antitrust laws, 18n, 119n, 189n; cited, 187n; co-chairman of Antitrust Committee, 18n, 119n, 254; on composition of Antitrust Committee, 191; efforts to revise antitrust laws, 26 and n, 251–55, 369–71; on implied conspiracy and trade associations, 86, 108–9, 112; endorsed rule of reason and workable competition, 190; on influence of Antitrust Report, 256–57, 372; on justification of restrictions on competition, 115, 125n, 254; on per se antitrust decisions, 25n; on rule of reason and workable competition, 26 and n, 137nn, 144n; *Tag* case a rule of reason decision, 108n; mentioned, 260

Organization: book clubs, 414; civil liberties, 415; dominates twentieth-century society, 408–15; by managements to meet united labor, 6; for philanthropy, 414; in religion, 413; in research, 412–13

"Organization Man," 412, 422

Organizational revolution, 408–15

O'Rourke, J. S., 332–33

Osborn, C. R.: quoted, 312nn

Pack, Charles D.: quoted, 315–16 and n

Parker (Chief Justice): quoted, 127n

Patents: abuse by dominant firm, 182; antitrust policy, 216–20; basis of public policy on, 217, 411; and business conduct, 278; in cellophane industry, 154–57, 284, 394–95; compulsory patent licensing, 383n; doctrine of patent misuse, 218–19; Du Pont's cellophane infringement settlement, 156–57 and n; Du Pont–General Motors–U.S. Rubber exchange agreement, 297n; exchange agreements, 11, 211, 220, 373; full-line forcing, 231; international cartel cases, 215; and market power, 217–18; modification of patent laws, 17; nonuse and restraint of trade, 219; price fixing by license, 219; in tin can industry, 169, 171 and n, 174, 178; titanium cartels, 373; tying clauses in licenses, 219–20, 232n; and United Shoe's market power, 383n

Patman, Wright: cited, 191n

Pearce, Charles A.: cited, 71nn, 76n; quoted, 209n

Pennsylvania Sugar Refining Company, 70n

Peppin, John C.: quoted, 129n

Per se antitrust violation: basing point pricing cases, 109–11, 249–50; businessmen disapprove principle, 25; decisions disapproved by Antitrust Committee, 256; Oppenheim on, 108–9, 254–55 and n, 370; price fixing, 114; *Socony-Vacuum* decision, 250–51; trade association cases, 110–11

Perelle, Charles W.: quoted, 313–14

"Perennial gale of creative destruction," 14, 260

Perfect competition, 279

Perkins, George W.: on advantages of large-scale companies, 22n; on creation of business court, 22n; on effect of Sherman Act prosecutions, 22

Peterson, V. H.: cited, 312n, 313

Phalen, Mary Bell: quoted 63n

Phelps, George E.: quoted, 103

Pierce, Frank W.: quoted, 419

Pillsbury Mills case, 205–7

"Pittsburgh Plus," 147 and n, 148n

Poor's Industry and Investment Surveys, 176n

Pope, Alexander: quoted, 9

Potential competition: *Aluminum* de-

443

cision (1950), 376; *American Can* decision, 168; Clark's view of, 28, 244, 367, 416; insufficient in tin can industry, 175; prevented in tobacco industry, 362

Powder Trust, 321*n*

Pratt, John L.: favored Du Pont's development of General Motors' chemical discoveries, 350 and *n*; on General Motors' duty to buy from Du Pont, 335; on General Motors' purchases, 301, 302*n*, 333*n*; link between Du Pont and General Motors, 300, 329, 330*n*, 334–37; member of General Motors general purchasing committee, 336*n*

Preconceptions: affect judgments on workable competition, 30, 70, 183, 246, 262, 373, 384; of Antitrust Committee on antitrust and foreign commerce, 212–13; and *Du Pont–General Motors* case, 323–24, 398–99; and economic theory, 401; about monopoly power, 274

Prices: reciprocity and stabilization of, 316

Price cutting: and cost-price relationships, 282; judgments differ as to effects of, 124; by a monopolist, 161; and oligopoly, 363–65; and profits in steel, 146; and Sugar institute, 73*n*; and Tag Manufacturers Institute, 106 and *n*; trade association methods of curbing, 31 and *n*

Price discrimination: by American Can Company, 174*n*, 175; brokerage payments, 224; and *Cement Institute* case, 66–67; Clayton Act provisions, 221; "competition with any person," 225; cost justification, 226–28, 230; freight absorption, 234; *Glucose* cases, 111*n*; good faith defense, 227–30; *Goodyear* case, 222; injury to buyers' competition, 74*n*, 221–22; may perform economic function, 74; by a monopolist, 161; monopolistic efficiency, 229–30; *Morton Salt* decision, 251; prohibited in 1950 Can decrees, 179; quantity discounts to chain stores, 222–23; Robinson-Patman Act, 97*n*, 223–31; in steel industry, 149; in sugar industry, 75; tin plate rebate, 230; when unlawful, 228–29

Price fixing: between corporation and subsidiary, 216; in patent licenses, 219; per se unlawful, 24–25, 114; *Socony-Vacuum* decision, 111*n*, 357–58; in sugar industry, 72; Supreme Court on, 111*n*; *Tag Institute* decision, 108; terms and conditions of sale, 64*n*; in tin can industry, 173; trade associations, 47*n*; *Trenton Potteries* case, 25*n*; through United States Maltsters Association, 80

Price leadership: in can industry, 174, 180; in steel industry, 147, 181; in tobacco industry, 365

Price movements and industrial structure, 153*n*

Price theory: cruel readjustments unavoidable, 73; effect of institutional changes on, 415–18; function of price in a competitive economy, 32–33, 115; inadequate to explain price behavior, 27; long-run stability impairs price functions, 176; originally concerned with competitive pricing, 187

Prices: in aluminum industry, 376; of cans increased consumers' living costs, 177; of cans stable, 175–76; of cans tied to price of tin plate, 173; of cellophane controlled, 163, 284–85; of cellophane and rivals moved independently, 161–63; Chamberlinian theory, 11; collaboration to stabilize, 73; in competitive markets, 159; competitive or monopolistic?, 80, 279–80; cross-elasticity of demand, 282, 389; effect of freight rate books on, 65; effect of open price reporting on, 116; function of, 32-33, 115; identical under Milk and Ice Cream Can Institute, 83; identical pricing encouraged by NRA tag code, 94; influence of trade association on, 47, 49–51, 55, 58–59, 82–83; of maple flooring, long-run movements, 56; of maple flooring, short-run behavior, 57, 59–61; monopolist's pricing policy, 161; monopoly not necessarily profitable, 75*n*; nonprice competition, 288*n*; not cut despite decline in demand, 58; in oligopolistic industries, 78*n*, 86–87, 360; significance of competition in terms and conditions of sale, 102; significance of uniformity, 81*n*; *Socony-Vacuum* decision, 250; in steel

Index

industry, 146, 148–51, 181; in tag industry, 95–96, 101, 106
Pricing policies and structure, 235
Priestley, Joseph, 406
Private enterprise: and *Aluminum* decision (1950), 377; ceasing to be free enterprise, 359; confidence in revived, 367; and liberal arts colleges, 421; and the modern corporation, 419; NRA an attempt at self-regulation of, 23; and rivalry of substitutes, 274; United States system admired, 183
Proctor, Edward W.: cited, 304n
Profits: of American Can Company, 177; in cellophane, 163–65, 267, 284–85; function of in competitive markets, 159; indicator of monopoly power, 267, 279; indicator of workable competition, 30; in rayon, 164–65, 285; trade association set ceiling on, 48
Protestant Reformation, 413
Public interest: *Aluminum* decision (1950), 376; antitrust goal, 252–54; and collective action, 252n; and contemporary industrial structure, 416; corporate welfare identified with, 367; and countervailing power, 15; dissolution of big can companies, 180n; early restraints of trade held contrary to, 126 and n; Mason on need of tests for, 30, 244; may be endangered by size and power, 168; and restrictions on competition, 70, 115–18, 127, 129, 137, 244, 261, 403; said to depend on willingness to lower prices, 121; standard in British trade regulation, 117, 360
Public policy: Adam Smith concerned with, 402; of antitrust laws, 271n; Blackwell Smith on, 252; toward business, issues in, 239, 422; controlled decision-making versus free market, 93n; decentralization of economic power, 16; does not forbid expansion, 142n; need for public interest tests, 244; and reasonable restrictions on competition, 128nn; should outlaw restrictions on competition, 117; significance of bigness, 12, 239; Stocking and Watkins on, 260; towards business cycle excesses, 33; workable competition a treacherous guide to, 69
Purdy, Harry Leslie: cited, 20n

Pure competition: growth of firm under, 287; and reciprocal buying, 290
Pure monopoly: prices in, 279

Ramseyer, Charles F., 145n
Raskob, John J.: approved Sloan's election, 328; director of both Du Pont and General Motors, 330n; on Du Pont's control of General Motors, 326–27, 398; on managers' securities plan, 329, member of General Motors finance committee, 350; planned General Motors–Du Pont cooperation in chemicals, 342; recommended Du Pont's purchase of General Motors stock, 322; vice president of General Motors, 333n
Raymond, Daniel: quoted, 408
Rayon, profits in: 164-65, 392
Reagan, John H.: 132n, 133n
Reciprocal buying: conditions conducive to, 290–93; in Great Depression, 296; by packers, 294–95; by railroads, 293–94, 313–14; U.S. Rubber's objectives and methods, 305–7. *See also* Business reciprocity
Reed, Stanley, 372
Relevant market: and business conduct, 278; *Cellophane* case, 158–61, 280–81, 355n, 385–93; concept narrowed in *Du Pont–General Motors* case, 320, 355 and n; and mergers, 204–6; "reasonably" interchangeable products, 388; and substitute products, 277
Republic Steel Corporation, 203, 315
Resale price maintenance, 232
Restraint of trade: common-law rules on, 129–30; in *Du Pont–General Motors* case, 323–24, 352–56; earliest cases, 126n; early distinction between reasonable and unreasonable, 127–30; meaning in Sherman Act, 130, 136; nonuse of patents, 219; in oligopolistic markets, 126n; restriction on competition, 126; and rule of reason in early American cases, 128n; and rule of reason in English cases, 127–28nn; technical meaning, 136
Restrictions on competition: of "appreciable part" of commerce, 249; congressional purpose to outlaw, 132; corporation-subsidiary relationships, 251; through delivered pricing, 233;

445

Du Pont's in gun powder, 320 and *n*, 321; and economic analysis, 244; by labor unions, 3–6, 236; Oppenheim on weighing justifications of, 254; in patent licenses, 218; political consequences of, 359; and public interest, 261; and rule of reason in English cases, 127–28; status at common law, 129–30, 132*n*; in steel industry, 148, 197; versus undue restrictions, 196

Retailing Daily, quoted, 31

Reyburn Manufacturing Company, 85*n*

Reynolds, Joshua, 405

Reynolds Metals Company, 375–77

Reynolds, R. J., Tobacco Company, 361–62, 365

Rhodes, J. C., Company, 382*n*

Rice, H. H., quoted, 334

Richardson, Samuel, 406

Rigid Steel Conduit case, 234–35, 364

Ripley, W. Z., 409*n*

Robertson, Ross M.: cited, 248, 274*n*, 384*n*; quoted, 277, 286

Robertson, William, 406

Robinson, David W., 194*n*

Robinson, E. A. G.: cited, 317

Robinson, Joan: cited, 27, 120*n*, 188, 360

Robinson-Patman Act: Antitrust Committee's recommendations emasculate, 230; background of, 221–23; and basing point pricing, 235; conflict with Sherman Act, 225; conflicting principles in, 226–27; injury to competition among customers, 74*n*, 111*n*; interpreted to protect little businessmen, 189; power of chain stores, 222–23 and *n*; provisions, 97*n*, 223–28, 230–31; purpose of, 225; reinterpretation, 228–30

Rochester and Pittsburgh Coal Company, 303

Rockefeller, John D., Jr., 325

Roebuck, John, 406

Rogers, William F.: cited, 400*n*; quoted, 356

Roosevelt, Franklin D.: quoted, 358, 359

Roosevelt, Theodore: cited, 23*n*

Rose, John C.: quoted, 166*nn*, 167–68

Rostow, Eugene V.: on *American Tobacco* decision (1946), 363; on Antitrust Report, 193; cited, 19*n*, 141*n*, 384*n*; on control of oligopoly, 249; dissents from Antitrust Report, 194 and *n*, 208; on international cartels, 212*n*

Roth, Almon E.: quoted, 6

Rottenburg, Irving: cited, 410*n*

Rubber Securities Company, 323

Rule of reason: aim of advocates of, 26, 143–44; *American Can* decision, 166–67; *American Tobacco* decision (1911), 21, 138–39, 268; Antitrust Committee endorsed, 140, 197–98, 208, 210, 215, 219, 256; *Appalachian Coals* decision, 250–51; Blackwell Smith on, 252–53, 370 and *n*; *Cellophane* decision, 264*n*; certain combinations inherently unreasonable, 25*n*; Chief Justice White on, 135–38, 268; in common-law cases, 128–30; Dirlam and Kahn on, 268; drift away from, 189; effect of adopting, 24, 139–40, 144, 180–81, 195, 262, 268; and elimination of competition, 129*n*; endorsed by Howery of FTC, 271*n*; exclusive dealing cases, 232; expounded by Justice Brandeis, 24*n*; FTC merger cases, 206–8; Federal Trade Commission Act, 210; foreign commerce cases, 215; *Hardwood Lumber* decision in harmony with, 38; legality of combinations tested by, 24; meanings of, 24–26, 136–39, 143–44, 189*n*; and monopoly, 134–40, 198; more liberal interpretation not needed, 115; 1911 decisions disturbing to Congress, 21; no economic standard of reasonableness, 24; not applied to price-fixing, 24–25; not applied in *Tag* decision, 108; not assessment of social desirability of combinations, 180–81; Oppenheim on, 26, 115, 254–55 and *n*, 370–71; origins of, 126–28; patent-antitrust cases, 219; standard endorsed by Business Advisory Council, 125, 190; public welfare criterion, 126*n*; refusal to write into Sherman Act, 20 and *n*, 135 and *n*; rejected in *Aluminum* decision, 361; and Sherman Act remedies, 372, 382–83; *Standard Oil* decision (1911), 21, 135–39, 268; *Sugar Institute* decision, 72–73, 75–76; trade association cases, 110–11; *Trans-Missouri Freight* decision, 134–35; unacceptable antitrust standard, 261; vali-

Index

dated new industrial structure, 139, 197
S. O. and O. C. Company, 382n
Sage, George H.: cited, 68n
Salt Producers Association, 77–79, 364
Sanborn, Walter H.: quoted, 129 and n
Schlatter, Hugo: cited, 321n
Schumpeter, Joseph A.: cited, 19n; competition theory irrelevant, 415; on monopoly and innovation, 278 and n; "perennial gale of creative destruction," 14, 248n, 417–18; theory criticized, 260
Schwartz, Louis B., 194, 208; quoted, 194n, 239
Seaton, S. B.: quoted, 104
Seaver Company, 379
Shea, George: quoted, 31
Sheehan, Robert; quoted, 169n, 170n
Sherman, John, 131, 132n, 133n
Sherman Act: *Aluminum* test of § 2 violation, 141, 181, 361; amendment of inadequate, 183; *American Tobacco* (1946) test of § 2 violation, 361–63; Antitrust Committee on foreign commerce provision of, 213–16; applicable to certain oligopoly conduct, 182; "appreciable part" of commerce, 249; attempt to stay within boundaries of, 54, 64; background of, 131–34; bans monopoly unlawfully acquired or maintained, 273; bans every contract that restrains trade, 105n, 134–35; and basing point pricing, 234–35; businessmen's attitude toward, 20–22; and Chamberlinian theory, 361; changes since enactment of, 185, 195; comprehensiveness, 132–36 *passim*; and compulsory royalty-free licensing, 219; and concept of cross-elasticity, 267, 277, 389, 396–97; and conduct due to structure, 235; conspiracy to eliminate price discrimination a violation of, 74–75; constitutional problem, 132, 134; and definition of the market, 272, 277, 278, 280, 286, 396–97; described in *Appalachian Coals* case, 357; Dirlam and Stelzer on test for violation of, 267–68; dissatisfaction with, 18–20, 185–86; *Du Pont–General Motors* case, 319–20, 352–56, 397–99; effect on of concept of workable competition, 166, 181, 183, 263, 372, 396; and Federal Trade Commission Act, 76n; failure of, 186, 196, 197, 199, 410; increase in maximum fine, 238n; international cartels, 212 and n; Judge Gary's views on, 21–22; Judge Knox on, 375; Judge Leahy's test of § 2 violation, 385; Judge Rose on purpose of, 167–68; Judge Wyzanski on interpretations of § 2, 308–81; *Knight* case, 8–9, 18, 70n, 136n, 186n; long-term requirements contracts illegal under, 175n; *National Lead* case, 373–74; no monopoly in cans under, 180n; penalties not corrective of structure, 365; and price fixing, 111n; proposal to reinterpret, 119; purpose of, 131–34, 144, 185, 194–96; realistic interpretation of, 182; remedies, 381–83; Robinson-Patman Act conflicts with, 225; Rostow on size and, 249, 363; and rule of reason, 136n, 138, 140, 189n, 197, 262, 269; rule of reason amendment rejected, 20 and n; subordinated to state law, 8–9; Thorelli's study of, 130n; tying clauses under 219–20, 231; violation of made synonymous with bad conduct, 138
Simon, William: cited, 23n
Size: abuse of feared, 168, 362; *Aluminum* decision (1950), 376–77; Business Advisory Council on, 253, 370; and business conduct, 288; and business reciprocity, 315–18; "community mindedness" a consequence of, 421; and competition, 142; condemned per se?, 143; corporate, and power, 418; of Du Pont as seller of automobile fabrics and finishes, 356; and efficiency, 7, 9, 379n, 422; external expansion, 8–10, 203–4, 218; in steel industry, 7–8, 145; and government contracts, 412; internal expansion, 9; optimum scale of production may require few sellers, 123; role of war, 10–11, 203, 218; Rostow on *American Tobacco* decision (1946), 249, 363; and Sherman Act, 24n, 139–40, 197; social and economic significance, 12, 422; through patents, 218; of tobacco companies, 362
Sloan, Alfred P., Jr.: approved organization of Kinetic, 350; director of General Motors and Du Pont, 330n;

447

favored Du Pont's antifreeze, 338; and General Motors' reciprocity with Du Pont, 299–301; "member of the Du Pont family," 328; opposed general chemical agreement, 342; on General Motors stock voted by Du Pont, 330n; opposed General Motors' manufacture of chemicals, 350; suggested general purchasing committee, 336; tetraethyl lead and Jersey Standard, 345–48

Smith, Adam: on appealing to benevolence, 419n; concerned with public policy, 402; on economic individualism, 402–3; "obvious and simple system of natural liberty," 131, 403; on reciprocal buying, 289n; skeptical of the corporation, 408; views a reflection of his times, 403–7; mentioned, 360, 401

Smith, Blackwell: on Antitrust Committee, 237–38; on Antitrust Report, 120n, 193n, 256, 371; cited, 19n, 119n, 189n, 384n; on concerted action, 116; counsel for NRA, 251n; endorsed rule of reason and workable competition, 190; on per se antitrust decisions, 25n; on revision of antitrust laws, 251–52; tests of effective competition, 253; on workable competition and antitrust, 369–72; mentioned, 261

Smithies, Arthur: cited, 68n

Social responsibility of corporate executives, 418-23

Société Industrielle de la Cellulose, 156n, 394

Spencer, Herbert, 2

Sraffa, Piero: quoted, 26, 415

Standard & Poor's Industry Surveys: cited, 169nn, 175n, 178n; quoted, 170n, 180n

Standard Oil case (1911), 21, 135–39, 195, 268

Standard Oil Company, 21, 137–38

Standard Oil Company of Indiana, 203, 325, 344

Standard Oil of Indiana case, 227, 233

Standard Oil Company (Louisiana), 344

Standard Oil Company (New Jersey), 20n, 196, 419; and tetraethyl lead, 344–48

Standard Oil Trust, 124, 131

Standard Stations case, 232, 251

Stanley Committee, 21

Steel: basing point pricing, 110n, 147–48; competition believed ruinous, 21, 147; conduct reflects structure, 146–51, 181; countervailing power in, 14; demand price-inelastic, 146; effect of mergers, 144; industry's performance, 149–52; large industry essential to military success, 7–8; 1952 strike, 15; price leadership, 147–48; price movements, 149–51; price stabilization policy, 147–51; reciprocal dealings in industry, 301, 307, 308, 314–17; structure of industry, 139, 144–46; uniform pricing of extras, 148

Steel case and rule of reason, 139, 197–98

Steel Code, 172n

Stelzer, Irwin M.: see Dirlam, Joel B., and Irwin M. Stelzer

Stevenson, Jordon & Harrison, 77–79

Stewart, R. W., 325

Stigler, George J.: cited, 29n, 32n, 122n, 151n, 190n, 275n; dissents from Antitrust Report, 194n; workable competition not an antitrust guide, 257–58

Stine, C. M., 341

Stocking, George W.: *Basing Point Pricing and Regional Development*, cited, 69n, 146n, 199n, 234n, 250n, declined to serve on Antitrust Committee, 260–61; "The Economics of Basing Point Pricing," cited, 70n, 86n, 109n; "The Law on Basing Point Pricing: Confusion or Competition," cited, 23n, 86n, 109n; preconceptions stated, 30n. See also Stocking and Mueller; Stocking and Watkins

Stocking, George F., and Mueller, Willard F.: "The Cellophane Case and the New Competition," cited, 164n, 241n, 280n, 354n, 391n, ibid., quoted, 264n, 266

Stocking, George W., and Myron W. Watkins: *Cartels in Action*, cited, 211n, 213n; *Cartels or Competition?*, cited, 45n, 117, 213n; *Monopoly and Free Enterprise*, cited, 19n, 74n, 86n, 87n, 210n, 241n, 275n

Stratton, Samuel S.: cited, 68n

Structure: see Industrial structure

Substitutes, 28, 123–24, 244, 274, 286, 367–68, 416; *Aluminum* decision (1945), 360; *Aluminum* decision

(1950), 376–77; for cellophane, 159–66, 266, 280–83, 285, 385–87, 396–97; and the relevant market, 276–77
Sugar Institute, 70–76; "Code of Ethics," 71; disbanded, 76n; open pricing, 72
Sugar Institute case, quoted, 73
Sugar Trust, 131
Sullivan, George F.: quoted, 317
Sunderland, Thomas E.: cited, 19n, 23n, 119n, 189n, 384n; on attack on big business, 143n; on per se antitrust decisions, 25n
Surplus Property Act, 374–75
Swett, Arthur H., Jr.: quoted, 96–99 *passim*
Swift & Company, 294
Sylvania Industrial Corporation of America: conduct in duopolistic industry, 384; Du Pont's patent infringement settlement, 156–58, 284, 393–96; only other producer of cellophane until 1951, 280, 393

Taft, William H.: on effect of *Knight* decision, 19n, 186n; on restraints of trade at common law, 129
Tag Manufacturers Institute, 87–108; agreements a result of NRA experience, 94; buyers' access to price information, 107 and n; cooperation among competitors, 96; counsel attacks integrity of FTC, 92; decision liberalizes earlier trade association cases, 92–93; defects of price-reporting system, 107; efforts to eliminate penny difference in prices, 103–4; "liquidated damages," 87n, 90–91n, 97–99n, 105–6n; nature of price information, 88–89n, 95–97n, 103n; off-list prices, treatment of, 97, 100n, 105; professed aim, 88
Tariff: effect of on aluminum prices, 361
Tariff Act of 1930, 155, 266n, 394
Taylor, Myron, 151–52
Technology: basis for broadening application of rule of reason, 26; causes of progress in are complex, 183; contributions of American Can Company, 178; a curb on monopoly by bringing substitutes, 244–45, 274; effect on concept of the market, 274; and the modern corporation, 7, 13, 218, 422; need for publicly supported research, 17; said to necessitate oligopoly, 28, 121

Temporary National Economic Committee: analysis of trade association activities, 209–10; purpose of, 187; reflected concern for decline of competition, 358–59
Temporary National Economic Committee Hearings: cited, 147n, 148n, 150n, 164n, 172n, 177n
Tennyson, Alfred: quoted, 14–15, 45
Theory of Monopolistic Competition: cited, 27, 120 and n; 122–23, 188 and n, 276n, 277n, 360n, 416; quoted, 27n, 188n
Thorelli, Hans B.: cited, 131n; on belief common law opposed monopolies, 130n; on divergence in English and American policy, 130; on purpose of Sherman Act, 133n
Thorp, Willard E.: cited, 120n; quoted, 88
Till, Irene, and Walton Hamilton: quoted, 217n
Timberlake, E. Compton: cited, 82n
Times-Picayune case, 231–32
Tin can industry, 166–80; industrial performance after 1950 decrees, 179–80; prices, 176; structure, 166n, 167–72
Tisdale, George M.: quoted, 305
Townshend (Lord), 405
Trade associations: affected by NRA experience, 86, 87, 92–95; Antitrust Committee's view of, 208–10; businessmen's attitude toward, 113, 114; court decisions on statistical activities contrasted, 93n; data distributed among sellers, not buyers, 65–66, 75; effects of general resort to statistical activities, 116–17; Federal Trade commission cases, 76–87; Gunpowder Trade Association, 320 n; *Hardwood Lumber* decision, 37–38; importance increases in a buyer's market, 31; legal "rules" for statistical activities, 93n; *Linseed Oil* decision, 38–39; *Maple Flooring* decision quoted, 43–44; in maple flooring industry, 39–61; membership has increased, 112; and price cutting, 31; rule of reason as to, 110–12, 208; shaken by per se decisions?, 108–12, 118; standardization of product, 41–42, 82–84; statistical activities, 35, 36, 43–44, 79, 114; sugar industry's "Code of Ethics," 71, 72n; *Sugar Institute*

449

case, 70–76; *Tag Institute* case, 87–108; and uniformity of pricing, 93n; useful activities, 113, 117–18; and workable competition, 31, 35–36, 38, 44, 69, 70, 72, 75, 77, 81, 84, 87, 88, 108, 115–18, 261

Trans-Missouri Freight Association case, 129, 134–35

Trevelyan, G. M.: quoted, 407

Triffin, Robert: quoted, 277n

Troll, John H., 412

Trusts: bills to outlaw, 133n; 1888 political platforms on, 131n; fear of, 131, 195; good and bad, 361; holding companies a form of, 199

Tull, Jethro, 405

Turpie, David, 133n

Tying clauses: Antitrust Committee approved law on, 231–32; "any substantial market," 25n, 231; and "monopolistic leverage," 232; in patent licenses, 219–20, 232n

Union Carbide and Carbon Corporation, 165n, 337

United Motors Company, 340

United Shoe Machinery case, 378–83

United Shoe Machinery Corporation, 20n, 197, 378–82

U.S. Bureau of Corporations, 139n, 186

U.S. Bureau of Labor Statistics: cited, 150

U.S. Department of Commerce: Business Advisory Council report, *Effective Competition,* cited, 18n, 119n, 125n, 189n, 370; *ibid.,* quoted, 144n, 253; sponsored trade association standardization of products, 82n; statistics on trade associations, 112n; study of trade association activities, 56n

United States Maltsters Association, 79–80

United States Rubber Company: *Du Pont–General Motors* case, 319–20, 323–24; reciprocal business plan, 305–7; reciprocity with Du Pont, 309nn; reciprocity with U.S. Steel Corporation, 307; stock bought by Du Ponts, 305n, 323; use of reciprocal buying, 296, 305–10

United States Steel Corporation: and basing point pricing, 69n, 110n, 147–48, 365–66; cause of steel industry's structure today, 144–45, 181; *Columbia Steel* case, 143; Du Pont's business with and reciprocity, 299n; efficiency of, 153n; inefficiency of, 151–52; ingot capacity, 7, 139, 144–45, 197; institutional advertising, 420; live-and-let-live policy, 148, 149n; organized to monopolize trade, 197; "Pittsburgh Plus," 147; price stabilization policy, 147–51; rebate on tin plate by subsidiary of, 167, 172, 230; reciprocity with U.S. Rubber, 307–8; role of mergers, 20n, 197, 203; size and 1920 decision, 139; and steel prices, 153n; *TNEC Papers* cited, 150n

Usher, A. P.: cited, 405n

Van Gelder, Arthur P.: cited, 321n

Vanderbilt, O. DeGray III: cited, 312n; quoted, 313

Vanderblue, Homer B., 57

Veblen, Thorstein: quoted, 401

Vertical integration, 355

Viner, Jacob: quoted, 69

Virginia Chemical Corporation, 373

Wagner Act, 5

Walker, Albert H.: cited, 131n

Wall Street Journal: cited, 31n, 145n, 325n

Walters, Adelaide: cited, 213n

War: effect on antitrust laws, 187; effect on industrial expansion, 10–11

Warner, Charles: quoted, 302–3

Warren, Earl, 400; quoted, 272, 384

Watkins, Myron W.: cited, 126n. *See also* Stocking, George W., and Myron W. Watkins

Watt, James, 405

Waugh Equipment Company, 294, 317

Wealth of Nations, The, 289n, 402–4, 407–8, 419n

Webb-Pomerene Act, 211–13

Webb, Sidney and Beatrice: quoted, 3

Weir, Ernest T., 145n

Wescott (of Du Pont): cited, 348n; quoted, 348n

Weston, J. Fred: analysis criticized, 202; methods of calculating external growth, 203n; on role of mergers, 9, 10, 202–3

Wharton, Don: cited, 414n

Whisky Trust, 131

White, Edward D.: on rule of reason,

Index

135, 136, 268; on Standard Oil combination, 137–38
White, Hugh E.: cited, 69n
Whitney, George, 329
Whittaker, Charles Evans, 319, 400
Whyte, William H., Jr.: quoted, 412
Wilcox, Clair: cited, 29n, 77n, 122n, 189n, 275n
Wilson, Charles E., 329; quoted, 400
Wilson, Woodrow: quoted, 21
Winslow, S. W., 378n
Winton Engine Company, 311 and n
Wood, Henry: cited, 131n
Wooden, Walter B.: cited, 69n
Woolley, Victor B.: quoted, 197n
Workable competition: Adelman on, 30, 123, 276; aim of advocates of, 143–44; Antitrust Committee's attitude toward, 119n, 255, 371; in antitrust decisions, 372–400; Blackwell Smith on, 116, 251–54 *passim*, 369–72; Business Advisory Council endorsed, 125, 190; business reciprocity and, 318; and *Cellophane* case, 165, 264n, 281, 388, 396; Clark's concept of, 28, 29n, 108n, 121, 123, 244–46, 318, 366–67, 369, 416; concept of, 28–30, 108, 121–25, 189–90, 242, 275–80, 366–69; correct application and antitrust enforcement, 180–84, 267; and cross-elasticity of demand, 124, 158; Dirlam and Kahn on, 258–60; Dirlam and Stelzer on, 242, 263–67 *passim*, 272; economists' evaluation of, 190, 241–42, 246, 257–60, 263–67, 272, 275–76, 369; Edwards' structural tests of, 318; environmental factors affecting concept, 367–68; and free enterprise, 117–18, 261; function of price and, 32–34, 115; gaining acceptance as antitrust standard, 367–69; Griffin on, 247, 369; Howery on, 271n; inappropriate antitrust guide, 69, 119n, 144, 153, 183, 242, 247, 255–67 *passim*, 272, 275–76, 383, 396–97, 400; Judge Knox on, 375–76; Judge Wyzanski on role of courts and, 381–82, 383; lawyers' adaptation of, 251–55, 369–72; Lewis on, 276; literature on, 121n, 189n, 248n, 275n; Markham on, 30, 246, 369; Mason on, 30, 70, 243–46, 369; and public interest test, 115, 254; Oppenheim on, 115, 144n, 251–55 *passim*, 369–72; Robertson on, 277, 286; Schumpeter on temporary monopoly, 278, 417–18; Stocking's position on, 122–25 *passim*, 152–53, 165–66, 180–84, 260–63, 275–76, 383, 396–97, 400; usefulness tested, 35–36, 180–84, 263, 372–400; a vague concept, 30, 116, 182, 373; various concepts of, 29–30, 115–16, 246–48, 369, 384
Workable monopoly, 29, 165, 258
Wright, David McCord: cited, 19n
Wright, Joseph S.: cited, 86n
Wyzanski, Charles E., 372; quoted, 142n; *United Shoe* decision, 378–83, 384

Yerkes, L. A.: on lowering price of cellophane, 163n, 391; on patents to protect cellophane, 157n, 284, 395n; on tariff on cellophane, 154n
Youngstown Sheet and Tube Company, 317–18

Zimmerschied, K. W., 341

451